Microsoft®

Microsoft® Visio® 2010

Step by Step

Scott A. Helmers

Published with the authorization of Microsoft Corporation by:

O'Reilly Media, Inc.
1005 Gravenstein Highway North
Sebastopol, CA 95472

Microsoft Press titles may be purchased for educational, business, or sales promotional use. Online editions are also available for most titles (*http://my.safaribooksonline.com*). For more information, contact our corporate/institutional sales department: (800) 998-9938 or *corporate@oreilly.com*.

6 7 8 9 10 11 12 13 14 LSI 8 7 6 5 4 3

Acquisitions and Developmental Editor: Kenyon Brown
Production Editor: Adam Zaremba
Editorial Production: Online Training Solutions, Inc.
Technical Reviewer: John Marshall
Illustrator: Robert Romano
Indexer: Lucie Haskins
Cover: Karen Montgomery

978-0-735-64887-6

[2013-07-19]

Contents

Introducing Visio 2010

Microsoft Visio 2010 is a bold new release. If you're new to Visio, your timing is excellent! This version of Visio is easier to use than ever before and yet the diagrams you create can have more impact and style, and can present more real-world data than in any previous version.

If you've used prior versions of Visio, you're in luck too. You'll find the features you love, but you'll see them presented with the new Visio ribbon. In addition, you'll discover that you can publish dynamically updateable diagrams to Microsoft SharePoint, where anyone can view them, even if they don't have Visio. You'll find new templates and stencils, faster methods for creating drawings, simple ways to add structure to your diagrams, improved integration with AutoCad drawings, diagram validation rules, and a wealth of other new features.

In short, whether you're a first timer or have been using Visio for years, this is the strongest and most exciting version of Visio yet.

Creating and Enhancing Diagrams More Easily

Quick Shapes, AutoConnect, AutoAdd, AutoDelete, AutoAlign, AutoSize... just the names of some of the new and enhanced features in Visio 2010 suggest that creating diagrams will be simpler. A few examples include the following:

- Want to add a new shape to the page? For commonly used shapes, there's no need to move the pointer to the stencil and drag a shape onto the page. Just point to a shape that's already on the page and the QuickShapes menu offers you four shapes. One click and you've not only added a new shape but it's already connected to the existing shape.
- Need to insert a shape between two existing shapes? Simply drop the new shape onto the connector between two existing shapes. Not only will AutoAdd insert the new shape but it will add a new connector. And if there isn't enough room for the new shape, Visio will even rearrange part of the diagram to make room.
- Want to delete a shape that's connected between two others? Just select the shape and press the Delete key. Self-healing connectors do the rest; the shapes on either side of the deleted shape will be connected to each other.

- Need to enlarge the drawing page and print the new diagram across multiple sheets of paper? Simply drag a shape into the space surrounding the drawing page and AutoSize will add a new page. That's it! No other adjustments or setting changes required.
- Don't like the way your shapes are aligned on the page? Click the Auto Align & Space button and Visio rearranges your diagram. Not quite happy with the result? Undo the changes, move a few shapes around, and then click Auto Align & Space again.
- Need to present your diagram to an audience but think the drawing is a bit boring? Open the Visio 2010 Themes gallery: one click applies a suite of coordinated colors, styles, fonts, line patterns, and effects to every shape. You can also apply predesigned page backgrounds or page borders by selecting one from a new gallery.

Visio 2010 also brings Live Preview to your diagrams. Many of the features listed above, along with most font, color, size, and style changes, take advantage of Live Preview to show you a potential change before you make it. Live Preview even extends to Visio ***Data Graphics***, letting you preview the dynamic presentation of the data behind your shapes.

Adding Structure to Visio Diagrams

Many types of Visio diagrams contain sets of shapes that are related to each other. In previous Visio versions, you could visually suggest the relationships by creating some combination of groups, colored background shapes, or borders.

Visio 2010 introduces a new type of shape called a *container* that provides more than just a visual grouping for a set of shapes. The container structure means that shapes in a container know they are contained, and the container knows the members that reside within it. Consequently, when you move, copy, or delete a container, all of the members go with it. However, unlike a group shape, the member shapes are accessible with a single click just as if the container were not there.

In most containers, you can place member shapes wherever you'd like. However, a *list* is a special type of container that maintains members in ordered sequence. Each list member knows exactly where it resides within the list.

Visio 2010 includes a third type of structured diagram component known as a *callout.* You still use new-style callouts to add annotations to other shapes, but both the callout and the target shape are aware of each other. Once again, this improves many user interface actions, but also allows Visio ***add-ins*** to work more intelligently with annotated shapes.

Containers, lists, and callouts are great for Visio users, but they also offer intriguing options to Visio developers for building location-aware shapes and for writing code that takes advantage of diagram structure.

Publishing to SharePoint

In Visio 2010, as in previous versions of Visio, you can save any Visio drawing as a set of webpages. This was, and is, a tremendously useful capability because it allows anyone with Windows Internet Explorer to view your web-published Visio diagram without needing Visio.

Although this publishing option has many advantages, it also has one fundamental drawback: the published drawings are static. If the diagram changes or the underlying data changes, you need to republish the drawing before users can see the changes.

The combination of Visio 2010 and SharePoint Server 2010 Visio Services introduces a new option that you can use to publish dynamically updateable Visio web drawings. You can publish drawings that contain live connections to external data sources and feature data graphics to visualize the data behind the diagram. When the underlying data changes, or certain aspects of the diagram change, Visio Services on SharePoint ensures that the web drawing is automatically updated.

You needn't stop with simply publishing a web drawing, either. You can create Web Parts to contain your Visio drawings and can even create interactions among Web Parts so that published Visio drawings interact with each other and with non-Visio Web Parts.

Managing Business Processes

The Premium edition of Visio 2010 adds several new templates that are specifically focused on business process and also adds a number of process-related features.

Using the Business Process Management Notation (BPMN) template, you can create process maps that conform to the BPMN 1.2 standard.

With the SharePoint Workflow template, you can create a visual layout of a SharePoint workflow, export it to SharePoint Designer for refinement and completion, and then execute the workflow in SharePoint. You can also bring a SharePoint Designer workflow back into Visio in order to see a graphical representation.

The Process tab in Visio Premium 2010 includes several new buttons for automatically creating and managing subprocesses within a process diagram.

Validating Diagrams

Visio 2010 validation rules, which are part of Visio Premium 2010, introduce a new level of quality to your Visio diagrams. You've always been able to create great looking diagrams with Visio, but now you can ensure that your diagrams meet a minimum set of predefined conditions before you publish or distribute them.

Four Visio 2010 templates—Basic Flowchart, Cross Functional Flowchart, Microsoft SharePoint Workflow, and Business Process Modeling Notation—include predefined validation rule sets that you can run in diagrams created from those templates. You can also import existing rule sets into other diagrams. For example, you can add the flowchart rules to a Visio 2003 flowchart to improve its quality. You can also create your own rules and rule sets to validate diagrams.

Summary

There's a lot to like about Visio 2010! This introduction has barely scratched the surface of some of the new features in the software. The exercises in this book will get you started with Visio 2010 and will give you hands-on experience with the best that Visio has to offer.

Modifying the Display of the Ribbon

The goal of the Microsoft Office working environment is to make working with Office documents, including Microsoft Word documents, Excel workbooks, PowerPoint presentations, Outlook e-mail messages, Access database tables, and Visio diagrams as intuitive as possible. You work with an Office document and its contents by giving commands to the program in which the document is open. All Office 2010 programs organize commands on a horizontal bar called the *ribbon*, which appears across the top of each program window whether or not there is an active document.

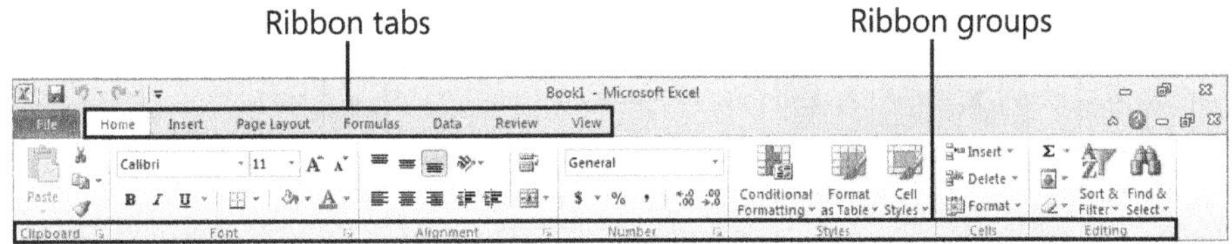

Commands are organized on task-specific tabs of the ribbon, and in feature-specific groups on each tab. Commands generally take the form of buttons and lists. Some appear in galleries. Some groups have related dialog boxes or task panes that contain additional commands.

Throughout this book, we discuss the commands and ribbon elements associated with the program feature being discussed. In this topic, we discuss the general appearance of the ribbon, things that affect its appearance, and ways of locating commands that aren't visible on compact views of the ribbon.

Dynamic Ribbon Elements

The ribbon is dynamic, meaning that the appearance of commands on the ribbon changes as the width of the ribbon changes. A command might be displayed on the ribbon in the form of a large button, a small button, a small labeled button, or a list entry. As the width of the ribbon increases or decreases, the size, shape, and presence of buttons on the ribbon adapt to the available space.

For example, when sufficient horizontal space is available, the buttons on the Review tab of the Word program window are spread out and you're able to see more of the commands available in each group.

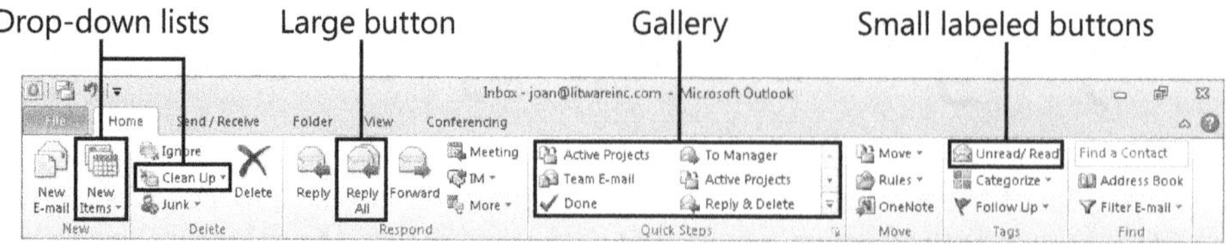

If you decrease the width of the ribbon, small button labels disappear and entire groups of buttons hide under one button that represents the group. Click the group button to display a list of the commands available in that group.

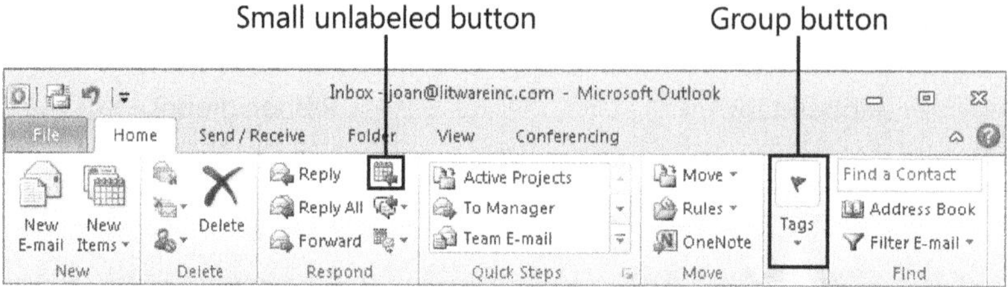

When the window becomes too narrow to display all the groups, a scroll arrow appears at its right end. Click the scroll arrow to display hidden groups.

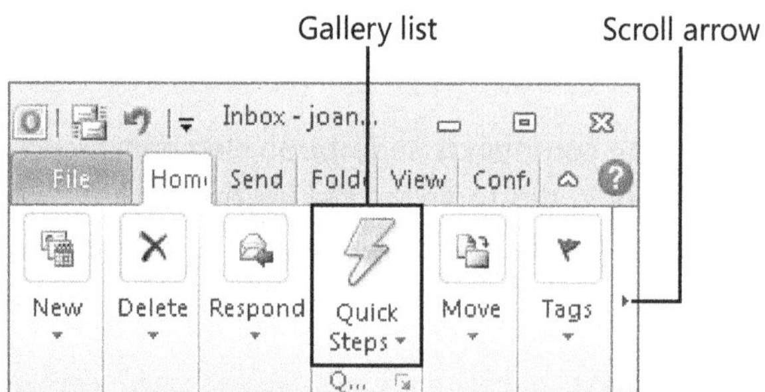

Changing the Width of the Ribbon

The width of the ribbon is dependent on the horizontal space available to it, which depends on these three factors:

- **The width of the program window** Maximizing the program window provides the most space for ribbon elements. You can resize the program window by clicking the button in its upper-right corner or by dragging the border of a nonmaximized window.

Tip On a computer running Windows 7, you can maximize the program window by dragging its title bar to the top of the screen.

- **Your screen resolution** Screen resolution is the size of your screen display expressed as pixels wide × pixels high. The greater the screen resolution, the greater the amount of information that will fit on one screen. Your screen resolution options are dependent on your monitor. At the time of writing, possible screen resolutions range from 800 × 600 to 2048 × 1152. In the case of the ribbon, the greater the number of pixels wide (the first number), the greater the number of buttons that can be shown on the ribbon, and the larger those buttons can be.

  On a computer running Windows 7, you can change your screen resolution from the Screen Resolution window of Control Panel. You set the resolution by dragging the pointer on the slider.

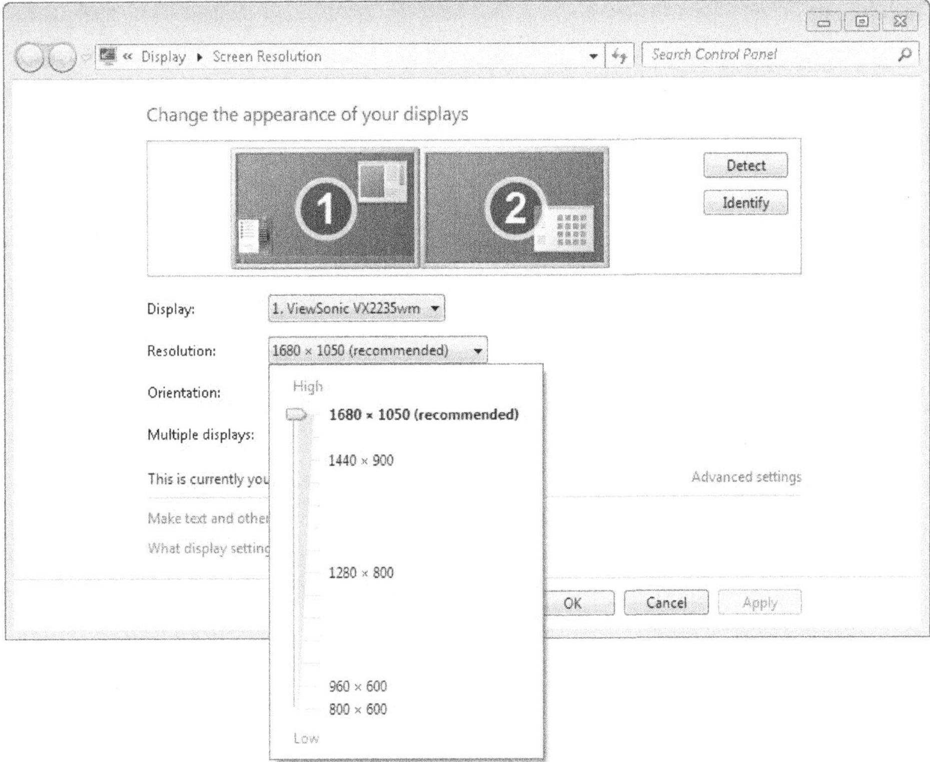

- **The density of your screen display** You might not be aware that you can change the magnification of everything that appears on your screen by changing the screen magnification setting in Windows. Setting your screen magnification to 125% makes text and user interface elements larger on screen. This increases the legibility of information, but means that less fits onto each screen.

On a computer running Windows 7, you can change the screen magnification from the Display window of Control Panel. You can choose one of the standard display magnification options, or create another by setting a custom text size.

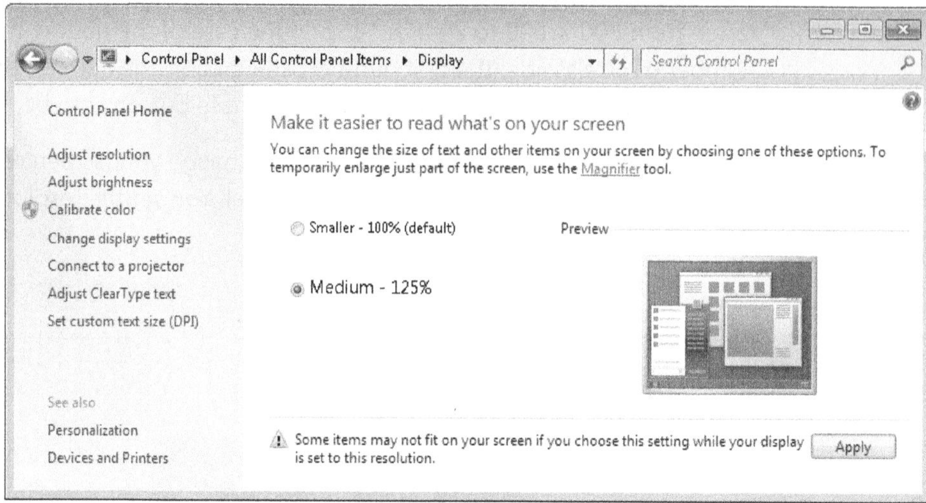

The screen magnification is directly related to the density of the text elements on screen, which is expressed in dots per inch (dpi) or pixels per inch (ppi). (The terms are interchangeable, and in fact are both used in the Windows dialog box in which you change the setting.) The greater the dpi, the larger the text and user interface elements appear on screen. By default, Windows displays text and screen elements at 96 dpi. Choosing the Medium - 125% display setting changes the dpi of text and screen elements to 120 dpi. You can choose a custom setting of up to 500% magnification, or 480 dpi, in the Custom DPI Setting dialog box. The list allows you to choose a magnification of up to 200%. You can choose a greater magnification by dragging across the ruler from left to right.

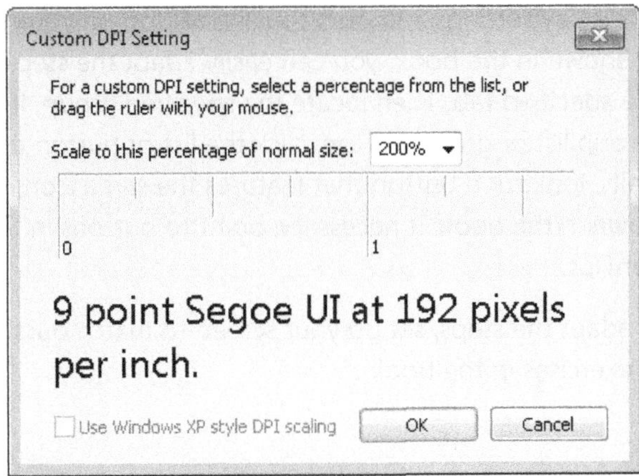

See Also For more information about display settings, refer to *Windows 7 Step by Step* (Microsoft Press, 2009), *Windows Vista Step by Step* (Microsoft Press, 2006), or *Windows XP Step by Step* (Microsoft Press, 2002) by Joan Lambert Preppernau and Joyce Cox.

Adapting Exercise Steps

The screen images shown in the exercises in this book were captured at a screen resolution of 1024 × 768, at 100% magnification, and the default text size (96 dpi). If any of your settings are different, the ribbon on your screen might not look the same as the one shown in the book. For example, you might see more or fewer buttons in each of the groups, the buttons you see might be represented by larger or smaller icons than those shown, or the group might be represented by a button that you click to display the group's commands.

When we instruct you to give a command from the ribbon in an exercise, we do it in this format:

- On the **Insert** tab, in the **Illustrations** group, click the **Chart** button.

If the command is in a list, we give the instruction in this format:

- On the **Page Layout** tab, in the **Page Setup** group, click the **Breaks** button and then, in the list, click **Page**.

The first time we instruct you to click a specific button in each exercise, we display an image of the button in the page margin to the left of the exercise step.

If differences between your display settings and ours cause a button on your screen to look different from the one shown in the book, you can easily adapt the steps to locate the command. First, click the specified tab. Then locate the specified group. If a group has been collapsed into a group list or group button, click the list or button to display the group's commands. Finally, look for a button that features the same icon in a larger or smaller size than that shown in the book. If necessary, point to buttons in the group to display their names in ScreenTips.

If you prefer not to have to adapt the steps, set up your screen to match ours while you read and work through the exercises in the book.

Features and Conventions of This Book

This book has been designed to lead you step by step through all the tasks you're most likely to want to perform in Microsoft Visio 2010. If you start at the beginning and work your way through all the exercises, you will gain enough proficiency to be able to create and work with many types of Visio diagrams. However, each topic is self-contained. If you have worked with a previous version of Visio, or if you completed all the exercises and later need help remembering how to perform a procedure, the following features of this book will help you locate specific information:

- **Detailed table of contents** Search the listing of the topics within each chapter.
- **Chapter thumb tabs** Easily locate the beginning of the chapter you want.
- **Topic-specific running heads** Within a chapter, quickly locate the topic you want by looking at the running heads at the top of odd-numbered pages.
- **Glossary** Look up the meaning of a word or the definition of a concept.
- **Detailed index** Look up specific tasks and features in the index, which has been carefully crafted with the reader in mind.

You can save time when reading this book by understanding how the *Step by Step* series shows exercise instructions, keys to press, buttons to click, and other information.

Convention	Meaning
SET UP	This paragraph preceding a step-by-step exercise indicates the practice files that you will use when working through the exercise. It also indicates any requirements you should attend to or actions you should take before beginning the exercise.
CLEAN UP	This paragraph following a step-by-step exercise provides instructions for saving and closing open files or programs before moving on to another topic. It also suggests ways to reverse any changes you made to your computer while working through the exercise.
1 2	Numbered steps guide you through hands-on exercises in each topic, as well as procedures in sidebars and expository text.

Convention	Meaning
See Also	This paragraph directs you to more information about a topic in this book or elsewhere.
Troubleshooting	This paragraph alerts you to a common problem and provides guidance for fixing it.
Tip	This paragraph provides a helpful hint or shortcut that makes working through a task easier.
Important	This paragraph points out information that you need to know to complete a procedure.
Keyboard Shortcut	This paragraph provides information about an available keyboard shortcut for the preceding task.
Ctrl+B	A plus sign (+) between two keys means that you must press those keys at the same time. For example, "Press Ctrl+B" means that you should hold down the Ctrl key while you press the B key.
	Pictures of buttons appear in the margin the first time the button is used in a chapter.
Bold	In exercises that begin with SET UP information, bold type displays text that you should type; the names of program elements, such as buttons, commands, windows, and dialog boxes; and files, folders, or text that you interact with in the steps.

Using the Practice Files

Before you can complete the exercises in this book, you need to copy the book's practice files to your computer. These practice files, and other information, can be downloaded from here:

oreilly.com/catalog/9780735648876/

Display the detail page in your web browser and follow the instructions for downloading the files.

Important The Microsoft Visio2010 program is not available from this website. You should purchase and install that program before using this book.

The following table lists the practice files for this book.

Chapter	File
Chapter 1: A Visual Orientation to a Visual Product	Size & Position_start.vsd
Chapter 2: Creating a New Diagram	Autoconnect and Quick Shapes_start.vsd Basic shapes_start.vsd
Chapter 3: Adding Sophistication to Your Drawings	Background Exercises_start.vsd Corporate Diagram International_start.vsd Corporate Diagram_start.vsd International Office.jpg Starfish.jpg Text Exercises_start.vsd
Chapter 4: Drawing the Real World: Flowcharts and Organization Charts	HR Recuiting Flowchart_start.vsd Org Chart Data_start.xlsx
Chapter 5: Adding Style, Color, and Themes	HR Recruiting Flowchart with labels_start.vsd Org Chart by Hand with data_start.vsd Org Chart via Wizard with data_start.vsd
Chapter 6: Entering, Linking to, and Reporting on Data	HR Process Data_start.xlsx HR Process Map with data_start.vsd HR Process Map_start.vsd
Chapter 7: Adding and Using Hyperlinks	HR Process Map_start.vsd Human Resources Policy Manual.docx Sample PDF Document.pdf Sample presentation.pptx Sample Project file.mpp Sample spreadsheet.xlsx

Chapter	File
Chapter 8: Sharing and Publishing Diagrams: Part 1	HR Process Map for Chapter08_start.vsd
Chapter 9: Drawing the Real World: Network and Data Center Diagrams	Network Diagram (Basic) with data_start.vsd Network Diagram (Basic)_start.vsd Network Diagram (Detailed)_start.vsd Network Diagram (Organized)_start.vsd Network Diagram with Rack_start.vsd Network Equipment Data (Basic)_start.xlsx
Chapter 10: Visualizing Your Data	Casino Floor.vsd HR Process Map with data_start.vsd Sales Proposal Process TaskMap.pdf
Chapter 11: Adding Structure to Your Diagrams	Containers, Lists and Callouts_start.vsd
Chapter 12: Creating and Validating Process Diagrams	HR Recruiting Flowchart Validation_start.vsd RuleSets -- BPMN.html RuleSets -- CFF.html RuleSets -- Flowchart.html RuleSets -- SharePoint Workflow.html Theatre Ticketing Process_start.vsd Theatre Ticketing with Subprocess_start.vsd Visio 2007 Flowchart_start.vsd
Chapter 13: Sharing and Publishing Diagrams: Part 2	HR Process Map Save as Web2_start.vsd Theater Ticketing Diagram_start.vsd
Appendix: Looking Under the Hood	ShapeSheet_start.vsd

Companion Content

Bonus content for this book, including a list of all templates included with Visio 2010 and a selection of Visual Basic for Applications programs, can be found here:

oreilly.com/catalog/9780735648876/

Please follow the directions for downloading.

Getting Support and Giving Feedback

Errata

We've made every effort to ensure the accuracy of this book and its companion content. If you do find an error, please report it on our Microsoft Press site at *oreilly.com*:

1. Go to *microsoftpress.oreilly.com*.
2. In the Search box, enter the book's ISBN or title.
3. Select your book from the search results.
4. On your book's catalog page, in the list of links under the cover image click View/ Submit Errata.

You'll find additional information and services for your book on its catalog page. If you need additional support, please send an email message to Microsoft Press Book Support at *mspinput@microsoft.com*.

Please note that product support for Microsoft software is not offered through the addresses above.

Getting Help with Visio 2010

If your question is about Visio, and not about the content of this Microsoft Press book, your first recourse is the Visio Help system. You can find general or specific Help information by clicking the Help button (labeled with a question mark) located in the upper-right corner of the Visio program window.

If your question is about Visio or another Microsoft software product and you cannot find the answer in the product's Help system, please search the appropriate product solution center or the Microsoft Knowledge Base at:

support.microsoft.com

You can post questions and search previously answered questions at the Microsoft Answers community-based forums at:

answers.microsoft.com

In the United States, Microsoft software product support issues not covered by the Microsoft Knowledge Base are addressed by Microsoft Product Support Services. Location-specific software support options are available from:

support.microsoft.com/gp/selfoverview/

We Want to Hear from You

At Microsoft Press, your satisfaction is our top priority, and your feedback our most valuable asset. Please tell us what you think of this book at:

www.microsoft.com/learning/booksurvey

The survey is short, and we read *every one* of your comments and ideas. Thanks in advance for your input!

Stay in Touch

Let's keep the conversation going! We're on Twitter: *http://twitter.com/MicrosoftPress*.

Your Companion eBook

The eBook edition of this book allows you to:

- Search the full text
- Print
- Copy and paste

To download your eBook, please see the instruction page at the back of this book.

Acknowledgments

First and foremost, my deepest thanks and love to Marilyn, Sara, and Julie for doing everything that I didn't do while I was in book-writing mode. It's over and I'm back!

A special thanks to my daughter Sara, who read every word of every chapter before it left the house for the first time. The end result is better for her effort.

Thanks to the Visio team at Microsoft for creating such an incredible product and for being such a welcoming and supportive group. I've had the pleasure of getting to know many team members over the last three years and look forward to continuing to work with them. Particular thanks to Stephanie Horn for getting answers to a long list of questions as I was writing the book.

The dozen or so Visio experts in the world who are part of the Microsoft Most Valuable Professional (MVP) program are an amazingly talented group, and it is a pleasure to count many of them as friends. In particular, thanks to: John Marshall for his astute and historically rich technical editing of this book; Chris Roth for maintaining the ever-useful collection of articles, ideas, and forums at the Visio Guy website (*www.visguy.com*); Al Edlund for advice on page scaling; and David Parker for the Rules Tools (*www.visiorules.com*) and for consultation on that subject.

Few people are more knowledgeable on the subject of BPMN than Dr. Bruce Silver (*www.brsilver.com*). I appreciate his candid review of, and improvements to, the BPMN sections of Chapter 12.

Thanks to the editorial teams at Microsoft Press, O'Reilly, and OTSI for their guidance and support throughout the development of this book. A very special thanks to copy editor Jaime Odell. It's difficult to imagine a more collaborative, professional, and yet downright pleasant editing experience. She's set the bar very high for the next book.

Thanks to eagle-eyed and thoughtful reader Wayne Dale for dozens of suggestions and corrections between the first and second printings of this book.

Finally, thanks to Kathy Brennan and Mike Cunningham. Our collective decision to build TaskMap as a Visio add-in started the journey of discovery that led to this book.

Chapter at a Glance

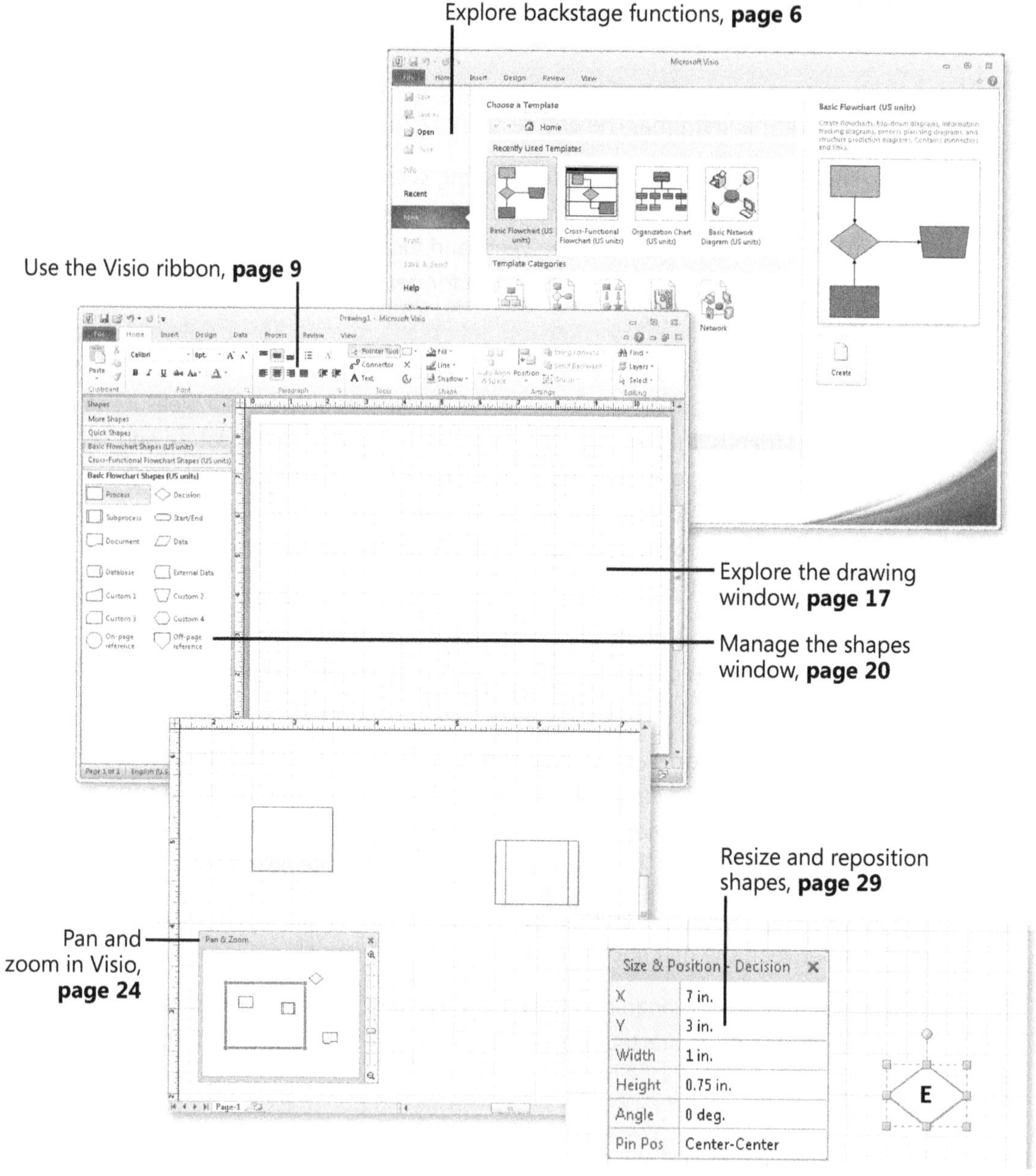
Explore backstage functions, **page 6**
Use the Visio ribbon, **page 9**
Explore the drawing window, **page 17**
Manage the shapes window, **page 20**
Resize and reposition shapes, **page 29**
Pan and zoom in Visio, **page 24**
Size & Position - Decision
X
7 in.
Y
3 in.
Width
1 in.
Height
0.75 in.
Angle
0 deg.
Pin Pos
Center-Center
E

1 A Visual Orientation to a Visual Product

In this chapter, you will learn how to

- ✔ Get started with Visio 2010.
- ✔ Explore the Backstage view.
- ✔ Use, resize, and minimize the Visio ribbon.
- ✔ Use contextual and add-in tabs.
- ✔ Understand shapes, masters, stencils, and templates.
- ✔ Explore the drawing window.
- ✔ Manage the Shapes window.
- ✔ Pan and zoom in Visio.
- ✔ Resize and reposition shapes.

Microsoft Visio 2010 looks different. *Very* different. That's because it's the first version of Visio to employ what Microsoft calls the ***fluent user interface*** (UI), otherwise known as the ***ribbon UI*** or just the ***ribbon***. Most products in the Microsoft Office suite adopted the ribbon in their 2007 versions, but Visio and a few others did not.

The good news for Visio users is that the Visio 2010 ribbon benefits from several additional years of development experience and millions of person-hours of user experience with the 2007 ribbons in other products. In addition, because the goal of a ribbon-style interface is a visual presentation of a related group of functions, the ribbon is very appropriate for Visio because Visio is, first and foremost, a visual product.

Consequently, the Visio ribbon is well-designed, logical, and quite easy to use. This doesn't mean you won't spend a few moments on occasion trying to figure out how to accomplish a particular task or hunting for a familiar tool. However, the vast majority of Visio functions are right where you would expect them to be after you've spent a few minutes exploring the ribbon layout and structure. Before you do that, though, you need to see how Visio looks when you start it, because that, too, is different in Visio 2010.

In this chapter, you will learn the differences among the three editions of Visio 2010. You will launch Visio and explore the Backstage view and will then explore the tabs on the Visio ribbon. You will compare the permanent tabs on the ribbon with contextual tabs and add-in tabs. You will learn about stencils, templates, masters, and shapes and how to manage the various windows that comprise the Visio user interface. Finally, you will practice moving and resizing Visio shapes.

Practice Files Before you can complete the exercises in this chapter, you need to copy the book's practice files to your computer. The practice files you'll use to complete the exercises in this chapter are in the Chapter01 practice files folder. A complete list of practice files is provided in "Using the Practice Files" at the beginning of this book.

Getting Started with Visio 2010

When you start Visio, it opens in the so-called ***Backstage view***. The Backstage view contains many of the items that were previously located on the File menu in Visio, and in fact, you'll notice that the blue tab at the top of the Backstage view is labeled File.

Tip Visio templates are provided in two different sets of measurement units. You might be offered a choice between the two when you select a template or you might not see a choice, as is the case for the following graphics. The two sets of measurement units are as follows:

- **US Units** Diagrams created with *US Units* use the 8.5-by-11-inch, letter-sized paper that is common in the United States and parts of Canada and Mexico. Templates created for US Units also include additional drawing and paper sizes that are common in those countries. The default measurement units are inches and feet.
- **Metric** *Metric* drawings are sized using International Standards Organization (ISO) specified paper sizes; the default size is usually A4. Metric templates also include other ISO drawing and paper sizes. All measurements are in millimeters or other metric measurement units.

Visio Standard

When you start Visio Standard 2010, the Backstage view opens to the New page.

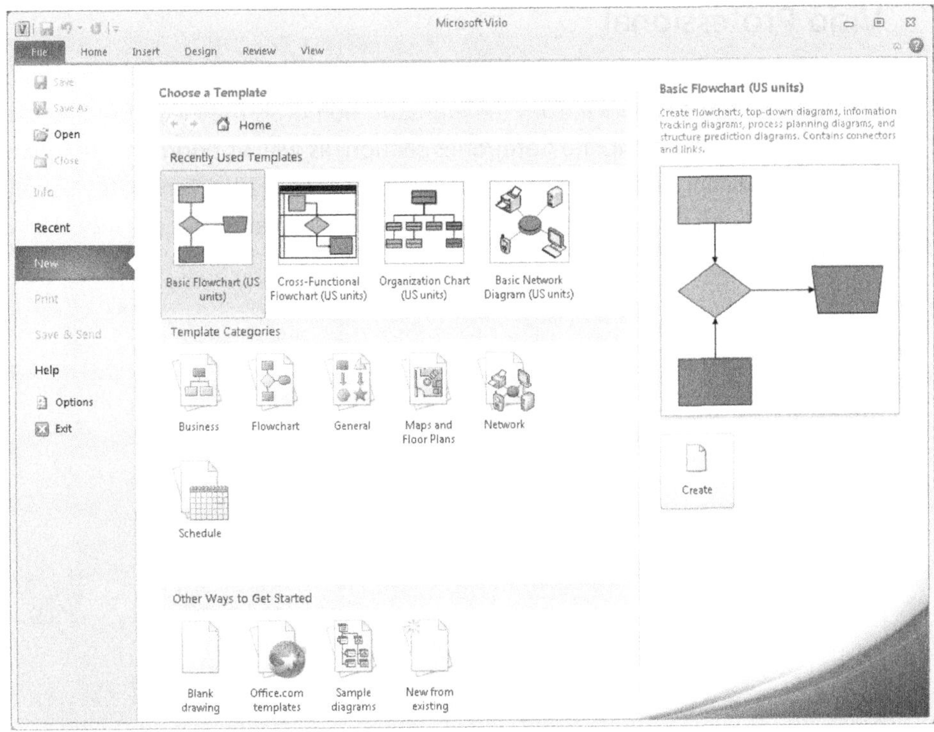

Key functions of the New page include the following:

- In the upper part of the screen, you see one or more Recently Used Templates.
- In the center of the screen you see icons representing Template Categories, each of which contains one or more templates. Refer to "Selecting Visio 2010 Templates" located with the companion content for this book for a list of the templates that are included with Visio Standard 2010. For more information about companion content, see the "Companion Content" section at the beginning of this book.
- In the lower part of the screen, you see Other Ways To Get Started, which contains links to online template collections and which you can use to create new drawings from a blank template, a sample diagram, or an existing Visio drawing.
- The right side of the Backstage view displays details about whichever item or collection you have selected in the center of the screen.

Visio Professional

When you start Visio Professional 2010, the Backstage view looks like the following graphic. The key difference from the Standard edition is the inclusion of additional template groups in the Template Categories section, as well as additional templates in several of the existing categories. Refer to "Selecting Visio 2010 Templates" located with the companion content for this book for a list of the templates that are included with Visio Professional 2010.

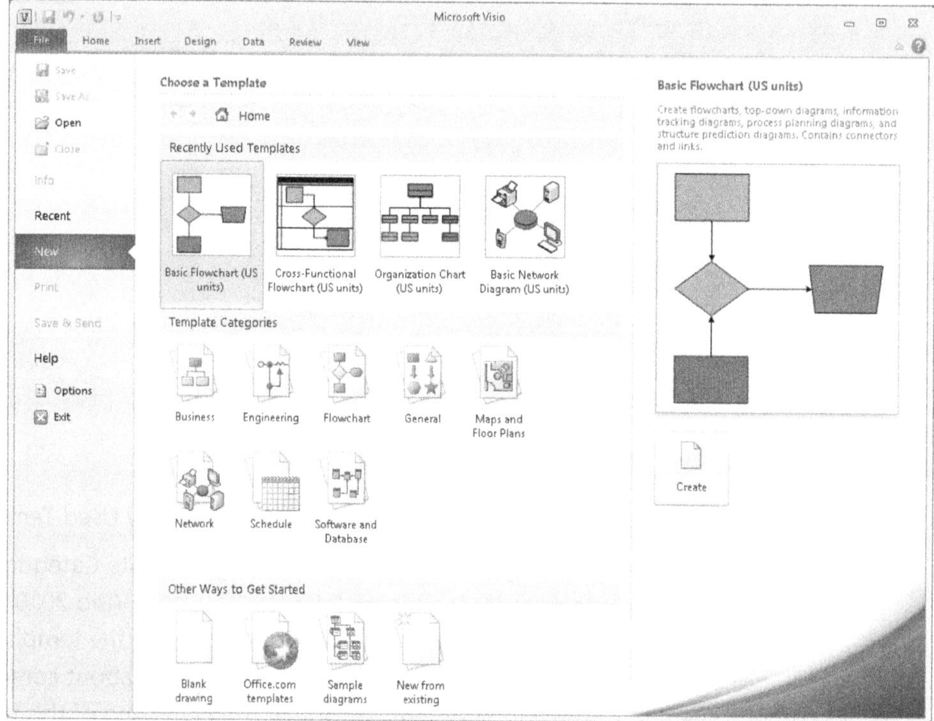

The Professional edition also includes one additional tab that is visible at the top of the previous graphic. The Data tab (situated between the Design and Review tabs) adds powerful data linking and data management features and is described in detail in Chapter 6, "Entering, Linking to, and Reporting on Data."

Visio Premium

When you start Visio Premium 2010, the main parts of the Backstage view look identical to the Professional edition. However, there is one subtle visible difference and one difference that is not visible on this screen:

- The visible difference is the addition of a Process tab, which you can see between the Data and Review tabs at the top of the following graphic. Business process functions are a key focus area for the Premium edition of Visio 2010 and will be covered in Chapter 4, "Drawing the Real World: Flowcharts and Organization Charts," and Chapter 12, "Creating and Validating Process Diagrams."
- The invisible difference is the inclusion of additional templates in the Business and Flowchart categories. Refer to "Selecting Visio 2010 Templates" located with the companion content for this book for a list of the templates that are included with Visio 2010 Premium.

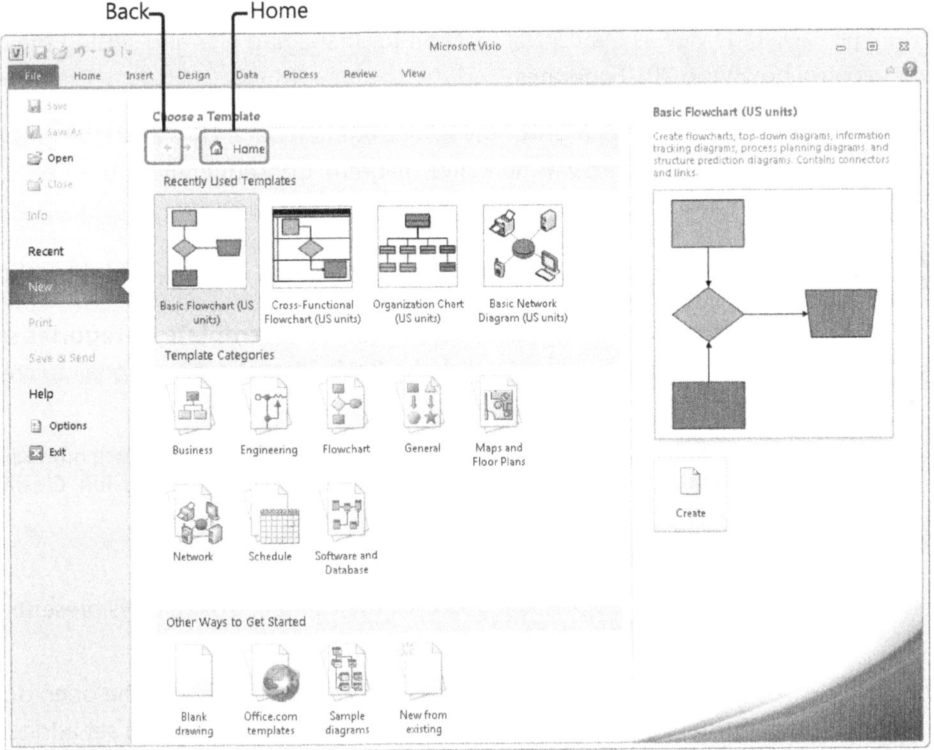

Regardless of your Visio edition, you can begin a new document by clicking a template category icon, and then double-clicking the thumbnail for a template.

Tip **If you have opened a template category but choose not to use a template in that category, you can return to the New page by clicking either the back arrow or the Home button at the top of the template area of the screen. Both buttons are shown in the preceding graphic.**

See Also The Visio Toolbox website (*visiotoolbox.com/2010/templates.aspx*), which is run by Microsoft, contains dozens of additional templates that you can use with Visio. Some are supplied by Microsoft, others by third-party vendors, and most are free.

Important Most of the screen shots in this book feature the Premium edition ribbon. Consequently, you might see tabs, buttons, or options in this book that don't apply to your edition of Visio. In general, you can ignore any buttons or tabs that do not appear on your computer screen. Where necessary, the text will distinguish those exercises or functions that can only be performed with a specific Visio 2010 edition.

Exploring the Backstage View

The Backstage view is the central location for managing files and setting the options that control how Visio 2010 operates.

In the preceding section, most of the left navigation pane choices in the graphics were unavailable because there was no active diagram. Consequently, in this exercise, you will start a new drawing so you can see the full Backstage view.

SET UP Start Visio, or if it's already running, click the File tab, and then click New.

1. On the **New** page of the Backstage view, in the **Template Categories** section, click **Flowchart**, and then double-click the **Basic Flowchart** thumbnail to create a new drawing.

   Tip Visio names your new drawing Drawing*n*, where *n* is a sequence number that is incremented for each new drawing created within one Visio session. Closing and restarting Visio always resets the sequence number to 1.

2. Click the **File** tab.

   When a drawing is open and you click the File tab, Visio always presents the Info page of the Backstage view.

   - The right side of the page provides information about the open document along with a Properties list that you can use to view and set additional document properties. You will use the Properties list in several places in this book, including Chapter 7, "Adding and Using Hyperlinks," and Chapter 8, "Sharing and Publishing Diagrams: Part 1."
   - The center of the page includes two command buttons. You will learn more about the Remove Personal Information button in Chapter 8. You can click the Reduce File Size button if document size is a major consideration.

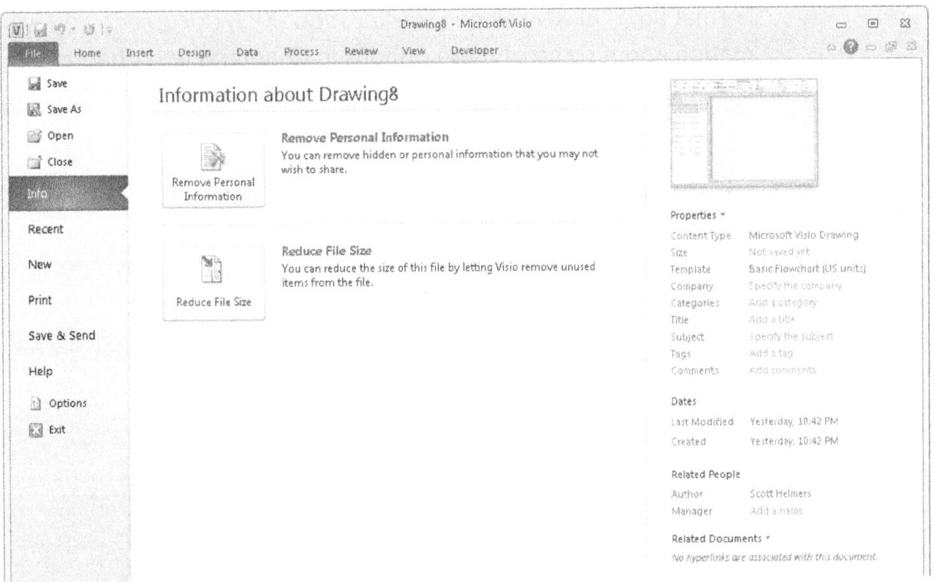

The buttons above the word *Info* on the left navigation bar provide basic file management functions that are the same in Visio as in any other Office application.

3. In the Backstage view, click **Recent**.

   Visio displays a list of the most recent files you've opened along with the preview graphic for each file. Clicking a file name opens that file in Visio. Right-clicking a file name offers several options for managing entries in the most recently used file list.

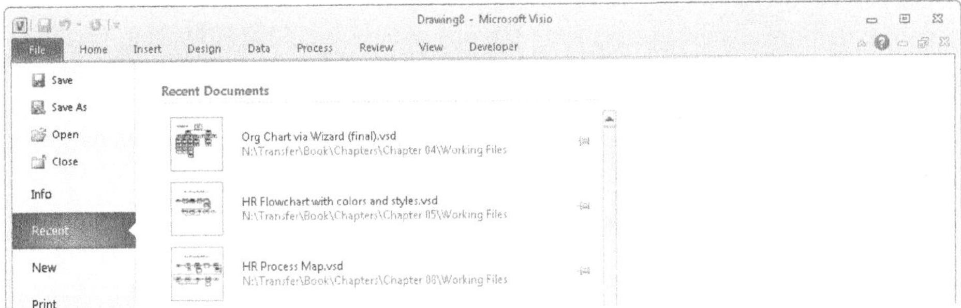

4. Click **New** to open the template selection page for your edition of Visio, as shown in the "Getting Started" section earlier in this chapter.

5. Click **Print** to obtain print preview and printing options. You will learn about print options in Chapter 8.

6. Click **Save & Send** to package a Visio drawing in various formats and send it via email, to save it to a Microsoft SharePoint server, or to create a Portable Document

Format (PDF) or XML Paper Specification (XPS) document. You will find more information about some of these options in Chapter 8 and Chapter 12.

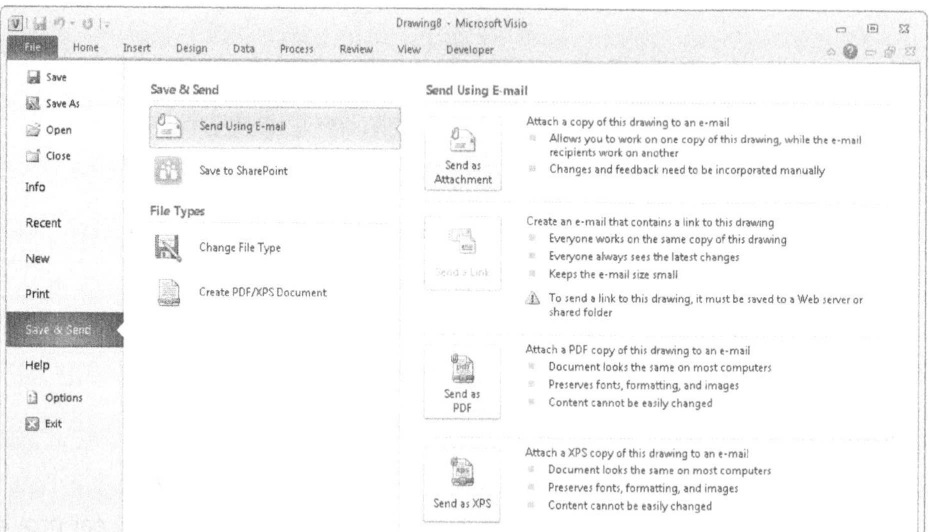

7. Click **Help** to view various ways to get assistance with Visio and to check for program updates. The right side of the Help page displays information about your copy of Visio, including which edition you are running.

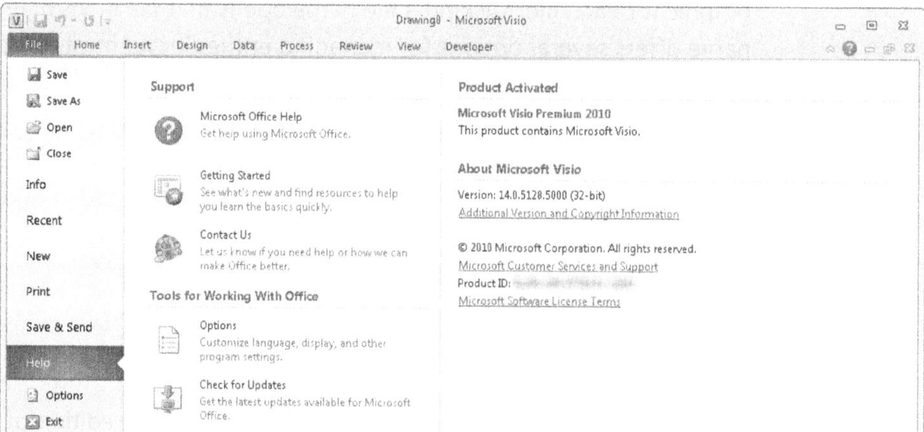

8. Click **Options**.

   The Visio Options dialog box contains dozens of settings you can use to customize the operation of Visio. Many people use Visio 2010 without ever needing to change any of these options, but it's a good idea to examine the option categories for potential future use.

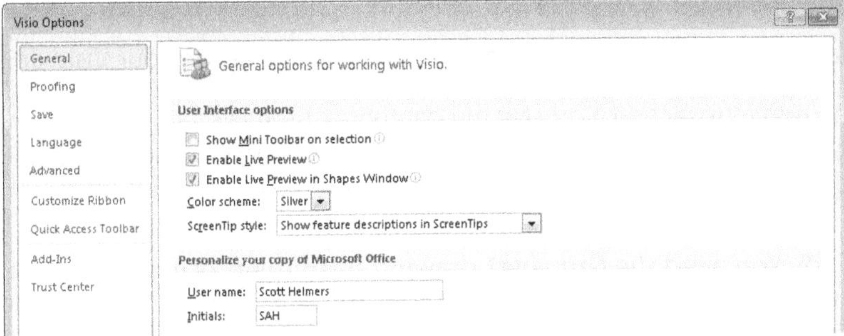

- **General** Enter your user name and initials as well as set various global options, including Live Preview and the Visio window color scheme.
- **Proofing** Set autocorrect, spelling, and grammar options.
- **Save** Set the default Visio save format (Visio 2007/2010; XML; Visio 2002) and the document management check out/check in options.
- **Language** Set editing, display, help, and ScreenTip language parameters.
- **Advanced** Set dozens of options in five categories: Editing, Display, Save/Open, Shape Search, and General.
- **Customize Ribbon** Add/rearrange commands on built-in ribbon tabs; create new tabs and commands.
- **Quick Access Toolbar** Add/remove command buttons on the ***Quick Access Toolbar***.
- **Add-ins** View and add/delete Visio add-ins.
- **Trust Center** View and edit macro settings and other trust-related options.

9. Click the **Home** tab to return to the Visio drawing.

CLEAN UP Leave the *Drawing1* drawing open if you are continuing with the next exercise.

Using the Visio Ribbon

The Visio ribbon consists of multiple tabs, each of which contains a set of related functions. The function buttons on any one tab are organized into named groups. Consequently, the instructions in the book that guide you to a specific function will include three parts, for example:

*On the **Home** tab, in the **Tools** group, click the **Pointer Tool** button.*

The specific tabs you see will depend on the edition of Visio you are using. In addition, certain buttons will be enabled or disabled depending on your Visio edition.

In the previous section, you saw the contents of the File tab, also known as the Backstage view. In this exercise, you will explore the remaining tabs. (Edition differences are described in the text.)

SET UP You need the *Drawing1* drawing from the preceding exercise. If it is not open, create a new drawing: on the File tab, click New; in the Template Categories section, click Flowchart, and then double-click the Basic Flowchart thumbnail.

1. Click the **Home** tab if it is not already selected.

   The Home tab is what it sounds like: a place where you will spend a considerable amount of time. The Home tab contains the largest number of buttons by far, because the Visio team at Microsoft tried to fit as many of the most frequently used functions as possible onto this tab. You'll find sets of related buttons organized into groups called Clipboard, Font, Paragraph, Tools, Shape, Arrange, and Editing.

   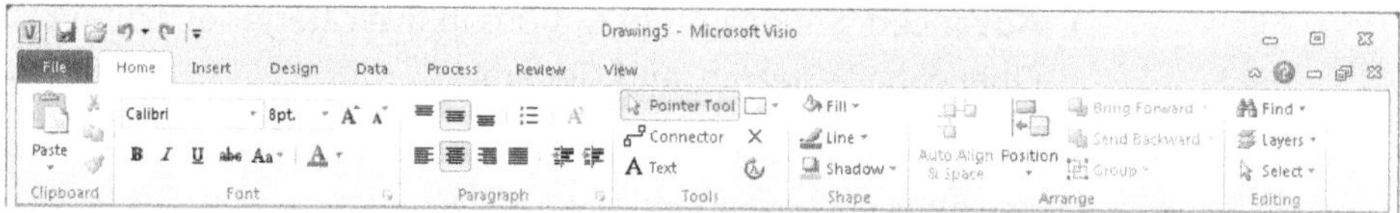

   You will use buttons on this tab in most of the exercises in this book.

   Tip Many of the groups on the Visio tabs include a small arrow in the lower-right corner of the group (refer to the Font and Paragraph groups above). The arrow button, known as the *dialog box launcher*, opens a dialog box that provides detailed control over multiple functions related to that group. In many cases, the dialog box that opens will look familiar to experienced Visio users because it is the same one that was used in previous Visio versions.

2. Click the **Insert** tab to access the **Pages**, **Illustrations**, **Diagram Parts**, **Links**, and **Text** groups. Many of the functions available on this tab mirror the items on the Insert menu in previous versions of Visio.

   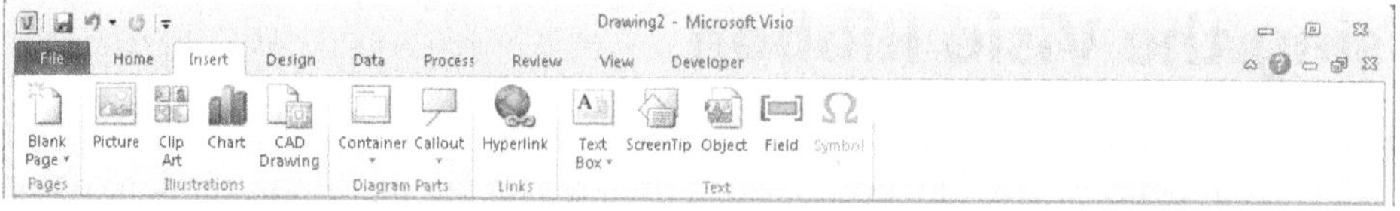

   You will use buttons on this tab in multiple chapters including Chapter 3, "Adding Sophistication to Your Drawings," and Chapter 11, "Adding Structure to Your Diagrams."

3. Click the **Design** tab to change **Page Setup**, select **Themes**, create or edit page **Backgrounds**, and change page **Layout**.

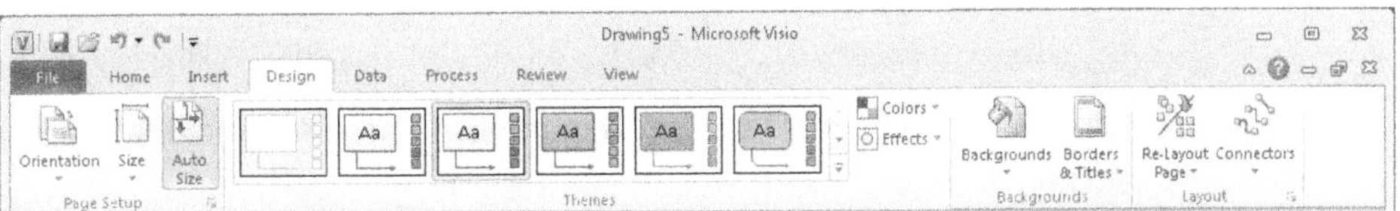

You will use buttons on this tab in various exercises, including those in Chapter 3 and Chapter 5, "Adding Style, Color, and Themes."

4. Click the **Data** tab.

Important This tab is only available in the Professional and Premium editions.

On the Data tab, you can establish and maintain links to External Data, Display Data using ***data graphics***, and Show/Hide both the Shape Data and External Data windows.

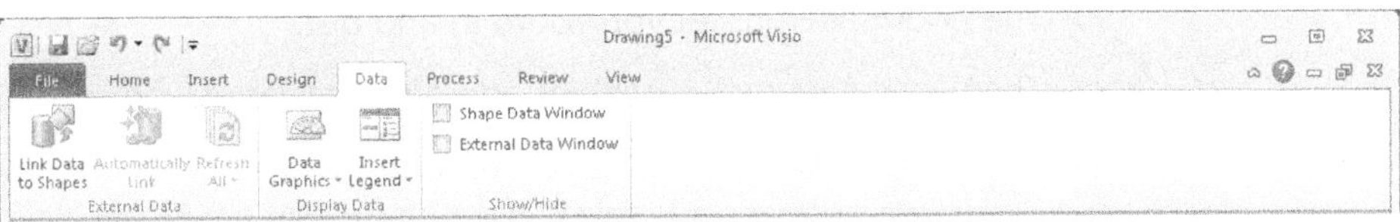

You will use buttons on this tab primarily in Chapter 6 and Chapter 10, "Visualizing Your Data."

5. Click the **Process** tab.

Important This tab is only available in the Premium edition.

In the Subprocess group, you can create a new ***subprocess*** or link to an existing one. In the Diagram Validation group, you can validate a drawing against a set of business rules and manage validation issues. You can also import or export a SharePoint Workflow from this tab.

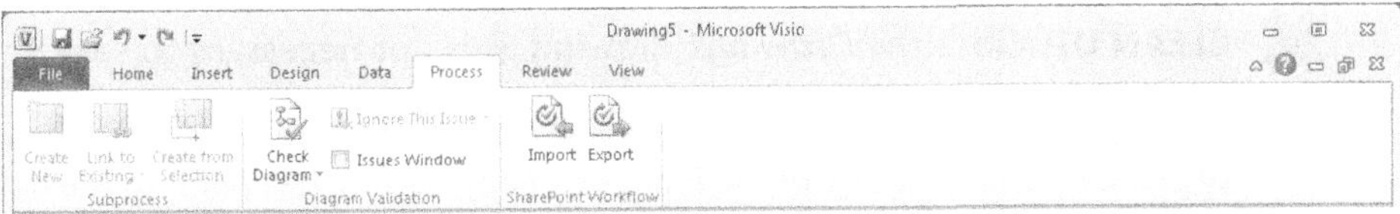

You will use buttons on this tab in Chapter 12 and Chapter 13, "Sharing and Publishing Diagrams: Part 2."

6. Click the **Review** tab for access to functions for **Proofing**, **Language**, **Comments**, **Markup**, and **Reports**.

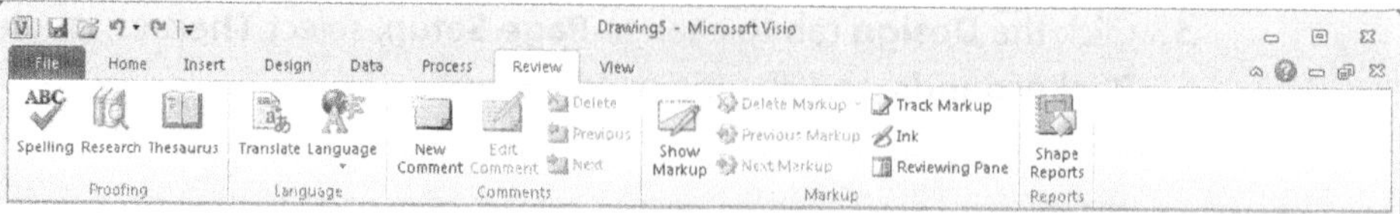

You will use buttons on this tab in various exercises, including those in Chapters 3 and 6.

7. Click the **View** tab.

   As the name suggests, most of the buttons on this tab affect what you see on the screen:

   - The lone button in the Views group sets Visio into full-screen display mode.

     Keyboard Shortcut **Press F5 to enter or exit full-screen view mode.**

   - The Show group controls which drawing window aids and task panes are visible.
   - The Zoom buttons let you zoom in and out.
   - The Visual Aids group enables and disables various on-screen drawings aids.
   - The Window buttons allow you to arrange or select among multiple windows when you have more than one drawing open.
   - The Macros group provides access to the Visio macro programming window and to a list of pre-programmed add-ons that enhance capabilities in Visio.

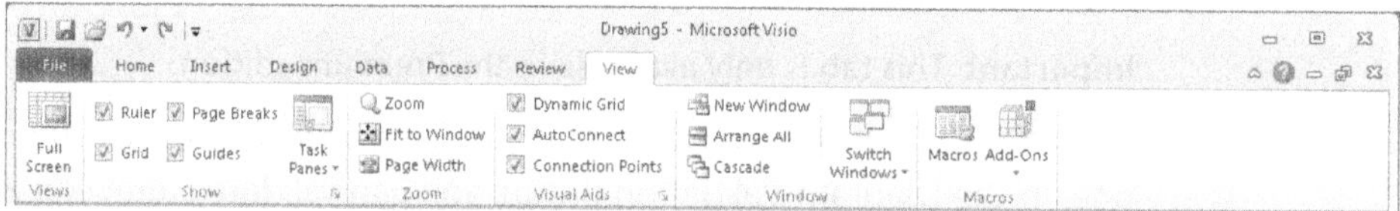

You will use buttons on this tab in exercises later in this chapter and throughout the rest of the book.

CLEAN UP **Close the *Drawing1* drawing. It is not necessary to save your changes.**

Tip **The buttons and controls on all ribbon tabs display pop-up tooltip text when you point to them. If you are unsure of the function of any button, just point to the button to view the tooltip.**

See Also **If you have used previous versions of Visio and would like help shifting from toolbars and menus to the ribbon, Microsoft has created an interactive guide to the ribbon for each product in the Office suite. When you click a toolbar or menu item in the guide, it will display the appropriate ribbon button. Look for the Visio guide at *office.microsoft.com/en-us/visio-help/learn-where-menu-and-toolbar-commands-are-in-office-2010-and-related-products-HA101794130.aspx*.**

Where Are the Keyboard Shortcuts?

If you are accustomed to using keyboard shortcuts, you'll be happy to know that they still exist in Visio 2010. Most shortcuts are the same as in previous versions of Visio, although some were changed to make them consistent with other applications in the Office suite.

To see the keyboard shortcut letters, press the Alt key. The following graphic shows the shortcut letter associated with each tab on the Visio 2010 ribbon. Notice, too, that each button on the Quick Access Toolbar has been assigned a shortcut number based on its position within the Quick Access Toolbar.

Quick Access Toolbar

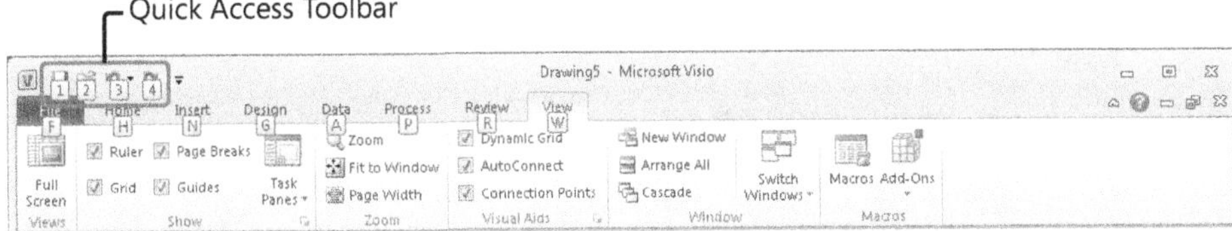

Pressing the letter or number for any displayed shortcut key opens the relevant tab and displays the shortcut keys for that tab. For example, pressing the N key when in the view shown in the previous graphic displays the Insert tab and the shortcut letters shown in the following graphic.

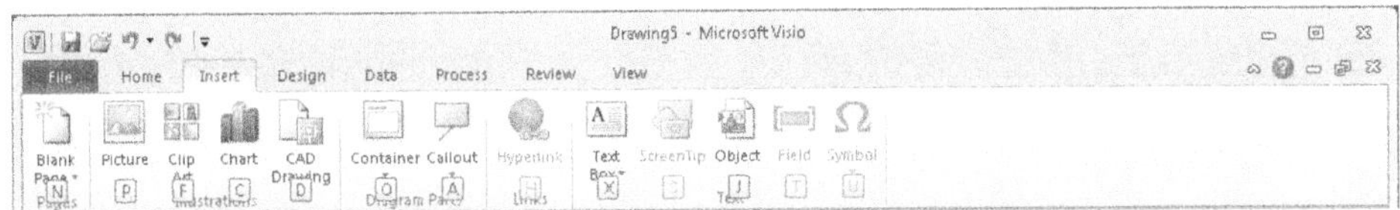

Tip **Previous versions of Visio used the capital letter *I* as the shortcut key for the Insert menu. Visio 2010 uses the keyboard shortcut *N* to be consistent with other Office applications.**

Resizing the Ribbon

The Office ribbon is a dynamic user interface element; its appearance changes if the width of the window in which it is being viewed changes. For example, if you are viewing the Visio Home tab in a window with a size of 1024 x 768 pixels, it will look like the following graphic.

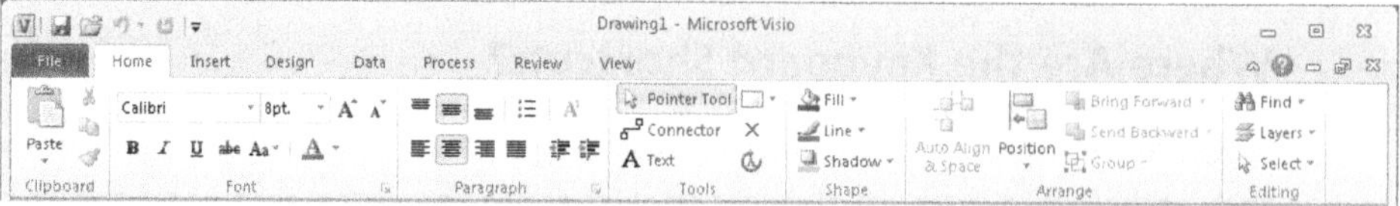

In a window that is only 800 pixels wide, various buttons and groups collapse. Notice the rearrangement of buttons in the Font and Paragraph groups, for example. Also, the captions of the rightmost buttons in the Arrange group have been hidden and the Editing group has been collapsed to a single button.

Collapsed buttons and groups retain all of their functions, as you can see from the submenu that appears when you click the Editing button.

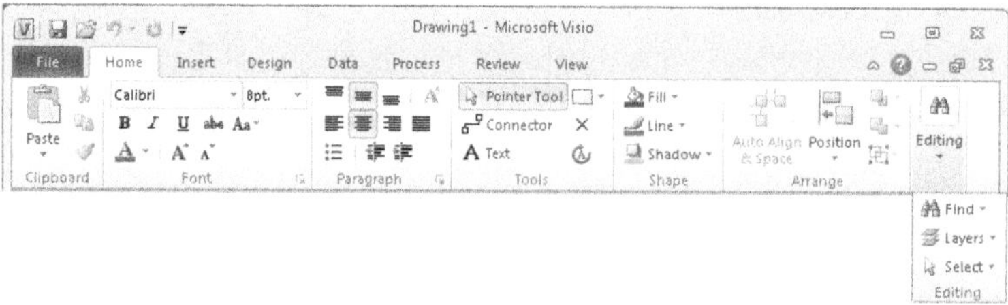

Although you would never try to run Visio in this narrow a window, the following graphic shows the ultimate collapsed form of the Home tab. However, notice that once again each collapsed group displays all of its functions on a drop-down menu, as illustrated by the Font group.

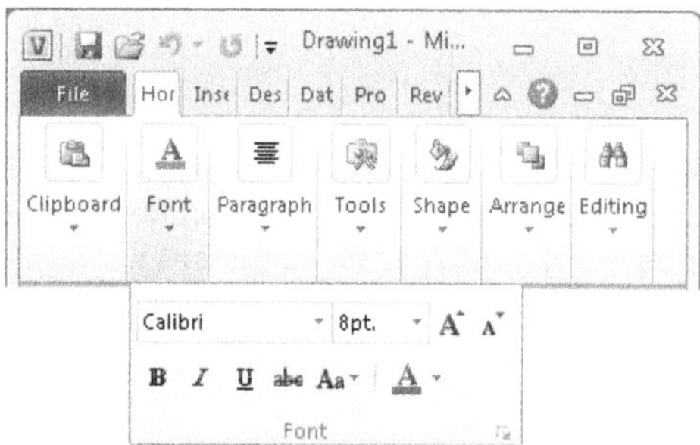

Minimizing the Ribbon

Because the ribbon takes a reasonable amount of space at the top of the Visio window, you may want to minimize it at certain times. The key to doing so is a very small up arrow located in the upper-right corner of the Visio window, just to the left of the Visio Help button.

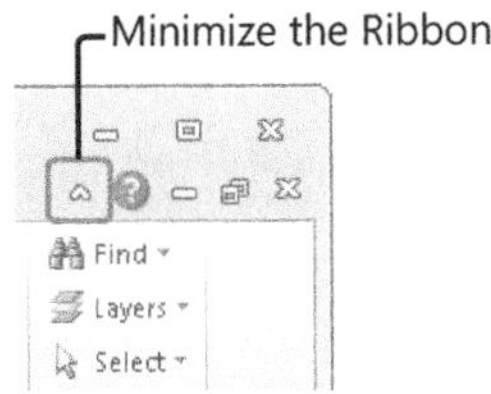

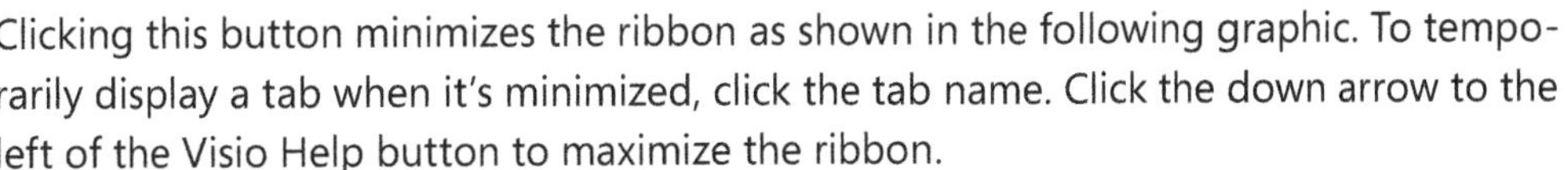

Clicking this button minimizes the ribbon as shown in the following graphic. To temporarily display a tab when it's minimized, click the tab name. Click the down arrow to the left of the Visio Help button to maximize the ribbon.

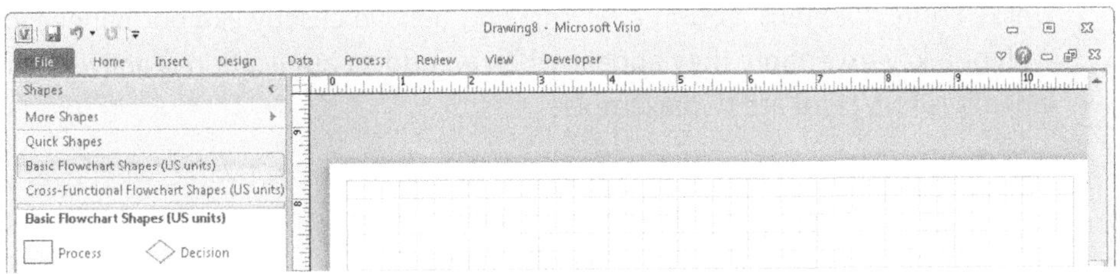

Understanding Contextual Tabs

All of the ribbon tabs shown in the preceding sections are visible 100 percent of the time as you run Visio. However, there are two types of tabs that only appear when necessary.

Contextual tab sets contain infrequently used functions and only appear when the use of those functions is possible. Contextual tab sets usually appear to the right of the View tab and are not activated automatically, that is, you must click the tab to view its contents. A contextual tab set includes a colored header and may contain one or more tabs under the header. Here are examples of two contextual tab sets:

- **Picture Tools** This contextual tab set appears whenever you insert or select a graphic on a Visio drawing page. The green Picture Tools header contains a Format tab, which includes buttons to crop, rotate, and otherwise modify a picture.

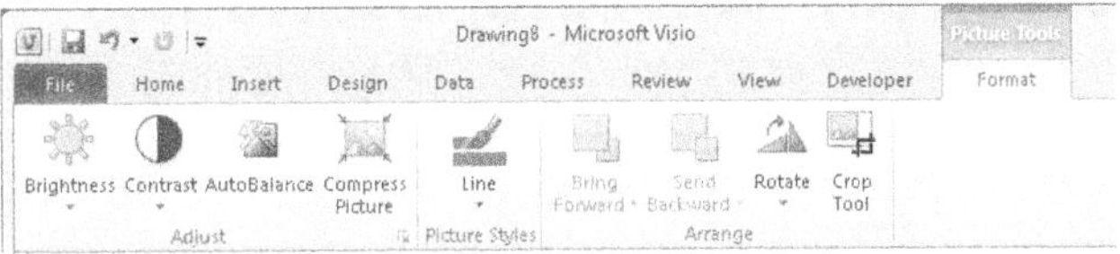

- **Container Tools** This contextual tab set appears whenever you insert or select a Visio ***container***. The orange Container Tools header contains a Format tab, which includes buttons to size and style containers, and to control container membership. You will learn about containers in Chapter 11.

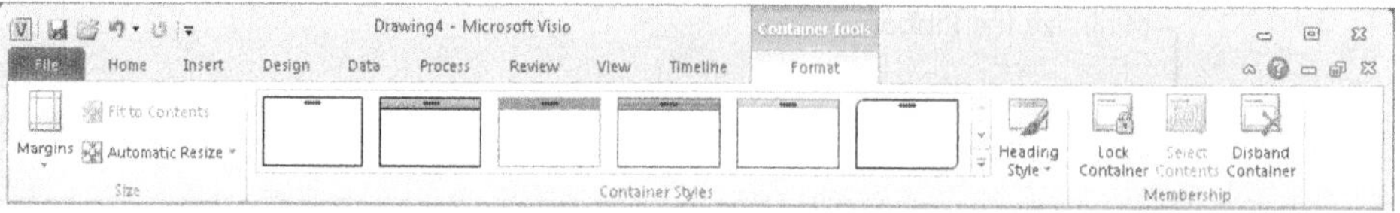

Understanding Add-in Tabs

Add-in tabs are associated with software that adds capabilities to Visio. Some add-ins are packaged with Visio by Microsoft; others are sold by third-party software vendors.

Unlike contextual tabs, add-in tabs look and behave exactly like permanent Visio tabs with one key exception: they appear when an add-in application is active and disappear when it is not. Here are two examples:

- **Org Chart** This add-in is included with Visio and is activated whenever you create or edit a drawing that uses either of the Visio organization chart templates. You will learn about organization charts in Chapter 4.

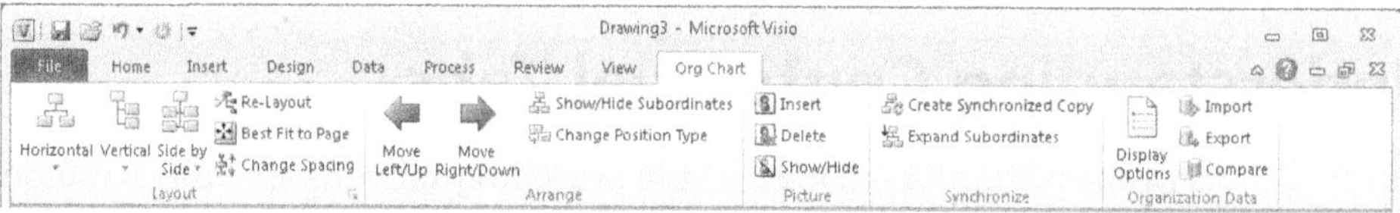

- **TaskMap** This third-party add-in provides easy-to-use process mapping, analysis, and improvement functions that can be used with any edition of Visio.

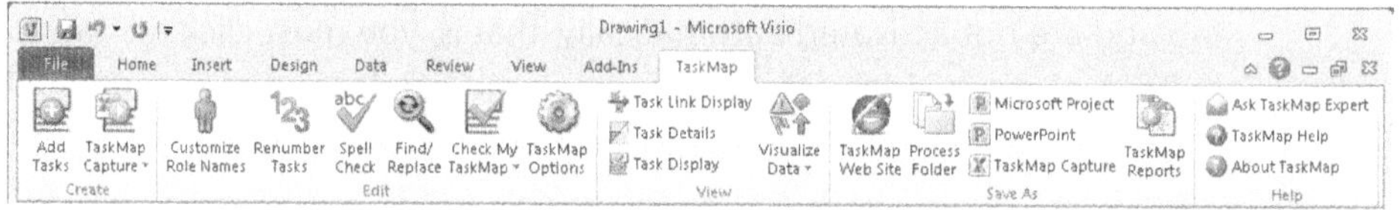

See Also **For more information about the TaskMap add-in, go to *www.taskmap.com*.**

Understanding Shapes, Masters, Stencils, and Templates

Before you explore the rest of Visio, it's helpful to understand a number of commonly used terms:

- ***Master*** An object in a Visio stencil. The vast majority of people who create diagrams with Visio use the masters that ship with Visio or that they download from the Internet. You can create new masters; however, the techniques for doing so are outside the scope of this book.

- ***Stencil*** A collection of masters.
- ***Shape*** An object on a Visio drawing page. Often you create shapes by dragging a master from a stencil to the drawing page; however, you can also create shapes in other ways. (You will learn more about shapes in Chapter 2, "Creating a New Diagram," and throughout this book.)

  A shape can be very simple: a line, a polygon, an image. A shape can also be a sophisticated object that changes appearance or behavior as data values change, as its position on the page changes, or as properties of another shape change—the possibilities are endless.
- ***Template*** A Visio document that includes one or more drawing pages with preset dimensions and measurement units. A template may also include one or more stencils; it may include background pages and designs; its pages may contain shapes or text. A template may also include special software that only operates in that template.
- ***Workspace*** A collection of Visio windows and window settings. At minimum, the workspace consists of the drawing window and the zoom settings for the pages in the drawing; frequently, it also includes a Shapes window containing one or more stencils. Unless you have changed the default action, Visio saves the workspace you see on the screen in any open document whenever you save the document. As a result, when you next open the same document, the workspace is restored.

Tip Despite the distinction made in this list between a master and a shape, you will find that many people refer to an object in a stencil as a shape. Indeed, when you think about it, the window that displays stencils is called the *Shapes* window! Consequently, unless the distinction is important in a specific context, the text in this book will refer to *shapes* in a stencil.

Exploring the Drawing Window

The primary Visio window in which you will work is called the drawing window because it contains the ***drawing page***. At various times, you may have additional, smaller windows open to assist in performing specific tasks.

In this exercise, you will examine the components of the drawing window. In subsequent exercises in this and other chapters, you will open and explore several subwindows.

SET UP Start Visio, or if it's already running, click the File tab, and then click New.

1. On the **New** page of the Backstage view, in the **Template Categories** section, click **Flowchart**, and then double-click the **Basic Flowchart** thumbnail to create a new drawing.

Below the ribbon are two windows:

- The ***Shapes window*** on the left contains one or more stencils, each represented by a gray header bar containing the name of the stencil. If there are many open stencils in the Shapes window, you might see a scroll bar at the right of the headers. You will investigate the Shapes window in the next section of this chapter.

  Tip The Shapes window on your system may be wider or narrower than the one that appears in the following graphic.

- The larger window on the right is the ***drawing window***. It displays all or part of the current drawing page. The drawing window is bounded on the top and left by rulers that display inches, millimeters, or whatever units you have selected (or your template has selected) for measuring page dimensions.

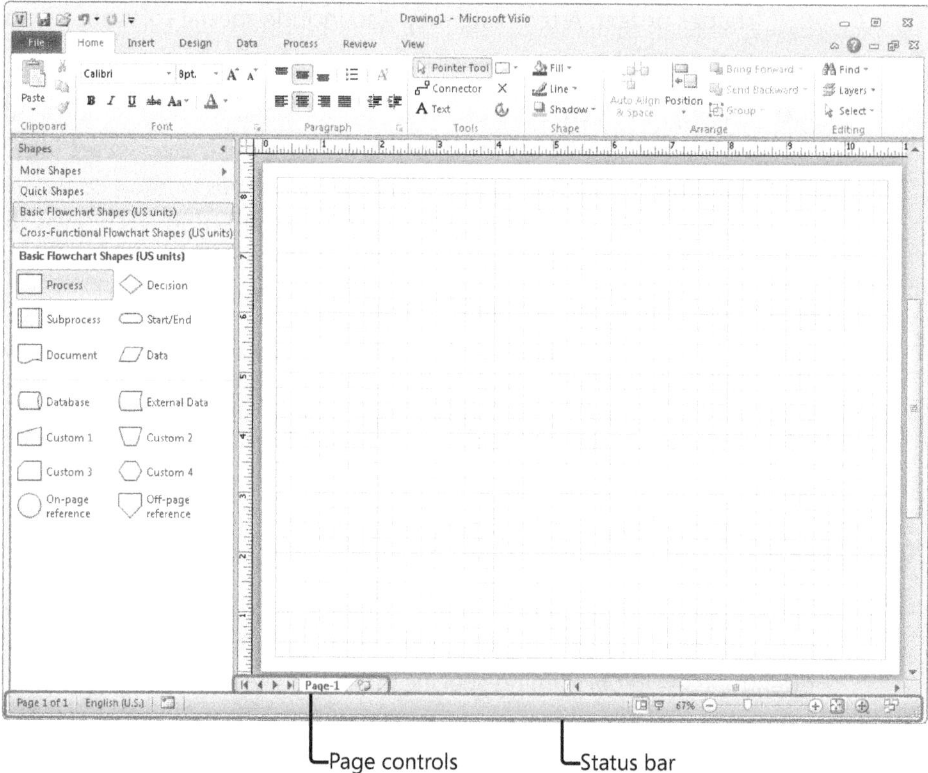

At the lower left of the drawing window is a set of ***page controls***.

- **A** Click these arrows to move between pages when the document contains more than one page. The first and last arrow move you to the first or last page of the document.
- **B** The ***page name tab*** displays the name of each page; in this case, Page-1 is the only page. Right-click the page name tab to access page management functions.
- **C** Click the Insert Page button to add a new page.

Below the Shapes and drawing windows is a ***status bar*** that contains a variety of indicators, buttons, and controls. The buttons and indicators on the left end of the status bar are context sensitive, so they will show different information depending on the state of the drawing.

If nothing is selected on the drawing page, the left end of the status bar looks like the following graphic.

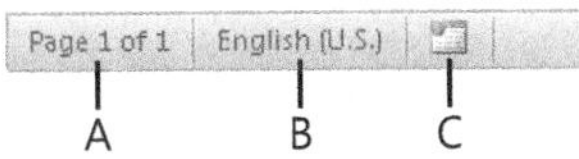

- **A** The Page Number button shows which page is active and displays the total number of pages in the current drawing; click this button to open the Page dialog box.
- **B** The Language area displays the language of the current drawing; the drawing language is normally derived from Windows or Visio language settings.
- **C** Click the Macros button to start the macro recorder.

If you have selected a shape on the drawing page, the left end of the status bar looks like the following graphic instead.

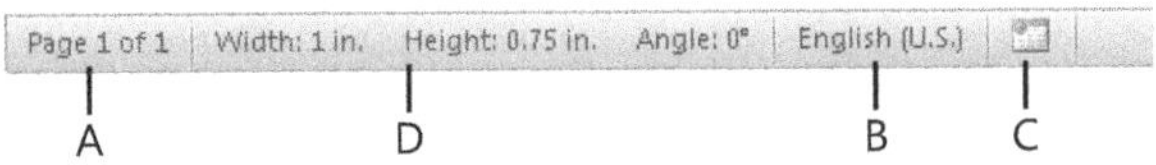

- **A** Same as previous A.
- **B** Same as previous B.
- **C** Same as previous C.
- **D** This area contains three buttons. The Width and Height buttons display the dimensions of the selected shape and the Angle button displays its angle of rotation; click any of the three buttons to open the Size & Position window.

The right end of the status bar contains a variety of useful buttons and controls.

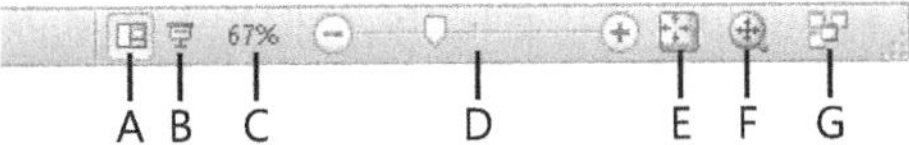

- A This button has no function in Visio 2010 (similar buttons in other Microsoft Office applications switch to specific screen views).
- B Click the Full Screen button to display the drawing page in full-screen view.
- C The Zoom Level button displays the current zoom percentage; click it to open the Zoom dialog box.
- D Move the Zoom slider to zoom in or out.
- E Click the Fit Page To Current Window button to resize the drawing page so the entire page is visible in the drawing window.
- F Click the Pan & Zoom Window button to open the Pan & Zoom window.
- G Click the Switch Windows button to switch to another Visio window.

Tip Most other Office applications require use of a button on the View tab of the ribbon to switch among multiple open windows. The Visio development team had the foresight to include the Switch Windows button (G) on the status bar where it is much more convenient.

2. Right-click anywhere in the status bar to view the **Customize Status Bar** menu.

   You can click any of the options in the Customize Status Bar menu to toggle the display of a button or control.

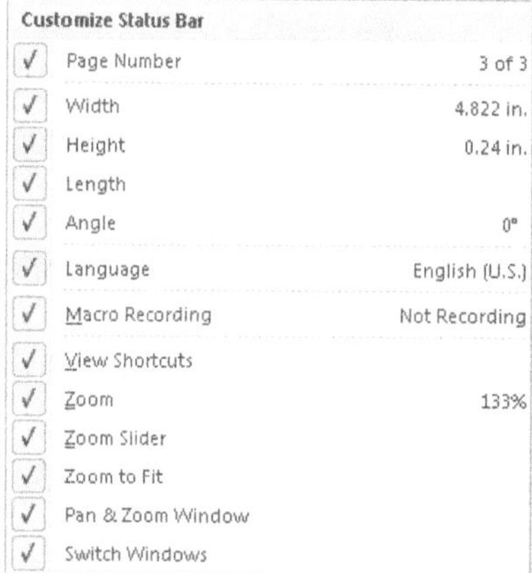

CLEAN UP Save your drawing as *Exploring Visio 2010*. Leave the drawing open if you are continuing with the next exercise.

Managing the Shapes Window

In this exercise, you will learn various ways to manipulate the Shapes window so it appears in the most useful size and position when you are working on a drawing.

SET UP If the *Exploring Visio 2010* drawing is still open from the preceding exercise, continue with this exercise. Otherwise, create a new drawing: on the File tab, click New; in the Template Categories section, click Flowchart, and then double-click the Basic Flowchart thumbnail. Save the new drawing as *Exploring Visio 2010.*

1. Change the width of the **Shapes** window by dragging the window boundary left or right.

   In the following graphic, you can see that the cursor turns to a double-headed arrow as the window border is dragged to a wider or narrower view. The cursor is to the right of the Decision shape.

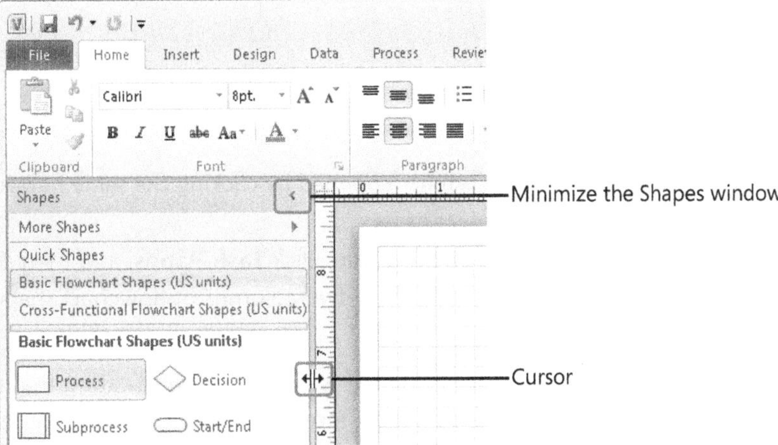

2. Minimize the **Shapes** window by clicking the **Minimize the Shapes window** button shown in the preceding graphic.

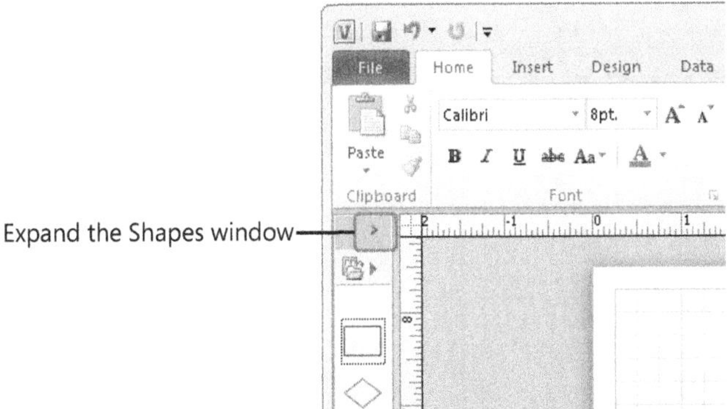

3. Return the **Shapes** window to its former size by clicking the **Expand the Shapes window** arrow highlighted in the preceding graphic.

Task Panes

4. To hide the **Shapes** window entirely, on the **View** tab, in the **Show** group, click the **Task Panes** button, and then click **Shapes**.

   Tip The various subwindows that can be opened or closed within the Visio window are sometimes referred to as *task panes*.

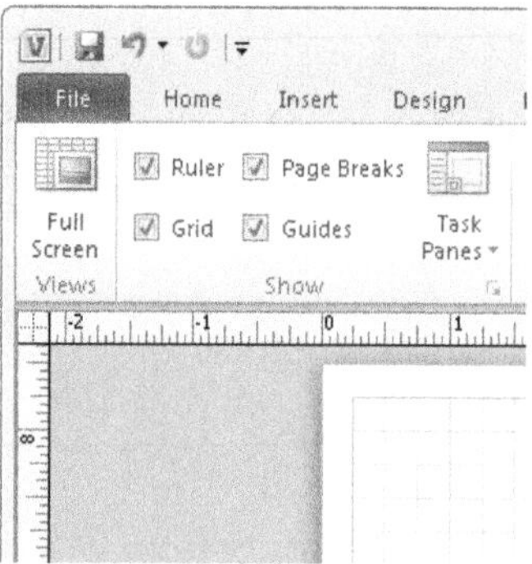

   Tip The Shapes window can be reopened by clicking the same button you used to close it.

5. On the **View** tab, in the **Show** group, click **Task Panes**, and then click **Shapes**. If the window does not already show two columns of flowchart shapes, adjust the width so it does.

   The Basic Flowchart Shapes title bar is highlighted, indicating that this is the active stencil. However, the flowchart template opens a second stencil called *Cross-Functional Flowchart Shapes*.

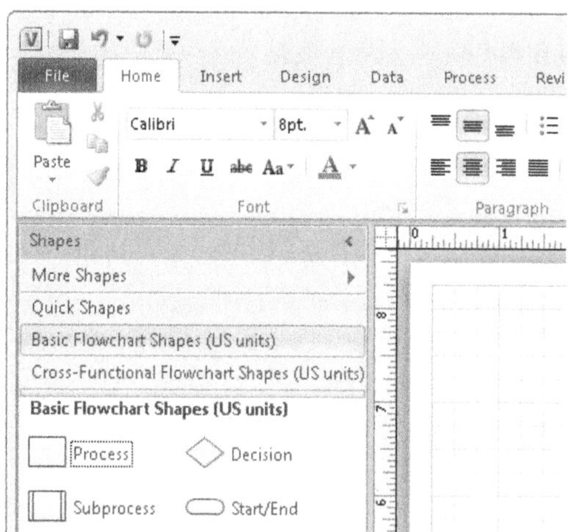

6. In the **Shapes** window, click **Cross-Functional Flowchart Shapes**.

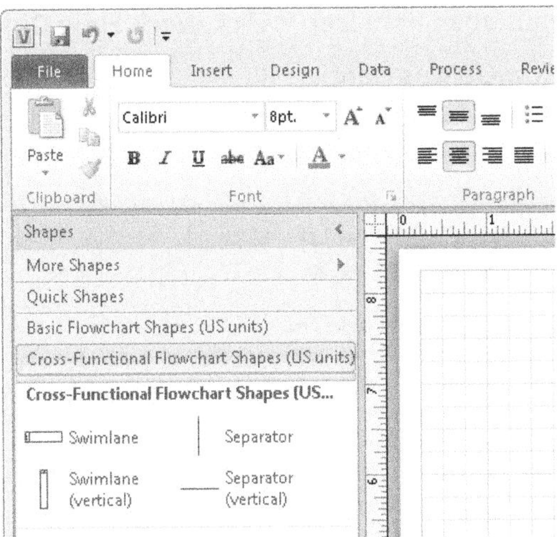

Tip When you click the title bar of any stencil, the title bars remain stationary and the stencil always opens in the same place, below all title bars. This is a significant improvement in behavior over previous versions of Visio.

You are not restricted to using just the stencils that open in a particular template, as you will see in the next step.

7. In the **Shapes** window, click **More Shapes**, and then point to **Flowchart**. (Do not click any stencils in the Flowchart group yet.)

   You now see a set of cascading menus. In the following graphic, you see the collection of stencils in the Flowchart group.

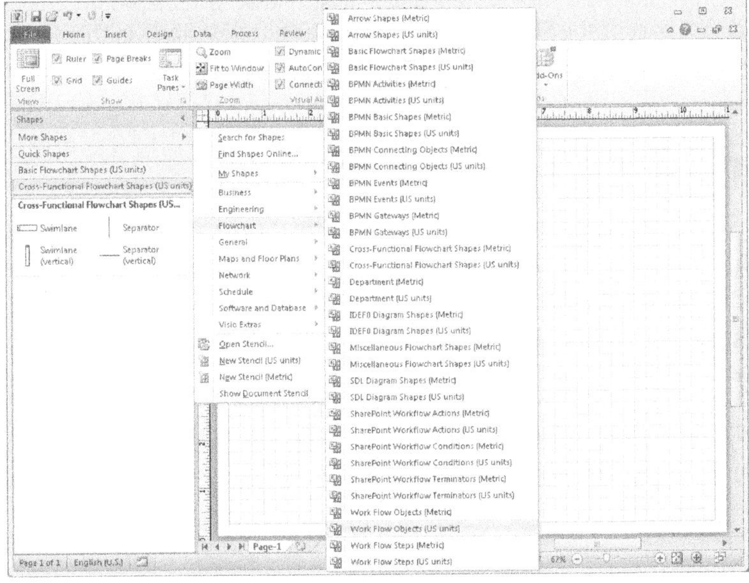

8. With the cascading menus open from Step 7, click **Work Flow Objects**.

   Visio opens the Work Flow Objects stencil.

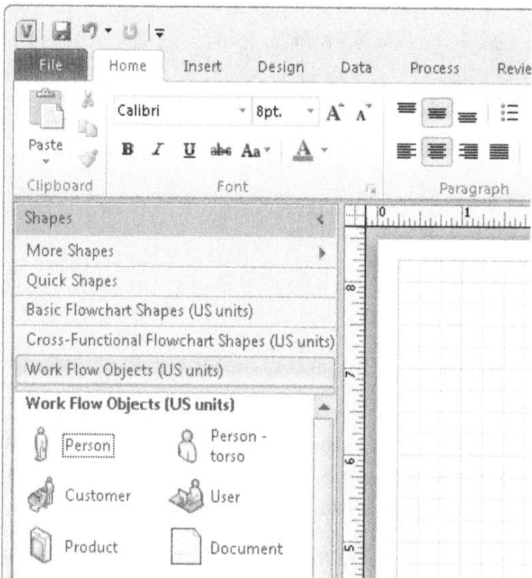

9. Right-click **Work Flow Objects**, and then click **Close**.

   Tip You can close any stencil by right-clicking its title bar and clicking Close.

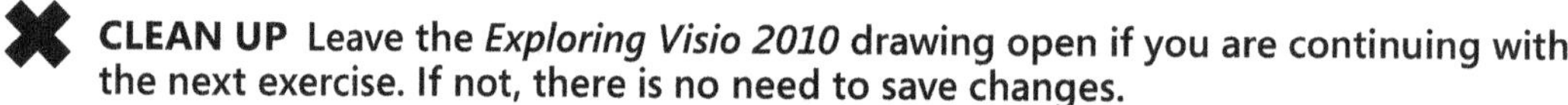

CLEAN UP Leave the *Exploring Visio 2010* drawing open if you are continuing with the next exercise. If not, there is no need to save changes.

Tip The Quick Shapes stencil, visible above Basic Flowchart Shapes in the previous graphics, is an important part of the Shapes window that was not described in this section. You will learn about Quick Shapes in Chapter 2.

Panning and Zooming in Visio

As you work with more detailed Visio diagrams, you will find that you frequently need to ***zoom*** in and out and ***pan***—move left-right and up-down—within the drawing window. Both can be accomplished using a variety of techniques, some of which rely on your mouse, some that use a special Pan & Zoom window, and others that use keyboard shortcuts.

In this exercise, you will learn several techniques to pan and zoom your diagram, beginning with keyboard shortcuts and ending with the Pan & Zoom window.

SET UP If the *Exploring Visio 2010* drawing is still open from the preceding exercise, continue with this exercise. Otherwise, create a new drawing: on the File tab, click New; in the Template Categories section, click Flowchart, and then double-click the Basic Flowchart thumbnail. Save the new drawing as *Exploring Visio 2010.*

1. Click **Basic Flowchart Shapes** if it is not already the active stencil, and then drag a **Process** shape onto the drawing page.
2. Drag a **Decision** shape onto a different part of the page.
3. Drag a **Document** shape onto yet another part of the page.
4. Drag any other shape of your choice onto the page. Space the shapes so they occupy at least half of the drawing page.

   Your diagram might look something like the following graphic.

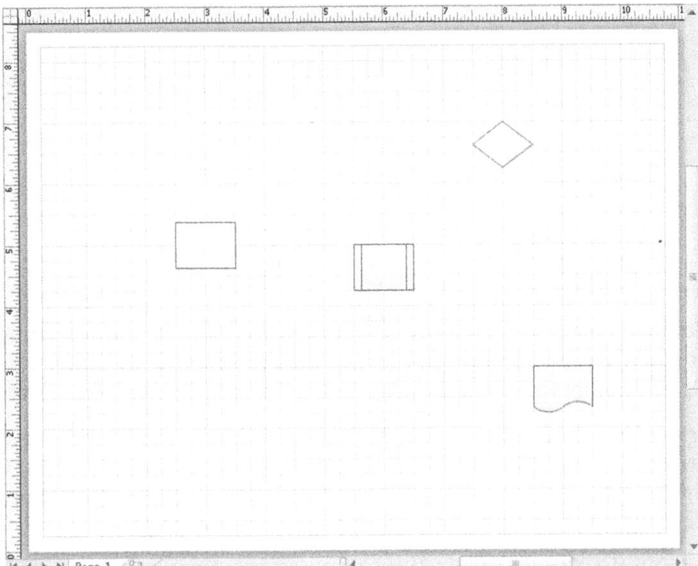

5. Hold down the Ctrl+Shift keys (the cursor will change to a magnifying glass with a plus sign), and then drag a rectangle around two of the shapes on the drawing page.

   Important You must press Ctrl+Shift *before* you click for this zoom technique to work.

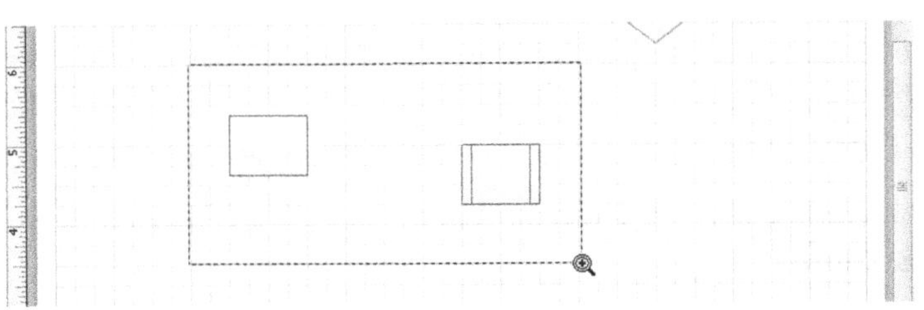

6. Release the mouse button and the keys.

   Visio sets the view in the drawing window to just the rectangle you outlined with the mouse.

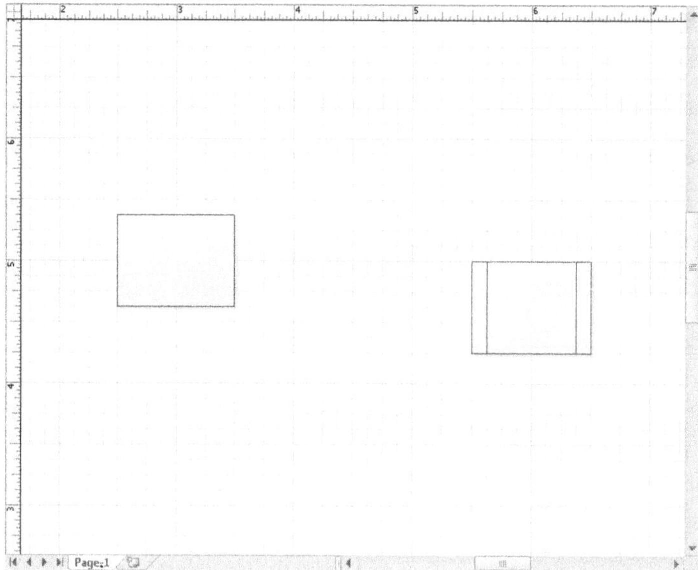

7. Press Ctrl+Shift+W to return to a view of the whole drawing page.

   Tip Ctrl+Shift+W is an incredibly useful keyboard shortcut to remember because you will frequently zoom in to part of a drawing and then want to return to full page view. To help remember this shortcut, just remember that *W* is the first letter of *whole page*.

   Important In previous versions of Visio, the keyboard shortcut to view the whole page was Ctrl+W. It may take a bit of retraining to get accustomed to using Ctrl+Shift+W instead. To make matters worse, in Visio 2010, Ctrl+W closes the active document (you will receive a warning if the document has unsaved changes).

8. Hold down the Ctrl key and rotate the mouse wheel.

   Important You can only perform this step if your mouse has a wheel.

   Visio zooms in or out as you rotate the mouse wheel.

   Tip Sometimes you may want to zoom in on a specific shape. Visio provides an option setting that makes this very easy to do. On the File tab, click Options, and then click Advanced. In the Editing Options section of the Visio Options dialog box, click Center Selection On Zoom. Now when you select a shape and press the Ctrl key while rotating the mouse wheel, Visio automatically zooms in and out on the selected shape.

9. Press Ctrl+Shift+W to return to a view of the whole drawing page.

Task Panes

10. On the **View** tab, in the **Show** group, click the **Task Panes** button, and then click **Pan & Zoom**.

The Pan & Zoom window opens. You can drag it to position it wherever you'd like.

Tip **You can also open the Pan & Zoom window by clicking the Pan & Zoom button on the right end of the status bar. (Refer to "Exploring the Drawing Window" earlier in this chapter for information about the Visio status bar.)**

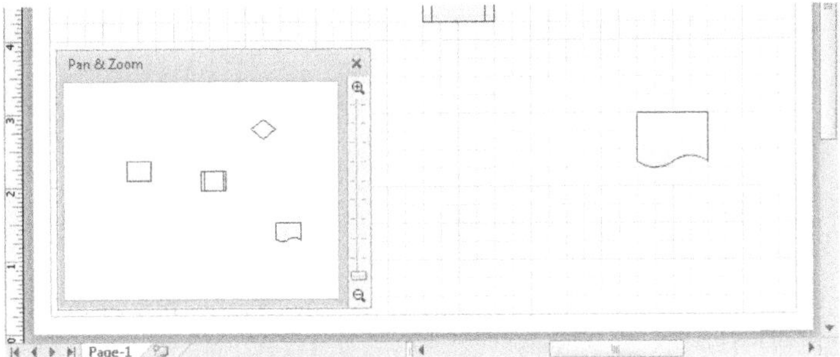

11. Click in the **Pan & Zoom** window, and then drag the cursor to create a rectangle that surrounds any two of the shapes.

    A red rectangle appears in the Pan & Zoom window and the drawing window shows only the selected portion of the page.

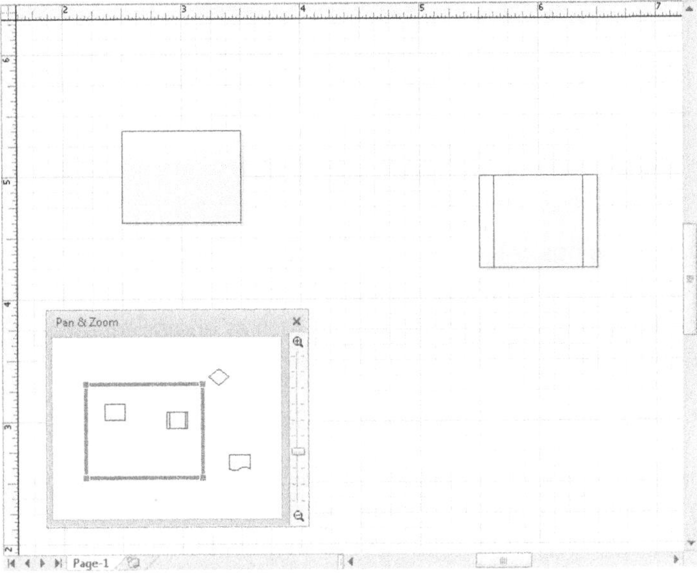

12. In the **Pan & Zoom** window, click in the interior of the red rectangle, and then drag into another part of the miniature drawing page.

    The drawing window now shows the newly selected area of the drawing page.

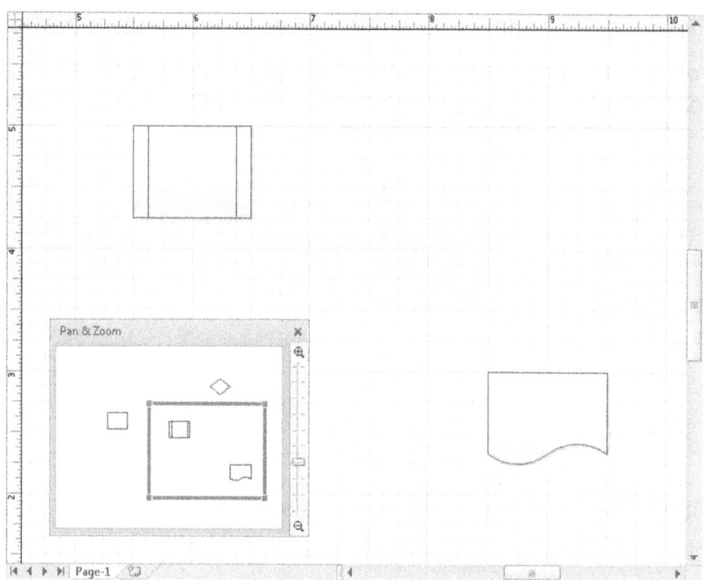

With the Pan & Zoom window open, you can:

- Continue to move the red rectangle to reposition what appears in the drawing window.
- Drag the edges or the corners of the red rectangle to resize it and change the zoom level.
- Drag the slider control on the right edge of the Pan & Zoom window to change the zoom level.

For many drawings, the Pan & Zoom window isn't necessary and may even be in the way. However, it is extremely helpful when your drawing page is very large, as it may be if you are working on diagrams such as engineering drawings, floor plans, or office layouts.

 **CLEAN UP Close the Pan & Zoom window. Save changes and close the drawing.**

Tip If you have a mouse with a wheel button, you can move the drawing page up and down in the drawing window by rotating the mouse wheel. You can reposition the drawing page to the left and right by holding down the Shift key while rotating the mouse wheel.

You can also move the drawing page using the arrow keys on your keyboard. Be sure that no shapes are selected before pressing the arrow keys, however, or you will move the selected shape(s) instead of moving the page.

Resizing and Repositioning Shapes

Visio shapes can be manipulated in a variety of ways using the mouse, the keyboard, or a combination of the two. Visio provides visual feedback about which shape properties you can alter, which is very helpful because seemingly identical shapes may have been designed with very different capabilities.

In this exercise, you will change the characteristics of several shapes by using the mouse, the keyboard, and the Size & Position window.

SET UP You need the *Size & Position_start* drawing located in the Chapter01 practice files folder to complete this exercise. Open the drawing in Visio and save it as *Size & Position*.

1. Click once (don't double-click) to select shape **A**.

The blue squares and circle that appear on a selected shape are referred to as ***selection handles*** or just ***handles***, and allow you to alter the shape in the following ways:

- Dragging the square handles in the center of each edge alter the width or height of the shape.
- Dragging the square handles on the corners adjust the width and height proportionally.

For example, if you drag the middle handle on the right edge to the right, you will increase the width of shape A, as shown in the following graphic on the left. If you drag the upper-right handle away from the shape, you will increase the size of the shape proportionally in both dimensions, as shown in the following graphic on the right.

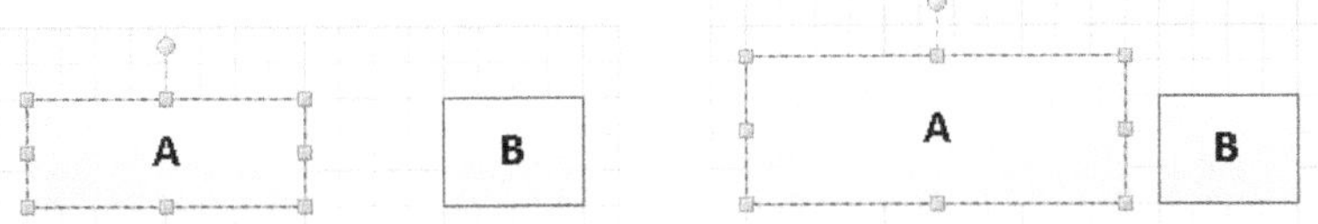

2. Click once (don't double-click) to select shape **B**.

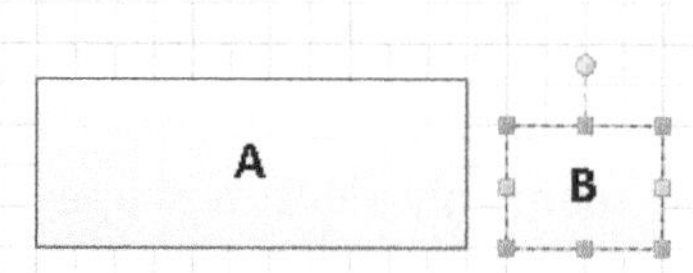

Notice that some of the handles on shape B are gray rather than blue. This indicates that the designer of this shape chose to lock certain attributes of this shape. In the case of shape B, you can drag the width resize handles but the height adjustment has been locked. You can confirm this by trying to drag any of the gray handles.

3. With shape **B** still selected, point to the blue circle above the shape.

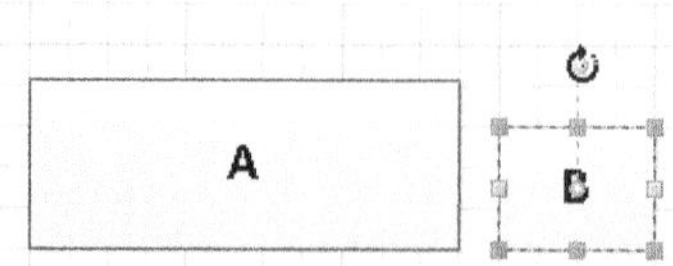

The blue circle is the ***rotation handle***. When you point to it, the cursor changes to a curved arrow and an additional selection handle appears in the center of the shape (it's on top of the letter *B* in the previous graphic). The new handle is the Center Of Rotation handle, commonly referred to in Visio as the ***pin***.

When you rotate a shape, it rotates around the pin. To envision the purpose of the pin, imagine that shape B is a piece of paper you've stuck on your wall with a pin. If you rotate the piece of paper, it will rotate around the pin.

4. Drag the rotation handle clockwise approximately 90 degrees.

5. Click once to select shape **C**.

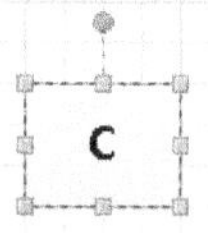

For this shape, the rotation handle is locked, which you can see because the rotation handle is grey.

Shape C also has another locked attribute but one that isn't visible. You'll see evidence of this in the next step.

6. Reposition shape **C** by dragging it up and down; it behaves quite normally. But try dragging it side to side and you'll see that you can't do it.

   Shape C was locked to prevent horizontal motion. A shape designer might lock shapes in this way if they must remain in a specific plane.

7. Click once to select shape **D**, which is a subprocess shape from the Basic Flowchart Shapes stencil.

   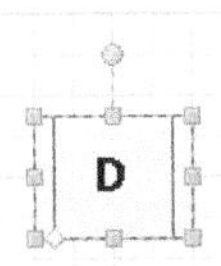

   All of the usual handles are blue, but there is a new style of control handle in the lower left of shape D. The yellow diamond indicates that you can drag that handle to alter a shape property other than the size and orientation of the shape itself.

8. Drag the yellow control handle to the right.

   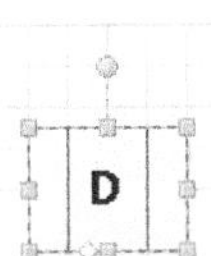

   The control handle moves the interior lines of the subprocess shape. You can drag the control handle back to the left, and the interior lines effectively disappear. They do still exist, as you can see by the continuing presence of the yellow diamond; if you drag the diamond back to the right, the lines will reappear.

   Tip **You will find yellow control handles on a variety of the shapes in Visio stencils. Whenever you select a shape and see a yellow handle, it's worth experimenting with it to see how you can alter the shape's appearance.**

9. Click once to select shape **E**.

Task Panes

10. On the **View** tab, in the **Show** group, click the **Task Panes** button, and then click **Size & Position** to open the **Size & Position** window.

Tip Whenever one or more shapes are selected, you can also open the Size & Position window by clicking Width, Height, or Angle in the status bar at the bottom of the Visio window.

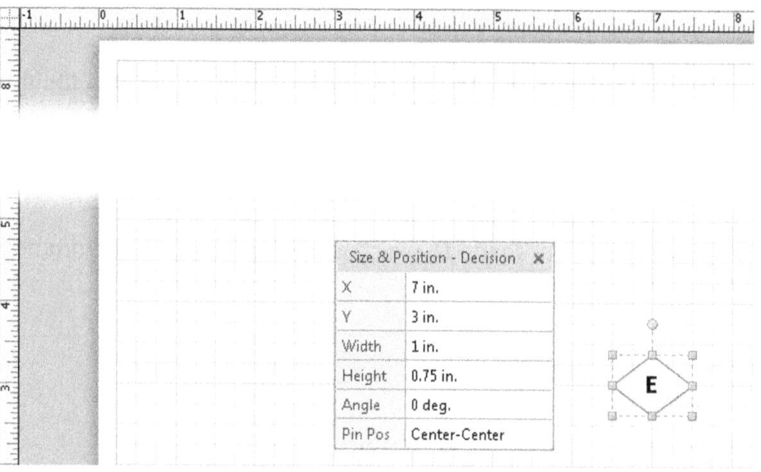

The Size & Position window displays current values for six shape attributes, but it also allows you to change those attributes.

11. Click in the **Width** cell, type **2**, and then press Enter.

    The width of the cell changes to reflect the new value. Notice that you didn't need to type a value for units because Visio uses the units displayed in the cell as the default. By comparing the width of shape E with the ruler shown at the top of the following graphic, you can confirm that the shape is, indeed, 2 inches wide.

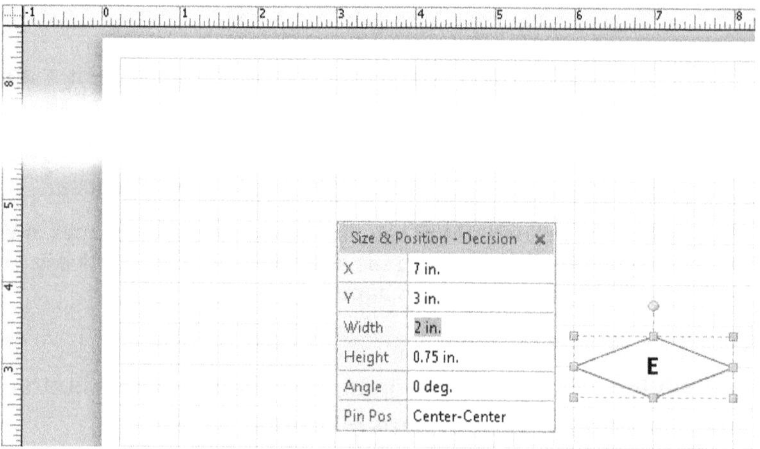

The X and Y cells in the Size & Position window reflect the location of the shape on the page with respect to the lower-left corner of the page. By comparing the values in the X and Y cells above with the rulers at the edge of the drawing page, you can see that the center of shape E is at X=7 inches and Y=3 inches.

12. Click in the **Y** cell, type **4**, and then press Enter.

By changing the Y value from 3 inches to 4 inches, you have moved the shape higher on the page. You can confirm the new position of the shape on the page by looking at the ruler shown on the left side of the following graphic.

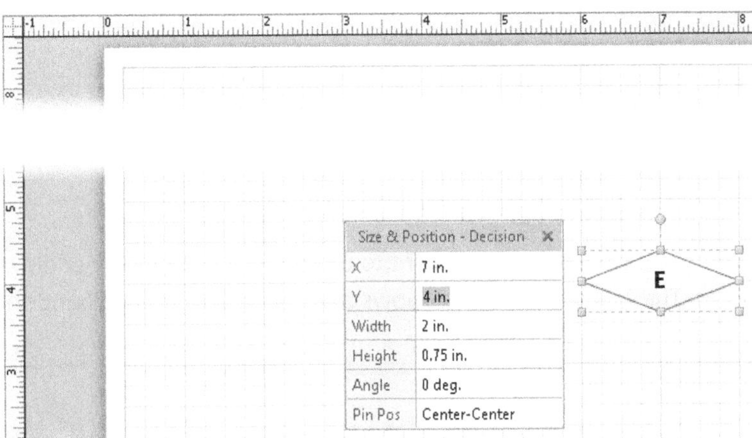

13. Click in the **Pin Pos** cell, click **Center-Left**, and then press Enter.

Changing this setting moves the pin for the selected shape. The following graphic shows the result of changing the pin to Center-Left. Notice two things:

- The rotation handle is now on the left edge of the shape.
- The shape has shifted to the right on the page. This is because the X and Y coordinates of the shape specify the location of the pin for the shape. Because you have moved the pin within the shape, the location of the shape on the page changes.

Tip Using the Pin Pos menu, you can relocate the pin based on a fixed set of pin positions. You can also make freeform changes to the pin location by dragging the Center Of Rotation handle described in Step 3 above.

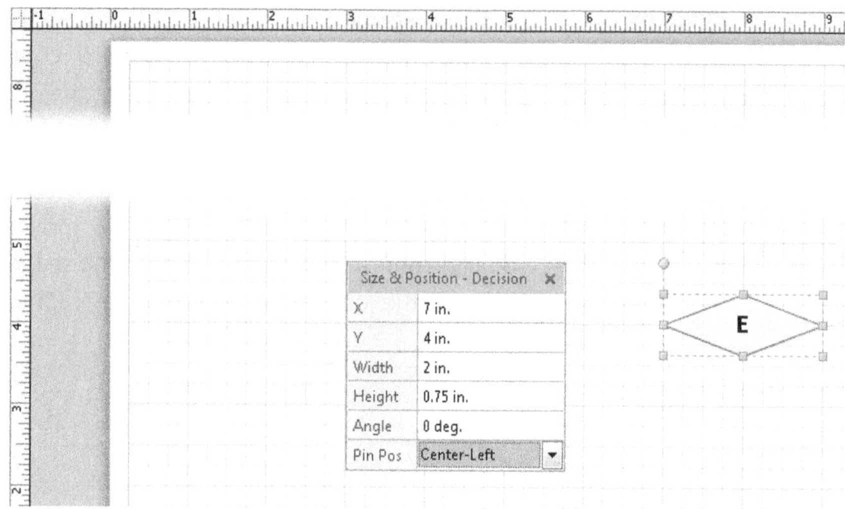

14. Click in the **Angle** cell, type **-90**, and then press Enter.

Typing -90 degrees is equivalent to dragging the rotation handle clockwise 90 degrees. The following graphic shows that shape E rotated around the new pin.

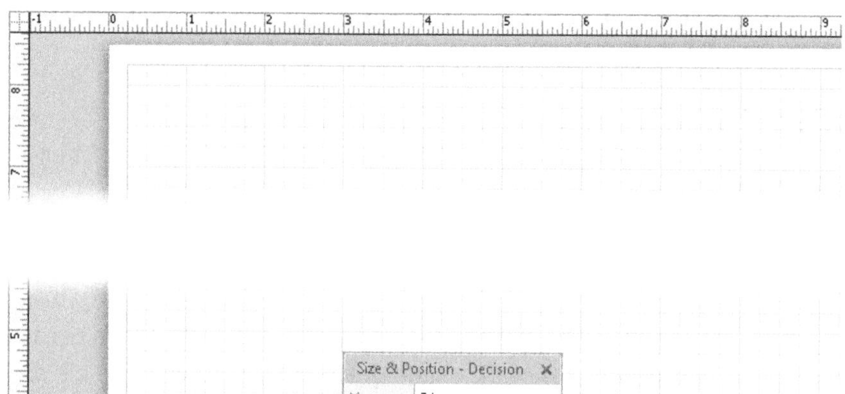

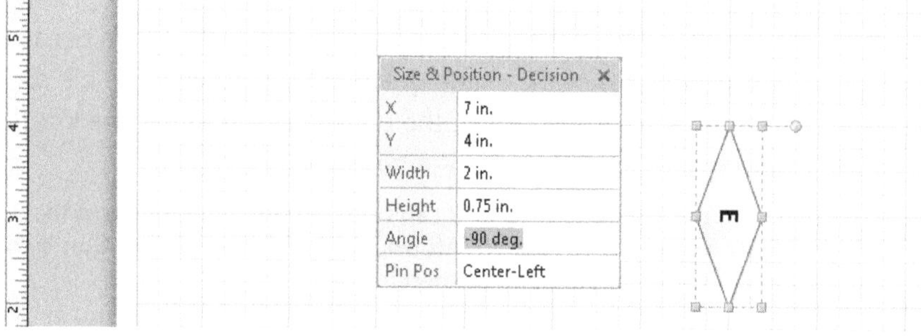

CLEAN UP Close the *Size & Position* drawing. It is not necessary to save changes unless you want to.

Tip If you select more than one shape before dragging a resize handle or making changes in the Size & Position window, the changes you make will affect all selected shapes.

Key Points

- Visio Professional contains templates, stencils, ribbon tabs, and functions that are not included in Visio Standard. A key focus for the additional features in Visio Professional is creating and managing Visio diagrams that are driven by data stored outside of Visio.
- Visio Premium includes features that are not part of either Standard or Professional. A key focus for the Premium edition is documenting and managing business processes.
- Visio 2010 is the first version of Visio to employ the Office fluent user interface, commonly known as the ribbon. The Visio ribbon is well-designed and easy to use, in large part because the goal of the ribbon is to present sets of related functions visually, and Visio is a visual product.
- Contextual tabs and add-in tabs provide unique features and are only visible when they are relevant and can be used. Most ribbon tabs are visible all of the time.
- The Backstage view provides file management and option settings for Visio 2010.
- The drawing window and the Shapes window are the primary windows you will use to create and manipulate Visio diagrams.
- Visio provides a variety of keyboard shortcuts, mouse techniques, and specialized subwindows for panning and zooming within a diagram and for sizing and positioning shapes.

Chapter at a Glance

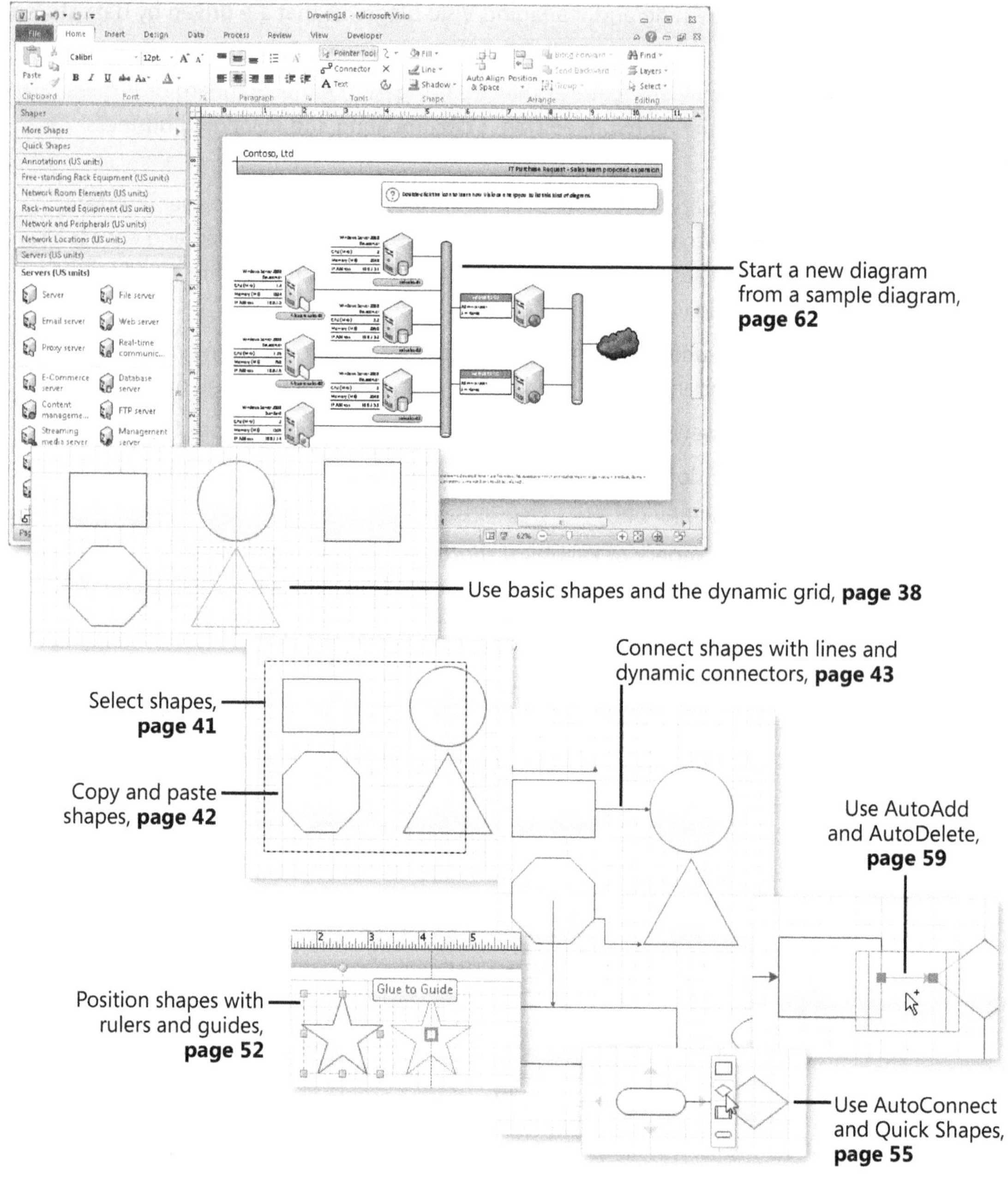
Start a new diagram from a sample diagram, **page 62**
Use basic shapes and the dynamic grid, **page 38**
Connect shapes with lines and dynamic connectors, **page 43**
Select shapes, **page 41**
Copy and paste shapes, **page 42**
Use AutoAdd and AutoDelete, **page 59**
Glue to Guide
Position shapes with rulers and guides, **page 52**
Use AutoConnect and Quick Shapes, **page 55**

2 Creating a New Diagram

In this chapter, you will learn how to

- ✔ Use basic shapes and the Dynamic Grid.
- ✔ Select, copy, and paste shapes.
- ✔ Connect shapes with lines and dynamic connectors.
- ✔ Identify 1-D shapes and types of glue.
- ✔ Position shapes with rulers and guides.
- ✔ Use AutoConnect and Quick Shapes.
- ✔ Use AutoAdd and AutoDelete.
- ✔ Start a new diagram from a sample diagram.

As you saw in Chapter 1, "A Visual Orientation to a Visual Product," Microsoft Visio 2010 includes a variety of templates in at least six categories (more in the Professional and Premium editions). One of the easiest ways to begin a new diagram is to start with one of the templates. Some templates include stencils that contain very simple shapes; others contain stencils with very complex, intelligent shapes.

In Chapter 4, "Drawing the Real World: Flowcharts and Organization Charts" and Chapter 9, "Drawing the Real World: Network and Data Center Diagrams," you will learn about templates in the latter category; you may even be surprised how sophisticated some of the shapes in those templates are.

In this chapter, you will explore some of the key features of Visio 2010 using a very basic template. Some of these features include the Dynamic Grid, AutoConnect, Quick Shapes, AutoAdd, and AutoDelete.

Practice Files Before you can complete the exercises in this chapter, you need to copy the book's practice files to your computer. The practice files you'll use to complete the exercises in this chapter are in the Chapter02 practice files folder. A complete list of practice files is provided in "Using the Practice Files" at the beginning of this book.

Using Basic Shapes and the Dynamic Grid

Visio 2010 provides an enhanced ***Dynamic Grid***. The purpose of the Dynamic Grid is to help you position a shape with greater accuracy as you drop it on the page, eliminating much of the need to drag and nudge the shape into alignment after you've placed it on the page.

In this exercise, you will create a drawing from a stencil containing basic Visio shapes. In the process of doing so, you will use the Dynamic Grid. You will also create several shapes using Visio's drawing tools.

SET UP Start Visio, or if it's already running, click the File tab, and then click New. In the Template Categories section, click General, and then double-click the Basic Diagram thumbnail. Save the drawing as *Basic shapes*.

1. Drag a **Rectangle** shape onto the drawing page and position it toward the upper-left corner of the page.
2. Drag a **Circle** shape onto the drawing page and position it to the right of the rectangle. Before you release the mouse button to drop the circle, move it up and down on the page.

   As you move the circle, you see an orange, horizontal line appear when the circle is in certain positions relative to the rectangle. This line is part of the Visio 2010 Dynamic Grid feature that assists you in aligning and spacing shapes.

   From left to right in the following graphics, you can see the Dynamic Grid line when the circle is aligned with the top, center, and bottom of the existing rectangle.

   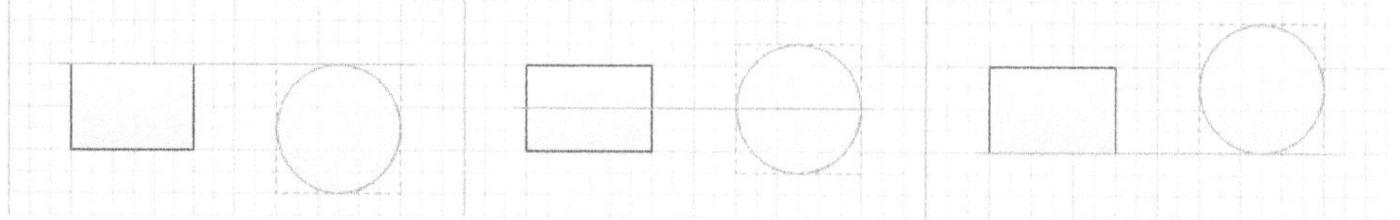

   Troubleshooting If the Dynamic Grid lines don't appear as you move shapes near others already on the page, it is probably because the feature is turned off for this drawing. To activate the Dynamic Grid, on the View tab, in the Visual Aids group, click the Dynamic Grid button.

3. Use the Dynamic Grid to align the circle with the center of the rectangle and drop it approximately 1 inch (2.5 cm) to the right of the rectangle.

   Tip **Use of the Dynamic Grid lines is not restricted to positioning new shapes as you drop them from the stencil. The Dynamic Grid lines also appear when you reposition existing shapes on the page.**

4. Click on the circle and drag it closer to the rectangle.

   The Dynamic Grid centerline appears, and if you've located the circle a certain distance from the rectangle, a second Dynamic Grid element will appear. When the distance between the two shapes matches the default spacing interval for this page, a double-headed arrow appears.

   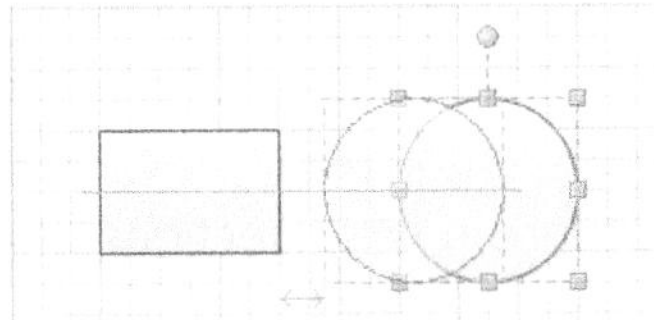

5. Press Ctrl+Z to undo the shape movement and position the circle back where you originally dropped it.
6. Drag a **Square** shape onto the page and position it on the right side of the circle but don't release the mouse button yet.
7. Use the Dynamic Grid to align the square with the center of the circle and then move the square left and right until the orange double-headed arrow appears.

   Notice that the double-headed arrow shown in the following graphic is longer than the double-headed arrow shown in the graphic after Step 4 and that there are two of them, not one. In Step 4, the double-headed arrow shows that the interval between your shapes matched the drawing's default spacing. In this example, the pair of double-headed arrows indicates that your new shape is the same distance from the circle that the circle is from the rectangle.

   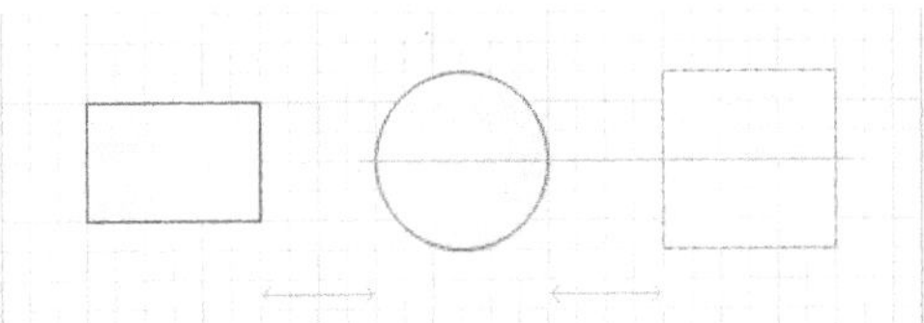

8. Release the left mouse button to drop the square.
9. Continue to experiment with the Dynamic Grid by dragging an **Octagon** shape below the rectangle on the drawing page.

As shown in the following graphic, the Dynamic Grid can provide guidance in two directions at once: the vertical line shows alignment with the rectangle; the pair of longer double-headed arrows shows horizontal spacing; the short double-headed arrow highlights vertical spacing.

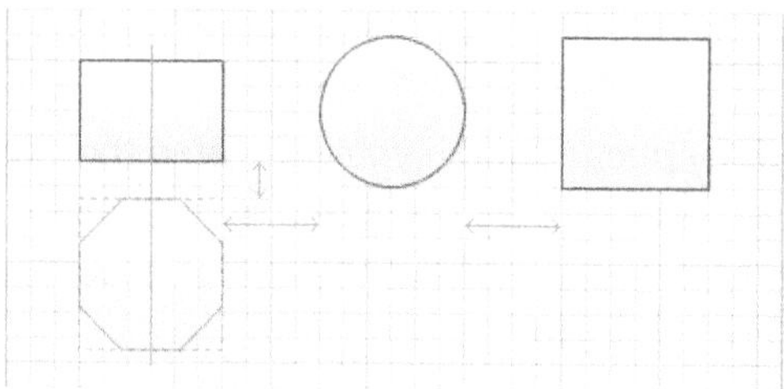

10. Release the left mouse button to drop the shape.
11. Drag a **Triangle** shape to the right of the octagon and below the circle. Once again, notice that the Dynamic Grid can work in two directions simultaneously.

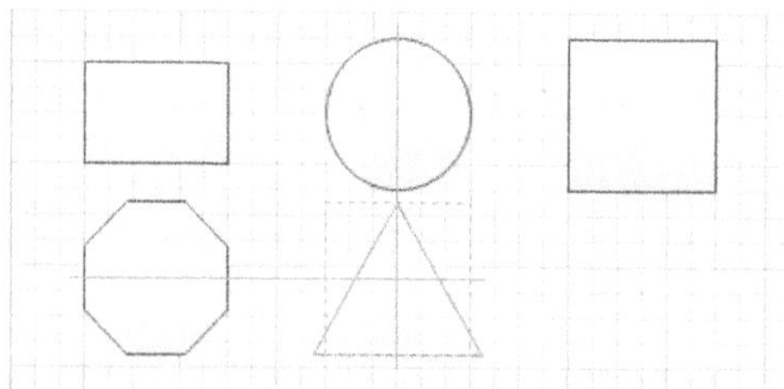

Now that you've added five shapes to the page by using a Visio stencil, it's time to create some shapes of your own using the Visio drawing tools.

Rectangle

12. On the **Home** tab, in the **Tools** group, click the **Rectangle** tool. Notice that the cursor changes to a plus sign with a rectangle to the lower right.

Important The Rectangle tool is one of six tools on the same menu that is located immediately to the right of the Pointer Tool. The button on this tool shows the Rectangle tool each time you start Visio. However, Visio always displays the most recently used tool on the button. Consequently, if you have previously used a different tool, the button and the popup tooltip text may show any one of the six tools. There are two tools that draw two-dimensional shapes: Rectangle and Ellipse. There are four tools that draw lines: Line, Freeform, Arc, and Pencil.

13. Click anywhere on the drawing page and drag down and to the right to draw a rectangle.

Tip You can constrain the Rectangle tool so it only draws squares by holding down the Shift key while dragging the mouse.

Ellipse

14. On the **Home** tab, in the **Tools** group, click the **Ellipse** tool, and then drag to create an ellipse to the right of your rectangle.

Tip You can constrain the Ellipse tool so it draws only circles by holding down the Shift key while dragging the mouse.

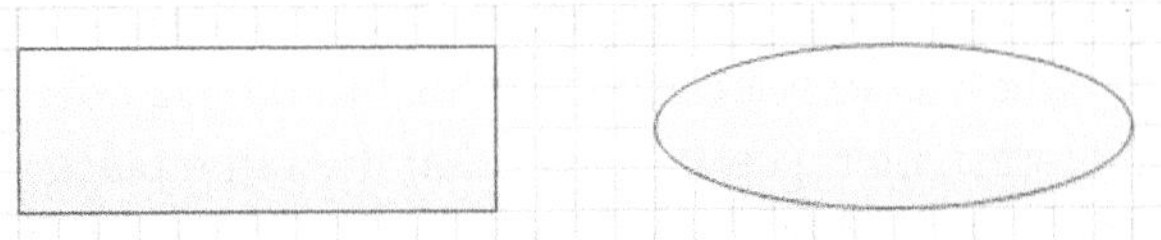

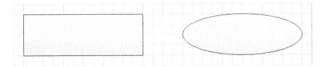

CLEAN UP Save your changes to the *Basic shapes* drawing but leave it open if you are continuing with the next exercise.

Tip To return Visio to normal operating mode after using one of the drawing tools, on the Home tab, in the Tools group, click Pointer Tool.

Dynamic Grid

Although you have used the Dynamic Grid in this exercise while working with simple, geometric shapes, it is also useful with more complex shapes. However, if at any time you prefer to work without the Dynamic Grid, you can turn it off: on the View tab, in the Visual Aids group, click the Dynamic Grid button.

Selecting Shapes

You can use several techniques for selecting shapes in Visio. The most obvious is that you can click once on a shape to select it. To select more than one shape using this method, hold down the Shift key or the Ctrl key while clicking additional shapes. You can remove shapes from an existing selection with the same method.

A second common technique is to draw a ***bounding box*** around one or more shapes. You draw a bounding box by clicking anywhere on the page background and moving the mouse while holding down the mouse button. The bounding box appears as a dashed rectangle.

The default behavior in Visio is to select any shapes that are fully surrounded by a bounding box. For example, in the following graphic on the left, the rectangle and octagon will be selected when you release the mouse button. In the graphic on the right, no shapes will be selected.

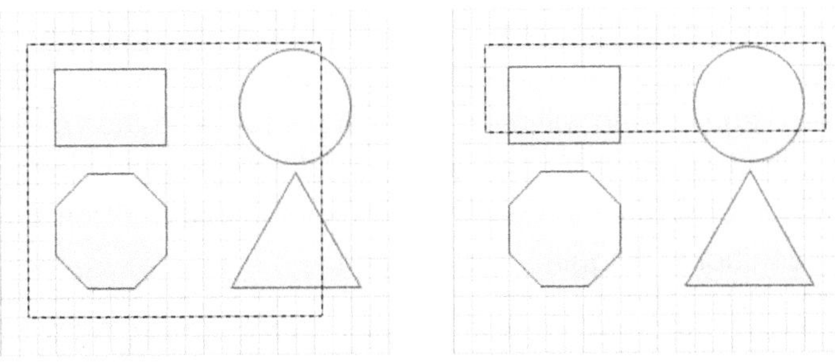

Visio offers an alternative to a bounding box that lets you select shapes with a freeform lasso. To change from ***area select*** (another name for the bounding box technique) to ***lasso select***, on the Home tab, in the Editing group, click the Select button, and then click Lasso Select. To create a lasso selection, click the left mouse button and drag a lasso around the shapes of interest, being certain to end at the same place you began. When you release the mouse button, the enclosed shapes will be selected. The lasso in the following graphic will select the circle and the octagon.

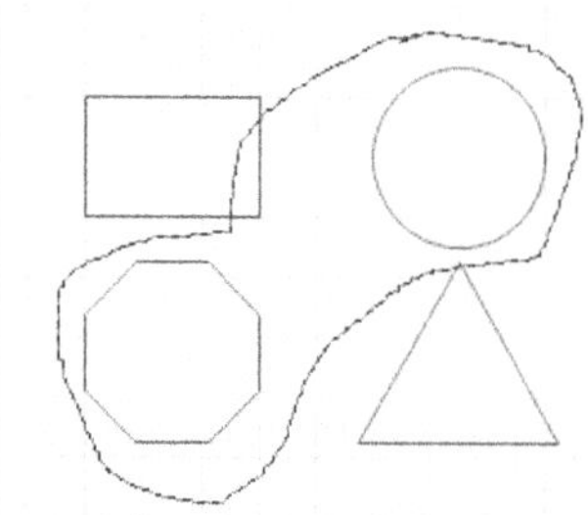

Tip **To revert to using bounding boxes, on the Home tab, in the Editing group, click the Select button, and then click Area Select.**

You can change selection behavior in Visio so it will select shapes that are partially enclosed by a bounding box or lasso. On the File tab, click Options, and then click Advanced; select the Select Shapes Partially Within Area check box.

Area/lasso selection and click selection are not mutually exclusive. You can select one or more shapes by clicking first, and then add additional shapes by holding down Shift or Ctrl while drawing a bounding box or lasso loop. The reverse works as well: you can start with a bounding box or lasso selection and add additional shapes with the same keyboard and mouse combination.

Keyboard Shortcut **You can select all shapes on a page by pressing the standard Windows keyboard shortcut Ctrl+A.**

Copying and Pasting Shapes

One of the simplest but nicest enhancements in Visio 2010 is that pasting copied shapes works more logically. For example, if you copy one or more shapes from Page-1 and then paste them onto Page-2, Visio will paste them in the same position on Page-2 that they were on Page-1. In previous versions, Visio always pasted shapes into the center of the drawing window. Occasionally this was what you wanted, but as often as not, this placement required additional dragging and nudging.

In this exercise, you will create a new page and copy the shapes from Page-1 to Page-2.

SET UP **If you completed the preceding exercise, continue working with the *Basic shapes* drawing. If not, you need the *Basic shapes_start* drawing located in the Chapter02 practice file folder to complete this exercise. Open the drawing in Visio and save it as *Basic shapes*.**

1. Select all of the shapes on **Page-1**, and press Ctrl+C to copy them.
2. To the right of the **Page-1** name tab below the drawing page, click the **Insert Page** button.

Insert Page

3. Press Ctrl+V to paste the shapes onto **Page-2**. Notice that they are placed in the identical position on the page that they occupy on Page-1.
4. Click the **Page-1** name tab to return to that page.

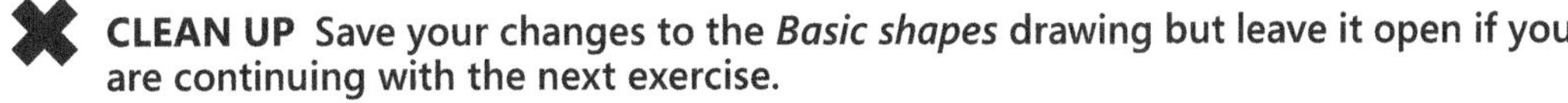

CLEAN UP **Save your changes to the *Basic shapes* drawing but leave it open if you are continuing with the next exercise.**

There are two other enhancements to the paste logic in Visio 2010.

- You can paste to a specific place: right-click at the location on the page where you would like to paste, and select Paste from the context menu. Visio will center the pasted shape(s) at the cursor location.
- It's easier to use Paste Special: right-click anywhere on the drawing page and select Paste Special from the context menu; Visio opens the Paste Special dialog box. (In previous versions of Visio, you were required to use the Edit menu to access the Paste Special dialog box.)

Keyboard Shortcut **Duplicating shapes is often faster and easier than copying and pasting, especially if you want to reproduce the same shape multiple times. To create duplicates: after selecting one or more shapes, type Ctrl+D or hold down the Control key while dragging the shape(s) with the mouse.**

Connecting Shapes with Lines

Visio shapes are either one dimensional (1-D) or two dimensional (2-D). ***1-D*** shapes act like lines, with endpoints that can be attached to other shapes. ***2-D*** shapes behave like polygons, with edges and an interior. However, appearances can be deceiving because some shapes that appear to be two-dimensional may actually be 1-D shapes in Visio; there's an example at the end of the section titled "Starting a New Diagram from a Sample Diagram" later in this chapter. The reverse can also be true.

In previous exercises, you worked primarily with 2-D shapes. In this exercise, you will connect a variety of 1-D shapes to 2-D shapes.

SET UP **You need the *Basic shapes* drawing from the preceding exercise.**

Line

1. On the **Home** tab, in the **Tools** group, click the **Line** tool. Notice that the cursor changes to a plus sign with a diagonal line to the lower right.

   Important **The Line tool is one of six tools located on a menu immediately to the right of the Pointer Tool. If the Line tool is not visible, click the arrow next to whichever tool is displayed on the button.**

2. Point near any of the five shapes toward the top of the page. Notice that little blue Xs appear on the edges and/or in the center of the shapes.

   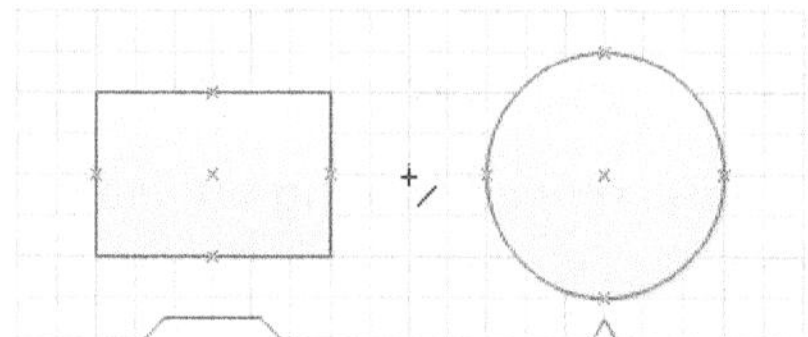

   The blue Xs are ***connection points***. They appear whenever you move near them with a 1-D shape or a tool like the Line tool.

3. Move the cursor near a connection point and notice that a red square appears. The square indicates that you can click on it to glue one end of the line to the connection point.

   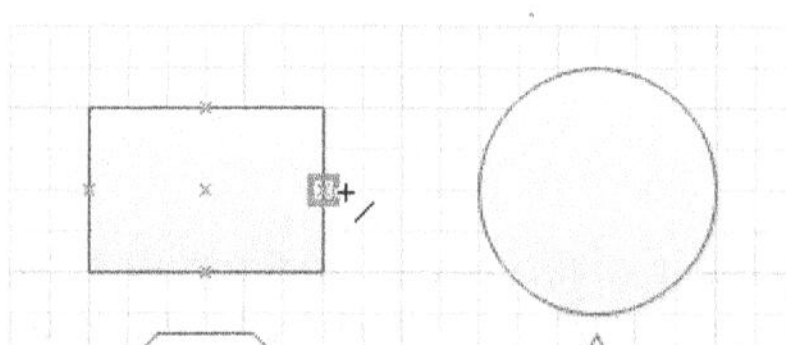

4. Drag from the connection point on the right end of the rectangle to the connection point on the left edge of the circle, and then release the mouse button.

   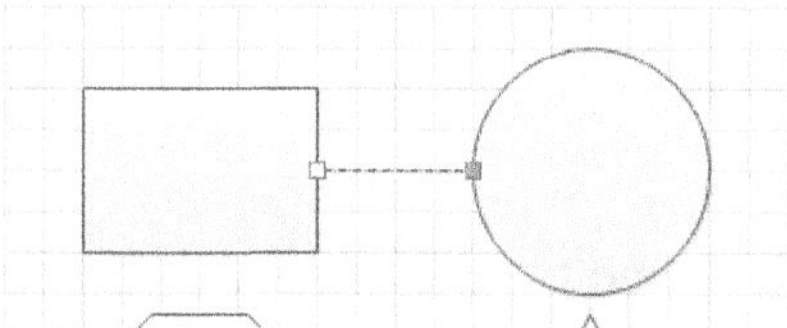

   You have drawn a line that is glued to the edges of the two shapes. Notice that the handle on the originating end of the glued line shows a white box with a red outline and the handle on the destination end shows a solid red box.

5. Draw another line above the rectangle but do not glue either end to a shape.

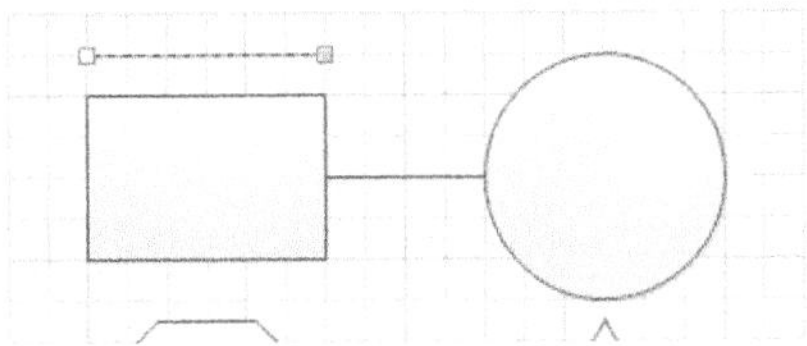

The line shows a white square with a blue outline on the originating end and a solid blue square on the destination end.

Tip **The color distinction between the unglued line ends in this step and the glued line ends in the previous step is an important one in Visio. Although it's quite obvious in these two examples whether the line ends are connected, in the next step, you'll see an example in which the color of the line end is very helpful in determining connectedness.**

6. Use the **Line** tool to draw a line from the connection point at the center of the octagon to the long rectangle below it.

The long rectangle that you created with the drawing tool in a previous exercise does not contain any connection points; consequently, you can only drop the end of the line onto the shape and can't glue it. You can confirm which ends are glued by comparing the color and pattern at each end of this line with the handles in the previous two examples.

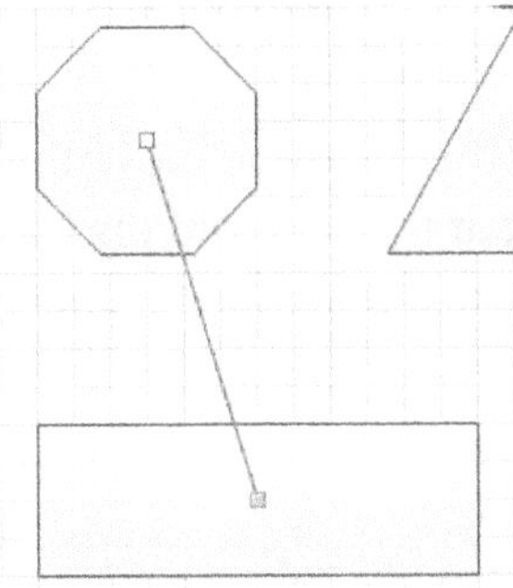

Pointer Tool

7. On the **Home** tab, in the **Tools** group, click the **Pointer Tool**.

8. Drag the circle up and to the right. Drag the long rectangle below the octagon down. The following two graphics show the before (left) and after (right).

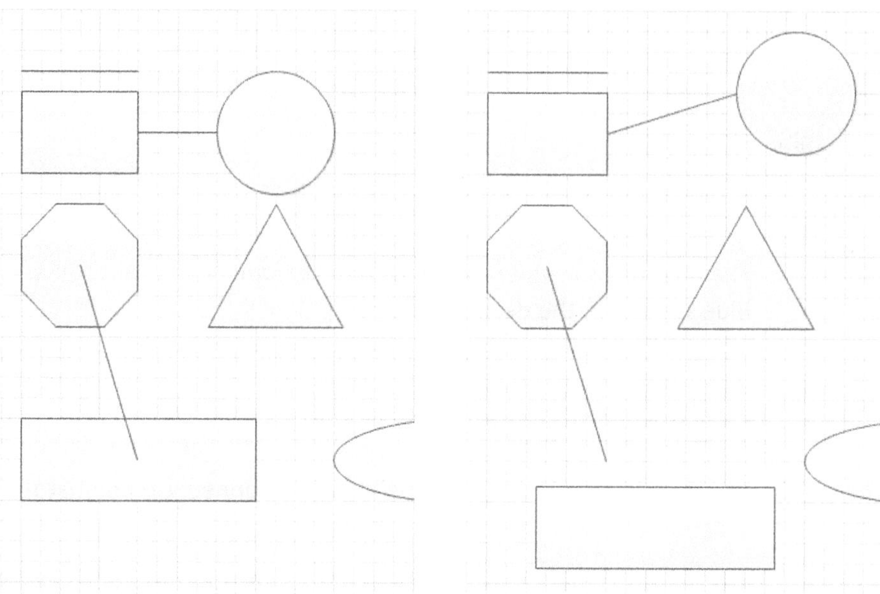

The line that is glued to the rectangle and circle stays attached at the connection points. The line that was touching the long rectangle but was not glued becomes separated when you move the rectangle.

Freeform

9. On the **Home** tab, in the **Tools** group, click the **Freeform** tool. Notice that the cursor changes to a plus sign with a squiggly line to the lower right.
10. Click the connection point in the center of the circle and move the cursor randomly, eventually arriving at the connection point at the center of the square. Notice that the line develops a bend each time you make a significant change in direction.

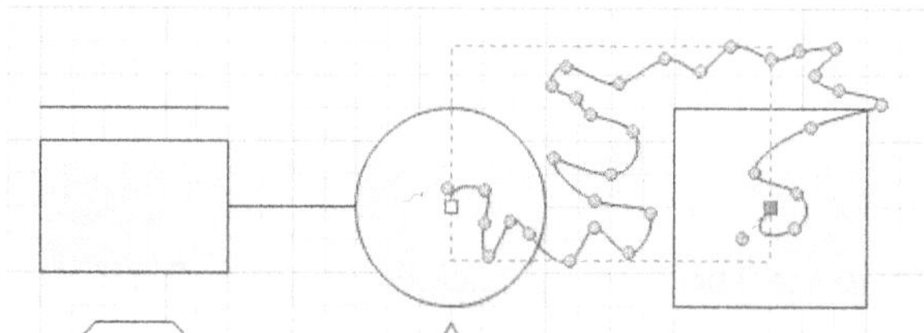

There are several important things to note about the line you've drawn:

- If you glued both ends of the line to connection points, the curved line behaves just like the straight line: if you move the shapes, the line will follow. In the case of the freeform line, the line will also retain its unique set of curves. (Try moving the shapes attached to your squiggly line; the results are often quite interesting.)

- There are blue circles at the key points of curvature along the line. These circles are actually handles that you can drag to reshape the line.
- The blue circles are only visible if you select the shape with one of the line tools (Line, Freeform, Arc, or Pencil). If you select it with the Pointer Tool or the Rectangle or Ellipse tools, only the endpoints are visible, as shown in the following graphic.

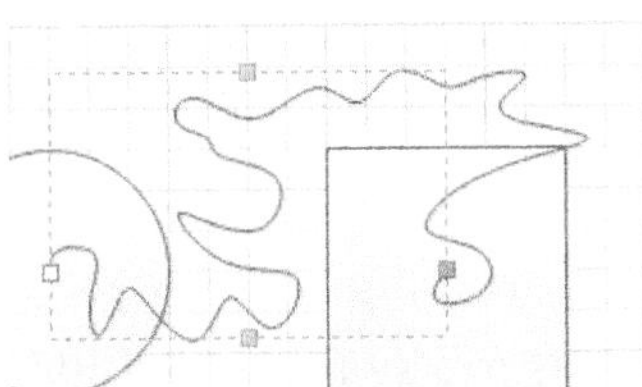

11. In a blank area of the drawing page, draw a freeform line but be sure to end it at exactly the same point that you started.

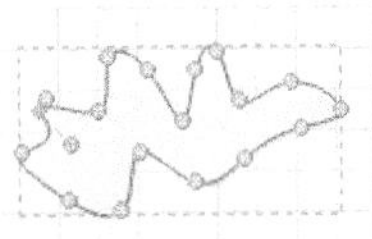

Notice the important difference from the line you drew in the previous step: as soon as you finish "closing the loop," Visio applies a fill to your new shape and no square handles appear at the beginning and end of the line. By ending your line at the same place you began, you've drawn a 2-D shape, not a 1-D shape.

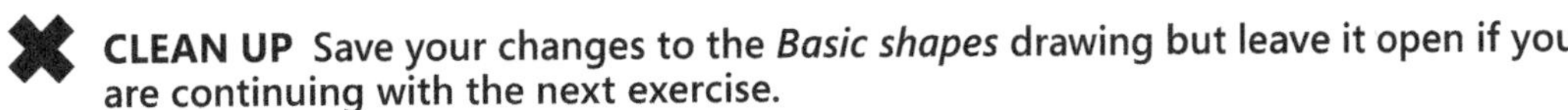

CLEAN UP Save your changes to the *Basic shapes* drawing but leave it open if you are continuing with the next exercise.

Though you didn't use them in this exercise, you can experiment with the Arc and Pencil tools to learn about their unique characteristics.

Connecting Shapes with Dynamic Connectors

In the previous exercise, you learned about four types of 1-D shapes that you can create with the Visio line tools. Although several of those line types can include curves or bends, those features are only present if you place them there. Visio also offers a line called a ***dynamic connector***. When you use a dynamic connector, Visio automatically adds and removes bends in the line based on the positions of the shapes to which it's glued.

In this exercise, you will perform some of the same steps you completed in the previous exercise but will use dynamic connectors in order to understand the differences in behavior.

SET UP You need the *Basic shapes* drawing from the preceding exercise.

1. Click the **Page-2** tab at the bottom of the drawing page to move to Page-2.

Connector

2. On the **Home** tab, in the **Tools** group, click the **Connector** button. Notice that the cursor changes to a black arrow and there is an arrow with two right-angle bends below it.

   Just as with the line tools you used in the preceding exercise, you'll see that connection points appear on various shapes as you point near them with the Connector Tool.

3. Drag from the connection point on the right center of the upper rectangle to the connection point on the left edge of the circle, and then release the mouse button.

   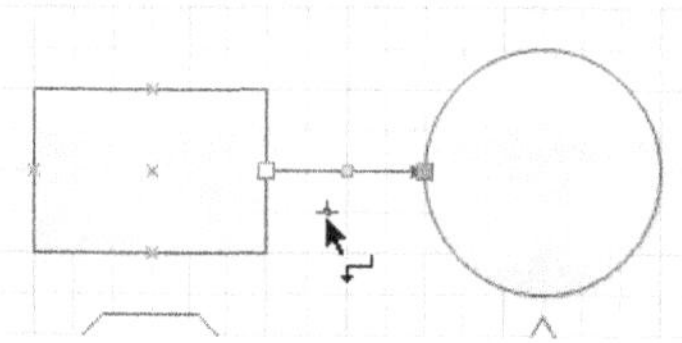

   Just as in the preceding exercise, the line you've drawn shows red handles at its endpoints. However, unlike the previous line, a dynamic connector has an arrowhead on its destination end by default. The arrowhead in this graphic is largely obscured by the red handle, but when the dynamic connector is deselected, as in the following graphic, the arrowhead is visible.

4. Draw another dynamic connector above the rectangle but do not glue either end to a shape. Even if you try to draw the connector as a straight line, notice that it appears to have a mind of its own. This will turn out to be one of the most useful characteristics of a dynamic connector, as you will see in subsequent steps in this exercise.

   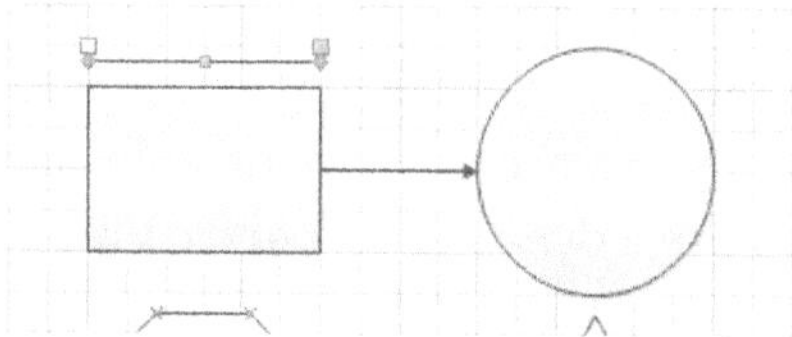

5. Use the dynamic connector to draw a line from the connection point at the center of the octagon to the center of the long rectangle below it.

Something very different happens compared to the preceding exercise where you performed the same step with the line tool. Even though the long rectangle does not contain any connection points, you can still glue a dynamic connector to the shape. Visio provides two visual cues: pop-up text appears above the rectangle, as shown in the following graphic on the left, and the border of the shape is outlined in red. When you release the mouse button, the connector appears as shown in the graphic on the right.

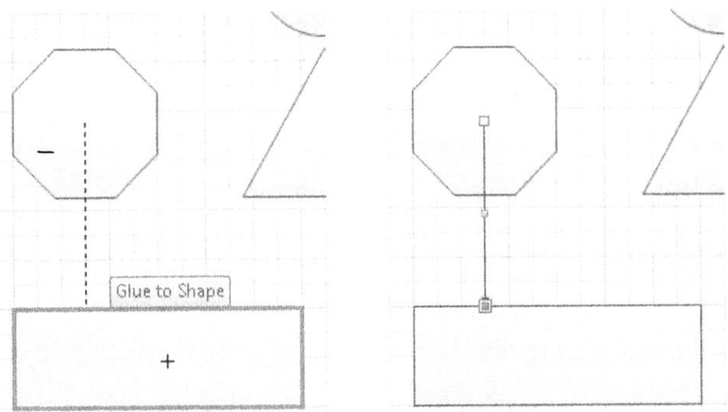

You've just used something Visio calls ***dynamic glue*** to attach a connector to a shape without any connection points. As you will discover in the next step, you can do the same thing even if a shape has connection points, merely by pointing to a part of the shape where there aren't any.

6. Point to the interior of the octagon until the border of the selection rectangle lights up in red (the following graphic on the left shows the cursor inside the selection rectangle). Drag until the border of the triangle turns red and the words *Glue to Shape* appear, as shown on the right. Don't release the mouse button yet.

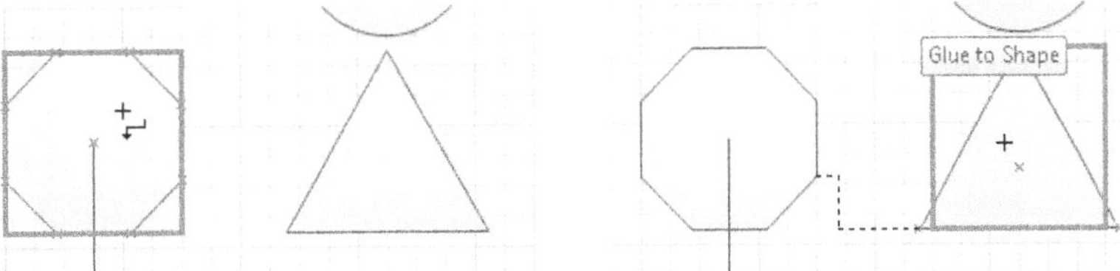

In the graphic on the right, even though the cursor (the plus sign) is above the center of the triangle, the dynamic connector once again seems to have a mind of its own and is connecting to the lower-left corner.

7. Release the mouse button to observe that the dynamic connector has glued itself to points along the edges of the two shapes.

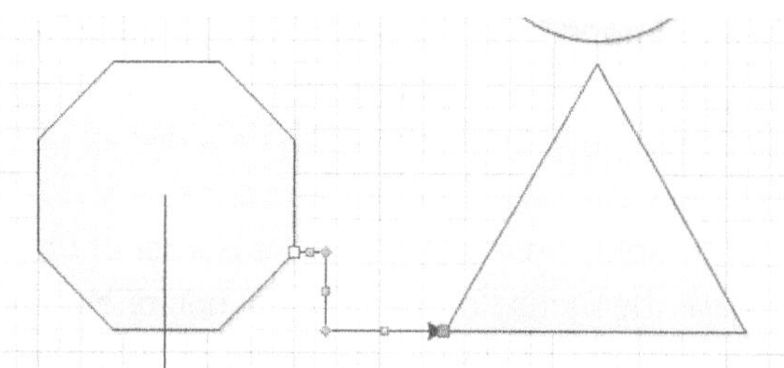

Tip **Notice the blue control handles at each bend and in the middle of each segment of a dynamic connector. You can drag any of these control handles to relocate individual segments of the dynamic connector.**

With a few final steps, you will see the real value of a dynamic connector and learn the difference between ***static glue*** and dynamic glue.

Pointer Tool

8. On the **Home** tab, in the **Tools** group, click the **Pointer Tool**.
9. Drag the circle up and to the right; drag the long rectangle below the octagon down and to the right; drag the triangle down until it touches the ellipse.

   The following graphics show the before (left) and after (right).

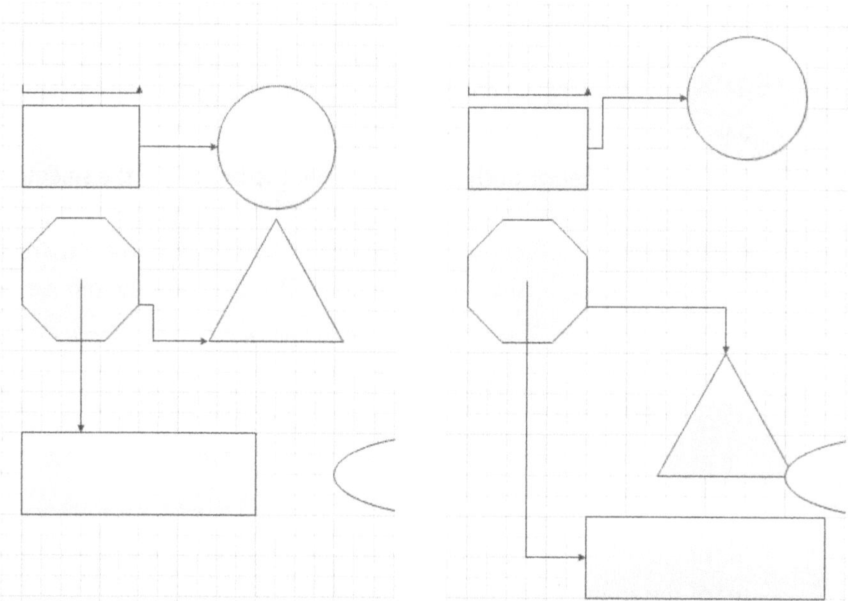

Here are three key observations after moving the three shapes:

- The connector between the upper rectangle and the circle has right angle bends but is still attached at exactly the same two connection points. This is an example of static glue, that is, glue that remains attached to a fixed point on a shape.

- The connector between the octagon and the long rectangle now contains a right-angle bend. The tail of the arrow remains glued to the center connection point, another example of static glue, but you now see evidence of dynamic glue: the head of the arrow is still attached to the long rectangle but it is connected at a different place along the edge of the shape.
- The connector between the octagon and the triangle is glued dynamically at both ends. Moving the triangle down caused the attachment point on the triangle to change. In this particular case, the connection to the octagon remained in the same place; however, a different set of shape movements can cause the dynamic glue to the octagon to change locations as well.

CLEAN UP Save your changes to the *Basic shapes* drawing, and then close it.

Adjusting Dynamic Connectors

By default, dynamic connectors use right-angle bends as you saw in this exercise. You can change the appearance of a dynamic connector by right-clicking it and selecting one of three options: Right-Angle Connector, Straight Connector, or Curved Connector.

As you move shapes that are linked by dynamic connectors, Visio adjusts the connector segments. In addition, as noted in the tip after Step 7, you can manually adjust individual connector segments by dragging control handles. If at any point, a dynamic connector has too many bends or becomes convoluted, you can right-click it and then click Reset Connector. Visio redraws the connector with the minimum number of bends and segments to fit in the required space.

Identifying 1-D Shapes and Types of Glue

In the preceding sections, you've seen several types of 1-D shapes and two forms of glue. This section summarizes the behavior of 1-D shapes and identifies the visual cues Visio provides to differentiate glue types:

- A 1-D shape drawn with any of the line tools (Line, Freeform, Arc, or Pencil) retains its original form when the shapes at the ends are moved.
- A 1-D shape created with the Connector Tool adds or removes bends in the line to accommodate shape movements.

- A line or dynamic connector attached to a connection point forms static glue; the 1-D shape remains attached at that fixed point on the 2-D shape no matter how the 2-D shape is moved.

  A 1-D shape connected with static glue shows these red handles.

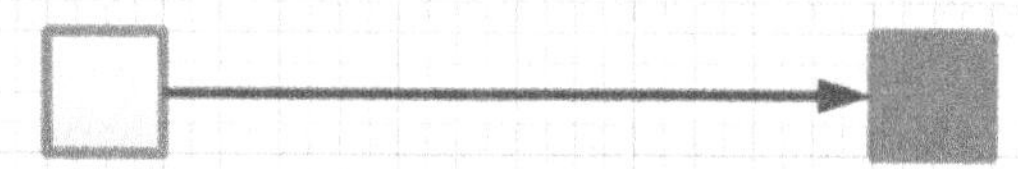

- A dynamic connector attached to a shape but not to a connection point forms dynamic glue; as the 2-D shape moves, the point at which the dynamic connector attaches to the shape moves.

  A dynamic connector connected with dynamic glue shows these red handles.

- When the ends of a 1-D shape are not glued to another shape, the handles at the ends of the line are light blue and look like these.

See Also Users of previous versions of Visio will recognize that line handles look different in Visio 2010. For a description of the historical differences plus a discussion of line directionality, go to *www.visguy.com/2010/03/22/1d-shape-handles-through-the-years/*.

Positioning Shapes with Rulers and Guides

In some of the preceding exercises, you have aligned shapes by using the Dynamic Grid feature of Visio 2010. However, the Dynamic Grid doesn't always do what you need. For example, if there are other shapes between the two you are trying to align, the Dynamic Grid doesn't help. Similarly, you may want to align shapes in ways that the Dynamic Grid doesn't provide.

In this exercise, you will align shapes by using other Visio features.

SET UP Click the File tab, and then click New. In the Template Categories section, click General, and then double-click the Basic Diagram thumbnail. Save the drawing as *Shape Alignment*.

1. Drag a **Rectangle** shape onto the page and position it about one fourth of the way down the page. Drop it so the left end is at the left margin of the page. Then use the resize handle on the right to stretch the right edge to the right margin.

   Tip As you drag a shape near the edge of the page and it becomes aligned with the page margin, an orange Dynamic Grid line appears.

2. Drag a **Star 5** shape above the left half of the rectangle.

   In the next step, you will try to align a second star with the one you just placed.

3. Drag a **Star 5** shape onto the page below the rectangle and observe that the Dynamic Grid does not help you align the two stars because of the intervening rectangle. Drop the star onto the page.

   To align the two stars, you can use the grid lines on the page; however a ***guide*** will make the task much easier.

4. Position the cursor over the vertical ruler on the left side of the page and observe that the cursor changes to a double-headed arrow. Click the ruler and drag into the middle of the drawing page.

   The guide appears as a vertical blue line on the page, but guides do not print.

   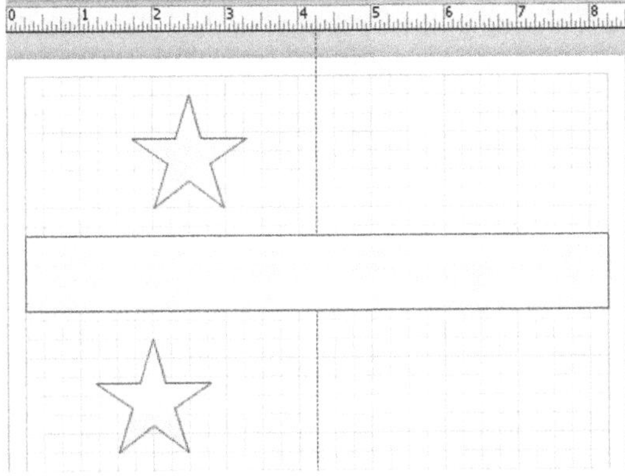

5. Drag the top star toward and over the guide and observe that you can glue the edges and center of the star shape to the guide.

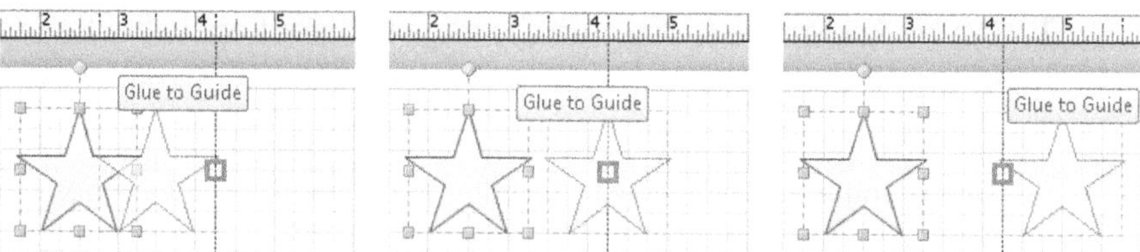

6. Glue the center of the star to the guide.
7. Drag the bottom star and glue its center to the guide.

Tip Remember that if you hold the Shift key while dragging a shape, you restrict it to moving only horizontally or vertically but not both.

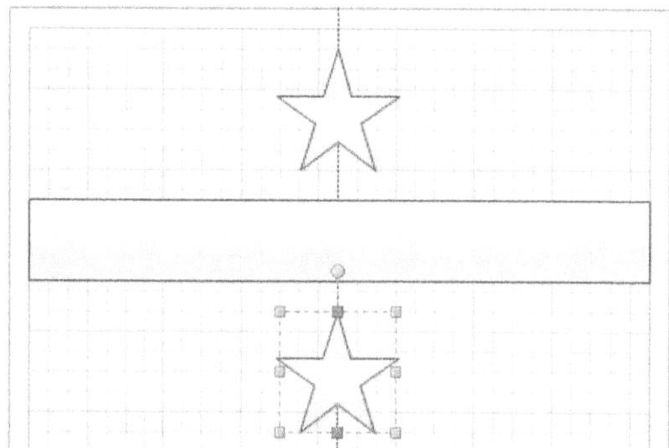

The two stars are now precisely aligned, despite the intervening shape.

Realize that the stars are actually glued to the guide just as lines were glued to shapes in previous exercises. If you move the guide, the stars will move also. If you don't need to move the aligned shapes as a unit, you can delete the guide as you would any other shape: just click to select it, and then press the Delete key.

Tip You can create more than one guide by dragging the ruler onto the page again. You can also create horizontal guides by dragging the ruler at the top of the page down.

The rulers provide another means for aligning shapes, as you will see in the next two steps.

8. Use the **Zoom** slider at the bottom of the drawing page to set the zoom level to **100%**. Then position the drawing page so you can see the upper-left corner.
9. Drag an **Octagon** shape into the upper-left corner of the page; before releasing the mouse button, observe that there are dashed lines in both the horizontal and vertical rulers (the lines are highlighted in the following graphic).

   The lines on the top ruler mark the left, center, and right of the octagon; the lines on the side ruler denote the top, middle, and bottom of the shape.

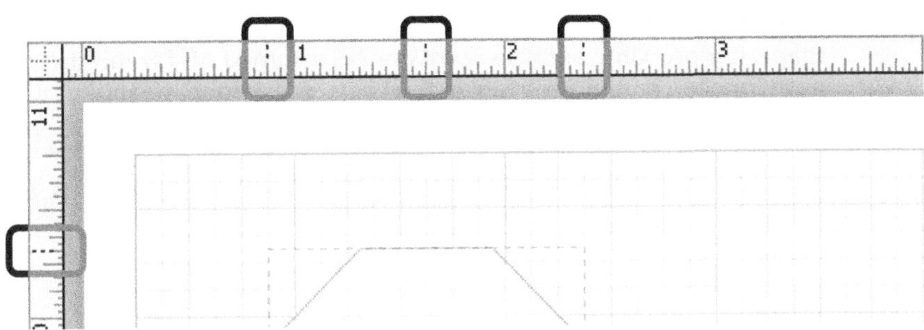

 **CLEAN UP** Save your changes to the *Shape Alignment* drawing, and then close it.

Using AutoConnect and Quick Shapes

AutoConnect was introduced in Visio 2007 and provides a fast means to connect shapes with dynamic connectors. ***Quick Shapes*** are a Visio 2010 innovation that builds on AutoConnect and lets you create drawings even more quickly.

In this exercise, you will use AutoConnect and Quick Shapes to create a new drawing.

SET UP Click the File tab, and then click New. In the Template Categories section, click Flowchart, and then double-click the Basic Flowchart thumbnail. Save the new drawing as *Autoconnect and Quick Shapes*.

1. Drag a **Start/End** shape into the upper-left corner of the drawing page.
2. Drag **Process** and **Decision** shapes onto the page to create a drawing like the one shown in the following graphic.

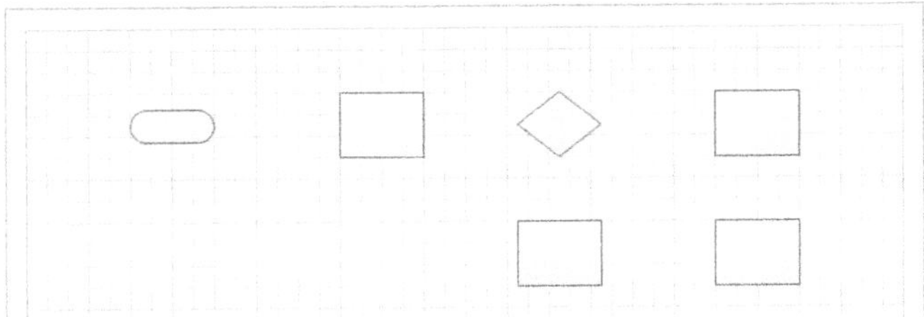

Notice that when you point to any shape on the page, blue AutoConnect arrows appear on the sides that are not yet connected to another shape.

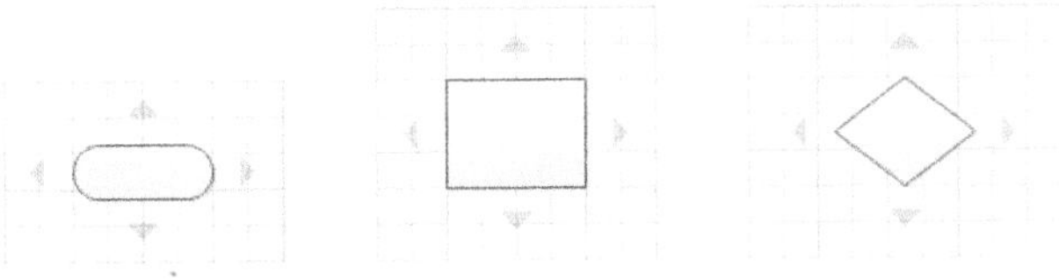

Troubleshooting If the AutoConnect arrows don't appear when you point to a shape, it is probably because AutoConnect is turned off for this drawing. To activate AutoConnect, on the View tab, in the Visual Aids group, select AutoConnect.

3. Point to the **AutoConnect** arrow on the right side of the **Start/End** shape. The Live Preview feature of Visio shows a dynamic connector linking the start/end to the process shape.

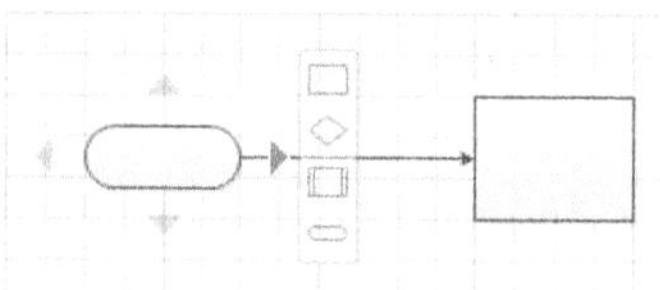

4. Click on the **AutoConnect** arrow to connect the shapes.
5. Continue clicking the appropriate **AutoConnect** arrows until the diagram looks like the following graphic.

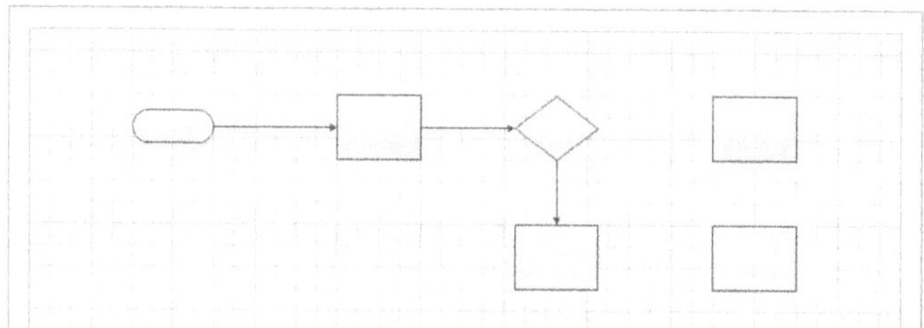

As you can see, AutoConnect makes short work of adding dynamic connectors to existing shapes. Each AutoConnect arrow seeks out a neighboring shape in the direction that the arrow points.

AutoConnect is also useful if the desired target shape is not in quite the right direction, as you'll see in the next two steps.

6. Point to the **Decision** shape until the **AutoConnect** arrows appear.
7. Click the **AutoConnect** arrow on the right of the **Decision** shape and drag it to the lower of the two rectangles on the right side of the page.

As you drag, the screen will look like the following graphic on the left. When you release the mouse button you'll see the connected shapes shown on the right.

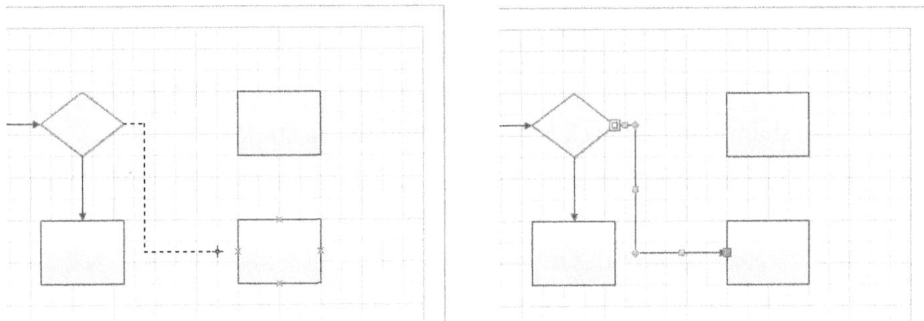

Now that you've used AutoConnect, you will work with a closely related feature to learn another way to create certain types of drawings quickly.

Before moving to the next step, look back at the picture in Step 3. In addition to the Live Preview image of a dynamic connector arrow, you also see four small shapes on a Mini Toolbar. These shapes are Quick Shapes. You will use Quick Shapes to create a drawing that is similar to the one you just built.

Insert Page

8. To the right of the **Page-1** name tab below the drawing page, click the **Insert Page** button. Visio adds a new page called Page-2.
9. Drag a **Start/End** shape into the upper-left corner of **Page-2**.
10. Point to the **AutoConnect** arrow on the right side of the **Start/End** shape.

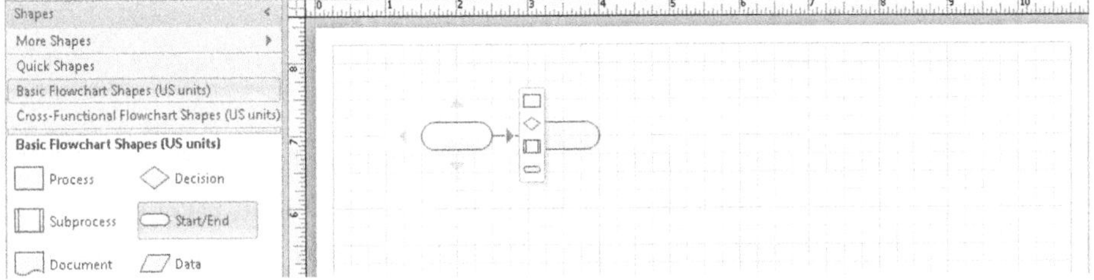

Live Preview shows more than just an arrow: it also displays a preview of the shape that is currently selected in the stencil, along with a Mini Toolbar containing four shapes.

If you want to add another Start/End shape to the current drawing, a single click will accomplish that and the new shape will be automatically spaced at the default interval for this page.

However, if you want to add a different shape, Quick Shapes provide an instant solution. Every open stencil in Visio 2010 includes a Quick Shapes section at the top of the stencil window pane, and most stencils include preselected Quick Shapes. If you look closely, you'll see a fine gray line that divides the Quick Shapes section from the rest of the stencil.

The shapes that appear in the Mini Toolbar shown in the previous graphic are the first four shapes in the Quick Shapes section. If you want different shapes to appear in the Quick Shapes Mini Toolbar, simply drag them to be among the first four shapes in the Quick Shapes section of the stencil.

Tip You can change the order of appearance of shapes in either the Quick Shapes section or the main part of a stencil merely by dragging them to a new location.

11. Point to any of the four shapes in the Quick Shapes Mini Toolbar and notice that the Live Preview image changes to reflect that shape.

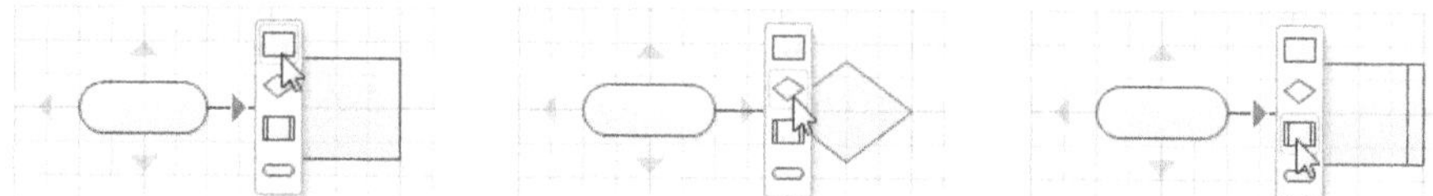

12. Click the **Process** shape in the Mini Toolbar to drop it on the page, then point to it to drop a **Decision** shape to its right.
13. Point to the **Decision** shape on the page and drop a **Process** shape below it.

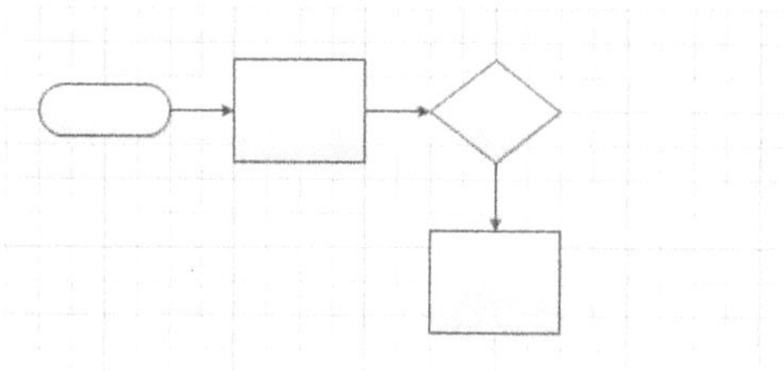

When you click a Quick Shape in the Mini Toolbar, Visio always adds a dynamic connector and spaces the new shape at the default interval for the page. Consequently, to finish reproducing the pattern you created on Page-1, it is necessary to place and connect the final two shapes manually.

14. Drag a **Process** shape from the stencil and drop it to the right of the **Decision** shape already on the page. Then drop another **Process** shape below it. Be sure to use the Dynamic Grid to ensure that spacing of the new shapes is consistent with the existing shapes.

Connector

15. On the **Home** tab, in the **Tools** group, click the **Connector** button, and then use the **Connector Tool** to link the **Decision** shape to the lower-right **Process** shape.

Tip You can also point to the Decision shape and drag a connector from the AutoConnect arrow to the Process shape as you did in Step 7.

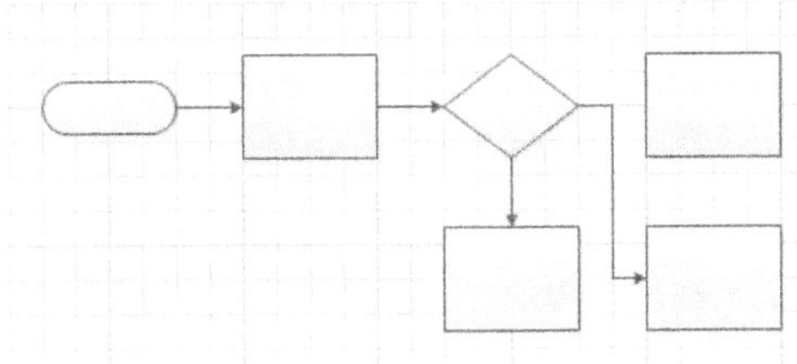

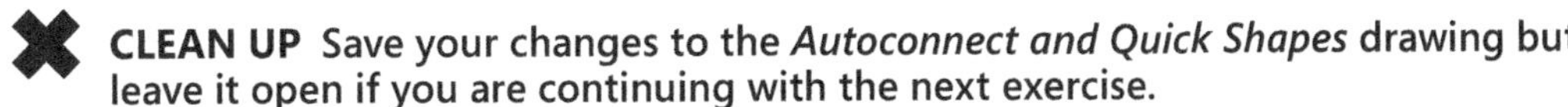

CLEAN UP Save your changes to the *Autoconnect and Quick Shapes* drawing but leave it open if you are continuing with the next exercise.

See Also The "Visio Insights" blog, written by the Visio development team at Microsoft, contains the following two posts that are relevant to the exercise in this section:

- *blogs.msdn.com/b/visio/archive/2009/09/22/autoconnect-in-visio-2010.aspx*
- *blogs.msdn.com/b/visio/archive/2010/12/08/flowcharts-in-under-a-minute.aspx*

Tip You can turn AutoConnect off for all drawings if you prefer to operate without it. On the File tab, click Options, and then click Advanced. In the Editing options section, clear the Enable AutoConnect check box.

Using AutoAdd and AutoDelete

Visio 2010 offers enhanced ways to add and delete shapes in a drawing:

- When you add a shape using AutoAdd, Visio rearranges the existing drawing to make the new shape fit. Sometimes the changes it makes are minor; other times they are more significant.
- When you delete a shape that is linked to one other shape with a dynamic connector, AutoDelete automatically removes the now superfluous connector. In addition, if you delete a shape that that is between two other shapes, Visio will delete one dynamic connector and reconnect the remaining one to both shapes.

In this exercise, you will alter a drawing by using AutoAdd and AutoDelete techniques.

SET UP If you completed the preceding exercise, continue working with the *Autoconnect and Quick Shapes* drawing. If not, you need the *Autoconnect and Quick Shapes_start* drawing located in the Chapter02 practice file folder to complete this exercise. Open the drawing in Visio and save it as *Autoconnect and Quick Shapes*.

1. Navigate to **Page-2** if you're not already there.
2. Drag a **Subprocess** shape from the stencil and position it on top of any existing dynamic connector.

Both ends of the connector display large red squares that are visible through the semitransparent subprocess shape. Don't release the mouse button yet.

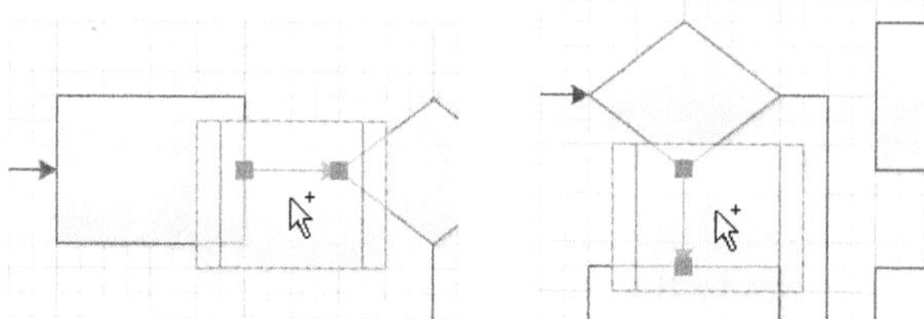

3. Drop the **Subprocess** shape on the connector below the **Decision** shape. Visio pushes the process shape down to make room for the new subprocess shape.

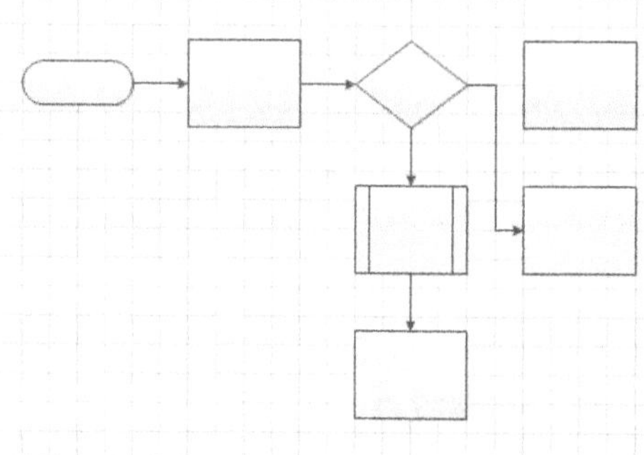

4. Drop a **Subprocess** shape on the connector between the **Start/End** shape and the first **Process** box. Visio makes more significant changes in order to accommodate the new shape and avoid the unconnected process shape in the upper right.

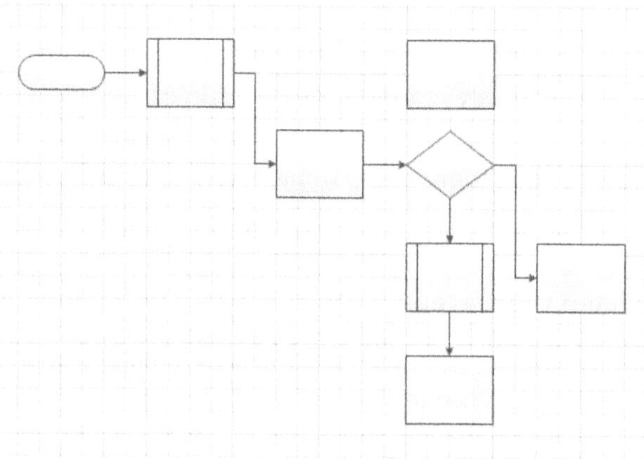

5. Select the **Process** shape at the very bottom of the diagram, and then press the Delete key to remove the shape.

   Notice that Visio also removes the dynamic connector that was linked to the Process shape.

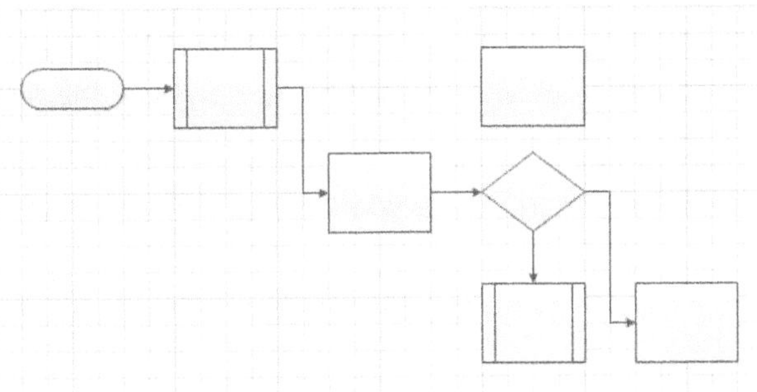

6. Select the **Subprocess** shape between the **Start/End** shape and the first **Process** shape, and then press the Delete key.

   In addition to deleting the subprocess shape, Visio removes one of the two dynamic connectors and reconnects the remaining one between the start/end and the process shapes.

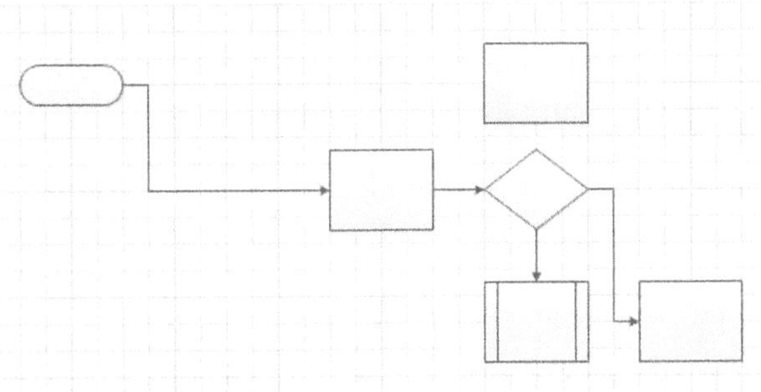

CLEAN UP Save your changes to the *Autoconnect and Quick Shapes* drawing, and then close it.

Tip If you prefer not to have Visio automatically delete connectors when you delete shapes, you can turn this feature off. On the File tab, click Options, and then click Advanced. In the Editing options section, clear the Delete Connectors When Deleting Shapes check box.

The Power of Undo

As you work on a diagram and make both small-scale and large-scale changes, one of your most powerful allies is the Undo feature in Visio. You can undo nearly any action in Visio. The program provides 20 undo levels, which means you can undo the most recent 20 actions in your diagram. You shouldn't hesitate to try anything with Visio because you will be able to undo it if you don't like the result.

If you prefer a larger or smaller number of undo levels, on the File tab, click Options, and then click Advanced, where you will find a setting for Maximum Number Of Undos.

Starting a New Diagram from a Sample Diagram

In addition to the Visio templates that you've used several times in this chapter, Visio 2010 includes five completed sample drawings that you can use as the basis for creating a drawing of your own. Each sample diagram contains shapes, text, and data on one or more pages.

The data that is included with each sample is stored in a Microsoft Excel file that is linked to the drawing using the Visio data linking feature that you will learn more about in Chapter 6, "Entering, Linking to, and Reporting on Data."

In this exercise, you will create a new drawing from one of the Visio 2010 sample diagrams.

SET UP Click the File tab, and then click New.

1. In the **Other Ways to Get Started** section, click **Sample diagrams**.

   In the center panel, you see the name and preview image of the five sample diagrams. The right panel displays additional information about the selected sample diagram and provides evidence of the underlying data in the form of a button labeled Open Sample Data. Clicking that button launches Excel and displays the data for the selected diagram.

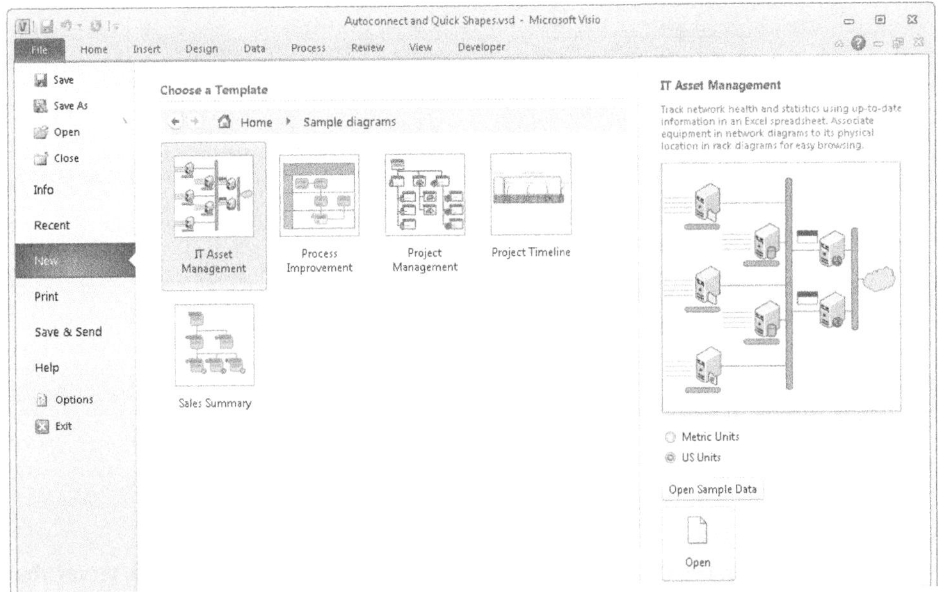

2. Double-click the **IT Asset Management** thumbnail.

   The sample diagram opens. Notice that the title of the Visio window is not *IT Asset Management* but is *Drawing1* (or *Drawing* followed by another number if you have created other new drawings during the same Visio session). Visio has not opened the sample document but has created a new diagram from it.

External Data Window

3. If you are running Visio Professional or Premium and see the **External Data** window, on the **Data** tab, in the **Show/Hide** group, click the **External Data Window** button to close it. If you are running Visio Standard, the External Data window does not appear.

   The first page of the sample diagram shows the network topology for Contoso, Ltd. The page name tabs below the drawing window indicate that there are three additional pages in the drawing.

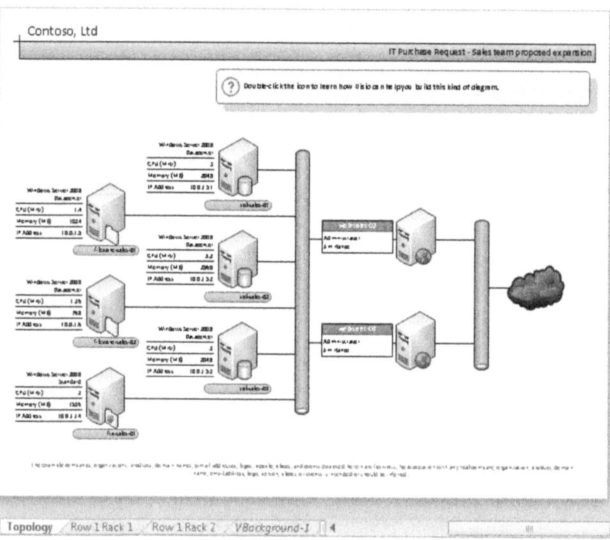

Tip The data you see displayed under and on the left of the server shapes in this and the following graphics is displayed by Visio *data graphics*. You will learn about data graphics in Chapter 10, "Visualizing Your Data."

4. Zoom in on the left half of the page.

   Each server is pictured with an icon representing the server type and also displays data about the server.

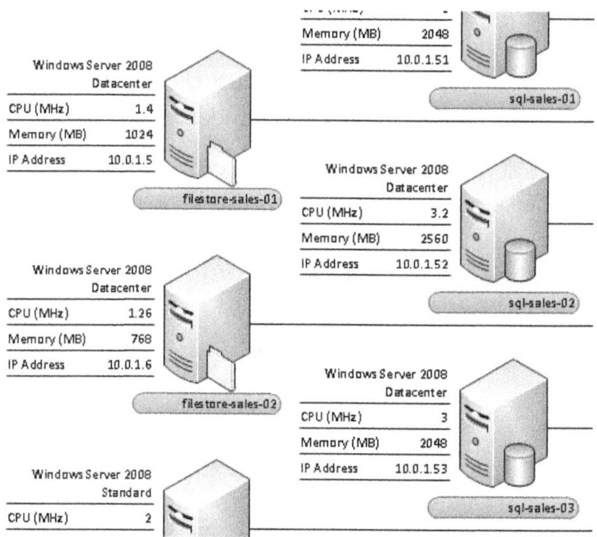

5. Point to **filestore-sales-02** on the left side of the diagram.

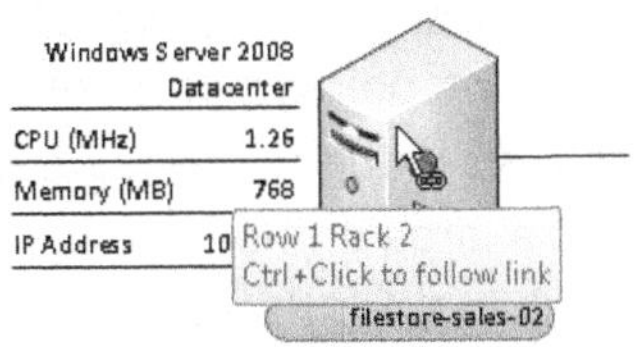

The cursor displays a hyperlink indicator attachment, and the pop-up text displays the name of the hyperlink target—in this case, a page name and the instructions "Ctrl+Click to follow link". (You will learn more about hyperlinks in Chapter 7, "Adding and Using Hyperlinks.")

6. While pressing the Ctrl key, click the server shape to follow the hyperlink. Visio displays page Row 1 Rack 2 with its representation of the rack containing server filestore-sales-02.

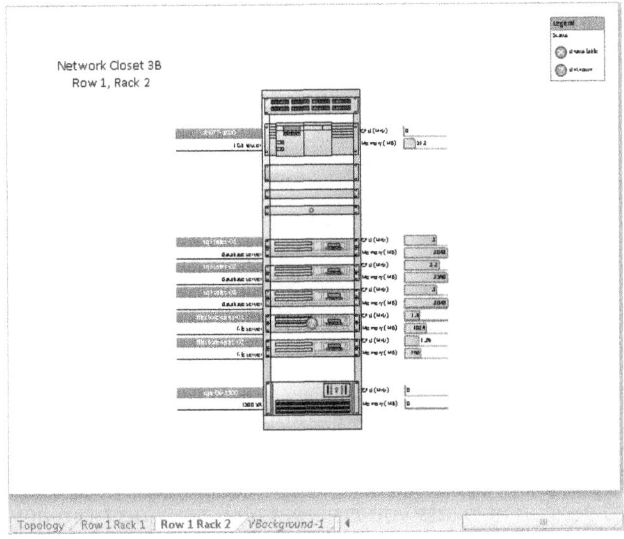

7. Zoom in to explore the rack diagram, and then click once to select the rack shape for **filestore-sales-02**.

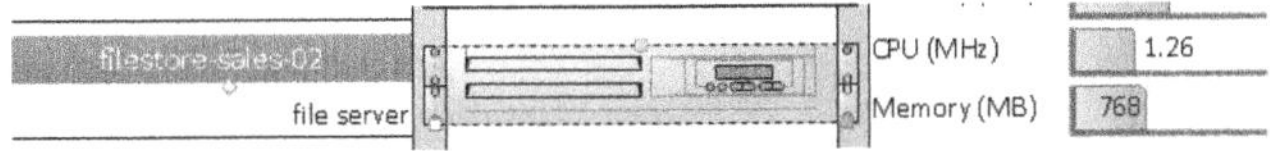

In "Identifying 1-D Shapes and Types of Glue" earlier in this chapter, you learned that 1-D shapes have symbols at their endpoints that indicate when they are glued to another shape. If you look at the shape in the rack on your screen or in the previous graphic, you see that it displays those symbols: a white square with a red outline on the left and a solid red square on the right. Despite the fact that it looks like a 2-D shape, the server is really a 1-D shape!

The server was designed as a 1-D shape so it would snap into the equipment rack, which was created with a series of connection points along both vertical side pieces (the connection points are the small blue X's in the following graphic). If you explore the rack-related stencils, you'll find a large number of shapes that appear to be 2-D shapes but that are actually 1-D shapes for this reason.

See Also **If you would like to learn how to create 2-D shapes that exhibit 1-D behavior, refer to "Creating Well Connected Assemblies with 1D Visio Shapes" at** ***www.visiozone.com/?p=83.***

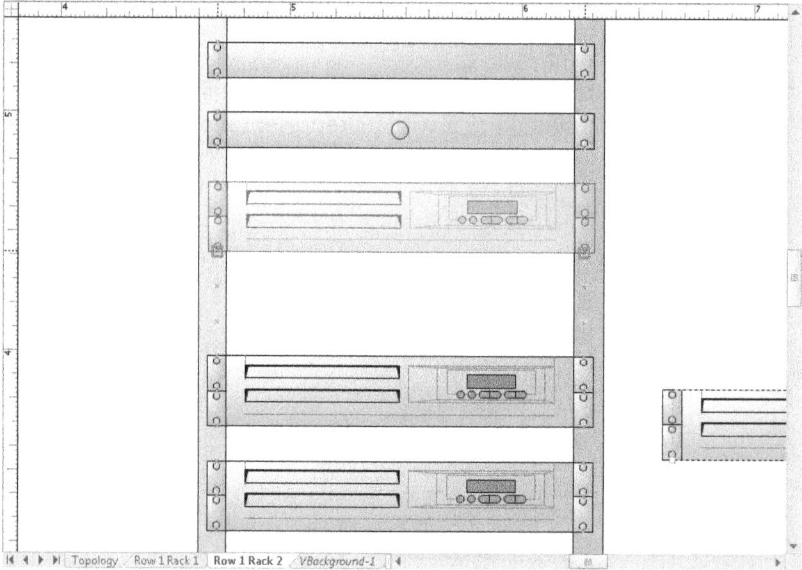

 **CLEAN UP Save your diagram as *Network Map*, and then close the file.**

In addition to creating a new drawing from one of the five sample drawings provided with Visio, the 2010 version also lets you create a new drawing from any existing drawing. This enables you to create a drawing by starting with existing content, knowing that any changes you make will not affect the original drawing.

Key Points

- The Visio 2010 Dynamic Grid facilitates aligning new and existing shapes on the drawing page and eliminates much of the need to drag and nudge shapes into alignment after you've placed them on the page. You can also use the rulers on the edges of the drawing page or drag guides onto the page to assist with shape positioning.
- Visio provides multiple shape selection techniques. Mouse-only techniques allow either selection by area or freeform selection using a lasso. Other techniques use a combination of keystrokes and mouse movements.
- The Visio 2010 paste function is smarter than in previous versions of the product. When you copy shapes from one page to another, the shapes are now pasted into the exact position they occupied on the source page. You can also select a specific paste location or use Paste Special by right-clicking.
- You can connect shapes by using either lines or dynamic connectors. Lines retain their shape characteristics when adjacent shapes are moved. Connectors, on the other hand, add or remove elbow bends to dynamically adjust their appearance in order to accommodate new shape positions.
- Lines and connectors can be glued either to a specific connection point on a shape or to the shape as a whole. The former is known as static glue; the latter is referred to as dynamic glue. When you reposition shapes that use dynamic glue, the attachment point of a line or connector can change.
- Visio shapes are one of two types: 1-D shapes, which behave like lines; and 2-D shapes, which behave like filled polygons.
- The Visio 2010 AutoConnect and Quick Shapes features can significantly reduce the time it takes to create a drawing consisting of connected shapes.
- With the Visio 2010 AutoAdd function, you can split dynamic connectors merely by dropping a new shape onto them. The reverse is also true: if you delete a shape that is linked by dynamic connectors, AutoDelete removes unneeded connectors.
- The Visio development team at Microsoft created a list of favorite tips and tricks for Visio 2010 that is an excellent companion to this chapter; go to *blogs.msdn.com/b/visio/archive/2010/12/21/our-favorite-visio-tips-amp-tricks.aspx.*

Chapter at a Glance

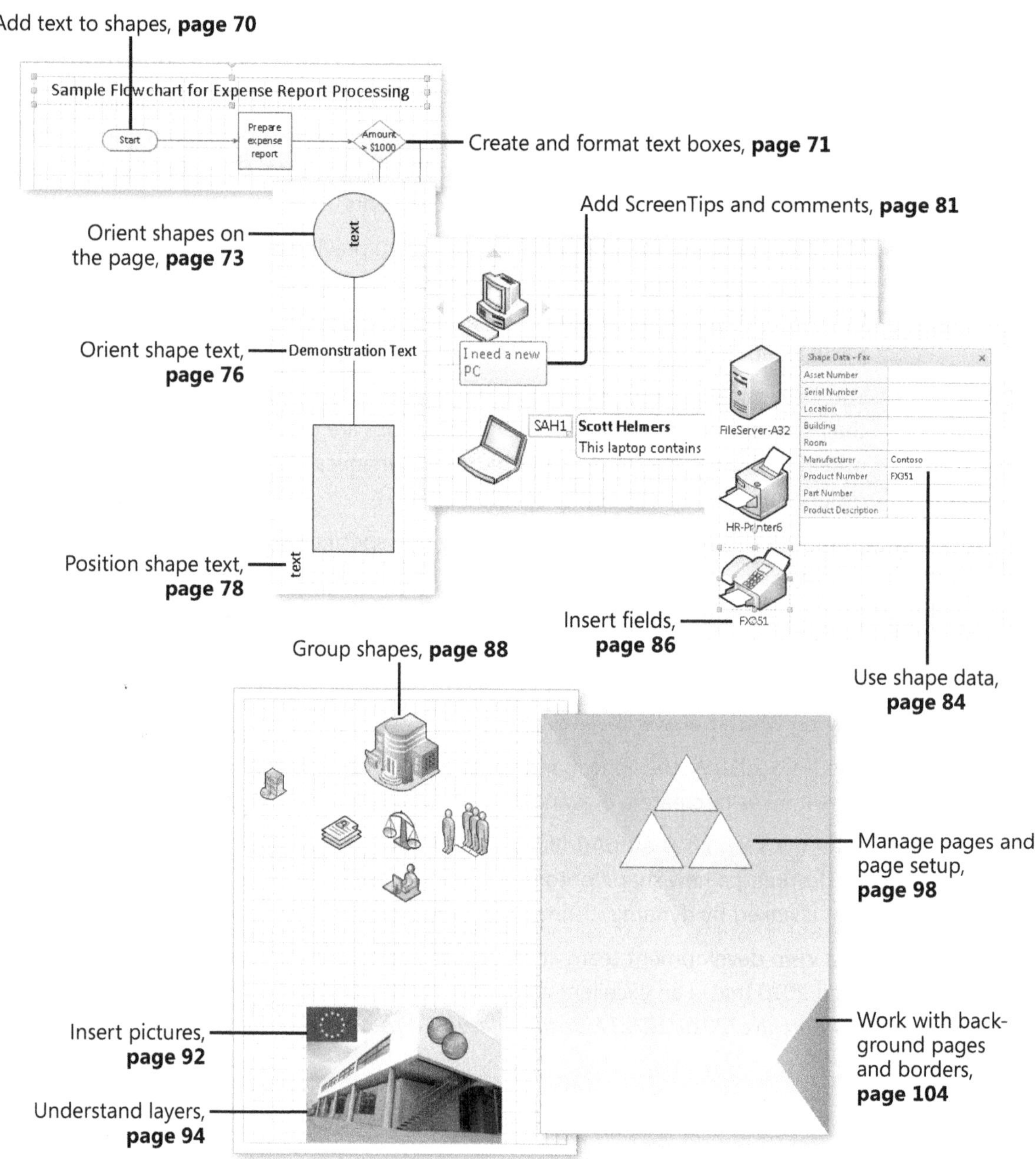

3 Adding Sophistication to Your Drawings

In this chapter, you will learn how to

- ✔ Add text to shapes.
- ✔ Create and format text boxes.
- ✔ Orient shapes on the page.
- ✔ Orient and position shape text.
- ✔ Add ScreenTips and comments.
- ✔ Use shape data.
- ✔ Insert fields.
- ✔ Group shapes.
- ✔ Insert pictures.
- ✔ Understand layers.
- ✔ Manage pages and page setup.
- ✔ Work with background pages and borders.

At this point in your Microsoft Visio 2010 journey, you know how to perform many basic tasks: create drawings from templates and sample diagrams, add shapes from stencils, create your own shapes, and connect shapes by using lines and dynamic connectors.

In this chapter, you will move beyond the basics and explore ways to add sophistication to your drawings. In addition to managing pages and page layouts, you will add text to shapes and manipulate shapes and text in new ways. You will also add fields, ScreenTips, and comments to shapes; insert pictures and other objects; learn about layers; and take the first steps in creating data-driven diagrams. (There's more on that last subject in Chapter 6, "Entering, Linking to, and Reporting on Data" and Chapter 10, "Visualizing Your Data.")

> **Practice Files** Before you can complete the exercises in this chapter, you need to copy the book's practice files to your computer. The practice files you'll use to complete the exercises in this chapter are in the Chapter03 practice files folder. A complete list of practice files is provided in "Using the Practice Files" at the beginning of this book.

Adding Text to Shapes

In some Visio diagrams, the shapes are self-explanatory. In many drawings, however, you need to label the shapes.

In this exercise, you will add text to existing shapes.

SET UP You need the *Text Exercises_start* drawing located in the Chapter03 practice file folder to complete this exercise. Open the drawing in Visio and save it as *Text Exercises.*

1. On the left side of the page, click once (don't double-click) on the start/end shape, type **Start**, and then click anywhere on the page background to finish text editing.

   Because the default font size is very small, in the next steps you will increase the size for all shapes on the page.

2. Press Ctrl+A to select all shapes.

Font Size

3. On the **Home** tab, in the **Font** group, in the **Font Size** list, click **14 pt.** The text in your start/end shape is more legible.
4. Double-click the process shape to the right of the start shape, type **Prepare expense report**, and then click anywhere on the background of the page.

   When you click outside of the shape, notice that the dimensions of the shape change—it grows taller. The process box is an example of a shape that expands automatically when the amount of text exceeds its size.

5. Click once (don't double-click) on the decision shape, press F2, type **Amount > $1000**, and then click outside of the shape.

   Tip F2 is a Visio keyboard shortcut that enters and exits text edit mode.

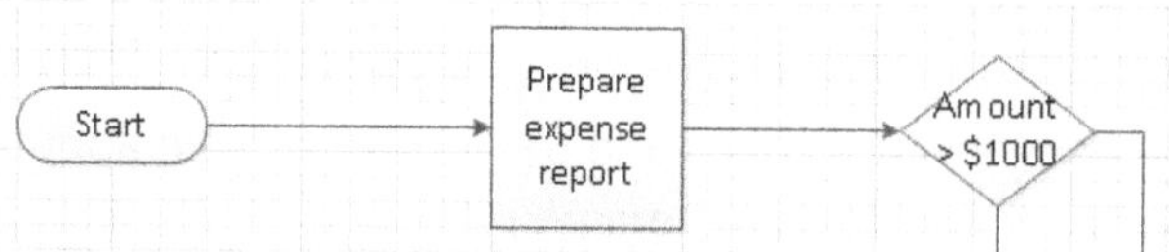

CLEAN UP Save your changes to the *Text Exercises* drawing but leave it open if you are continuing to the next exercise.

Tip You added text to shapes in Steps 1, 4, and 5 in this exercise. You may have noticed that you were instructed to use a different method each time. For most Visio shapes, the three methods of entering text edit mode—single-click and start typing; double-click; and select the shape and press F2—are interchangeable. You will find exceptions to this rule, but most shapes behave as you saw in this exercise.

Creating and Formatting Text Boxes

Although a picture can be worth a thousand words, sometimes you still need a few words.

In this exercise, you will create and format a text box to use as a page title.

SET UP You need the ***Text Exercises*** drawing that you created in the previous exercise.

Text

1. On the **Home** tab, in the **Tools** group, click the **Text** button. The cursor changes to a plus sign with a page icon below it.
2. Click in the upper-left corner of the drawing page and drag to create a text box that is approximately 6 inches (150 mm) long. Visio automatically zooms in so you can type in the text box.

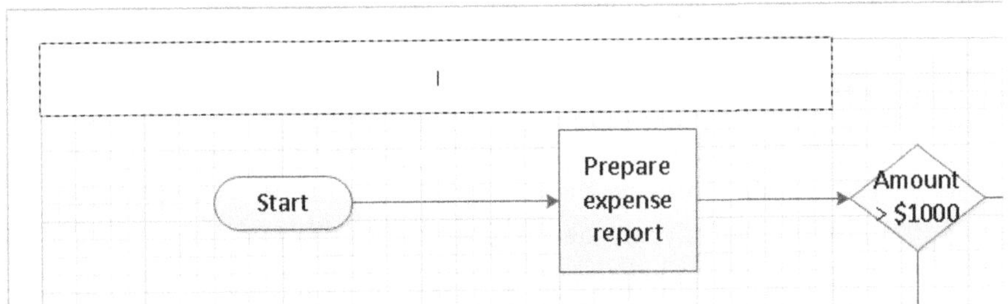

3. Type **Sample Flowchart for Expense Report Processing**.

Pointer Tool

4. On the **Home** tab, in the **Tools** group, click the **Pointer Tool** button. Visio closes the text box, returns to the previous zoom level, and leaves the text box selected.

   Tip If you want to continue working with the Text tool to create another text box, you can close the current text box by pressing the Esc key.

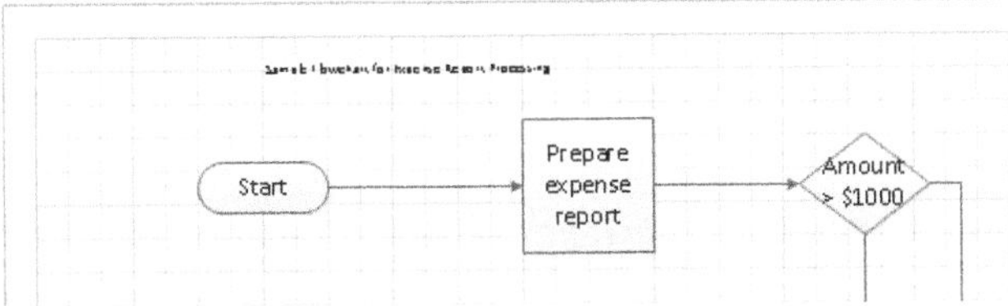

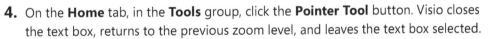

The text in the page title box is a bit small!

8pt.

Font Size

5. On the **Home** tab, in the **Font** group, click the **Font Size** arrow. As you point to various font sizes, notice that Visio provides a live preview of the results on the drawing page.

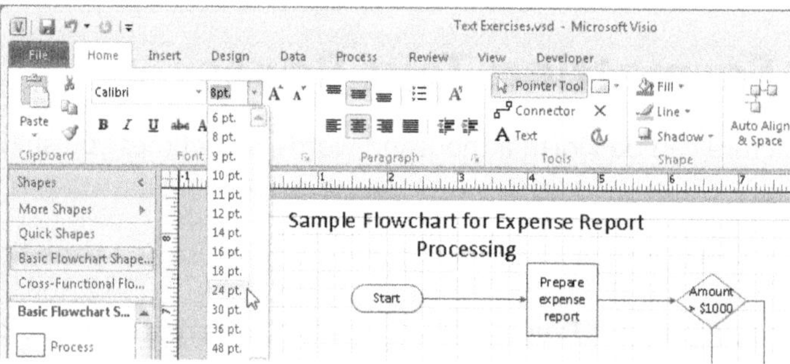

6. Select **24 pt.** as the new font size.

7. Because the text wraps inside the text box at this font size, drag the right resize handle to the right until the text no longer wraps.

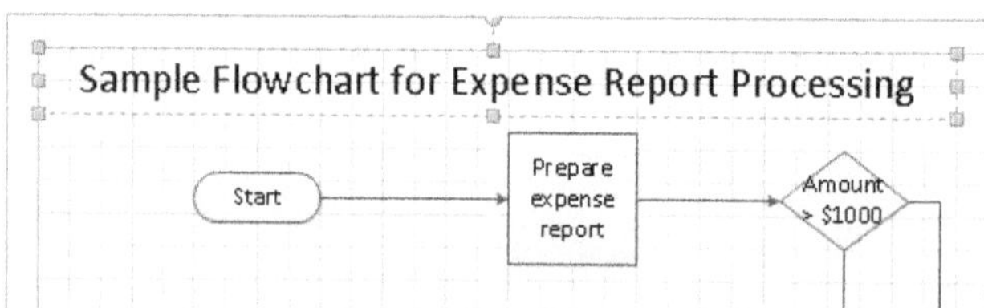

At this point, you can use all of the usual text manipulation tools in the Font and Paragraph groups on the Home tab to apply other fonts, colors, and text styles or to add bullets or numbers and reposition the text within the text box.

8. Right-click on the text box, and then click the **Bold** button on the Mini Toolbar to make the title text bold.

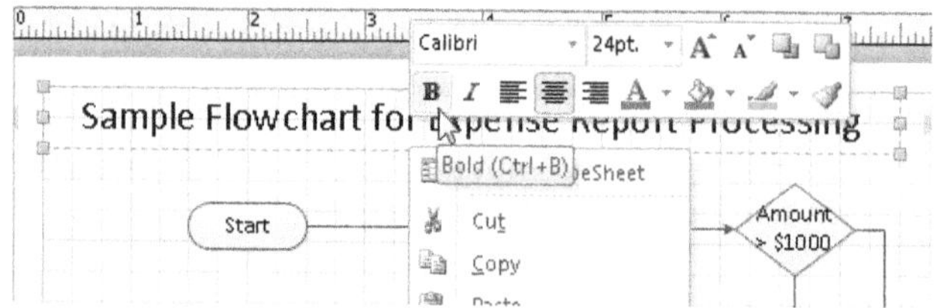

Tip The Mini Toolbar functions that include menus—text color, fill color, and line color—all include Live Preview.

CLEAN UP Save your changes to the *Text Exercises* drawing, and then close it.

In this exercise, you created a page title text box manually, but Visio offers a number of preformatted text boxes that are designed as page titles. You will see an example in "Working with Background Pages and Borders" later in this chapter.

Tip **If you are a long-time Visio user and prefer to use the legacy text formatting dialog boxes, they are still available. Just click the dialog box launcher in the Font and Paragraph groups on the Home tab (refer to the following graphic).**

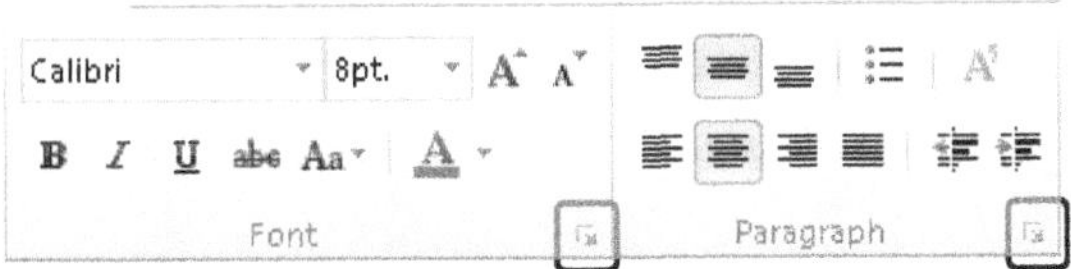

Tip **To apply changes to all of the text in a text box, select the box by using the Pointer Tool before making changes. To change only part of the text, double-click the text box to enter edit mode, and then select the specific text you want to change. (As an alternative to double-clicking the text box, you can select the text box by using the Text tool, which automatically enters edit mode.)**

Orienting Shapes on the Page

When you drop shapes onto the Visio drawing page, they are usually oriented the way you want them to be. However, there are times when you want the shapes to appear at a different angle. Visio provides several ways to accomplish this.

In this exercise, you will add several shapes to the Visio drawing page and rotate the shapes to different angles.

Tip **The font size for some of the graphics in this exercise has been increased for readability. The font in your shapes may be smaller.**

SET UP **Start Visio, or if it's already running, click the File tab, and then click New. In the Template Categories section, click General, and then double-click the Block Diagram thumbnail. Save the drawing as *Orient Shapes and Text.***

Page Width

1. On the **View** tab, in the **Zoom** group, click the **Page Width** button, and then position the page so you can see the top edge.
2. Drag a **Box** shape from the **Blocks** stencil and drop it so the center is approximately 8 inches (200 mm) up from the bottom and 3 inches (75 mm) in from the left side of the page.

Tip Use the ruler on the left and top edges of the drawing page to guide shape placement.

The shapes in the US Units version of the Block Diagram stencil contain the word *text*, whereas the same shapes in the Metric Units version of the stencil do not. Because the examples in this chapter were created using the U.S. version, you will see the word *text*. If you are using the Metric stencil, add the word *text* to each shape.

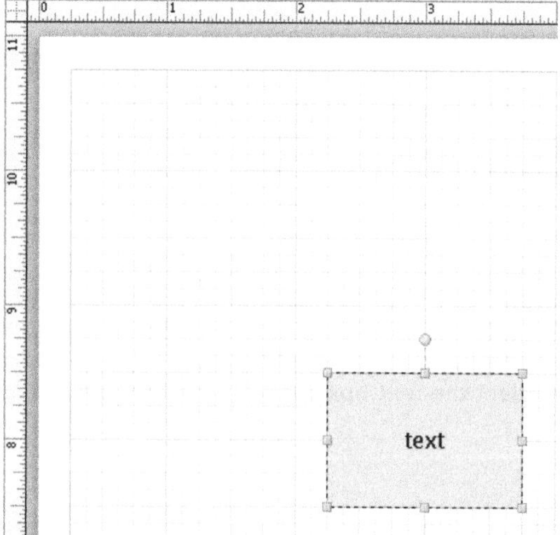

In addition to the regular selection handles surrounding the box, notice the rotation handle at the top center just above the box.

When you point to the rotation handle, the cursor changes from an arrow to a circular arrow. Notice also that a dot appears in the center of the rectangle. This dot shows the geometric center of the shape, that is, the point around which the shape will rotate when you drag the rotation handle.

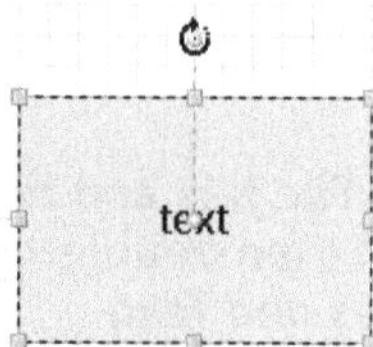

Tip If you do not see a rotation handle above a shape, it's because the shape designer has turned off the rotation feature.

3. Grab the rotation handle and rotate the shape 90 degrees to the left (counterclockwise). Both the shape and the text rotate.

4. Drag the rotation handle counterclockwise another 90 degrees so the box is inverted.

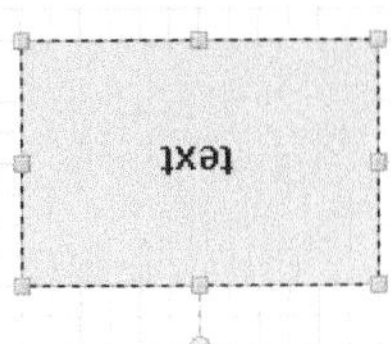

Notice that the text is also upside down—more about that in the next exercise.

5. Return the box to its original upright position to continue with this exercise. As you can see, you are able to rotate the shape freely through 360 degrees of arc.
6. Drag a **Circle** onto the page so its center is approximately 3 inches (75 mm) to the right of the center of the box, using the **Dynamic Grid** to align it with the box.
7. On the **Home** tab, in the **Tools** group, click the **Connector** button.

Connector

8. Draw a connector from the right side of the box to the left side of the circle.
9. On the **Home** tab, in the **Tools** group, click the **Pointer Tool** button.

Pointer Tool

10. Click the new connector and type **Demonstration Text**. Then press Esc.
11. Draw a bounding box around all three shapes to select them, and then right-click on any of the shapes.
12. In the Mini Toolbar, set the font size to **14 pt.** to make it easier to read the text in the steps that follow.

Tip Note that you can apply the same change to multiple shapes at one time.

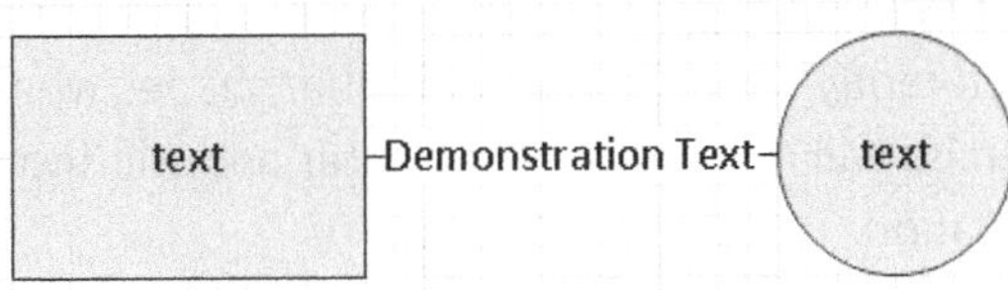

13. Draw a bounding box around all three shapes to select them, and then rotate the entire selection 90 degrees clockwise.

Tip You can rotate selections of shapes as easily as you can rotate individual shapes.

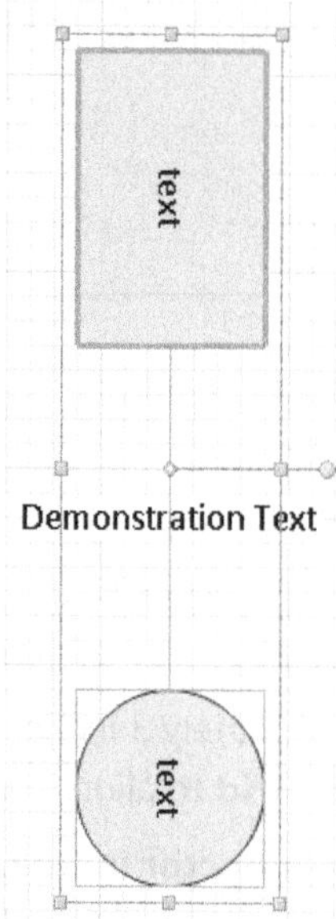

Notice the difference in behavior between the text in the box or circle and the text on the connector.

14. Rotate the selection another 90 degrees clockwise so the shapes are inverted.

At this point, it's quite obvious that the text in some shapes seems to behave better—or at least differently—than the text in other shapes when the shapes are rotated. The next exercise will make this even clearer and will show you how to change the text orientation.

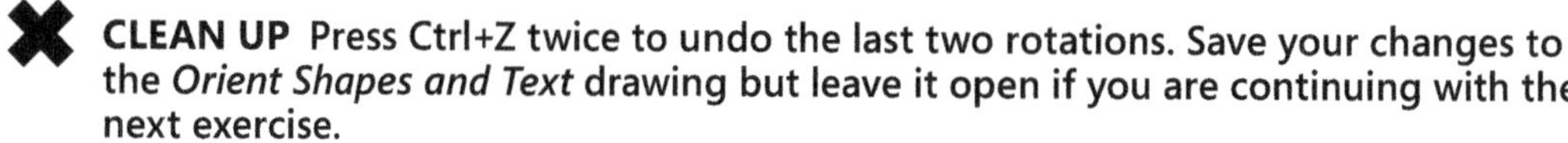

CLEAN UP Press Ctrl+Z twice to undo the last two rotations. Save your changes to the *Orient Shapes and Text* drawing but leave it open if you are continuing with the next exercise.

Orienting Shape Text

As you observed in the preceding exercise, shape text does not always rotate as you rotate the containing shape. Whether it does depends on how the underlying shape was designed.

In this exercise, you will see additional examples of automatic text rotation. You will also rotate text manually and reposition text blocks on shapes.

SET UP You need the *Orient Shapes and Text* drawing that you created in the preceding exercise. Open the drawing in Visio if it is not already open.

1. Drag a **2-D single** arrow shape from the **Blocks** stencil onto the drawing page and position it below the box shape from the preceding exercise.
2. While the arrow is still selected, type **ABC**.
3. In the **Shapes** window, click **Blocks Raised**, drag a **Right arrow** onto the page, and position it below the arrow you placed in the previous step.
4. While the arrow is still selected, type **ABC**.
5. Draw a bounding box around both arrows to select them, and change the font size to **14 pt.** (See the graphic on the left following Step 7.)
6. Select the upper arrow and use the rotation handle to rotate it 180 degrees.
7. Select the lower arrow and use the rotation handle to rotate it 180 degrees.

The graphic on the left shows the results of Step 5. The graphic on the right shows the results of Steps 6 and 7.

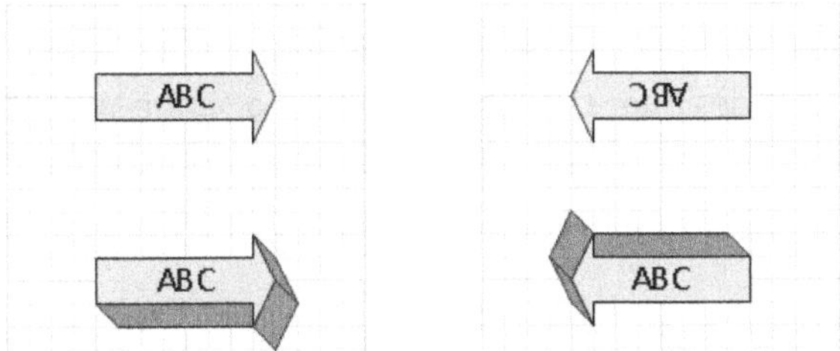

Although the two arrow shapes are similar in some respects, their designers made different choices for how text should be handled. In the upper arrow, the text rotates along with the shape. In the lower arrow, the text responds to ***gravity***, or more correctly, it responds to a mathematical function that sets the text angle based on the shape angle so that it appears to be responding to gravity.

Tip For the technically inclined, if you look in the TxtAngle cell in the Text Transform section of the ShapeSheet for the lower arrow, you will actually see a function named GRAVITY(). You will learn the basics of the ShapeSheet in the Appendix.

To get a better sense of how the gravity function works, rotate the lower arrow in several steps from its current position to its original position.

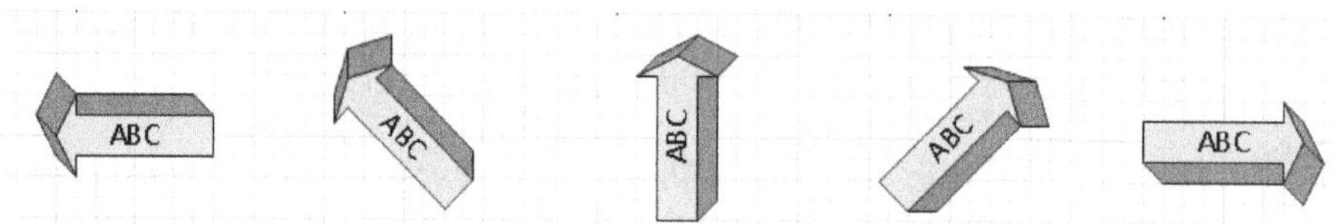

You can see that some shapes are designed so the text will be upright as the shape is rotated, but what do you do with shapes that aren't designed that way? Enter the Text Block tool...

Text Block

8. On the **Home** tab, in the **Tools** group, click the **Text Block** button.
9. Click once on the upper arrow and notice that the selection handles appear as usual.
10. Drag the selection handle clockwise. Notice that because you are using the Text Block tool and not the Pointer Tool, only the text rotates. Stop when you have rotated the text 180 degrees.

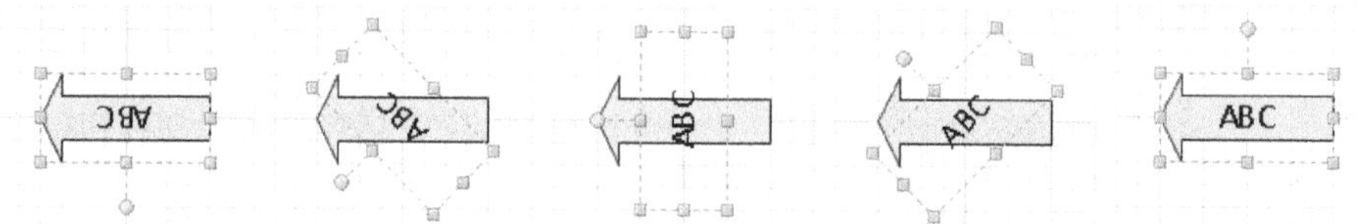

You can use the Text Block tool to reorient the text in virtually any shape. However, be aware that a shape designer can lock the text in a shape so that the text can neither be altered nor repositioned. If you click with the Text Block tool on a shape whose text is locked, the handles will be grayed out as shown in the following graphic.

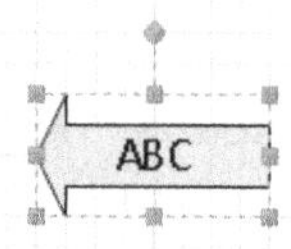

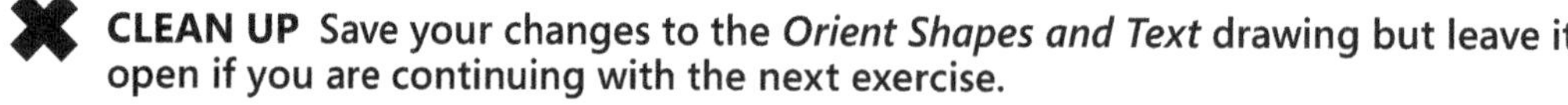

CLEAN UP Save your changes to the *Orient Shapes and Text* drawing but leave it open if you are continuing with the next exercise.

Positioning Shape Text

The text on a Visio shape is located in a ***text block***. You can reposition the text within a text block with several buttons located on the Visio ribbon. You can also reposition the entire text block by using the Text Block tool you learned about in the previous exercise.

In this exercise, you will reposition text within a text block and you will move the text block to a new location.

SET UP **You need the *Orient Shapes and Text* drawing that you used in the preceding exercise. Open the drawing in Visio if it is not already open.**

1. Click once on the rectangle that contains the word *text*.

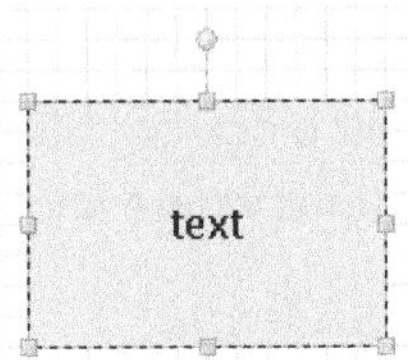

Tip **When you select a shape, the illuminated buttons in the Paragraph group show the current text alignment for that shape. For example, after clicking the rectangle, the Paragraph group should look like the following graphic, indicating that the text is centered both vertically and horizontally.**

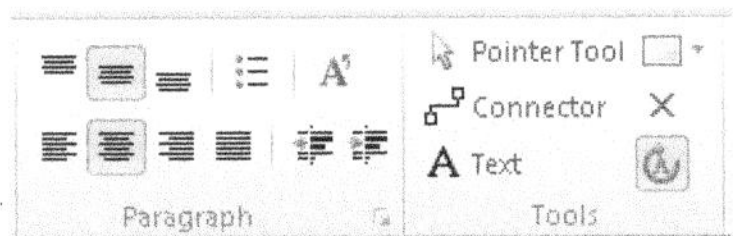

2. On the **Home** tab, in the **Paragraph** group, click any of the buttons to observe the effect. For example, if you click the Align Top button and then the Align Left button, the shape will look like the following graphic.

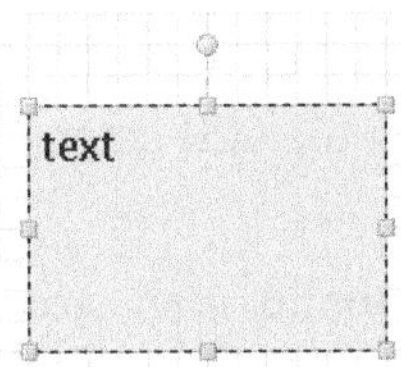

Text Block

3. On the **Home** tab, in the **Tools** group, click the **Text Block** button, and then click once on the rectangle that contains the word *text*.
4. Click anywhere on the edge of the text block (the blue dashed lines) and drag the text block up and to the left.

   When the Text Block tool is active, the text block moves independently from the underlying shape. If you use the Pointer Tool and move the underlying shape, the text block also moves and remains in the same position relative to the shape.

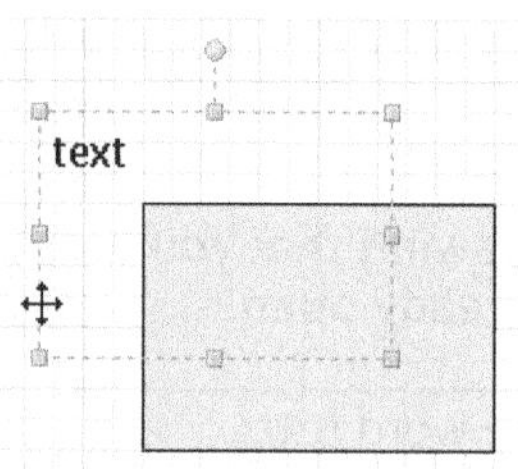

You can also resize the text block whenever the Text Block tool is active by dragging any of the resize handles. Although moving the text block on this particular shape may not make a lot of sense, there are other situations where knowing how to move and rotate text can be very helpful.

5. In the **Shapes** window, click **More Shapes**, point to **Network**, and then click **Computers and Monitors**. The Computers And Monitors stencil opens.
6. Drag an **LCD monitor** shape onto the page, drop it below the circle shape, and type **Hello**. Notice that this shape was designed so that the text block is located below the shape.

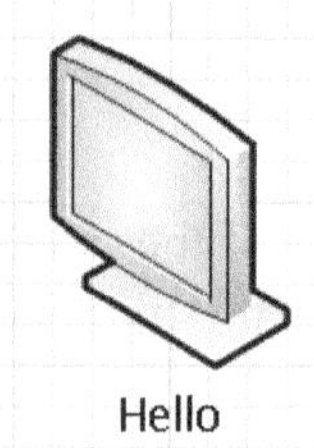

7. On the **Home** tab, in the **Tools** group, click the **Text Block** button. Reposition and rotate the text block so the word *Hello* appears on the LCD screen at approximately the same angle as the screen itself.

Tip Repositioning and rotating the text in the LCD monitor is an excellent situation in which to use the zoom feature in Visio. Zoom in to enlarge the shape before attempting to relocate and rotate the shape, and you will be able to complete this step more easily and more precisely.

 **CLEAN UP** Save your changes to the *Orient Shapes and Text* drawing, and then close it.

See Also For another perspective on text block positioning, go to *www.visguy.com/2007/11/07/text-to-the-bottom-of-the-shape/.*

Adding ScreenTips and Comments

In some drawings, you want to provide your reader with additional information that doesn't need to be visible at all times. Visio provides two convenient options with very different characteristics:

- ***ScreenTips*** display pop-up text when you point to a shape but they are otherwise invisible. Indeed, there is no way to know that a ScreenTip exists unless you point to a shape containing one and a pop-up appears.

  Important ScreenTips are part of a shape. Consequently, they move with a shape and are deleted when you delete a shape.

- ***Comments*** provide a visible indication of their presence but require you to click on them to see the text of the comment. The comment indicator displays the initials of the person who created the comment, along with a unique sequence number. Each comment also stores and displays the name of the comment author and the date on which it was created.

  Important It is important to understand that comments, unlike ScreenTips, are attached to the drawing page and not to specific shapes. Consequently, they may appear near shapes in some circumstances but they bear no relationship to, and operate independently from, Visio shapes. You will see evidence of this in the exercise in this section.

In general, use ScreenTips to provide useful but noncritical information about a shape. You should make the assumption that the reader may happen upon a ScreenTip but also may not. Use comments when it is vital that the reader know that they exist and when it is important to know who created the comment and when.

In this exercise, you will add a ScreenTip to a shape. You will also add and edit a comment.

SET UP Click the File tab, and then click New. In the Template Categories section, click Network, and then double click the Basic Network Diagram thumbnail. Save the drawing as *Text and Data on Shapes.*

1. In the **Shapes** window, click **Computers and Monitors**. The Computers And Monitors stencil opens.
2. Drag a **PC** shape onto the page.

Screen Tip

3. On the **Insert** tab, in the **Text** group, click the **ScreenTip** button. The Shape ScreenTip dialog box opens.

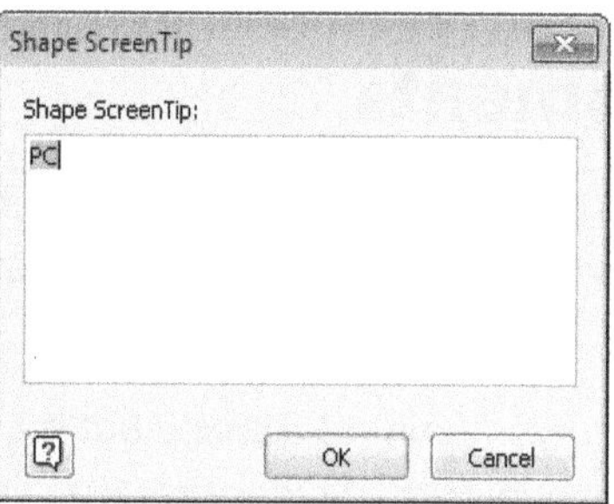

4. Type **I need a new PC** to overwrite the text in the dialog box, and then click **OK**.
5. Point to the PC and observe the pop-up text that you've created.

6. Drag a **Laptop** shape from the **Computers and Monitors** stencil onto the page.

New Comment

7. On the **Review** tab, in the **Comments** group, click the **New Comment** button.

Tip Comments are part of the review feature set in Visio. Consequently, you will find comment buttons on the Review tab and not on the Insert tab where you found ScreenTips.

Visio drops a comment indicator and an edit box for the comment body onto the page. The indicator contains the author's initials (taken from the Visio settings) and a sequence number. In the following example, the comment indicator shows *SAH1*.

The comment edit box displays the author's name and the current date. The insertion point just below the author's name indicates that you can start typing the body of the comment.

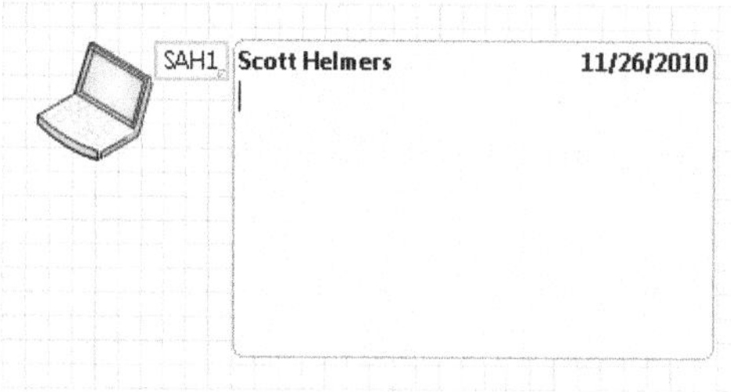

8. Type **This laptop contains Visio Premium 2010.**

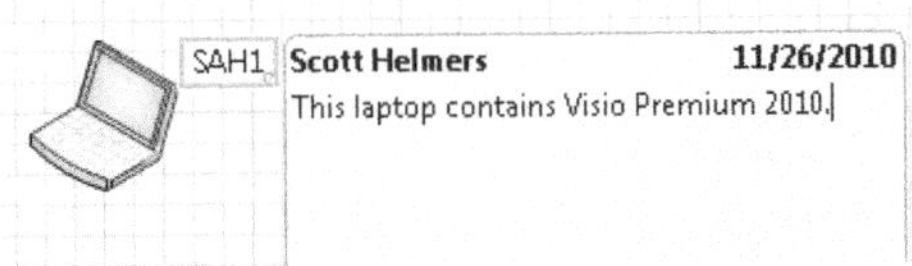
SAH1
Scott Helmers 11/26/2010
This laptop contains Visio Premium 2010.

9. Click anywhere on the background of the page to close the comment edit box. The border of the comment indicator has dimmed to show that it is not selected.

SAH1

10. Point to the comment **SAH1** but don't click the shape.

    Visio displays the author and the creation date of the comment. The pop-up text remains on the screen only as long as you continue to point to the indicator.

SAH1
Scott Helmers 11/26/2010

11. Click once on the comment **SAH1**.

    Visio displays the comment header as in the previous step but it also displays the body of the comment in the minimum required space. The comment body remains on the screen until you click elsewhere on the page or press Esc.

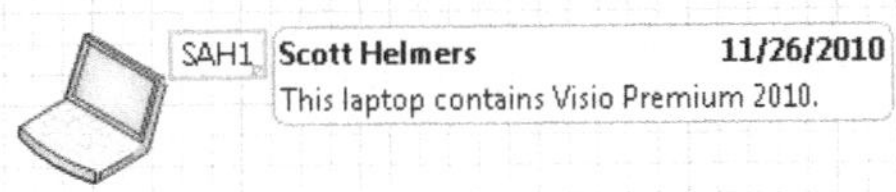
SAH1
Scott Helmers 11/26/2010
This laptop contains Visio Premium 2010.

12. Click anywhere outside the comment balloon to close it.
13. Double-click the comment **SAH1**, and type **It also contains Office 2010.**

    Visio opens the comment in edit mode so you can make changes to the text. The comment body remains on the screen until you click elsewhere on the page or press Esc.

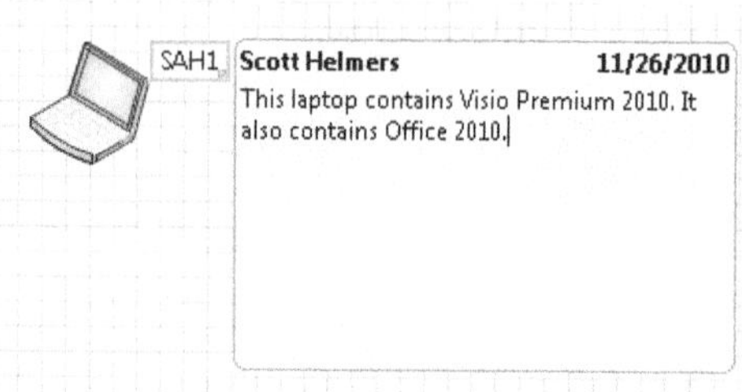

14. Click anywhere outside the comment balloon to close it.

Important Visio placed the comment *SAH1* near the laptop only because the shape was selected when you clicked the New Comment button in Step 7. However, the shape and the comment are not connected in any way, as the next steps in this exercise will illustrate. If no shape is selected when you click the New Comment button, Visio places the comment in the center of the drawing window.

15. Drag the laptop to the left. Note that the comment indicator does not move. Similarly, neither selecting nor deleting the laptop affects the comment, and vice versa.

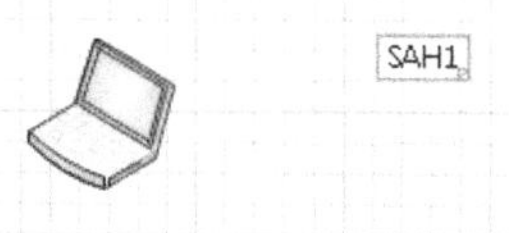

16. Right-click comment **SAH1**, and then click **Delete Comment**.

 **CLEAN UP** Save your changes to the *Text and Data on Shapes* drawing, and then close it.

Tip If your Visio diagram contains more than one comment, you can navigate among them using the Previous and Next buttons in the Comments group on the Review tab.

You can turn all comment indicators in your drawing on or off by clicking Show Markup in the Markup group on the Review tab.

Using Shape Data

A significant part of what gives Visio diagrams uniqueness and value is the data that resides inside Visio shapes. Called ***shape data*** in Visio 2010 and Visio 2007, data fields were known as ***custom properties*** in previous versions of Visio.

Many of the masters in the built-in Visio stencils already contain shape data fields. In this exercise, you will work with existing data fields. In Chapter 6, you will work with data in more detail, including creating new shape data fields.

In this exercise, you will add and edit values in computer and network shapes.

SET UP Click the File tab, and then click New. In the Template Categories section, click Network, and then double-click the Basic Network Diagram thumbnail. Save the drawing as *Shape Data*.

1. In the **Network and Peripherals** stencil, drag a **Server**, a **Printer**, and a **Fax** shape onto the page, arranging them from top to bottom on the page.
2. Click once on the server to select it.
3. On the **View** tab, in the **Show** group, click the **Task Panes** button, and then click **Shape Data**.

Task Panes

The Shape Data window appears and displays the names and current values, if any, for data fields that are contained within the server shape.

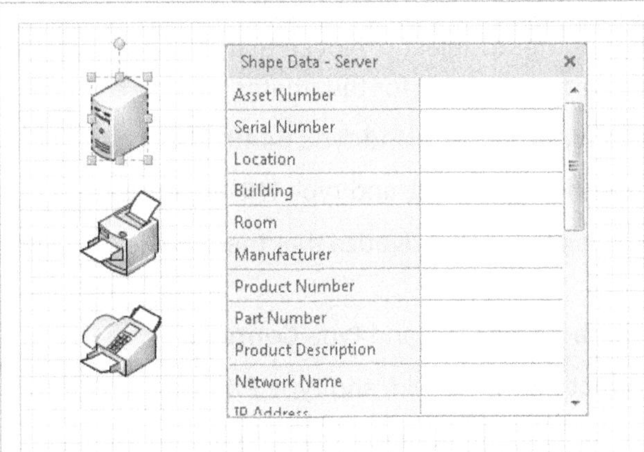

Tip The Shape Data window can appear anywhere on the screen but you can relocate it by dragging the gray window header. The graphic shows a floating window. If you drag the Shape Data window close to the edges of the drawing window, it will attach to the edge of the drawing window or dock itself in a fixed location. If this happens, but you want the window to be somewhere else, you can drag the header bar to relocate it. You can also resize the window to show a larger or smaller number of data fields.

4. Click in the **Asset Number** field, and type **6789-001**.
5. Click in the **Serial Number** field, and type **13579**.
6. Click in the **Network Name** field, and type **FileServer-A32**.

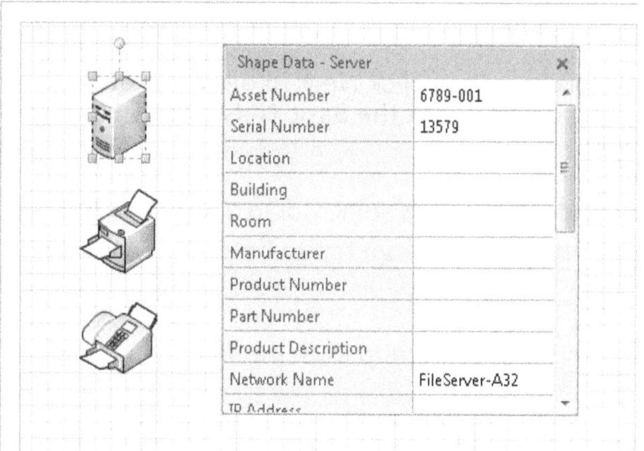

Tip Note the scroll bar on the right side of the Shape Data window. This shape has additional data fields that are not visible in the graphic.

7. Click once on the printer to select it. Notice that the Shape Data window now shows the fields that are defined for the printer.
8. Click in the **Asset Number** field, and type **6449-001**.
9. Click in the **Network Name** field, and type **HR-Printer6**.
10. Click once on the fax to select it. Notice that there are fewer fields defined for the fax machine.
11. Click in the **Manufacturer** field, and type **Contoso**.
12. Click in the **Product Number** field, and type **FX351**.

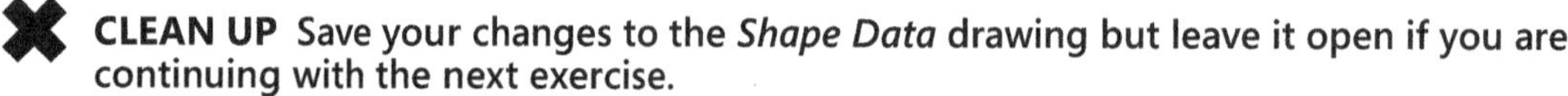
CLEAN UP Save your changes to the *Shape Data* drawing but leave it open if you are continuing with the next exercise.

Inserting Fields: The Basics

Now that you have entered data into several shapes, wouldn't it be nice to see some of it on the drawing?

In this exercise, you will insert a field onto a shape and link the field to shape data.

SET UP You need the *Shape Data* drawing that you created in the preceding exercise.

1. Click once on the server shape to select it.
2. On the **Insert** tab, in the **Text** group, click the **Field** button.

Field

The Field dialog box opens and displays eight categories of field data that can be inserted into a shape.

3. In the **Category** section of the **Field** dialog box, click **Shape Data**. The Shape Data fields for this shape appear in the Field name section.

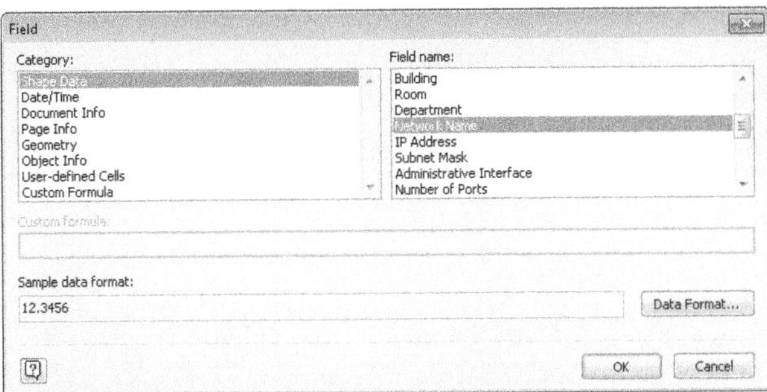

4. Scroll down in the **Field name** section, click **Network Name**, and then click **OK**. The field you inserted appears under the server.

Tip For the server shape and the other shapes on this page, the default text position is centered below the shape. As you saw in previous sections in this chapter, shape text may appear in the middle of a shape or somewhere else. You've also learned how to reposition shape text if you prefer a different location.

5. Click once on the printer to select it, and then repeat Steps 2–4 to display the network name for the printer.

6. Click once on the fax to select it, and repeat Steps 2 and 3, but this time click the **Product Number** field.

Your diagram should look like the following graphic.

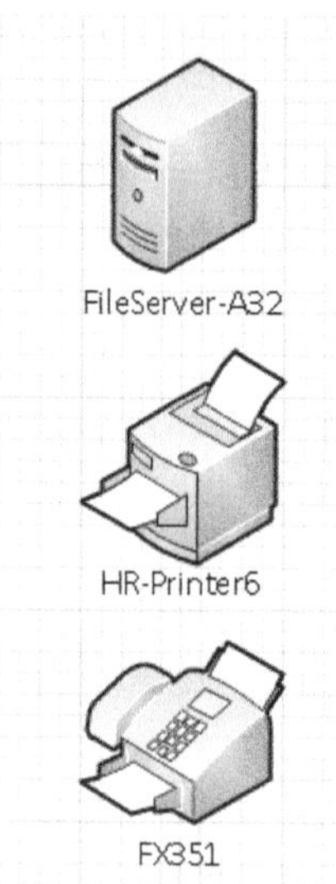

CLEAN UP Save your changes to the *Shape Data* drawing, and then close it.

There is a lot more that you can do with fields than simply displaying the contents of one field. You will learn more about fields in the Appendix.

Grouping Shapes

Most of the exercises you've done in this book so far have involved using or manipulating individual shapes. Sometimes it's more convenient to work with a set of shapes as a single unit.

In this exercise, you will create and work with a group shape.

SET UP Click the File tab, and then click New. In the Template Categories section, click Flowchart, and then double-click the Work Flow Diagram thumbnail. Save the drawing as *Corporate Diagram*.

1. In the **Shapes** window, click the **Department** stencil if it is not already selected.
2. Drag a **Headquarters** shape to the top center of the drawing page.
3. On the status bar, click either the **Width** or **Height** button to open the **Size & Position** window.

See Also For more information about the status bar and the Size & Position window, see Chapter 1, "A Visual Orientation to a Visual Product."

4. In the **Size & Position** window, double both the **Width** and **Height** to 2 in. for U.S. units or 60 mm. for metric.
5. Position the resized shape in the center of the page at the top margin.

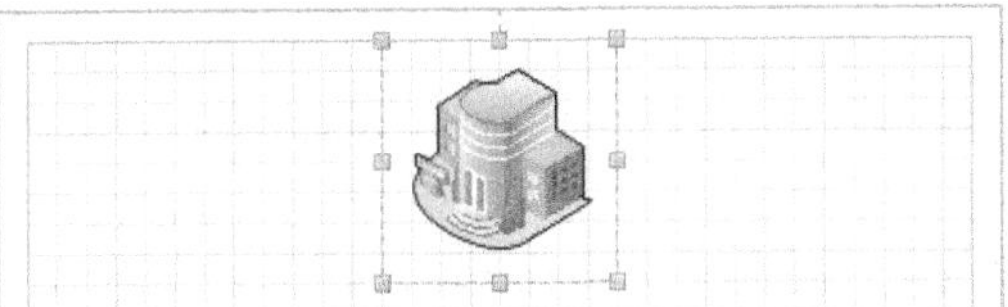

6. Drag the following shapes onto the page and position them in any arrangement below the headquarters icon: **Human resources**, **Legal department**, **Management**, **Customer service**.

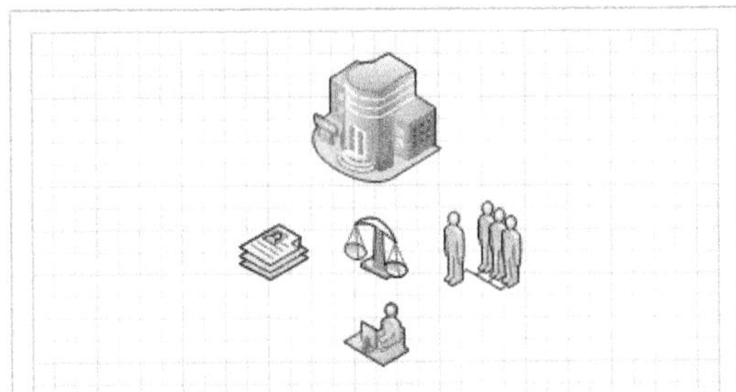

7. Draw a bounding box around all five shapes.

Group

8. On the **Home** tab, in the **Arrange** group, click the **Group** button, and then click **Group**. Notice that the magenta selection rectangles around the individual shapes have disappeared, indicating that the group operation was successful.

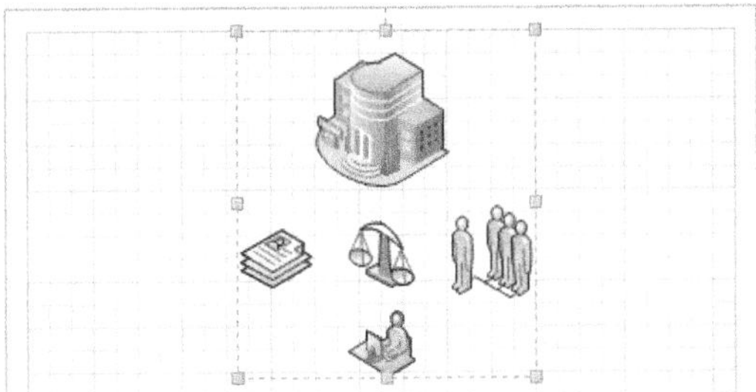

Tip You can also group shapes by right-clicking on a shape within the selection rectangle and clicking the Group menu entry.

Like the individual shapes that comprise it, a group is also a shape. You can apply borders or fills, add fields and text, add shape data—in short, you can do anything with a group shape that you can with any other shape.

9. Drag the group to the upper-left corner of the page. All shapes that are part of the group move together.
10. Click anywhere on the page background to deselect the group.
11. Click once on any shape in the group. Notice that the entire group is selected.
12. With the group still selected, click once on the management shape.

    The selection rectangle around the group changes from a blue dashed line with resize handles to a gray dashed line to indicate that the group no longer has the focus. The management shape, on the other hand, now displays resize handles and a rotation handle because it is now the selected shape.

    The default behavior for grouped shapes is what you have observed in the preceding two steps: the first click selects the group; the second click selects a shape within the group. It is possible to change this behavior but you won't do that in this exercise.

    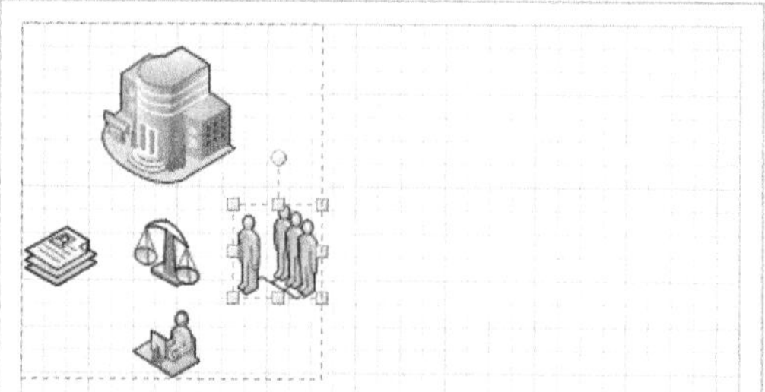

13. Click the dashed line surrounding the group to change the focus back to the group.
14. Drag the lower-right resize handle to enlarge the group. Notice that all shapes within the group resize proportionally.

    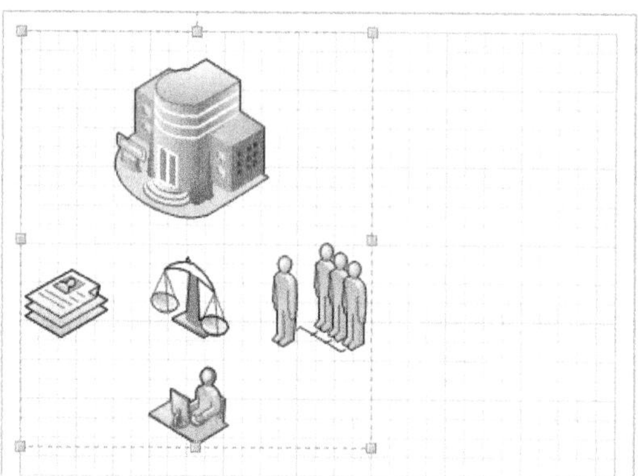

15. Drag a **Cafeteria** shape from the **Department** stencil and drop it somewhere within the boundary of the group.

16. Select and drag the group back to the center of the page. You can see that dropping a shape onto a group does not add it to the group.

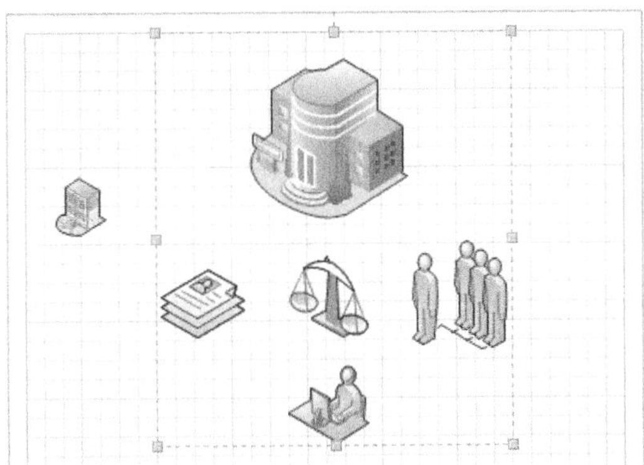

Tip By default, shapes dropped on a group are not added to the group. However, if you run Visio in developer mode, you can change the behavior of a group so it will accept dropped shapes. You will learn about developer mode in the Appendix.

17. On the **Home** tab, in the **Arrange** group, click the **Group** button, and then click **Ungroup**.

    The shapes remain on the page but Visio removes the group. Any styles, text, or data associated with the group are now gone as well. As you can see, each shape now shows its own selection rectangle.

Important Ungrouping the shape in this step is perfectly safe. In general though, ungrouping a shape can be very destructive unless you know exactly what you're doing. The reason is that to Visio, a group is just another shape and it can have its own data and properties. Compounding the problem, the shapes in many groups derive some of their own behavior and data from the group. Consequently, when you ungroup the parent shape, you destroy the shape properties that were derived from the group.

Tip You can also ungroup shapes by right-clicking on a shape within a group and clicking the Group menu entry.

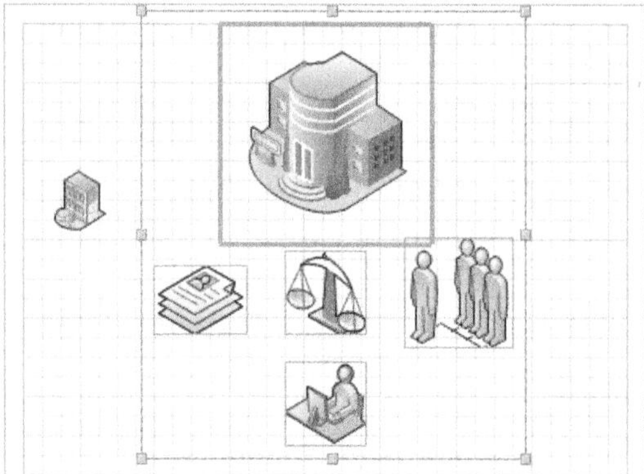

CLEAN UP Save your changes to the *Corporate Diagram* drawing but leave it open if you are continuing with the next exercise.

Inserting Pictures

As is true for Microsoft Word, PowerPoint, and many other programs, Visio lets you import pictures of various types into a drawing. You may want to add a picture of a specific object, a piece of clip art or a general background image—either way, you can import almost any type of image or picture into Visio.

In this exercise, you will import several pictures to add value to and enhance the appearance of your drawing.

SET UP You need the *International Office* image and the *Corporate Diagram* drawing for this exercise. Either continue with the open copy of the drawing from the previous exercise or open the *Corporate Diagram_start* drawing located in the Chapter03 practice file folder and save it as *Corporate Diagram*.

1. Drag an **International division** shape from the **Department** stencil and drop it in the lower-left corner of the drawing page.

Picture

2. On the **Insert** tab, in the **Illustrations** group, click the **Picture** button.
3. Navigate to the Chapter03 practice file folder, click **International Office.jpg**, and then click **Open**. (This image originated in the Microsoft Office Clip Art gallery.)
4. Drag the inserted photo to the bottom center of the page next to the International division icon.

Clip Art

5. On the **Insert** tab, in the **Illustrations** group, click the **Clip Art** button. The Clip Art task pane opens.
6. In the **Search for** box, type **EU flag**, select the **Include Office.com content** checkbox, and then press Enter. Several flag images appear.
7. Double-click one of the flag images to add it to your drawing.
8. Reduce the size of the flag image, and then position it in the upper-left corner of the building image.
9. Drag the International division icon and drop it on the right face of the building.
10. Close the **Clip Art** task pane. Your drawing now includes an iconic representation of various headquarters' functions at the top of the page, and images that represent the international division office at the bottom.

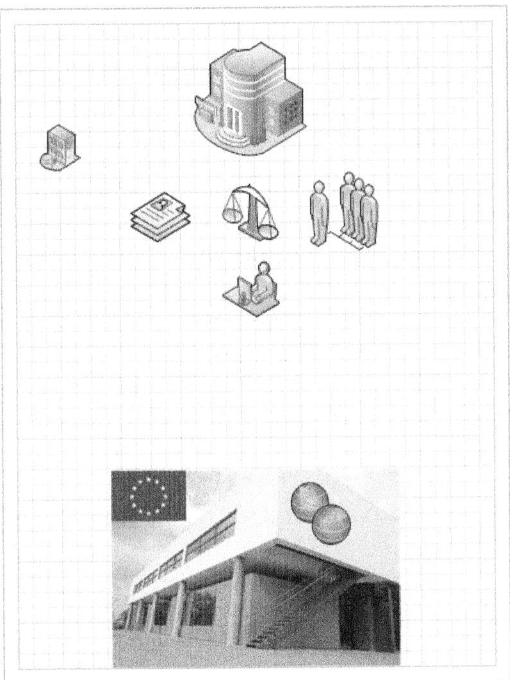

CLEAN UP Save your changes to the *Corporate Diagram* drawing but leave it open if you are continuing with the next exercise.

Once inserted into your drawing, an image becomes a shape, much like the group did in the preceding exercise. Consequently, you can use any of the various tools in Visio to alter or adjust the shape's properties. You can also add data to the image shape by using a technique you will learn in Chapter 6.

As you completed the steps in this exercise, you may have noticed that when you selected an image, the Picture Tools contextual tab set appeared. You can use the buttons on the Format contextual tab to alter the properties of an image.

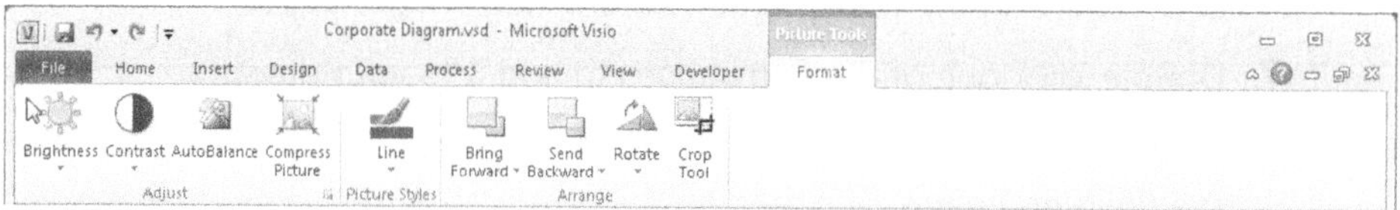

Tip Like most of the other applications in the Microsoft Office suite, you can insert more than just pictures into a Visio drawing. On the Insert tab, click Object, and you will find a list of 25 document and object types.

Understanding Layers

You can organize objects in a Visio drawing into layers and control various properties of all layer members at once. For example, you can control whether layer members will print, be visible on the drawing page, or be selectable. In a town map, for instance, you might put roads on one layer, sewer lines on a second, water pipes on a third, and buildings on a fourth. Organized this way, you can lock certain layers to prevent accidentally moving or selecting that collection of objects while working with shapes on other layers. Similarly, you could print a map showing roads and buildings, but not pipes.

Layers offer considerable flexibility in managing the parts of a sophisticated drawing. However, working with layers requires some planning because things can get complex: a drawing page can have multiple layers; each layer has multiple properties; and any shape can be on zero, one, or multiple layers.

In this exercise, you will assign shapes to a layer and change the layer properties to see the effects on the drawing.

SET UP **You need the *Corporate Diagram* drawing for this exercise. Either continue with the open copy from the previous exercise or open the *Corporate Diagram International_start* drawing located in the Chapter03 practice file folder and save it as *Corporate Diagram*.**

1. Select the globe symbol and the flag at the bottom of the page (do not select the photo of the building).

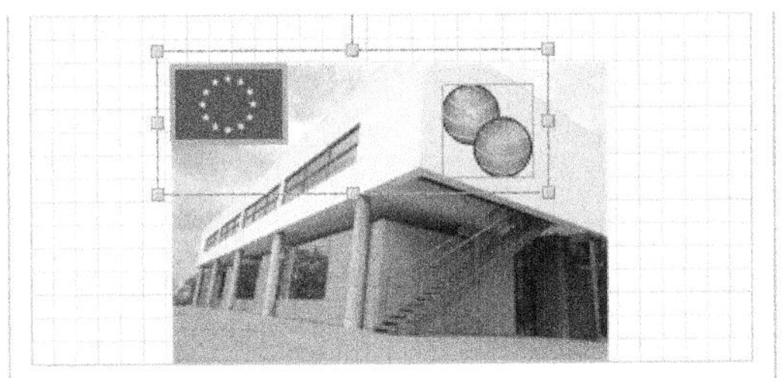

Layers

2. On the **Home** tab, in the **Editing** group, click the **Layers** button, and then click **Assign to Layer**. The Layer dialog box opens, followed immediately by the New Layer dialog box.

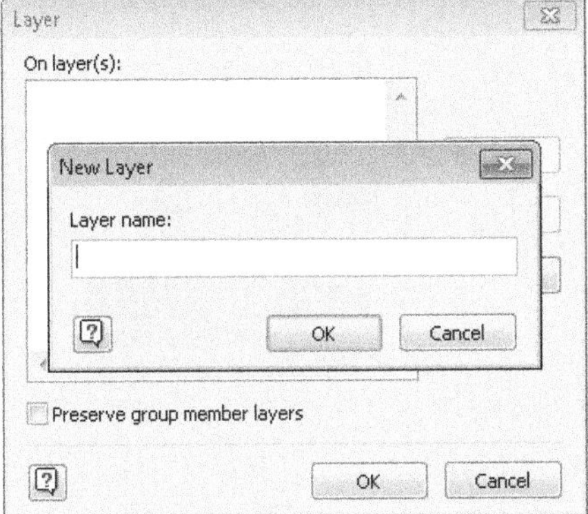

3. In the **New Layer** dialog box, type **International**, and then click **OK**.

   The International layer is added to the Layer dialog box as shown in the following graphic, and the selected shapes are added to the new layer. You can continue using this dialog box to create more layers and to add the selected shapes to other existing layers.

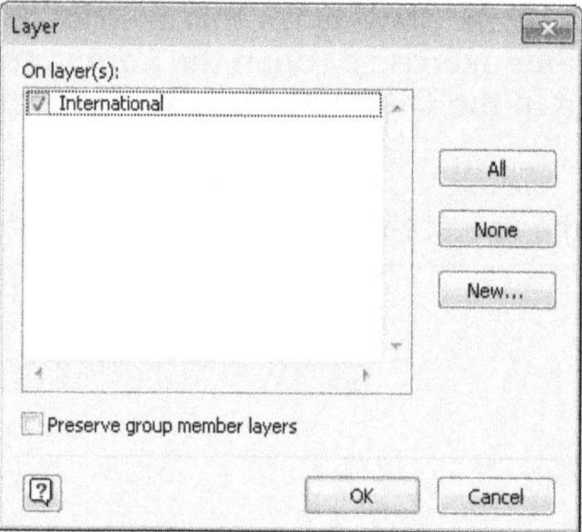

4. Click **OK**. The drawing doesn't look any different at this point but you will see evidence of the new layer in subsequent steps.

   Tip Putting shapes on a layer is not the same as putting them in a group. Unlike a group, the shapes on a layer can be selected, moved, and sized independently.

5. On the **Home** tab, in the **Editing** group, click the **Layers** button, and then click **Layer Properties**.

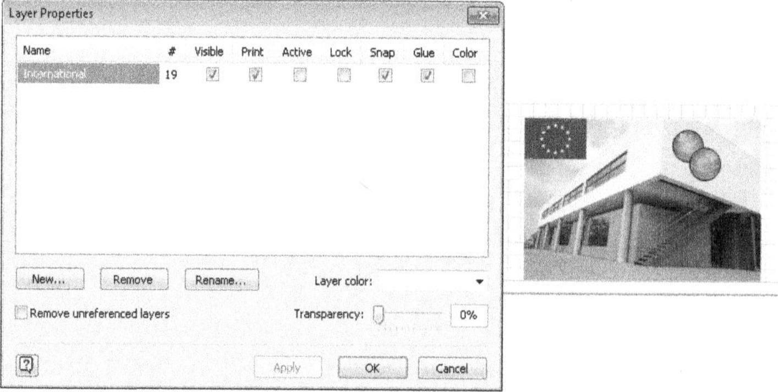

The Layer Properties dialog box includes seven check boxes for setting layer properties. The properties are described in the following paragraphs; default settings for each property are shown in the previous graphic.

The Visible check box controls whether a layer's shapes are visible on the drawing page.

The Print check box includes or excludes a layer's members from printing.

Tip Because the Visible and Print check boxes are separate, you can create a drawing in which members of a layer are visible in the drawing but do not print, and vice versa.

When you set a layer to be Active, all new shapes added to the page are automatically added to the layer. More than one layer can be active at once, in which case new shapes are added to all active layers.

Adding a check mark to Lock prevents you from selecting, moving, or editing any shapes on the layer. In addition, you cannot add shapes to a locked layer.

The Snap and Glue settings allow/disallow snapping or gluing other shapes to the shapes on this layer.

With the Color option, you can temporarily override the colors of all objects on a layer; clearing this option returns layer members to their original colors. When you select the Color property for a layer, the Layer Color and Transparency settings in the lower right of the dialog box are activated.

Tip **Every layer belongs to exactly one page. When you create a new layer, it is added to the current page. If you copy layer members to a different page, the layer is added to the destination page. (If a layer of the same name already exists on that page, the copied shapes are added to the existing layer.)**

6. In the **Layer Properties** dialog box, clear the check box below **Visible**, and then click **Apply**.

   Tip **The Apply button provides a preview of the intended change without closing the Layer Properties dialog box. If you make a change in the Layer Properties dialog box and want that change to affect your drawing immediately, it is not necessary to click Apply—just click OK.**

   In the graphic on the right, you can see that the two shapes on the International layer are no longer visible. Compare this graphic to the one following Step 5.

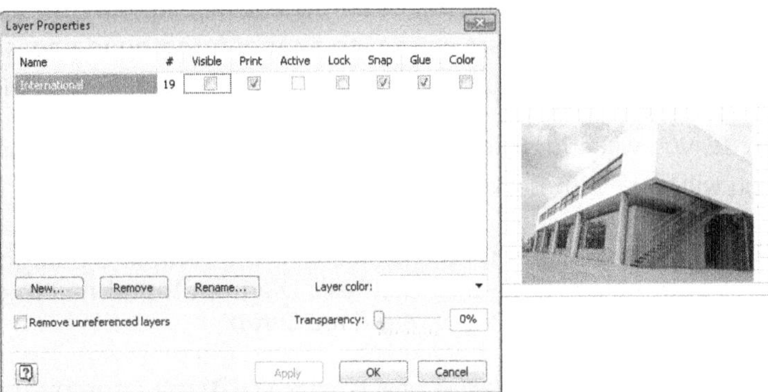

7. Click **OK** to close the **Layer Properties** dialog box.

CLEAN UP **Save your changes to the *Corporate Diagram* drawing, and then close it.**

The shapes in certain Visio stencils include pre-assigned layers. The flowchart shapes and the building design shapes are two examples. In addition, dynamic connectors are always on a layer, so dropping the first one onto any page creates a layer called *Connector*.

Tip **Although they both help you organize sets of shapes, groups and layers serve different purposes. In addition, groups and layers are not mutually exclusive—you can use both in the same drawing.**

Managing Pages and Page Setup

A Visio drawing can contain any number of pages and each page can have its own dimensions, measurement units, and other characteristics. In addition, the on-screen drawing page can have different dimensions from the physical printer page.

Setting the drawing page size to be different from the physical page lets you do things like:

- Compress a large drawing to fit on a smaller sheet of paper.
- Print a drawing on a very large sheet of paper.
- Print a drawing across multiple sheets of paper.

Indeed, Visio gives you remarkable flexibility in setting page attributes that are useful for virtually any diagram type and any form of printed or electronic output.

Visio drawings also support two types of drawing pages:

- ***Foreground pages*** contain the active drawing content and are typically the pages that are printed or published in some form.
- ***Background pages*** contain page elements that can appear on one or more pages.

By associating a background page with a foreground page, all text and graphics on the background page appear on the foreground page. One common use for background pages is to add consistent borders or titles to a set of foreground pages. Another is to include the company logo, a legal notice, or any other graphic or text on multiple pages.

In this exercise, you will add, delete, and reorder pages as well as change various page settings. You will work with background pages in the next exercise.

SET UP Click the File tab, and then click New. In the Template Categories section, click General, and then double-click the Basic Diagram thumbnail to create a new drawing. Save the drawing as *Pages and Page Setup*.

Blank Page

1. On the **Insert** tab, in the **Pages** group, click the **Blank Page** button.

   Visio adds a page called Page-2. Clicking the Blank Page button is equivalent to clicking the Insert Page button that you learned about in Chapter 2, "Creating a New Diagram" (it's the button to the right of Page-2 in the following graphic).

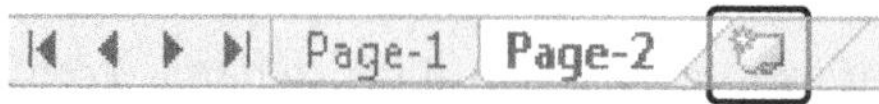

Next you'll change some of the attributes of Page-2 using convenient new features of Visio 2010.

Landscape

Zoom Level

2. On the **Design** tab, in the **Page Setup** group, click the **Orientation** button, and then click **Landscape**. Clicking this button changes the orientation of both the drawing page and the printer page.
3. On the status bar, click the **Zoom Level** button, and set the zoom level to **50%**.

   You are changing the zoom setting so you can see the entire drawing page plus part of the surrounding ***drawing canvas*** for use in the next step.

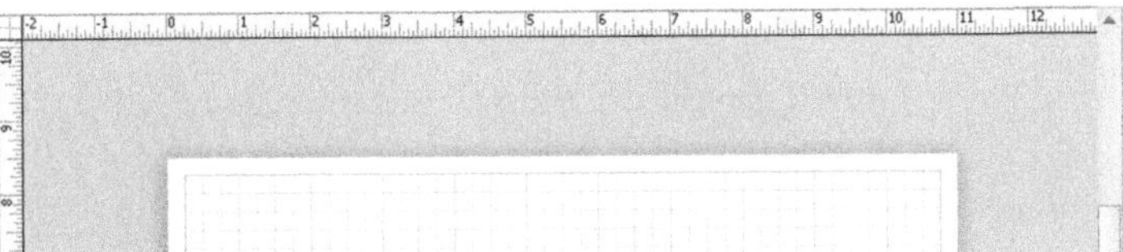

4. Drag a **Square** from the **Basic Shapes** stencil onto the top edge of the page so that part of it is on the page and part is on the canvas.

   The Visio 2010 Auto Size feature is on by default in many templates. As you can see in the following graphic, if you place a shape partly or entirely off the drawing page, Visio adds a page for you. The dashed line is the boundary between ***tiles***, each of which represents the portion of the drawing page that will print on a single physical page.

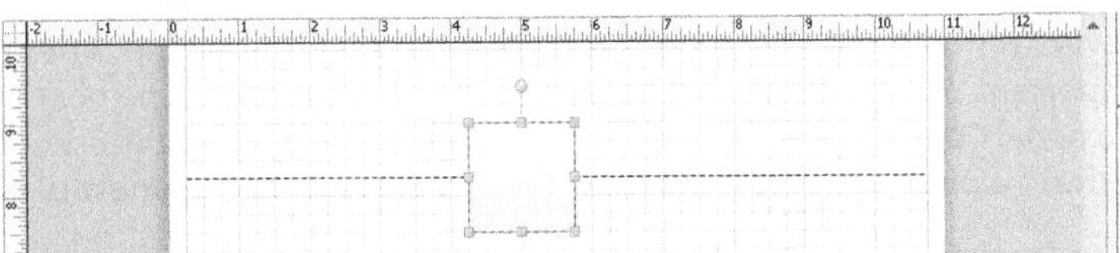

5. Drag the square down so it is below the dashed line. Visio removes the added page because it is no longer needed.

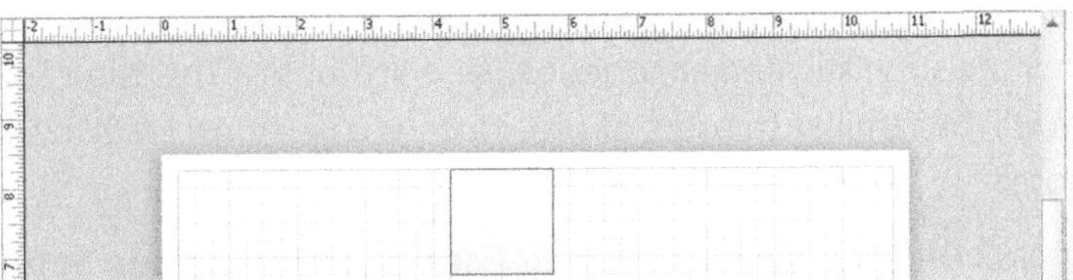

You can turn off the Auto Add feature if you want to use the drawing canvas to store shapes temporarily that you don't want to be on the drawing page.

Auto Size

6. On the **Design** tab, in the **Page Setup** group, click the **Auto Size** button.

   The Auto Size button, which was illuminated to indicate that the Auto Size was enabled, is no longer illuminated after you click it.

   Tip The Auto Size option is applied per page. Consequently, changing the setting for the current page does not affect other pages.

7. Drag a **45 degree double** arrow from the **Basic Shapes** stencil onto the canvas just above the square. The arrow remains on the canvas and Visio does not expand the drawing page.

   Tip Items on the drawing canvas do not print.

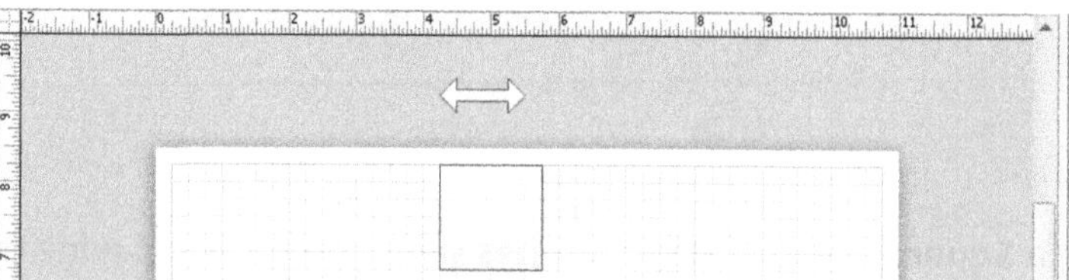

Size

The remaining button on the Design tab in the Page Setup group is the Size button. Selecting a new page size from the list resets both the drawing page and printer page sizes.

8. On the **Insert** tab, in the **Pages** group, click the **Blank Page** button. Visio adds a new page.

   Important When you added a page in Step 1, the new page had portrait orientation; however, this time the new page has landscape orientation. The difference demonstrates an important point: when you add a page, Visio copies all of the characteristics of the *active page*. Consequently, if the pages in your drawing have different attributes, be sure to activate a page with the desired attributes before adding a new page.

9. On the **Design** tab, in the **Page Setup** group, click the **Auto Size** button. This action turns Auto Size behavior back on for this page.

   You've now used three buttons in the Orientation group on the Design tab that simplify some page-related functions. There are times, however, when you need to make more sophisticated changes to page attributes. The Page Setup dialog box, which will be familiar to users of previous Visio versions, is still available for that purpose.

10. Right-click on the page name tab for **Page-3**, and click **Page Setup**. The Page Setup dialog box opens to the Page Properties tab.

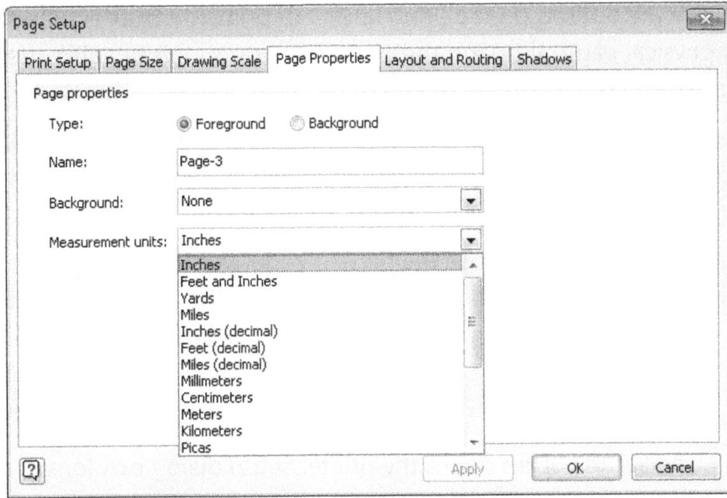

In addition to selecting the page type and changing the page name, you can assign a background page (refer to the next exercise) and select from a large number of measurement units. Be sure to notice the scroll bar in the measurement units menu—you have a total of 20 choices. If you change the measurement units, you will see the result in the rulers on the top and left of the drawing page.

11. In the **Page Setup** dialog box, click the **Print Setup** tab.

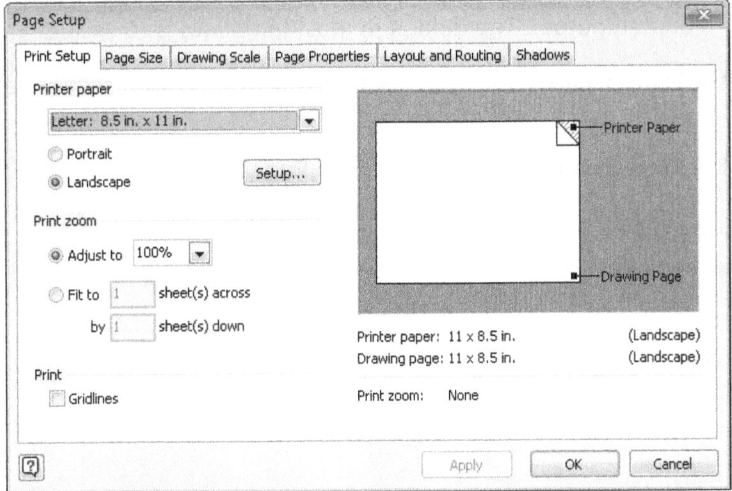

You use the options on the Print Setup tab primarily to affect the size and layout of the physical page, although the zoom settings on this tab also affect the drawing page size.

The Print Setup tab contains three configuration sections on the left and a preview pane on the right. The preview pane changes dynamically to reflect your current print settings and displays them in both visual and text form:

- **Printer paper** Choose the paper size for your desired printer. Most U.S. Units templates default to letter-sized paper as shown in the previous graphic. Metric templates typically default to A4. Regardless of the default, there is a long list of alternate, predefined paper sizes available in the list at the top of this section. You can also select Portrait or Landscape orientation.

  The Setup button opens the printer setup dialog box for the current printer.

- **Print zoom** Adjust To 100% is the default zoom for many templates but you can select a different zoom level if you want your drawing to print larger or smaller than normal. Choosing a zoom setting greater than 100% causes your drawing to be split across multiple sheets of paper; choosing a setting less than 100% scales your drawing down to fit onto a portion of the printer page.

  Fit To provides an alternate way to scale your drawing for printing.

- **Print** The single setting in this section includes or excludes Gridlines from printed output. The default in most templates is to exclude gridlines.

12. In the **Printer paper** section, click **Portrait**. The preview section reflects your choice.
13. In the **Page Setup** dialog box, click the **Page Size** tab.

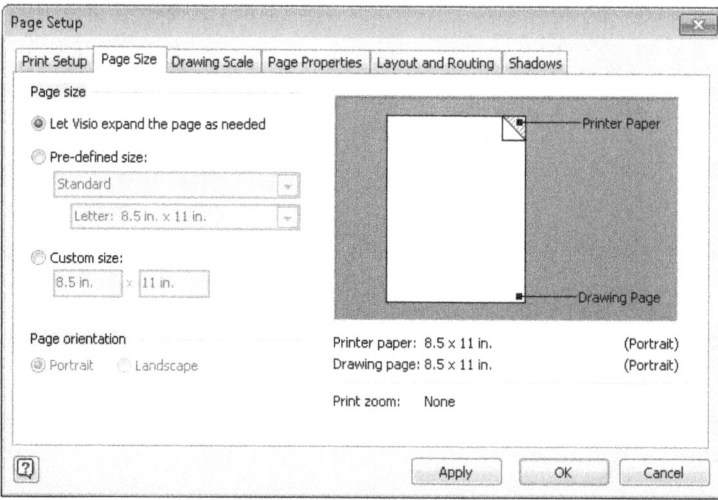

You use the Page Size tab to change attributes of the drawing page; changes you make on this tab do not directly affect the printed page.

The Page Size tab includes two configuration sections plus a preview pane:

- **Page size** The first option in this section enables the dynamic Auto Size behavior you used in Steps 6 and 9. As an alternative, the second and third options let you set a fixed page size, either from a list of preset sizes or by typing specific dimensions.
- **Page orientation** The options in this section are only active if you choose Pre-defined Size or Custom Size in the Page Size section. You can use these options to set a different orientation for the physical page than the one that is set for the drawing page.

14. Click **OK**. The dialog box closes and Page-3 now has portrait orientation.
15. Double-click the page name tab for **Page-2** (not Page-3), type **Landscape with Square**, and then press Enter.

As you saw in Step 10, you can change the page name on the Page Properties tab in the Page Setup dialog box, but double-clicking the page name tab is usually more convenient.

In addition to changing page names, you can also change the sequence of pages in a drawing.

16. Drag the page name tab for **Page-3** to before **Page-1**.

As you drag the page name tab, the cursor displays a page icon and a black down arrow points to the junctions between pages.

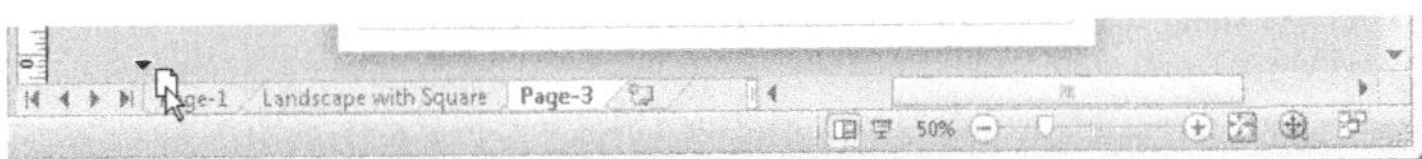

When you release the mouse button, the page tabs reflect the new page sequence.

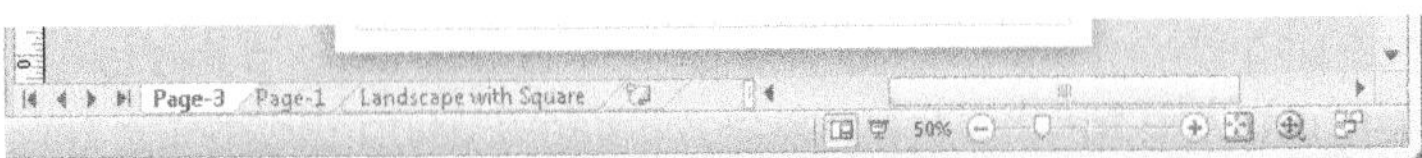

Tip Dragging page name tabs is an easy way to resequence pages when the destination tab location for your page is visible. When the destination is not visible, it's often easier to right-click on any page name tab and select Reorder Pages. In the Reorder Pages dialog box that opens (shown in the following graphic), use the Move Up or Move Down buttons.

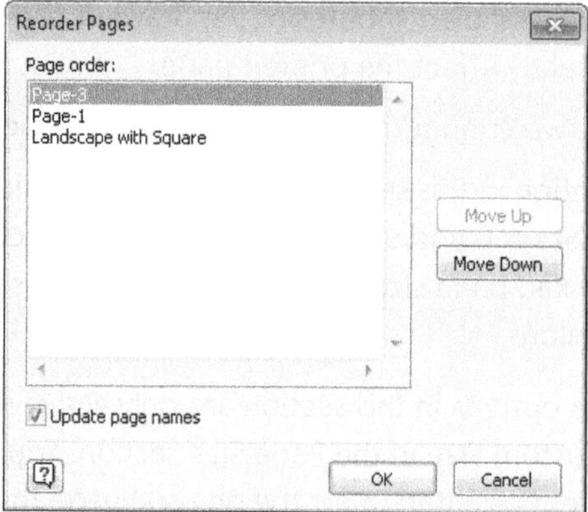

CLEAN UP Save your changes to the *Pages and Page Setup* drawing, and then close it.

Keyboard Shortcut Visio provides two convenient shortcuts for navigating back and forth among the foreground pages in your drawing: Ctrl+Page Up and Ctrl+Page Down.

Working with Background Pages and Borders

You can create background pages manually and assign them to selected foreground pages. You can also take advantage of several Visio features that automatically create and assign background pages. In this exercise, you will do both.

Tip In the previous section, you adjusted the sizes and attributes of foreground pages. You can use the same techniques to resize and adjust attributes of background pages.

SET UP You need the *Starfish* image and the *Background Exercises_start* drawing located in the Chapter03 practice files folder to complete this exercise. Open the drawing in Visio and save it as *Background Exercises.*

1. Take a look at the drawing you just opened to see that it contains four pages, each of which has a collection of identical or similar shapes. In addition, each page name reflects the contents of the page. The shapes on each page exist so you can quickly tell one page from another as you complete the steps in this exercise. Notice, also, that the drawing for this exercise was created using the metric template.
2. At the bottom center of the drawing page, move the slider to the right to make more space to display page names.

Blank Page

3. On the **Insert** tab, in the **Pages** group, click the **Blank Page** arrow (not the button), and then click **Background Page**.

   The same Page Setup dialog box that you saw in the previous exercise opens to the Page Properties tab. Notice that the Type is preset to Background and that the default page name is Background-1.

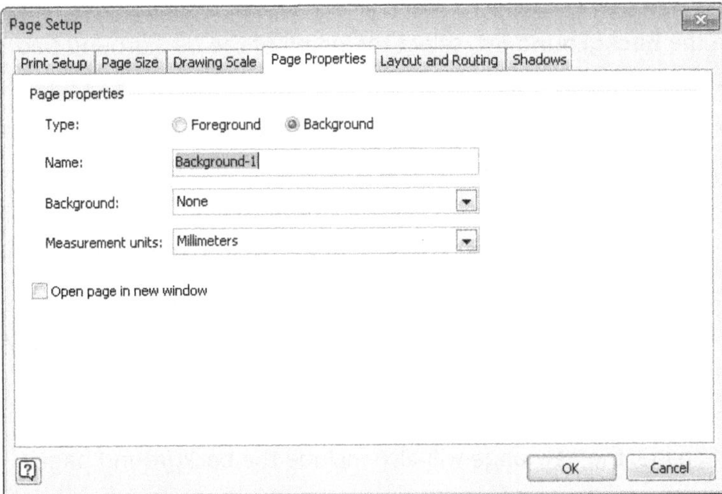

4. Click **OK**. Visio creates the background page.

   Squares Circles Triangles Arrows *Background-1*

   Tip Remember that the attributes of the active page determine the attributes of each new page. If your drawing contains pages with different orientations or settings, activate the page that is like, or most like, your desired background page before creating the new page.

Picture

5. On the **Insert** tab, in the **Illustrations** group, click the **Picture** button, navigate to the **Starfish.jpg** in the Chapter03 practice files folder, and then click **Open**.

   Visio inserts the picture into the center of the drawing window. You will use this picture as a stand-in for a company logo.

6. Drag the starfish picture to the upper-right corner of the page, and then resize it so it is approximately 25 mm (1 inch) wide.

   Tip Remember that when you have selected a shape, its current width and height are displayed in the status bar at the bottom of the Visio window. As you drag the corner resize handle, the status bar updates dynamically to show the current size.

Tip You can include "Company Confidential" or other text on the pages in your diagram by adding a text box to the background page.

Now that you've created a background page, you can apply it to one or more foreground pages.

7. Right-click on the **Squares** page name tab, and then click **Page Setup**. The Page Setup dialog box opens to the Page Properties tab.
8. Use the **Background** list, select the name of the background page, **Background-1**, and then click **OK**.

   The Squares page now includes the "logo" and any other objects or text you placed on that page. Three important notes:

   - Because the starfish is on a background page, you cannot select, change, or relocate it on this page. You must go to the background page to make changes.
   - Applying background pages is done per page. If you navigate to the Circles or Triangles pages, you'll see that they do not show the background.
   - If you create a new page from an active page that includes a background page, the new page will also include the background page.

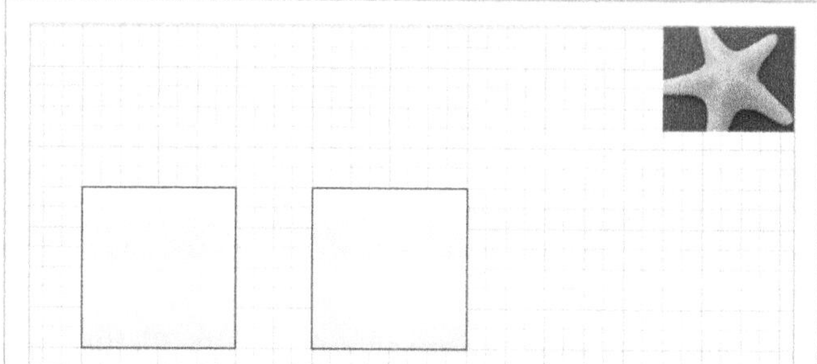

9. Go to the **Circles** page. Notice that the background was not applied to this page.

Borders & Titles

10. On the **Design** tab, in the **Background** group, click the **Borders & Titles** button.

    The Borders & Titles gallery opens, giving you a preview of each gallery selection. If you point to any thumbnail image in the gallery, you will see its name. Be sure to notice that there is a scroll bar at the right giving you access to additional selections.

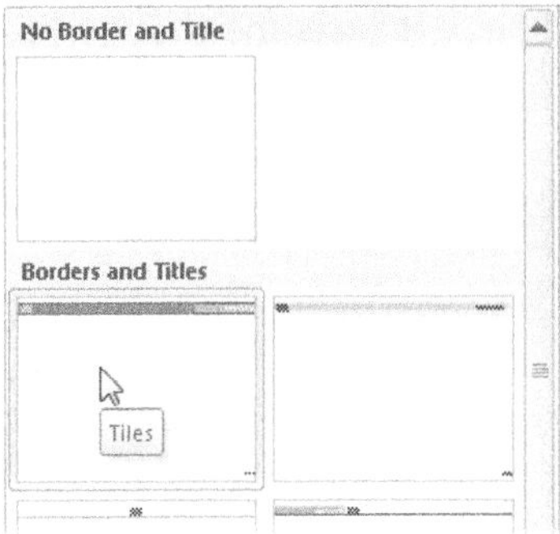

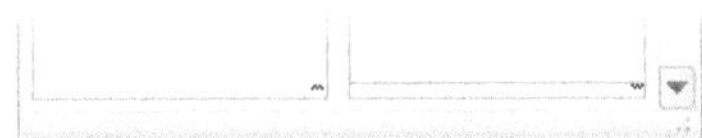

11. Click the **Tiles** thumbnail, which should be toward the upper left.

    Visio creates a background page containing the title shapes and applies it to the Circles page. Most of the title box you see across the top of the page is reserved for the document title but the right portion contains today's date. There is also a page number in the lower-right corner.

    Tip The page number will be updated dynamically if you add, delete, or reorder pages.

    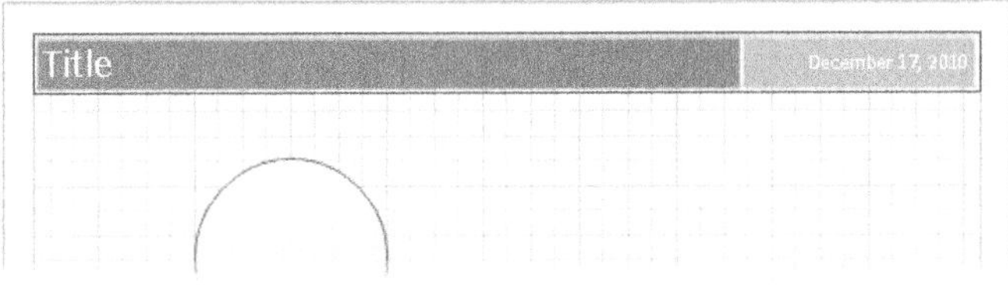

    Tip The automatically generated background page is called VBackground-1. Visio includes the letter *V* to distinguish the background page it created from the one you created manually.

12. Go to **VBackground-1**, double-click in the **Title** text box, and then type **Tailspin Toys**.

13. Go to **Circles**. The Circles foreground page reflects the change you made on the background page.

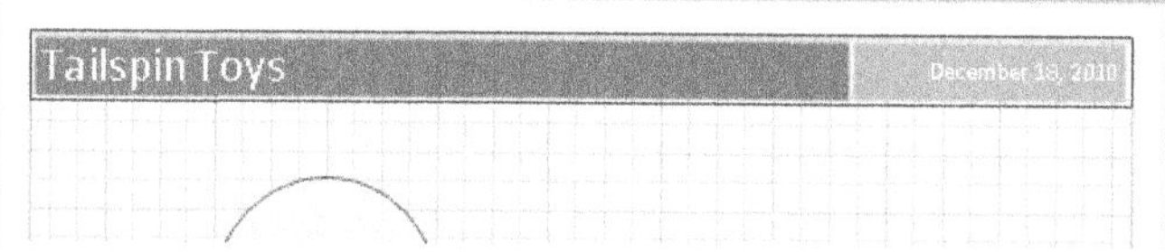

14. Go to the **Triangles** page.

Backgrounds

15. On the **Design** tab, in the **Background** group, click the **Backgrounds** button.

    The Backgrounds gallery provides a preview of available backgrounds, and if you point to any background, you will see its name.

16. Click once on the **Verve** background. Visio creates a new background page called VBackground-2, and applies it to Triangles.

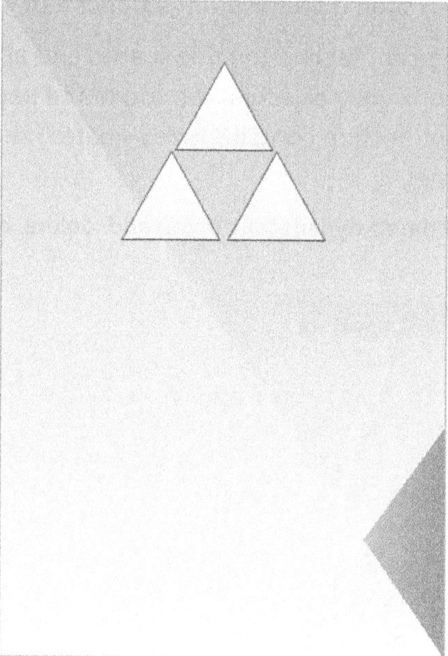

17. Go to the **Arrows** page. Note that it does not include any of the backgrounds you've created for other pages in the drawing.
18. Right-click on the **Arrows** page name tab, and then select **Page Setup**.
19. In the **Background** list, select **Vbackground-2**, and then click **OK**.

You have now assigned the same background page to both Triangles and Arrows.

 **CLEAN UP** **Save your changes to the *Background Exercises* drawing, and then close it.**

To look at examples of finished diagrams that use background pages, click the File tab, and then click New. In the Other Ways To Get Started section, click Sample Diagrams, and then double-click IT Asset Management, Process Improvement, Project Timeline, or Sales Summary. All have one or more background pages.

Four final thoughts about background pages:

- Changes you make to a background page appear on all pages using that page.
- Background pages can have background pages. It is possible, therefore, to build a set of foreground pages that all display shapes from a common background page. (Think of it as the "deep background" page.) Those same foreground pages can also display the contents of other background pages that are unique to an individual page or to a group of pages.
- If you have foreground pages with different orientations or sizes, you are likely to need multiple background pages with matching attributes.
- The page name tabs for background pages always appear to the right of all foreground pages and cannot be reordered.

Key Points

- You can add text to almost any Visio shape. In addition, you can create "text only" shapes to add titles, labels, and other information to a drawing.
- Visio provides a set of tools for changing the size, position, and orientation of shapes on a page. There is a complementary set of tools for altering the size, position, and orientation of the text displayed on a shape.
- ScreenTips and Comments are two different ways to add text comments to a drawing. Each behaves differently and is suited for a different purpose.
- Many Visio shapes contain one or more data fields. Shape data can turn a drawing into far more than just a "pretty picture"—the drawing can become the single source for viewing structure, content, form, and function.
- You can display shape data on the drawing page by inserting a field into a shape and linking that field to shape data.
- Visio provides several ways to organize collections of shapes. You can use groups to tie a set of shapes together so you can move, resize, and work with them as a unit. You can use layers to hide, print, recolor, or lock a set of shapes, while allowing each shape to retain its individuality in ways that aren't true in a group. In Chapter 11, "Adding Structure to Your Diagrams," you will learn about another option called ***containers***.

Chapter at a Glance

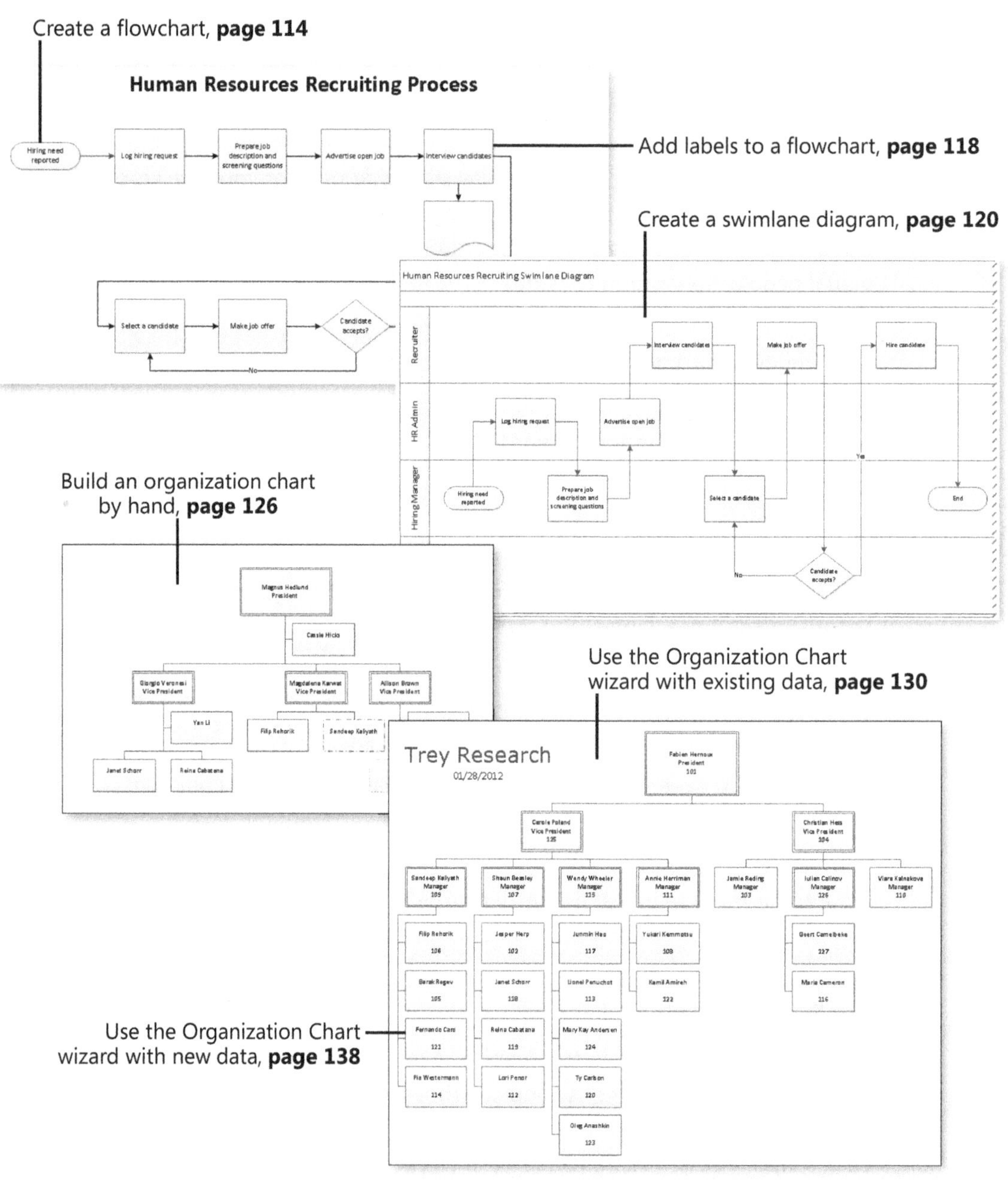

Create a flowchart, **page 114**
Human Resources Recruiting Process
Add labels to a flowchart, **page 118**
Create a swimlane diagram, **page 120**
Human Resources Recruiting Swimlane Diagram
Recruiter
HR Admin
Hiring Manager
Build an organization chart by hand, **page 126**
Use the Organization Chart wizard with existing data, **page 130**
Trey Research
01/28/2012
Use the Organization Chart wizard with new data, **page 138**

4 Drawing the Real World: Flowcharts and Organization Charts

In this chapter, you will learn how to

- ✔ Select a flowchart type.
- ✔ Create flowcharts.
- ✔ Add labels to flowcharts.
- ✔ Understand and create swimlane diagrams.
- ✔ Understand organization charts.
- ✔ Build an organization chart by hand.
- ✔ Use the Organization Chart Wizard with existing or new data.
- ✔ Enhance org charts with pictures.

In the first three chapters, you learned many of the basic capabilities of Microsoft Visio 2010. In this chapter, you will apply that knowledge to creating real-world diagrams. There is no better place to start than with the humble ***flowchart***, because creating flowcharts is one of the most common tasks for which people use Visio. In fact, according to Microsoft, one-third of all Visio diagrams are based on templates from the flowchart category.

Whether the end goal is to diagram the logic of a current or future software module, or to document the way that a work procedure is, or could be, performed, Visio flowcharts are the standard. Visio is also used to create an alternative type of flowchart called a ***cross-functional flowchart*** or ***swimlane diagram***.

Another common application for Visio is to create ***organization charts***, often known as ***org charts***. You can create org charts manually by dragging the intelligent organization chart shapes from the Visio stencil onto the drawing page, or you can run the Organization Chart Wizard to automate the work of creating your drawing.

In this chapter, you will learn about different types of flowcharts and will create both conventional flowcharts and swimlane diagrams. You will also learn how to add text to Visio flowchart shapes. Finally, you'll learn how to build an organization chart by hand as well as by using the wizard, and how to enhance organization charts with pictures.

Practice Files Before you can complete the exercises in this chapter, you need to copy the book's practice files to your computer. The practice files you'll use to complete the exercises in this chapter are in the Chapter04 practice files folder. A complete list of practice files is provided in "Using the Practice Files" at the beginning of this book.

Selecting a Flowchart Type

Visio provides different flowchart templates, depending on the edition that you use.

Visio Standard

Visio Standard 2010 includes three flowchart templates, as shown in the following graphic. You will work with the Basic Flowchart and Cross-Functional Flowchart templates in this chapter.

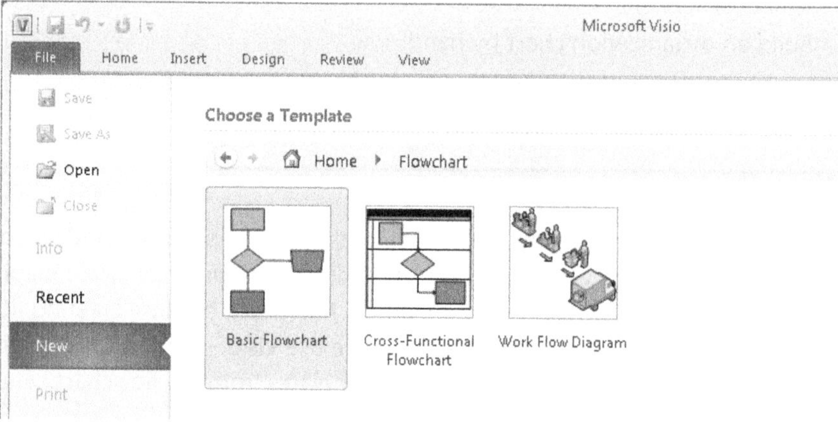

Visio Professional

Visio Professional 2010 includes the same three flowcharts as the Standard edition but also includes two additional flowchart templates: IDEF0 and SDL Diagram.

See Also For additional information about IDEF0, go to *en.wikipedia.org/wiki/IDEF0*. For additional information about SDL, go to *en.wikipedia.org/wiki/Specification_and_Description_Language*.

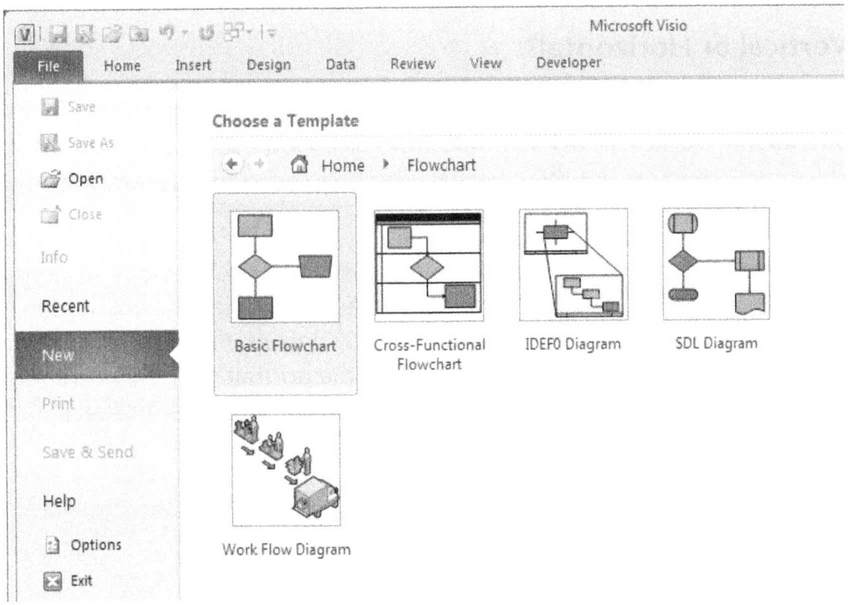

Visio Premium

Visio Premium 2010 adds two workflow templates beyond those available with the Professional edition. You will learn more about the BPMN Diagram and Microsoft SharePoint Workflow templates in Chapter 12, "Creating and Validating Process Diagrams."

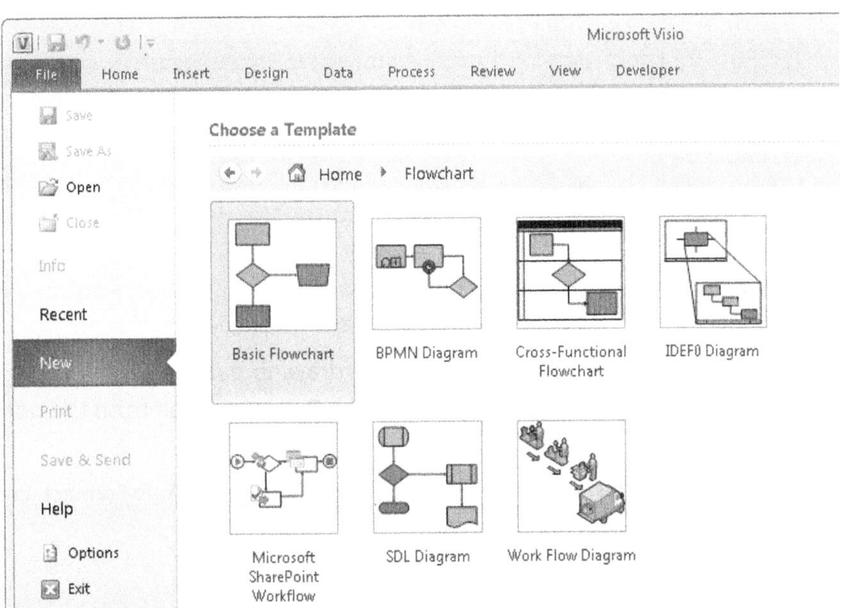

Vertical or Horizontal?

Should you draw your flowcharts with vertical (portrait) or horizontal (landscape) orientation? Vertical flowcharts, with tasks arranged from top to bottom, are probably more common, but there have always been advocates for the left-to-right, horizontal view.

One interesting note if you have created flowcharts with previous versions of Visio: the Visio 2010 Basic Flowchart template defaults to horizontal orientation, whereas previous versions presented a vertical view by default. Although this may frustrate people with a long-standing preference for the portrait view, there is some logic to this choice because computer screens have grown wider over the years.

Creating Flowcharts

In this exercise, you will create a new flowchart for a simple human resources recruiting process. The flowchart will have seven process steps and one decision.

SET UP Start Visio, or if it's already running, click the File tab, and then click New. In the Template Categories section, click Flowchart, and then double-click the Basic Flowchart thumbnail. Save the new drawing as *HR Recruiting Flowchart*.

1. Drag a **Start/End** shape from the **Basic Flowchart Shapes** stencil onto the drawing page.

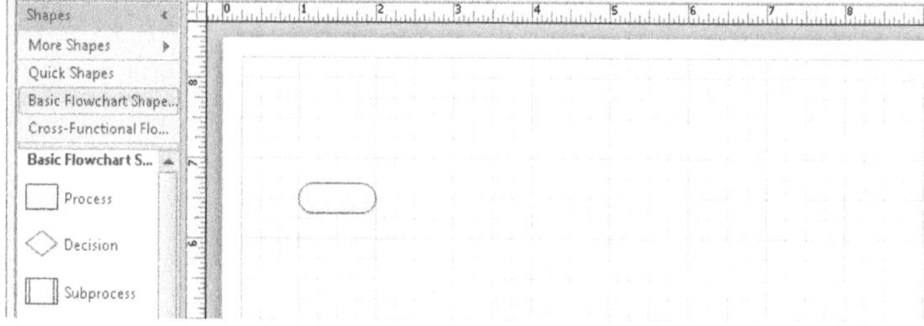

2. Click once on the **Process** shape in the stencil to select it.
3. Point to the start shape you added to the drawing page, and click the right-facing blue triangle that appears in order to add a **Process** shape from the pop-up **Quick Shapes** menu.

   See Also For a refresher on using Quick Shapes, see "Using AutoConnect and Quick Shapes" in Chapter 2, "Creating a New Diagram."

4. Use the same technique to add three more **Process** shapes to the page.

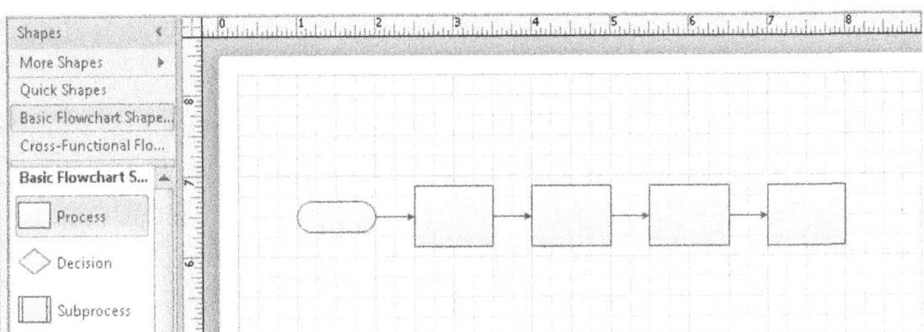

5. Drag a **Process** shape onto the drawing page. Then use the Dynamic Grid to position the new process shape below the left-most process shape.

   See Also For more information about the Dynamic Grid in Visio, see "Using Basic Shapes and the Dynamic Grid" in Chapter 2.

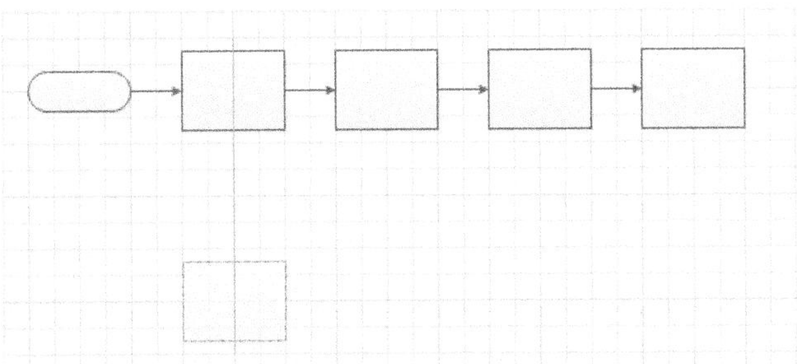

6. From the **Quick Shapes** menu, add the following four shapes:
   - Another **Process** shape to the right of the one from Step 5.
   - A **Decision** diamond to the right of the previous process shape.
   - Another **Process** shape to the right of the decision diamond.
   - A **Start/End** shape to the right of the final process shape.

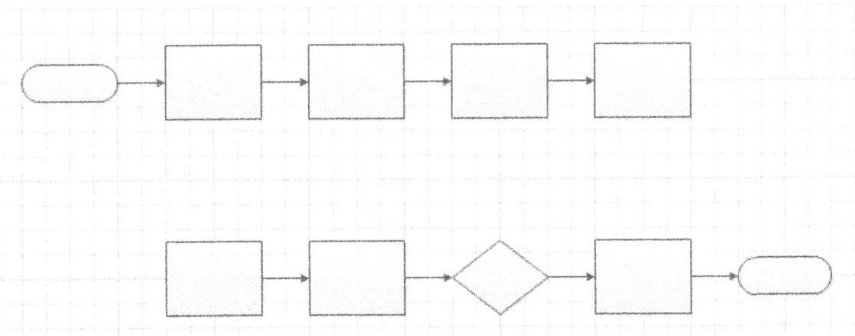

At this point, the flowchart is nearly complete with the exception of two connectors: one that links the end of the first row to the beginning of the second row, and one that links the decision diamond back to a previous step in the flowchart.

Connector

7. On the **Home** tab, in the **Tools** group, click the **Connector** button, and then move the cursor near the last shape in the first row.

   Notice two things:

   - The cursor has changed from a white arrow with a black outline (the ***Pointer Tool***) to a black arrow with a connector beneath it (the ***Connector Tool***).
   - When you move the Connector Tool near a shape, small blue Xs, called ***connection points***, appear at various places on the shape.

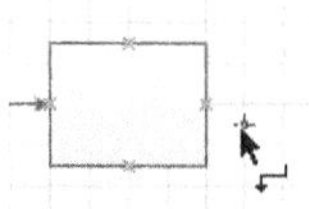

8. Click the connection point on the right of the process shape, and then drag to the leftmost connection point on the first process shape in the second row.

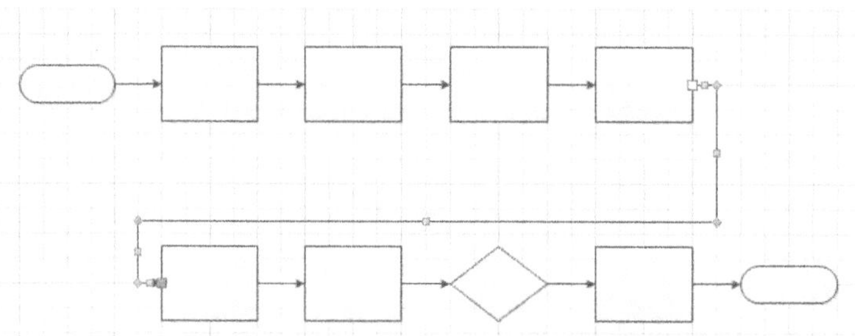

9. Click the connection point on the bottom of the decision diamond, and then drag to the connection point on the bottom of the process shape two shapes to the left.

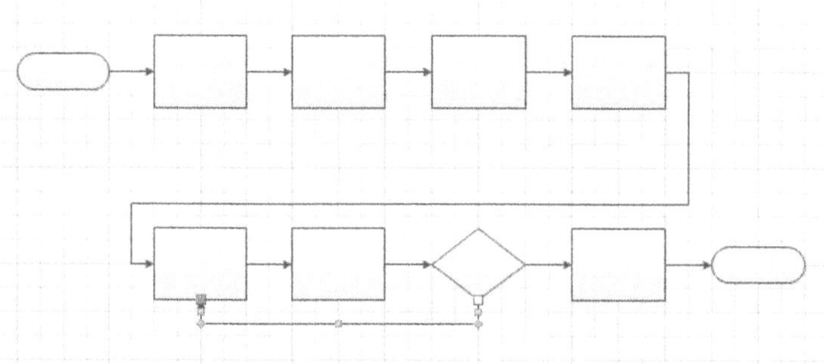

Pointer Tool

10. On the **Home** tab, in the **Tools** group, click the **Pointer Tool** button to return the cursor to its normal operating mode.
11. Drag a **Document** shape to just below the last process shape in the top row.

Important Do not drop the document shape on the connector line or Visio will break the connector in two and connect your document shape to both lines. This feature is called *AutoAdd* and is described in Chapter 2.

Notice that Visio automatically moved the connector line out of the way, which is generally good. However, because the new positioning isn't desirable for your flowchart, you will rearrange some of the shapes in the next step.

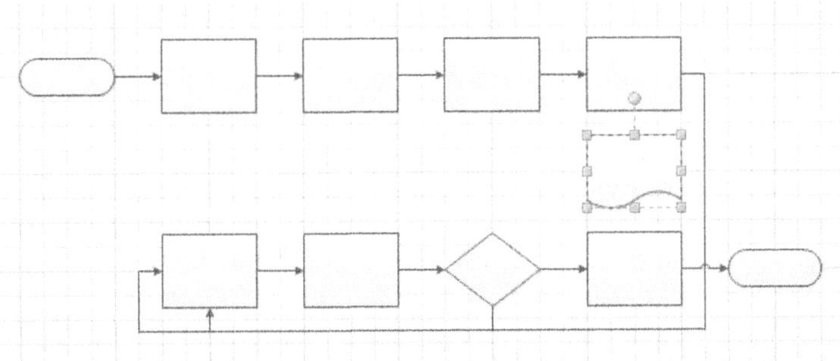

12. Drag a bounding box around all of the shapes in the bottom row. Then hold down the Shift key while you drag that row down to make more room.

    Tip Holding down the Shift key constrains Visio to moving the selected shapes only vertically or horizontally, whichever is the first direction you move the cursor.

    Once again, Visio will reposition the connector line to accommodate the new location of the bottom row.

13. Click the blue AutoConnect arrow under the upper-right process shape to connect it to the document shape.

    The layout of your flowchart is now complete.

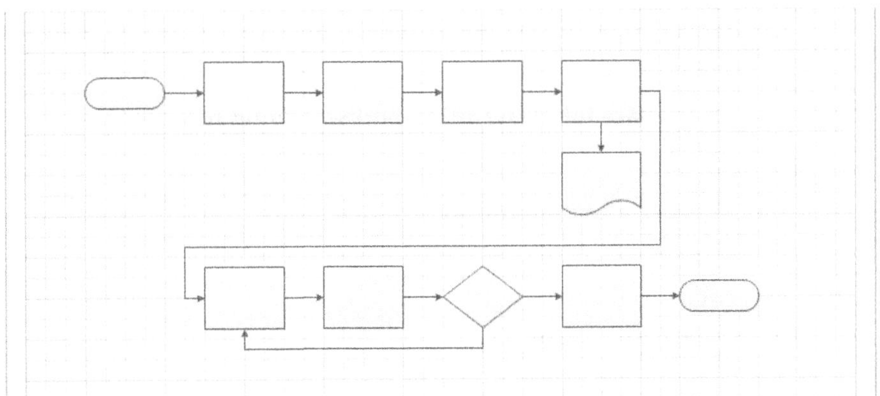

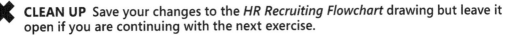

 **CLEAN UP** Save your changes to the *HR Recruiting Flowchart* drawing but leave it open if you are continuing with the next exercise.

Adding Labels to Flowcharts

In the preceding exercise, you learned the mechanics of creating a flowchart, but your diagram isn't very useful yet because your shapes have no labels, data, or identifying information.

See Also For information about adding data to your shapes, see Chapter 6, "Entering, Linking to, and Reporting on Data."

In this exercise, you will add text labels to your flowchart shapes.

SET UP If you completed the preceding exercise, continue working with the *HR Recruiting Flowchart* drawing. If not, you need the *HR Recruiting Flowchart_start* drawing located in the Chapter04 practice file folder to complete this exercise. Open the drawing in Visio and save it as *HR Recruiting Flowchart*.

1. Double-click the start shape in the upper-left of your diagram, and then type **Hiring need reported**.
2. Double-click the first process shape in your flowchart, and then type **Log hiring request**.

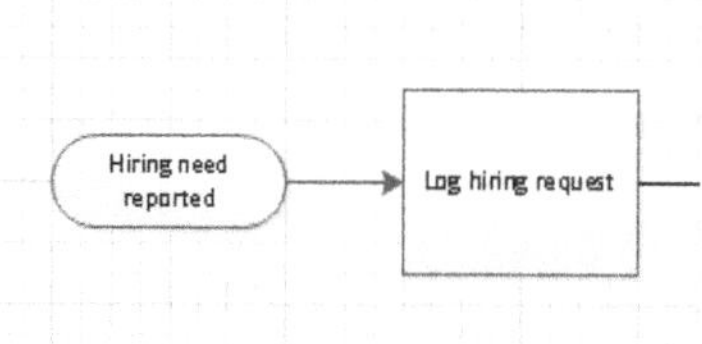

Tip You can also add text to most Visio shapes by clicking once to select the shape and then starting to type. That technique will work with the flowchart shapes.

3. Continue from left to right across the top row and add the following labels to the process shapes:
   - **Prepare job description and screening questions**
   - **Advertise open job**
   - **Interview candidates**
4. Double-click and type the following text into the five shapes in the bottom row, moving from left to right:
   - **Select a candidate**
   - **Make job offer**
   - **Candidate accepts?**
   - **Hire candidate**
   - **End**

5. Double-click the connector between the **Candidate accepts?** shape and the **Hire candidate** shape and type **Yes**.
6. Double-click the connector between the **Candidate accepts?** shape and the **Select a candidate** shape and type **No**.
7. Add a text box to the top of the page and type **Human Resources Recruiting Process** as a title for the flowchart.
8. Select the title text box, and then set the font size to **24 pt.** and make the text bold.

   Your finished flowchart should look something like the following graphic.

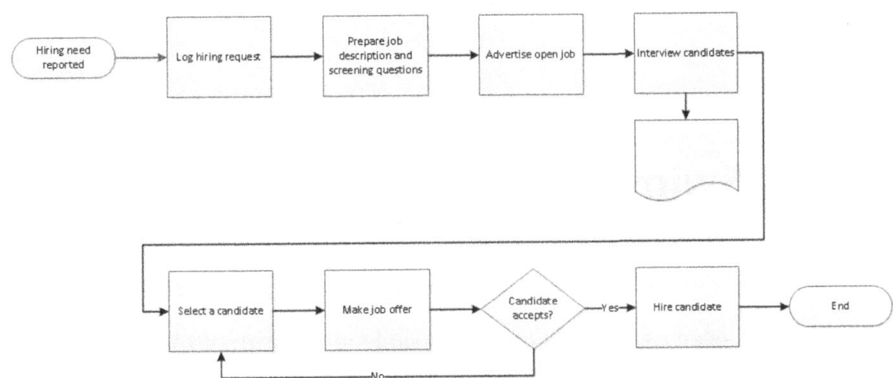

CLEAN UP Save your changes to the *HR Recruiting Flowchart* drawing, and then close it.

Understanding Swimlane Diagrams

Swimlane diagrams are a popular variation on flowcharts because they correct one significant failing of flowcharts: very few flowcharts show who is responsible for each of the steps or who makes the key decisions.

A swimlane diagram, on the other hand, is specifically organized by role, function, or department. Each process step is placed into a specific lane based on who does the work or who has the responsibility for that process step. For example, a swimlane diagram with a focus on roles might include lanes marked *Accounts Payable Clerk*, *Accounting Supervisor*, and *Chief Financial Officer*. Similarly, a department-focused swimlane drawing might show lanes labeled *Sales*, *Marketing*, *Order Processing*, and *Manufacturing*.

Swimlane diagrams are also known as *cross-functional flowcharts* because they show work steps as they cross the functional boundaries in an organization. In this context, individual swimlanes are usually referred to as ***functional bands***.

Regardless of the terminology, swimlane diagrams can be laid out with horizontal or vertical lanes. Using Visio, you can choose the orientation you prefer, as you'll see in the exercise in the following section.

Tip Some Visio templates employ additional software, outside of Visio itself, to perform their functions. The cross-functional flowchart diagram is an example of this type of Visio add-in. And, as is typical for this type of add-in, cross-functional flowcharts present a custom tab on the ribbon. The ribbon shown in the following graphic includes the Cross-Functional Flowchart tab.

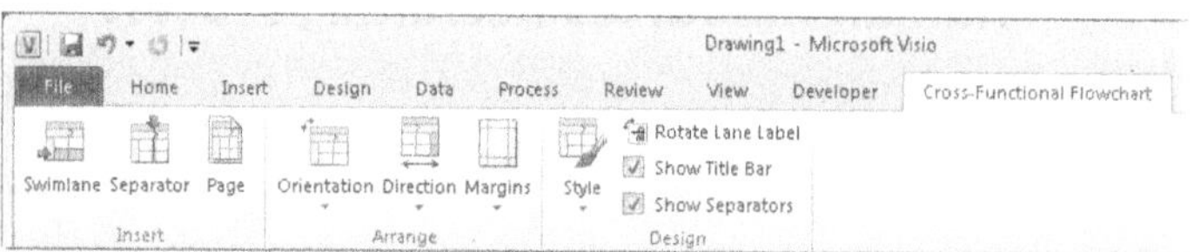

Creating Swimlane Diagrams

In the preceding exercises, you created a flowchart of a human resources recruiting process. However, the flowchart does not indicate who is responsible for each task.

In this exercise, you will create a swimlane diagram of the same process. In doing so, you will organize the work steps into role-based lanes to make responsibilities clear.

SET UP Click the File tab, and then click New.

1. In the **Template Categories** section, click **Flowchart**, and then double-click the **Cross-Functional Flowchart** thumbnail. The orientation selection dialog box opens.

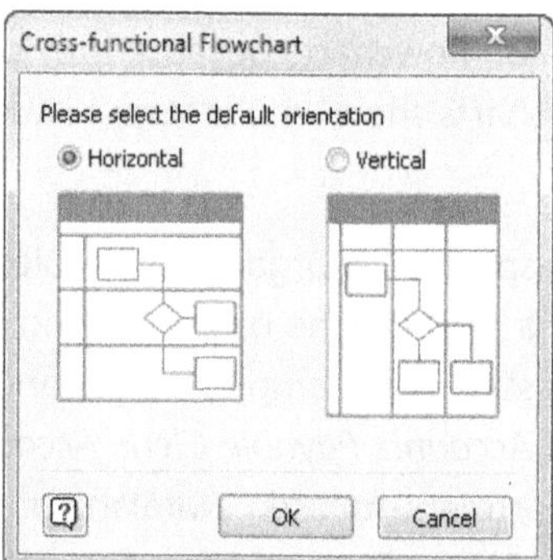

Tip If you have previously selected a default orientation, this dialog box will not appear again. However, you can still change both the orientation of a single diagram and the default for future diagrams. On the Cross-Functional Flowchart tab, in the Arrange group, click the Orientation button and make your selection.

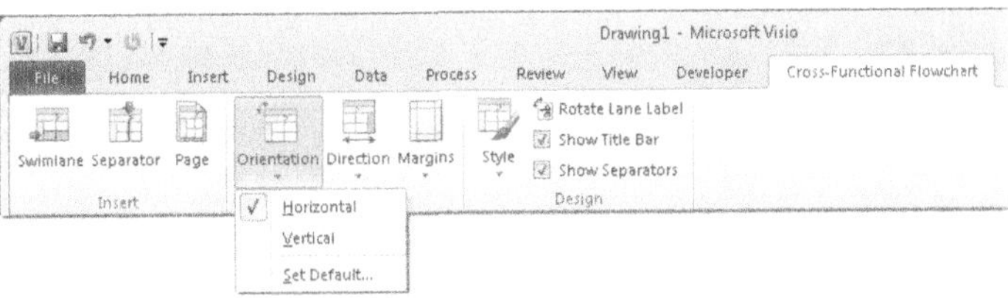

2. Click **OK** to select a **Horizontal** layout. The swimlane add-in places a title band and two swimlanes onto the drawing page.

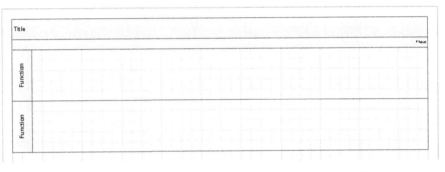

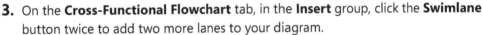

Swim Lane

3. On the **Cross-Functional Flowchart** tab, in the **Insert** group, click the **Swimlane** button twice to add two more lanes to your diagram.

   Tip There are three other ways to add swimlanes, each of which is useful at various times:

   - Right-click the header of an existing lane, and Visio offers you a choice of adding a new swimlane above or below the one you've selected.
   - Drag a Swimlane shape from the stencil and drop it on top of an existing lane.
   - Point to the boundary between lanes, with the cursor just outside the swimlane structure, and click the blue insertion triangle. (You will learn about the final method in Chapter 11, "Adding Structure to Your Diagrams.")

   You've probably already figured this out, but swimlane diagrams are so named because they resemble a swimming pool viewed from above.

4. Double-click the **Title** bar and type **Human Resources Recruiting Swimlane Diagram**.
5. Double-click the **Function** title bar for the top swimlane and type **Recruiter**.
6. Type **HR Admin** as the title for the second swimlane, **Hiring Manager** for the third swimlane, and **Candidate** for the bottom swimlane.

Human Resources Recruiting Swimlane Diagram

Recruiter

HR Admin

Hiring Manager

Candidate

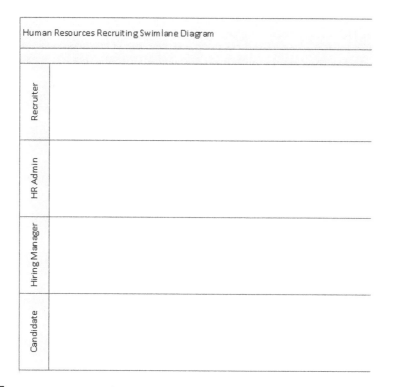

7. Drag a **Start/End** shape from the **Basic Flowchart Shapes** stencil onto the drawing page and use the Dynamic Grid to position it in the **Hiring Manager** lane.

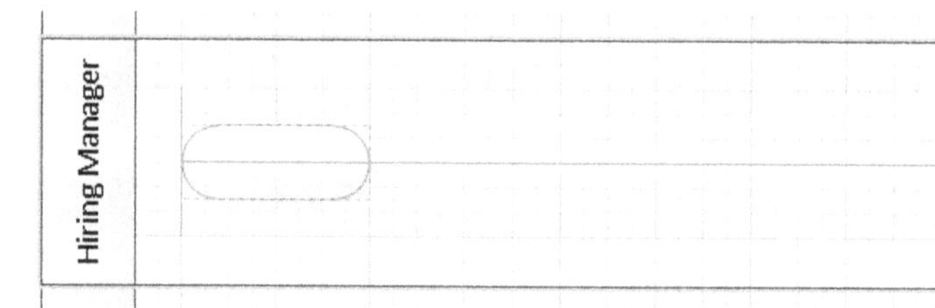

8. Click the start/end shape and type **Hiring need reported**.

9. Drag a **Process** shape into the **HR Admin** lane, dropping it to the right of the start/end shape, and then type **Log hiring request**.

Connector

10. On the **Home** tab, in the **Tools** group, click the **Connector** button, and then draw a connector from the top of the **Hiring need reported** shape to the left side of the **Log hiring request** shape.

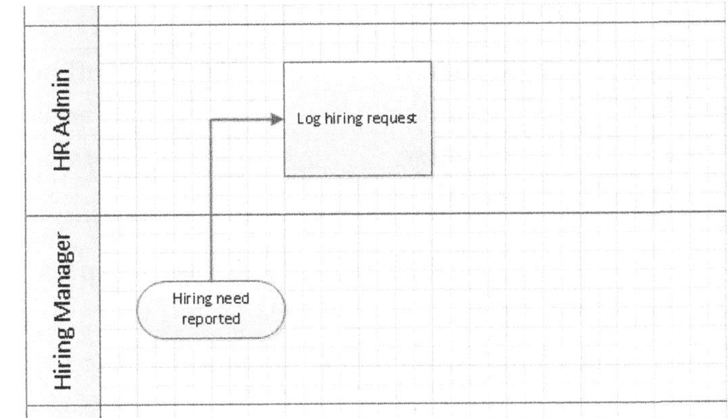

11. Drag a **Process** shape into the **Hiring Manager** lane, and then type **Prepare job description and screening questions**.
12. Use the **Connector** tool to link the previous process step to your new task.

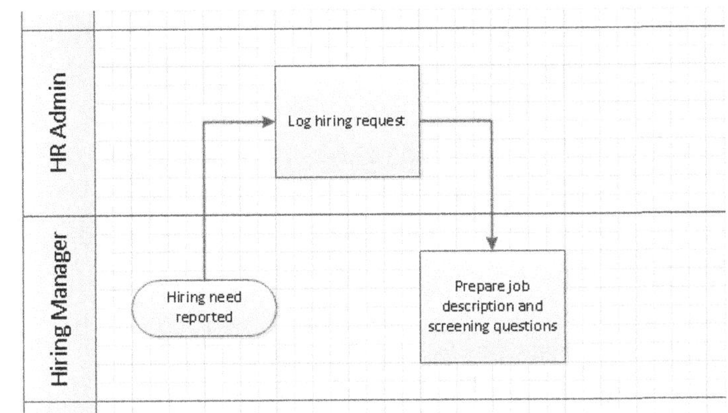

13. Continue adding flowchart shapes to your diagram using the information in rows 4-10 of the following table. (Rows 1-3 represent the shapes you've already added.) As you add each shape, draw a connector from the previous row's shape to the new shape.

	Shape	Swimlane	Shape text
1	**Start/End**	**Hiring Manager**	**Hiring need reported**
2	**Process**	**HR Admin**	**Log hiring request**
3	**Process**	**Hiring Manager**	**Prepare job description and screening questions**
4	**Process**	**HR Admin**	**Advertise open job**
5	**Process**	**Recruiter**	**Interview candidates**
6	**Process**	**Hiring Manager**	**Select a candidate**

	Shape	Swimlane	Shape text
7	**Process**	**Recruiter**	**Make job offer**
8	**Decision**	**Candidate**	**Candidate accepts?**
9	**Process**	**Recruiter**	**Hire candidate**
10	**Start/End**	**Hiring Manager**	**End**

14. Add a connector from the bottom of the **Candidate accepts?** shape to the bottom of the **Select a candidate** shape.
15. Click the connector from the **Candidate accepts?** shape to the **Hire candidate** shape and type **Yes**.
16. Click the connector from the **Candidate accepts?** shape to the **Select a candidate** shape and type **No**.

    Your swimlane diagram should look something like the following graphic. It's unlikely that your drawing will look exactly like this one because you probably made different decisions about placing and connecting shapes. However, after you have the general placement and connectivity correct, you can adjust and tweak your diagram to make it look the way you'd like.

    If you think your diagram is too crowded, realize that the cross-functional flowchart template used the default paper size for your region. If you need more space, you can increase the drawing page size as described in Chapter 3, "Adding Sophistication to Your Drawings."

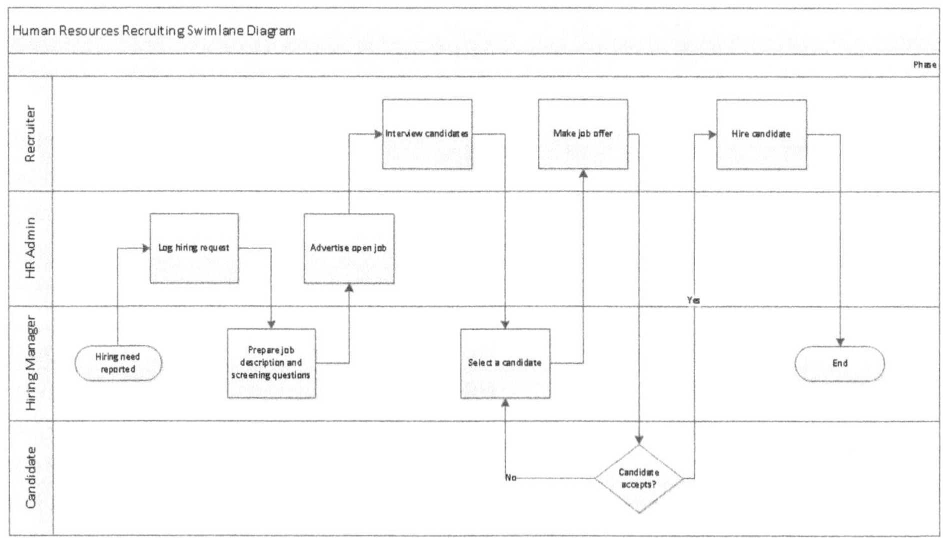

 **CLEAN UP** Save the drawing as *HR Recruiting Swimlane*, and then close it.

One final note about the Visio 2010 take on cross-functional flowcharts: although the end result looks very much as it has in previous versions of Visio, the underlying structure is very different. In fact, structure is the operative word in the previous sentence. In Visio 2010, each swimlane is a ***container***, and the overall framework is a ***list***. Containers and lists are key components of Visio 2010 structured diagrams and are described in Chapter 11.

Understanding Organization Charts

An organization chart is typically used to reflect the structure of an organization by showing who reports to whom. The Visio organization chart solution is based on a hierarchical model in which each employee has one boss. Consequently, it doesn't lend itself to organizations that use a matrix or other nonhierarchical structure. However, it is well-suited for most organizations.

Some org charts are simple and unadorned, showing just names and titles. Other org charts are more sophisticated and might display additional departmental or personal information, including photographs. Like most Visio templates, the org chart template includes a set of intelligent shapes. However, the org chart shapes are assisted by add-in software that is packaged with Visio. The combination of the two simplifies the creation of org charts by handling nearly all of the sizing and spacing chores when you do things like drop an employee shape on top of a manager shape. In addition, the add-in software includes a wizard that you can use to import organization data from Microsoft Excel or other data sources.

The org chart add-in also displays an add-in tab on the Visio ribbon whenever an org chart is the active drawing.

See Also **For more information about add-in tabs, see "Understanding Add-in Tabs" in Chapter 1, "A Visual Orientation to a Visual Product."**

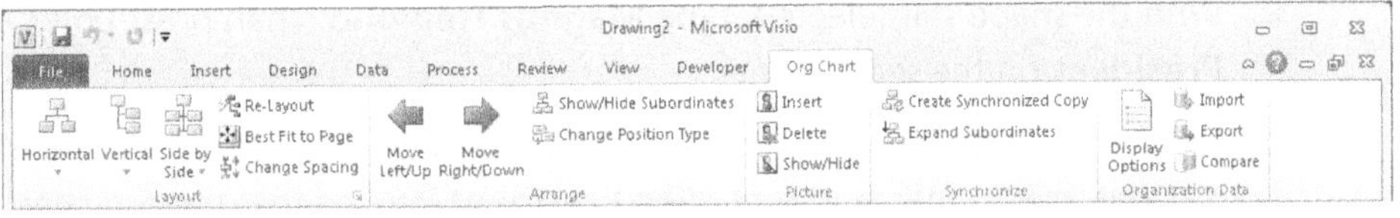

In the sections that follow, you will create a simple org chart manually and a more complex org chart by using data in an Excel workbook.

Building an Organization Chart by Hand

You will use the Organization Chart Wizard in the next two exercises, but it's important to understand first how easy it is to create org charts by hand.

In this exercise, you will create a new org chart by dragging shapes onto the page and using the org chart template's auto-positioning features. You will also enter data for each shape in the chart.

SET UP Click the File tab and then click New. In the Template Categories section, click Business, and then double-click the Organization Chart thumbnail. Save the new drawing as *Org Chart by Hand*.

> **Tip The only difference between the template called Organization Chart and the one called Organization Chart Wizard is that the latter automatically starts a wizard when you open a new document. If you select the Organization Chart Wizard by mistake for this exercise, just cancel the wizard and you can continue.**

1. Drag the **Executive** shape from the **Organization Chart Shapes** stencil to the top center of the drawing page.

   The org chart add-in presents an animated dialog box showing how to add additional shapes to the chart unless you have previously turned it off. You can select the check box in the lower-left of the dialog box to suppress future display of the animated help.

   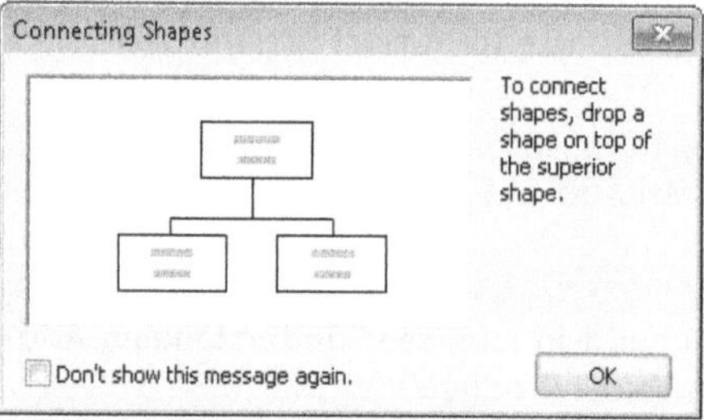
   Connecting Shapes
   To connect shapes, drop a shape on top of the superior shape.
   Don't show this message again.
   OK

2. With the shape still selected, type **Magnus Hedlund**. Then press Enter and type **President** on the second line.

3. Drag a **Manager** shape onto the **Magnus Hedlund** shape. Then type **Magdalena Karwat**, press Enter, and type **Vice President**. Notice that the org chart software automatically positions the new shape below the *Hedlund* shape.

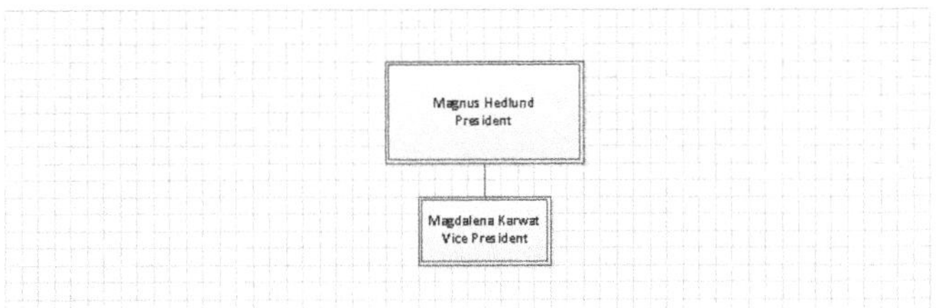

4. Repeat Step 3 and notice that the org chart add-in has positioned the second manager shape to the side of the first one. With the new shape still selected, type **Allison Brown**, press Enter, and then type **Vice President**.

5. Drag one more **Manager** shape onto the **Hedlund** shape. Type **Giorgio Veronesi**, press Enter, and then type **Vice President**.

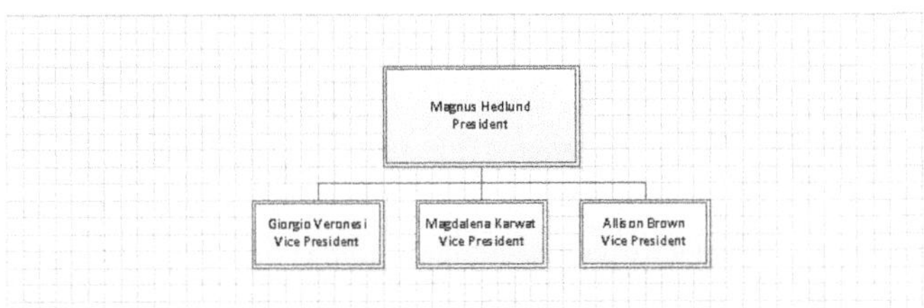

6. Drag two **Position** shapes onto the **Giorgio Veronesi** shape, then type **Janet Schorr** into the first one and **Reina Cabatana** into the second.

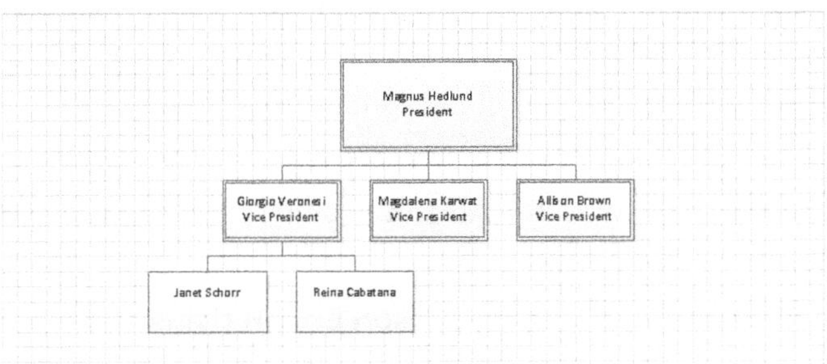

7. Drag one **Position** shape onto the **Magadalena Karwat** shape and type **Filip Rehorik**.

   The org chart's shape placement mechanism has hidden part of the Reina Cabatana shape behind the Filip Rehorik shape.

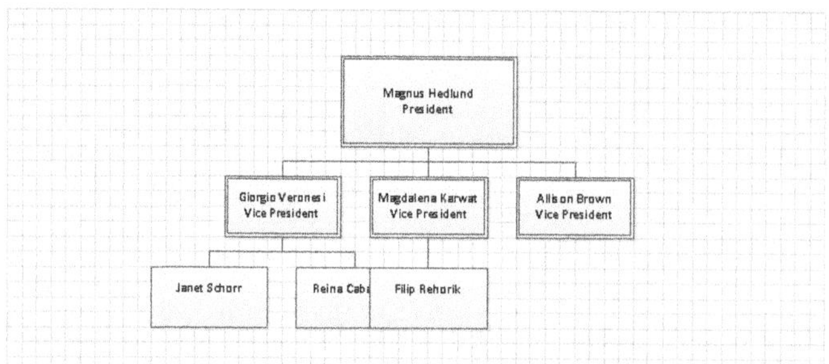

Re-Layout

8. On the **Org Chart** tab, in the **Layout** group, click the **Re-Layout** button to solve the problem.

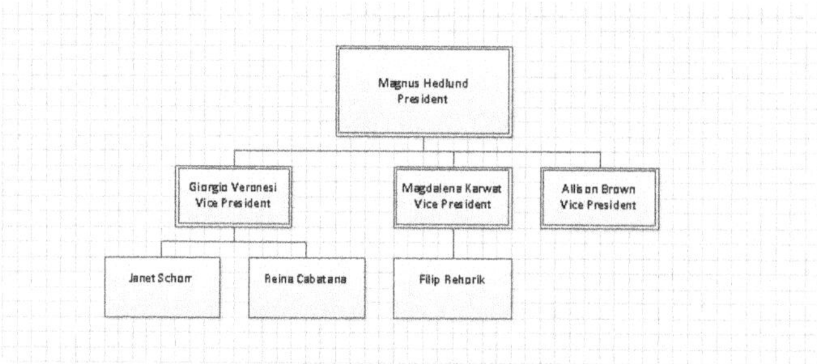

Tip There may be times when you don't like the changes made by the re-layout function. If that's the case, simply press Ctrl+Z or click the Undo button on the *Quick Access Toolbar*. No matter how extensive the changes, a single undo will return the diagram to its previous layout.

9. Drag a **Consultant** shape onto the **Magadalena Karwat** shape and type **Sandeep Kaliyath**. Notice that consultant shapes have a dash-dot outline.
10. Drag a **Vacancy** shape onto the **Allison Brown** shape and type **Open**. Notice that vacancy shapes have a dotted outline.
11. Drag an **Assistant** shape onto the **Allison Brown** shape and type **Gabe Frost**.
12. Drag an **Assistant** shape onto the **Giorgio Veronesi** shape and type **Yan Li**.
13. Drag an **Assistant** shape onto the **Magnus Hedlund** shape and type **Cassie Hicks**.
14. On the **Org Chart** tab, in the **Layout** group, click the **Re-Layout** button.

Tip You can also initiate page layout by right-clicking anywhere on the background of an org chart page and selecting Re-layout from the context menu.

The org chart add-in has rearranged your drawing to position all of your shapes. Take note of the dash-dot consultant, the dotted vacancy, and the placement of the assistant shapes under Magnus Hedlund, Allison Brown, and Giorgio Veronesi.

At this point, you've built a reasonably sophisticated organization chart by doing little more that dragging shapes and typing text.

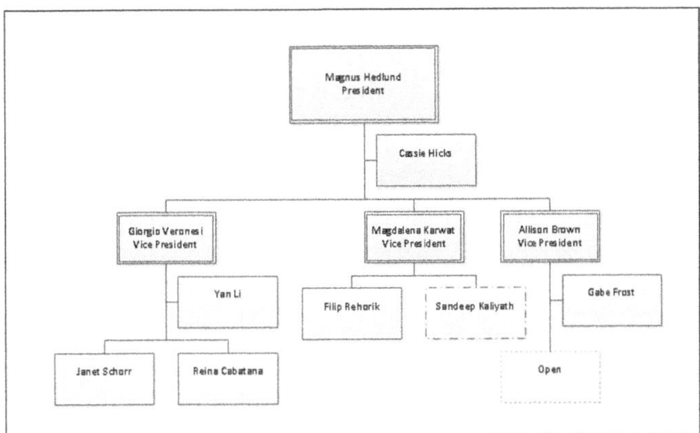

 **CLEAN UP** Save your changes to the *Org Chart by Hand* drawing, and then close it.

Altering Org Chart Shapes

Whether you create an organization chart manually, as you've just done, or automatically using the wizard, you might want to modify the appearance and attributes of the org chart shapes after they're on the page. The Visio organization chart add-in provides a number of easy ways to make changes.

Type

You can right-click any org chart shape to change its type. For example, in the organization chart you created in the preceding exercise, you identified a vacancy in Allison Brown's group, symbolized by a dotted outline around the position box. When Allison hires a person to fill that vacancy, simply right-click the vacant position shape, click Change Position Type, click Position, and then click OK.

Appearance

You can change the appearance of the org chart shapes by adding a dividing line between the position and the title. To do so, select some or all of the shapes on the page, right-click any of the shapes, and then click Show Divider Line.

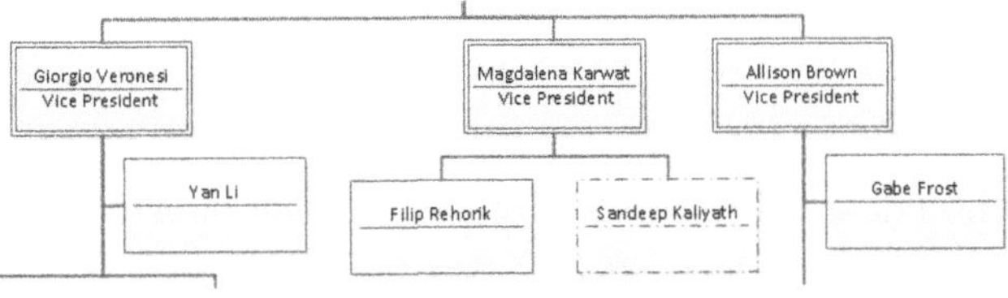

You can also affect the appearance of org chart shapes by showing additional data on each shape. For examples of what is possible, on the Org Chart tab, in the Organization Data group, click the Display Options button. In the resulting Options dialog box, click the Fields tab to see your choices.

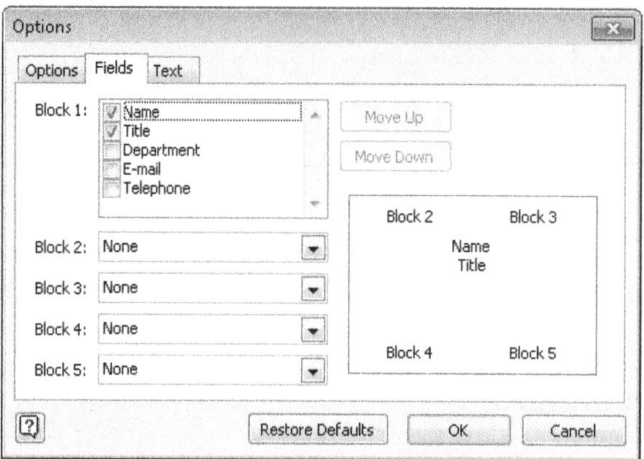

On the other tabs in this dialog box, you can change the size and spacing of org chart shapes and the size and formatting of the text.

See Also **You can change the appearance of an organization chart quite dramatically by applying *themes*. For details and examples, see "Applying Themes to Your Diagrams" in Chapter 5, "Adding Style, Color, and Themes."**

Using the Organization Chart Wizard with Existing Data

What if you already have your organization data available in electronic form? For example, you might have:

- An Excel workbook that already contains names and reporting information.
- A Human Resources or Enterprise Resource Planning (ERP) system that can generate an Excel file or a text file.
- Organization data in a Microsoft Exchange Server directory.
- Organization data in a Microsoft Access, dBase, or other database.

In all of those situations, the org chart wizard can help you to create your chart.

In this exercise, you will use data in an Excel workbook to build an organization chart.

SET UP You need the *Org Chart Data_start* workbook located in the Chapter04 practice file folder to complete this exercise.

1. Start Excel, open the *Org Chart Data_start* workbook, and save it as *Org Chart Data*. While the workbook is open, look at the data that will be used in this exercise. In particular, notice that there are columns for Name, Title, Reports To, Employee Number, and Extension.

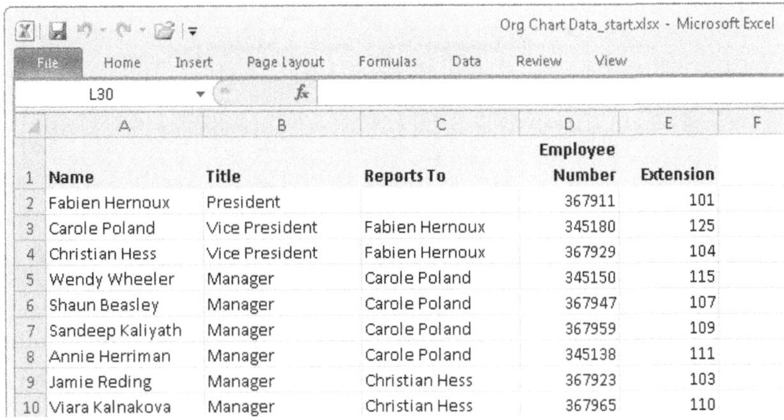

	A	B	C	D	E
1	Name	Title	Reports To	Employee Number	Extension
2	Fabien Hernoux	President		367911	101
3	Carole Poland	Vice President	Fabien Hernoux	345180	125
4	Christian Hess	Vice President	Fabien Hernoux	367929	104
5	Wendy Wheeler	Manager	Carole Poland	345150	115
6	Shaun Beasley	Manager	Carole Poland	367947	107
7	Sandeep Kaliyath	Manager	Carole Poland	367959	109
8	Annie Herriman	Manager	Carole Poland	345138	111
9	Jamie Reding	Manager	Christian Hess	367923	103
10	Viara Kalnakova	Manager	Christian Hess	367965	110

2. Close Excel, and then start Visio.
3. In the **Template Categories** section, click **Business**, and then double-click the **Organization Chart Wizard** thumbnail.

   Tip The only difference between the template called Organization Chart Wizard and the one called Organization Chart is that the former automatically starts a wizard when you open a new document. If you select Organization Chart by mistake for this exercise, just click the Import button in the Organization Data group on the Org Chart tab to launch the wizard.

   The first page of the wizard appears.

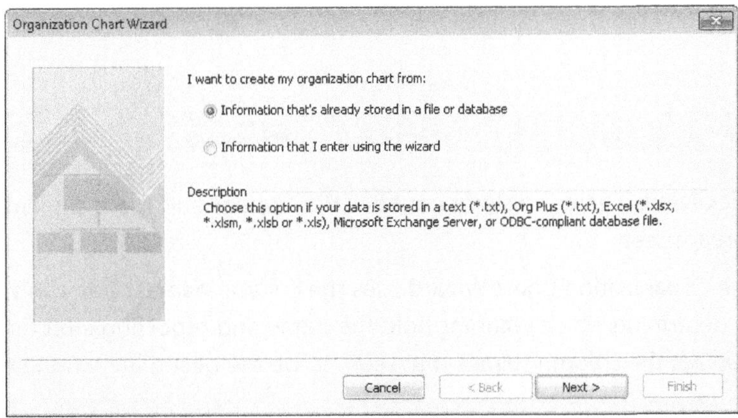

4. Click **Next**. The data source type page appears.

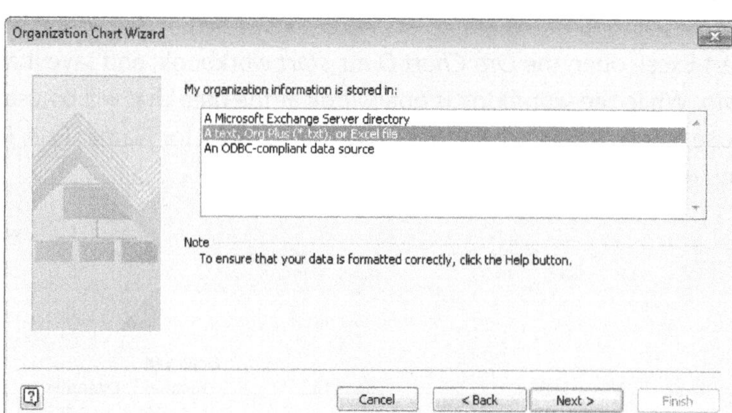

5. Click **A text, Org Plus (*.txt), or Excel file**, and then click **Next**. The file selection page appears.
6. Click the **Browse** button on the file selection page, and then, in the resulting file open dialog box, navigate to the *Org Chart Data* workbook. After selecting the correct file, click the **Open** button.

   The file name you selected appears in the Locate The File That Contains Your Organization Information box.

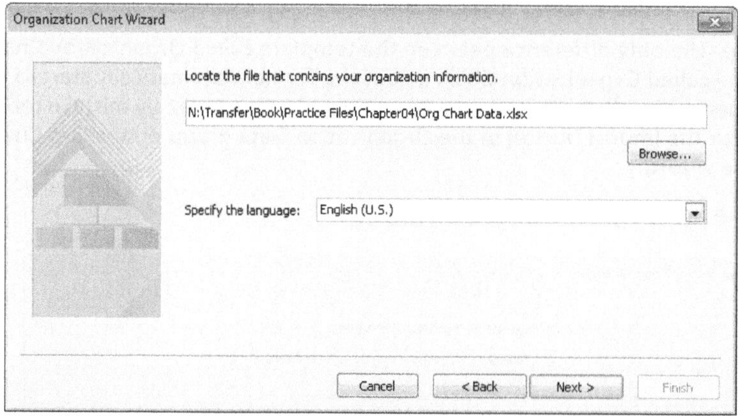

7. Click **Next**. There is a slight pause as Visio opens and reads the data in your spreadsheet.

   The Organization Chart Wizard uses the column names, if any, in your spreadsheet to determine which columns hold the name and reporting structure information. It displays the column names that seem to be the best match in the next wizard page.

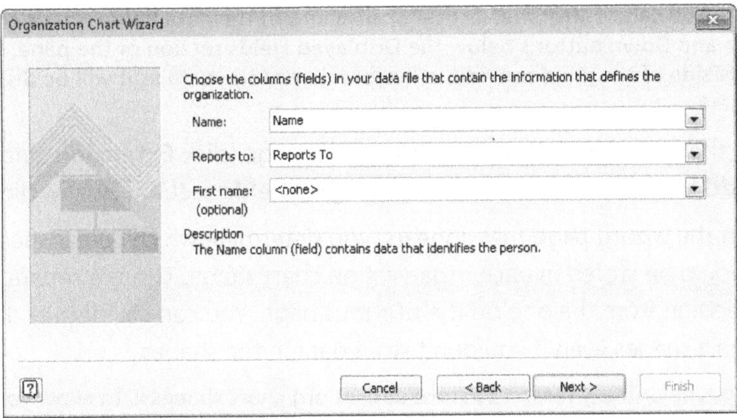

Because the *Org Chart Data* workbook contains columns called *Name* and *Reports To*, the assumptions made by Visio are correct as shown. If the assumptions are not correct, click the arrows to the right of Name and Reports To in order to select the correct columns.

Notice you can specify that a separate column contains employees' first names, if that is the case.

8. Click **Next**.

   The next Organization Chart Wizard page provides an opportunity for you to select which employee data will be displayed on each shape in the chart. The wizard assumes that you want to display the name and title fields, so those fields are preselected on the right side of the page.

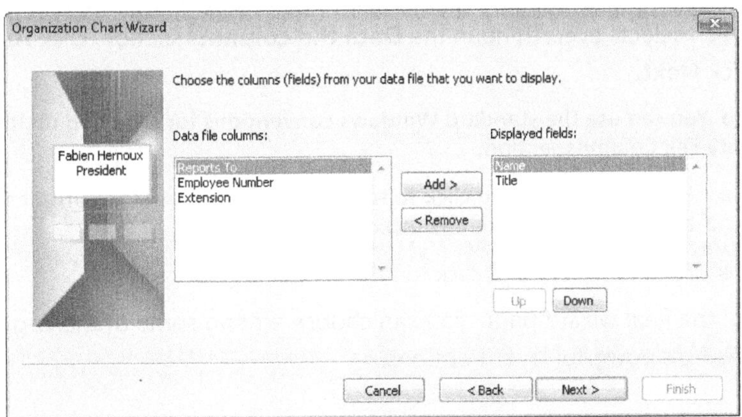

Tip You can control the vertical positioning of the data fields you've chosen with the Up and Down buttons below the Displayed Fields section of the page. The pane on the left side of the page provides a live preview of the data as it will be displayed in the org chart.

9. In the **Data file columns** section of the page, click **Extension**, and then click the **Add** button to move it to the **Displayed fields** section. Finally, click **Next**.

   On the wizard page that appears, you determine which spreadsheet data, if any, should be stored in each organization chart shape. This is a separate and unrelated decision from the one on the previous page. You can still display data on the org chart shapes even if you don't store data in the shapes.

   Tip The primary reason to store data in org chart shapes is to allow you to run reports or use the data in other ways without the need to revert to your original data source.

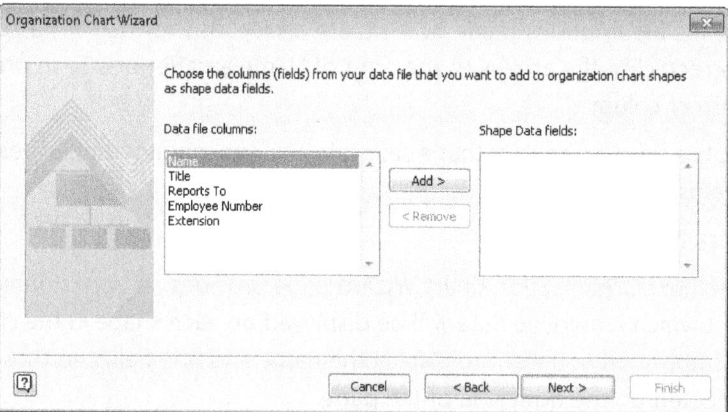

10. To add all fields to the shape, hold down the Shift key while clicking **Extension**, which selects everything in the **Data file columns** section, click **Add**, and then click **Next**.

    Tip You can use the standard Windows conventions for selecting multiple items in the Data File Columns section:

    - Hold down Shift and click to select everything from the current selection up to and including the item you click.
    - Hold down Ctrl and click to select noncontiguous items.

    On the final wizard page, you can choose among some of the Organization Chart Wizard's powerful layout options.

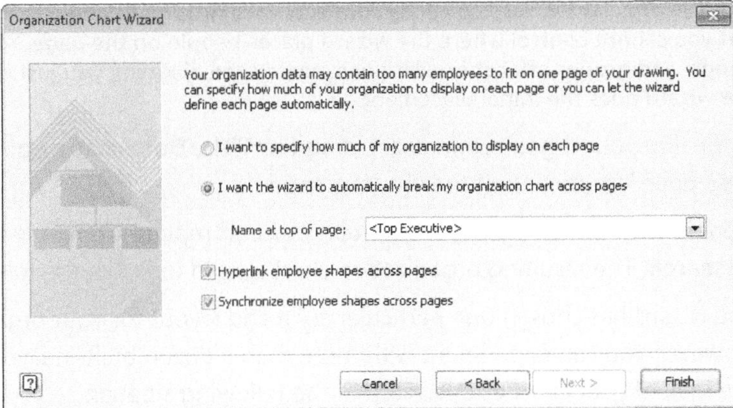

Accepting the default selection of I Want The Wizard To Automatically Break My Organization Chart Across Pages lets the wizard figure out how much to fit on each Visio page. The <Top Executive> option tells Visio to select the person who doesn't report to anyone else as the top shape on the first page of the org chart. If you prefer to select a specific person (like a department head), you can click the arrow to choose anyone in your list.

Clicking I Want To Specify How Much Of My Organization To Display On Each Page takes you to a wizard page not shown here, and allows you to control more directly how much to fit on each org chart page.

The Hyperlink Employee Shapes Across Pages check box specifies whether the wizard should add hyperlinks when org charts consist of multiple pages. For example, if a manager's direct reports don't fit on the page with the manager, the wizard will leave the manager shape on the original page and also place it on a subsequent page along with that manager's direct reports. A check mark in this option tells Visio to add links in both manager shapes, making page-to-page navigation simpler.

The Synchronize Employee Shapes Across Pages check box also applies to the scenario described in the preceding paragraph. A check mark in this option tells Visio to update the second shape if you change the data in the first one.

11. Click **Finish**. The completed organization chart appears in the Visio drawing window.

Tip **The org chart wizard correctly connects each group of people to its respective boss, but you cannot control where the wizard places people on the page. You can relocate people and groups after the wizard has created the diagram; you just can't control how the wizard does the initial placement.**

12. To finalize your organization chart, drag the **Title/Date** shape from the stencil into the upper-left portion of the drawing page.

13. Double-click the **Company Name** text box and replace *Company Name* with **Trey Research**. The resulting organization chart should look like the following graphic.

    The wizard has chosen one particular style and layout for your organization chart. However, you can experiment with more than a dozen built-in layouts to change the look of your chart as described in the following sidebar.

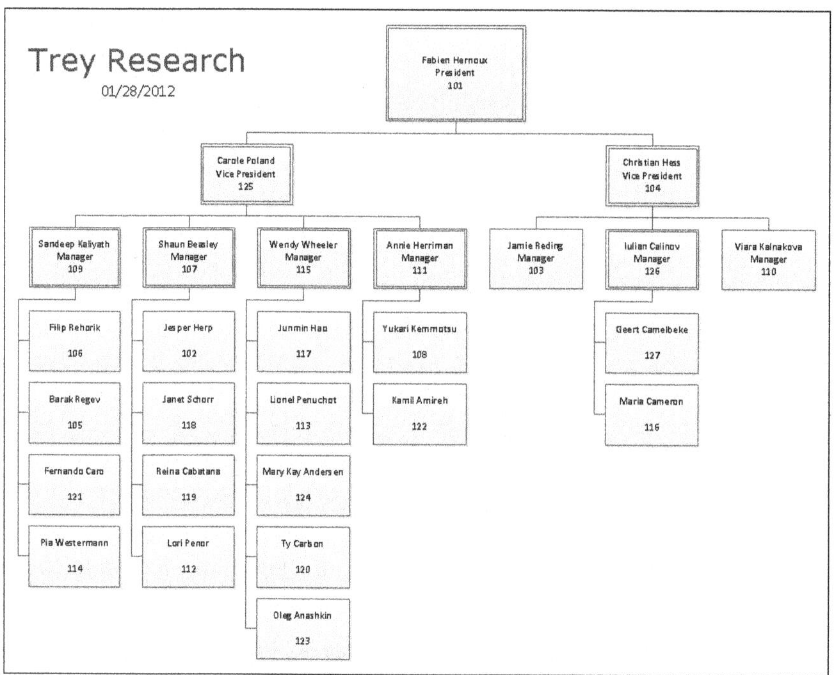

CLEAN UP Save your drawing as *Org Chart using Wizard* and then close it.

Altering Org Chart Layout

Although the org chart wizard has used a default layout for your chart, you can change the layout, move shapes and groups of shapes, and hide parts of the chart.

Rearrange

You can change the layout of an org chart by using more than a dozen predefined layouts supplied with Visio. On the Org Chart tab, in the Layout group, click Horizontal, Vertical, or Side By Side to select from a variety of options.

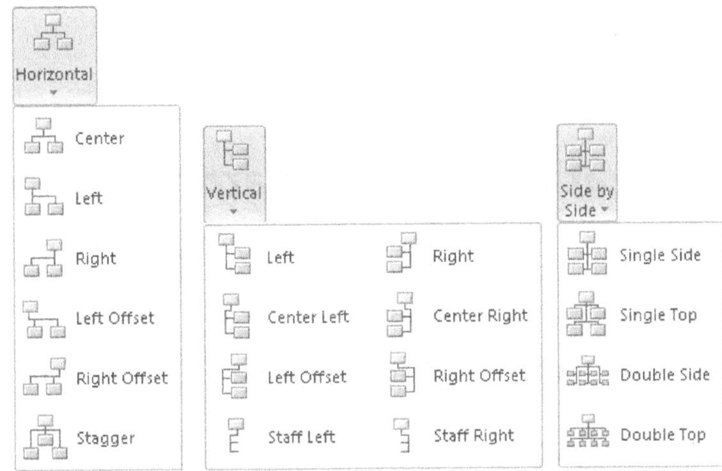

As an alternative, right-click any shape with subordinates, and then click Arrange Subordinates. Visio opens a dialog box showing all of the built-in layouts.

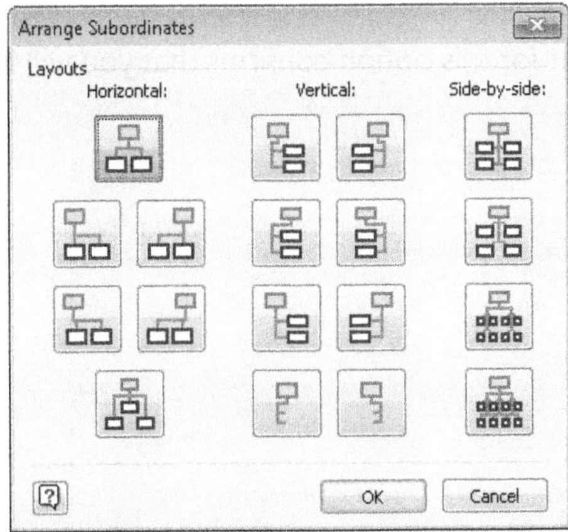

Tip **If you don't like the results of any re-layout operation—no matter how radical the changes—you can restore the previous layout with a single undo.**

Move

You can adjust the layout of an organization chart by moving shapes or groups of shapes left/right or up/down. Look for the Move buttons in the Arrange group on the Org Chart tab. For example, in the completed *Org Chart using Wizard* drawing from the preceding exercise, select the vice president named *Christian Hess*, and then click the Move Left/Up button to see the effect.

Hide

If you want to hide some sections of your org chart, click the Hide Subordinates or Show Subordinates options on a shape's shortcut menu or the Show/Hide Subordinates button in the Arrange group on the Org Chart tab.

Using the Organization Chart Wizard with New Data

If your organization data is not in a format that Visio can read and you would like to type it into a spreadsheet but don't want to start from scratch, the Organization Chart Wizard can create a preformatted spreadsheet for you.

In this exercise, you will use the Organization Chart Wizard to create an Excel workbook into which you will enter your organization data.

SET UP Click the File tab, and then click New. In the Template Categories section, click Business, and then double-click the Organization Chart Wizard thumbnail.

1. On the first page of the **Organization Chart Wizard**, click **Information that I enter using the wizard**.

   Notice that the description text for this option confirms that you will be creating a new data source.

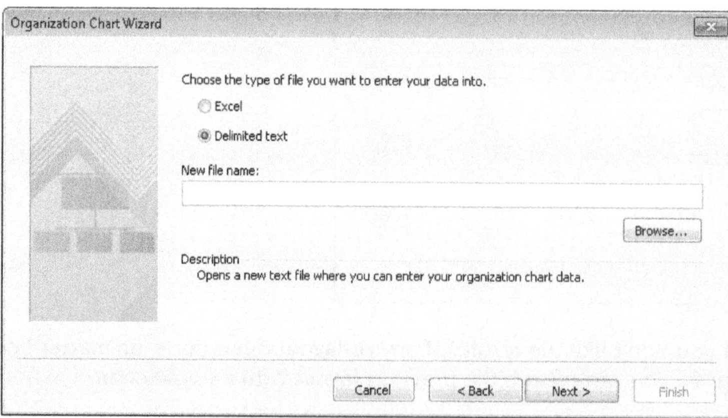

2. Click **Next**. The file type selection page appears.
3. On the file type selection page, click **Excel**, and then click the **Browse** button. In the resulting dialog box, select a folder in which to save the file, type **Org Chart Data via Wizard** in the **File name** box, and then click the **Save** button.

   The selected file name appears in the New File Name box on the next wizard page.

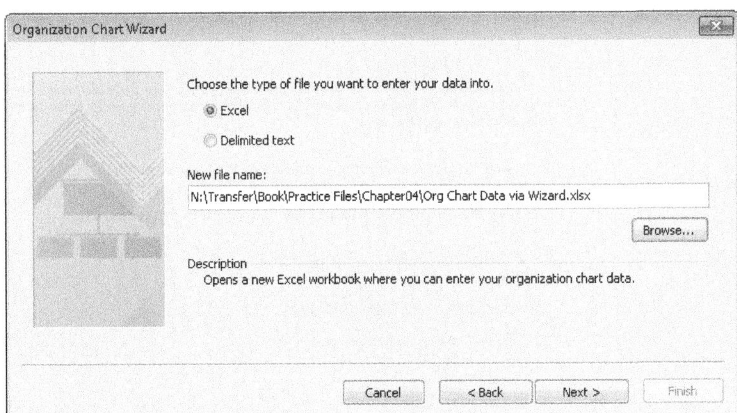

4. Click **Next**. Visio instructs you to type your data over the sample data provided in the Excel workbook it has created.

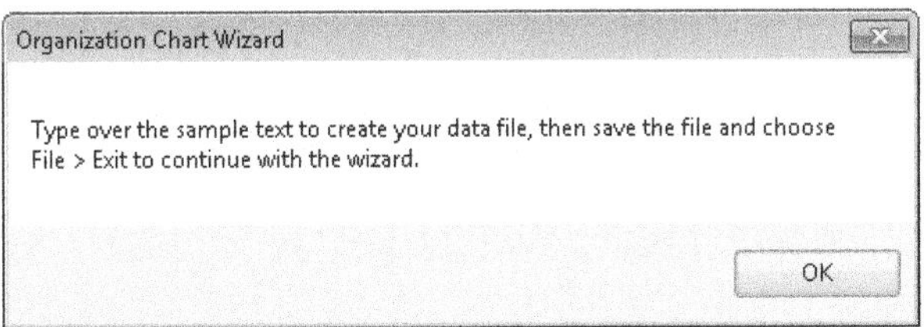

5. Click **OK**. Excel opens to display the formatted workbook. As shown in the following graphic, notice that each column heading includes a comment with instructions for entering data in that column.

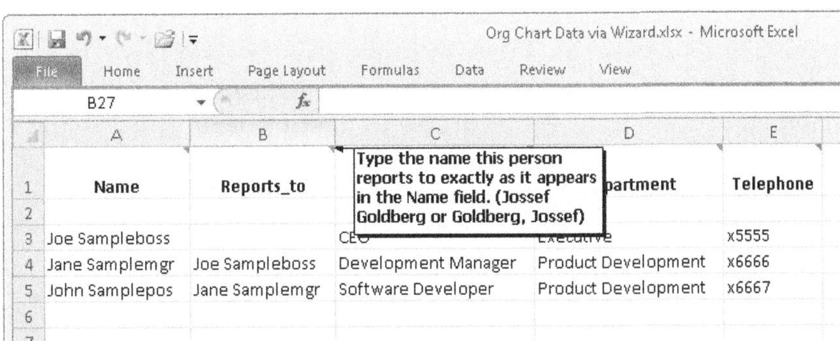

6. Ordinarily, you would type your data into the worksheet at this point; however, for this exercise you will use the sample data, so just close Excel.

   Important **Closing the worksheet isn't sufficient; you must close the Excel application.**

   When you close Excel, Windows returns the focus to Visio, where you will see the final page of the Organization Chart Wizard.

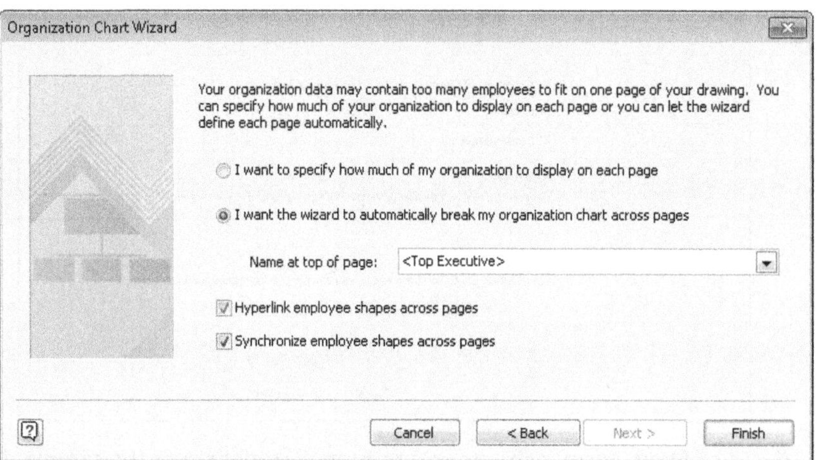

7. Click **Finish** to display your org chart.

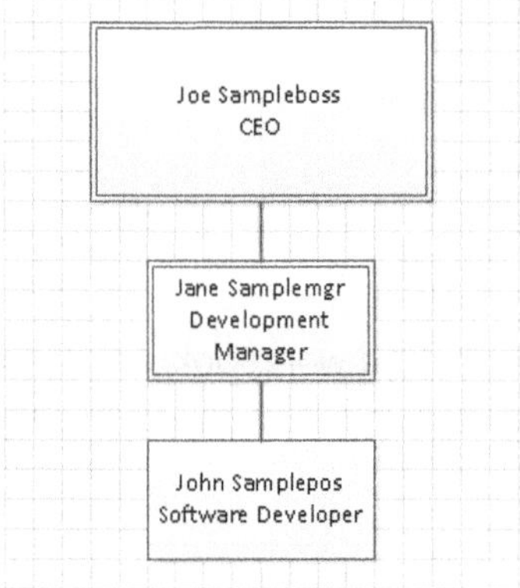

CLEAN UP **Save the sample file if you want to keep it.**

Enhancing Org Charts with Pictures

Visio 2010, like previous versions, gives you the option to add images to organization chart shapes. You can right-click a shape to add a picture or you can click the buttons in the Picture group on the Org Chart tab.

However, Visio only allows you to add or delete pictures one shape at a time. If you would like to add pictures to multiple shapes at once, check out an article and code sample provided by Visio MVP John Goldsmith at *visualsignals.typepad.co.uk/vislog/2008/06/linking-org-chart-images.html.*

An Unconventional Use for Organization Charts

Occasionally, you find a use for a Visio template that its designers might not have envisioned. The author of this book and another Visio expert did exactly that with the org chart wizard by using it to display the folder structure on a Windows computer. After all, groups of people and folders on a disk drive are both organized hierarchically, so it seemed like a logical thing to do.

See Also **To read an article about viewing the Windows disk drive as an "organization chart," go to** ***www.experts-exchange.com/viewArticle.jsp?articleID=2802.***

Key Points

- Creating flowcharts is one of the most common uses for Visio. The built-in templates make it very easy for you to create both conventional flowcharts and swimlane diagrams.
- Swimlane diagrams, also known as cross-functional flowcharts, offer one key advantage over regular flowcharts: each process step resides in a swimlane that identifies which role, department, or function is responsible for that step.
- You can create organization charts manually by dragging shapes from the org chart stencil onto the drawing page.
- The Organization Chart Wizard automates most of the creation of org charts by letting you import data from Excel spreadsheets, text files, and databases. In addition, the wizard can provide you with a preformatted spreadsheet that you can use to enter your organization's data prior to running the wizard.

Chapter at a Glance

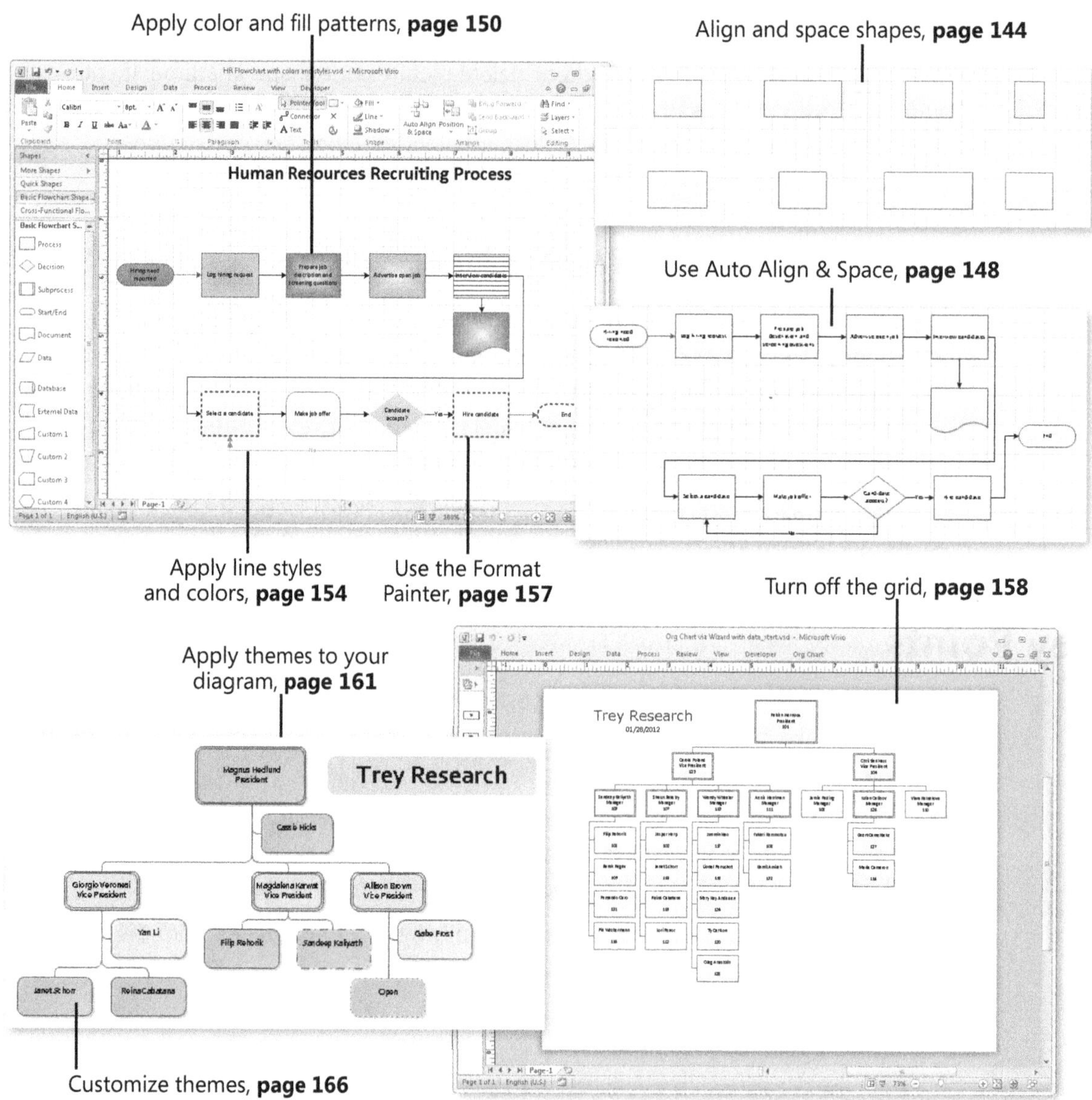

Apply color and fill patterns, **page 150**
Align and space shapes, **page 144**
Human Resources Recruiting Process
Use Auto Align & Space, **page 148**
Apply line styles and colors, **page 154**
Use the Format Painter, **page 157**
Turn off the grid, **page 158**
Apply themes to your diagram, **page 161**
Trey Research
Customize themes, **page 166**

5 Adding Style, Color, and Themes

In this chapter, you will learn how to

- ✔ Align and space shapes.
- ✔ Use the Auto Align & Space feature.
- ✔ Apply color and fill patterns.
- ✔ Apply line styles and colors.
- ✔ Use the Format Painter.
- ✔ Turn off the grid.
- ✔ Apply themes to your diagrams.
- ✔ Customize themes.
- ✔ Set theme options.

In Chapter 4, "Drawing the Real World: Flowcharts and Organization Charts," you created flowcharts, swimlane diagrams, and organization charts. They were functional and, perhaps, moderately pleasing to the eye, but they lacked style.

In this chapter, you will add style and aesthetic appeal to Microsoft Visio 2010 drawings by learning some tips and tricks for aligning and spacing shapes, applying style and color to individual shapes, and applying style and color themes to an entire drawing.

> **Practice Files** Before you can complete the exercises in this chapter, you need to copy the book's practice files to your computer. The practice files you'll use to complete the exercises in this chapter are in the Chapter05 practice files folder. A complete list of practice files is provided in "Using the Practice Files" at the beginning of this book.

Aligning and Spacing Shapes

Parents and teachers often admonish children by saying, "Neatness counts!" Although children tire of hearing that phrase, neatness is an important factor when you create Visio drawings. It is remarkable how much more effective your diagram can be if the viewer isn't distracted by lines that cross unnecessarily or shapes that are almost, but not quite, aligned.

Chapter 1, "A Visual Orientation to a Visual Product," and Chapter 2, "Creating a New Diagram," explored many of the ways that Visio helps you create neat drawings—rulers, guides, the dynamic grid—so that you can drag and nudge individual shapes to your heart's content. However, Visio includes additional tools that make it even easier to position and align multiple shapes at once.

What's on Top?

When you drop shapes onto a Visio drawing page, their horizontal (X-axis) and vertical (Y-axis) positions are obvious. Less obvious is each shape's position on the Z-axis. You see evidence of the placement on the Z-axis when you drop shapes on top of each other, because some shapes appear to be "in front of" or "behind" other shapes.

Even when shapes are not on top of each other, however, Visio keeps track of the ***Z-order***, that is, the position of each shape along the Z-axis. The first shape you drop on a page is at the back, and every subsequent shape you add is one step in front of the previous one. If you're in doubt, try the following experiment:

1. Drop three shapes in separate parts of the drawing page so none of the shapes are touching.
2. Drag the second shape you dropped so it partially overlaps the third. Notice that it appears behind the third shape.
3. Drag the first one so it overlaps part of the second and part of the third. The first shape will maintain its Z-order and appear behind the other two.

You can alter the Z-order of any shape or shapes by using the Bring Forward or Send Backward buttons in the Arrange group on the Home tab. You can also right-click a shape and select Bring To Front or Send To Back from the context menu.

Tip The buttons on the Home tab default to moving a shape one step forward or backward, but you can use commands on each button's menu to move the full distance in either direction. The right-click context menus have the opposite default: they move the shape(s) the full distance in one direction, but they contain drop-down menus to move one step at a time.

In this exercise, you will work with several valuable Visio tools that align and distribute shapes on the drawing page. After creating a collection of randomly placed shapes, you will rearrange them into neat rows and columns without dragging a single shape.

SET UP Start Visio, or if it's already running, click the File tab and then click New. In the Template Categories section, click Flowchart, and then double-click the Basic Flowchart thumbnail. Save the new drawing as *Align and Space BEFORE*.

1. Drag four **Process** shapes into a row but deliberately space them very irregularly and don't align them with each other. Repeat with four additional shapes in a second row. Finally, drag the resize handles so some shapes are wider than others.

   Tip Your diagram doesn't need to look exactly like the one shown here, but this is an example of the type of "messy diagram" you should create.

   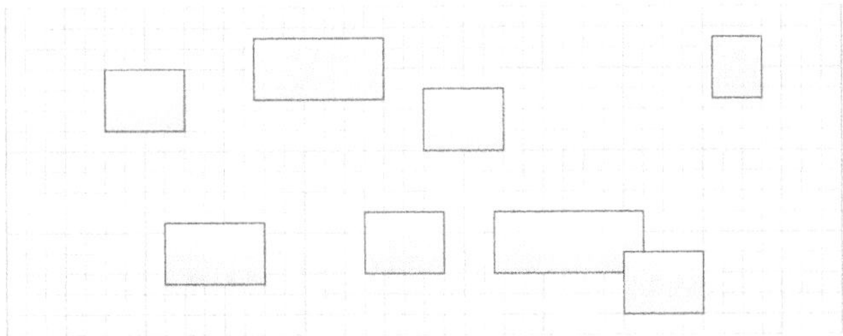

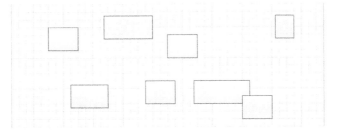

   Your first task is to rearrange the shapes in the upper row so they are vertically aligned.

2. Draw a bounding box around the shapes in the top row.

   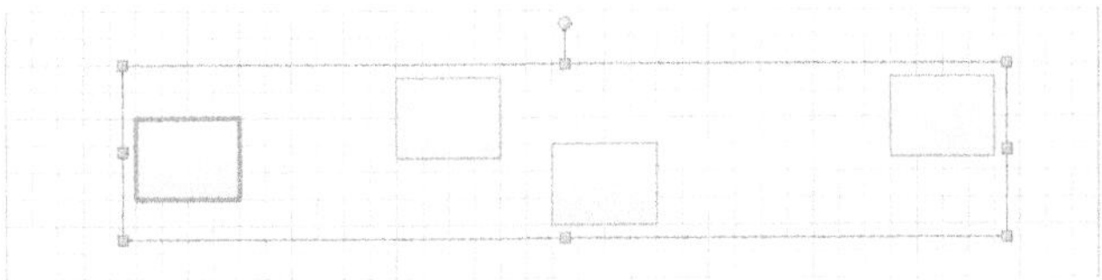

   Important The leftmost shape in the previous graphic has a bolder selection outline than the others. This is the shape Visio will use as the *anchor shape* for the operations you will perform in this exercise. Just as its name suggests, the anchor will stay in place—the other shapes will move relative to it.

   It's important to notice which shape is the anchor because the results can be very different with different anchor shapes. For that reason, it's also important to understand how Visio selects the anchor shape so you can change it if you want to:

   - **If you use a bounding box or another technique to select multiple shapes at once, the anchor will be the shape that is farthest to the back. This will usually be the shape that you placed on the page first unless you have changed the Z-order by using the Send Backward or Send Forward functions.**

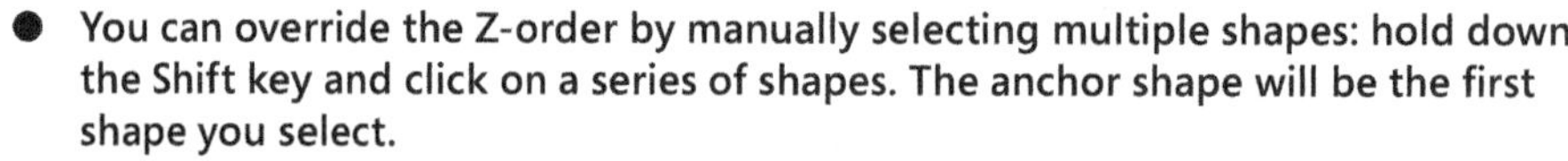

- **You can override the Z-order by manually selecting multiple shapes: hold down the Shift key and click on a series of shapes. The anchor shape will be the first shape you select.**

Position

3. On the **Home** tab, in the **Arrange** group, click the **Position** button, and then move the cursor over a series of entries on the menu to observe the Live Preview results. For example, point to **Align Left**, **Align Center**, and then **Align Right** to see shapes aligned along their left edges, centers, or right edges.

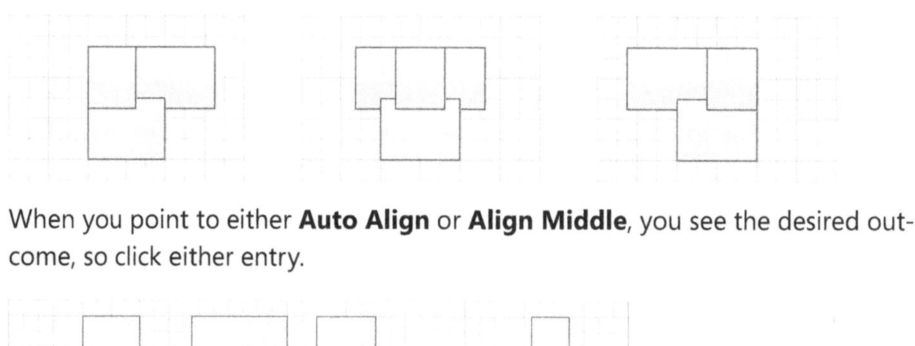

When you point to either **Auto Align** or **Align Middle**, you see the desired outcome, so click either entry.

Tip **If you want to prove to yourself that your choice of anchor shape does make a difference, try this experiment: Undo the alignment action so the shapes in the top row are back where they started; click any shape so it will be the anchor; hold down Shift and click the remaining shapes in the row; align the shapes. You'll see that the row has been aligned to your chosen anchor.**

4. Repeat Step 3 with the second row, using **Align Middle**.

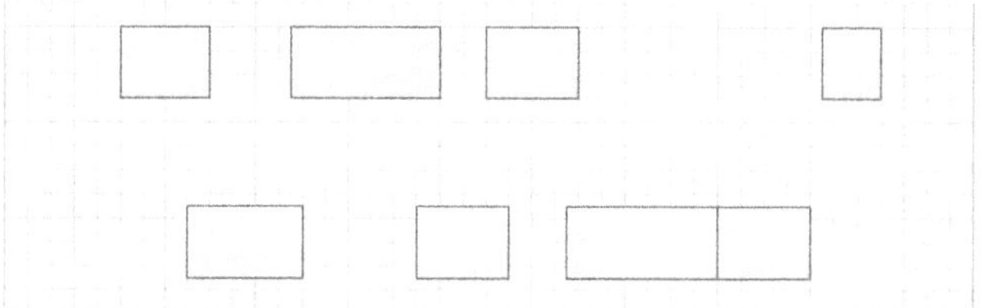

Now that the alignment looks better, you can correct the irregular spacing between shapes.

5. Select all of the shapes in the top row. Then on the **Home** tab, in the **Arrange** group, click the **Position** button. In the **Space Shapes** section of the menu, point to **Auto Space** and note that Visio leaves the anchor shape in place and arranges the remaining shapes so the distance between the edges of each pair of shapes is identical.

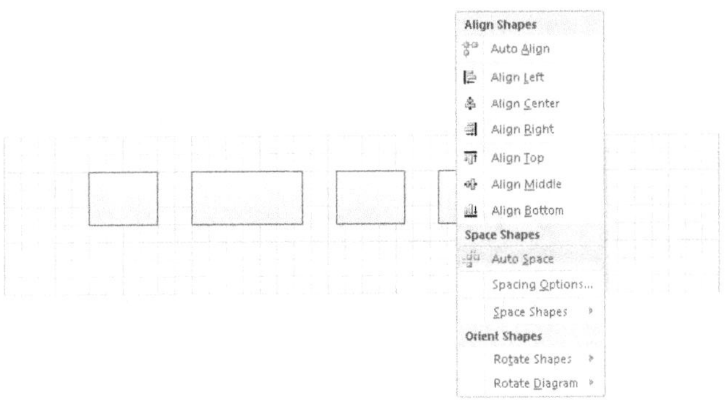

6. Although Auto Space can be useful, point to **Space Shapes** in the **Space Shapes** section to see other options. Then click **Distribute Horizontally**.

   Whereas Auto Space leaves only the anchor in place and sets equal spacing between pairs of shapes, Distribute Horizontally leaves the two outermost shapes in place prior to adjusting the inter-shape spacing.

7. Select the leftmost shape in the top row. Then hold down Shift and click the leftmost shape in the bottom row.
8. On the **Home** tab, in the **Arrange** group, click the **Position** button, and then click **Align Center**.
9. Hold down Shift and click the next shape to the right in each row, and then repeat Step 8.
10. Use the same technique to align the third and fourth pair of shapes in each row.

    Keyboard Shortcut In Visio you can press F4 to repeat the previous operation. For example, after clicking Align Center in Step 8, you can complete Steps 9 and 10 by selecting a pair of shapes and then pressing F4 to align them.

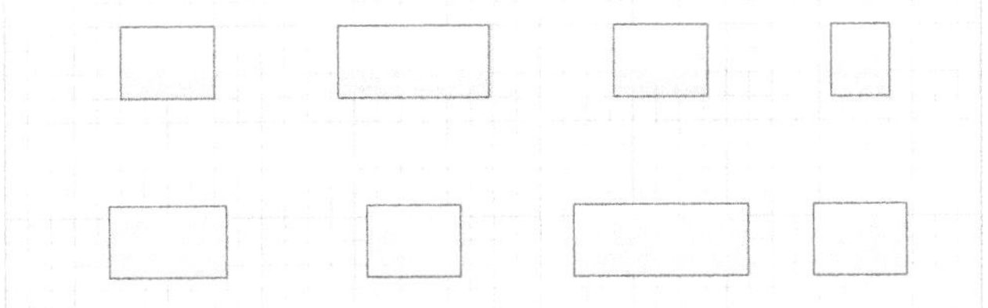

CLEAN UP Save your modified drawing as *Align and Space AFTER*.

In this exercise, you aligned and spaced the shapes on the page by using one particular combination of options. You may find it worthwhile to experiment with other combinations so you understand the full range of choices provided by Visio.

Using the Auto Align & Space Feature

Visio 2010 includes a powerful new Auto Align & Space feature that makes a best effort to position the shapes in your drawing for you.

In this exercise, you will use the flowchart you created in Chapter 4 to better understand the Visio 2010 auto-arrange features.

SET UP You need the *HR Recruiting Flowchart with labels_start* drawing located in the Chapter05 practice file folder to complete this exercise. Open the drawing in Visio.

1. Move various shapes around to make the flowchart less understandable. The graphic below shows one "messy diagram" arrangement.

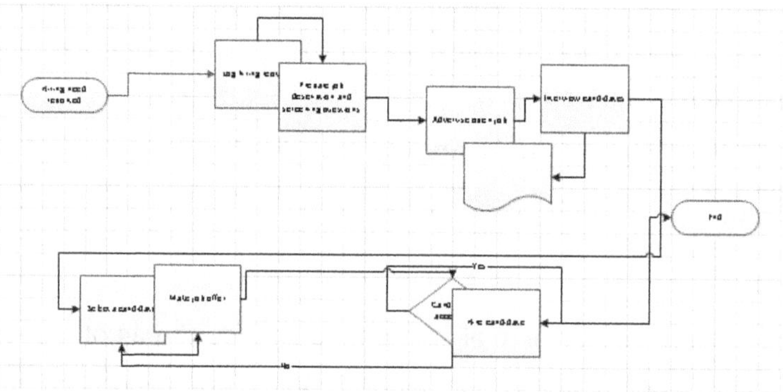

Auto Align & Space

2. On the **Home** tab, in the **Arrange** group, click the **Auto Align & Space** button.

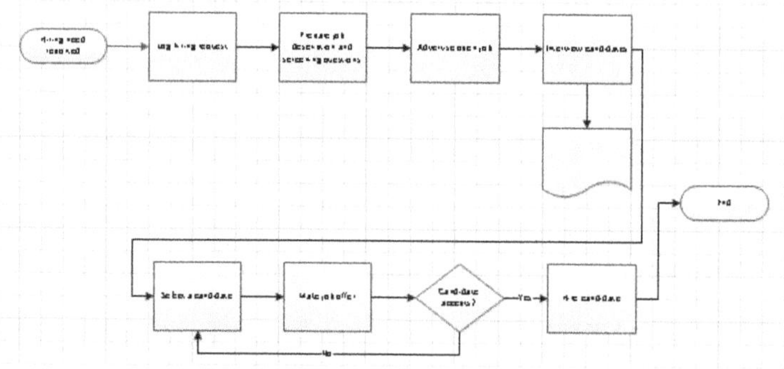

The auto-arrange feature made a significant improvement in the diagram, although you may still want to do some fine tuning. It's important to understand that the results you achieve using Auto Align & Space are closely tied to the locations of each shape on the page before you click the button. Sometimes, if you move just one shape a short distance before clicking Auto Align & Space, you will get very different results. Consequently, if your Auto Align & Space results are not satisfactory, press Ctrl+Z to undo the operation, move a shape or two, and try again.

CLEAN UP Close the Visio drawing; it is not necessary to save it first.

What Other Arrangements Are Possible?

In addition to the spacing and distribution functions you used in the preceding exercises, Visio offers other auto-arrange options.

If you would like to see how these other options work, open the Align and Space BEFORE drawing that you created in a previous exercise. Select all shapes in the top row. On the Home tab, in the Arrange group, click Position, and then in the Space Shapes area, click More Distribute Options. The Distribute Shapes dialog box that opens may take a moment to understand but does provide multiple options for horizontal and vertical spacing.

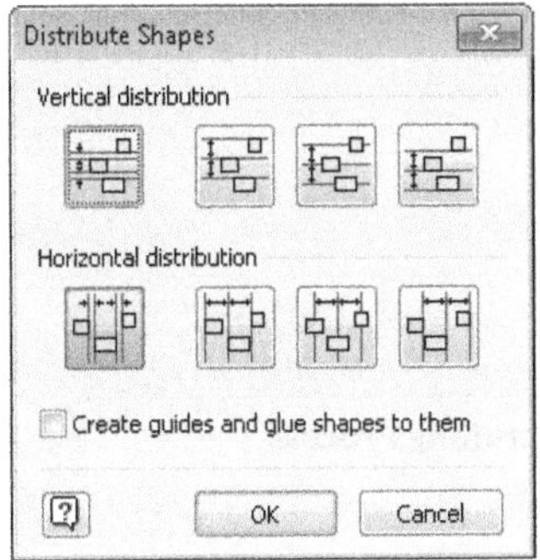

You can change the vertical and horizontal spacing used by any Visio auto-arrange options from the Spacing Options dialog box. To open this dialog box, on the Home tab, in the Arrange group, click Position, and then click Spacing Options.

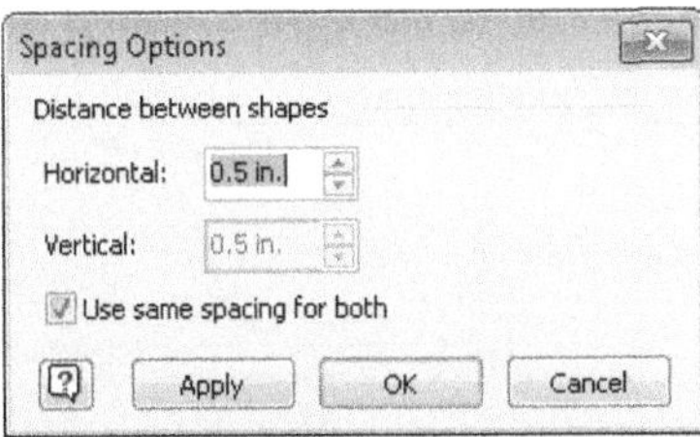

Applying Color and Fill Patterns

The judicious use of color and fill patterns can add considerable value to your Visio drawings. For example, you might add color or patterns to differentiate among similar shapes, call attention to specific features, highlight patterns or trends, or simply to make a drawing more attractive.

You can use several techniques to add color and style in Visio. Some apply a change to a single shape attribute, and others change multiple characteristics at once. In the next several sections, you will find out how to change one or two color/fill attributes at a time. Then in the "Applying Themes to Your Diagrams" sections later in this chapter, you will learn how to apply a coordinated set of changes with one click.

In this exercise, you will add color and fill patterns to individual shapes. Note that the results of this exercise won't be a diagram you would want to provide to anyone—it will be aesthetically challenged; however, it will let you experiment with many different colors, patterns, and styles.

SET UP You need the *HR Recruiting Flowchart with labels_start* drawing located in the Chapter05 practice file folder to complete this exercise. Open the drawing in Visio and save it as *HR Flowchart with colors and styles.*

1. Narrow the **Shapes** window to one column as described in Chapter 1.
2. Set the zoom level to **100%** and center the drawing on the screen to make all flowchart shapes visible.

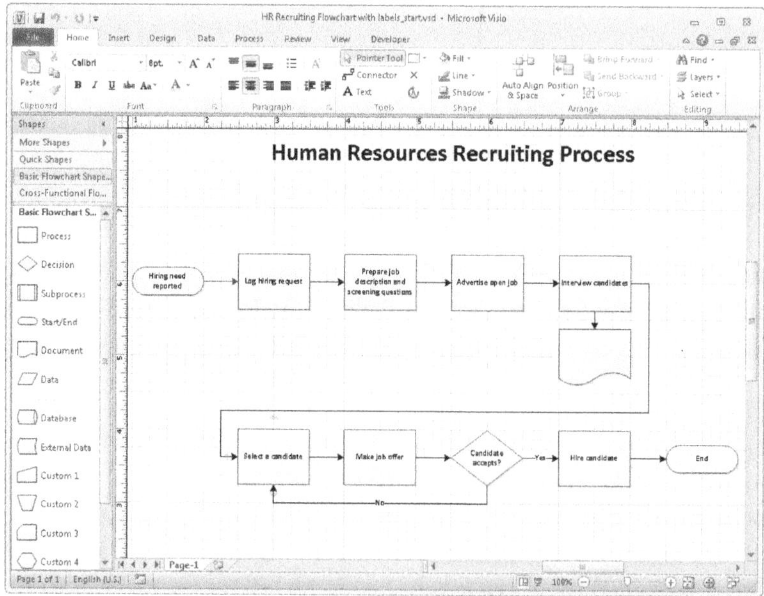

3. Right-click the **Hiring need reported** shape, click the arrow to the right of the **Fill** button on the Mini Toolbar, and then click any shade of green for this start shape.

   Tip Note that Live Preview is active in the color picker dialog box, so you can preview each color before selecting one.

4. Right-click the **Log hiring request** shape, click the arrow to the right of the **Fill** button on the Mini Toolbar, and then click **More Colors**.

   Tip In this exercise, you will be selecting fill colors and patterns using the Mini Toolbar that appears when you right-click a shape. You can access all of the same functions by clicking the Fill button in the Shape group on the Home tab.

   The resulting Colors dialog box offers two tabs, Standard and Custom, from which you can choose virtually any color to add to your shape.

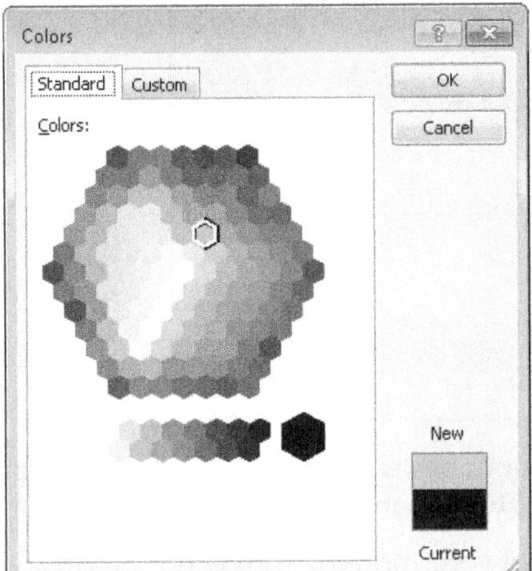

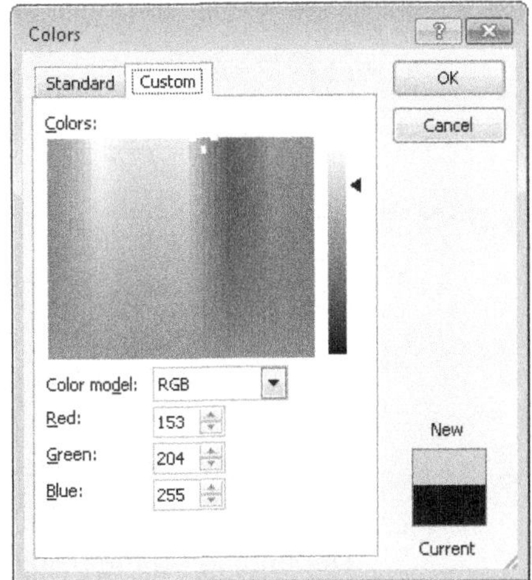

5. On the **Standard** tab of the **Colors** dialog box, click a light blue color, and then click **OK**. Your first two shapes should look something like the following graphic.

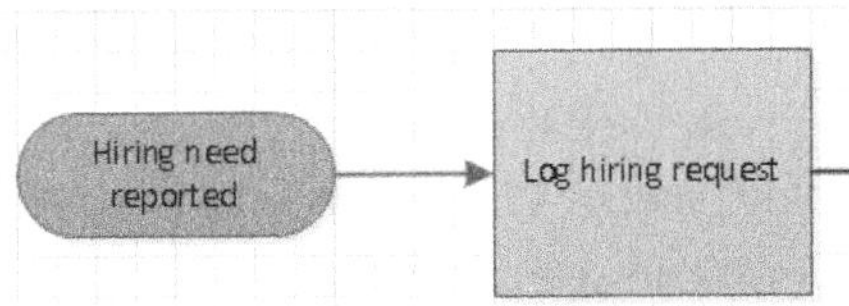

6. Right-click the **Prepare job description and screening questions** shape, click the arrow to the right of the **Fill** button on the Mini Toolbar, and then click **Fill Options** to open the **Fill** dialog box.

All of the preceding steps allowed you to change exactly one attribute at a time. With the Fill dialog box, you can change multiple attributes at once. For example, in this dialog box, you can create two-color shapes with various fill patterns, as well as set partial or full transparency. On the right side of the dialog box, you can set shadow attributes.

Tip **You can also open this dialog box by right-clicking a shape, selecting Format, and then clicking Fill.**

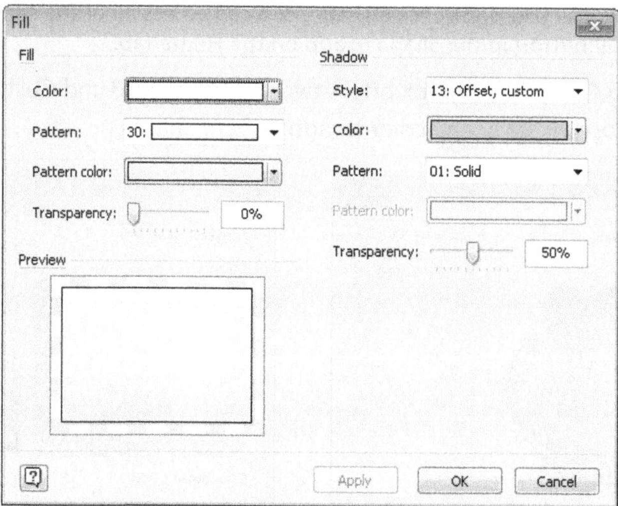

Tip **If you've used previous versions of Visio, you may recognize this dialog box because it has been brought into Visio 2010 unchanged.**

Depending on the resolution of your monitor, it may not be obvious that the flowchart shape you've selected has a fill pattern. However, the 30 in the Pattern field indicates that it uses pattern number 30. The pattern is difficult to see because the primary fill color is white and the pattern color is gray. You will make the pattern more obvious by changing one of the two colors in the next step.

7. In the **Fill** section of the dialog box, click the **Color** arrow, and select the violet color in the upper-right of the color palette. (This color is labeled *Accent5* if you point to it.) Having selected a color, you can see in the Preview section of the dialog box that there is indeed a fill pattern that fades from top to bottom.

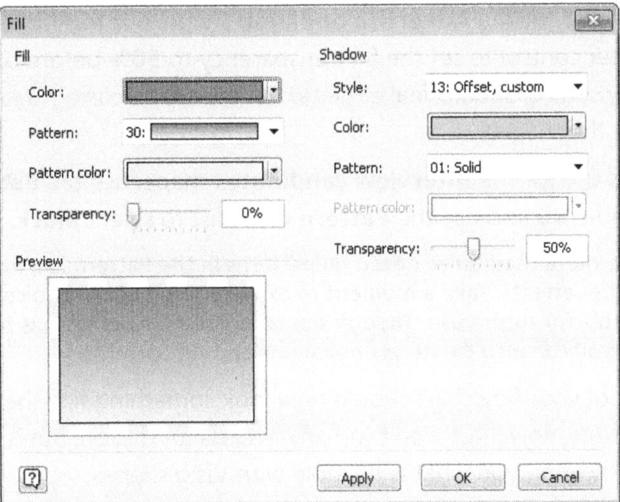

8. In the **Pattern** list, select fill pattern **35**. This pattern fades from the outside toward the center, which should allow the text in the shape to remain legible.

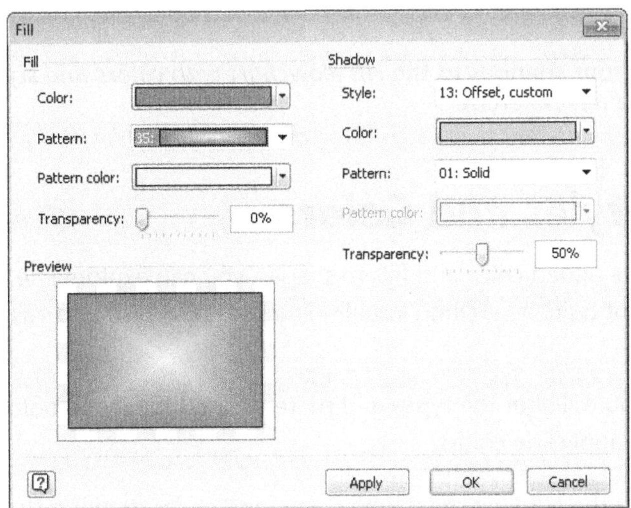

Tip If you want to reverse the fill pattern, that is, to have the shape darker in the center and lighter toward the edges, simply swap the color selections for Color and Pattern Color.

9. Click **OK**.

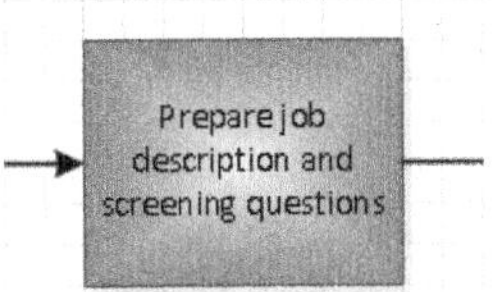

10. Repeat Steps 6-8 for the **Advertise open job** shape, but this time, use the **Transparency** slider control to set the fill transparency to **50%** before clicking **OK**. The transparency setting should make the text in the shape easier to read but still add a bit of flair to the shape.
11. Repeat Steps 6-8 for the **Interview candidates** shape; use the **Pattern** list to select pattern number **06** and use the **Pattern color** list to select **Black**. Then click **OK**.

Tip There are more than three dozen fill patterns in the Pattern list, involving lines, fades, and other effects. Take a moment to explore some of the choices so you will know what is available for future use. Though the technique for doing so is beyond the scope of this book, you can also create your own line and fill patterns.

The top row of your flowchart should now look something like the following figure. It's clear that this flowchart won't win any awards for design, but it has served its purpose by showing you what is possible with Visio shapes.

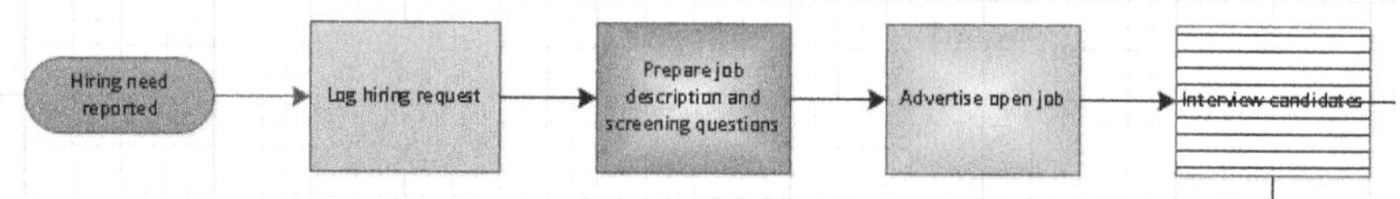

CLEAN UP Save your changes to the *HR Flowchart with colors and styles* drawing and continue with the next exercise.

Applying Line Styles and Colors

Now that you have added color and fills to shapes, you can explore line formatting options. Although not quite as exciting visually, line styles can also add value and meaning to your drawings.

In this exercise, you will alter the types and patterns used for shape borders and connectors. You will also apply line colors.

SET UP You need the *HR Flowchart with colors and styles* drawing that you created in the preceding exercise. Open the drawing in Visio if it is not already open.

Line

1. Right-click the **Select a candidate** shape, click the arrow to the right of the **Line** button on the Mini Toolbar, point to **Weight**, and then click **2¼ pt** on the submenu. The selected shape now shows a bold border.

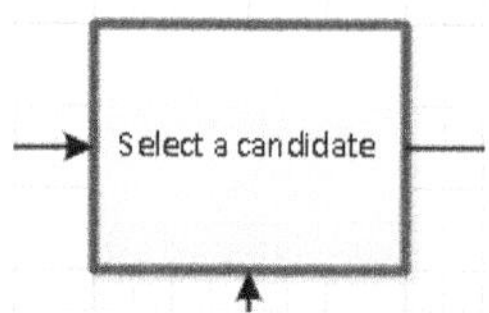

Tip In this exercise, you will be selecting line colors and patterns by using the Mini Toolbar that is available when you right-click a shape. You can access all of the same functions by clicking the Line button in the Shape group on the Home tab.

2. Right-click the same shape again and click the arrow to the right of the **Line** button on the Mini Toolbar, but this time point to **Dashes** and click the fourth line pattern from the top.

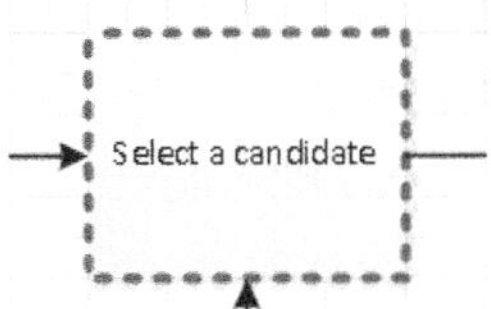

3. Right-click the **Make job offer** shape, click the arrow to the right of the **Line** button on the Mini Toolbar, and then click **Line Options** to open the **Line** dialog box.

   In the preceding steps, you changed exactly one attribute at a time. With the Line dialog box, you can change multiple attributes at once. In addition, using this dialog box, you can change the rounding of the corners on a shape or the arrows at the ends of a line.

   Tip You can also open this dialog box by right-clicking a shape, selecting Format, and then clicking Line.

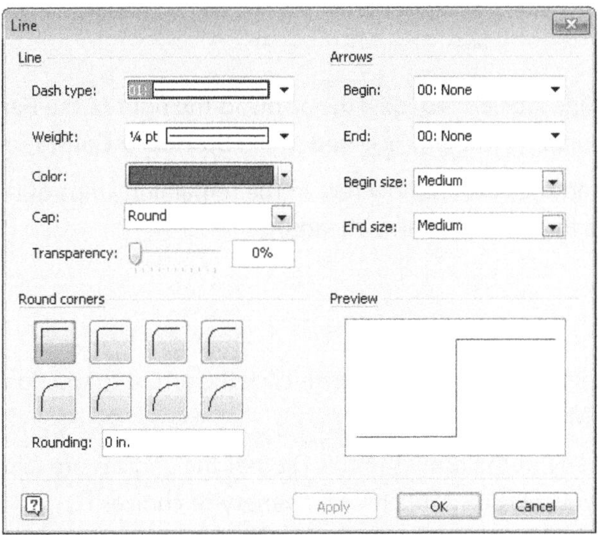

Tip If you've used previous versions of Visio, you may recognize this dialog box because it has been brought into Visio 2010 unchanged.

4. In the **Round corners** section of the dialog box, click the upper-right button, and then click **OK**.

Tip Although this dialog box does not provide Live Preview, the Preview section in the lower-right corner of the dialog box shows the results of your choices.

5. Right-click the **Candidate accepts?** shape, click the arrow to the right of the **Line** button on the Mini Toolbar, and then click **No line**.
6. Because it no longer has a border, apply a light gray fill color to the **Candidate accepts?** shape to make it more visible.

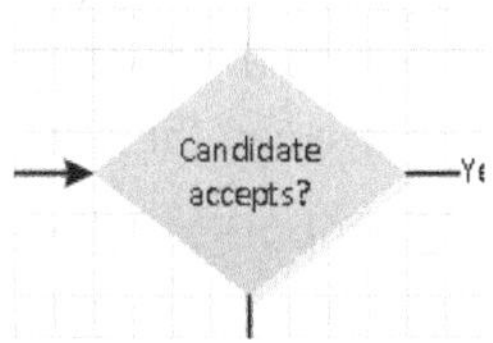

7. Right-click the line labeled **No**, click the arrow to the right of the **Line** button on the Mini Toolbar, and then click **Red** in the **Standard Colors** section.

   Notice that the line has turned red but the color of the text label has not changed.

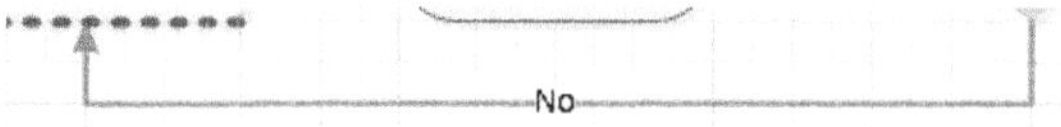

Font Color

8. Right-click the line labeled **No**, click the arrow to the right of the **Font Color** button on the Mini Toolbar, and then click **Red** in the **Standard Colors** section.

   Both the line and the text are now red. In the remaining steps of this exercise, you will change the format of the arrowhead.

9. Right-click the line labeled **No**, and then click the arrow to the right of the **Arrows** button on the Mini Toolbar.

   You can select any of the arrows in this list, but the choices are fairly standard. In the next step, you will see a much wider variety of choices.
10. Click **More Arrows**, which opens the same **Line** dialog box you used in Step 3.

    Notice that you see the current arrow type, number 05, in the End box in the Arrows section of the dialog box. You also see the current line color, rounding style, and other line attributes.

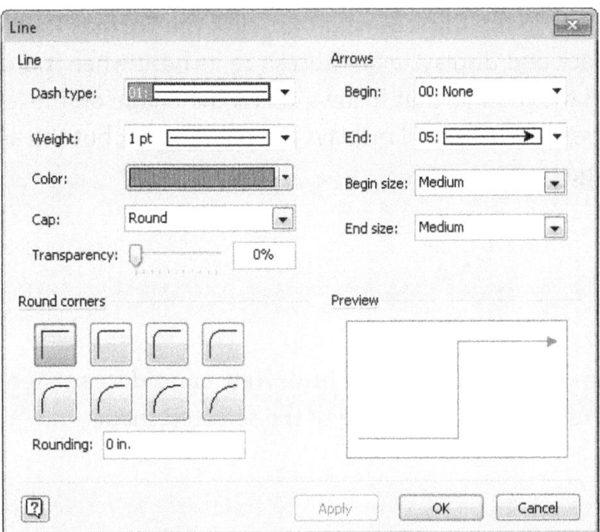

11. Click the arrow to the right of the **End** box, and click arrow style **14**. Notice the amazing selection of arrow styles both before and after number 14.

    Your line now has an open-headed arrow, and the bottom row of your flowchart looks like the following figure.

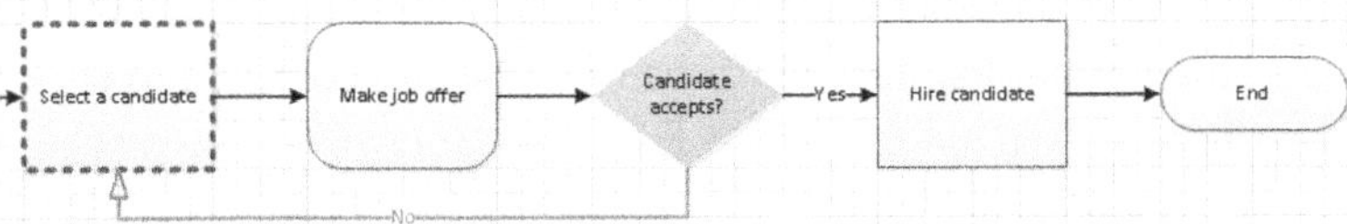

CLEAN UP **Save your changes to the *HR Flowchart with colors and styles* drawing and continue with the next exercise.**

Using the Format Painter

Like many other applications in the Microsoft Office suite, Visio includes a Format Painter feature, which is an easy way to transfer the formatting from one shape to another.

In this exercise, you will copy a shape's formatting.

SET UP **You need the *HR Flowchart with colors and styles* drawing that you worked with in the preceding exercise. Open the drawing in Visio if it is not already open.**

1. Click to select the **Prepare job description and screening questions** shape.

Format Painter

2. On the **Home** tab, in the **Clipboard** group, click the **Format Painter** button. The cursor turns black and displays a paintbrush to its right when it is over the page background (in the graphic that follows, this is the image on the left). When you point to a shape, the cursor still displays the paint brush, but the arrow turns white again (the image on the right).

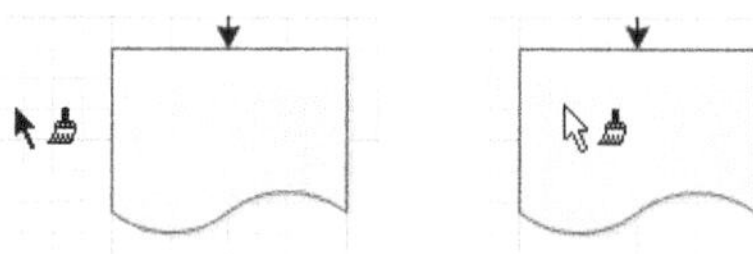

3. Click the document shape below the **Interview candidates** shape once. The document shape takes on the appearance of the selected shape.

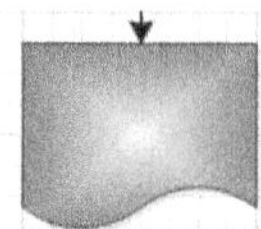

4. Click the **Select a candidate** shape, and then double-click the **Format Painter** button. Double-clicking causes the Format Painter to be persistent—you can click several shapes in a row to apply the same style to all of them.
5. Click the **Hire candidate** and **End** shapes once each. Notice that the cursor still shows the Format Painter paintbrush, so you can continue to click additional shapes if you want.

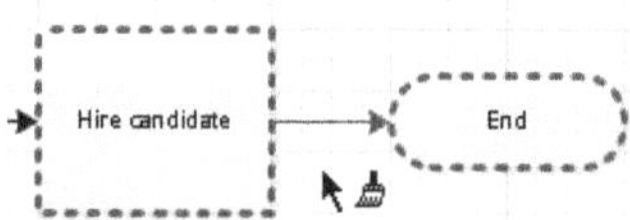

6. Press Esc to return the cursor to pointer mode.

Tip **You can also click either the Format Painter button or the Pointer Tool button to resume normal Visio operation.**

CLEAN UP Save your changes to the *HR Flowchart with colors and styles* drawing and close the drawing.

Turning Off the Grid

For the majority of Visio users, the background grid is invaluable for aligning and positioning shapes on the page. However, just because it's vital for creating and editing Visio drawings, don't assume that people looking at your drawings also need to see it.

In fact, turning the grid off can be a surprisingly effective way to make your drawings more attractive even if you're just showing someone a work in progress. Consider these two points when debating whether the grid is relevant for your audience:

- The full-screen viewing mode in Visio, which was designed for presenting Visio drawings, automatically removes the grid.
- The default behavior for printing is to remove the grid.

The designers of Visio clearly think of the grid as a design-time device, and you should too.

In this exercise, you will remove the grid and maximize screen real estate to show your Visio drawing more effectively, while still retaining the ability to edit the drawing.

SET UP You need the *Org Chart via Wizard with data_start* drawing located in the Chapter05 practice file folder to complete this exercise. Open the drawing in Visio.

Grid

1. On the **View** tab, in the **Show** group, clear the **Grid** check box.

   Selecting or clearing the grid check box turns the grid on and off.

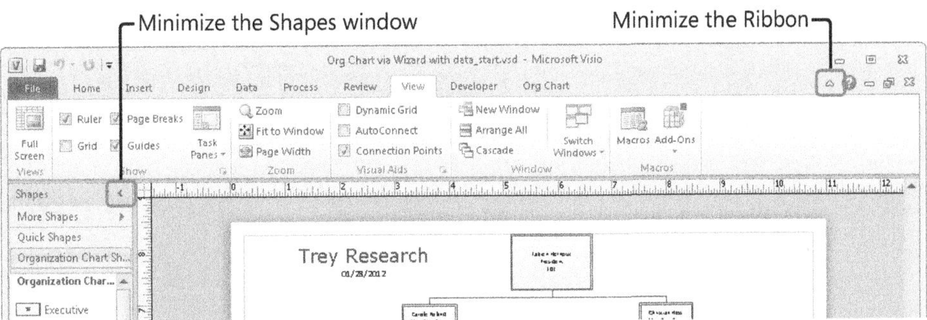

Tip **It's useful to realize that you haven't deactivated the grid or the snap-to-grid function just by making the lines invisible. You can tell this quite easily by dragging a shape across the page. For example, slowly drag the *Kamil Amireh* shape from the center of the page toward the lower-right corner. It will look like the shape is bumping down stairs as it snaps to successive vertical and horizontal grid lines.**

   You can make your drawing even more visible with a few additional steps.

2. Click the **Minimize the Ribbon** button located in the upper-right corner of the Visio window, as shown in the graphic after Step 1.

3. Click the **Minimize the Shapes window** button located in the upper-left corner of the **Shapes** window, as shown in the graphic after Step 1.

Page Breaks

4. On the **View** tab, in the **Show** group, select the **Page Breaks** check box. This option removes the page boundary line around the edges of the drawing.

   As the following graphic shows, you now have a clean view of the drawing page: the ribbon is hidden; the shapes window has been minimized; the grid is gone. However, even though you've minimized everything surrounding the drawing page, this is not a presentation view—you can still edit the drawing.

   Tip **The Show group on the View tab also includes an option to turn off the rulers.**

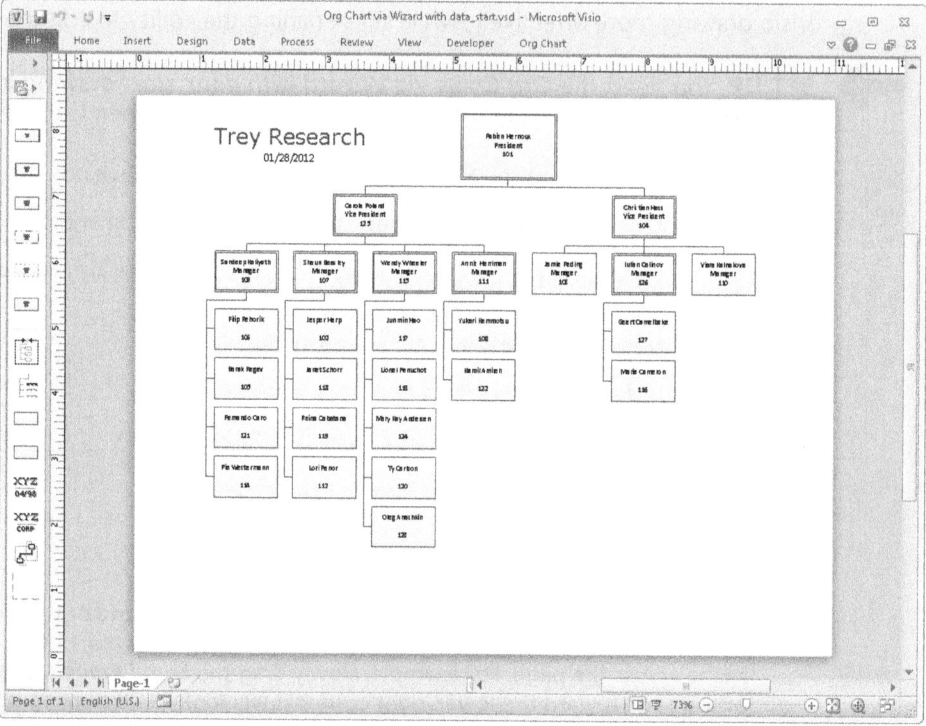

CLEAN UP **Close the *Org Chart via Wizard with data_start* drawing. It is not necessary to save it because you've only changed the view of the chart and not the chart itself.**

Applying Themes to Your Diagrams: Part 1

Visio 2007 introduced the idea of themes. A ***theme*** is a coordinated set of background, fill, line, and accent colors. Visio 2007 also introduced ***theme effects***, which can include specific fonts, fill patterns, shadows, and line styles. The Visio 2010 themes are very similar to those in 2007 but are easier to use because they take advantage of Live Preview.

Whether used individually or together, themes and theme effects are a fast and powerful way to alter the appearance of a Visio drawing. Well-chosen themes can add a distinctive and professional appearance.

In this exercise, you will apply themes to an organization chart you created in Chapter 4.

SET UP You need the *Org Chart by Hand with data_start* drawing located in the Chapter05 practice file folder to complete this exercise. Open the drawing in Visio and save it as *Org chart with themes*.

1. Turn off the grid lines as described in the preceding exercise.
2. Set the zoom level to approximately **75%** and position the organization chart on the right side of the Visio window. This combination of size and position settings looks odd, but it enables you to see Live Preview effects in most of the chart when you use the Themes gallery in subsequent steps.

A Text

3. On the **Home** tab, in the **Tools** group, click the **Text** tool, and then use it to add a text block to the right of the **Magnus Hedlund** shape.
4. In the new text block, type **Trey Research**, and press Esc. Then on the **Home** tab, in the **Font** group, set the font to **24 pt.** and **Bold**. You will use this text block later in this exercise as you work with theme colors.

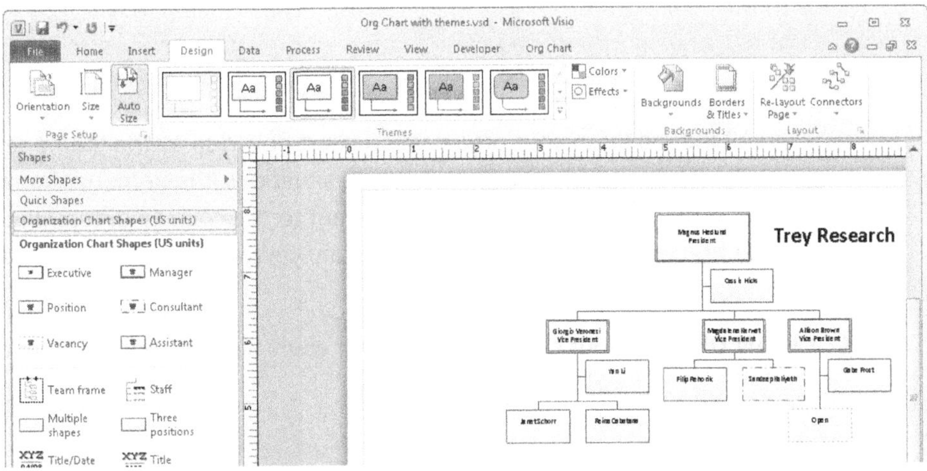

5. On the **Design** tab, in the **Themes** group, point to a few of the displayed themes and observe the Live Preview effects in the drawing. Notice the tooltip text that contains a name and description for each theme color set.

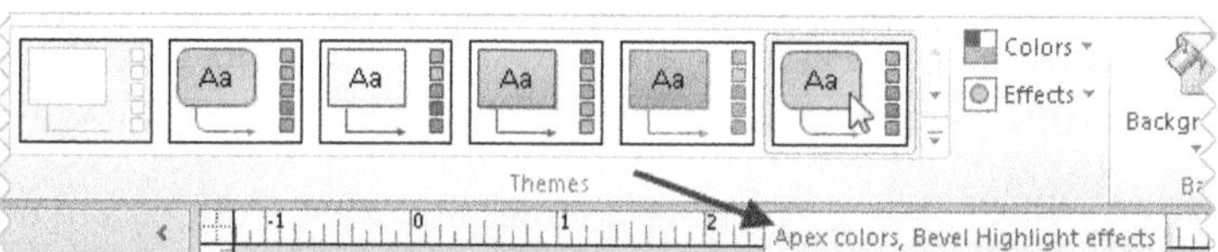

Tip The theme color names (*Apex* in the previous example) are fabricated names that serve merely to distinguish one set of colors from another. Don't look for any significance or meaning in the names.

6. Click the Apex colors theme to apply it to your organization chart and notice that it includes rounded corners, a bevel effect on each shape, curved connector lines, and a beige color. (You may need to zoom in to see the beveled edges.)

Tip Notice that Visio has changed the colors of the masters in the Shapes window to reflect the color and style of the theme you've chosen.

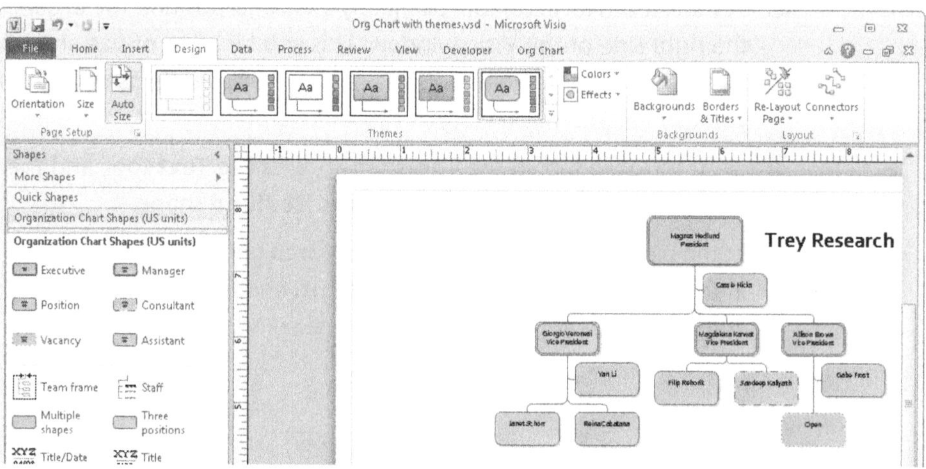

All the shapes in your organization chart now display the theme settings, and they all look essentially the same. In some situations, the homogenous appearance is fine, but in many cases, you might want to use color to differentiate among different types of shapes. In the next section, you will see one technique for accomplishing this.

 **CLEAN UP** Save your changes to the *Org chart with themes* drawing and continue with the next exercise.

Applying Themes to Your Diagrams: Part 2

Now that you know the basics of applying a theme, you are ready to explore more sophisticated ways to use themes to differentiate among various shapes on a page. The exercise in this section will walk you through one technique for applying different colors to different shapes. You will see another technique, called ***color by value***, in Chapter 10, "Visualizing Your Data."

To get started, you will manually apply a fill color to selected shapes. However, the key to taking advantage of the color schemes that are built into themes is to restrict your choices to ***theme colors***. To see the distinction between theme colors and other colors, look more closely at the color picker menu shown in the following graphic.

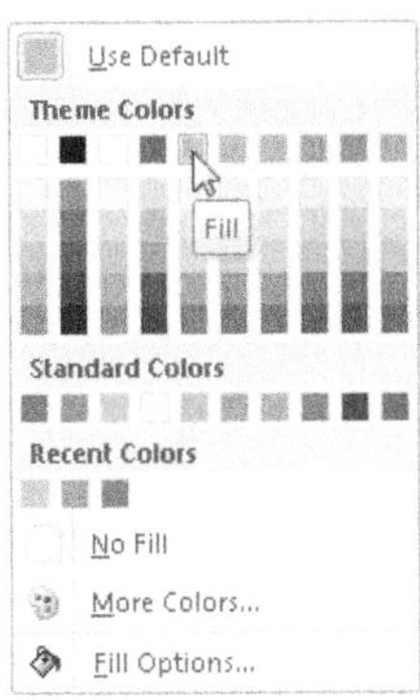

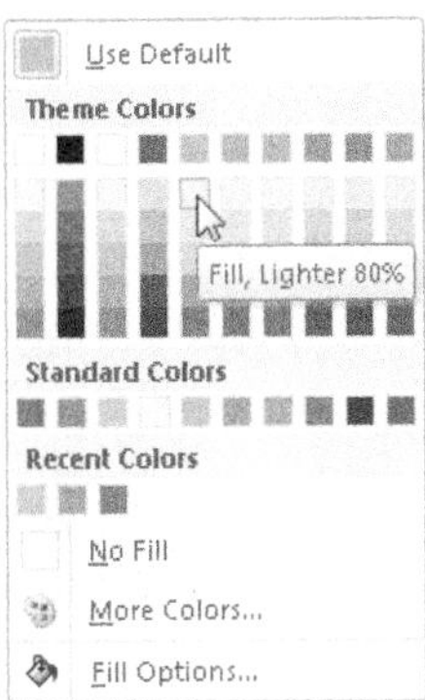

Notice that the color choices are grouped into Theme Colors and Standard Colors. If you choose a fill color from the Theme Colors section, the fill in your shape will change color as you change themes. However, if you pick a Standard Color or use the More Colors option, you have locked the color of your shape; it will not be affected by themes.

You can use this knowledge to your advantage: set fixed colors in shapes you always want to look the same; set theme colors in shapes you want to look different as you switch themes.

The leftmost columns in the Theme Colors section contain color choices for five diagram attributes. The columns from left to right are for White, Black, Background, Line, and Fill. Below the primary color for each column are five color shades, both darker and lighter than the color at the top of the column.

Pointing to any color box will display a tooltip that includes the column function. For example, in the previous graphic, the menu on the left shows the tooltip when you point to the top of the Fill column. The menu on the right shows the cursor pointing to a lighter shade of the fill color.

The following graphic shows how accent colors fit into themes. The rightmost five color columns show accent colors 1 to 5, respectively. As a specific example, the left menu shows a tooltip for *Accent1*. Below each accent color are color shades, both darker and lighter, that are derived from the accent color. The right menu shows one of the lighter shades of accent color 5.

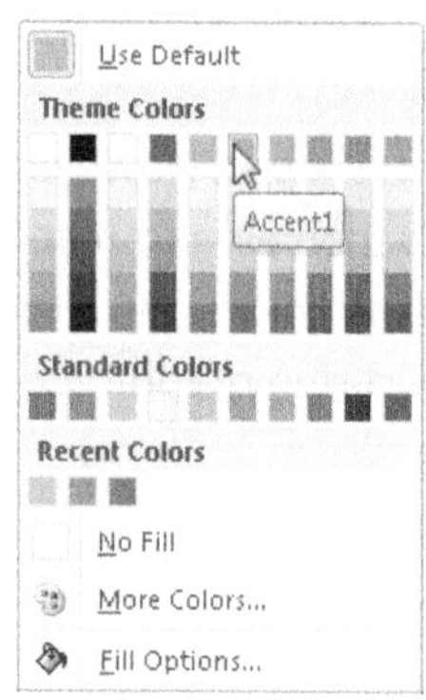

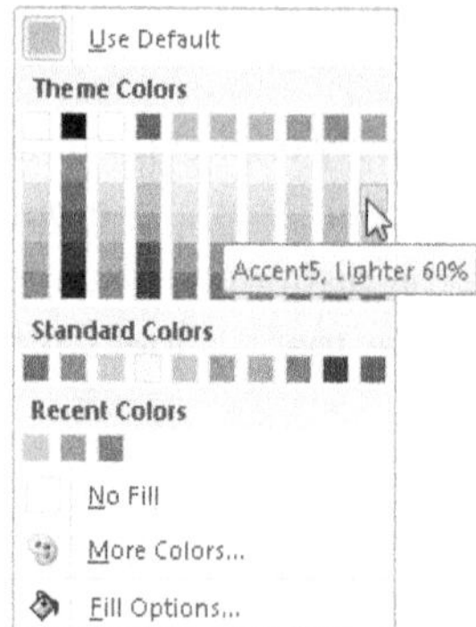

In this exercise, you will apply fill colors and then apply different themes to see the effects.

SET UP You need the *Org chart with themes* drawing that you created in the preceding exercise. Open the drawing in Visio if it is not already open.

1. Right-click the *Trey Research* title block, click the arrow to the right of the **Fill** button on the Mini Toolbar, and then click and apply the light green color from the **Standard Colors** section of the color picker.

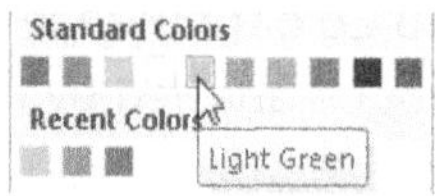

2. Hold down Shift and click the three shapes containing the title **Vice President** to select them. Open the color picker, and then click **Fill, Lighter 60%**.

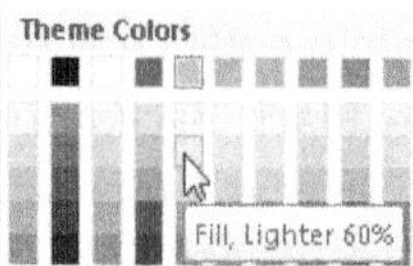

3. Hold down Shift and click the **Yan Li** and **Gabe Frost** shapes. Open the color picker, and then click **Accent5, Lighter 80%**.

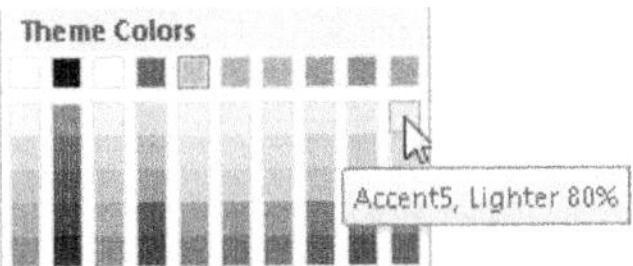

You can see that the shapes for the vice presidents are a lighter shade and the two assistants are a different color.

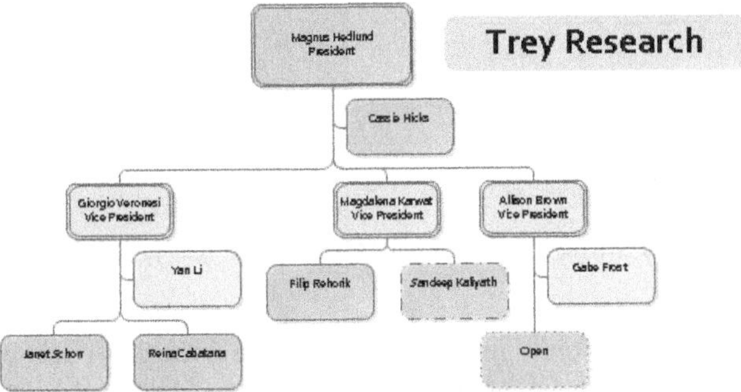

4. On the **Design** tab, in the **Themes** group, click the down arrow at the right end of the theme selection pane to view another row of themes.

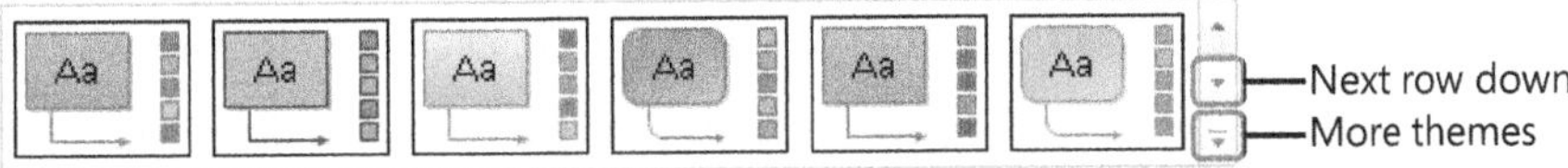

5. On the **Design** tab, in the **Themes** group, click the **More** button to open the entire **Themes** gallery, then point to various theme icons to see the results.

   As you point to the theme icons, you will notice two things that are the direct result of the color changes you made in Steps 1, 2, and 3:

   - The background color of the *Trey Research* title block does not change (though its font and other effects do change for some themes).
   - There are three distinct colors for the organization chart shapes, regardless of which theme you select.

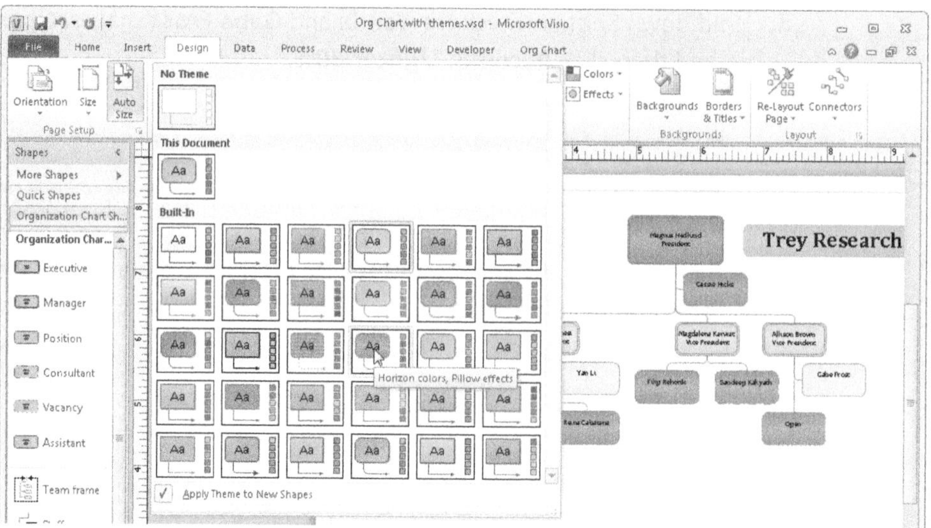

The Themes gallery shows you the current theme for This Document as well as all Built-In themes.

Tip The themes that are built into Visio contain the same color sets that are used in the 2010 versions of other Office applications, such as Microsoft Word and Microsoft PowerPoint.

The next step is not required but is included here so you know that it is as easy to remove a theme as it was to apply it.

No Theme

6. On the **Design** tab, in the **Themes** group, click the **No Theme** button.

   Tip You can revert to your previous theme by pressing Ctrl+Z to undo the change.

   The shapes to which you manually applied a fill color in steps 1, 2 and 3 will still have a fill color after you select No Themes. The text block will retain its Standard Color. The org chart shapes will contain fill colors from the diagram's default color palette.

CLEAN UP Save your changes to *Org chart with themes* and close your drawing.

Customizing Themes

In the preceding exercise, you learned how to use the built-in themes of Visio. You can also create new themes by creating a customized combination of colors and styles.

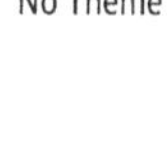
Colors

To create a custom theme, on the Design tab, in the Themes group, click Colors to open the theme Color gallery. The Color gallery is shown on the left in the following graphic.

From this gallery, you can select an existing color set to create your custom theme or you can create a new color set by clicking Create New Theme Colors at the bottom of the Color gallery.

If you choose to create your own set of colors, Visio presents a dialog box in which you select colors for fills, lines, and other objects. Your custom color set will appear under the Custom heading in the Color gallery similar to the custom effects example shown on the right in the previous graphic.

Tip **It's a subtle effect, but when you select or create a theme color set, the colors on the Colors button in the Themes group on the Design tab change to reflect your choice.**

You can select an existing set of effects to create your custom theme or you can create a new set by clicking Create New Theme Effects at the bottom of the Effects gallery.

Effects

To open the Effects gallery, on the Design tab, in the Themes group, click Effects. The Effects gallery is shown on the right in the previous graphic.

If you choose to create your own custom effects, Visio presents a dialog box in which you can create the desired effects. Your custom effect will appear under the Custom heading as shown in the graphic.

Tip **It's a subtle effect, but when you select or create a theme effect, the appearance of the Effects button in the Themes group on the Design tab changes to reflect your choice.**

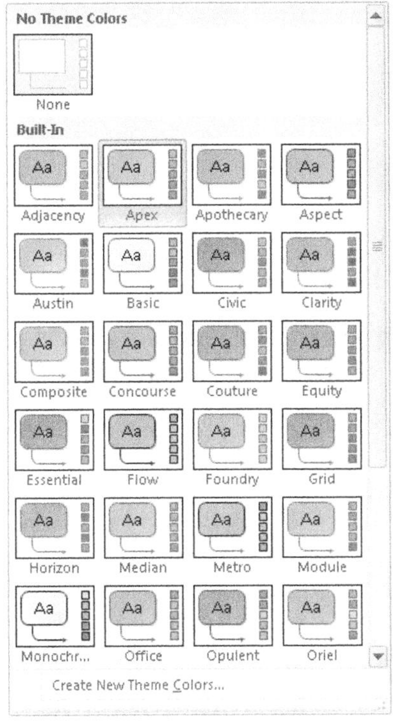

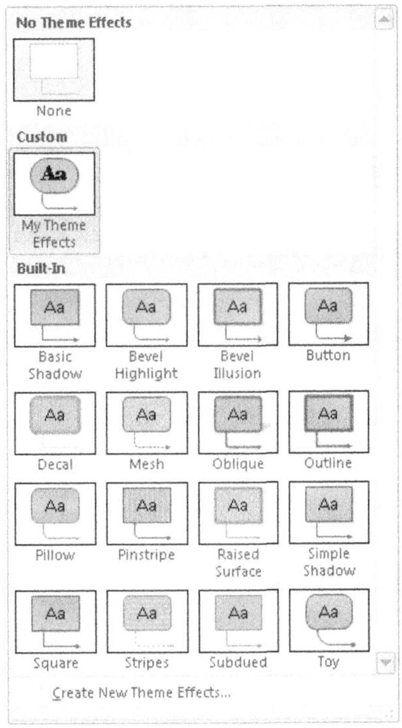

Setting Theme Options

When you apply a theme, you can apply it to the current page or to all pages in your drawing. The default action when you click the thumbnail for a theme is for Visio to apply it the same way the previous theme was applied. If you're not sure how that was done, right-click the theme thumbnail instead of left-clicking it and you can make an explicit choice from the menu.

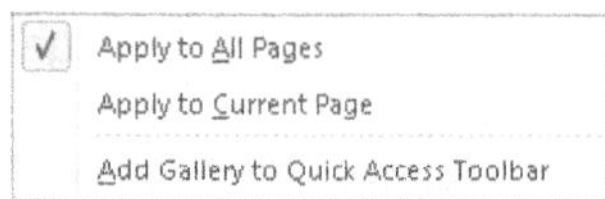

You can choose whether Visio should automatically apply a theme to shapes as they are dropped on the page. You set your preference by selecting or clearing the check box at the bottom of the Themes gallery. If the check box is cleared, as shown in the upper graphic of the following pair of graphics, the current theme will not be applied; the selected check box shown in the lower graphic indicates that the selected theme will be applied to new shapes.

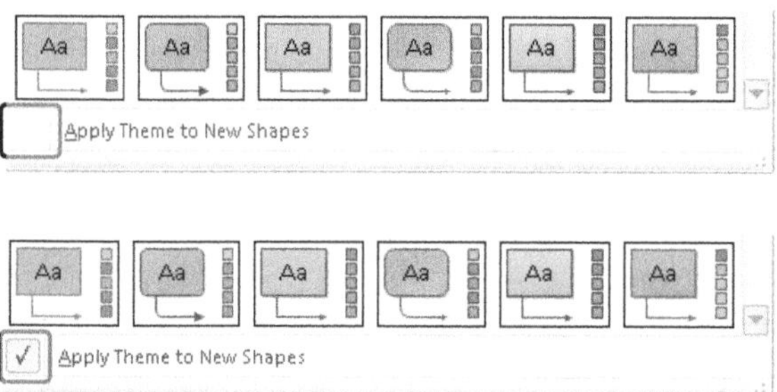

If you choose the option to apply a theme to new shapes, Visio also applies your theme settings to the masters in the current stencil, as you can see in the following graphic.

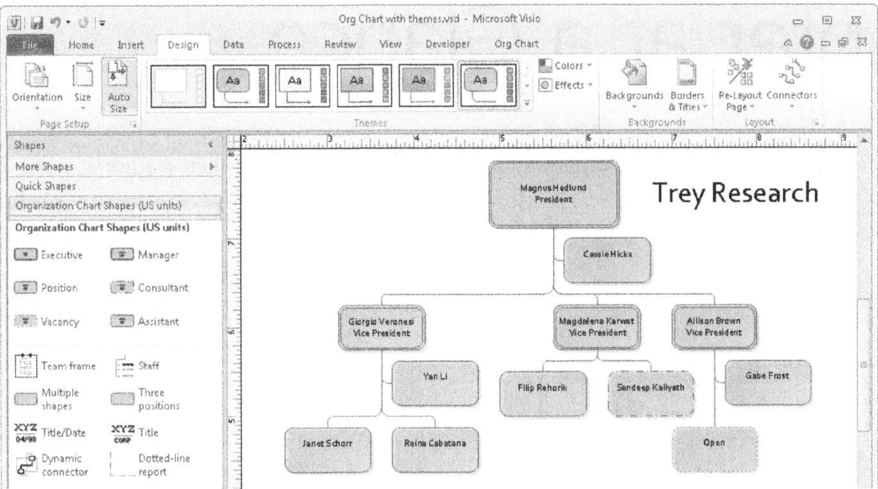

Tip If you want to copy a theme from one Visio drawing to another, merely copy a shape containing the theme from the first drawing and paste it into the second one. You can then delete the shape—the theme will remain behind. Your copied theme will not appear in the Theme gallery but will appear under the Custom heading in the Colors gallery, the Effects gallery, or both, depending on what your theme contains.

You cannot delete the built-in colors, effects, or themes. However, you can delete custom colors and effects. To do so, open the appropriate gallery, right-click the custom object, and then click Delete.

Key Points

- Visio 2010 includes powerful tools for aligning shapes and setting the spacing between them. Some tools are semi-automated, allowing you to select among various alignment and spacing options. Others are fully automated and attempt to enhance your drawing for you.
- You can apply an enormous variety of theme colors and standard colors to any Visio shape. If you want your shapes to change appearance automatically when you apply different themes, be sure to use theme colors in your shapes.
- You can enhance the appearance of shapes by applying any of several dozen predefined fill patterns and line patterns, or you can create your own. You can also add shadows.
- Visio themes are a powerful way to add visual appeal and professionalism to your diagrams. Each theme is a predesigned collection of colors, patterns, fonts and styles.
- Visio includes 30 built-in themes, and you can design your own custom themes.

Chapter at a Glance

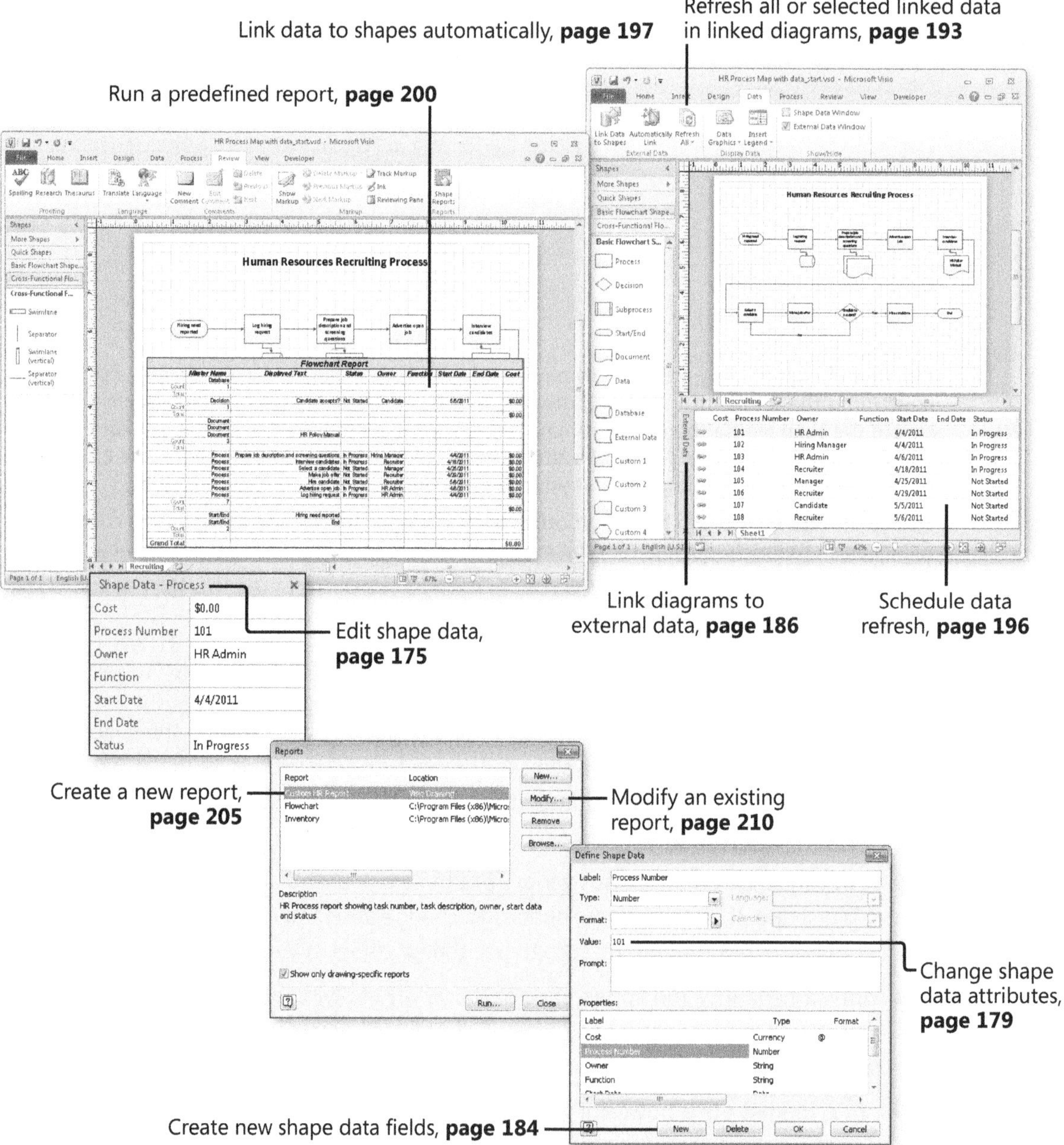

Link data to shapes automatically, **page 197**
Refresh all or selected linked data in linked diagrams, **page 193**
Run a predefined report, **page 200**
Edit shape data, **page 175**
Link diagrams to external data, **page 186**
Schedule data refresh, **page 196**
Create a new report, **page 205**
Modify an existing report, **page 210**
Change shape data attributes, **page 179**
Create new shape data fields, **page 184**

6 Entering, Linking to, and Reporting on Data

In this chapter, you will learn how to

- ✔ Understand shape data.
- ✔ Edit shape data.
- ✔ View and change shape data attributes.
- ✔ Create new shape data fields.
- ✔ Link diagrams to external data.
- ✔ Refresh all or selected data in linked diagrams.
- ✔ Schedule data refresh.
- ✔ Link data to shapes automatically.
- ✔ Run a predefined report.
- ✔ Create a new report.
- ✔ Modify an existing report.

One of the most significant ways you can add value to your Microsoft Visio drawings is to store relevant data in the shapes on the drawing page. Although this capability has been a part of Visio since the beginning, Visio 2010 and Visio 2007 have added a significant level of sophistication to the program's ability to import, store, manipulate, visualize, and report on critical business data.

In this chapter, you will discover ways to make your drawings even more valuable by creating data-driven diagrams. You will learn how to use, create, and edit shape data fields. You will also learn techniques for linking shapes in a Visio drawing to data stored in spreadsheets, databases, and other sources. Finally, you will learn to extract data from a Visio diagram by creating, modifying, and running reports.

Practice Files Before you can complete the exercises in this chapter, you need to copy the book's practice files to your computer. The practice files you'll use to complete the exercises in this chapter are in the Chapter06 practice files folder. A complete list of practice files is provided in "Using the Practice Files" at the beginning of this book.

Understanding Shape Data

Many Visio shapes contain data fields, referred to collectively as ***shape data***, that you can use to quantify and describe various properties of the shape.

Tip The data fields that are called *shape data* in Visio 2010 and Visio 2007 were called *Custom Properties* in Visio 2003 and earlier.

Visio 2010 supports eight types of shape data:

- **String** Free-form text
- **Number** Any numeric data; can be restricted to integers or a specific number of decimal places
- **Fixed List** A drop-down list from which users can make a selection; users cannot add additional values to the list
- **Variable List** A drop-down list from which users can make a selection; users can add additional values to the list by typing in the text box
- **Duration** Time value expressed in one of five time units supported by Visio: seconds (es.), minutes (em.), hours (eh.), days (ed.), weeks (ew.); users enter a number followed by one of the time unit abbreviations shown
- **Date** Calendar date; users can either type a date or use a drop-down calendar to select a date
- **Currency** Currency value in currency units based on user's Region and Language settings in Windows
- **Boolean** True or False

Viewing Shape Data

To view the shape data for any Visio object, right-click the shape, and click Data, which displays the data submenu. Then click Shape Data on the submenu.

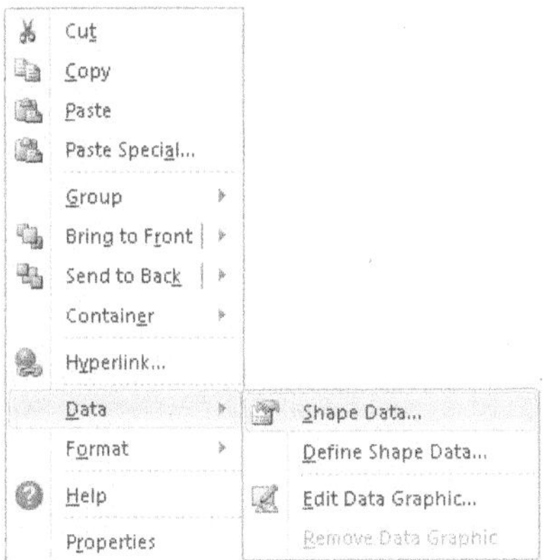

The Shape Data window typically appears somewhere within the main Visio window, usually in whatever position it was located the last time it was opened. The following graphic shows the data associated with a pump/motor 1 shape from the Fluid Power template in the Engineering template that is provided with Visio.

You can position the floating Shape Data window (shown on the left) wherever you would like it. Note that you can also resize the window or dock it in a fixed position by dragging it to an edge of the drawing window (shown in the center).

Tip **The pushpin button in the docked window lets you turn AutoHide on or off for the docked window. If you turn AutoHide on, the window "rolls up" into the header when you're not using it (shown on right).**

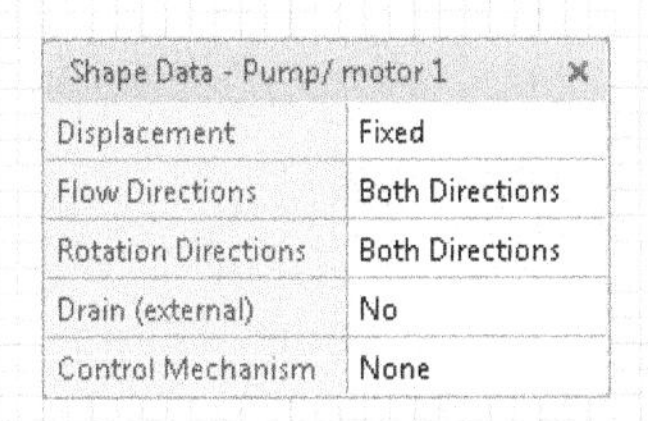

Displacement	Fixed
Flow Directions	Both Directions
Rotation Directions	Both Directions
Drain (external)	No
Control Mechanism	None

Shape Da...

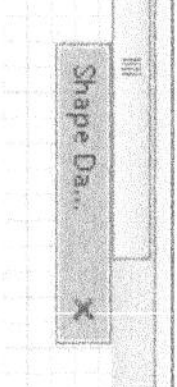

Tip **If the Shape Data window is already open when you right-click a shape, click Data, and then click Shape Data, Visio will close it. This may not be what you expect, especially if you didn't notice that the window was already open and can't figure out why it didn't appear.**

If you look closely at the following two graphics, you'll notice a subtle difference. It turns out that the Shape Data menu entry is actually a toggle that alternately shows and hides the window. In the graphic on the left, the window is closed so the icon to the left of Shape Data looks normal. However, in the one on the right, the icon is highlighted, indicating that the window is open.

Other Ways to View Shape Data

Because shape data is so vital to Visio diagrams, there are several additional ways to view a shape's data.

When you right-click some shapes, you can click Properties instead of Data. Although the Properties menu entry usually opens the same Shape Data window as the Data submenu technique, in some Visio templates, it opens a Shape Data dialog box instead. Although their appearance is a bit different, you can edit data in either one.

Tip **The Properties entry is usually at the very bottom of the context menu.**

For example, compare the following Shape Data dialog box for the Fluid Power pump/motor 1 with the corresponding Shape Data window, shown previously.

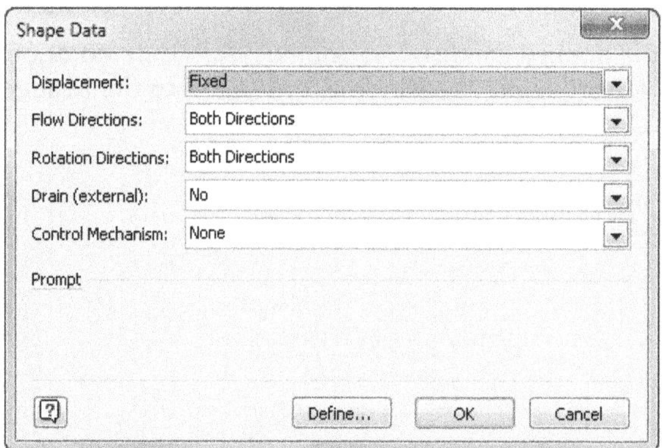

You can also open the Shape Data window from the Visio ribbon. On the Data tab, in the Show/Hide group, select the Shape Data Window check box.

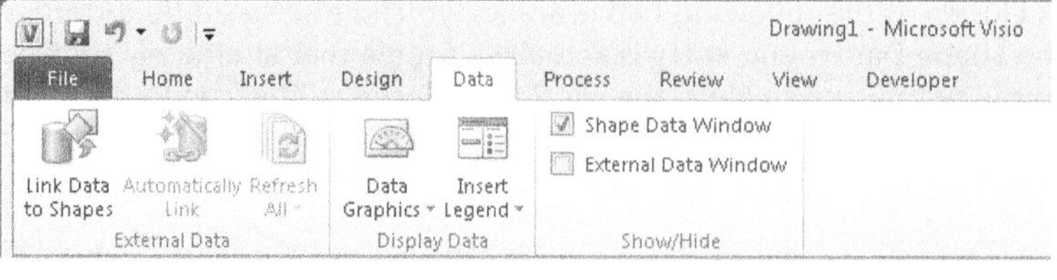

Editing Shape Data

After you have the Shape Data window open, you can change a shape's data. As you do so, you'll notice that some shape data fields behave differently than others. Visio enforces various rules based on the data type and formatting applied to each shape data field.

See Also For a list of the shape data types supported by Visio, see "Understanding Shape Data" earlier in this chapter.

As a simple example, you cannot enter text into a number or currency field. Similarly, Visio prevents you from entering anything other than a number and one of the five valid time unit abbreviations in a duration field.

In this exercise, you will edit some of the data associated with the Human Resources Recruiting Process you worked with in Chapter 4, "Drawing the Real World: Flowcharts and Organization Charts." There are two differences between this map and the one from Chapter 4: the spacing between shapes has been expanded to open up the drawing; and additional shapes have been added to represent a database and several documents.

SET UP You need the *HR Process Map_start* drawing located in the Chapter06 practice file folder to complete this exercise. Open the drawing in Visio and save it as *HR Process Map*. Then open the Shape Data window.

1. Click on the shape labeled **Log hiring request**. Its data appears in the Shape Data window.
2. To see an example of data validation based on field type, type **abc** into the **Cost** field, and then press either the Tab or Enter key to move to the next field.

   Visio displays an error dialog box, indicating that your entry is not valid for this field because the Cost field expects a currency entry.

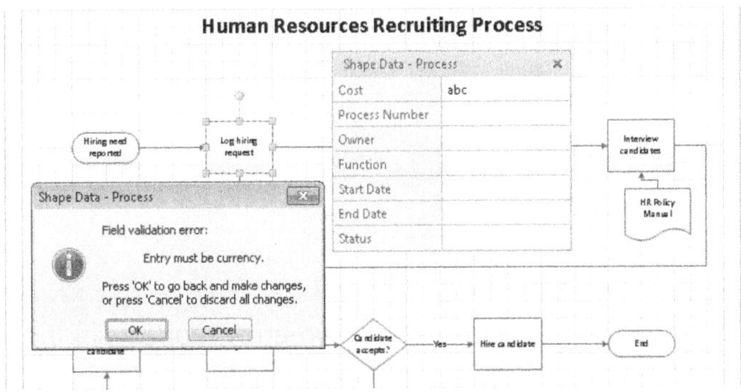

3. Click **OK** to close the error dialog box.
4. Type **5** and then press either the Tab or Enter key to move to the next field.

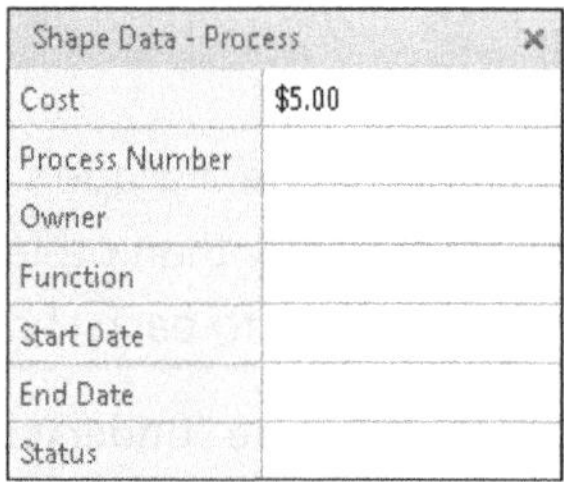

Tip Because the copy of Windows on which these graphics were made uses United States Region and Language settings, the currency amount appears in dollars. Your computer will display currency values based on your regional settings.

5. Type **101** in the **Process Number** field.
6. Press either the Tab or Enter key to move to the **Owner** field, and then type **John Smith**.
7. Click in the **Start Date** field. Notice that a browse button appears in the right end of the field.

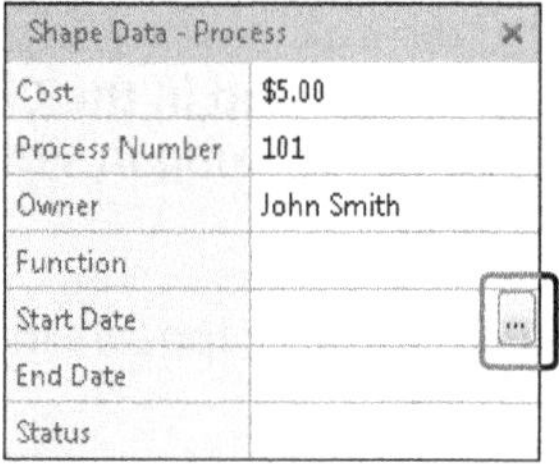

Tip In a Visio date field, you can either type a date or use the calendar field browse button to select a date.

8. Click the calendar field browse button and click a date in the pop-up calendar. The calendar closes and the selected date appears in the Shape Data window.

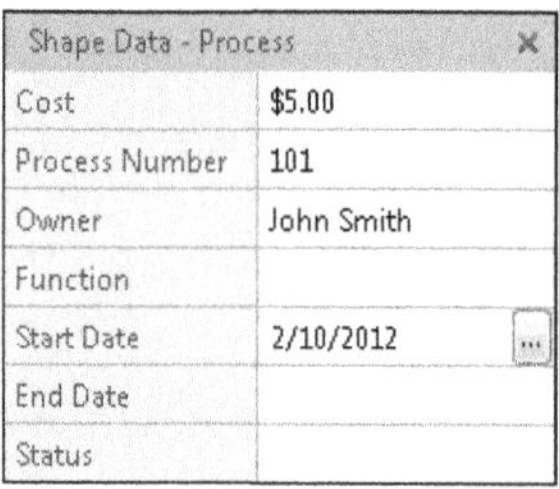

9. Click in the **Status** field. Notice that a down-arrow appears in the right end of the field. This is an example of a Visio list field.

10. Click the arrow to reveal the predefined choices for this list.

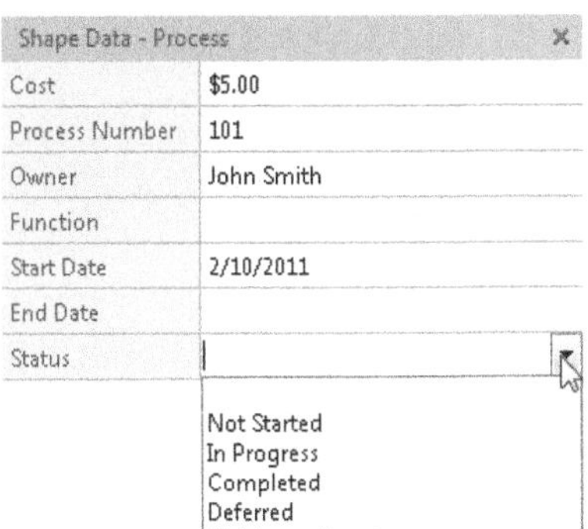

11. Click **In Progress** in the list.

Tip Visio supports two types of list fields: *fixed lists* and *variable lists*. In a fixed list field, you must select an entry from the list. In a variable list field, you have the option to select one of the list entries, or you can type your own text into the field if you prefer. If you type your own text, it gets added to the bottom of the list. The Status field in the preceding graphic is an example of a variable list field, so you can either select or type an entry in the field.

You can continue to enter or edit data for this process step, or you can select a different shape and edit its data.

CLEAN UP Save your changes to the *HR Process Map* drawing but leave it open if you are continuing with the next exercise.

Tip Though it is not advertised in any obvious way, you can edit data for more than one shape at a time. If you select multiple shapes before opening the Shape Data window, the changes you make will be applied to *all* selected shapes. This feature can be very powerful or very destructive, so it pays to be cautious.

Note that if you do select multiple shapes prior to opening the Shape Data window, you will only see the fields that all selected shapes have in common.

Viewing Shape Data Attributes

When you want to add data fields to a Visio shape, you need to open the Define Shape Data dialog box. To do so, right-click a shape, point to Data, and then click Define Shape Data.

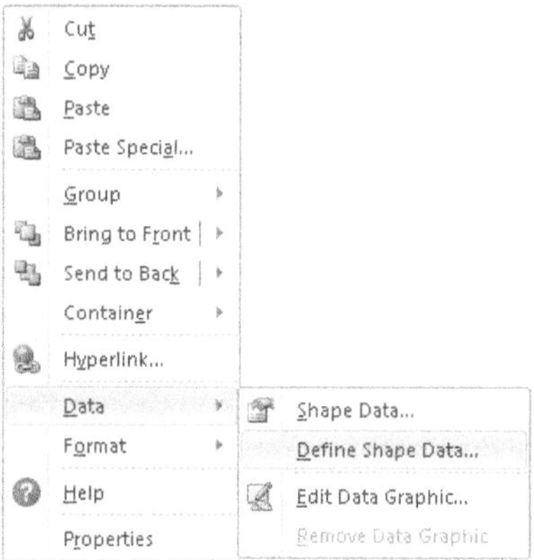

Tip **You can also open the Define Shape Data dialog box by right-clicking anywhere in the Shape Data window and then clicking Define Shape Data.**

The Define Shape Data dialog box looks like one of the following two samples. The one on the left appears for most Visio users. The one on the right appears if you are running Visio in developer mode, and offers several additional options.

See Also **For information about developer mode, see the Appendix.**

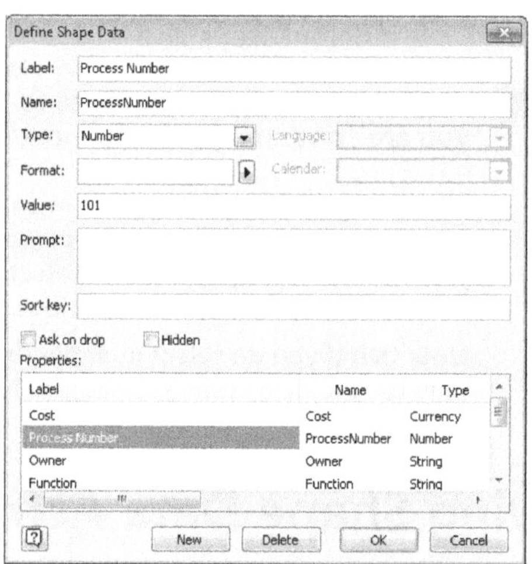

In both variations of the dialog box, notice that each data field has multiple attributes:

- **Label** Field name
- **Type** One of the eight types described in "Understanding Shape Data" earlier in the chapter
- **Format** Determines how data entered by the user will be presented; different field types have different format options

- **Value** The data value entered when a shape was defined or entered by the user
- **Prompt** Tooltip text that appears when the user points to the shape's name in the Shape Data window

In developer mode, you will see the additional attributes described in the following list. Although some of them are primarily for use by programmers, one or two may be of value even if you are not a programmer:

- **Name** An internal name used by Visio programmers; can be the same as Label except that Name cannot contain spaces or most special characters (an underscore character is OK).
- **Sort key** Visio uses the alphanumeric value in this field to determine the sequence in which fields will be presented in the Shape Data window.

  Important Visio treats the contents of the Sort key field as text even if you enter a number, which means that it arranges fields based on alphabetic sequence rather than numeric sequence. For example, if field A has a sort key of "1", field B has a sort key of "2", and field C has a sort key value of "10", Visio will place them in the Shape Data window in the sequence A, C, B, because the first character "1" in field C is less than the "2" in field B.

- **Add on drop** If selected, Visio opens the Shape Data dialog box whenever the user drops a shape containing this field onto a page.
- **Hidden** If selected, Visio hides this field; that is, the field does not appear in either the Shape Data window or Shape Data dialog box. Fields like this are often used by programmers to hold intermediate calculations or results that the user does not need to see.

Tip The shape data exercises that follow all use the regular Define Shape Data dialog box and not the developer version.

Although it is not advertised in any obvious way, you can create, edit, or delete shape data fields for more than one shape at a time. If you select multiple shapes before opening the Define Shape Data window, the changes you make will be applied to *all* selected shapes. This feature can be very powerful or very destructive, so it pays to be cautious.

Changing Shape Data Attributes

In previous sections of this chapter, you edited shape data and learned about the attributes that comprise each shape data field. In order to appreciate just how flexible and powerful the data features of Visio really are, it's helpful to do two more things: change the attributes of several existing data fields (this exercise), and create new data fields (the following exercise).

In this exercise, you will explore and change the attributes of the data fields in one of the process shapes in the Human Resources Recruiting Process map.

SET UP You need the *HR Process Map* drawing for this exercise. Either continue with the open copy from the previous exercise or open the *HR Process Map_start* drawing located in the Chapter06 practice file folder and save it as *HR Process Map*. Open the Shape Data window.

1. Click on the **Advertise open job** shape to view its shape data. Spend a moment looking at the names of the data fields for this shape.
2. Right-click in the **Shape Data** window, and then click **Define Shape Data**.

   Visio displays the attributes of the first data field, *Cost*. Notice that the Label field displays *Cost*, which is the label that appears in the Shape Data window. Notice, also, that the Type field is set to *Currency*.

   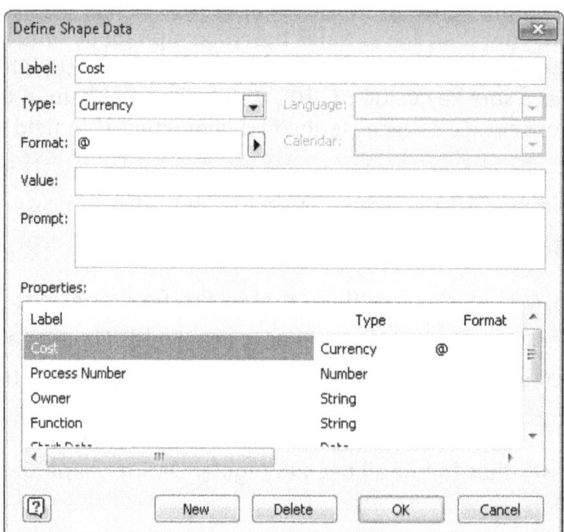

3. Click the right-facing arrow next to the **Format** field.

   Visio provides a list of alternate formats in which the currency value can be displayed. (The list you see depends on the Region and Language settings for your copy of Windows.) It usually makes sense to leave the format set to *System Setting*, especially if your diagram will be opened in countries that use other currencies than the one you use.

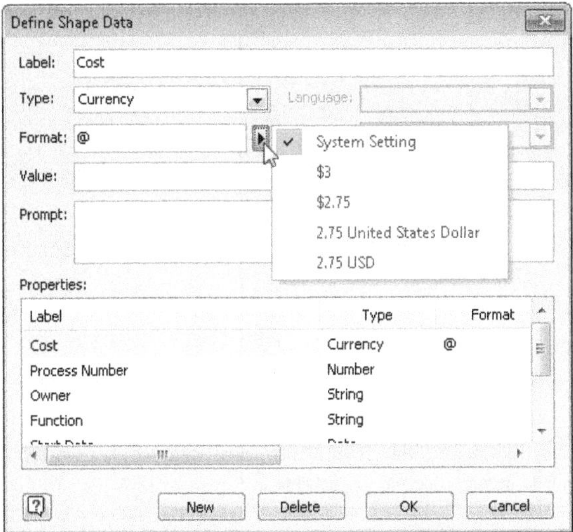

4. Click in the **Value** field and then type **125**. This value will appear as the default value for the Cost field the next time you open the Shape Data window for this shape. You can still change the value via the Shape Data window, but this provides a way for you to specify default values.

5. Type **Enter cost for this process step** into the **Prompt** field. These words will appear as a tooltip for this field later in this exercise.

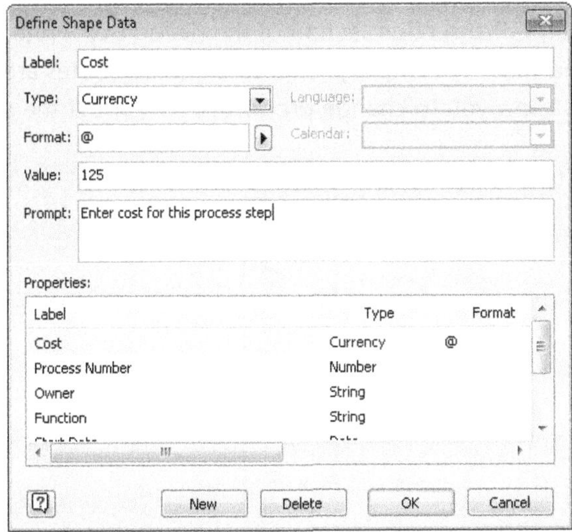

6. In the **Properties** section of the dialog box, click **Process Number**. Visio displays the attributes of this field in the upper half of the dialog box.

   Note that this is a *Number*-type field.

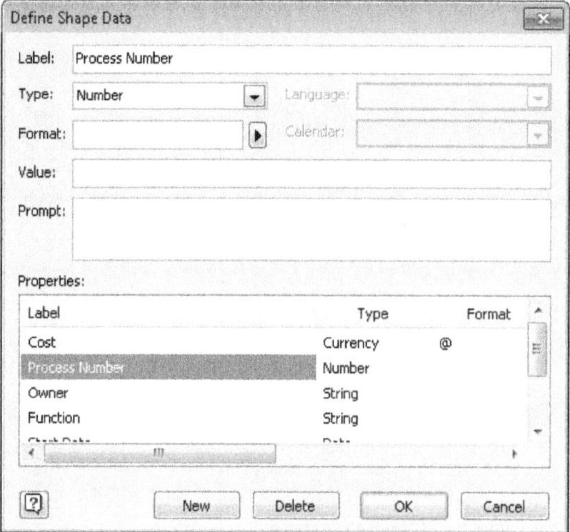

7. Click the arrow next to the **Format** field to explore the various formatting options Visio provides for numeric data.

8. Click **Owner** in the **Properties** section of the dialog box. Note that the Language field is now enabled, allowing you to specify the preferred language for this text field.

9. Click the arrow next to the **Format** field to explore the various formatting options Visio provides for text data.

10. Click **Start Date** in the **Properties** section of the dialog box. Note that this field has a Date type and that the Language and Calendar attributes are now enabled. These two settings allow you to change properties that affect the presentation of the date.

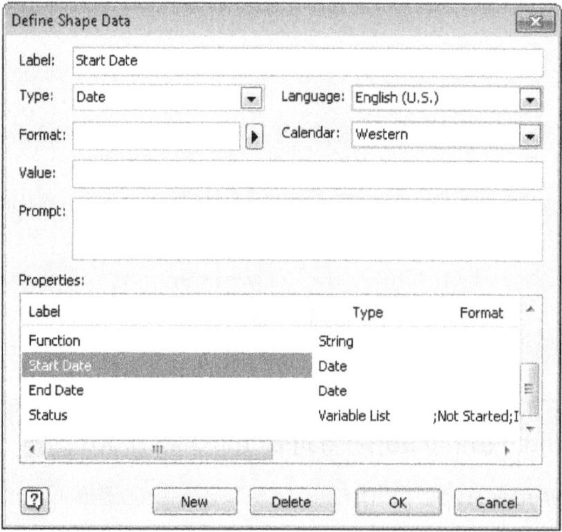

11. Click the arrow next to the **Format** field to explore the various formatting options Visio provides for date fields.

12. Click **Status** in the **Properties** section of the dialog box. Note that Status is a Variable List-type field.

    The Format field is used quite differently for Variable and Fixed List fields than for the other field types you've explored thus far. For list fields, Format holds a semicolon-separated list of values that will appear in the drop-down list in the Shape Data window.

    In the case of the Status field, the Format field holds the following string of characters:

    ;Not Started;In Progress;Completed;Deferred;Waiting on Input

    Important The semicolon at the very beginning of the list causes a null (blank) entry to appear at the top of the list. If you do not include a null entry, the user will not be able to leave the field blank after he or she has clicked something in the list. Both options may be appropriate in different situations: in some cases, a blank entry is not acceptable, so you want to force the user to select an entry from the list; in other cases, a blank entry is fine.

13. Type **;Waiting Manager Approval** at the end of the character string in the **Format** field.

    Important List entries are delimited by semicolons (";"). Be sure to type the semicolon before *Waiting Manager Approval* so that the new text becomes a separate entry in the list.

14. Type **In Progress** in the **Value** field.

    Tip If you want a value from the list to appear as the default for this field whenever the Shape Data window is opened, type it in the Value field. Be sure that the entry you type exactly matches a list item in the Format field, including upper and lower case letters.

15. Click **OK**.

    The Shape Data window reflects the changes you made to the fields: there is a default dollar amount in the Cost field and the Status is preset to *In Progress*.

Shape Data - Process.4	
Cost	$125.00
Process Number	
Owner	
Function	
Start Date	
End Date	
Status	In Progress

16. Point to the label for the **Cost** field. *Enter cost for this process step* appears as tooltip text because you typed it in the Prompt field in Step 5 of this procedure.
17. Click in the **Status** field and then click its arrow to display the list. Note that Waiting Manager Approval appears at the end of the list.

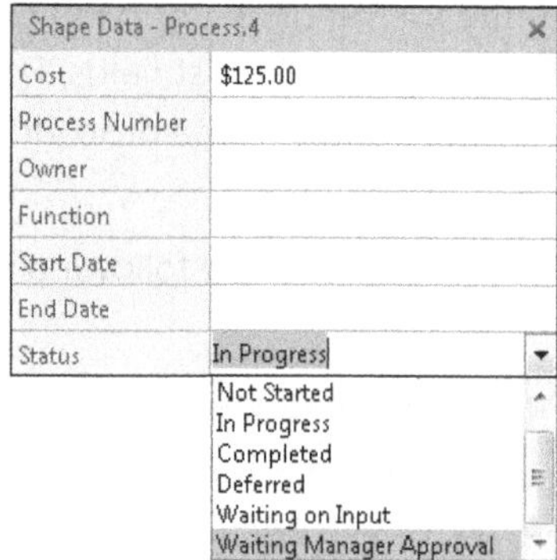

CLEAN UP Save your changes to the *HR Process Map* drawing, but leave it open if you are continuing with the next exercise.

Creating New Shape Data Fields

Now that you have successfully modified data fields for Visio shapes, you are ready to create a new shape data field.

In this exercise, you will add a new field to a shape that already contains other data fields.

SET UP You need the *HR Process Map* drawing for this exercise. Either continue with the open copy from the previous exercise or open the *HR Process Map_start* drawing located in the Chapter06 practice file folder and save it as *HR Process Map*. Open the Shape Data window.

1. Click the **Advertise open job** shape to view its shape data.
2. Right-click anywhere in the **Shape Data** window, and then click **Define Shape Data**.
3. Click the **New** button at the bottom of the **Define Shape Data** dialog box. The focus shifts to the Label field, allowing you to type a label for this field.

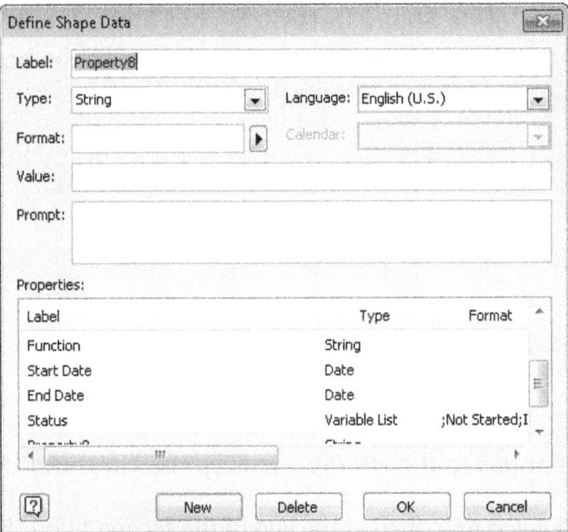

4. Type **Estimated duration**.
5. Click the down arrow to the right of **Type**, and then click **Duration**.
6. Click the right arrow next to **Format**.

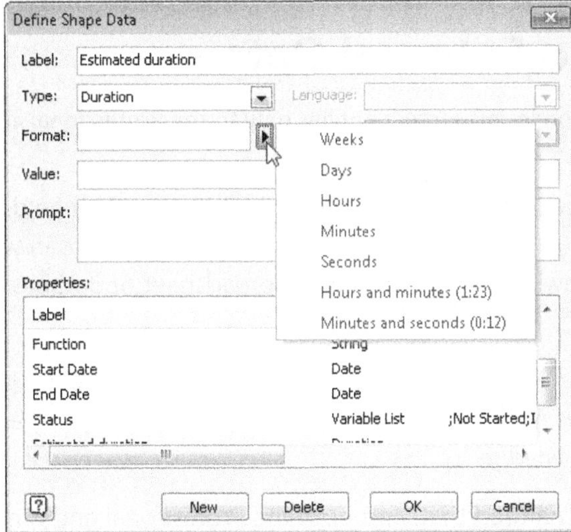

7. Click **Days**.

Tip You can set the format for a duration field to display the time in any of the standard Visio durations, ranging from seconds to weeks, or you can display the duration in one of the two listed time formats.

8. Click **OK** to close the **Define Shape Data** dialog box and return to the **Shape Data** window. Note that the field you created has been added to the bottom of the window.

Shape Data - Process.4	
Cost	$125.00
Process Number	
Owner	
Function	
Start Date	
End Date	
Status	In Progress
Estimated duration	

 **CLEAN UP** Save your changes to the *HR Process Map* drawing, and then close it.

Tip In a similar manner that was described at the end of the section titled "Editing Shape Data" earlier in this chapter, you can add, edit, or delete data fields for more than one shape at a time. To do so, select multiple shapes before opening the Define Shape Data dialog box.

If you select multiple shapes prior to opening the Shape Data window, you will see only the fields that all selected shapes have in common.

Linking Diagrams to External Data

Important The information in this section applies only to the Professional and Premium editions of Visio 2010.

Earlier in this chapter, you learned how to add and edit shape data fields. It's convenient to be able to do so manually, but it's also easy to imagine situations in which you would like to populate your drawings with data from a spreadsheet or database or other external source.

Prior to Visio 2007, it was possible to link Visio shapes to external data, but it was rather cryptic, somewhat confusing, and the procedures often required programming or at least some technical knowledge.

Visio 2007 Professional changed that, and both the Professional and Premium editions of Visio 2010 include the same ***data linking*** facility. In general, there are two steps involved in data linking:

1. Link the drawing to a data source.
2. Link the data to individual shapes.

In this exercise, you will link the process steps in the *Human Resources Process Map* drawing to data in an Excel spreadsheet.

SET UP You need the *HR Process Map_start* drawing and the *HR Process Data_start* workbook located in the Chapter06 practice file folder to complete this exercise. Open the drawing in Visio and save it as *HR Process Map with data.* Then open the *HR Process Data_start* workbook and save it as *HR Process Data.*

1. In the Excel workbook, examine the data it contains. In particular, notice the column headings.

HR Process Data_start.xlsx - Microsoft Excel

	A	B	C	D	E	F	G
1	Cost	Process Number	Owner	Function	Start Date	End Date	Status
2		101	HR Admin		4/4/2011		In Progress
3		102	Hiring Manager		4/4/2011		In Progress
4		103	HR Admin		4/6/2011		In Progress
5		104	Recruiter		4/18/2011		In Progress
6		105	Manager		4/25/2011		Not Started
7		106	Recruiter		4/29/2011		Not Started
8		107	Candidate		5/5/2011		Not Started
9		108	Recruiter		5/6/2011		Not Started
10							

Data Graphics

2. In Visio, on the **Data** tab, in the **Display Data** group, click the **Data Graphics** button, and then clear the **Apply after Linking Data to Shapes** check box.

   Visio will not apply a data graphic to shapes after you link them to data later in this exercise.

   See Also You will learn about data graphics in Chapter 10, "Visualizing Your Data."

   Tip Although you are turning data graphic activation off for this exercise, in many situations, it is valuable to turn it on so you can immediately see the results of your data linking operation.

Link Data to Shapes

3. In Visio, on the **Data** tab, in the **External Data** group, click the **Link Data to Shapes** button. The first page of the Data Selector wizard appears.

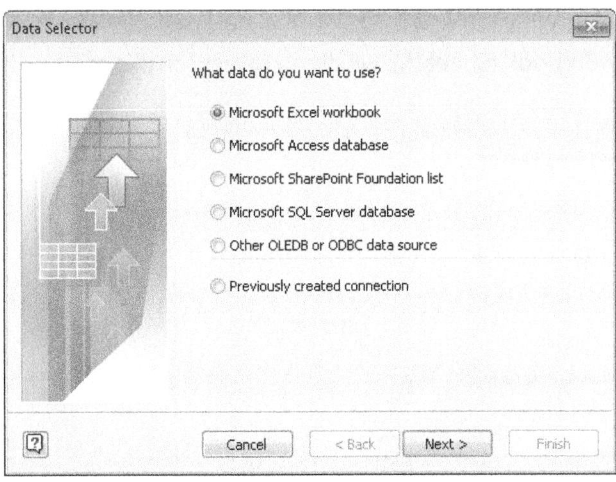

Tip **The default data type on the first page of the Data Selector wizard is Microsoft Excel Workbook, which is the one you will use for this exercise. However, notice that you can link to data stored in Microsoft Access, Microsoft SharePoint,, Microsoft SQL Server, or almost any other database.**

4. Click **Next**.

5. On the next **Data Selector** wizard page that appears, click the **Browse** button, and in the resulting file open dialog box, navigate to the **HR Process Data** Excel workbook. After selecting the correct file, click the **Open** button.

   The file name you selected appears in the What Workbook Do You Want To Import box.

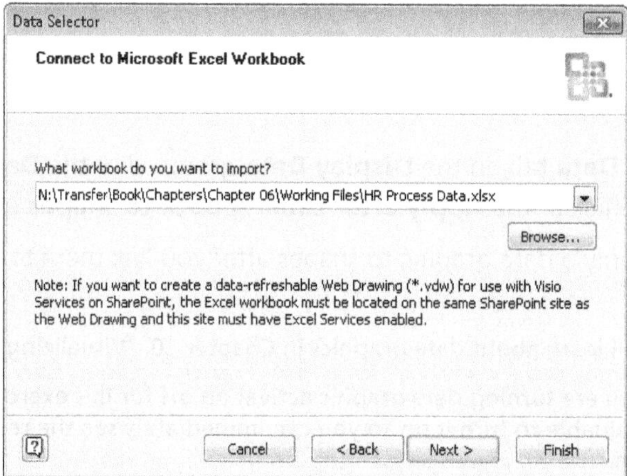

6. Click **Next**.

   On this page of the wizard, you will choose which worksheet contains the data to which you want to link. The Data Selector wizard usually defaults to the first worksheet in the workbook (Sheet1$), which is correct for this exercise.

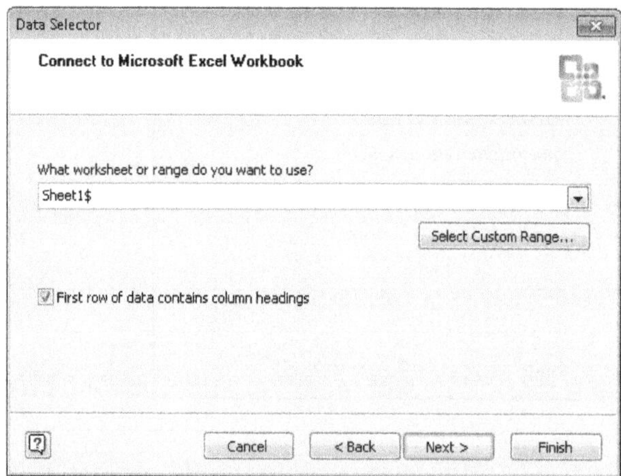

7. Select the **First row of data contains column headings** check box to indicate that the worksheet data includes column headings.

   Tip It is very helpful if your Excel workbook contains column headings, and if they match exactly to the names of the shape data fields in Visio. If the names match, Visio will know exactly how to map the data from the data source to the shapes.

8. Click **Next** to accept the defaults for both settings on this page of the wizard.

   On the Connect To Data page of the wizard you can customize the columns and rows from the selected worksheet that will be linked. As you can see in the following graphic, the default is all columns and all rows, which works for this exercise.

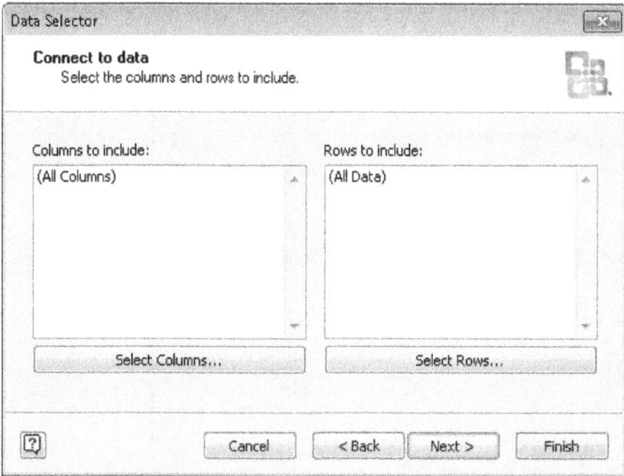

9. Click **Next**.

   On this page, Visio recommends a field that appears to uniquely identify each row of data based on its analysis of your data. You can change to a different field if there is a better choice.

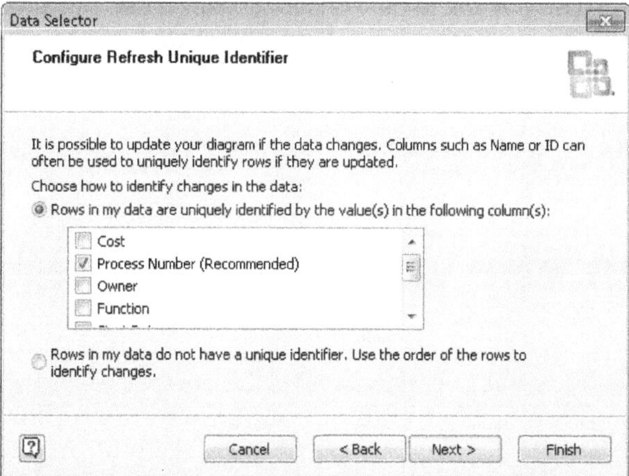

Tip You can select more than one field to constitute the unique ID if a single field is not sufficient.

The guesses Visio makes for the unique ID are generally pretty good. However, you should always think about the recommendation to determine whether there is a different field or combination of fields that is a better choice.

If your data does not contain a unique value for each row, you can click the option at the bottom of this page of the wizard to signify this, allowing Visio to use the sequence of the rows to identify them. Although this choice will work fine for reasonably stable data sets, be aware that using this option has potentially serious consequences later on if you reorder, add, or delete columns.

10. Click **Next** to display the final page of the wizard.

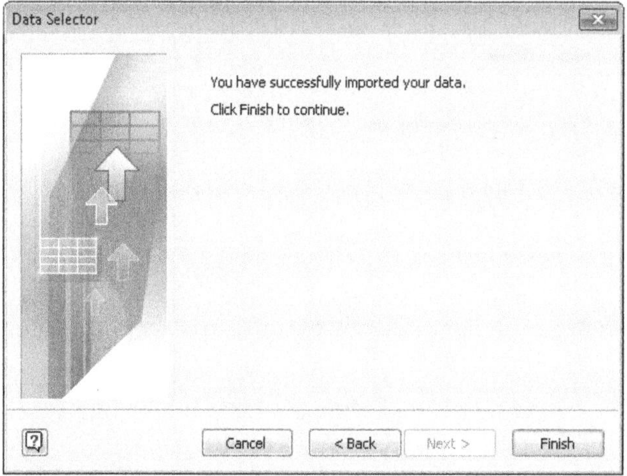

11. Click **Finish**.

Visio now displays the External Data window under the drawing pane. The External Data window contains one row for each row of data in your spreadsheet.

Tip In this exercise, you will link to only one Excel worksheet. However, it is possible to link a single diagram to more than one data source whether the sources are all of the same type or consist of a mix of databases, spreadsheets, and SharePoint lists.

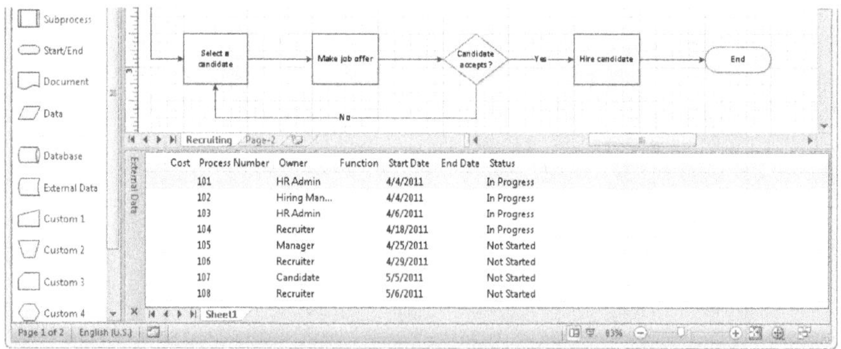

12. Drag data row **101** onto the **Log hiring request** process shape.

As you drag the data row, notice that the cursor appears to be dragging an outline of a shape across the page (see the following graphic on the left). Also, notice that the cursor is accompanied by a plus sign (+). This is the method Visio uses for letting you know that you are dragging the data for a specific shape type across the page.

Tip If you are dragging a data row onto a shape that is already on the page, as you are in this exercise, it doesn't matter whether the shape under the cursor matches the target shape. Visio will add the data to the existing shape.

In addition to dragging data rows onto existing shapes, you can create new shapes by dragging a data row onto a blank area of the drawing page. To do this, click once on the desired master in the stencil to select it, and then drag a data row onto the page. The shape under the cursor will reflect the master you've selected.

As the cursor moves onto the target shape, the plus sign is replaced by a linking symbol. In addition, the outline shapes take on a thicker, blue border (see the graphic on the right).

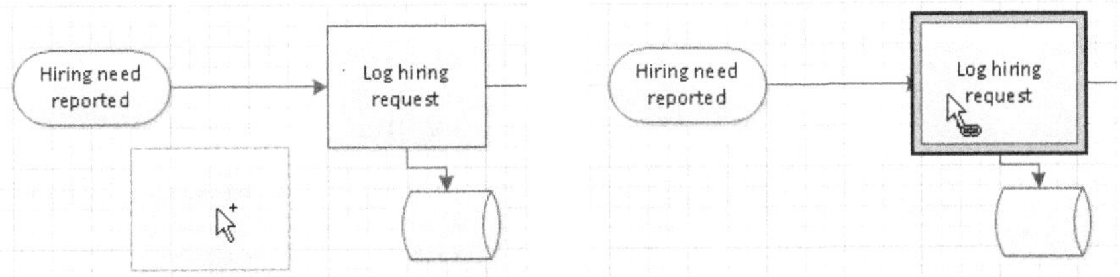

The end result of the drag and drop doesn't change the appearance of the shape on the page but you'll notice the addition of a linking symbol at the left end of the top data row, as shown in the following graphic.

Tip If you need to know which row is linked to which shape, right-click on the row, and then click Linked Shapes to see the answer. If you need to remove the link between a data row and a shape, right-click on the row, and then click Unlink.

External Data

	Cost	Process Number	Owner	Function	Start Date	End Date	Status
🔗		101	HR Admin		4/4/2011		In Progress
		102	Hiring Man...		4/4/2011		In Progress
		103	HR Admin		4/6/2011		In Progress
		104	Recruiter		4/18/2011		In Progress
		105	Manager		4/25/2011		Not Started
		106	Recruiter		4/29/2011		Not Started
		107	Candidate		5/5/2011		Not Started
		108	Recruiter		5/6/2011		Not Started

Sheet1

13. Open the **Shape Data** window for the **Log hiring request** shape.

As you can see, the data from the Excel spreadsheet now resides in the Visio shape. And even more important, potentially, is that this is a live link, as you'll see in the next section.

Shape Data - Process	
Cost	$0.00
Process Number	101
Owner	HR Admin
Function	
Start Date	4/4/2011
End Date	
Status	In Progress

14. Drag the remainder of the data rows onto the shapes on the page. Shape 102–104 are left-to-right in the top row, and shapes 105–108 are left to right across the bottom row. (The End shape does not have a data row.)

    The final result is a fully linked set of data rows.

Cost	Process Number	Owner	Function	Start Date	End Date	Status
	101	HR Admin		4/4/2011		In Progress
	102	Hiring Man...		4/4/2011		In Progress
	103	HR Admin		4/6/2011		In Progress
	104	Recruiter		4/18/2011		In Progress
	105	Manager		4/25/2011		Not Started
	106	Recruiter		4/29/2011		Not Started
	107	Candidate		5/5/2011		Not Started
	108	Recruiter		5/6/2011		Not Started

External Data — Sheet1

Tip The name on the tab at the bottom of the External Data window is the name of the worksheet in the linked Excel workbook. If you will be linking a diagram to more than one worksheet or even to worksheets in more than one workbook, it is useful to give each worksheet a unique name.

CLEAN UP Save your changes to the *HR Process Map with data* drawing in Visio and save your changes to the *HR Process Data* workbook in Excel. Leave both files open if you are continuing to the next exercise.

Tip When you populate shapes with data from the External Data window, Visio matches the external data column names with the names of the shape data fields in the target shape. If there are no matching shape data fields, Visio creates new shape data fields to accommodate the external data.

Refreshing All Data in Linked Diagrams

Important The information in this section applies only to the Professional and Premium editions of Visio 2010.

After you have linked data to a Visio drawing, there is a live connection between the two files. In fact, you can make changes to the data source and have those changes appear either manually or automatically in the Visio drawing. This is true whether the drawing is linked to a single data source or to multiple sources.

In this exercise, you will update cells in the Excel data source and see those changes in the Visio shapes.

SET UP If they are not already opened, open the *HR Process Map with data* Visio drawing and the *HR Process Data* Excel workbook that you created in the previous exercise.

1. In the Excel spreadsheet, type **Hiring Manager** in the **Owner** cell for process number **104** that currently contains **Recruiter**.
2. Type **4/15/2011** in the **Start Date** cell for process step **104** that currently contains **4/18/2011**.
3. Type **In Progress** in the **Status** cell for process step **105** that currently contains **Not Started**.

   The following graphic highlights the three changes you've just made.

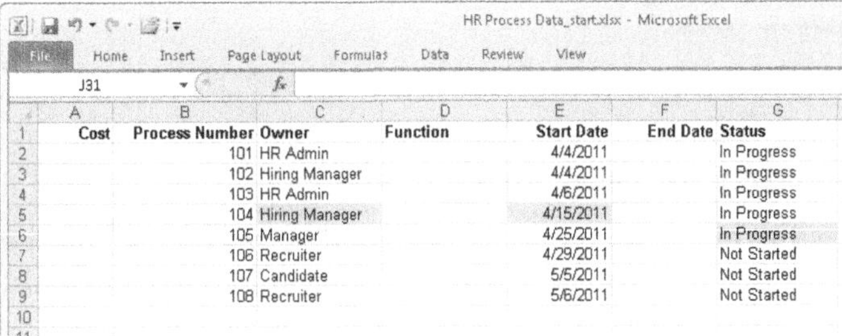

Cost	Process Number	Owner	Function	Start Date	End Date	Status
	101	HR Admin		4/4/2011		In Progress
	102	Hiring Manager		4/4/2011		In Progress
	103	HR Admin		4/6/2011		In Progress
	104	Hiring Manager		4/15/2011		In Progress
	105	Manager		4/25/2011		In Progress
	106	Recruiter		4/29/2011		Not Started
	107	Candidate		5/5/2011		Not Started
	108	Recruiter		5/6/2011		Not Started

Refresh All

4. Switch to Visio. Then on the **Data** tab, in the **External Data** group, click the **Refresh All** button (do not click the arrow).

   Tip As an alternative, you can also right-click in the External Data window and click Refresh Data.

Visio reads data from all linked data sources and shows the result in the Refresh Data dialog box.

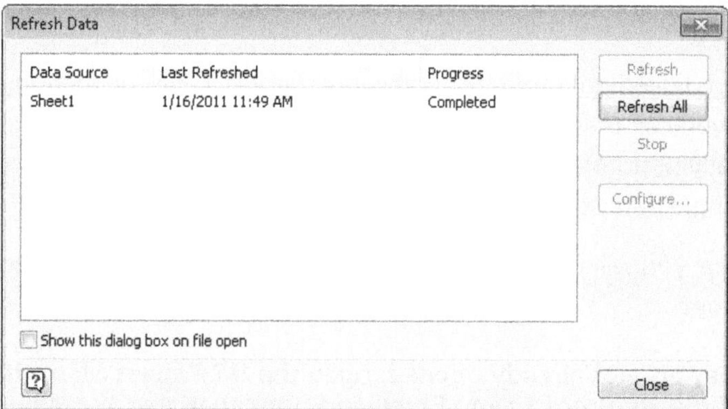

Tip It is not necessary to close the spreadsheet or other data source in order to update the Visio drawing.

Occasionally, Visio may display the following dialog box. If you know that the data links in your drawing are correct and safe, click OK. You can prevent future display of this dialog box by selecting the Don't Show This Message Again check box.

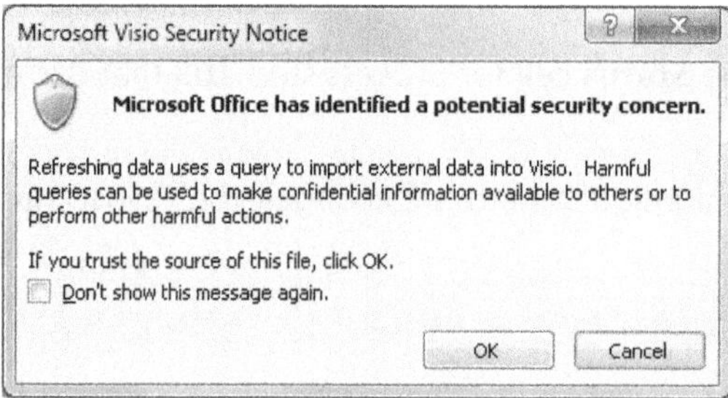

5. In the **Refresh Data** dialog box, click **Close**.

   Compare the data in the External Data window with the spreadsheet in Step 3 and you can see that the changes have been applied to the data in the drawing. For final proof, you should examine one of the shapes whose data you've changed.

6. Open the **Shape Data** window for the shape titled **Interview candidates**. The shape correctly reflects the new data in the Excel workbook.

Shape Data - Process.12	
Cost	$0.00
Process Number	104
Owner	Hiring Manager
Function	
Start Date	4/15/2011
End Date	
Status	In Progress

CLEAN UP Save changes to the *HR Process Map with data* drawing and the *HR Process Data* workbook but leave them open if you are continuing with the next exercise.

Important The data linking mechanism of Visio is designed for one-way data transfer, that is, for importing data *into* a Visio diagram. The opposite does not work. In other words, you can refresh the data in a drawing after making changes in a linked data source, but you cannot make changes to data in Visio and then push those changes to the linked data source.

Refreshing Selected Data in Linked Diagrams

Important The information in this section applies only to the Professional and Premium editions of Visio 2010.

The procedure in the previous exercise automatically refreshes data from all linked data sources. Many times, this is exactly what you want to do. However, if your Visio diagram is linked to several data sources, there may be times when you want to update the drawing from a subset of the linked repositories.

In this exercise, you will refresh data from some but not all active data sources.

SET UP If they are not already opened, open the *HR Process Map with data* Visio drawing and the *HR Process Data* Excel workbook that you worked with in the previous exercise.

Refresh All

In Visio, on the **Data** tab, in the **External Data** group, click the **Refresh All** arrow (below the button), and then click **Refresh Data** to open the **Refresh Data** dialog box.

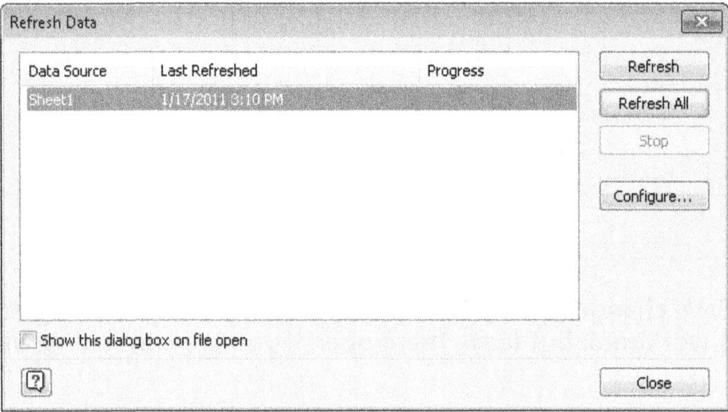

2. Select one or more data sources.

   Tip **There is only one data source in this exercise, but if you've linked a drawing to more than one, they will all be listed in this dialog box.**

3. Click the **Refresh** button, and then click **Close**.

CLEAN UP **Save changes to the *HR Process Map with data* Visio drawing and the *HR Process Data* Excel workbook but leave them open if you are continuing with the next exercise.**

Scheduling Data Refresh

Important **The information in this section applies only to the Professional and Premium editions of Visio 2010.**

The preceding two exercises showed you how to manually update the data in your diagram by rereading the data sources. It's easy to imagine situations in which you would like to have Visio update the data without manual intervention. Each scenario in the following list would be a good candidate for this feature:

- A network or rack diagram that is used to display near real–time network and server status
- A call center seating chart that shows which agents are on the phone and which are available
- A process map that shows up-to-date task status
- A factory floor plan that displays production statistics, performance threshold warnings, and safety issues

In this exercise, you will set a schedule so Visio will refresh your drawing automatically.

SET UP **If they are not already opened, open the** ***HR Process Map with data*** **Visio drawing and the** ***HR Process Data*** **Excel workbook that you worked with in the previous exercise.**

1. In Visio, right-click anywhere in the **External Data** window, and then click **Configure Refresh** to open the **Configure Refresh** dialog box.

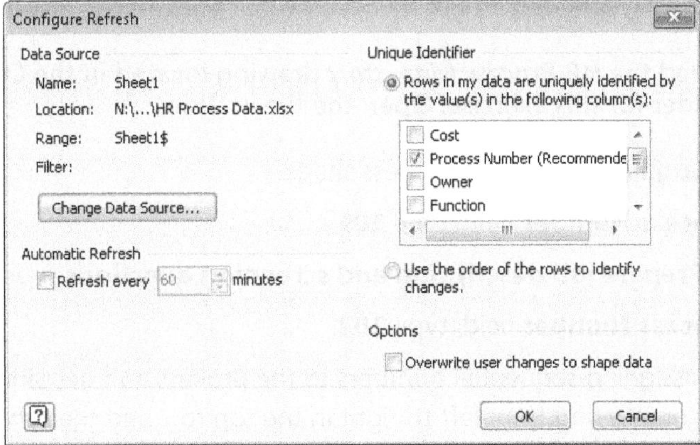

Tip **As an alternative to Step 1, you can open the Refresh Data dialog box shown in the previous two sections, select one or more data sources, and then click the Configure button.**

2. In the **Configure Refresh** dialog box, select the **Refresh every nnn minutes** check box.
3. Type **10** or use the spinner control to set the desired refresh interval, and then click **OK**.

   From this point forward, whenever your drawing is open, the data will refresh automatically at the specified time interval. The data will not refresh when the drawing is closed.

CLEAN UP **Save and close the** ***HR Process Map with data*** **Visio drawing and the** ***HR Process Data*** **Excel workbook.**

Linking Data to Shapes Automatically

Important **The information in this section applies only to the Professional and Premium editions of Visio 2010.**

After completing Steps 12-14 in the section titled "Linking Diagrams to External Data" earlier in this chapter, you were probably thinking "There must be a better way to link data to shapes!" Fortunately, there is. Visio includes an automatic linking facility that works very nicely when both the data and the shapes contain matching unique identifiers. The key to the automatic linking facility is in the previous sentence: the shapes on the drawing page and the data in your spreadsheet or other data source must have matching IDs.

In this exercise, you will first prepare your drawing by adding IDs to the shapes, and then you will automatically link the data to the shapes.

SET UP You need the *HR Process Map_start* drawing located in the Chapter06 practice file folder for this exercise. Open the file in Visio.

1. Click the **Log hiring request** process shape.
2. In the **Process Number** field, type **101**.
3. Click the **Prepare job description and screening questions** process shape.
4. In the **Process Number** field, type **102**.
5. Continue assigning sequential numbers to the process and decision shapes in the flowchart, numbering from left to right in the top row and then the bottom row.
6. Save the drawing as **HR Process Map with IDs**.

   Now that you've prepared the drawing, it is easy to link data to shapes automatically.
7. Follow Steps 2–11 in the section "Linking Diagrams to External Data" earlier in this chapter. This will connect your drawing to the spreadsheet and open the External Data window.

Automatically Link

8. On the **Data** tab, in the **External Data** group, click the **Automatically Link** button.

   If you did not select specific shapes before performing this step, you will see the following page of the wizard exactly as shown. If you did select one or more shapes before performing this step, the Selected Shapes option will be available so that you can automatically link just those shapes.

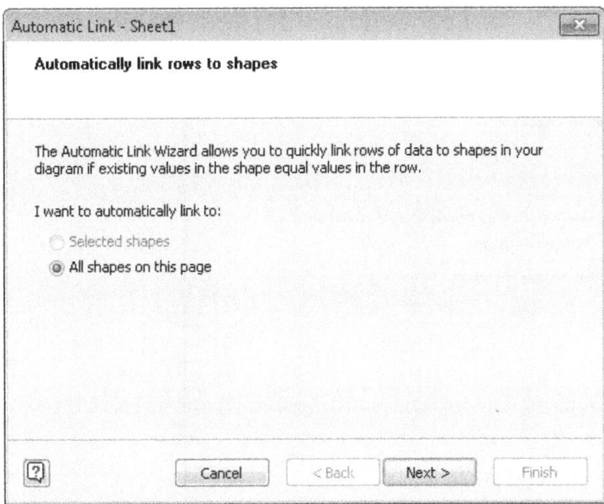

9. Click **Next**.

   On this page of the wizard, you tell Visio how to match data with shapes by indicating the column name in the data and the field name in the shapes that are equivalent.

10. Under the **Data Column** heading, click **Process Number** in the list.
11. Under the **Shape Field** heading, click **Process Number** in the list.

    Tip If you need to specify multiple conditions for matching data to shapes, click the And button and enter additional conditions.

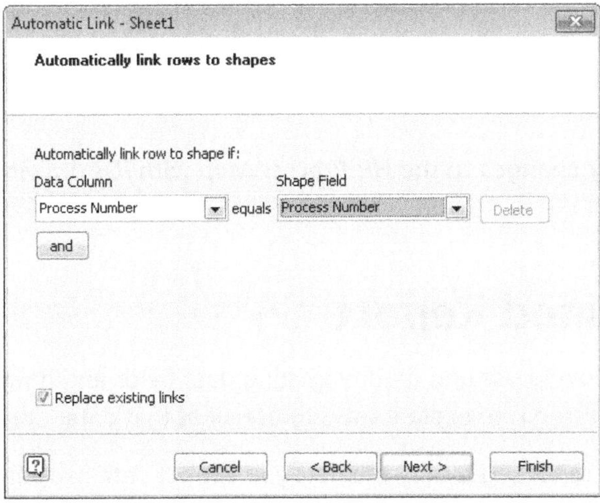

12. Click **Next**. The final wizard page summarizes your choices.

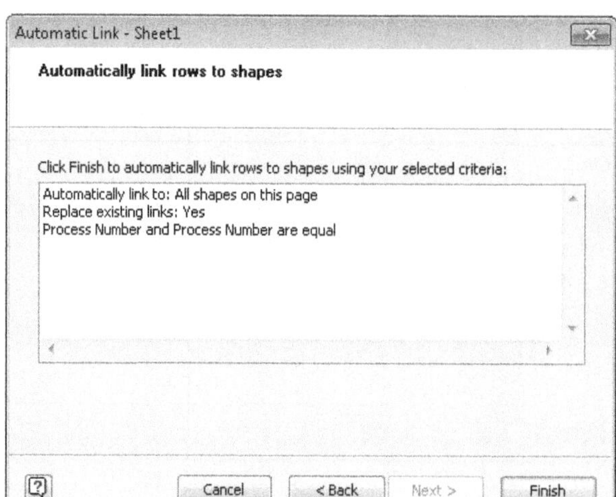

13. Click **Finish**.

    The data has now been linked to all matching shapes as you can see from the link symbols in the External Data window.

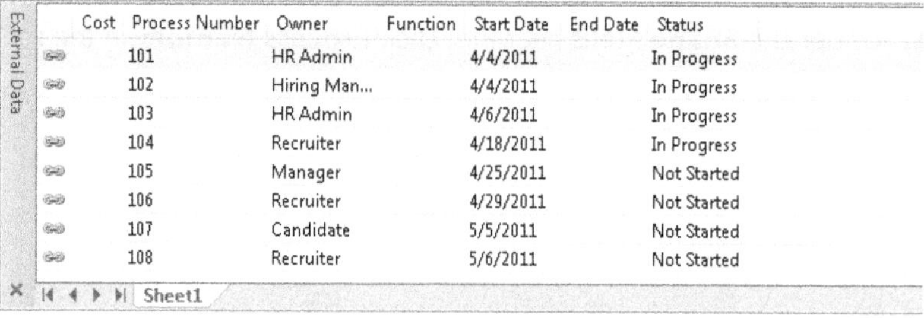

Cost	Process Number	Owner	Function	Start Date	End Date	Status
	101	HR Admin		4/4/2011		In Progress
	102	Hiring Man...		4/4/2011		In Progress
	103	HR Admin		4/6/2011		In Progress
	104	Recruiter		4/18/2011		In Progress
	105	Manager		4/25/2011		Not Started
	106	Recruiter		4/29/2011		Not Started
	107	Candidate		5/5/2011		Not Started
	108	Recruiter		5/6/2011		Not Started

 **CLEAN UP** Save your changes to the *HR Process Map with IDs* drawing, and then close it.

Running a Predefined Report

Now that you know how to use and modify existing data fields and how to create new fields, the next logical step is to explore ways to use all of that data.

Visio 2010 provides a reporting facility that lets you extract data in a variety of ways in order to summarize and present it. Many of the built-in Visio templates include predefined reports. You can also design your own reports by stepping through the provided report definition wizard.

In this exercise, you will run one of the built-in reports.

SET UP You need the *HR Process Map with data_start* drawing located in the Chapter06 practice file folder to complete this exercise. Open the drawing in Visio and save it as *HR Process Map Reports*.

Shape Reports

1. On the **Review** tab, in the **Reports** group, click the **Shape Reports** button. The Reports dialog box opens.
2. In the **Reports** dialog box, click once on **Flowchart** in the list of reports.

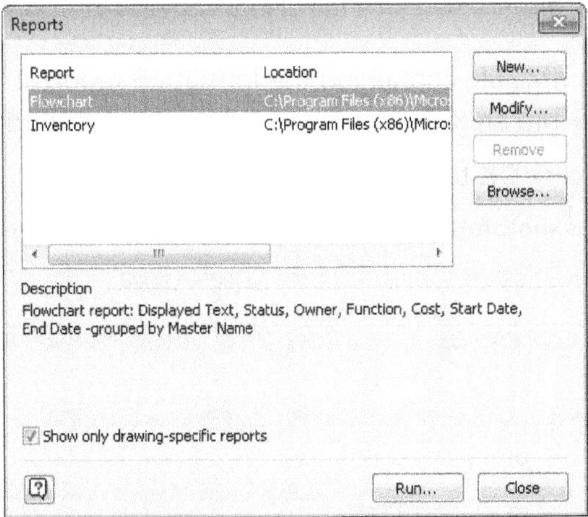

At the top of the Reports dialog box, there are two predefined reports: Flowchart and Inventory. The Flowchart report is part of the flowchart template in Visio and will appear whenever you create a diagram using that template. The Inventory report is a generic Visio report that counts shapes and is present every time you open the Reports dialog box.

Because you selected the Flowchart report, notice that there is a description of the report in the center of the dialog box.

3. Click **Run**. The Run Report dialog box opens.

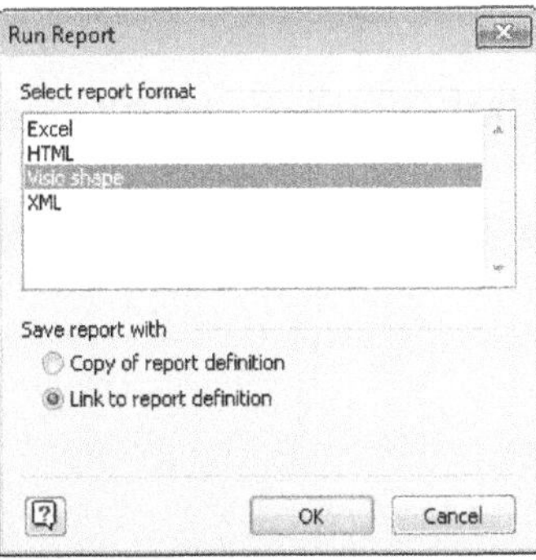

The Run Report dialog box offers four different report output options:

- **Excel** Drops the formatted report data into Microsoft Excel. The report data can be edited.
- **HTML** Drops the report into Windows Internet Explorer. This report format is read only.
- **Visio shape** Creates a new Visio shape that contains the report data. (For the technically inclined: this shape is actually an embedded Excel object, so after creating it, you can double-click the report shape and edit the data as though you were using Excel.)
- **XML** Creates an XML file containing the formatted report. The report data can be imported into an XML-aware application or can be edited.

4. Click **Excel**, and then click **OK** to open the Flowchart report.

   Tip This report includes subtotals for each entry in the Master Name column.

	A	B	C	D	E	F	G	H	I
1			**Flowchart Report**						
2		*Master Name*	*Displayed Text*	*Status*	*Owner*	*Function*	*Start Date*	*End Date*	*Cost*
3		Database							
4	Count	1							
5	Total								
6		Decision	Candidate accepts?	Not Started	Candidate		5/5/2011		$0.00
7	Count	1							
8	Total								$0.00
9		Document							
10		Document							
11		Document	HR Policy Manual						
12	Count	3							
13	Total								
14		Process	Prepare job description and screening questions	In Progress	Hiring Manager		4/4/2011		$0.00
15		Process	Interview candidates	In Progress	Recruiter		4/18/2011		$0.00
16		Process	Select a candidate	Not Started	Manager		4/25/2011		$0.00
17		Process	Make job offer	Not Started	Recruiter		4/29/2011		$0.00
18		Process	Hire candidate	Not Started	Recruiter		5/6/2011		$0.00
19		Process	Advertise open job	In Progress	HR Admin		4/6/2011		$0.00
20		Process	Log hiring request	In Progress	HR Admin		4/4/2011		$0.00
21	Count	7							
22	Total								$0.00
23		Start/End	Hiring need reported						
24		Start/End	End						
25	Count	2							
26	Total								
27	Grand Total								$0.00

5. On the **Review** tab, in the **Reports** group, click the **Shape Reports** button. Then click **Flowchart** and the **Run** button in the **Reports** dialog box to run the Flowchart report again.
6. In the **Run Report** dialog box, click **HTML**, and then click **OK**. Internet Explorer opens and displays the report.

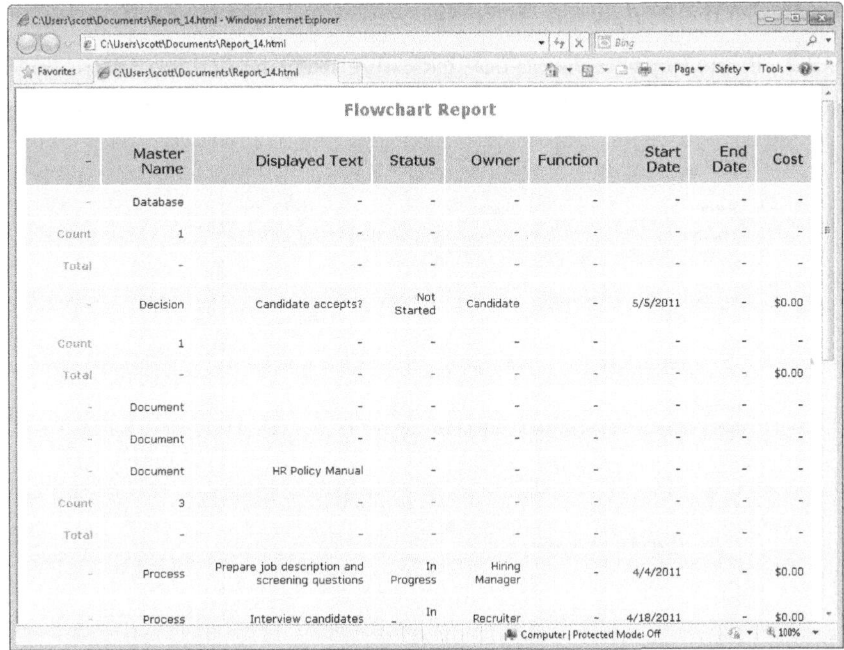

Flowchart Report

-	Master Name	Displayed Text	Status	Owner	Function	Start Date	End Date	Cost
-	Database	-	-	-	-	-	-	-
Count	1	-	-	-	-	-	-	-
Total	-	-	-	-	-	-	-	-
-	Decision	Candidate accepts?	Not Started	Candidate	-	5/5/2011	-	$0.00
Count	1	-	-	-	-	-	-	-
Total	-	-	-	-	-	-	-	$0.00
-	Document	-	-	-	-	-	-	-
-	Document	-	-	-	-	-	-	-
-	Document	HR Policy Manual	-	-	-	-	-	-
Count	3	-	-	-	-	-	-	-
Total	-	-	-	-	-	-	-	-
-	Process	Prepare job description and screening questions	In Progress	Hiring Manager	-	4/4/2011	-	$0.00
-	Process	Interview candidates	In	Recruiter	-	4/18/2011	-	$0.00

7. On the **Review** tab, in the **Reports** group, click the **Shape Reports** button. Then click **Flowchart** and the **Run** button in the **Reports** dialog box to run the Flowchart report again.
8. In the **Run Report** dialog box, click **Visio shape**, and then click **OK**. As you can see in the following graphic, the new shape object can be quite large, depending on the amount of data in your drawing, so you'll probably want to cut and paste it onto a separate page.

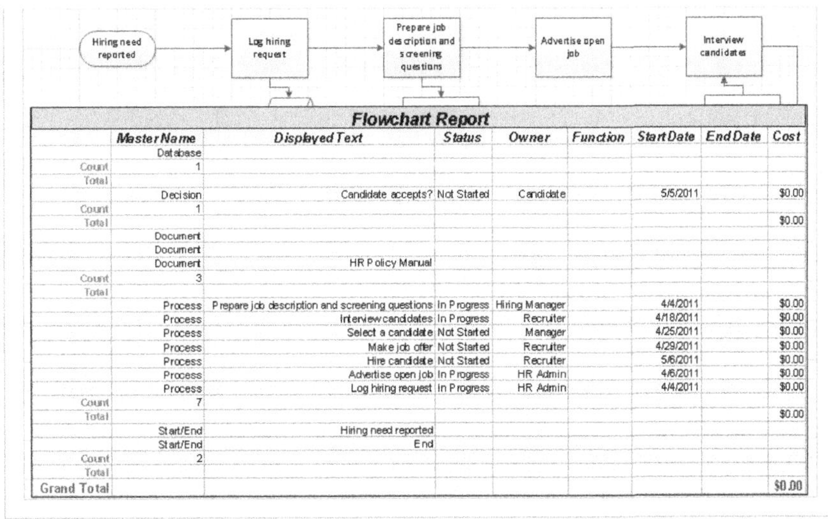

Flowchart Report

	Master Name	Displayed Text	Status	Owner	Function	Start Date	End Date	Cost
	Database							
Count	1							
Total								
	Decision	Candidate accepts?	Not Started	Candidate		5/5/2011		$0.00
Count	1							
Total								$0.00
	Document							
	Document							
	Document	HR Policy Manual						
Count	3							
Total								
	Process	Prepare job description and screening questions	In Progress	Hiring Manager		4/4/2011		$0.00
	Process	Interview candidates	In Progress	Recruiter		4/18/2011		$0.00
	Process	Select a candidate	Not Started	Manager		4/25/2011		$0.00
	Process	Make job offer	Not Started	Recruiter		4/29/2011		$0.00
	Process	Hire candidate	Not Started	Recruiter		5/6/2011		$0.00
	Process	Advertise open job	In Progress	HR Admin		4/6/2011		$0.00
	Process	Log hiring request	In Progress	HR Admin		4/4/2011		$0.00
Count	7							
Total								$0.00
	Start/End	Hiring need reported						
	Start/End	End						
Count	2							
Total								
Grand Total								$0.00

9. On the **Review** tab, in the **Reports** group, click **Shape Reports**.

10. In the **Reports** dialog box, click **Inventory**. Notice the description of this report—essentially, it just counts all occurrences of every shape on the page.

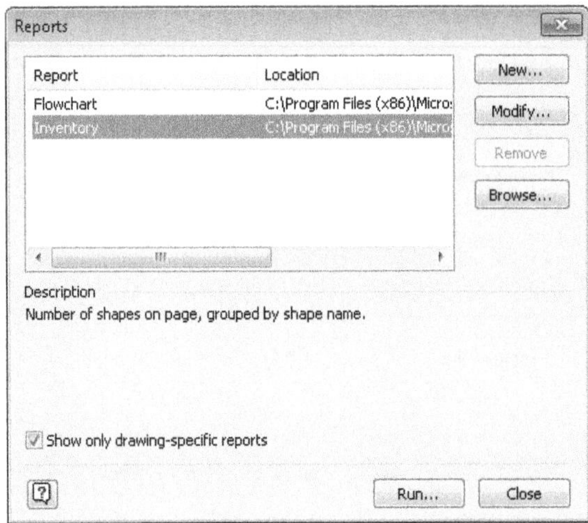

Tip The Show Only Drawing-Specific Reports option at the bottom of the dialog box is selected by default. Generally, this is a good thing because it prevents Visio from showing you a list of extraneous reports. However, if you're looking for a report that doesn't appear on the list when this option is selected, you can clear it. Doing so for the previous dialog box produces a long list of reports.

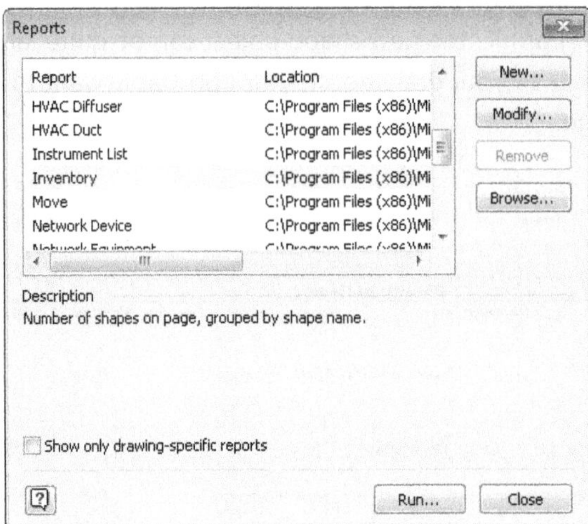

11. Click **Run**.

12. Double-click **Visio shape** in the **Run Report** dialog box to execute the report and create a new Visio shape.

    In the portion of the drawing page shown in the following graphic, the inventory report displays a simple count of each shape type.

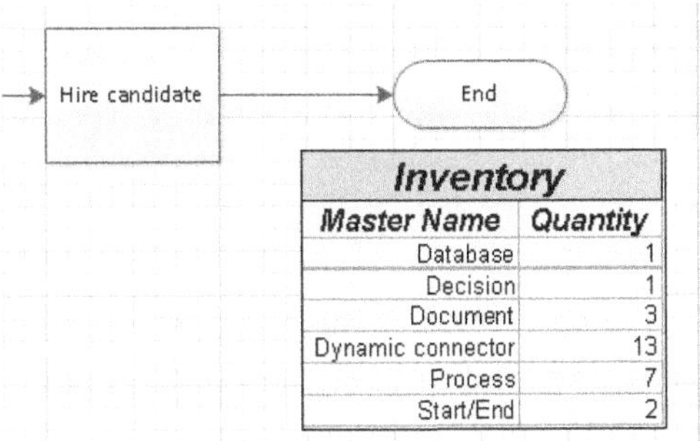

Inventory	
Master Name	Quantity
Database	1
Decision	1
Document	3
Dynamic connector	13
Process	7
Start/End	2

CLEAN UP Save your changes to the *HR Process Map Reports* drawing but leave it open if you are continuing with the next exercise.

Creating a New Report

Visio provides a Report Definition wizard so you can create new reports or modify existing reports. In this exercise, you will create a new report for the Recruiting Process.

SET UP You need the *HR Process Map Reports* drawing for this exercise. Either continue with the open copy from the previous exercise or open the *HR Process Map with data_start* drawing located in the Chapter06 practice file folder and save it as *HR Process Map Reports.*

Shape Reports

1. On the **Review** tab, in the **Reports** group, click the **Shape Reports** button. The Reports dialog box opens.

2. In the **Reports** dialog box, click the **New** button. The Report Definition Wizard opens.

   The Report Definition Wizard lets you select a set of shapes to include in the report.

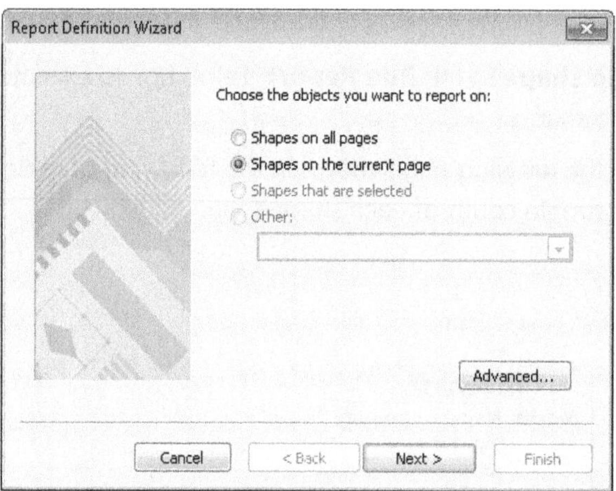

3. Click **Shapes on the current page** if it's not already selected, and then click **Next**.

   This page of the Report Definition Wizard shows the fields that you are most likely to want in your report. If you don't see the field you're looking for, select the Show All Properties check box.

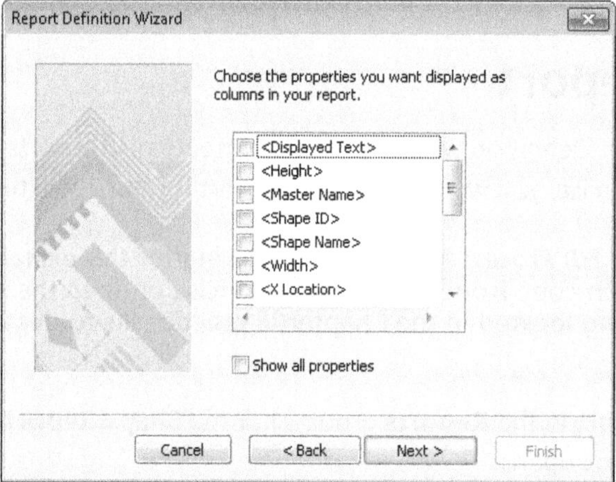

4. Select the **<Displayed Text>** check box, scroll down and select the check boxes for **Owner**, **Process Number**, **Start Date** and **Status**, and then click **Next**. The next wizard page opens.

5. Type **HR Report** in the **Report Title** text box.

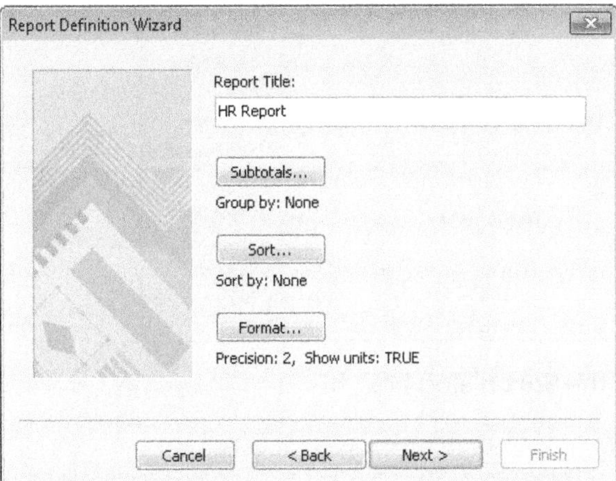

6. Click the **Sort** button so you can specify the order in which you want the data to appear in the report.

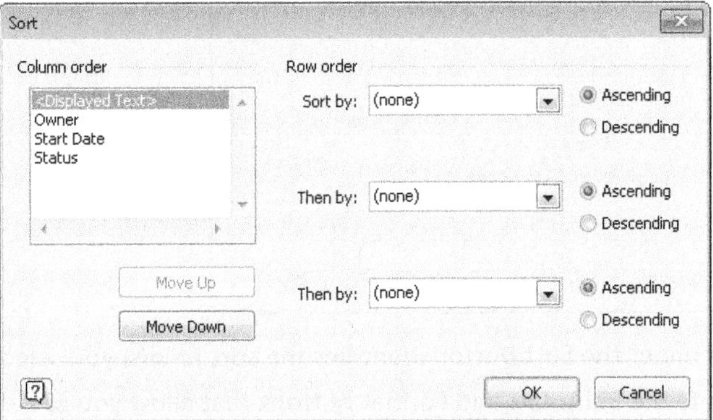

7. In the **Sort** dialog box, in the **Row Order** section, click the arrow next to **Sort by**, and then select **Process Number**.

   Tip You can sort by as many as three fields in the Row Order section.

8. In the **Column Order** section, click once on **Process Number**, and then click the **Move Up** button twice to set the column sequence as shown in the following graphic.

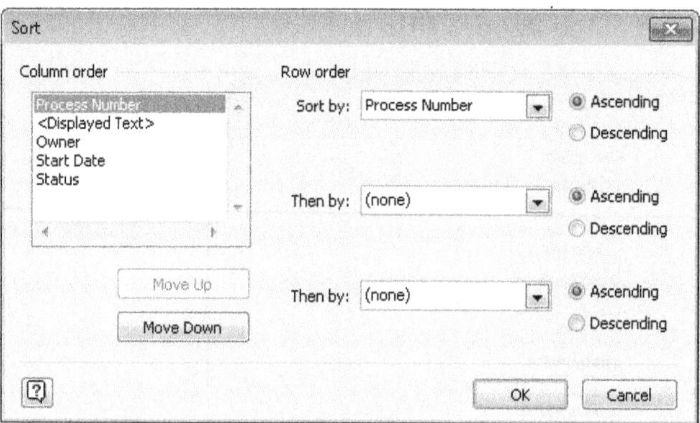

9. Click **OK** to close the **Sort** dialog box.

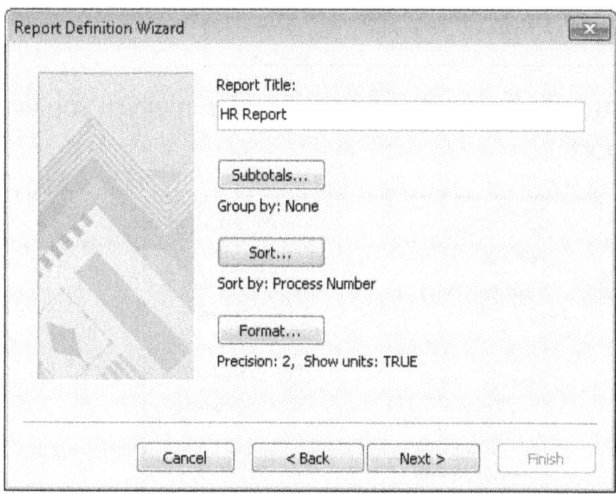

Tip The text under the Sort button identifies the sort field(s) you selected.

Be sure to note the Subtotals and Format buttons that allow you to customize the report output in additional ways beyond what you will use for this sample report.

10. Click **Next** to open the final page of the **Report Definition Wizard**.
11. Type **Custom HR Report** in the **Name** text box.
12. Type **HR Process report showing task number, task description, owner, start data and status** in the **Description** text box.

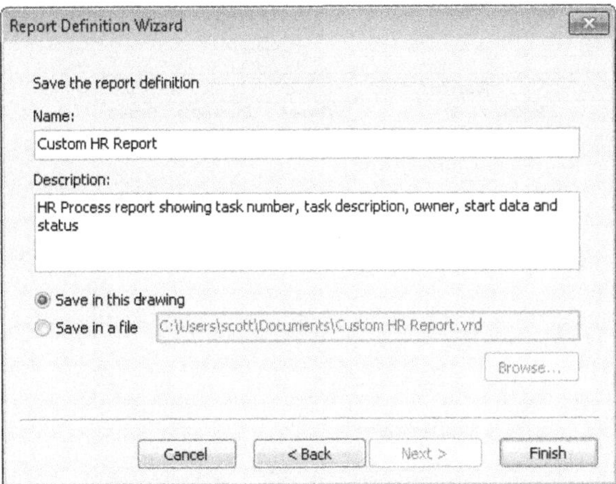

You can save the report definition in the current Visio drawing, which is the default, or you can save it to an external file.

Tip Save the report definition to an external file if you think you'll want to use it with multiple drawings. If you do, you can retrieve the report definition by clicking the Browse button in the Reports dialog box shown in the following graphic.

13. Click **Finish**. Your report appears in the list of available reports in the Reports dialog box and you can run it in the usual way.

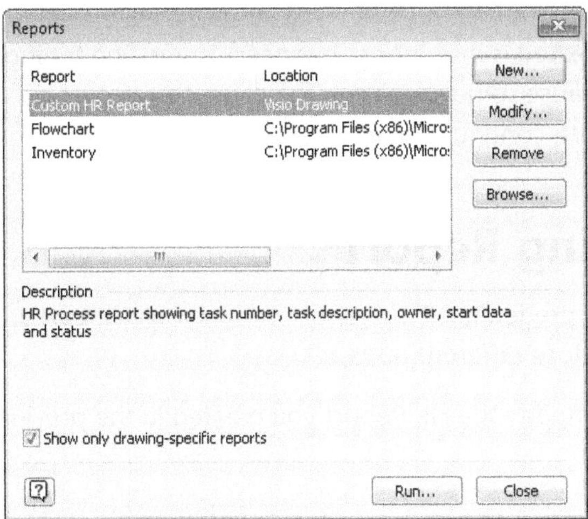

14. Click **Run** in the **Reports** dialog box.
15. Double-click **Visio shape** in the **Run Report** dialog box. Your custom report appears on the drawing page.

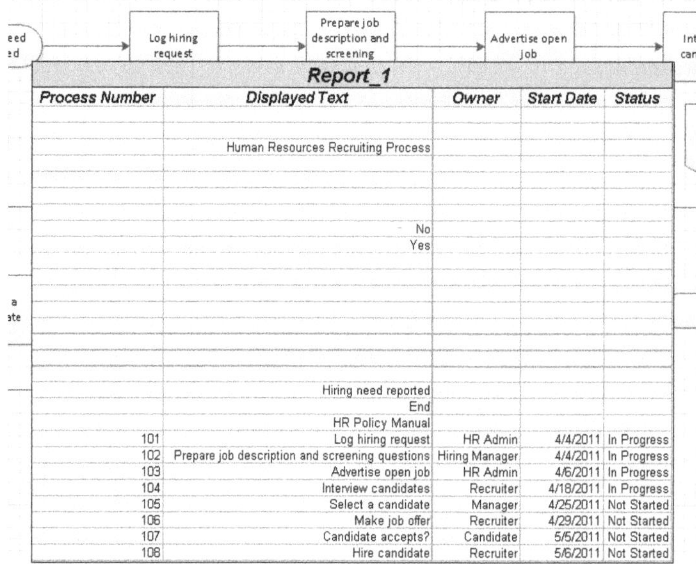

Report_1				
Process Number	**Displayed Text**	**Owner**	**Start Date**	**Status**
	Human Resources Recruiting Process			
	No			
	Yes			
	Hiring need reported			
	End			
	HR Policy Manual			
101	Log hiring request	HR Admin	4/4/2011	In Progress
102	Prepare job description and screening questions	Hiring Manager	4/4/2011	In Progress
103	Advertise open job	HR Admin	4/6/2011	In Progress
104	Interview candidates	Recruiter	4/18/2011	In Progress
105	Select a candidate	Manager	4/25/2011	Not Started
106	Make job offer	Recruiter	4/29/2011	Not Started
107	Candidate accepts?	Candidate	5/5/2011	Not Started
108	Hire candidate	Recruiter	5/6/2011	Not Started

When you save the changes to this file, your report definition will be saved with your drawing.

CLEAN UP Save your changes to the *HR Process Map Reports* drawing but leave it open if you are continuing with the next exercise.

The report you've just created is interesting, but needs some fine tuning. For example, there are blank rows because some shapes on the page, the arrows, do not contain any data. To modify the report, continue reading in the next section.

Modifying an Existing Report

Whether you are using a predefined Visio report or one you've created, there are times when you want it to produce different output.

In this exercise, you will modify the HR Report you created in the previous section to eliminate the blank rows.

SET UP Open the *HR Process Map Reports* drawing that you saved in the previous exercise, if it is not still open. If the HR Report is still on the drawing page, click it once to select it, and then press Delete.

Shape Reports

1. On the **Review** tab, in the **Reports** group, click the **Shape Reports** button.
2. In the **Reports** dialog box, click **Custom HR Report** in the list of reports.
3. Click the **Modify** button. The Report Definition Wizard appears.

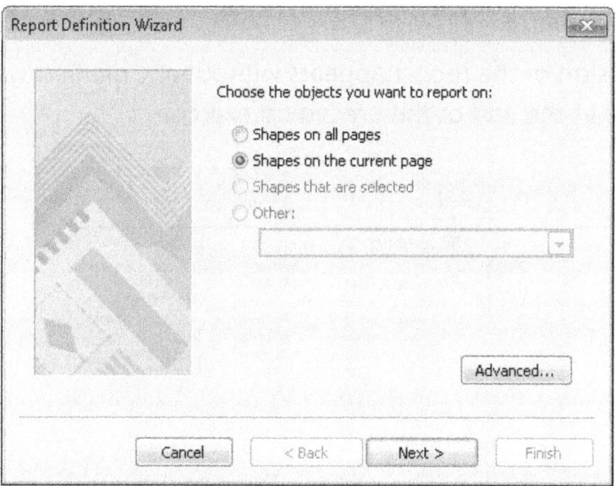

4. On the first page of the **Report Definition Wizard**, click the **Advanced** button. The Advanced dialog box opens.

   In the Advanced dialog box, you can limit the number of rows in the report by setting selection criteria.

5. Under the **Property** heading, click the arrow, and then click **Process Number**.
6. Under the **Condition** heading, click the arrow, and then click **is greater than**.
7. Under the **Value** heading, type **0**.
8. Click the **Add** button to add your selections to the **Defined criteria** list.

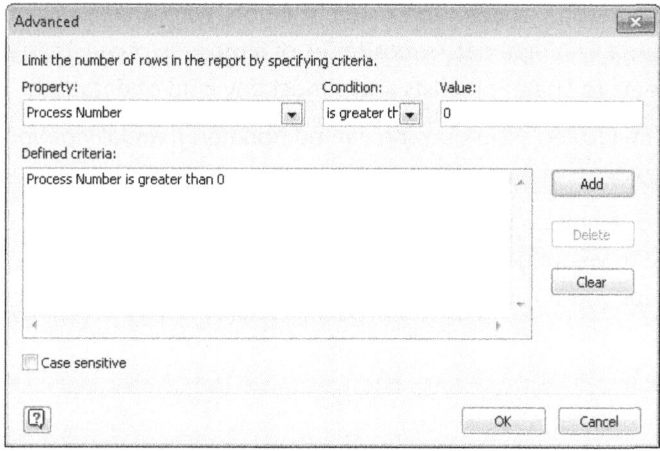

9. Click **OK**.
10. Click **Next** three times in the wizard, and then click **Finish** to save the updated report definition.
11. In the **Reports** dialog box, click **Run**.

12. Double-click **Visio shape**.

The modified version of the report appears without any blank rows. Compare this report to the one at the end of the preceding exercise.

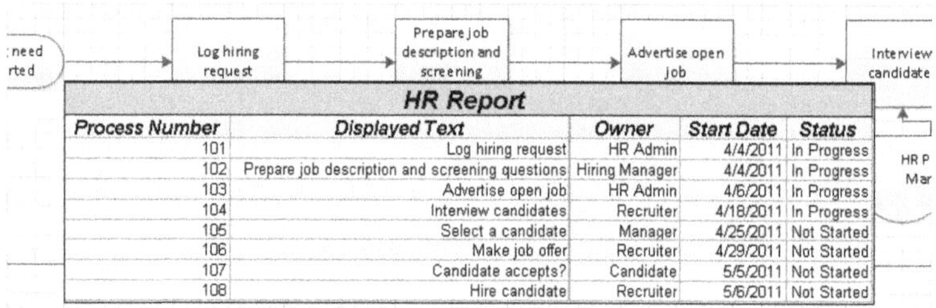

HR Report

Process Number	Displayed Text	Owner	Start Date	Status
101	Log hiring request	HR Admin	4/4/2011	In Progress
102	Prepare job description and screening questions	Hiring Manager	4/4/2011	In Progress
103	Advertise open job	HR Admin	4/6/2011	In Progress
104	Interview candidates	Recruiter	4/18/2011	In Progress
105	Select a candidate	Manager	4/25/2011	Not Started
106	Make job offer	Recruiter	4/29/2011	Not Started
107	Candidate accepts?	Candidate	5/5/2011	Not Started
108	Hire candidate	Recruiter	5/6/2011	Not Started

CLEAN UP Save and close the *HR Process Map Reports* drawing.

Tip It would be a good idea to experiment with the other buttons and option settings in the Report Definition Wizard while everything is fresh in your mind. There are many other ways that you can customize Visio reports.

Key Points

- Shape data exists in, or can be added to, any shape on a Visio drawing page. A growing percentage of Visio drawings are valuable not just because they are attractive pictures, but because they are visual representations of real-world data.
- Visio diagrams do not need to exist in isolation. You can link your drawings to personal or organizational data repositories of almost any type, ranging from simple spreadsheets to SharePoint lists and almost any kind of database.
- The data in a linked Visio drawing can be updated manually or you can schedule updates to occur at a preset time interval.
- Many Visio templates include predefined reports that you can run to export summarized data to webpages, Excel files, and other formats. In addition, the Visio Report wizard steps you through editing existing reports or creating your own.

Chapter at a Glance

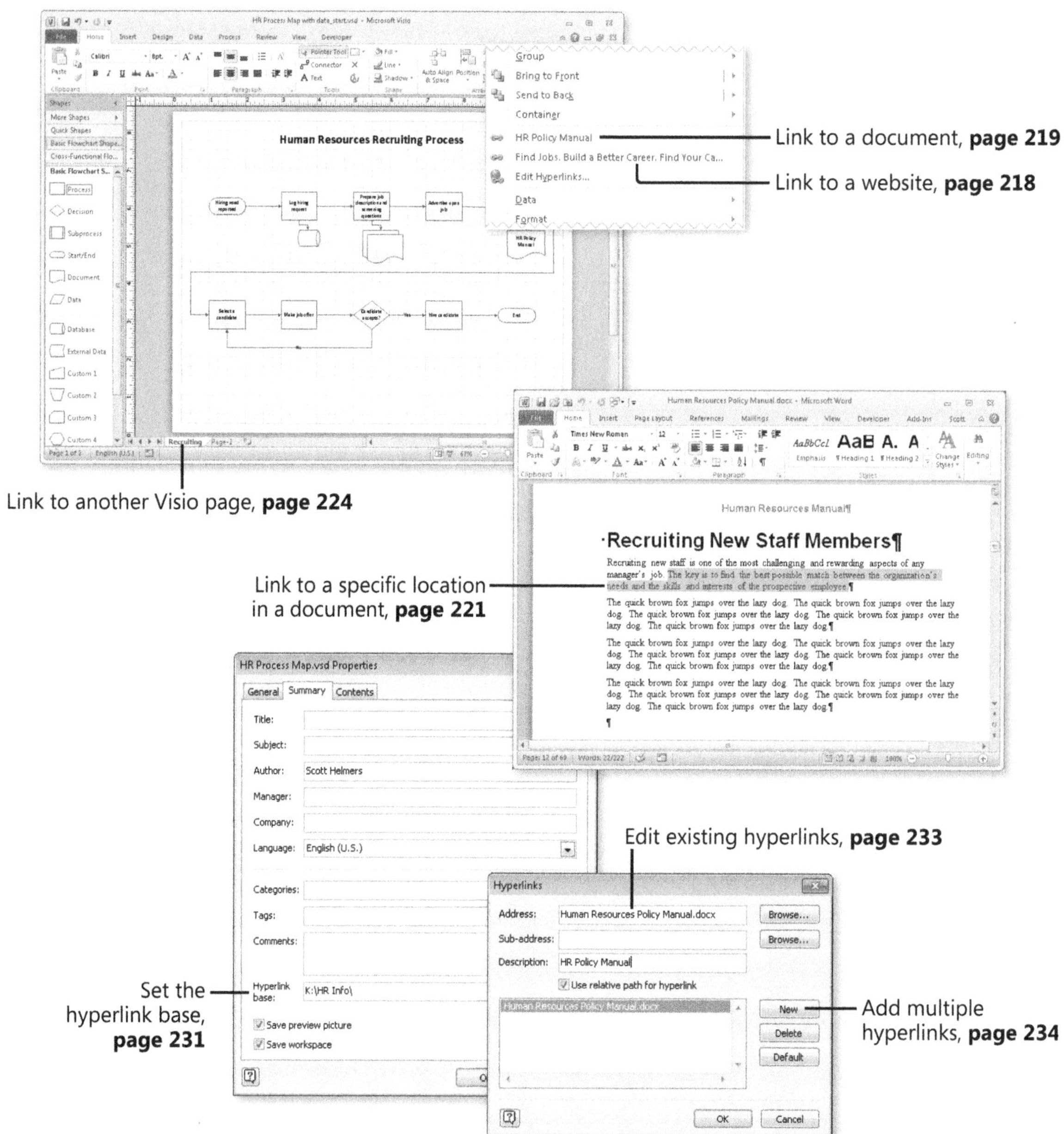

Link to a document, page 219
Link to a website, page 218
Link to another Visio page, page 224
Link to a specific location in a document, page 221
Edit existing hyperlinks, page 233
Set the hyperlink base, page 231
Add multiple hyperlinks, page 234
Human Resources Recruiting Process
Recruiting New Staff Members¶
HR Process Map.vsd Properties
Hyperlinks

7 Adding and Using Hyperlinks

In this chapter, you will learn how to

- ✔ Enhance diagrams by adding hyperlinks.
- ✔ Use hyperlinks.
- ✔ Link to a website, a document, a specific location in a document, or to another Visio page.
- ✔ Understand relative and absolute hyperlinks.
- ✔ Set the hyperlink base.
- ✔ Edit existing hyperlinks.
- ✔ Add multiple hyperlinks.

Aside from adding and using data in your drawings, one of the most significant ways to add value to a Microsoft Visio 2010 diagram is by adding hyperlinks. As you create or edit a drawing, try to anticipate what other resources your reader will require. With that in mind, create hyperlinks that lead the reader to documents, to webpages, to specific shapes elsewhere in the same or another Visio drawing—in short, to any location that will enhance the viewer's experience with your diagram.

A simple form of hyperlink might lead to another page in the same drawing, much like the off-page connector in the flowcharts you learned about in Chapter 4, "Drawing the Real World: Flowcharts and Organization Charts." More sophisticated hyperlinks can lead the reader to a specific cell in a Microsoft Excel spreadsheet, or to a particular phrase in a Microsoft Word document.

In this chapter, you will learn how to create both simple and sophisticated hyperlinks. You will learn how to use both relative and absolute links and to set the hyperlink base. You will also find out how to edit links and attach more than one link to the same shape.

Practice Files Before you can complete the exercises in this chapter, you need to copy the book's practice files to your computer. The practice files you'll use to complete the exercises in this chapter are in the Chapter07 practice files folder. A complete list of practice files is provided in "Using the Practice Files" at the beginning of this book.

Enhancing Diagrams by Adding Hyperlinks

Many business diagrams can be enhanced by adding hyperlinks. For example, if a step in your flowchart refers to a policy manual, add a link to the associated Word document or PDF. If your office layout is derived from a list of employees in Microsoft Access, link to the database. If the map of your new data center includes a move-in budget, link to the spreadsheet containing the budget.

One of the simplest ways to add a hyperlink to a Visio shape is to right-click the shape and click Hyperlink on the resulting context menu, which opens the Hyperlinks dialog box.

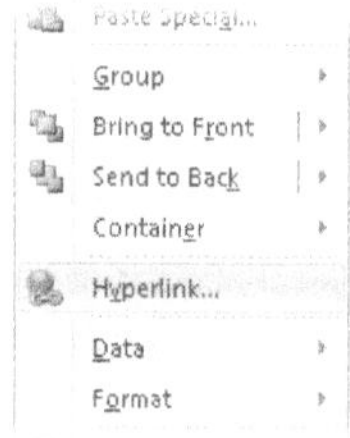

Hyperlink

Tip You can also open the Hyperlinks dialog box from the ribbon after selecting a Visio shape. On the Insert tab, in the Links group, click the Hyperlink button.

Keyboard Shortcut After selecting a Visio shape, you can open the Hyperlinks dialog box by pressing Ctrl+K. (This shortcut only works with the Ctrl key on the left side of the keyboard.)

In the exercises that follow, you will use the Hyperlinks dialog box to create multiple types of hyperlinks.

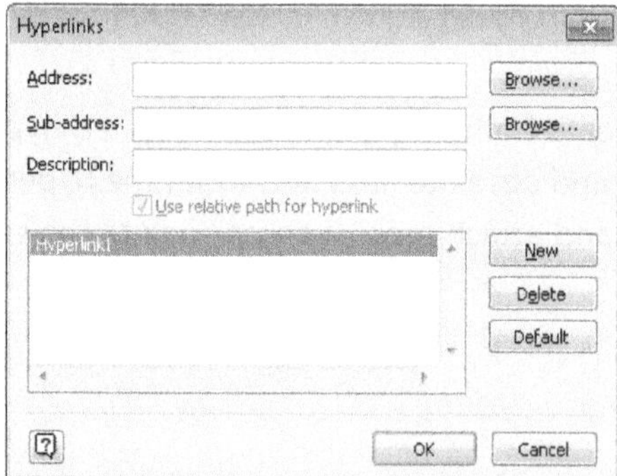

Using Hyperlinks

After you've created any type of hyperlink in a Visio drawing, you will notice several things:

- Moving the cursor over a hyperlinked object causes a hyperlink symbol to appear below the cursor (on the left in the following graphic).
- Pausing on a hyperlinked object displays a tooltip containing a description of the hyperlink (center graphic).
- Right-clicking a hyperlinked object displays the context menu, which includes a description of the hyperlink (right graphic).

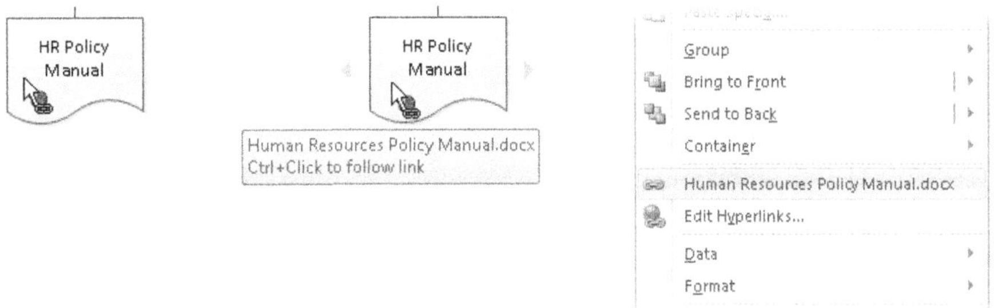

To follow a Visio hyperlink, simply right-click any hyperlinked shape, and then click the name of the hyperlink.

Keyboard Shortcut **You can also follow a hyperlink on a Visio shape by holding down the Ctrl key and clicking the shape, as indicated in the tooltip text shown in the middle of the previous graphic.**

If Visio warns that you are about to leave Visio and open another application, click Yes or OK as appropriate.

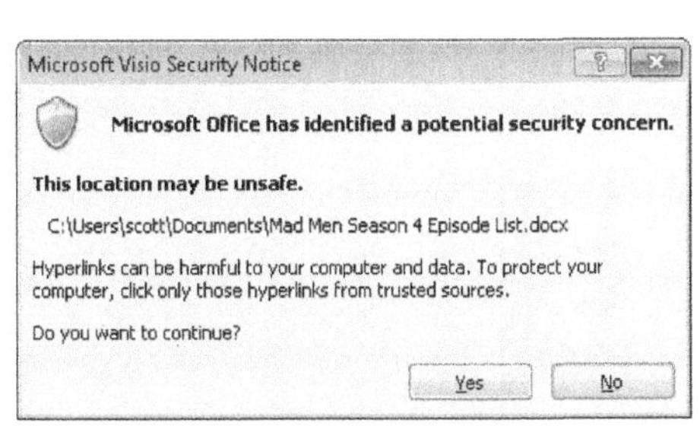

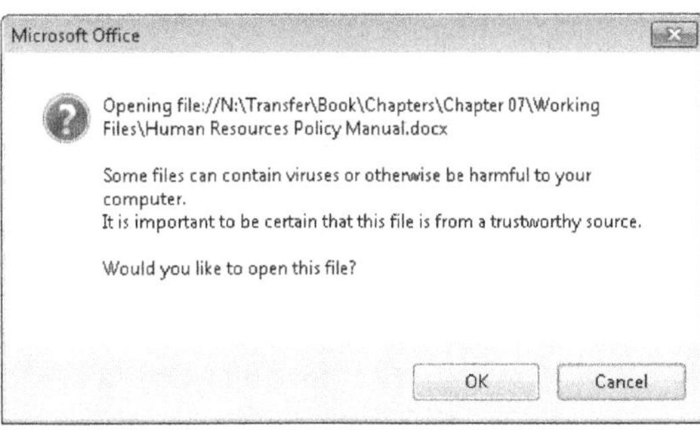

Tip **The dialog box on the left appears if the drawing containing the hyperlink has not yet been saved; the dialog box on the right appears when the file has been saved.**

Linking to a Website

In this exercise, you will create a hyperlink to a commercial website. You can use the same technique to create links to any website on the public World Wide Web as well as to sites on your organization's intranet.

SET UP You need the *HR Process Map_start* drawing located in the Chapter07 practice file folder to complete this exercise. Open the drawing in Visio and save it as *HR Process Map*. Then select the shape titled *Advertise open job* and open the Hyperlinks dialog box.

1. Click **Browse** to the right of **Address**.

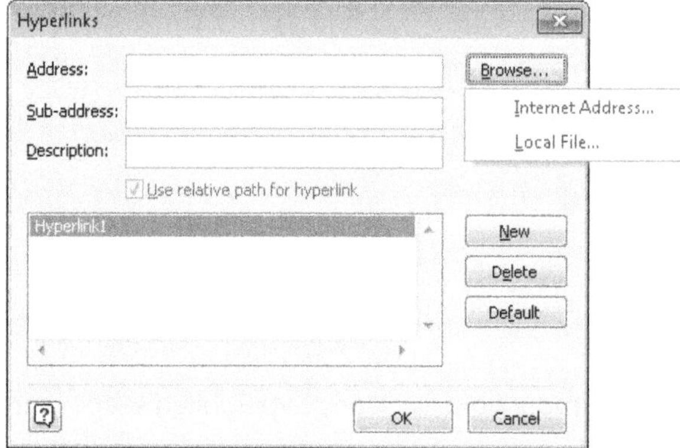

2. From the menu that appears, click **Internet Address.** Visio opens your web browser so you can provide the address of a website.
3. Navigate to www.monster.com.
4. Click the Visio icon on the Windows Task Bar to see that Visio has inserted the correct URL into the **Address** box.

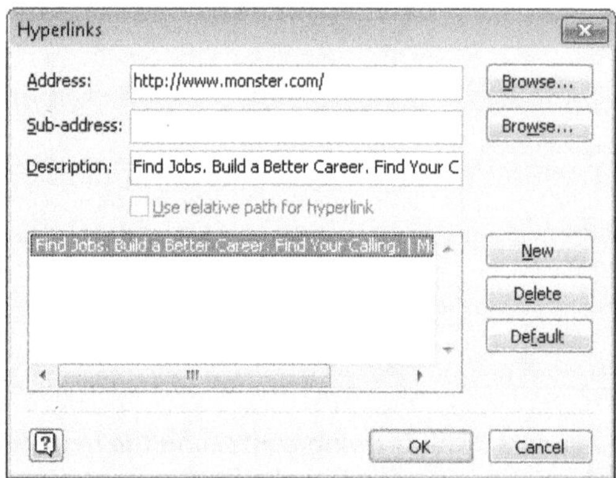

5. Click **OK**.

CLEAN UP Save your changes to the *HR Process Map* drawing but leave it open if you are continuing with the next exercise.

Now you can enjoy the result of the hyperlink by following the instructions in the "Using Hyperlinks" section earlier in this chapter.

Tip If your target webpage contains HTML bookmarks, you can include a bookmark in the address for the page. Clicking on this type of hyperlink will take the user directly to the part of the page containing the bookmark.

In addition to creating links to websites, you can also create hyperlinks to email addresses by prefixing the email address with *mailto:*.

Linking to a Document

In this exercise, you will create a link to a Microsoft Word document.

SET UP You need the *HR Process Map* drawing that you created in the preceding exercise. Either continue with the open copy of that file or open the *HR Process Map_start* drawing located in the Chapter07 practice file folder and save it as *HR Process Map*. When the map is open, select the document shape titled *HR Policy Manual* and then open the Hyperlinks dialog box.

1. Click **Browse** to the right of **Address**, and then click **Local File**.

   Tip The use of Local File by Visio is a bit of a misnomer. You can select files on your local hard drive, but you can also select files on a server, file share, or other nonlocal device.

2. Navigate to the Chapter07 practice files folder.

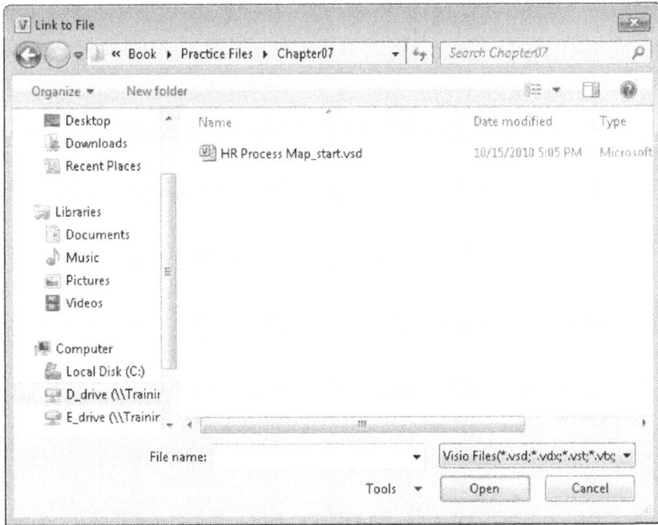

Important Note that Visio shows you only Visio files by default in the Link To File dialog box.

3. Click the box showing **Visio Files** to display a list of other file types.

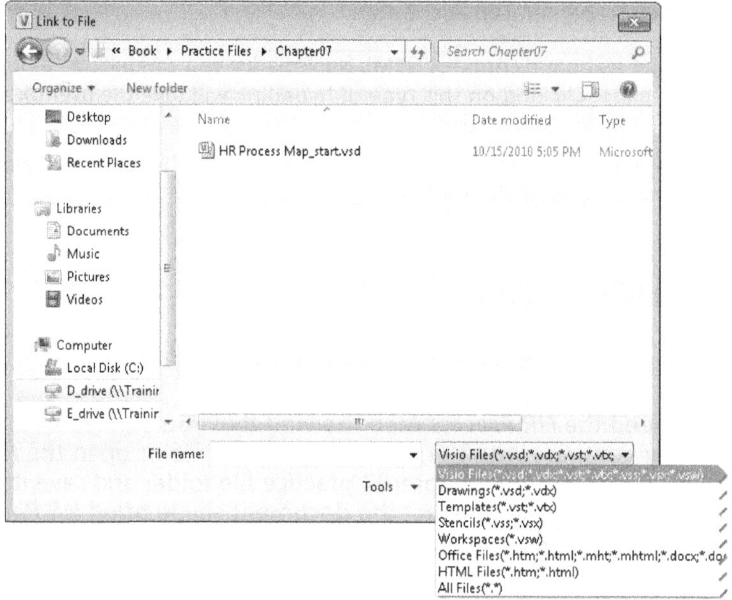

Tip Click All Files (*.*) in the list to see non-Visio and non–Microsoft Office files.

4. Click **Office Files** to display all types of Office documents located in this folder.

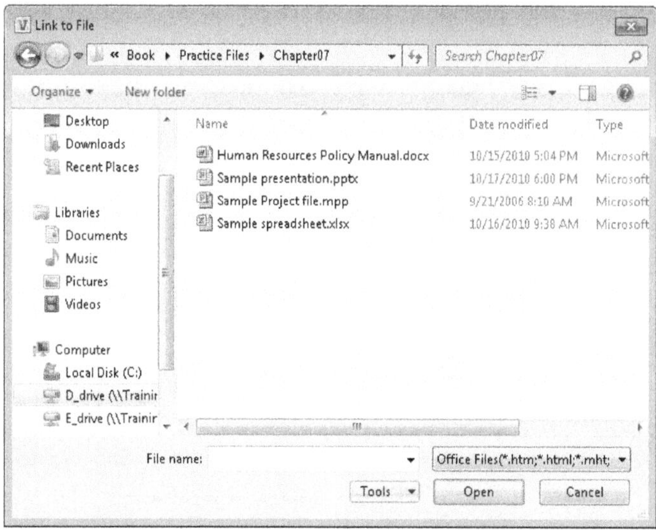

5. Click **Human Resources Policy Manual.docx**, and then click **Open**.

Visio shows the path to the target file in the Address box and places the target file name in the Description box.

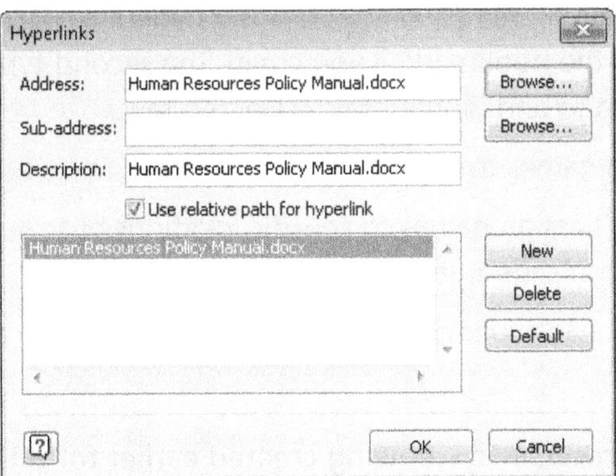

Tip **The text in the Description box will appear whenever the user points to the hyperlinked object in your Visio drawing. If the file name shown in the Description box is not what you want users to see, you can type any other text you prefer.**

6. Click **OK**.
7. Follow the hyperlink you've just created to prove that the Word document opens, and take note that it opens at the top of the document.

CLEAN UP **Save your changes to the *HR Process Map* drawing but leave it open if you are continuing with the next exercise. Close Word.**

Linking to a Specific Location in a Document

One of the underused but incredibly valuable features in Visio is the ability to link not just to a document, but to a specific location inside a document. Imagine a process map that refers to a policy manual at 17 different steps in the process. If each of those 17 hyperlinks merely opens the document at the cover page, you will leave the reader wondering where the relevant material resides in the document.

Imagine instead that each of the 17 hyperlinks moves the reader to a specific page or even to a particular word or phrase on that page. Accomplishing this is quite easy from Visio when you are armed with key knowledge about Word, Excel, and Microsoft PowerPoint. Keep in mind the following guidelines:

- For Word, the key is knowing that you can create named bookmarks in either of two ways:
  - You can assign a name to the location of the insertion point.

    - You can assign a name to a range of text—anything from one character to multiple paragraphs.

  If you create a bookmark in the first way, your Visio hyperlink will jump to the part of the page containing the bookmark; if you create the second type of bookmark, your hyperlink will jump to and highlight the selected text.

- In Excel, you can assign names to individual cells or to cell ranges.
- In PowerPoint, you can't assign names to specific locations but you can refer to slides either by number or slide title.

In this exercise, you will create and follow a hyperlink to a bookmark in a Word document.

SET UP You need the *HR Process Map* drawing created earlier for this exercise. Either continue with the open copy of that drawing or open the *HR Process Map_start* drawing located in the Chapter07 practice file folder and save it as *HR Process Map*. Drag a new document shape from the Basic Flowchart Shapes stencil in Visio and place it below the process box labeled *Hire candidate*. Finally, open the Hyperlinks dialog box.

1. Repeat Steps 1-5 in the preceding section titled "Linking to a Document."

   Important Do not close the Hyperlinks dialog box.

2. In the **Sub-address** text box, type **Recruiting**.

   Tip *Recruiting* is the name of a bookmark that already exists in the *Human Resources Policy Manual* document.

   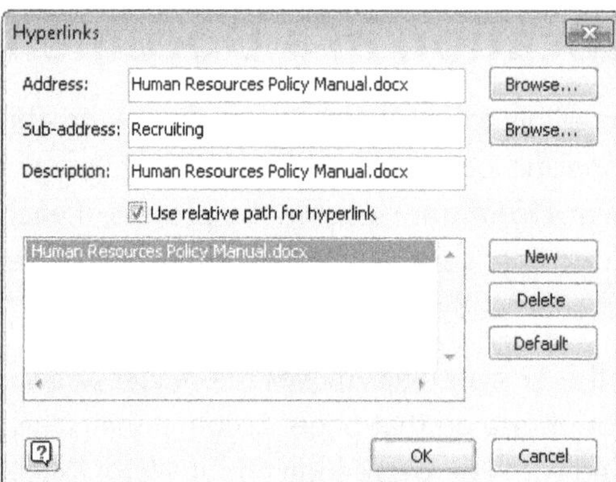

3. Click **OK**.
4. Follow the hyperlink you just created.

When you follow the hyperlink, you'll see that the bookmarked text is highlighted automatically in the resulting document window. In this example, notice that the highlighted text is located on page 12 (the page number is displayed in the status bar at the bottom of the Word window), a clear indication that you can guide the user of your Visio drawing to any part of a document.

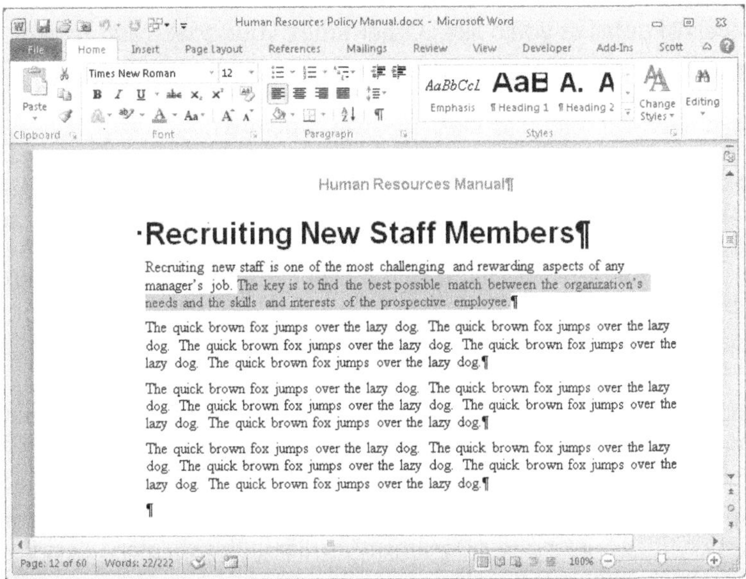

 **CLEAN UP Save your changes to the *HR Process Map* drawing but leave it open if you are continuing with the next exercise. Close Word.**

By using targeted hyperlinks, you can bring users of your Visio drawings directly to the one place in the document that is relevant to them at this moment.

Tip To link to a location in a Word document, create one or more bookmarks in the document first, and then use the bookmark name in the Sub-address field. For information about creating bookmarks in Word documents, refer to *Microsoft Word 2010 Step by Step* by Joyce Cox and Joan Lambert (Microsoft Press, 2010).

To link to a location in an Excel workbook, create one or more named cells or named cell ranges first, and then use the cell or range name in the Sub-address field. For information about creating named cells or ranges in Excel documents, refer to *Microsoft Excel 2010 Step by Step* by Curtis Frye (Microsoft Press, 2010).

To link to a location in a PowerPoint presentation, type either the slide number or slide title in the Sub-address field.

Linking to Another Visio Page

It is often helpful to link from a Visio shape on one page to another Visio page, whether the target page is in the same drawing or in a different drawing. Sometimes your goal is to achieve "drilldown," that is, to allow the reader to click a shape in a high-level view and be taken to the next lower level of detail. (You can continue to do this through as many levels of detail as you'd like.) Other times, your goal is just to take the reader to the next page or to related information on another page.

In this exercise, you will build Visio-to-Visio hyperlinks.

SET UP You need the *HR Process Map* drawing for this exercise. Either continue with the open copy of that drawing or open the *HR Process Map_start* drawing located in the Chapter07 practice file folder and save it as *HR Process Map*. When the drawing is open, select the process shape called *Hire candidate* and then open the Hyperlinks dialog box.

1. Leave the **Address** field blank.

   Important To link to another page in the Visio drawing you are currently editing, you *must* leave the Address field blank. If you do not leave this field blank and later decide to publish this map as a webpage, your hyperlink may not work.

   Tip If you want to link to a page in a different Visio diagram, complete Steps 1-3 in the section titled "Linking to a Document" earlier in this chapter, select the target Visio document, and then click OK.

2. Click **Browse** to the right of the **Sub-address** field. The Sub-address dialog box opens.
3. Click the arrow to the right of **Page**, and then click **Page-2** to select it as the name of the target page.

   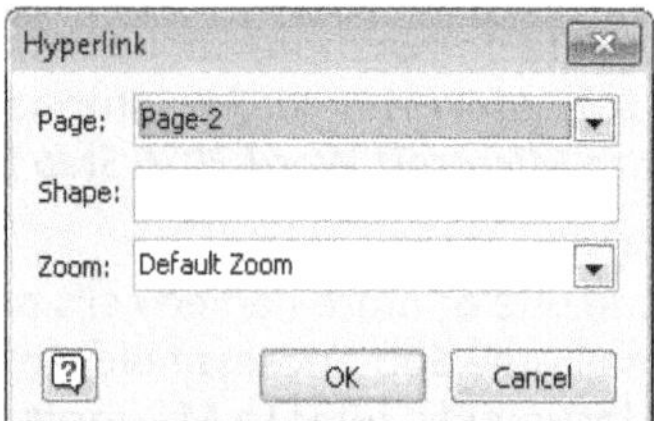

4. If you want to link to a specific shape on the target page, enter the shape name in the **Shape** text box.

   See Also For information about finding and using Visio shape names, see the sidebar titled "What Is a Shape Name? Where Do I Find It?" later in this chapter.

5. If you want to guide your reader to a specific page view, click the arrow to the right of **Zoom**, and then click a zoom level.

Tip The Zoom setting ensures that every time someone follows your hyperlink, that person will see the same view of the page. Select Page to show a full-page view, Width to show the full width of the page regardless of its height, and a percentage value to zoom in to that level of detail. If you don't select a zoom level, the user will see the target page at the same zoom level as the last time the page was viewed.

6. Click **OK**.

CLEAN UP Save your changes to the *HR Process Map* drawing but leave it open if you are continuing with the next exercise.

What Is a Shape Name? Where Do I Find It?

Every shape in a Visio drawing is referred to internally as a ***sheet***. Consequently, Visio shape names are often in the form *Sheet* or *Sheet.n*, where *n* is a number. Some shapes have names other than Sheet, so you will come across shapes names like *Process* or *Process.12*.

The easiest way to determine a shape's name is to run Visio in ***developer mode***, which adds the Developer tab to the ribbon. Follow these steps to determine a shape's name:

1. Turn on developer mode as described in the Appendix, and then select the target shape.

Shape Name

2. On the Developer tab, in the Shape Design group, click the Shape Name button to open the Shape Name dialog box.

3. Make note of, or copy, the text to the right of the Name text box, and then close the Shape Name dialog box.

Tip Another way to see the shape name is in the Shape Data window, which is described in the section titled "Viewing Shape Data" in Chapter 6, "Entering, Linking to, and Reporting on Data." As an example, look for the name *Process.4* in the title bar of the Shape Data window shown in the following graphic.

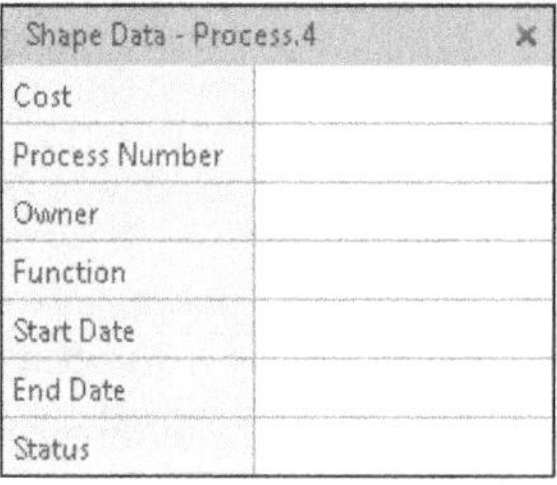

Understanding Relative and Absolute Hyperlinks

You may have noticed a Use Relative Path For Hyperlink check box in the Hyperlinks dialog box. If you're *very* observant, you may also have noticed that this check box is unavailable if you haven't yet saved your drawing, but is available and selected by default if your current drawing has been saved. What's this all about?

With Visio, you can build two types of links:

- **A relative link** provides a path to a resource by assuming a known starting location.

  As an analogy in the physical world, let's say you need to attend a meeting in room 216 at Lucerne Publishing. If you're standing at the reception desk in the lobby of the company's office and ask where the meeting is located, the receptionist might say, "Go up to the second floor and it's the second door on the right." Based on the known starting location you share with the receptionist, the lobby, that information is sufficient to get you to the intended location.

  Relative links in a Visio drawing work in a similar way. The folder containing the Visio drawing serves as "the lobby," and hyperlink targets on the same disk drive are found relative to that starting point.

  For Visio drawings, relative links work very nicely when the relationship between the starting point and the hyperlink targets remains fixed. Problems can arise, however, if you need to move the Visio drawing file to another computer or even to another location on the same computer. In this case, you must preserve the relative relationships from the new location of the Visio file to the target folders and files. One way you can accomplish this is by copying the entire directory structure containing the Visio drawing and its hyperlink targets.

- **An absolute link** contains all of the information required to locate a linked resource, regardless of the starting point.

  Returning to our meeting analogy, if you're at home and need directions to the conference room at Lucerne Publishing, you need a lot more information to arrive at your destination. An absolute address for the meeting room would look more like the following:

  Lucerne Publishing, Room 216, 3456 Elm St., San Francisco, CA 94117 USA

  Armed with an absolute address, you can get to the meeting from your home, or for that matter, from any starting location in the world.

  For Visio hyperlinks, absolute links work regardless of where your Visio drawing is located. You can move the drawing to a different computer and the links will continue to function without requiring any other changes.

Tip Relative and absolute hyperlinks are not mutually exclusive in a single drawing. In fact, many Visio drawings contain a mix of the two link types.

What does all of this have to do with the check box in the Visio Hyperlinks dialog box?

For a saved drawing, Visio assumes that the path to the target of a hyperlink begins in the same folder that contains the Visio drawing. Thus, the default behavior in Visio is to create a relative hyperlink using the location of your Visio drawing as the starting point for the path. When someone clicks your hyperlink, Windows figures out where the target object is by navigating from the location of the Visio drawing.

Just knowing this much explains why the Use Relative Path For Hyperlink check box is unavailable if you haven't yet saved your drawing—Visio can't create a relative link yet because there is no known starting point for the Visio drawing. Consequently, the only option is to use an absolute path that contains all of the information Windows will need to track down the target object.

Although there are no absolute guidelines on when to use relative links rather than absolute links, it's a good idea to think about your environment and the nature of your document collection before creating very many links in Visio. If all of your target documents are in their final resting place, on a network server, for example, then absolute links probably make the most sense. However, if your environment is more volatile, or you know in advance that you'll be moving your Visio drawing and its hyperlink targets to another computer or to a CD or DVD, then carefully constructed relative links are a good choice.

In addition to that advice, the following examples will help you to understand when Visio creates relative or absolute links.

Important **When you use the Hyperlinks dialog box to browse to and select a target document, Visio fills in the Address box and selects the Use Relative Path For Hyperlink check box based on the locations of the Visio drawing and the target document.**

For the examples that follow, assume that the *HR Process Maps* drawing, is saved in C:\Human Resources\Process Maps\ and that the hyperlink target is one of the Word documents shown in the following directory listing.

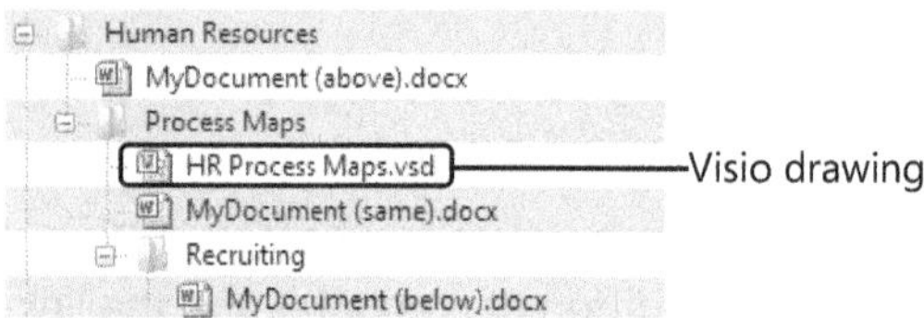

Tip **The file name of each Word document includes a parenthetical note to indicate whether it is in a directory above or below the Visio document, or is in the same directory.**

- When the target document is in the same folder as *HR Process Maps.vsd*, which obviously means that it is on the same disk drive as the Visio drawing, Visio creates a relative hyperlink and the Address box contains the following:

  MyDocument (same).docx

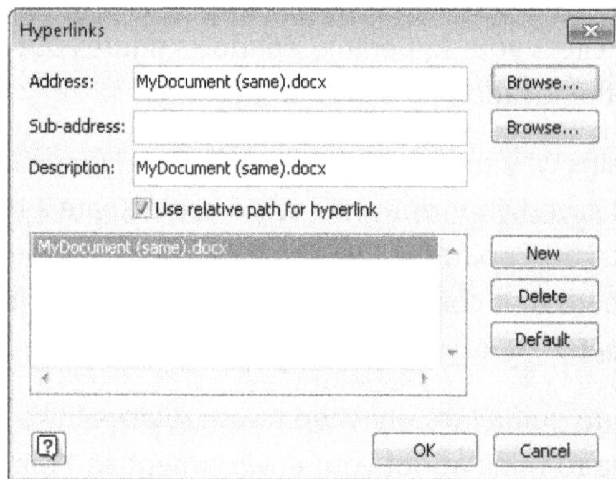

If you now clear the Use Relative Path For Hyperlink check box, the link becomes an absolute link that begins at the root of drive C. The Address box displays the full path to the document:

C:\Human Resources\Process Maps\MyDocument (same).docx

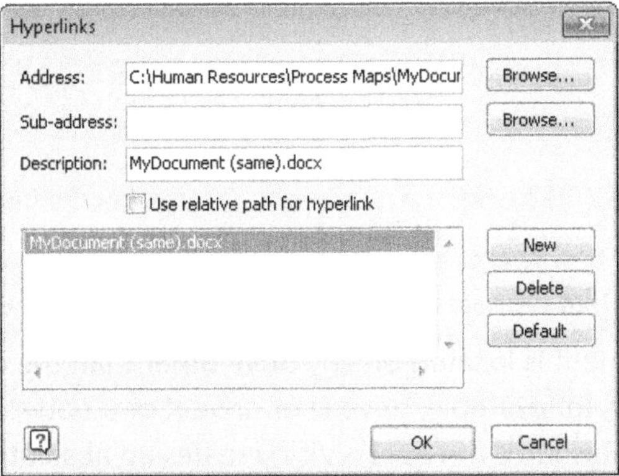

- When you link to a document located in C:\Human Resources\Process Maps \Recruiting\, which is a subfolder of the one containing the Visio drawing, Visio creates a relative hyperlink and the Address box contains the following:

  Recruiting\MyDocument (below).docx

  This indicates that the target document is in a folder called *Recruiting*.

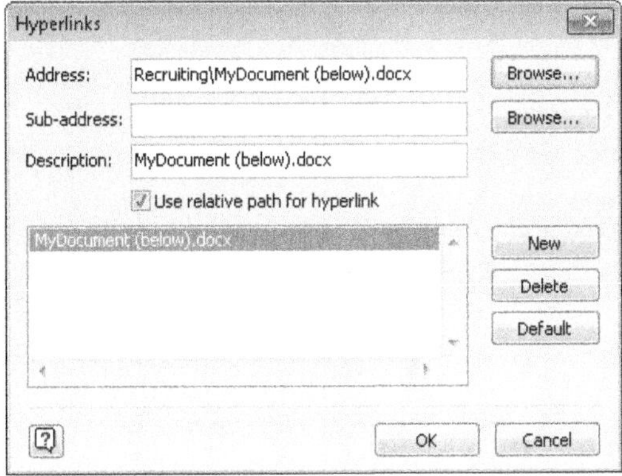

- When the target document is located in C:\Human Resources\, which is above the folder containing the Visio document, Visio creates a relative hyperlink and the Address box contains the following:

  ..\MyDocument (above).docx

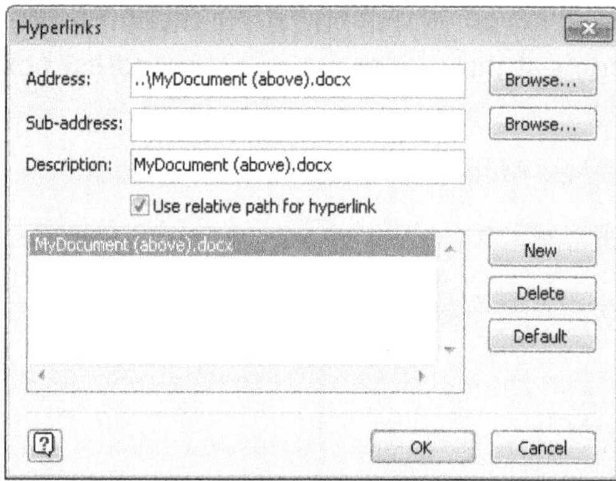

Tip "..\" is arcane syntax that predates Windows. It means "go up one directory level."

- When the target document is located on any drive other than the one containing the Visio document, for example, drive D or drive K or a network share such as \\MyServer\Human Resources\FY2011\, Visio creates an absolute link and the Address box contains something like the following:

  D:\SomeFolder\MyDocument.docx

  or

  \\MyServer\Human Resources\FY2011\MyDocument.docx

  The following figure shows a target document on drive N.

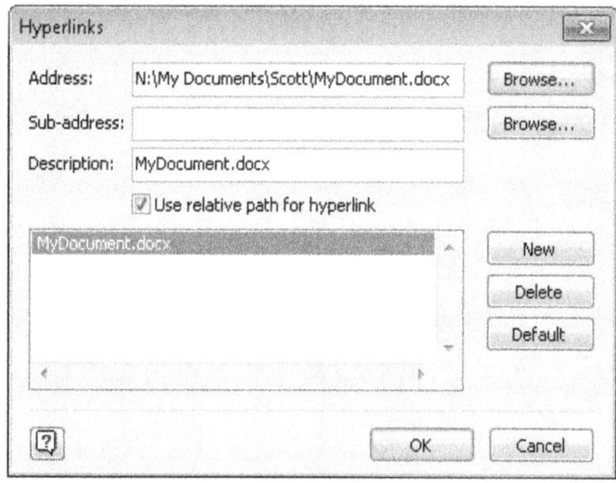

Tip Although the link shown in the previous graphic is an absolute link because the target object is located on a network drive, the Use Relative Path For Hyperlink check box still appears with a check mark. Just to confuse things further, if you try to clear the check box, you will find that you can't do so.

Important You can only create relative links to files that are located on the same physical hard drive as the saved Visio drawing.

Tip Visio always creates an absolute link if you begin your address with a server name, drive letter, or web protocol. All of the following will create absolute links regardless of the location of the Visio drawing:

- C:\SomeFolder\MyWorkbook.xlsx
- \\MyServer\Presentations\MySlideShow.pptx
- *http://MyWebSite.com/Somepage.html*

Setting the Hyperlink Base

One additional factor affects relative links in Visio: each Visio drawing has a property called the ***hyperlink base*** that is blank by default. Its purpose is to allow you to shift all relative links in a document from one location to another, perhaps because you want to move an entire collection of documents to a new server. If you enter a value for the hyperlink base, Visio will prepend all relative links in the document with the value in that field.

You set the hyperlink base using options in the Backstage view. For the sake of the next exercise, let's assume you want to change the hyperlink base to the following because your drawing contains relative links and you've moved all hyperlinked resources to that folder:

K:\HR Info

In this exercise, you will change the hyperlink base for a Visio drawing.

SET UP **You need the *HR Process Map* drawing for this exercise. Either continue with the open copy of that map or open the *HR Process Map_start* drawing located in the Chapter07 practice file folder and save it as *HR Process Map.***

1. Click the **File** tab to display the Backstage view.

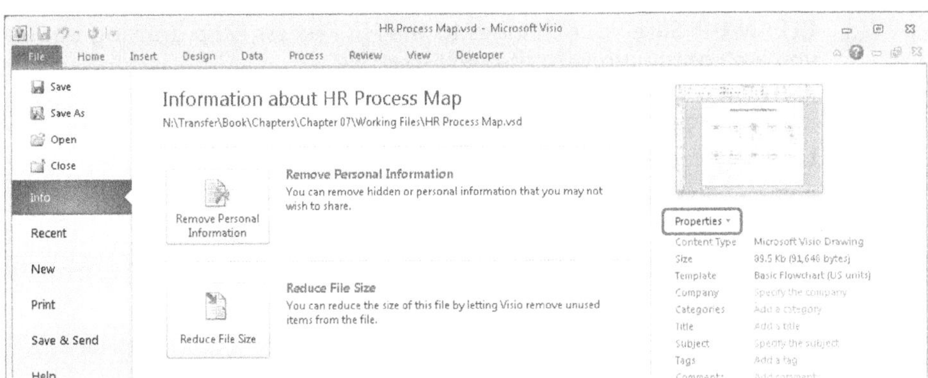

2. On the right side of the screen, under the diagram thumbnail in the upper right of the page, click the **Properties** button. On the menu that appears, click **Advanced Properties**.
3. In the **Hyperlink base** text box, type **K:\HR Info**.

Important Be sure to include a trailing backslash when you enter a hyperlink base.

4. Click **OK**.

   From now on, the physical location of your Visio drawing is no longer the starting point for relative hyperlinks. Instead, Visio will construct each hyperlink from the combination of K:\HR Info\ plus the path portion of the relative hyperlink.

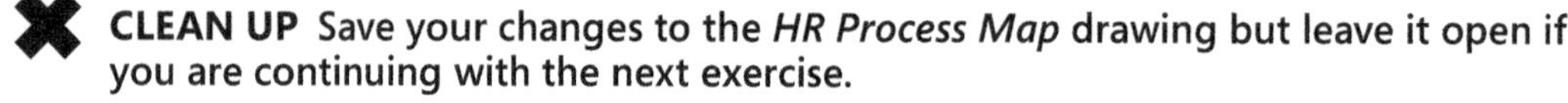

CLEAN UP Save your changes to the *HR Process Map* drawing but leave it open if you are continuing with the next exercise.

In this exercise, you created a hyperlink base for a location on a disk drive. The hyperlink base field can also be used to establish a base for web hyperlinks. For example, if you enter a hyperlink base such as the following:

http://OurIntranet/Finance/

and create a relative hyperlink of:

AuditInfo.html

Visio will combine the two to create a link of:

http://OurIntranet/Finance/AuditInfo.html

Tip There is only one hyperlink base per Visio document. Consequently, if you create either a directory path hyperlink base or a web-based hyperlink base, Visio will use it for *all* relative links in your document. You must be extremely careful when establishing a hyperlink base in a diagram.

Editing Existing Hyperlinks

You can both edit and delete existing hyperlinks.

In this exercise, you will change the description of an existing hyperlink.

SET UP You need the *HR Process Map* drawing for this exercise. Either continue with the open copy of that map or open the *HR Process Map_start* drawing located in the Chapter07 practice file folder and save it as *HR Process Map*. When the drawing is open, select the document shape called *HR Policy Manual* and then open the Hyperlinks dialog box.

Tip If you use the right-click method to open the Hyperlinks dialog box, you might notice that the menu entry that formerly said Hyperlink now says Edit Hyperlinks.

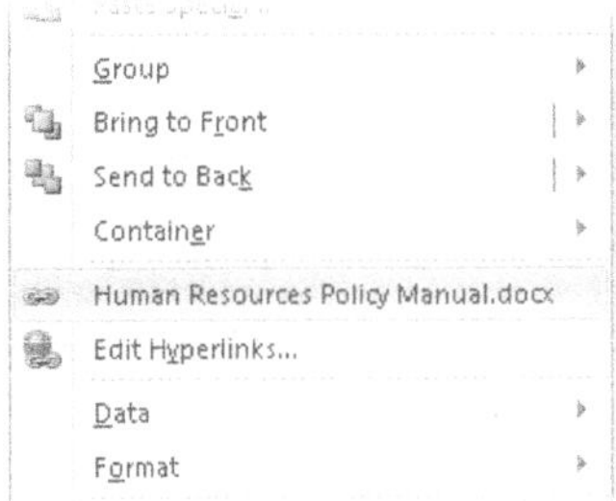

1. Select the hyperlink you want to change if it is not already selected. When it is selected, the hyperlink's details will appear in the appropriate boxes at the top of the **Hyperlinks** dialog box.
2. In the **Description** text box, type **HR Policy Manual**.

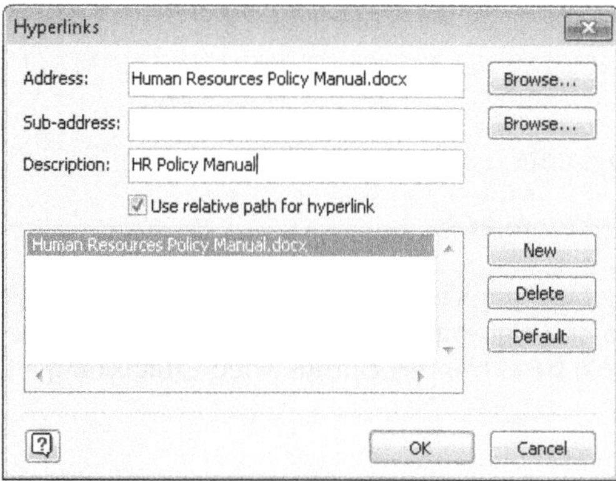

3. Click **OK**.

   The next time you point to or right-click the hyperlinked shape, you will see the new description text.

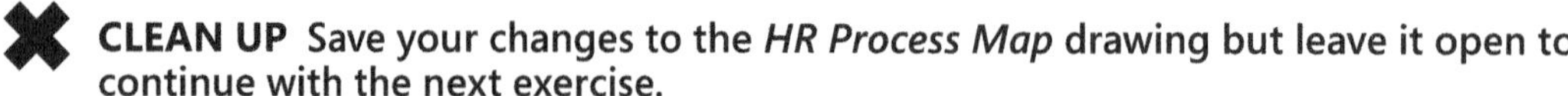

CLEAN UP **Save your changes to the *HR Process Map* drawing but leave it open to continue with the next exercise.**

Tip You can change the hyperlink destination for any existing link by clicking the Browse button to the right of the Address text box whenever you have the Hyperlinks dialog box open.

You can delete a hyperlink by selecting it in the Hyperlinks dialog box, and then clicking the Delete button.

Adding Multiple Hyperlinks

You can add more than one hyperlink to any object in Visio, offering your reader a choice of places to go or documents to view.

In this exercise, you will add a second hyperlink to a shape that already contains a hyperlink.

SET UP **Open the copy of the *HR Process Map* drawing that you saved in the previous exercise if it is not still open. After opening this drawing, select the document shape called *HR Policy Manual* and then open the Hyperlinks dialog box.**

1. Click the **New** button.

   Hyperlink2 appears below HR Policy Manual in the Hyperlinks dialog box.

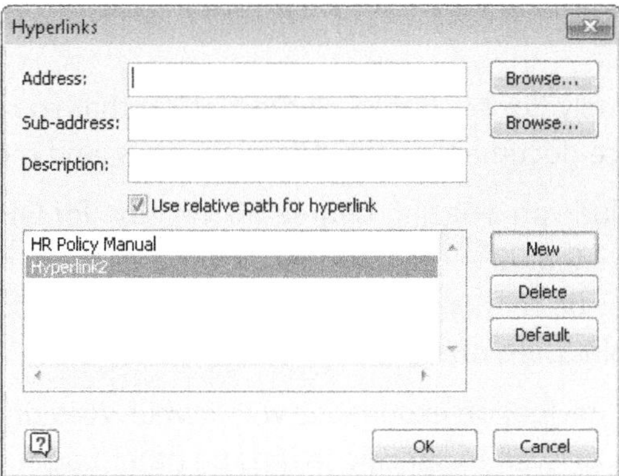

2. Create a hyperlink using any of the techniques described earlier in this chapter, and then click **OK**.

   If you've added more than one hyperlink to a shape, Visio notifies you of their existence when you pause on the linked shape.

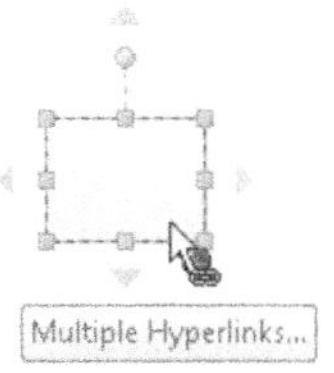

   Visio also displays the description of each hyperlink when you right-click a linked object. Notice that the previous link, HR Policy Manual, is now followed by the title of a web hyperlink.

 **CLEAN UP** Save and close the *HR Process Map* drawing.

Key Points

- Visio contains an extremely flexible hyperlink mechanism that you can use to create links to webpages, Office documents, other Visio drawings, and more.
- Your hyperlinks can include an amazing degree of precision for Office documents. You can easily build links that take users to specific phrases or sections of text in a Word document; to specific cells or cell ranges in an Excel workbook; and to specific slides in a PowerPoint presentation.
- You can enhance users' navigation experience within your Visio drawings by building links to other pages or even to specific shapes on other pages. This allows users to do things like "drill down" to a lower level of detail in a network diagram, or easily flip from page to page in a multipage drawing.
- Visio supports both relative and absolute hyperlinks, allowing you to create drawings that are connected to resources in a fixed location, or to create a portable Visio library that can be moved to another disk drive or be copied to a CD or DVD.
- Any Visio shape can include multiple hyperlinks, making it simple for you to build content-rich drawings that guide your readers to a variety of relevant resources.

Chapter at a Glance

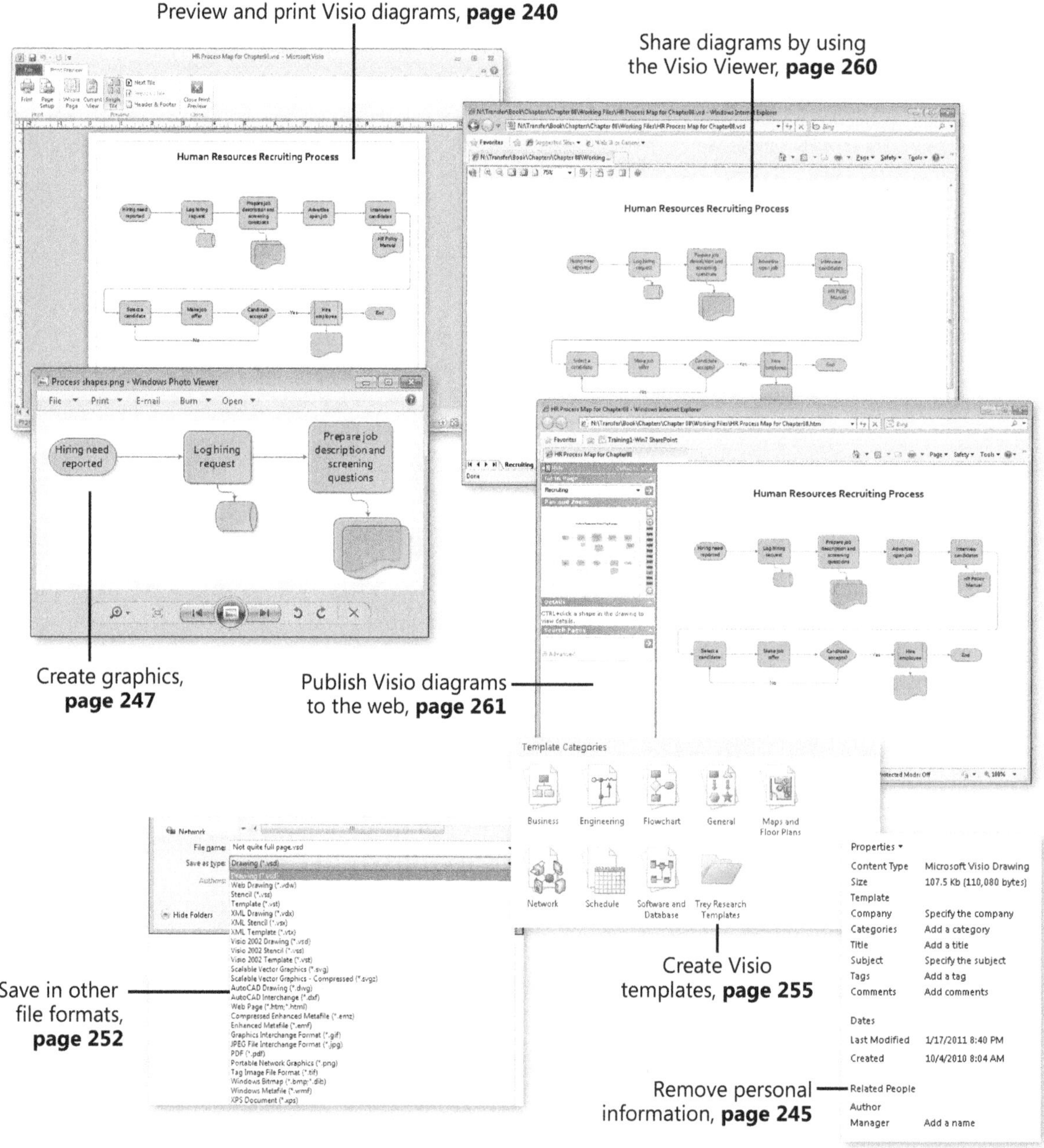

Preview and print Visio diagrams, **page 240**
Share diagrams by using the Visio Viewer, **page 260**
Create graphics, **page 247**
Publish Visio diagrams to the web, **page 261**
Save in other file formats, **page 252**
Create Visio templates, **page 255**
Remove personal information, **page 245**

8 Sharing and Publishing Diagrams: Part 1

In this chapter, you will learn how to

- ✔ Preview and print Visio diagrams.
- ✔ Remove personal information.
- ✔ Create graphics.
- ✔ Save in other file formats.
- ✔ Create Visio templates.
- ✔ Share diagrams by using the Visio Viewer.
- ✔ Publish Visio diagrams to the web.

When you've worked hard to create a Microsoft Visio 2010 diagram, the chances are extremely good that you want to share it with other people. Sometimes you may just want to share a printout, but in many cases, you want to share all or part of your diagram in electronic form. Visio has long provided an extensive list of "save as" alternatives, and the list is even longer with Visio 2010.

In this chapter, you will learn how to use the diagram preview mode in Visio and then how to print Visio diagrams. You will learn about the private information that Visio stores and discover how to remove it from diagrams you want to share electronically. Then you'll create graphics from all or some of the shapes on a drawing page and will save drawings in various file formats, including creating a new Visio template. Finally, you'll learn how people without Visio can view your drawings by using the Visio Viewer and by using a web browser when you publish diagrams as webpages.

Practice Files Before you can complete the exercises in this chapter, you need to copy the book's practice files to your computer. The practice files you'll use to complete the exercises in this chapter are in the Chapter08 practice files folder. A complete list of practice files is provided in "Using the Practice Files" at the beginning of this book.

Previewing and Printing Visio Diagrams

In this exercise, you will explore several options for previewing and printing your document.

SET UP You need the *HR Process Map for Chapter08_start* drawing located in the Chapter08 practice file folder to complete this exercise. Open the drawing in Visio and save it as *HR Process Map for Chapter08*.

1. On the **File** tab, click **Print** to display the **Print** page of the Backstage view.

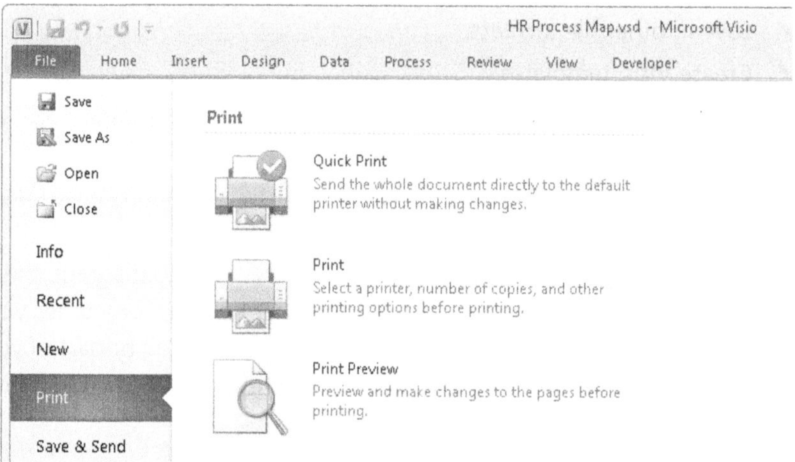

Tip Though you won't use it in this exercise, note that the Quick Print button prints the entire current document to the default printer.

Print Preview

2. On the **Print** page, click **Print Preview**.

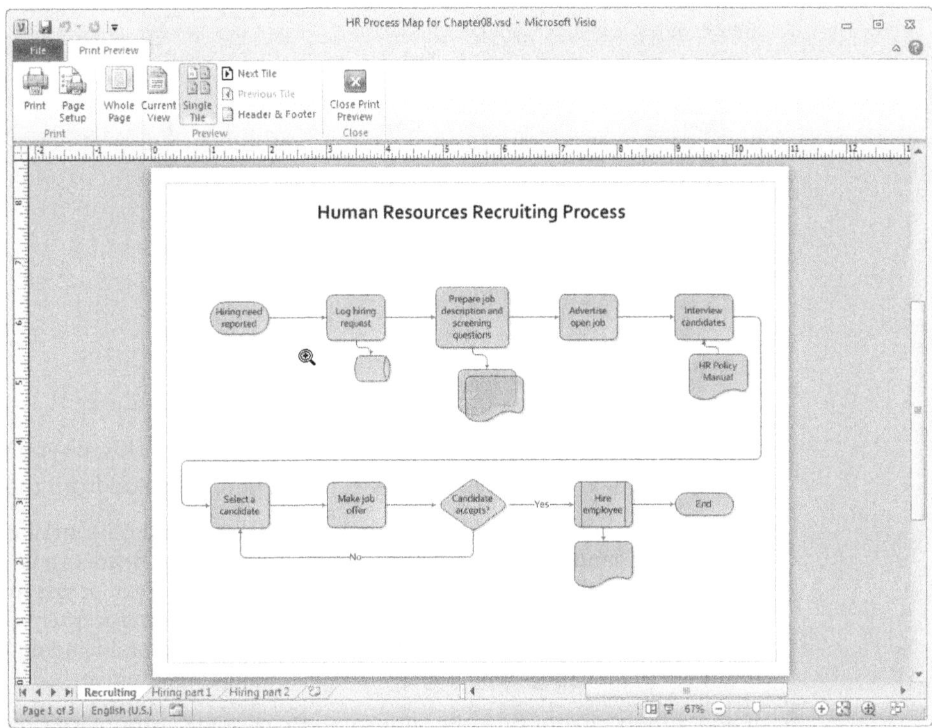

If you like what you see in the preview window, click the Print button in the Print group.

Tip Notice that the cursor, located between *Hiring need reported* and *Log hiring request*, has turned into a magnifying glass with a plus sign, indicating that when you click anywhere on the preview page, Visio will zoom in. After zooming in, the magnifying glass will contain a minus sign, indicating that the next click will zoom out.

Next Tile

3. In the **Preview** group, click the **Next Tile** button to view the next page of the drawing in preview mode.

   Tip The use of the word *tile* in this context will become clearer in Step 9.

   You can also move among pages by clicking the page name tabs at the bottom of the print preview window.

Header & Footer

4. In the **Preview** group, click the **Header & Footer** button to open the **Header and Footer** dialog box, which allows you to set a three-part header or footer for this document.

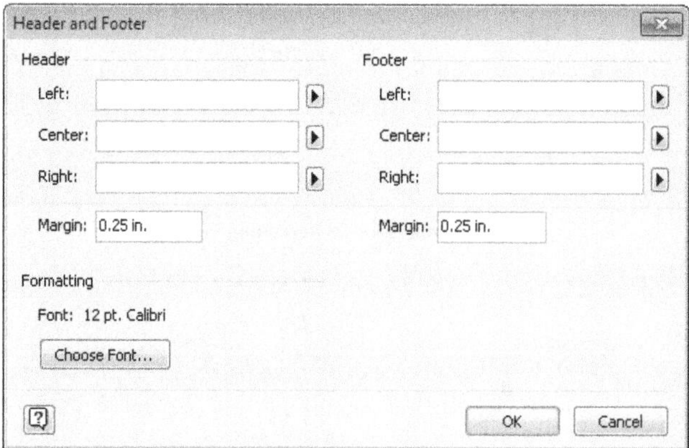

You can type text into any of the Header and Footer fields, or you can click the right arrow next to each field to select a predefined value from the list.

Tip Headers and footers print information on the top and bottom of each printer page and are independent of the drawing page. Consequently, headers and footers can be useful for Visio diagrams in which the drawing page is spread across multiple printer pages. They are used infrequently for the majority of Visio documents where each drawing page prints on a single printer page. In those cases, including header or footer information on background pages is a more common technique.

5. If you added header or footer information, click **OK**; otherwise click **Cancel**.

Close Print Preview

6. On the **Print Preview** tab, in the **Close** group, click the **Close Print Preview** button.

   Keyboard Shortcut You can also close the print preview by pressing the Esc key.

7. Click the **End** shape and drag it off the page to the right, causing Visio to create a new page.

   Important Performing the actions in this step and the next one creates a Visio diagram that is larger than one printer page so you can see the effect this has on print preview and printing.

8. Click the document shape below the **Hire employee** shape and drag it off the bottom of the page. Visio expands the drawing page to accommodate the new location.

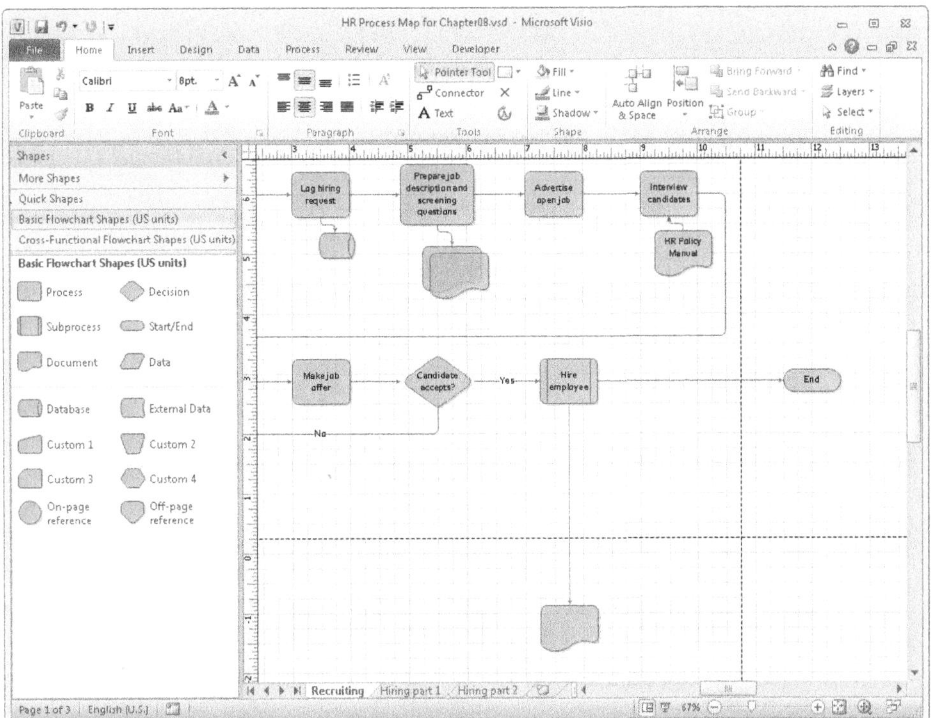

9. On the **File** tab, click **Print**, and then click **Print Preview**.

Keyboard Shortcut You can also open the print preview window by typing Alt+F, P, V (File, Print, Preview).

The default view shows the full drawing page divided into printer page–sized ***tiles***. As you move the cursor over any ***print tile***, Visio highlights it with a red border.

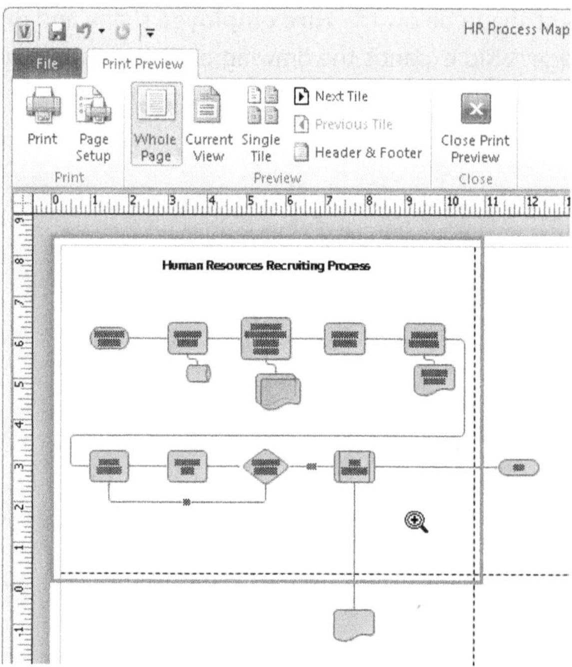

Tip Depending on the ratio between drawing page size and printer page size, you will see either multiple tiles per drawing page (as in the previous graphic) or a single tile per page (as shown in the graphic on page 241).

You can adjust what you see in the preview window by using several buttons on the ribbon:

Single Tile

- Click the **Single Tile** button in the **Preview** group to view just one print tile.
- Click the **Next Tile** or **Previous Tile** button to move forward or backward in the collection of print tiles.

Current View

- Click the **Current View** button in the **Preview** group to change the print preview to reflect the location and zoom setting of the ***active page*** in the Visio drawing.

Whole Page

- Click the **Whole Page** button to see all tiles for a single drawing page.

10. On the **Print Preview** tab, in the **Close** group, click the **Close Print Preview** button.

Print

11. On the **File** tab, click **Print**, and then click the **Print** button to open a standard print dialog box.
12. Click **OK** to print or click **Cancel** to close the dialog box without printing.

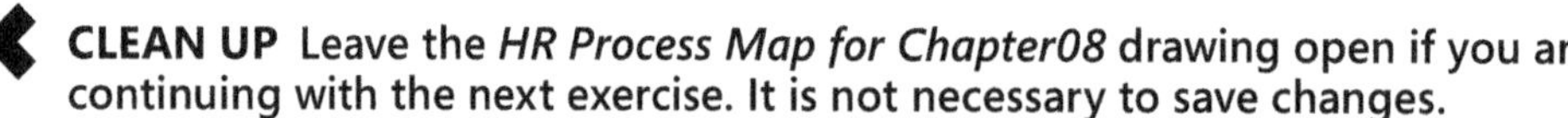
CLEAN UP Leave the *HR Process Map for Chapter08* drawing open if you are continuing with the next exercise. It is not necessary to save changes.

Removing Personal Information

Every Visio document contains a collection of metadata about the document itself. Some of the data fields are supplied by Visio; some are prefilled based on the template from which you create a document; most are blank. You examine and change metadata fields in a document's Properties dialog box, which is accessed by clicking the Properties button on the Info page of the File tab. The Properties dialog box is shown in the following graphic.

When you plan to share your Visio drawing in electronic form, you may want to remove personally identifiable information first.

In this exercise, you will remove personal information from a Visio diagram.

SET UP If the *HR Process Map for Chapter08* drawing is not open from the preceding exercise, open the *HR Process Map for Chapter08_start* drawing located in the Chapter08 practice file folder and save it as *HR Process Map for Chapter08*.

1. Click the **File** tab.

   By default, Visio opens to the Info page when you click the File tab (as described in Chapter 1, "A Visual Orientation to a Visual Product.") The Info page shows the location of the current drawing on disk, the document properties, and the Remove Personal Information and Reduce File Size buttons. The outlined section in the lower right of the following graphic contains the Company, Author, and Manager's names.

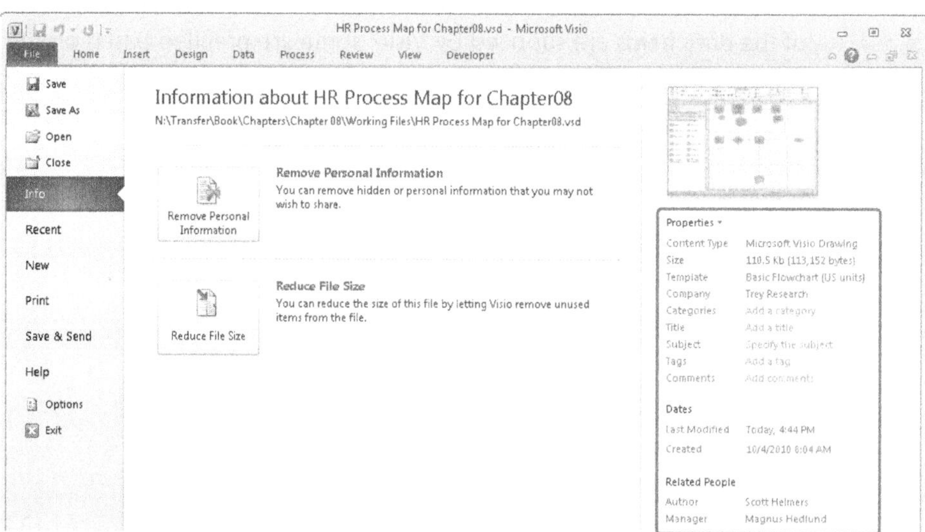

Remove Personal Information

2. Click the **Remove Personal Information** button. The Remove Hidden Information dialog box opens.

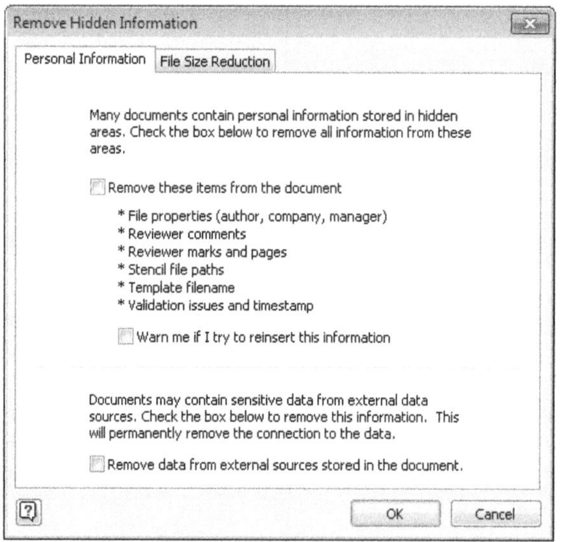

This dialog box offers three check boxes:

- **Remove these items from the document** Removes author, company, and other information shown in the Properties area of the Info page

- ❍ **Warn me if I try to reinsert this information** Protects you if you inadvertently add personal details back to the document after removing them
- ❍ **Remove data from external sources stored in the document** Removes private information from data sources to which this diagram has been linked using the techniques described in Chapter 6, "Entering, Linking to, and Reporting on Data"

3. Select **Remove these items from the document**, and then click **OK**.

   Compare the following graphic with the outlined area of the graphic shown in Step 1. You'll see that the Company, Author, and Manager names have all been removed.

Properties ▾	
Content Type	Microsoft Visio Drawing
Size	107.5 Kb (110,080 bytes)
Template	
Company	Specify the company
Categories	Add a category
Title	Add a title
Subject	Specify the subject
Tags	Add a tag
Comments	Add comments
Dates	
Last Modified	1/17/2011 8:40 PM
Created	10/4/2010 8:04 AM
Related People	
Author	
Manager	Add a name

CLEAN UP **Leave the *HR Process Map for Chapter08* drawing open if you are continuing with the next exercise; otherwise, close it without saving your changes.**

Creating Graphics

The collection of "Save As" file types in Visio is extensive and includes options to create the following image types:

- **JPEG** Joint Photographic Experts Group
- **GIF** Graphic Interchange Format
- **PNG** Portable Network Graphic
- **TIFF** Tagged Image File Format

- **SVG** Scalable Vector Graphics
- **WMF** Windows Metafile
- **EMF** Enhanced Metafile
- **BMP** Bitmapped Picture

Tip If you need a detailed description of any of these file formats, you can find plenty of information on the Internet. For example, the Wikipedia article at *en.wikipedia.org/wiki/Image_file_formats* describes most of the formats in the previous list.

Creating images in Visio is a shape-oriented, not a page-oriented, operation. To say that another way, Visio does not provide a built-in method to create an image of an entire page. If you create a graphic by clicking Save As for the current page, Visio will create an image that is only as big as the rectangle surrounding all shapes on the page. White space between that shape rectangle and the page boundaries will not be included. You will see an example of this behavior in the first steps of the following exercise and will also learn an easy workaround for this limitation.

In this exercise, you will create JPEG and PNG images from a Visio drawing.

SET UP If the *HR Process Map for Chapter08* drawing is not open from the preceding exercise, open the *HR Process Map for Chapter08_start* drawing located in the Chapter08 practice file folder and save it as *HR Process Map for Chapter08*. Set the Recruiting page to whole page view.

Save As

1. On the **File** tab, click **Save As**.

   Keyboard Shortcut You can also open the Save As dialog box by pressing Alt+F, A.

2. In the **File name** field, type **Not quite full page**.
3. Click the **Save as type** arrow to display the list of file formats in which you can save all or part of a Visio drawing. The list includes the image file types mentioned in the list prior to this exercise, along with additional file types that will be discussed in subsequent exercises.

   Tip Visio uses a standard Windows Save As dialog box. Although it is not shown in the following graphic, in the upper part of the dialog box, you can change the folder in which the image file will be saved. The default save location is the same folder that contains the Visio drawing.

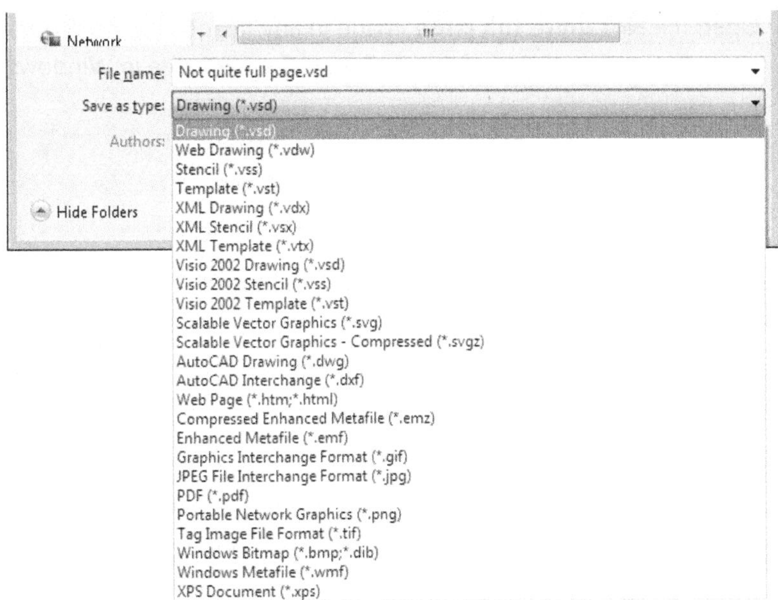

4. Click **JPEG File Interchange Format**, and then click **Save**. The JPG Output Options dialog box opens.

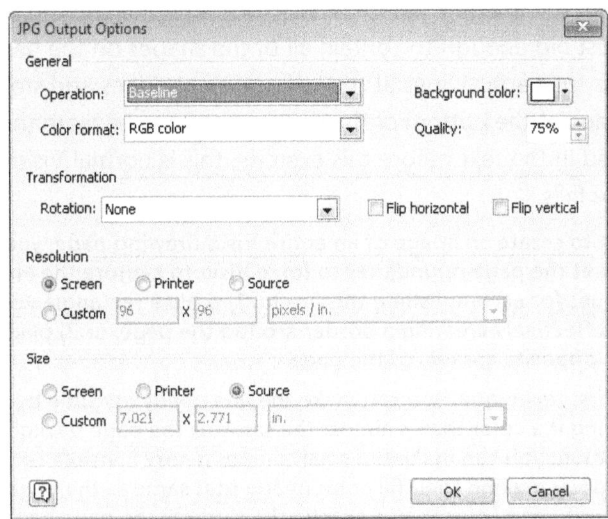

For most situations you can accept all default settings by clicking OK. However, if you require a specific JPG file format that differs from the defaults shown in the previous graphic, use the various drop-down lists, text boxes, and options to satisfy your needs.

5. Click **OK**.

6. Open the **Not quite full page** image in any image viewing program. On most systems, you can do this by double-clicking the file name in Windows Explorer.

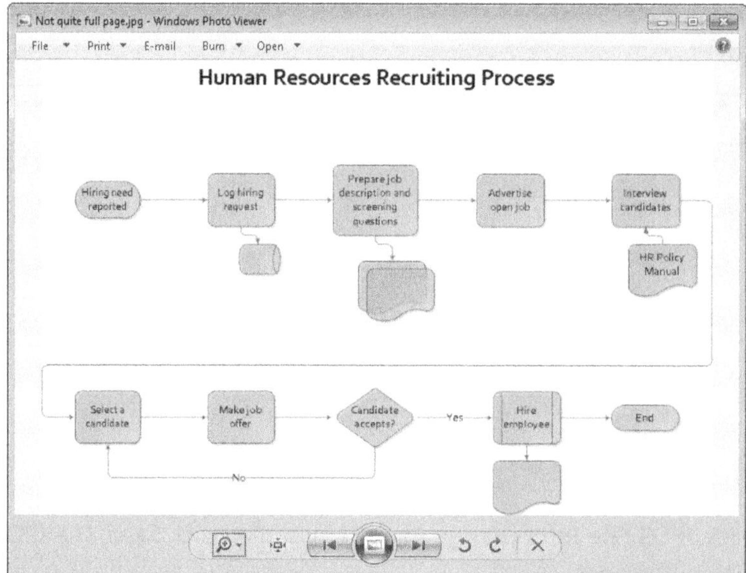

You can see that the image created by Visio does not include the full drawing page, but rather is just big enough to contain all of the shapes on the page. The image barely includes the vertical lines at the left and right edges and stops at the top of the page title and at the bottom of the document shape beneath the *Hire employee* shape. As noted in the text before this exercise, this is normal Visio behavior when creating image files.

Tip **If you want to create an image of an entire Visio drawing page, you must place one or more shapes at the page boundaries to force Visio to capture the entire page. The easiest techniques for accomplishing this are to: 1) draw a rectangle with no fill at the page margins, effectively creating a border around the page; or 2) place a pair of very small shapes in opposite corners of the page.**

If you use the first technique, you can make the line nearly invisible by making it very thin and/or giving it a color that is almost the same as the page background. If you use the second method, you can make the small shapes nearly invisible by making them very, very tiny or by making their fill color nearly that same as the page background. In either case, do not use a color that is exactly the same as the page background. If your shapes and the background are the same color, Visio will not "see" your added shapes and will not include them, so you will fail to capture the full page.

Next you will create a PNG image of a portion of the Visio recruiting diagram.

7. Use a bounding box to select the **Hiring need reported**, **Log hiring request**, and **Prepare job description and screening questions** shapes. Include the database and document shapes below the latter two shapes.

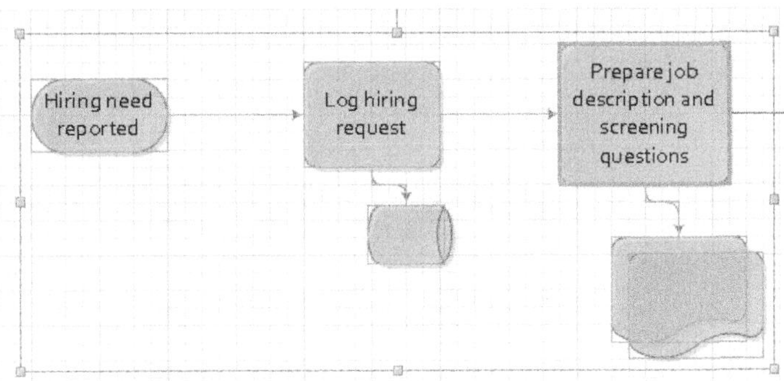

8. On the **File** tab, click **Save As**.
9. In the **File name** field, type **Process shapes**.
10. In the **Save as type** list, click **Portable Network Graphics**, and then click **Save**.

    The PNG Output Options dialog box opens.

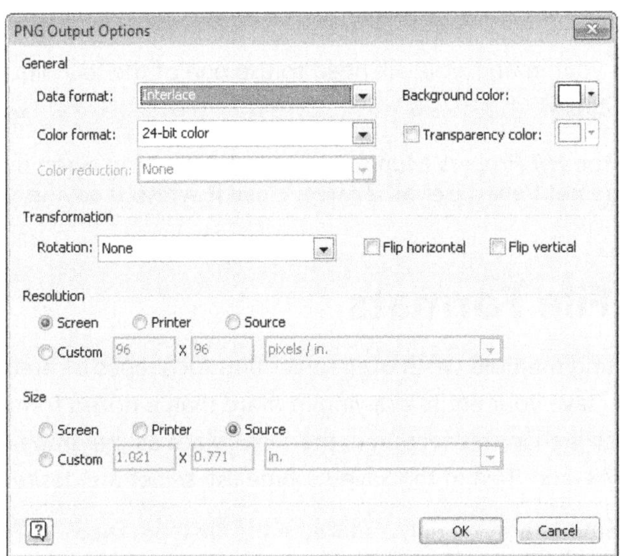

    As with JPEG images, you should be able to accept the default settings for PNG images unless you have specific requirements that mandate other settings.

11. Click **OK** in the **PNG Output Options** dialog box to create the PNG file.
12. Open the **Process shapes** image in any image viewing program.

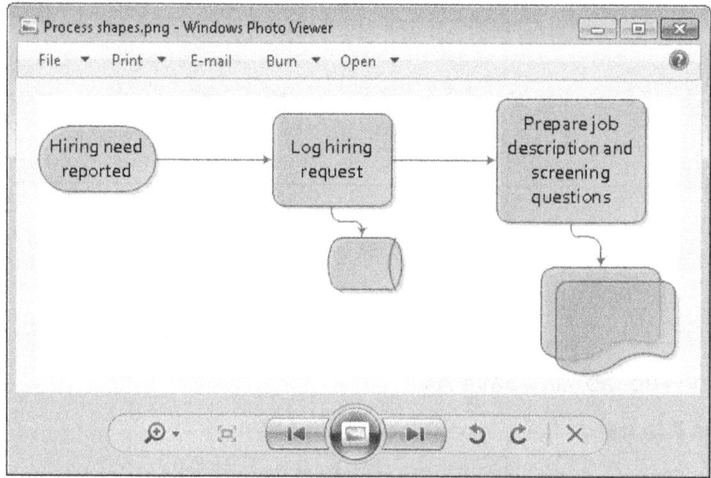

Notice that this image of a set of selected shapes exhibits the same behavior you saw when you created an image that contained all of the shapes on the page: the image is exactly as large as the set of shapes. If you require white space at the outside edges of your image, you will need to use one of the techniques described in the tip after Step 6.

CLEAN UP Leave the *HR Process Map for Chapter08* drawing open if you are continuing with the next exercise; otherwise, close it without saving your changes.

Saving in Other File Formats

In addition to creating multiple types of graphics files for shapes located on a single page, Visio lets you save your entire drawing in more than a dozen formats. You access the file formats described in this section in the same place as the graphic formats: on the File tab, click Save As, and then in the Save As Type list, select the desired file type.

Tip Some editions of Visio provide only a subset of the file types shown in the following tables. For edition details, go to *office.microsoft.com/en-us/visio/visio-edition-comparison-FX101838162.aspx.*

Table 1 **Visio File Types**

Save As format name	File extension	Description
Drawing	.vsd	Visio 2010 drawing
Stencil	.vss	Visio 2010 stencil
Template	.vst	Visio 2010 template
XML Drawing	.vdx	Visio drawing in Visio-specific XML format

Save As format name	File extension	Description
XML Stencil	.vsx	Visio stencil in Visio-specific XML format
XML Template	.vtx	Visio template in Visio-specific XML format
Visio 2002 Drawing	.vsd	Visio drawing in Visio 2002–compatible format
Visio 2002 Stencil	.vss	Visio stencil in Visio 2002–compatible format
Visio 2002 Template	.vst	Visio template in Visio 2002–compatible format

You may notice that the only previous version of Visio that appears in the Save As list is Visio 2002. This is because the last new Visio file format was introduced with Visio 2003. Because the file format used by Visio 2010 is the same as that used in Visio 2007 and Visio 2003, Visio 2010 drawing files are fully interchangeable with those versions of Visio without any special action. However, if a document contains features that are unique to Visio 2010, those features will not be available in prior versions.

Table 2 Non-Visio File Types

Save As format name	File extension	Description
AutoCAD Drawing	.dwg	AutoCAD drawing format; file can be opened directly by AutoCAD and other CAD systems that use this file format
AutoCAD Interchange	.dxf	AutoCAD drawing exchange format; intended to provide greater interoperability among systems that do not use DWG
PDF	.pdf	Adobe Portable Document Format; accurate rendering of a Visio drawing, including most hyperlinks, that is intended to be read-only; requires free PDF viewer
XPS Document	.xps	XML Paper Specification; an alternative to PDF for creating high-quality, read-only renderings of a document; requires free XPS viewer

Save As format name	File extension	Description
Web Page	.htm	HTML rendering of a Visio drawing that is viewable with a web browser
Web Drawing	.vdw	Microsoft-specific file format for storing and viewing Visio drawings in Microsoft SharePoint

All of the entries in Table 1 and the first two entries in Table 2 always save the entire Visio drawing in the new format. However, the last four entries in Table 2—PDF, XPS, Web Page, and Web Drawing—give you the choice of saving a subset of your pages into the desired format. Each offers an options dialog box, similar to the one for PDF shown in the following graphic, in which you can select a range of pages along with other format-specific options.

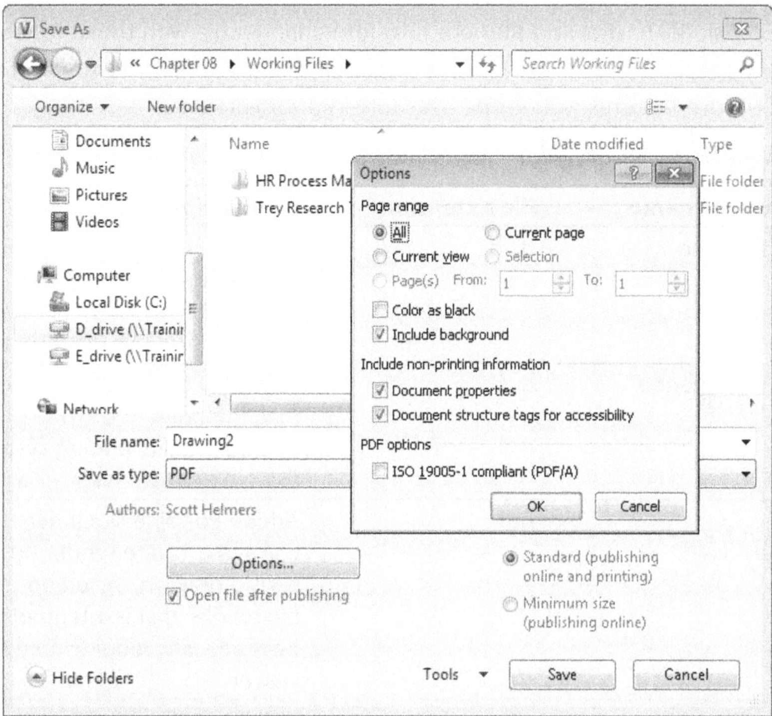

The inclusion of PDF as a built-in file format in Visio 2010 is a big advantage for many people. In previous versions of Visio, it was necessary to download PDF-creation software from Adobe, Microsoft, or another vendor in order to share Visio drawings in this popular file format.

XPS is an alternative to PDF that includes most of the same capabilities. Visio summarizes the benefits of PDF and XPS in the Backstage view: on the File tab, click Save & Send, and then click Create PDF/XPS Document to see the text shown on the far right in the following graphic.

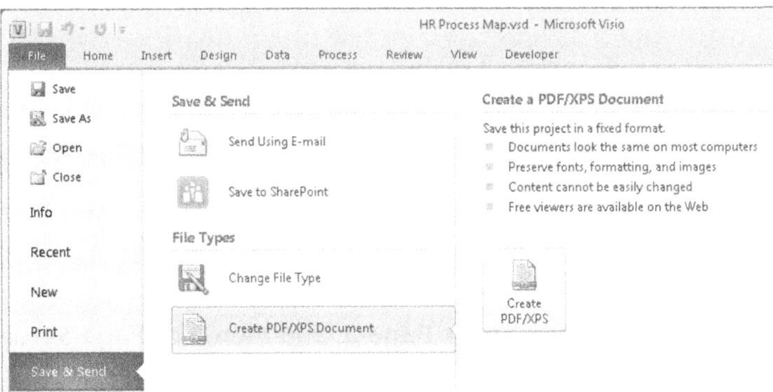

Creating Visio Templates

If you have created a drawing that other people will use as a starting point for creating their own drawings, you may want to save your drawing as a Visio ***template***. The advantage of sharing a template over sharing a drawing is that your document is not modified when someone uses it. Just like the templates that are packaged with Visio, whenever a user selects your template, Visio creates a new drawing. The new drawing inherits all of the attributes of your original document, including specific stencils, foreground and background pages, and even preset shapes on one or more pages.

In this exercise, you will add a background page to a drawing, add several objects to the background page, and save the Visio diagram as a template.

SET UP Click the File tab, and then click New. In the Template Categories section, click Maps And Floor Plans, and then double-click the Office Layout thumbnail to create a new drawing.

Blank Page

1. On the **Insert** tab, in the **Pages** group, click the **Blank Page** arrow (not the button) to display the submenu.
2. Click **Background Page**, and then in the **Page Setup** dialog box, click **OK**.
3. In the **Shapes** window, click **More Shapes**, point to **Visio Extras**, and then click **Title Blocks**.
4. Drag a **Drawn by** shape into the lower-right corner of the background page.

Tip The Drawn By shape automatically displays the contents of the Author field from the Visio document's properties.

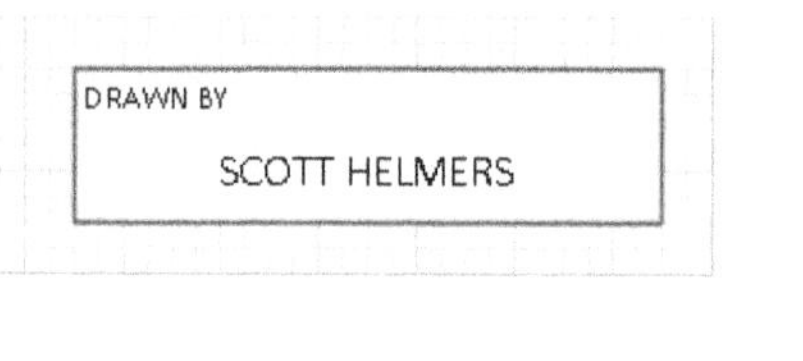

5. Add a text box to the upper-left corner of the page, type **Trey Research**, and apply the following attributes to the text box: **30 pt.**, **Bold**, **Align left**.

   You've created a background page and can now apply it to the foreground page in your document.

6. Right-click on the page name tab for **Page-1**, and then click **Page Setup**.
7. Click the **Background** arrow, and then click **Background-1**.

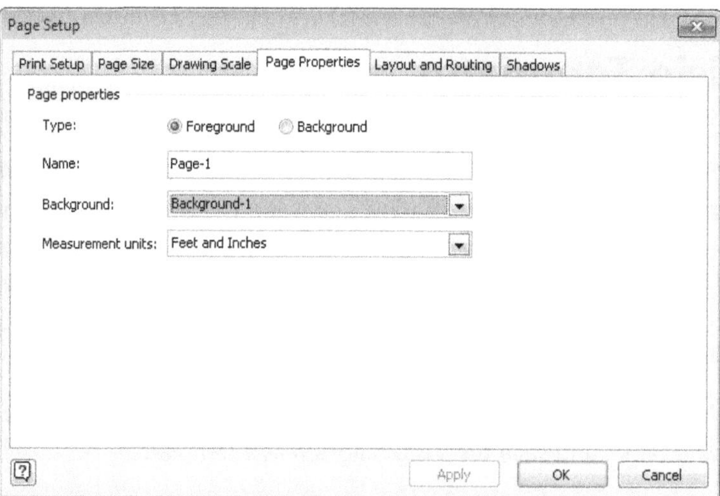

8. Click **OK**.
9. In the **Shapes** window, click the heading for **Walls, Doors and Windows** to activate that stencil.

   Your drawing page now displays the company name and a *Drawn by* information block from the background page.

Save

10. On the **File** tab, click the **Save** button.
11. In the **Save As** dialog box, navigate to the folder in which you'd like to save the template, and in the **File name** field, type **Trey Research Office Layout**.
12. In the **Save as type** list, click **Template**.

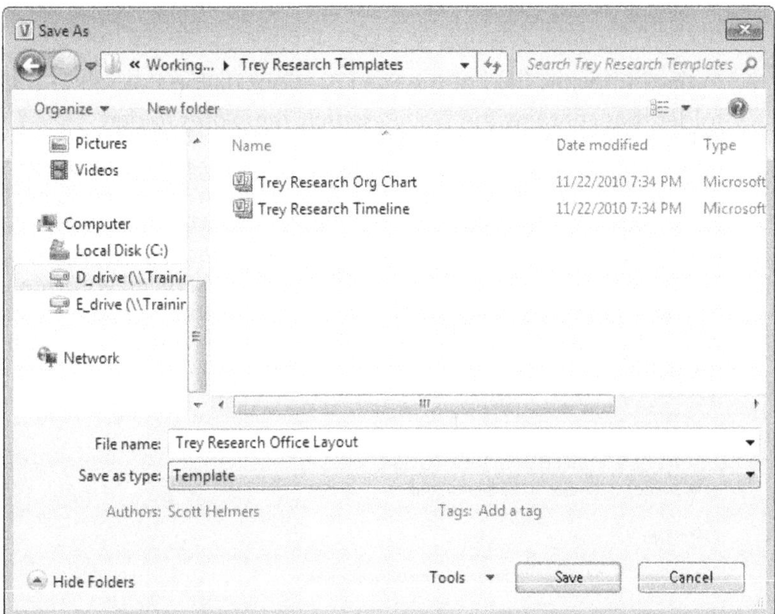

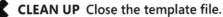

13. Click **Save**.

You have created a template that can be used by other people to create office floor plans for Trey Research. Each drawing will automatically show the name of the author of the document.

CLEAN UP **Close the template file.**

Where Do I Store Custom Templates?

You can store custom templates in any location that you like. You might store them on your own system if you're the only person who will use them, or you might place them on a server so you can share them with others.

Regardless of their location, you need to tell Visio where you've put your templates in order for them to show up on the New page in the ***Backstage view***. You will probably find it helpful to organize your templates by placing them in a folder. The following example uses a folder called *Trey Research Templates*.

To inform Visio of the location for your template folder:

1. On the File tab, click Options, and then click Advanced. Scroll to the bottom of the Advanced settings, and click the File Locations button.
2. In the Templates field of the File Locations dialog box, enter the path to the folder that contains the *Trey Research Templates* folder.

   Important Be sure to note the wording in the preceding sentence: "enter the path to the folder that contains the *Trey Research Templates* folder." In other words, do *not* include your template folder name in the template path. Stop one folder *above* your folder. This ensures that your folder name appears in the Template Categories panel along with the Visio-supplied template folders. For example, in the following graphic, the Trey Research Templates folder is located within the Working Files folder, so *Trey Research Templates* is not included in the path.

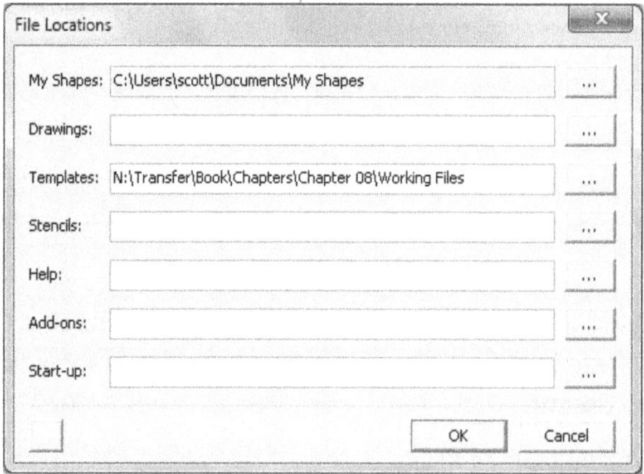

3. After entering the template path, click OK twice. The next time you start Visio, the Template Categories section of the New page on the Home tab should look something like the following graphic.

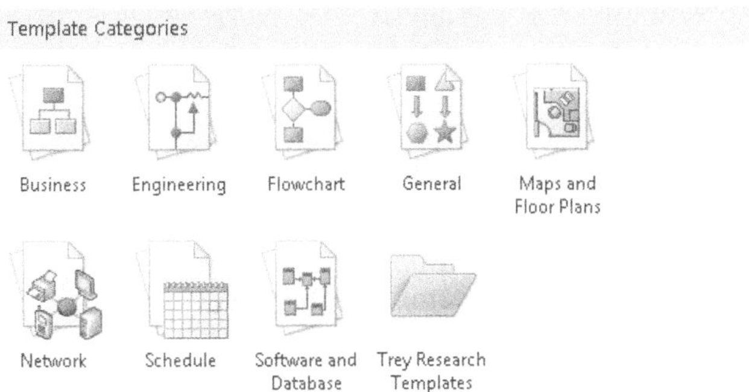

Troubleshooting If the *Trey Research Templates* folder doesn't appear as shown, see the important note following Step 2 in this sidebar.

4. Double-click *Trey Research Templates* to display the templates in that folder.

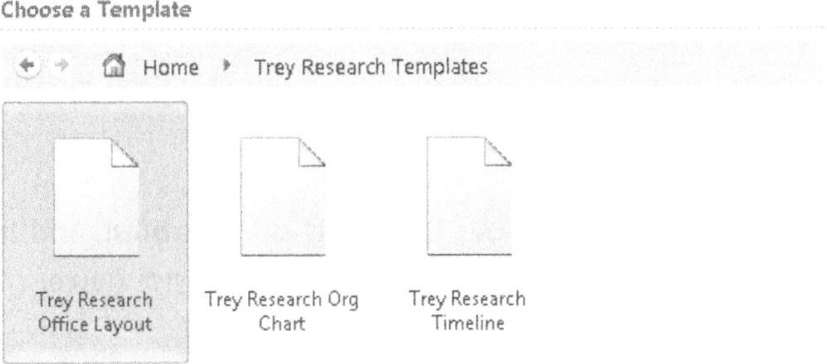

See Also You may have noticed that neither your template folder nor your custom templates display fancy graphics like the built-in templates. The blog post at *blogs.msdn.com/b/chhopkin/archive/2008/10/29/create-perfect-previews-for-your-templates.aspx* not only provides instructions for creating a preview graphic for your template, but also unlocks the secret of creating previews that contain high-quality images.

Sharing Diagrams by Using the Visio Viewer

Microsoft Office 2010 includes the Visio Viewer as a default installation option. Consequently, on a system that includes Office but not Visio, you can view any Visio diagram in Windows Internet Explorer (the Viewer runs as an Internet Explorer add-on).

On a system that includes both Office and Visio, Visio drawings will always open in Visio and not in the Visio Viewer.

In this exercise, you will use the Visio Viewer to examine a Visio drawing.

SET UP You need the *HR Process Map for Chapter08_start* drawing located in the Chapter08 practice file folder to complete this exercise.

1. On a system that includes Microsoft Office 2010 but not Visio, double-click the *HR Process Map for Chapter08_start* drawing in Windows Explorer.

   If this is the first time you have used the Visio Viewer on this system, you may see a warning like the one shown in the following graphic.

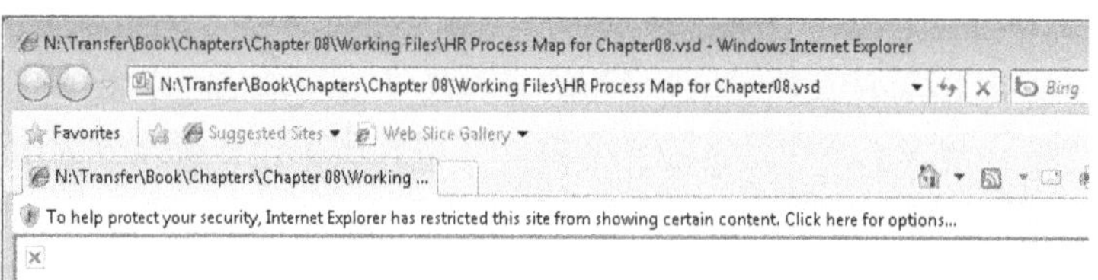

2. Click the yellow information bar, click **Add-on Disabled**, and then click **Run Add-on**. Internet Explorer asks permission to run the Visio Viewer control.

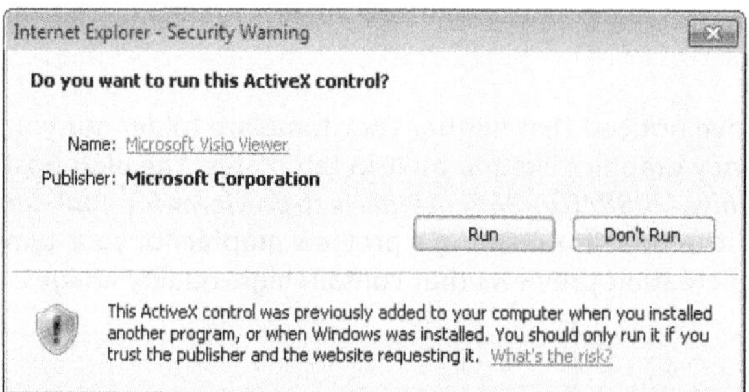

3. Click **Run**. The Visio drawing appears in the Internet Explorer window.

   The Internet Explorer view includes a set of zoom controls in the upper left and familiar-looking page navigation controls in the lower left. There are also three buttons that give you control over display, layer, and markup information for the Visio Viewer rendering of your drawing.

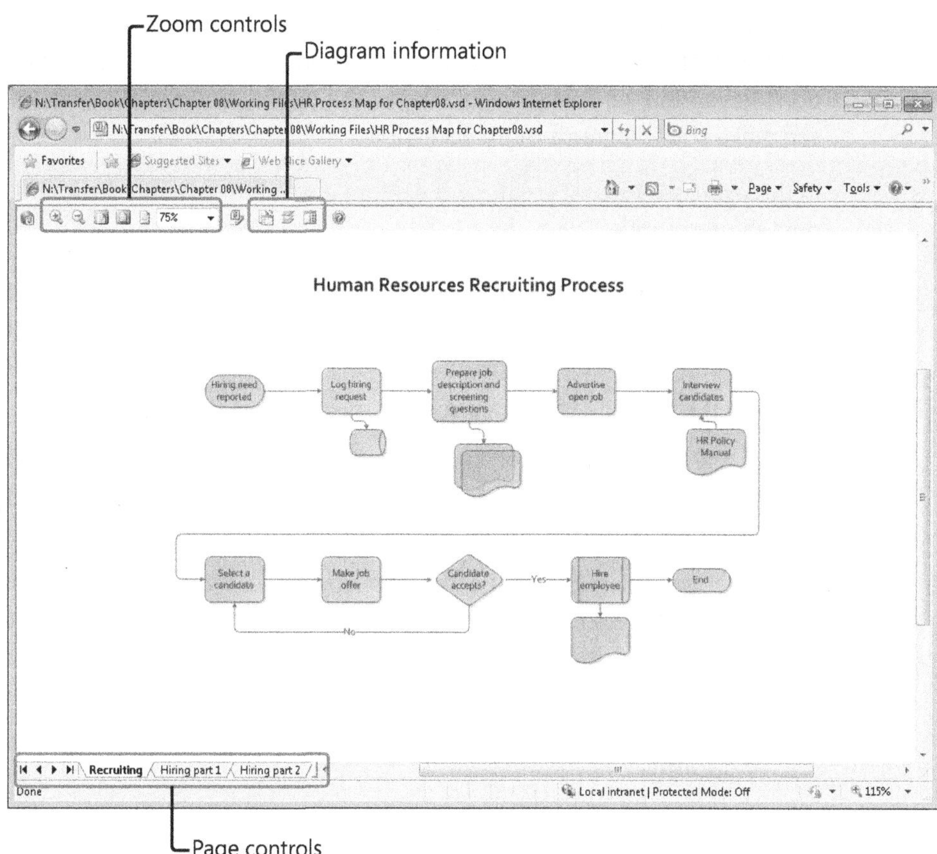

CLEAN UP Close Internet Explorer.

Tip After you have given Internet Explorer permission to run the Visio Viewer add-on, it will do so in the future without requiring any intervention.

Publishing Visio Diagrams to the Web

One of the most useful and powerful features in Visio for sharing diagrams is its ability to create a website from a Visio document. The Visio-generated website includes all foreground pages, preserves both page-to-page and external hyperlinks, and includes the following bonus features:

- A table of contents that allows you to jump to any page
- A pan-and-zoom pane that lets you click and drag to zoom and navigate around any page
- A details window to present shape data for any shape
- Full-text search for all text in the entire drawing

If you haven't explored the Save As Web Page option in Visio, you owe it to yourself to do so. Whether you want to share drawings on your intranet site with colleagues who don't have Visio, or publish diagrams on the public World Wide Web, this Visio feature can make your diagrams more accessible.

In this exercise, you will create and explore a website generated with default Visio web publishing settings.

SET UP You need the *HR Process Map for Chapter08_start* drawing located in the Chapter08 practice file folder to complete this exercise. Open the diagram and save it as *HR Process Map for Chapter08*.

Save As

1. On the **File** tab, click **Save As**.
2. In the **Save as type** list, click **Web Page**. (Do not click Web Drawing; you will learn about Save As Web Drawing in Chapter 13, "Sharing and Publishing Diagrams: Part 2.")

   After you select Web Page, the bottom of the Save As dialog box changes to offer additional choices related to creating a website. For this exercise, you will accept the default settings that lie behind the Change Title and Publish buttons. In Chapter 13, you will investigate the settings those buttons offer.

   Important The Change Title and Publish buttons do not exist in the Standard edition of Visio 2010.

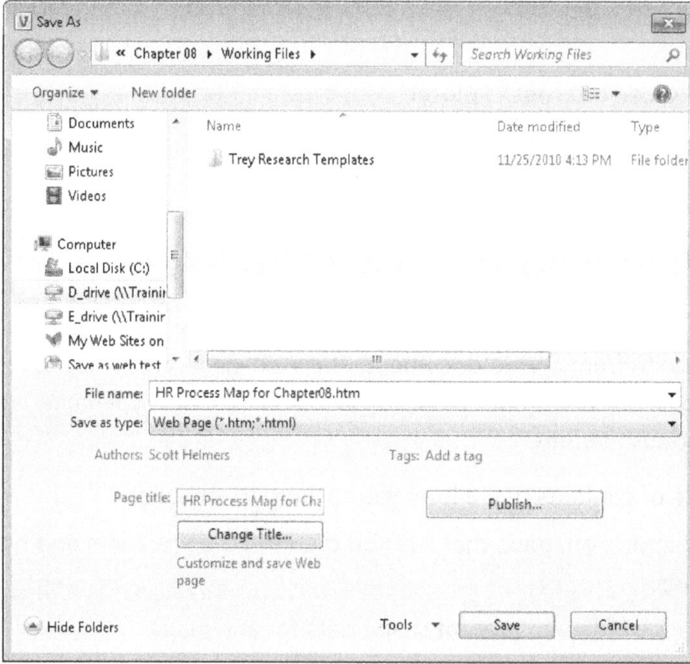

3. Click **Save**. One or more progress indicators appears.

   Your Visio-generated website appears automatically in Internet Explorer. In addition to a viewing pane, notice the four-part navigation pane on the left side of the browser window.

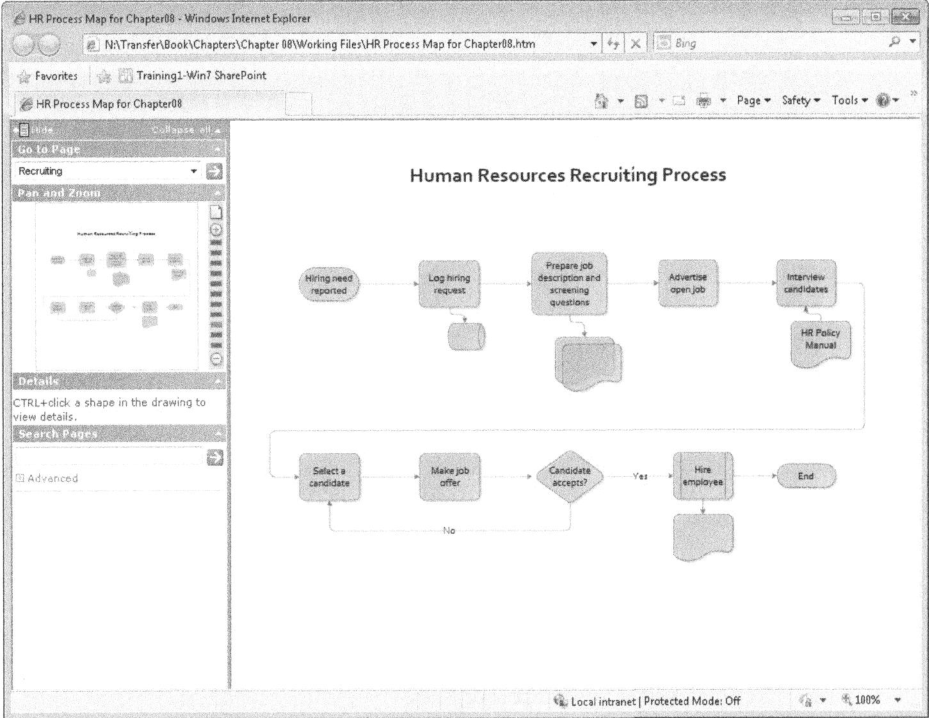

Important The website produced by Visio uses software that does not work well in browsers other than Internet Explorer. In Firefox, for example, you will see the image of each page, but the additional capabilities described in the remaining steps of this exercise will probably not be available. Consequently, even if you use Firefox or other software as your primary web browser, you will want to view your Visio-created websites in Internet Explorer.

See Also For the best browser viewing experience, you need to install Microsoft Silverlight. Information about Silverlight is available at *www.microsoft.com/silverlight/*. If you do not install Silverlight, you will have fewer viewing options.

4. Point to the **Hire employee** *subprocess* shape. Because this shape contains a hyperlink, Internet Explorer displays a pop-up that contains up to three entries:

   - The shape text, if any
   - Instructions to hold down the Ctrl key and click to see shape details
   - Instructions to click to follow the hyperlink

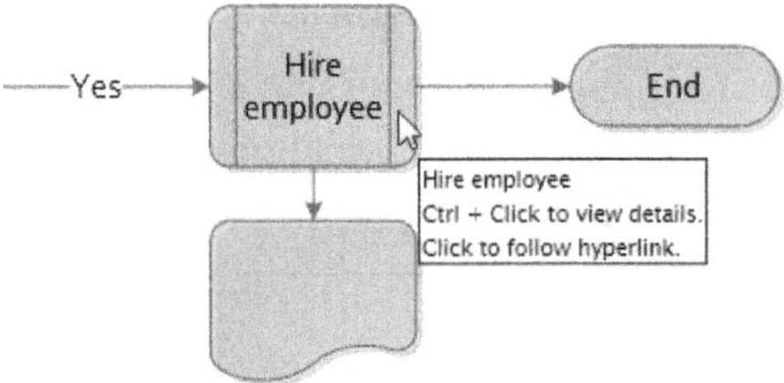

5. Click the **Hire employee** shape. Internet Explorer follows the hyperlink to the subprocess page.

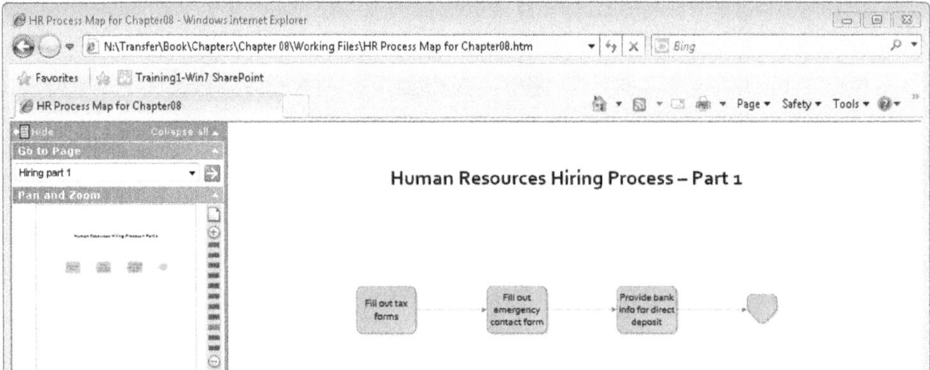

6. Click the browser's **Back** button to return to the first page.

7. Click the **Advertise open job** shape. This shape contains a hyperlink to monster.com, so that webpage appears.

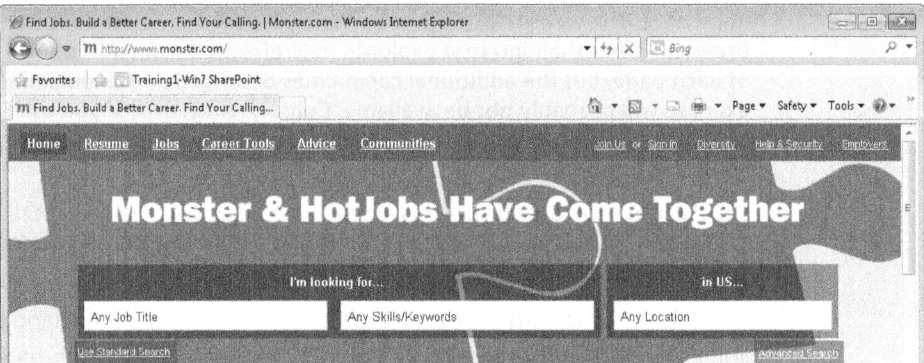

8. Click the browser's **Back** button to return to the first page.
9. In the **Go to Page** section of the navigation pane, click the down arrow, and then click **Hiring part 2**. Finally, click the green button containing the white arrow to go to the page you've selected.

   The viewing pane displays the selected page.
10. Click the browser's **Back** button to return to the first page.
11. In the **Pan and Zoom** section of the navigation pane, drag from the upper-left edge of the **Hiring need reported** shape to the upper right of the **Prepare job descriptions and screening questions** shape. As you drag the cursor, you'll see a blue box appear; it will follow your cursor to the right and will also expand downward. When you let go of the mouse, the box you've drawn turns from blue to red and the viewing pane shows just that portion of the drawing page.

   Important You can't control the shape of the box you draw in the Pan And Zoom pane. It will maintain the same aspect ratio as the viewing pane to the right. With Internet Explorer opened to full screen on a system with resolution of 1024×768, the result looks like the following diagram.

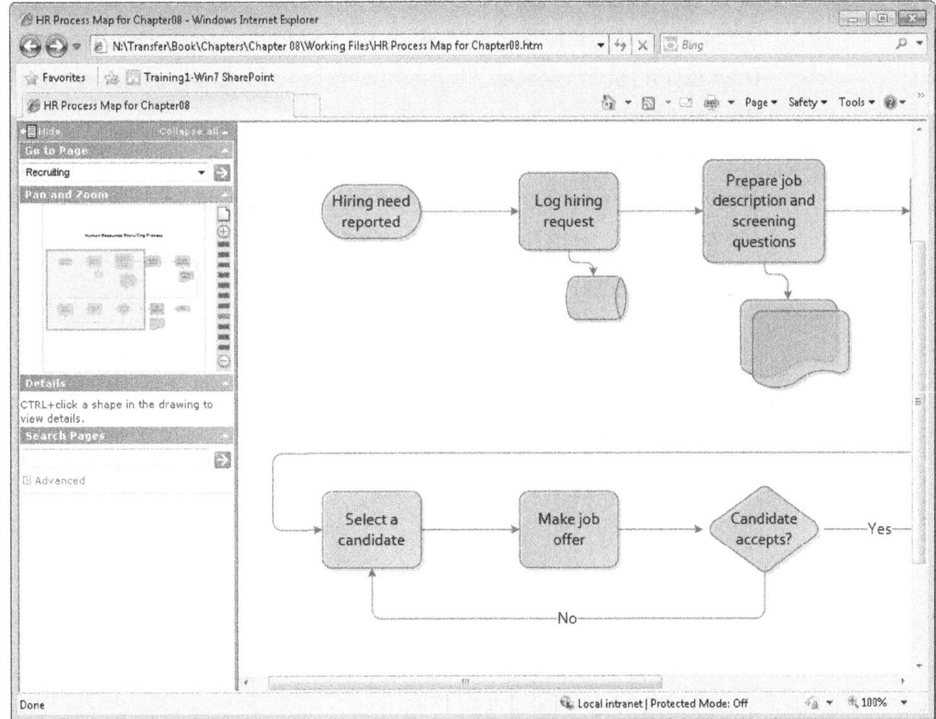

After you've drawn a zoom box, you can drag it left, right, up, and down within the Pan And Zoom pane to move the image in the viewing pane. You can also click the buttons and bars at the right edge of the Pan And Zoom pane to zoom in or out.

12. In the upper-right corner of the **Pan and Zoom** pane, click the icon that looks like a piece of paper to return the viewing pane to full page view.

13. Hold down Ctrl and click the **Hire employee** shape. The shape data for this shape appears in the Details pane, which is located just below the Pan And Zoom pane.

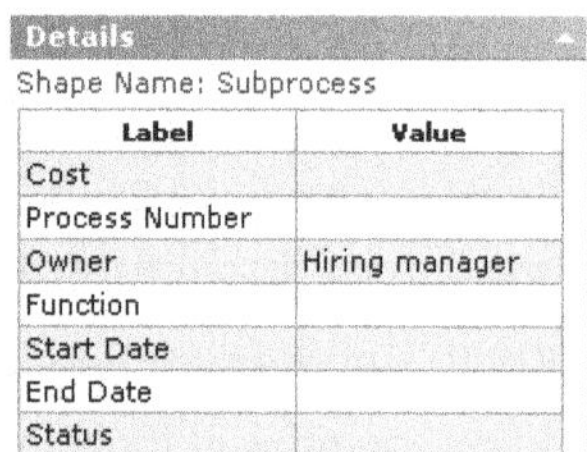

Details
Shape Name: Subprocess
Label
Value
Cost
Process Number
Owner
Hiring manager
Function
Start Date
End Date
Status

14. In the **Search Pages** pane, type **candidate**, and then click the arrow in the green square to execute the search. A list of all shapes that contain any form of the word *candidate* appears below the search box.

    What is particularly impressive about the full text search is that it presents more than just a list; it creates a hyperlinked list of search results, as you will discover in the next step.

15. Click the **Select a candidate** link in the **Search Pages** pane. Notice that an orange arrow appears over that shape for several seconds to show you exactly where on the page your search result is located.

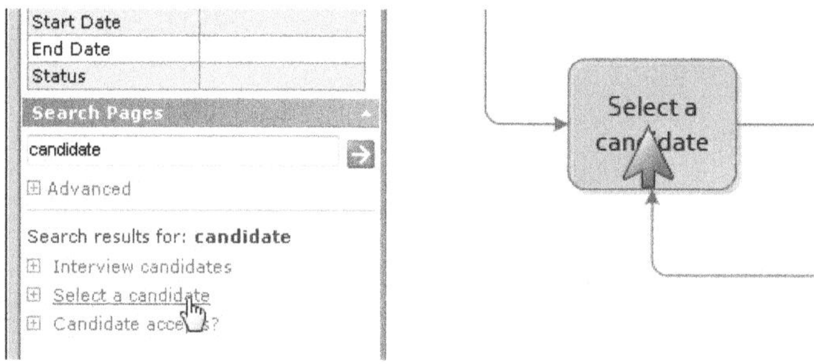

Try clicking the other entries in the search results list to see that the arrow points to each of them.

16. In the **Search Pages** pane, type **manager**, and then press Enter to execute the search.

At first glance, the search results look incorrect because two of the three listed items don't contain the word *manager*. However, it's important to understand that the search function is looking at the shape data inside the shapes as well as the text on the shapes. Consequently, if you click the first or second entry and then hold down Ctrl and click on the designated shape, you'll see that the shape data in the Details pane does, indeed, include the word *manager*.

Tip **You can also see the shape data associated with a search result by clicking the plus sign to the left of the search result.**

17. Click **Meet hiring manager** in the search results list. Even though the designated shape is located on another page, the target page will first appear in the viewing pane and then the orange arrow will appear.

 **CLEAN UP Close Internet Explorer and the *HR Process Map for Chapter08* drawing.**

Important **There is a known issue in the interaction between the network and computer shapes in several Visio stencils and the Save As Web Page function in Visio 2010. If you save a drawing containing those shapes to the web, the text in those shapes will not be found by the full-text search function, even though it should be.**

Key Points

- A significant part of the value of creating a Visio drawing comes from sharing it with others. Visio allows you to print diagrams as well as share them in a large variety of other formats.
- With Visio 2010, you can remove personal metadata from documents with a couple of clicks prior to sharing them electronically.
- Visio makes it extremely simple to save one or more shapes on a page in eight different graphic formats.
- You can save Visio diagrams, stencils, and templates in three different Visio formats: the native format that is compatible with Visio 2010, 2007, and 2003; an XML format that is compatible with the same three versions; and the native Visio format that is backward-compatible with Visio 2002 and 2000.
- You can create Visio templates that contain any document and page elements that you would like to have present every time you create a new diagram. Typical items to include in a template include company logos or other required graphics; legal notices or copyright statements; page numbering placeholders; customized background pages; and title blocks.
- The Visio Viewer that is included with every copy of Office 2010 lets anyone view Visio diagrams using nothing more than Internet Explorer.
- One of the most useful features in Visio is the ability to create an entire website from a Visio drawing. All graphic and text elements, all hyperlinks, and nearly every other Visio feature is preserved in the web rendering. In addition, a Visio-created website includes pan-and-zoom, shape data display, and full-text search capabilities.

Chapter at a Glance

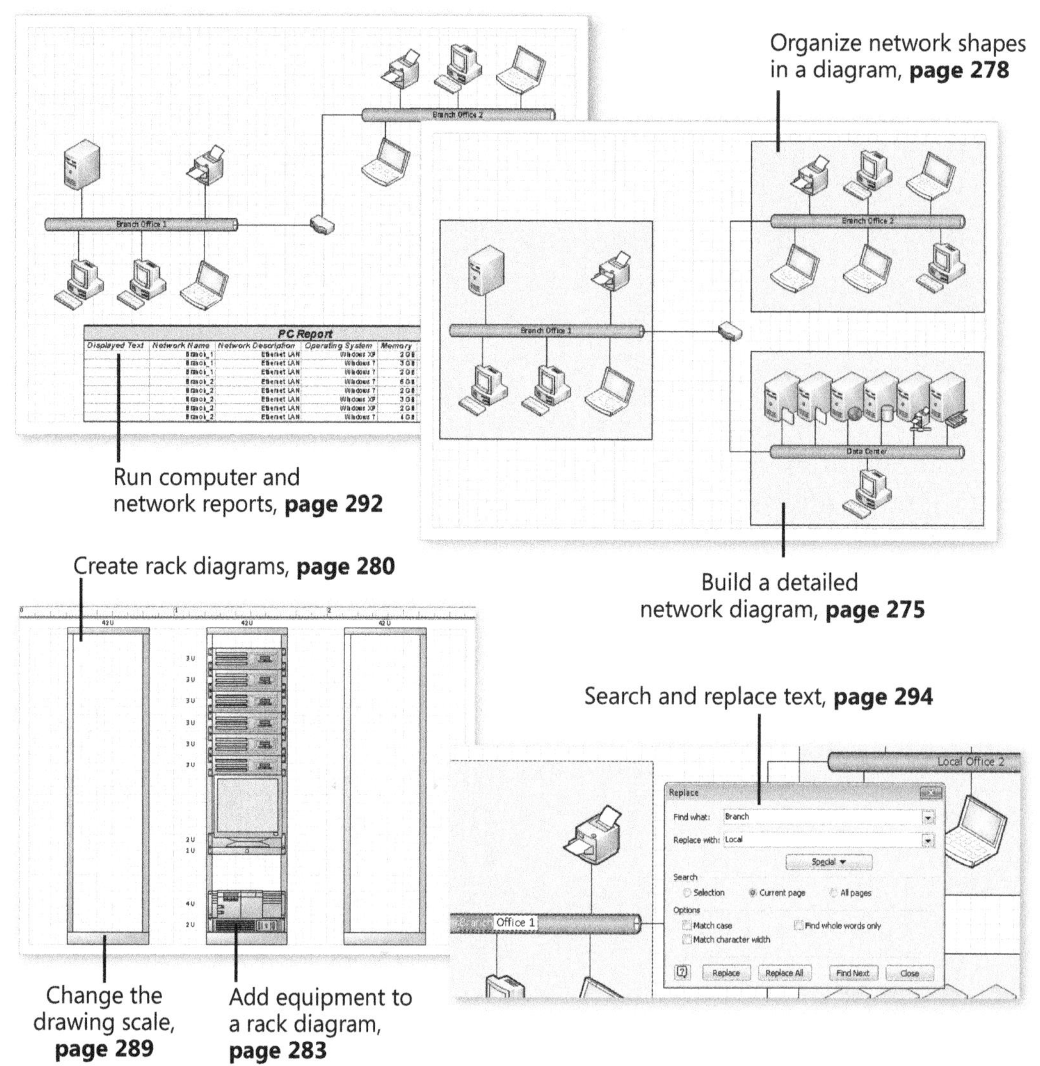

9 Drawing the Real World: Network and Data Center Diagrams

In this chapter, you will learn how to

- ✔ Build basic and detailed network diagrams.
- ✔ Organize network shapes in a diagram.
- ✔ Create rack diagrams.
- ✔ Add equipment to rack diagrams.
- ✔ Change the drawing scale.
- ✔ Run computer and network reports.
- ✔ Search and replace text.
- ✔ Map Active Directory and LDAP.

This chapter describes one of the more common uses for Microsoft Visio: creating network and data center diagrams. Whether your goal is to create a simple, stylized representation of network connectivity or to create a photo-realistic rack diagram that shows real-time equipment status, you can accomplish your goal with Visio 2010.

The network and computer stencils in Visio include hundreds of shapes for just about any type of device or equipment you might want to include in your diagrams. In addition, there are thousands of downloadable shapes, many of which were designed to look exactly like specific brands and models of equipment. You will find links to many sources of Visio shapes later in this chapter.

Early versions of Visio—Visio 2000 and before—included a network discovery and auto-mapping capability. In essence, you could point those early versions of Visio at a network and it would figure out what was out there and build a map for you. Although that capability no longer exists in Visio, several vendors provide Visio add-ins that have this capability. One place to look for Visio add-ins is a Microsoft website called the Visio Toolbox located at *www.visiotoolbox.com.*

In this chapter, you will build basic and detailed network diagrams and learn one technique for organizing network shapes. You will create rack diagrams using equipment shapes designed to fit in the racks and will learn how to set the page properties so that all shapes on the page are drawn to scale. You will run computer and network reports from your diagrams and find out how to search and replace text in a drawing. Finally, you'll learn about two templates that help you create maps for an Active Directory and an LDAP Directory.

Practice Files Before you can complete the exercises in this chapter, you need to copy the book's practice files to your computer. The practice files you'll use to complete the exercises in this chapter are in the Chapter09 practice files folder. A complete list of practice files is provided in "Using the Practice Files" at the beginning of this book.

Building Basic Network Diagrams

All three editions of Visio 2010 include a network diagram template called Basic Network Diagram.

In this exercise, you will use that template to create a diagram of a simple corporate network.

SET UP Start Visio, or if it's already running, click the File tab, and then click New. In the Template Categories section, click Network, and then double-click the Basic Network Diagram thumbnail. Save the drawing as *Network Diagram (Basic).*

1. Drag an **Ethernet** shape from the **Network and Peripherals** stencil onto the drawing page and position it a couple of gridlines in from the left edge of the page.
2. Drag the resize handle on the right end of the Ethernet shape until the network segment is approximately 100 mm (4 inches) long.

   Tip Remember that the Width button on the *status bar* displays the current length of any selected shape, so you can use it as a guide as you drag the resize handle.

   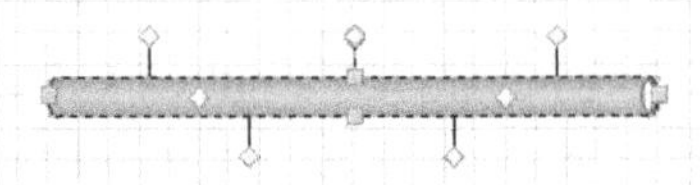

3. With the Ethernet shape still selected, type **Branch Office 1** to label the network segment, and then click anywhere on the background of the page.
4. Drag a **Server** shape onto the page and place it above and toward the left end of the Ethernet shape.
5. Click once on the Ethernet shape to select it, and then drag any yellow control handle toward the center of the server until a red square appears around the control handle (there's a connection point in the center of all of the computer and network shapes you will use in this exercise).

   Notice that the connector line remains attached to the Ethernet as you drag the control handle left or right.

   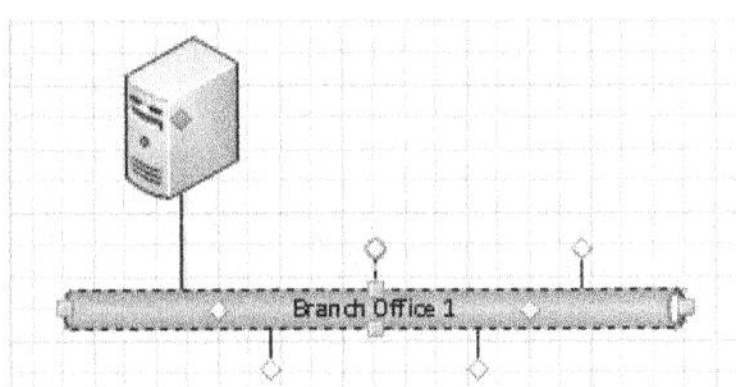

   Important Because there are only seven yellow handles on the Ethernet shape, you might think that you can only connect seven devices. However, each of the two control handles in the middle of the Ethernet segment actually hides more than two dozen additional handles. In fact, the Ethernet shape can accept up to 64 connections.

6. Drag a **Printer** shape above and toward the right end of the Ethernet, and then connect the printer to the network by dragging a yellow handle and gluing it to the printer.
7. Drag two **PC** shapes and one **Laptop computer** shape from the **Computers and Monitors** stencil and drop them below the Ethernet shape.
8. Drag a yellow control handle and glue it to the first PC.
9. Repeat Step 8 with the second PC.

   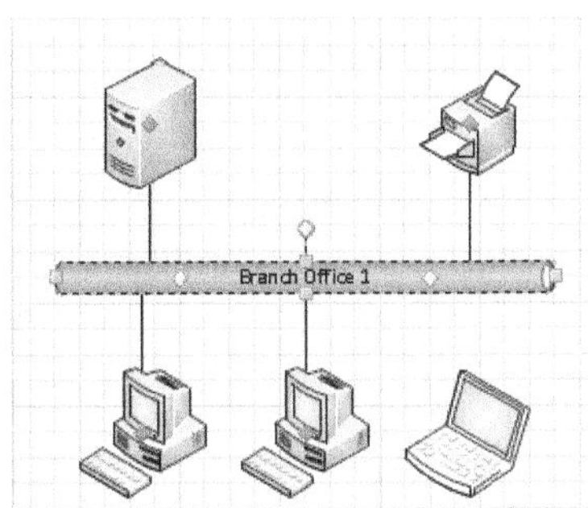

Your next task will be to connect the laptop to the network but there aren't any more control handles below the Ethernet segment.

10. Drag a control handle from the middle of the Ethernet shape and glue it to the laptop.

    As you can see in the following figure, dragging a control handle from the middle of the Ethernet segment successfully connected the laptop to the network, but there are still additional control handles available for future use.

    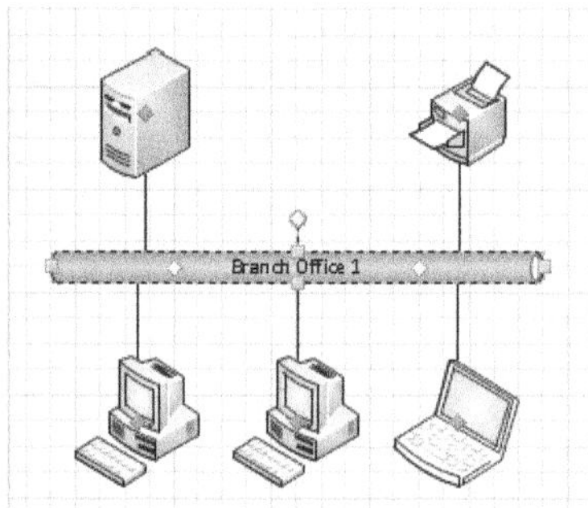

    Tip In this graphic, there is an unused control handle/connector line just above the center of the Ethernet segment. If you don't want it there, don't try to delete it—you'll end up deleting the entire Ethernet segment. Instead, if you want to hide the unused connection, drag its control handle back into the interior of the Ethernet shape. Then it won't be visible unless the network segment is selected.

11. Drag another **Ethernet** shape into the upper-right corner of the page, leaving enough room to add shapes above it.

12. While the Ethernet shape is still selected, type **Branch Office 2**, and then click anywhere on the background of the page.

13. Drag a **Printer** shape, two **PC** shapes, and three **Laptop computer** shapes, and attach them to the new network segment so you have a network that looks like the one on the right side of the graphic in Step 16.

14. Drag a **Router** shape from the **Network and Peripherals** stencil into the center of the page.

15. Drag the remaining unused connector from the **Branch Office 1** network and glue it to the router. Notice that the connector repositions itself so the end attached to the Ethernet is closer to the router.

16. Drag a connector from the **Branch Office 2** network and glue it to the router.

    The connector bends as you drag it toward the router—it behaves more like a ***dynamic connector*** than just a line. Your finished network diagram should look something like the following graphic.

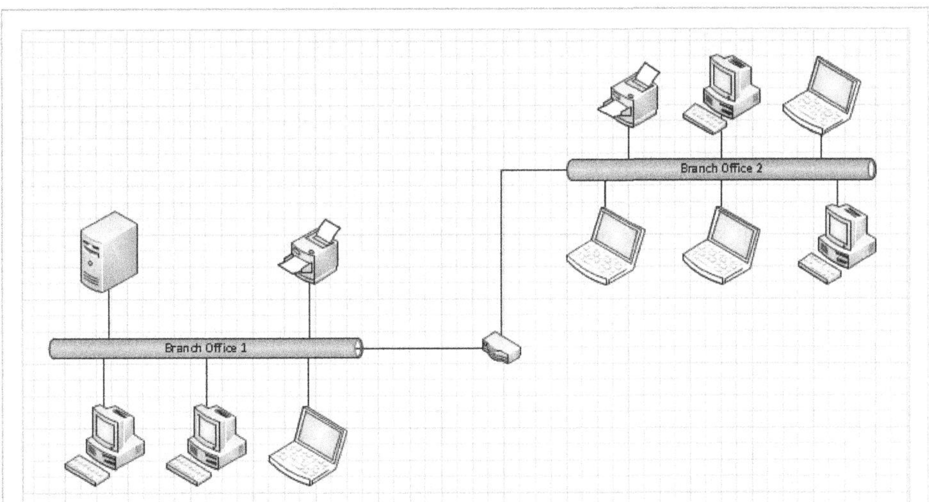

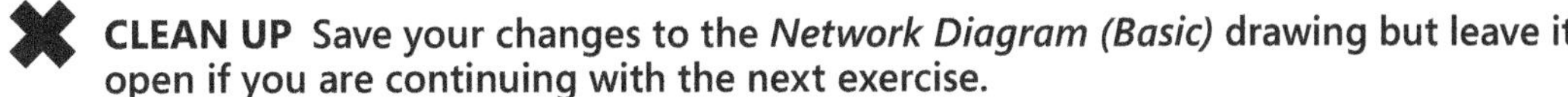
CLEAN UP Save your changes to the *Network Diagram (Basic)* drawing but leave it open if you are continuing with the next exercise.

Building Detailed Network Diagrams

Important The information in this section applies only to the Professional and Premium editions of Visio 2010.

The Professional and Premium editions of Visio 2010 include an advanced network diagram template that offers additional stencils you can use to create more sophisticated diagrams.

In this exercise, you will create a new drawing from the Detailed Network Diagram template. Then you will paste a copy of the network diagram you created in the previous section into the new drawing. Finally, you will add a network segment to the diagram by using shapes from the Detailed Network Diagram stencils.

SET UP If you completed the preceding exercise, continue working with the *Network Diagram (Basic)* drawing. If not, you need the *Network Diagram (Basic)_start* drawing located in the Chapter09 practice file folder to complete this exercise. Open the drawing in Visio.

1. Click the **File** tab, and then click **New**. In the **Template Categories** section, click **Network**, and then double-click the **Detailed Network Diagram** thumbnail to create a new drawing. Save the drawing as **Network Diagram (Detailed)**.

Important If the Shapes window opens with a scroll bar in the stencil titles section, drag the separator between the title bars and the shapes down to reveal all of the stencil titles.

Tip The primary differences between the Basic and Detailed network templates are visible in the Shapes window. The Basic template (on the left in the following graphic) includes just two stencils: Network And Peripherals and Computers And Monitors. The Detailed template (on the right) includes those two, plus six additional stencils you can use to create more sophisticated diagrams.

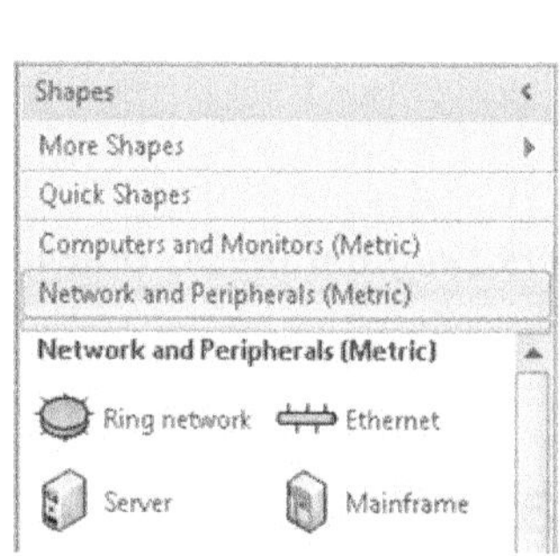

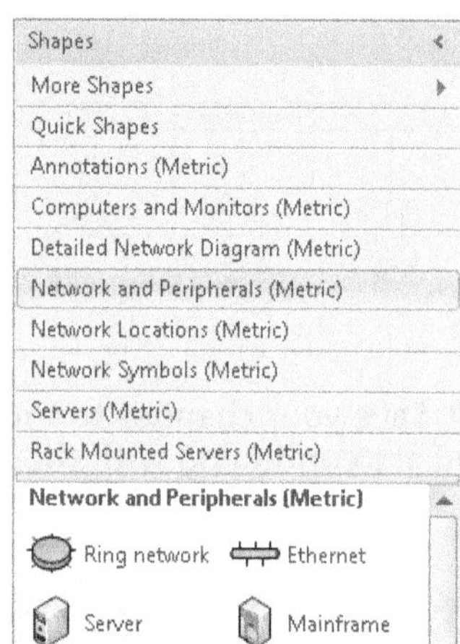

2. Switch to the Visio window that contains the Network Diagram (Basic) drawing that you opened to set up this exercise.
3. Press Ctrl+A to select all shapes on the page, and then press Ctrl+C to copy them.
4. Switch Visio windows to return to the Network Diagram (Detailed) drawing and press Ctrl+V to paste the basic network diagram onto **Page-1**.

   Tip The enhanced paste function in Visio 2010 places the copied network shapes into the same location on the new page that they occupied on the original page.

5. Drag an **Ethernet** shape from the **Network and Peripherals** stencil onto the drawing page and position it in the lower-right corner of the page.
6. Drag the left resize handle until the Ethernet segment is approximately 100 mm (4 inches) long, and then type **Data Center** to label the network segment.
7. Drag and glue a yellow control handle from the **Data Center** network to the router in the center of the page.
8. Drag a **File server** from the **Servers** stencil onto the page and position it on the left end and above the **Data Center** network segment.

9. Drag one of each of the following server shapes from the **Servers** stencil: **File server**, **Web server**, **Database server**, **Print server**, and **Directory server**. Position each server to the immediate right of the previous one.
10. Drag and glue a yellow control handle from the **Data Center** Ethernet to each server.
11. Drag a **PC** shape from the **Computers and Monitors** stencil; position it below and attach it to the **Data Center** network segment. Your new network segment should look something like the following graphic.

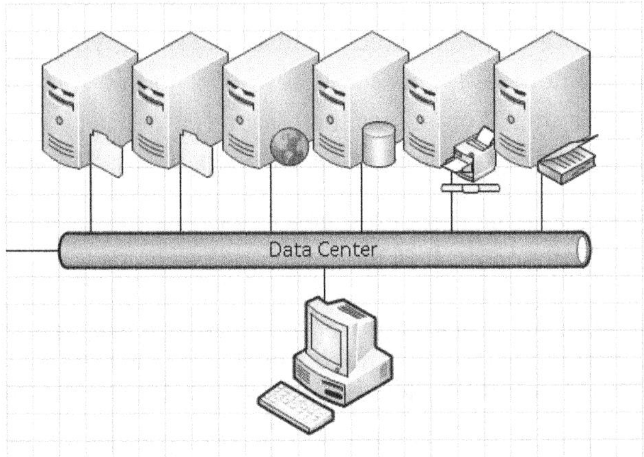

CLEAN UP Save your changes to the *Network Diagram (Detailed)* drawing but leave it open if you are continuing with the next exercise.

You have created a stylized view of the equipment attached to the Data Center network. In all likelihood, the actual equipment in the data center does not consist of stand-alone PCs, but consists of equipment mounted in racks. In two upcoming exercises, you will build a data center rack that contains equipment that is equivalent to the previous graphic.

Tip The stencils that are part of the Detailed Network Diagram template include many more shapes than just the ones you used in this exercise. If you work with networks, it would be a good idea to spend a few minutes exploring the shapes in the other stencils before moving on to the next exercise.

The Servers stencil you used in this exercise contains 16 customized shapes that you can use to represent specific server types. The Rack Mounted Servers stencil, which is also opened with the Detailed Network Server template, contains a corresponding set of 16 rack-mounted server shapes.

If you would like to create your own customized server shapes, see the article on the Visio Guy website at *www.visguy.com/2009/09/11/visio-server-shape-icon-customization-tool*.

Microsoft created a collection of server and network shapes for use in wall posters depicting product deployment scenarios. Though you may not need to create posters containing network shapes, the free, downloadable stencils offer an alternative to the usual shapes. To download these stencils, go to *www.microsoft.com/downloads/en/details.aspx?FamilyID=88e03d22-8f42-4c9d-94ef-d8e48322d677.*

See Also In Chapter 10, "Visualizing Your Data," you will learn additional methods for enhancing network and data center diagrams.

Organizing Network Shapes in a Diagram

It's quite common that once you've created a network drawing, you want to organize subsets of the shapes. Sometimes the reason is aesthetic: you want to create visual groupings within your diagram. Sometimes the reason is practical: you want to rearrange the drawing and it's easier if certain shapes are grouped.

In this exercise, you will add a background shape to each section of your network diagram and then group the shapes in that part of the network.

SET UP If you completed the preceding exercise, continue working with the *Network Diagram (Detailed)* drawing. If not, you need the *Network Diagram (Detailed)_start* drawing located in the Chapter09 practice file folder to complete this exercise. Open the drawing in Visio.

1. Save your drawing as **Network Diagram (Organized)**.

Rectangle Tool

2. On the **Home** tab, in the **Tools** group, click the **Rectangle** tool.
3. Draw a rectangle surrounding the equipment in **Branch Office 1**.

Fill

4. On the **Home** tab, in the **Shape** group, click the **Fill** tool and select a light-colored background color.
5. Right-click on the rectangle you've drawn, and then click **Send to Back** to place it behind the network shapes.

   See Also For information about the front-to-back positioning of Visio shapes, see the sidebar "What's on Top?" in Chapter 5, "Adding Style, Color, and Themes."

Pointer Tool

6. On the **Home** tab, in the **Tools** group, click the **Pointer Tool**.
7. Draw a bounding box around the new rectangle and the shapes within it.

Group

8. On the **Home** tab, in the **Arrange** group, click the **Group** button, and then click **Group**.

   See Also See Chapter 3, "Adding Sophistication to Your Drawings," for more information about grouping and ungrouping shapes.

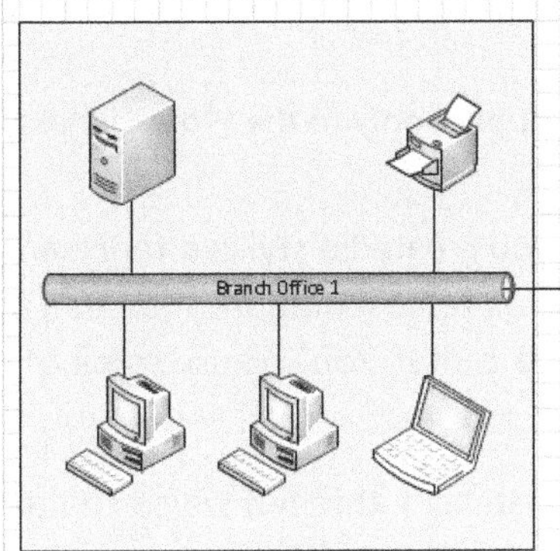

9. Repeat Steps 2–8 for **Branch Office 2** but select a different fill color in Step 4.
10. Repeat Steps 2–8 for **Data Center** but select a different fill color in Step 4.

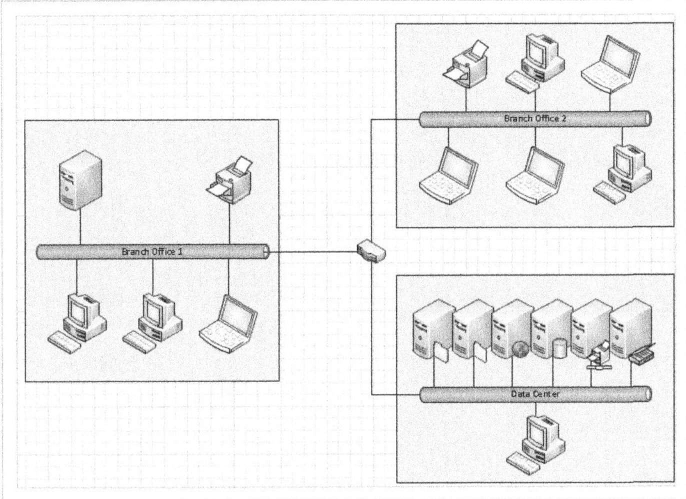

The approach you used in this exercise for grouping network shapes is very common. It offers the advantages, but also the disadvantages, of working with grouped shapes that were described in Chapter 3. In Chapter 11, "Adding Structure to Your Diagrams," you will learn about a new feature of Visio 2010—containers—that offers most of the advantages of grouping shapes but few of the disadvantages.

CLEAN UP Save the changes to the *Network Diagram (Organized)* drawing but leave it open if you are continuing with the next exercise.

Creating Rack Diagrams

Important **The information in this section applies only to the Professional and Premium editions of Visio 2010.**

In the previous exercises in this chapter, you created a stylized representation of your network. To build a more complete network representation, you need to add a diagram of the network equipment rack in the data center. You will use some of the stencils from the Rack Diagram template to create that picture.

The Rack Diagram template includes four stencils, three of which contain equipment and rack shapes (the fourth contains annotation shapes). The three equipment stencils are shown side by side in the following graphic.

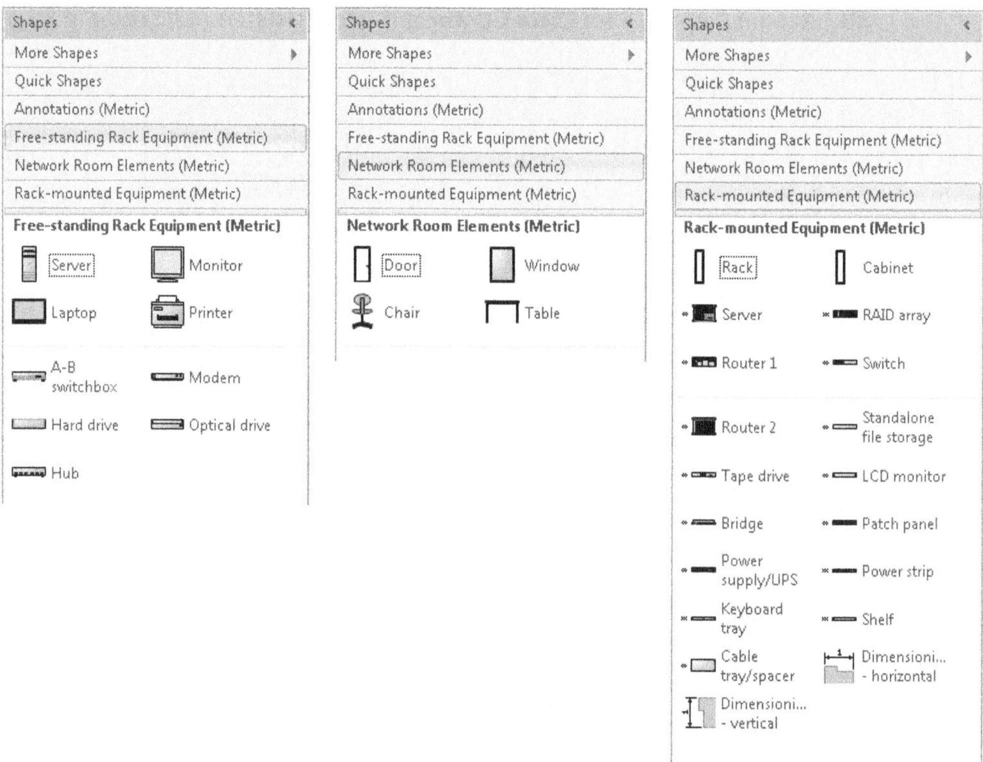

In this exercise, you will create the foundation for building a rack diagram by adding two stencils from the Rack Diagram template to your current drawing. You will also add a new page and will set the page attributes so you can create a drawing whose shapes are drawn to scale. Finally, you will add a rack shape to the new page.

SET UP If you completed the preceding exercise, continue working with the *Network Diagram (Organized)* drawing. If not, you need the *Network Diagram (Organized)_start* drawing located in the Chapter09 practice file folder to complete this exercise. Open the drawing in Visio.

1. Save your drawing as **Network Diagram with Rack**.
2. In the **Shapes** window, click **More Shapes**, point to **Network**, and then click **Free-standing Rack Equipment**.

   Tip You are not restricted to using just the stencils that are packaged with a Visio template. As you can see in this step and the next, you can open any Visio stencil in any diagram.

3. In the **Shapes** window, click **More Shapes**, point to **Network**, and then click **Rack-mounted Equipment**. The upper part of the Shapes window now shows the original stencils plus the two you've just opened.

   Next you will add a page that has the dimensions and drawing scale to hold an equipment rack.

4. Double-click the **Page-1** name tab, type **Network Overview**, and then press Enter.
5. Right-click the **Network Overview** name tab, and then click **Insert**.
6. Type **Data Center Detail**, click the **Measurement units** drop-down arrow, and then select **Meters**.

   Tip Changing measurement units is not required. However, a standard equipment rack is just over 2 meters (6.5 feet) tall. By selecting Meters as the measurement unit, the rulers on the left and top of the drawing page will show dimensions in meters, which is likely to be more useful than showing thousands of millimeters.

   If you are working in U.S. units, select either Feet And Inches or Feet (decimal).

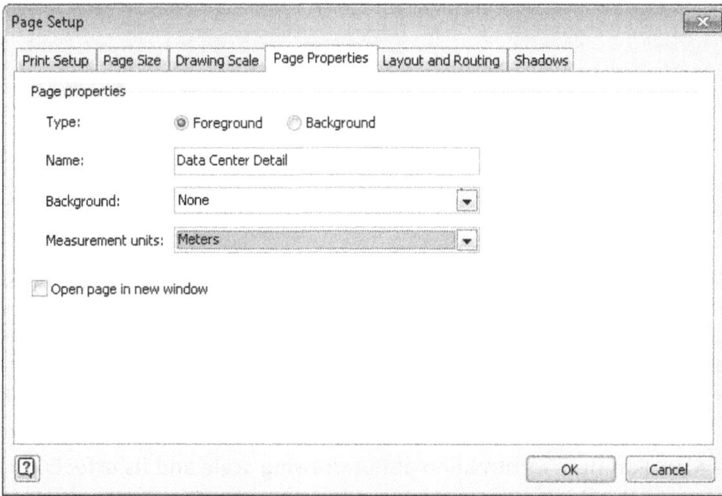

7. Click the **Drawing Scale** tab, click **Pre-defined scale**, and then select **Metric** in the first list and **1 : 10** in the second list.

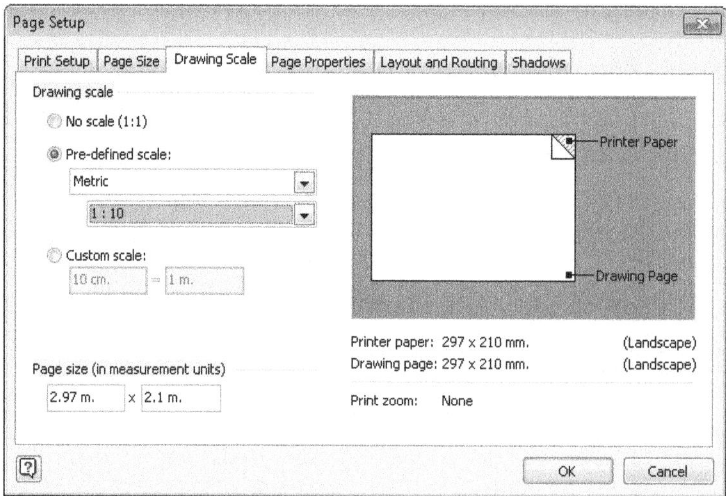

Tip If you are working in U.S. units, select Architectural in the first list and then select 1" = 1' 0" in the next list. See the following graphic.

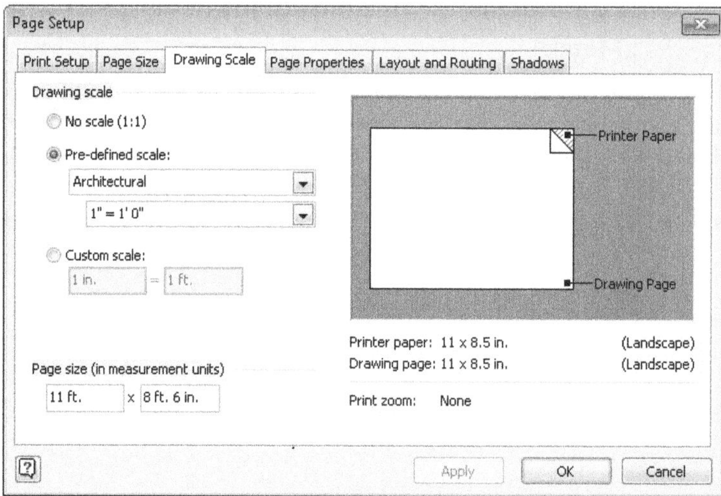

Important Visio rack shapes were created so that their size on the page reflects the drawing scale of the page. At a page-to-rack ratio of 1:1, each shape would be "life sized," that is, each shape would take as much space on the page as the real object does in a rack. By setting the scale to 1:10, each unit of measurement in your drawing represents 10 units in the real world. For U.S. units, a ratio of 1"=1'0" means that each inch on the page represents one foot in the real world.

See Also For more information about drawing scale and its effects on shapes, see "Changing the Drawing Scale" later in this chapter.

8. Click **OK**.

9. Drag a **Rack** shape from the **Rack-mounted Equipment** stencil onto the center of the drawing page.

   Because of the measurement units and page scale you've set in the preceding steps, the rack will occupy the entire space between the top and bottom margins of the page. (If you are using U.S. units, there will be some free space between the top and bottom margins.)

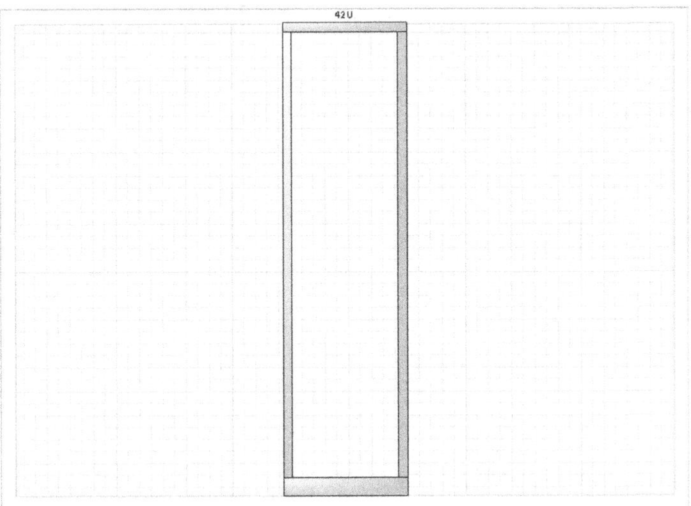

CLEAN UP **Save your changes to the** ***Network Diagram with Rack*** **drawing but leave it open if you are continuing with the next exercise.**

In the next exercise, you will add equipment shapes to your rack diagram.

Adding Equipment to Rack Diagrams

Important **The information in this section applies only to the Professional and Premium editions of Visio 2010.**

In the previous exercise, you built the foundation for a rack diagram by adding a drawing page with suitable dimensions and drawing scale to hold an equipment rack.

In this exercise, you will use that foundation to create a detailed representation of a data center equipment rack by adding the following equipment: six servers, one PC, a router, and a power supply. In addition, you will build a "drill-down" hyperlink to the equipment rack from your stylized network drawing.

SET UP You need the *Network Diagram with Rack* drawing from the preceding exercise in order to complete this exercise.

1. Drag a **Power supply/UPS** shape from the **Rack-mounted Equipment** stencil and drag it toward the bottom of the rack.

   The power supply shape, like all equipment shapes intended to be used within a Visio rack, is a 1-D shape. You will glue its end points to the connection points that appear on the side rails of the rack as you get close to the rack shape.

   See Also For more information about 1-D shapes and connection points, see Chapter 2, "Creating a New Drawing."

   Important In the following graphic, you see "2U" to the left of the power supply shape. You may also have noticed "42U" above the rack shape in the last graphic in the previous exercise.

   U is the abbreviation for one *rack unit*. Rack-mountable equipment is designed in multiples of 1U, which is 1.75 inches or 44.45 mm. Each piece of equipment you drag into the rack will display its height in U's.

   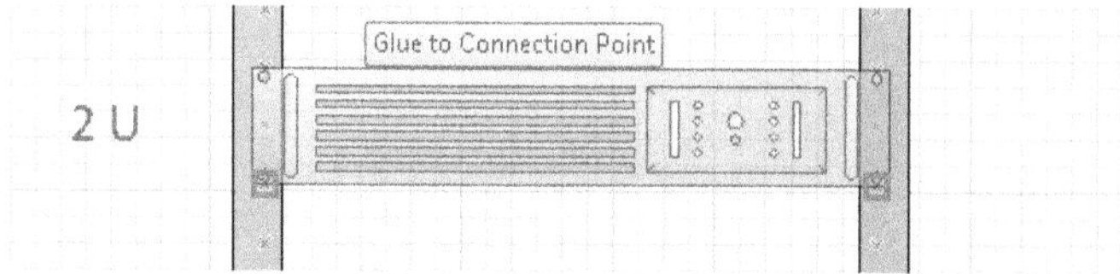

2. Glue the **Power supply/UPS** to the connectors at the bottom of the rack.
3. Drag a **Server** shape from the **Rack-mounted Equipment** stencil and drag it to the center of the rack.

   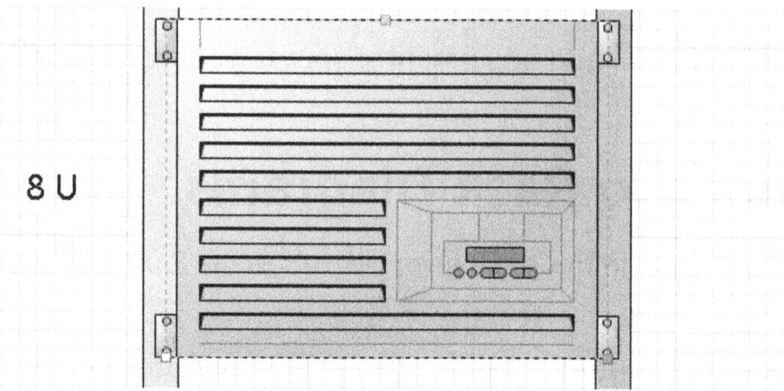

   The default server shape is very large—8U—but it's actually an interesting shape. Like many rack-mounted shapes, you can change its height, but this shape actually adjusts its appearance as you resize it; you will see this in the next step.

4. Drag the resize handle at the top of the server shape downward until the label at the left says **3U**.

Tip As you drag the handle, notice that at 7U, 6U, and 5U, the bottom half of the shape remains unchanged as the upper half of the shape gets smaller. However, at 4U and below, the lower part of the shape begins to adjust as well. As you can see, even a seemingly simple Visio shape can have reasonably sophisticated behavior.

5. Copy the 3U server shape and paste five copies onto the page. Drag each copy so it sits just above or below another server in the rack.

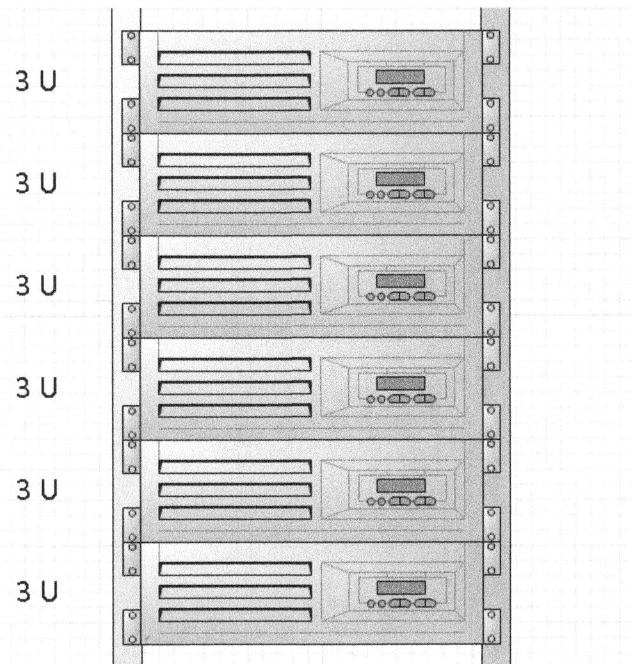

6. Drag a **Router 1** shape from the **Rack-mounted Equipment** stencil and position it at the bottom of the rack just above the power supply.
7. Drag an **LCD Monitor** shape from the **Rack-mounted Equipment** stencil and attach it to the rack between the bottom server and the router.

   This shape is not the actual monitor—that comes next—but is a shelf to hold the monitor.
8. Drag a **Monitor** shape from the **Free-standing Rack Equipment** stencil and position it below the servers. Adjust the position of the shelf you dropped in the previous step, if necessary, so the monitor appears to be sitting on the shelf.
9. Drag a **Keyboard tray** shape from the **Rack-mounted Equipment** stencil and attach it to the rack just below the monitor shelf. Your finished rack should look like the graphic on the left.

Tip If you prefer to see the rack without the "U" dimensions, right-click on the rack or any rack-mounted shape and click Hide U Sizes. The result is shown in the graphic on the right. You can turn U sizes back on by right-clicking and selecting Show U Sizes.

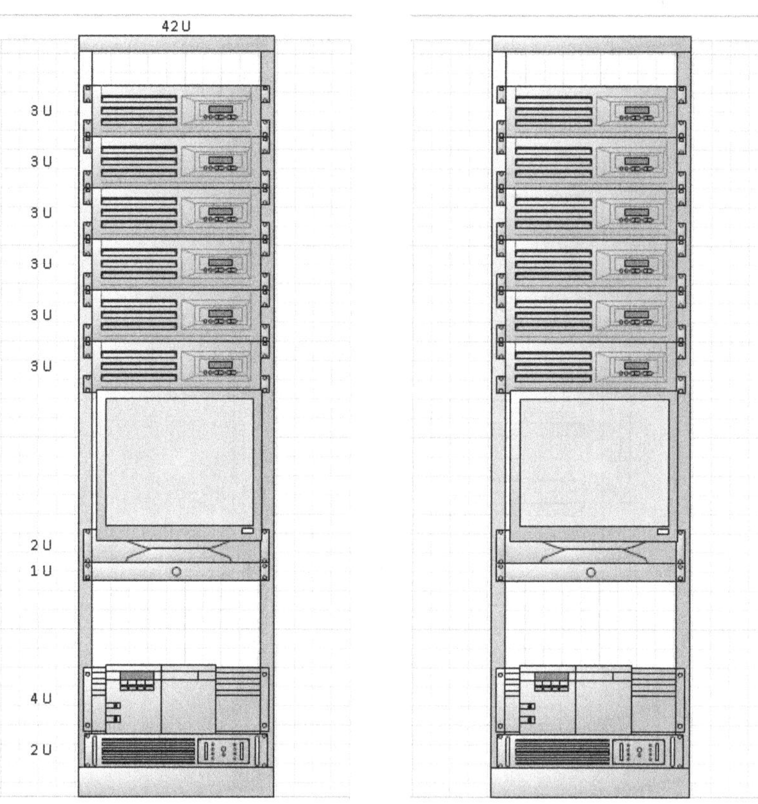

At this point your rack reflects the same equipment shown in your stylized diagram on the Network Overview page. In the final steps for this exercise, you will create a "drill-down" hyperlink from the overview page to the rack.

10. Return to the **Network Overview** page and draw a bounding box around the router and the **Data Center** group in the lower-right corner of the page.
11. Press Ctrl+K to open the **Hyperlinks** dialog box.

    See Also If you need a refresher on hyperlinks, see Chapter 7, "Adding and Using Hyperlinks."

12. In the **Hyperlinks** dialog box, click the **Browse** button to the right of **Sub-address**. The Hyperlink dialog box opens.
13. In the **Hyperlink** dialog box, select **Data Center Detail** from the **Page** list and select **Page** from the **Zoom** list.

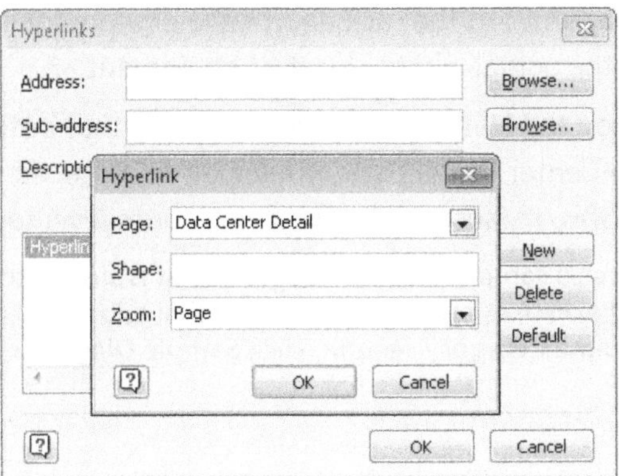

14. Click **OK**.
15. In the **Description** text box of the **Hyperlinks** dialog box, type **Drill down to Data Center**, and then click **OK**.

    Important It's very important to understand that you've just applied the identical hyperlink to all selected shapes in one step. The hyperlink is not attached to the part of the page you selected with the bounding box, but is attached to each selected shape individually. Visio makes it very easy to apply the same change to multiple shapes, which is great if that's what you want to do. However, you do need to be careful that you don't inadvertently apply a change to multiple shapes.

16. Right-click on any of the hyperlinked shapes, and then click **Drilldown to Data Center**.

    You will see a full-page view of the rack diagram on the Data Center Detail page.

CLEAN UP Save your changes to the *Network Diagram with Rack* diagram but leave it open if you are continuing with the next exercise.

The rack diagram you've created shows the key equipment in this simple data center. What might you do to enhance your rack drawing? Consider these ideas:

- Use ***data linking*** (Chapter 6, "Entering, Linking to, and Reporting on Data") to link the equipment in your rack to a spreadsheet or database containing asset IDs, serial numbers and other inventory information.
- Link your rack equipment to a real-time or near-real-time data source so the equipment in your rack contains status information.
- Use data visualization techniques (Chapter 10) to help the user of your diagram understand the data "behind the shapes."
- Add a patch panel and network cabling. Consider putting the cabling on a separate layer (see Chapter 3) so you can easily show or hide it.
- Add data to the rack shape so its location and other information is part of your network inventory reports.

- Add hyperlinks (see Chapter 7) to the rack and/or the equipment in the rack and link to photographs of the actual wiring closet or equipment.
- Change the hyperlinks on the Network Overview page so that instead of linking each server to the Data Center Detail page, you link it to a specific server shape in the rack. When you do this, try setting the hyperlink zoom level to 150% or 200%.

See Also **If you would like to see a sample network diagram that is similar to the one you've created in the previous several exercises but that also has several additional features, on the File tab, click New; in the Template Category section, click Sample Diagrams, and then double-click IT Asset Management.**

Where Can I Get Shapes That Look Like My Equipment?

In the exercises in this and preceding sections, you built network and rack diagrams using stock shapes that are delivered with Visio. The shapes probably look something like your servers, routers, and other equipment, but they can't match exactly because they are generic shapes.

If you want to create more realistic diagrams, there are thousands of downloadable Visio stencils and shapes from various sources, such as the following:

- Network and computer equipment vendors often provide shapes for their equipment.
- Some companies design and sell both product-specific and generic Visio shapes.
- Individuals have created network and computer equipment shapes. Many provide them for free; some charge for their artwork.

For large collections of links to various stencil sources (most are free), go to the following sites:

- *visio.mvps.org/3rdparty.htm*
- *www.visiocafe.com*

You can also try the following commercial stencil vendors:

- *www.visiostencils.com*
- *www.shapesource.com*

Examples of shapes provided by equipment manufacturers are located at the following sites:

- **Cisco** *www.cisco.com/en/US/products/hw/prod_cat_visios.html*
- **Dell** *www.dell.com/us/en/esg/topics/segtopic_visio.htm*

Changing the Drawing Scale

Important **The drawing scale concepts in this section apply to all editions of Visio. However, the exercise in this section uses rack shapes that are only available with the Professional and Premium editions of Visio 2010.**

In "Creating Rack Diagrams" earlier in this chapter, you used options on the Drawing Scale tab in the Page Setup dialog box to change the ratio between the dimensions for the images on the page and their real-life counterparts. The ability to create scaled drawings is a very powerful feature in Visio.

Occasionally, after you have created a scaled drawing, you need to adjust the scale. As a simple example, you might have created a diagram containing a single rack. What happens when you want to add additional racks and there isn't enough room on the page?

In this exercise, you will add additional racks to a diagram and rescale the page as required.

SET UP **If you completed the preceding exercise, continue working with the *Network Diagram with Rack* drawing. If not, you need the *Network Diagram with Rack_start* drawing located in the Chapter09 practice file folder to complete this exercise. Open the drawing in Visio and save it as *Network Diagram with Rack*.**

1. Drag a **Rack** shape from the **Rack-mounted Equipment** stencil and drop it to the right of the existing rack. Then drop another one on the left side.

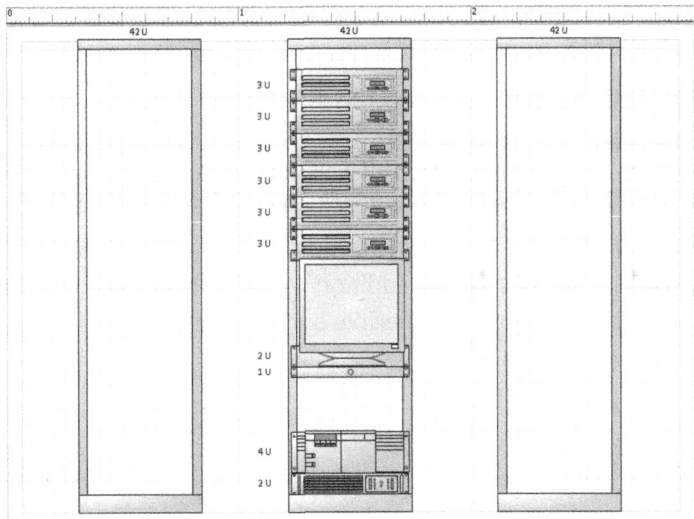

You could squeeze one or possibly two more racks onto this page but it would get very crowded. You could create a new page and add more racks there. But what if you want to fit one or two more racks onto this page without overcrowding? The trick lies in adjusting the drawing scale.

Tip When you create a scaled drawing page, it's a good idea to include a shape on the page that shows the page scale.

2. Right-click the **Data Center Detail** page name tab, and then select **Page Setup**.
3. Click the **Drawing Scale** tab, and then select **1 : 20** in the list under **Metric**.

   Tip If your drawing uses U.S. units, select ½"=1'0" under Architectural.

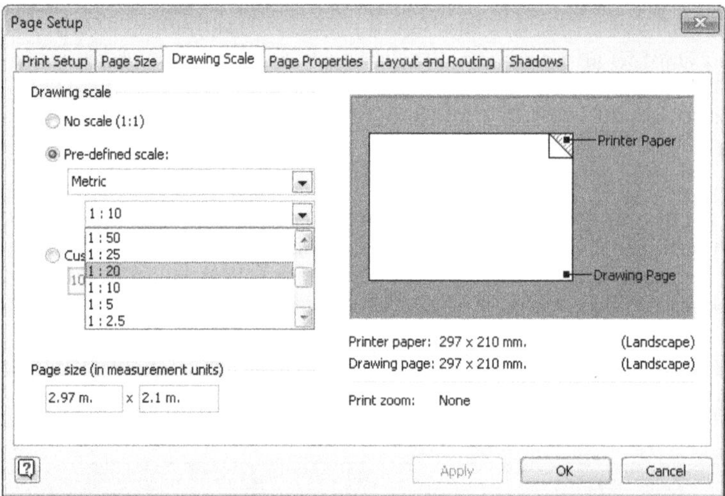

4. Click **OK**, and then press Ctrl+Shift+W to view the whole page.

   Important Look at the ruler at the top of the graphic in Step 1 to see that that drawing represents approximately 3 meters of wall space in your data center. Now look at the ruler in the following graphic; your drawing page now represents 6 meters of wall space.

   After cutting the page scale by half, you can certainly fit more racks onto the page, but the racks are very small. In addition, you may not need this much space. The good news is that Visio is very flexible and you can specify your own scale factor to achieve the ideal balance.

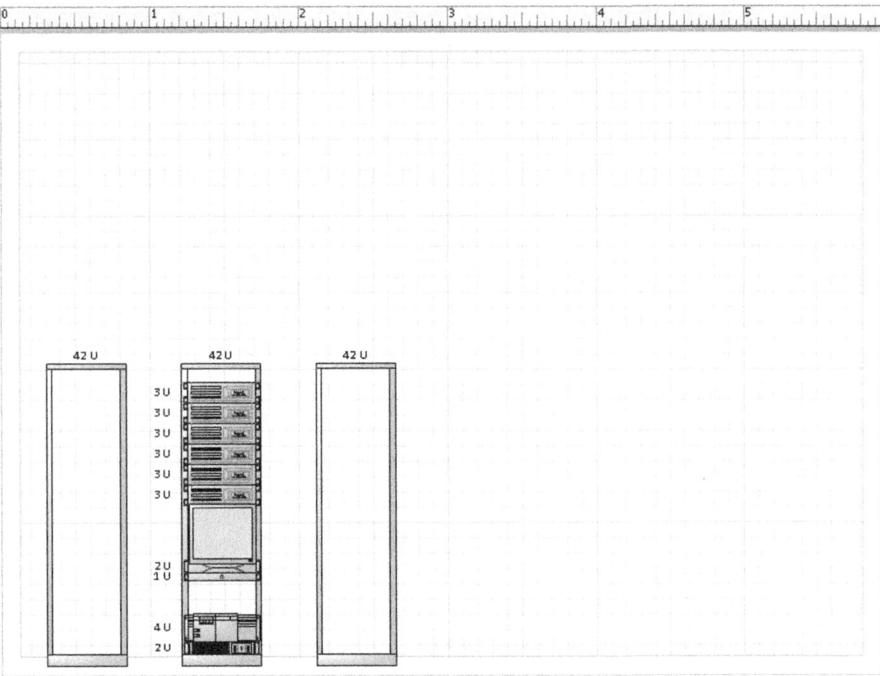

5. Right-click the **Data Center Detail** page name tab, and then select **Page Setup**.
6. In the **Page Setup** dialog box, click **Custom scale**.

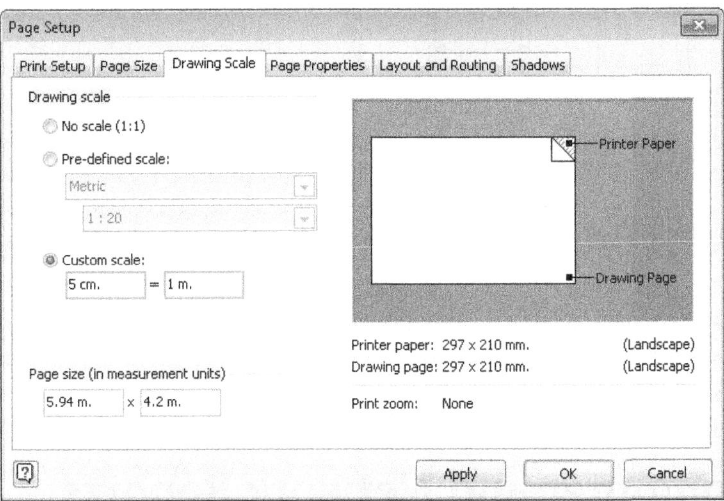

You see that a scale of 1:20 means that 5 cm. on the page equals 1 meter on the ground. If you had looked when the scale was 1:10, you would have seen settings of 10 cm = 1 m. You need to create a scaling ratio that is in between the two values you've already tried.

7. Type **7 cm.** in the first box under **Custom scale**, and then click **OK**.

   The resulting page size represents just over 4 meters of data center wall space and is appropriate for adding several additional racks. You can enter any other scale factors in the future to enlarge or reduce the working area of the page.

   Tip If your drawing uses U.S. units, try selecting ¾"=1'0" under Architectural.

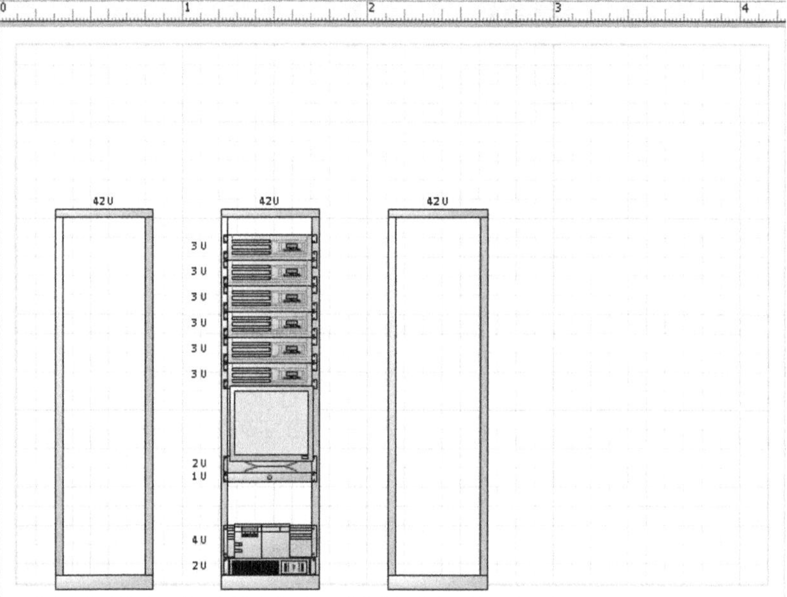

CLEAN UP Save your changes to the *Network Diagram with Rack* drawing and close the file.

Important Not all shapes were designed to respond to changes in the drawing scale of the page. If you change the page scale and the shapes don't respond appropriately, either you're out of luck or you'll need to find replacement shapes.

Running Computer and Network Reports

Many of the templates provided with Visio include predefined reports. Both the Basic and Detailed Network Diagram templates that were described earlier in this chapter include three reports that highlight different subsets of the ***shape data*** in the various computer and network shapes.

The following three graphics show part of the output available in the three network and computer equipment reports. The sample reports were created by adding data to the network diagram you created in the preceding exercise. If you would like to run these reports yourself, you can open the *Network Diagram (Basic) with data_start* drawing located in the Chapter09 practice file folder. (Refer to Chapter 6, for a refresher on Visio reports.)

If you prefer to add data to your own diagram and then run the reports, use the network map from the previous exercise and link it to the *Network Equipment Data (Basic)_start* workbook in the Chapter09 practice file folder. (Refer to Chapter 6 for a refresher on data linking.)

Tip **The Displayed Text column in the reports shows the text typed onto the shapes. In this network diagram, the only two shapes that contain text are the Ethernet segments.**

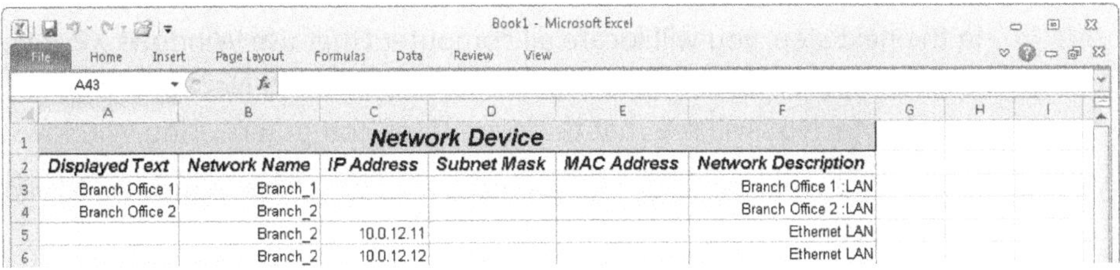

Network Device					
Displayed Text	Network Name	IP Address	Subnet Mask	MAC Address	Network Description
Branch Office 1	Branch_1				Branch Office 1 :LAN
Branch Office 2	Branch_2				Branch Office 2 :LAN
	Branch_2	10.0.12.11			Ethernet LAN
	Branch_2	10.0.12.12			Ethernet LAN

Network Equipment							
Building	Room	Displayed Text	Network Name	Network Description	IP Address	Manufacturer	Product Description
			Corporate	WAN	10.0.5.1	A. Datum Corporation	Router
Coolidge	476		Branch_2	Ethernet LAN	10.0.12.15	A. Datum Corporation	Laptop
Coolidge	478		Branch_2	Ethernet LAN	10.0.12.14	Contoso, Ltd	Laptop
Coolidge	544		Branch_2	Ethernet LAN	10.0.12.16	Contoso, Ltd	PC
East Atwater	216		Branch_1	Ethernet LAN	10.0.5.104	Contoso, Ltd	PC
East Atwater	311		Branch_1	Ethernet LAN	10.0.5.105	A. Datum Corporation	Laptop

Tip **Only part of the Network Equipment report is shown above; there are additional fields to the right of the Product Description column.**

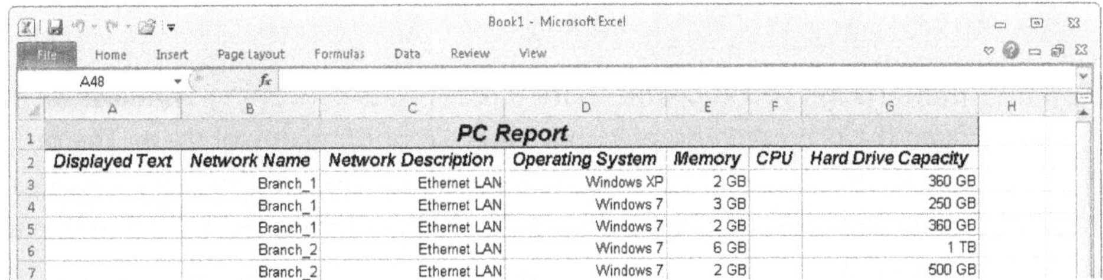

PC Report						
Displayed Text	Network Name	Network Description	Operating System	Memory	CPU	Hard Drive Capacity
	Branch_1	Ethernet LAN	Windows XP	2 GB		360 GB
	Branch_1	Ethernet LAN	Windows 7	3 GB		250 GB
	Branch_1	Ethernet LAN	Windows 7	2 GB		360 GB
	Branch_2	Ethernet LAN	Windows 7	6 GB		1 TB
	Branch_2	Ethernet LAN	Windows 7	2 GB		500 GB

Searching and Replacing Text

Although the need to search and replace text isn't directly related to network diagrams, the subject is included in this chapter because network diagrams provide a useful case for text search.

In this exercise, you will use the Visio find/replace features to locate and alter text in a drawing.

SET UP You need the *Network Diagram (Organized)_start* drawing located in the Chapter09 practice file folder to complete this exercise. Open it in Visio.

Find

1. On the **Home** tab, in the **Editing** group, click the **Find** button, and then click **Find**. The Find dialog box opens and allows you to type the search text as well as to define various search parameters.

   In the next step, you will locate all computers that use Windows XP. If you look at the PC Report mentioned in "Running Computer and Network Reports" earlier in this chapter, you will see that there are three computers using Windows XP.

2. In the **Find what** text box of the **Find** dialog box, type **Windows XP**, and then click **Find Next**.

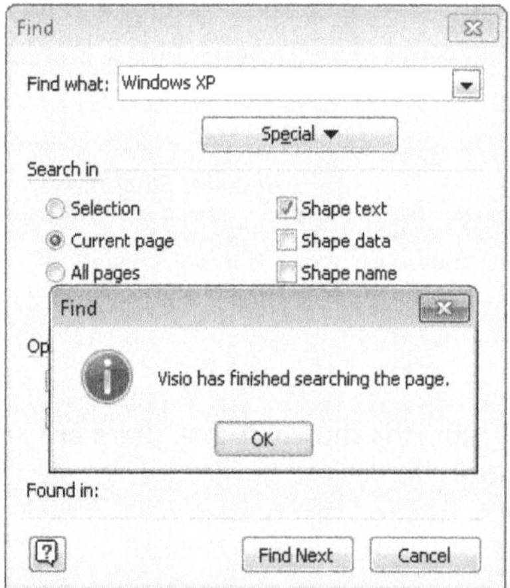

   Even though you know there are three shapes containing *Windows XP*, it's clear from the preceding graphic that Visio did not find any of them. The problem lies in the default search parameters that you see behind the search results message box: Visio only searched the ***shape text*** (the text displayed on a shape) and not the shape data.

3. Click **OK** to close the information dialog box, and then select **Shape data** in the **Find** dialog box.

4. Click **Find Next** again. This time the Find function identifies a PC with Windows XP in its shape data (look for the laptop that is selected in the Branch Office 2 network).

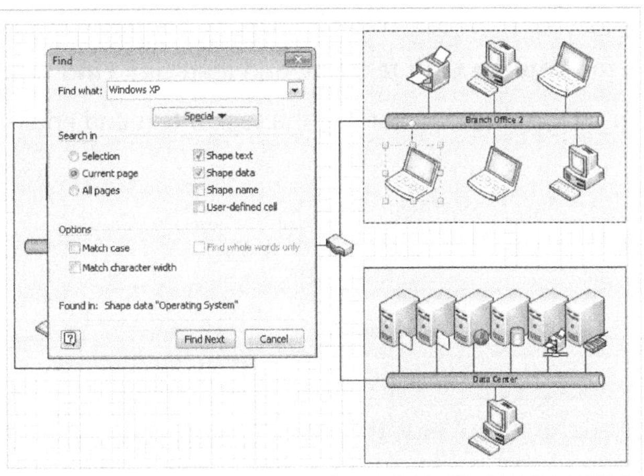

Continuing to click Find Next will identify other shapes that contain the search text *Windows XP*. Eventually, clicking Find Next will display a dialog box indicating that Visio has finished searching the page.

Tip **By using additional settings in the Find dialog box, you can limit a search to just those shapes that are currently selected or you can expand the search to all shapes on all pages. You can also search *shape names* and *user-defined cells*. The Options section of the Find dialog box lets you limit search results based on text case and other text attributes.**

5. Click **Cancel** to close the **Find** dialog box.
6. On the **Home** tab, in the **Editing** group, click **Find**, and then click **Replace**.

Tip **Both the Find and the Replace dialog boxes display the most recently used search string when you open them (see *Windows XP* in the following figure). In addition, both the Find What text box and the Replace With text box contain a drop-down arrow. Clicking the arrow displays recently used text strings.**

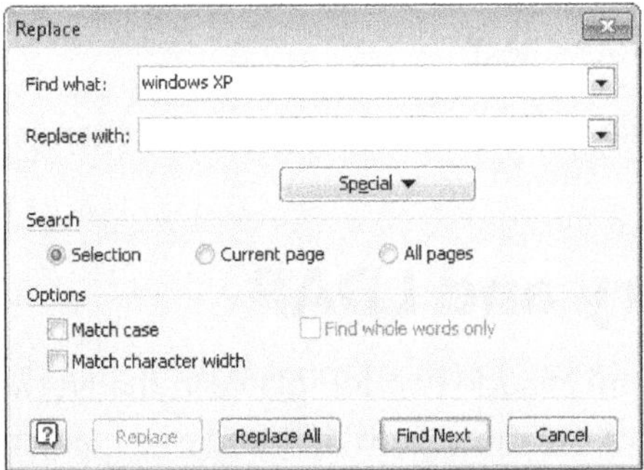

Important Notice that the Replace dialog box does not include check boxes for Shape Text, Shape Data, Shape Name, or User-Defined Cell as the Find dialog box does. This means that you can use the Replace function to change shape text and but cannot replace the text found in the other three locations.

7. In the **Replace** dialog box, type **Branch** in the **Find what** text box.
8. Type **Local** in the **Replace with** text box, and then click **Find Next**.

   Visio zooms in on the shape containing the search text and enters text-edit mode.

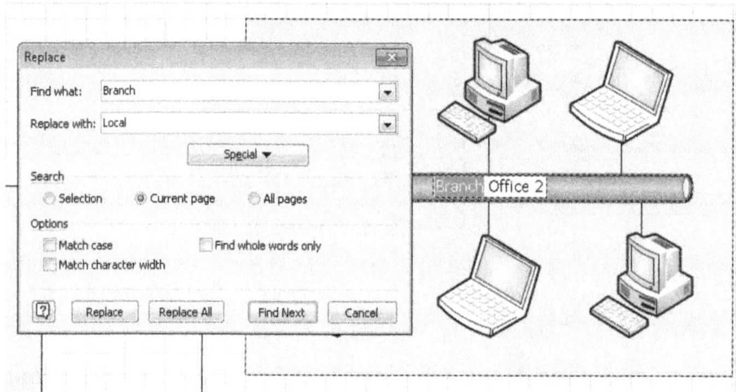

9. Click the **Replace** button. Visio makes the change, finds the next match, and enters edit mode.

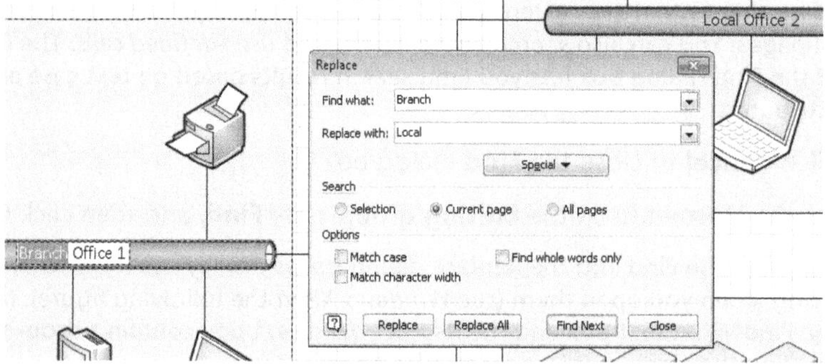

At any time, you can click Replace to make the next change, or Replace All to replace all occurrences of the found text.

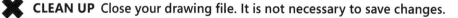

CLEAN UP Close your drawing file. It is not necessary to save changes.

Mapping Active Directory and LDAP

Visio Professional and Visio Premium include two templates in the Network category that help you create logical maps of the directories that underlie many networks:

- The Active Directory template provides shapes that represent common Active Directory objects, sites, and services.
- The LDAP Directory template includes shapes that represent common LDAP (Lightweight Directory Access Protocol) objects.

Neither template creates a drawing for you automatically. However, Microsoft offers a free download called the Microsoft Active Directory Topology Diagrammer that automatically builds a Visio diagram from an Active Directory. You can download this add-in from *www.microsoft.com/downloads/details.aspx?familyid=cb42fc06-50c7-47ed-a65c-862661742764*.

Key Points

- Visio offers up to five templates and more than a dozen stencils targeted at creating network, data center, and computer equipment diagrams.
- You can create both stylized network drawings and extremely realistic diagrams by using shapes supplied with Visio or that are available for download. Many equipment vendors provide stencils containing shapes for their products. In addition, other companies and individuals have created product-specific artwork.
- The Visio rack and equipment shapes were drawn to scale so that if you change the scale of the drawing page, the rack/equipment shapes will resize accordingly.
- One common way of organizing related sets of shapes in a network diagram is to group them together with a colored background shape. This creates a visually distinct group but also inherits some of the disadvantages of grouping shapes (see Chapter 3). Visio 2010 offers another option for grouping shapes, called containers, which will be discussed in Chapter 11.
- The Visio text search feature is very flexible and allows significant control over how the search will be conducted. You can use it to locate text on and inside shapes. The text replace function is more limited and does not allow replacing any text other than that which is displayed on a shape.
- Visio Professional and Visio Premium include templates for manually creating maps of Active Directory, Microsoft Exchange Server, and LDAP directories. In addition, Microsoft offers a free Active Directory Topology Diagrammer that automatically creates a Visio map from an Active Directory.

Chapter at a Glance

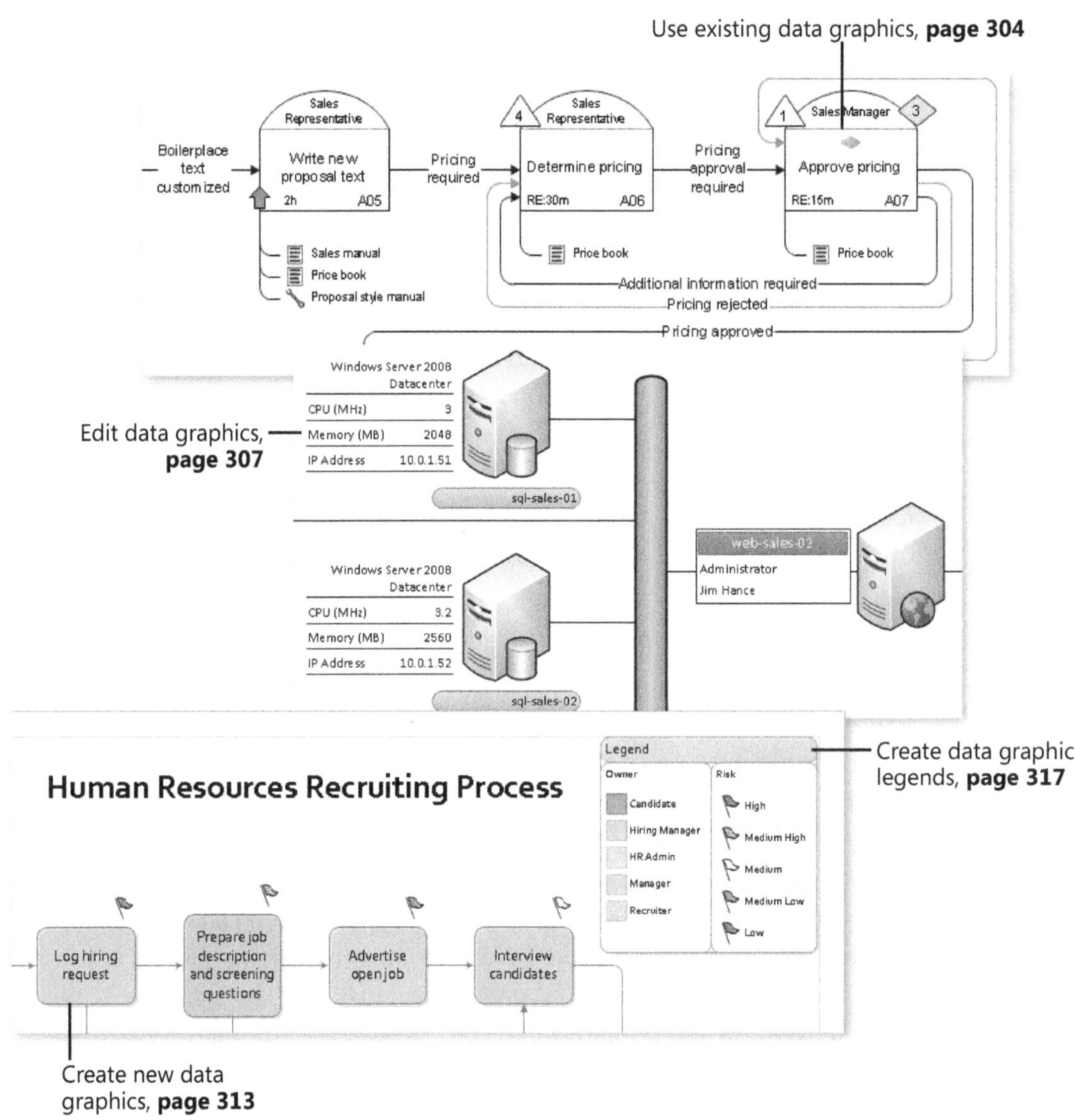

10 Visualizing Your Data

In this chapter, you will learn how to

- ✔ Enhance diagrams with data-driven graphics.
- ✔ Use existing data graphics.
- ✔ Edit data graphics.
- ✔ Create new data graphics.
- ✔ Create data graphic legends.

In Chapter 6, "Entering, Linking to, and Reporting on Data," you learned how to enter data into Microsoft Visio shapes and how to integrate data from external sources into your diagrams. After you have data in your Visio diagram, you need techniques to make that data visible. With a Visio ***data graphic***, you can do just that by displaying text or a graphic on a Visio shape based on the data inside the shape.

Data graphics are even more powerful when a diagram is connected to data that is dynamically refreshed from an external data source. In that situation, your Visio drawing becomes a dashboard showing near real–time status for your network, a business process, a restaurant seating chart, a manufacturing assembly line... the possibilities are endless.

In this chapter, you will use Visio 2010 data graphics to present shape data in a variety of attractive and useful ways.

Important The information in this chapter applies only to the Professional and Premium editions of Visio 2010.

Practice Files Before you can complete the exercises in this chapter, you need to copy the book's practice files to your computer. The practice files you'll use to complete the exercises in this chapter are in the Chapter10 practice files folder. A complete list of practice files is provided in "Using the Practice Files" at the beginning of this book.

Enhancing Diagrams with Data-Driven Graphics

A person using a Visio diagram you create can learn a lot about the subject of the diagram based on your choice of shapes, their positions on the page, how they are connected, and many other visual cues. However, if your diagram is connected to an external data source, it can convey so much more information.

In this section, you will see four examples of diagrams that use data graphics to tell even more of the story behind the picture.

Network Equipment Diagram

The first example continues the network and rack diagram theme from Chapter 9, "Drawing the Real World: Network and Data Center Diagrams." The story behind this diagram is as follows:

- You are a data center manager and have created rack diagrams for each rack in your computer room.
- You've populated your drawing with data by using the techniques you learned in Chapter 6 to connect your diagram to a Microsoft Excel spreadsheet or a database.
- The data for each rack-mounted server includes the data shown in the following graphic.

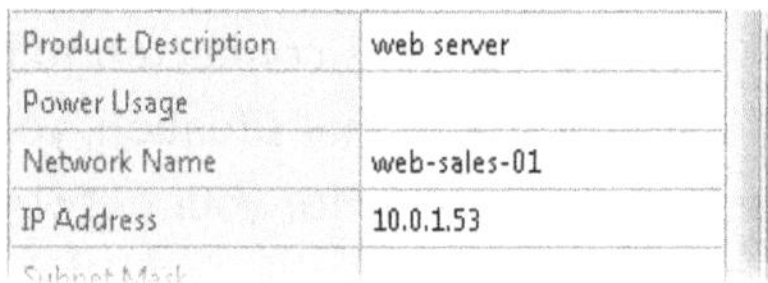

Product Description	web server
Power Usage	
Network Name	web-sales-01
IP Address	10.0.1.53

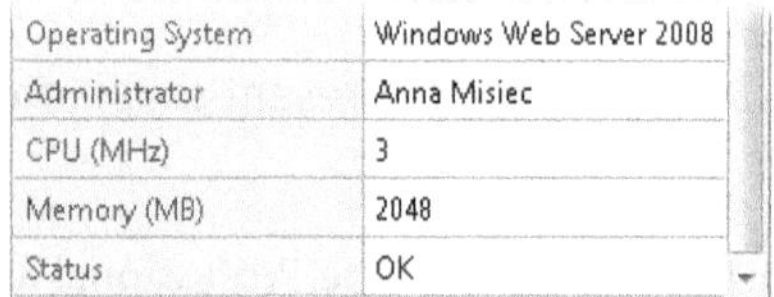

Operating System	Windows Web Server 2008
Administrator	Anna Misiec
CPU (MHz)	3
Memory (MB)	2048
Status	OK

- The spreadsheet or database contains some static data about your equipment, but it also contains live status information that is updated periodically.
- You have configured your Visio diagram to automatically read the data source and refresh the drawing at a preset time interval.

The result is that you can use data graphics to turn your Visio drawing into a dashboard for viewing network and equipment status. In the following graphic, several data graphics have been applied to the equipment rack to highlight the following:

- Server name and type (left)
- Server status (center)
- CPU and memory (right)

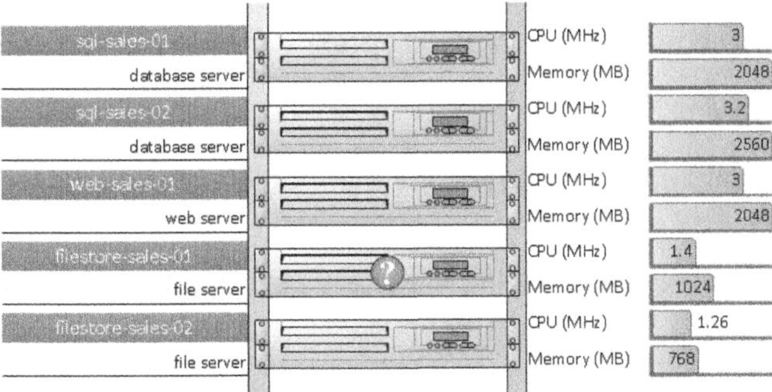

The following graphic shows the same equipment rack, at the same moment in time, but it uses different data graphics to highlight different information. In this version of the rack diagram, you see the following:

- Server name and IP address (left)
- Operating system name (right)

In addition, the status of the server is made even more evident by applying a color to the entire server shape rather than using an icon as in the previous example.

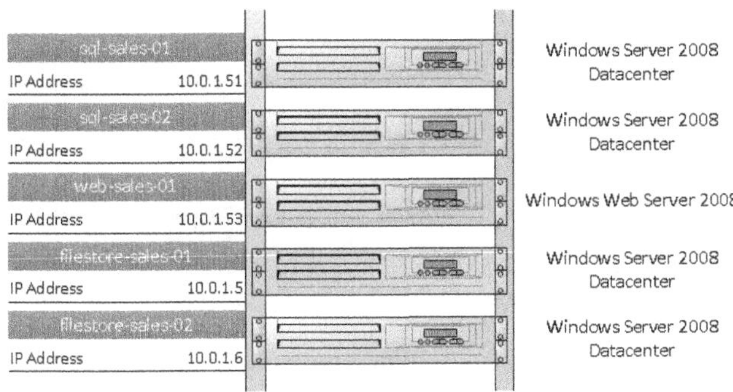

Part of the appeal of data graphics is represented by these two examples—you can apply different graphics at different times depending on what you need to know.

Tip **If you would like to work with a very similar diagram to the preceding example, click the File tab, and then click New. In the Other Ways To Get Started section, click Sample Diagrams, and then double-click the IT Asset Management thumbnail.**

Process Improvement Workflow

In this example, data graphics have been applied to process steps in a swimlane diagram in order to show several process quality measurements. In the upper right of the diagram, you also see a ***data graphic legend.*** (You will learn more about legends in "Creating Data Graphic Legends" later in this chapter.)

The metrics in this diagram:

- Show the duration of each step (look for a thermometer bar across the bottom of each task shape).
- Display a warning if the step is taking either 5-9 days or 10 or more days (lower-left corner of each step).
- Indicate whether each step is improving or being investigated (shape color).

The symbolism used for each of these metrics is explained in the legend that appears in the upper-right corner of the page.

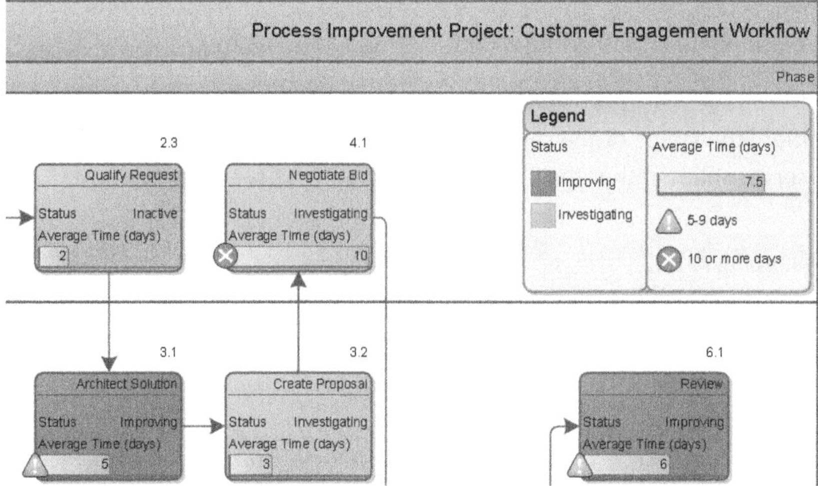

Tip **If you would like to work with a very similar diagram to the preceding example, click the File tab, and then click New. In the Other Ways To Get Started section, click Sample Diagrams, and then double-click the Process Improvement thumbnail.**

Casino Operation

The third example illustrates the types of near real–time information that a casino manager might view in Visio with the goal of monitoring critical operations. In all likelihood your job doesn't involve managing a casino, but you can probably think of important operations that you do need to monitor.

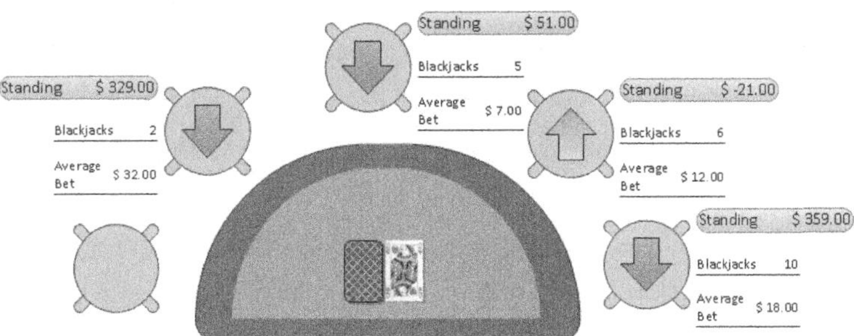

You see text callouts that highlight each bettor's recent history, including current dollar standing, average bet, and number of blackjacks. There is also a red or green arrow showing how each player is trending.

Tip If you would like to work with a very similar diagram to the preceding example, open the Casino Floor drawing in the Chapter10 practice file folder. Be sure to notice that the diagram has multiple pages showing different parts of the casino floor.

Risk Management

In the final example, you are viewing part of a process map that was created using a Visio add-in called TaskMap (www.taskmap.com). The following graphic shows three tasks in the middle of a sales proposal process.

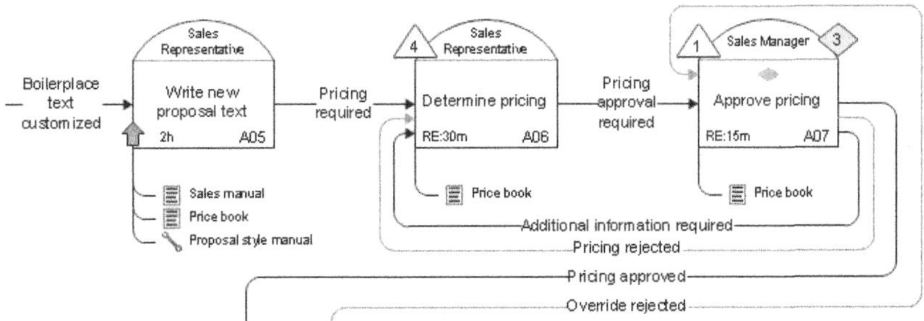

In this diagram, the data graphics depict two aspects of risk management:

- Yellow triangles identify risks; the number in each triangle relates to an entry in a master list of risks. Green diamonds show the corresponding control that the organization has put in place to mitigate the risk. (An organization might maintain the master list of risks and controls in something as simple as a spreadsheet, or they might employ a formal risk management system.)

  In a task like the one in the center, the organization has identified a risk but not a control, so the risk is more significant.
- The red arrows identify tasks that exceed a defined time threshold—30 minutes in the case of this example.

There is a third data graphic in this example: the task on the right displays a red diamond to indicate that it is a decision point in the process.

Tip **If you would like to look at the full page from which the excerpt above was taken, open the Sales Proposal Process TaskMap PDF in the Chapter10 practice file folder. In addition, a web-published version of this TaskMap that includes hyperlinks to Word and Excel documents, is available at *www.taskmap.com/Scott/Visio2010SBS/RiskManagement.htm*.**

The examples in this section highlight the importance of the data behind a diagram and suggest a variety of creative ways you can add value to your data-connected diagrams.

Using Existing Data Graphics

Now that you've seen examples showing how varied and useful data graphics can be, it's time to work with them.

In this exercise, you will work with the data graphics that are built into a sample diagram that is included with Visio 2010. First, you will learn how to turn data graphics off, then you will learn how to apply them to selected shapes.

SET UP Start Visio, or if it's already running, click the File tab and then click New. In the Other Ways To Get Started section, click Sample Diagrams, and then double-click the IT Asset Management thumbnail. When the drawing opens, close the External Data window and save the drawing as *Network with Data Graphics*.

1. Press Ctrl+A to select all shapes on the page.

   Tip **You must select one or more shapes *before* opening the data graphics gallery because you can only apply or remove data graphics on preselected shapes.**

Data Graphics

2. On the **Data** tab, in the **Display Data** group, click the **Data Graphics** button. The Data Graphics gallery opens and displays available data graphics along with several menu entries. When you point to a data graphic, popup text will display its name.

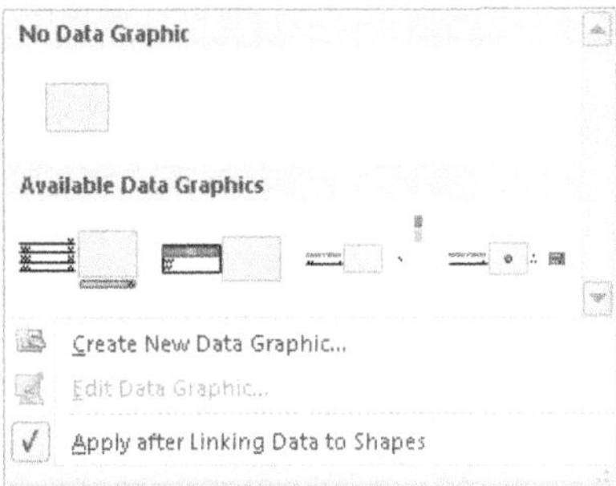

Tip **The selected Apply After Linking Data To Shapes check box at the bottom of the data graphics gallery causes the currently active data graphic to be applied each time you link data from the External Data window to one or more shapes on the drawing page. If you do not want a data graphic to be applied automatically, clear the check box to turn this option off. (See Chapter 6 for more information about data linking.)**

3. In the **Data Graphics** gallery, click the thumbnail below **No Data Graphic** to turn off data graphics on all shapes. The drawing page now shows the unadorned network diagram.

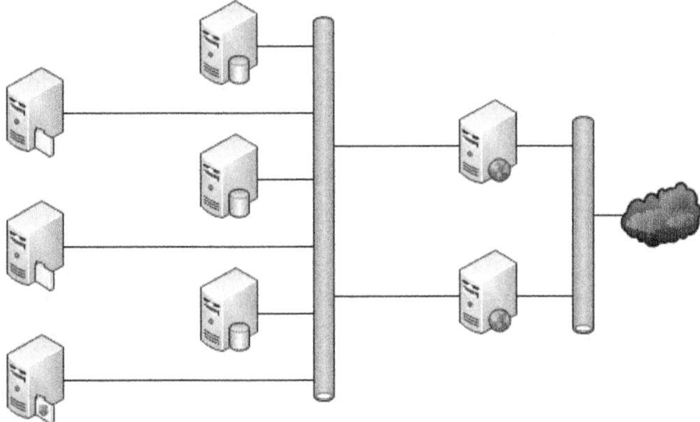

4. Select the six servers to the left of the longer network segment. (Do not include the network segment in your selection.)
5. On the **Data** tab, in the **Display Data** group, click the **Data Graphics** button to open the gallery, and then click the **Topology 1** thumbnail to apply that data graphic to the six servers.
6. Select the pair of web servers located between the two network segments.
7. On the **Data** tab, in the **Display Data** group, click the **Data Graphics** button to open the gallery, and then click the **Topology 2** thumbnail to apply that data graphic to the two servers.
8. Zoom in to view several servers in the center of the diagram.

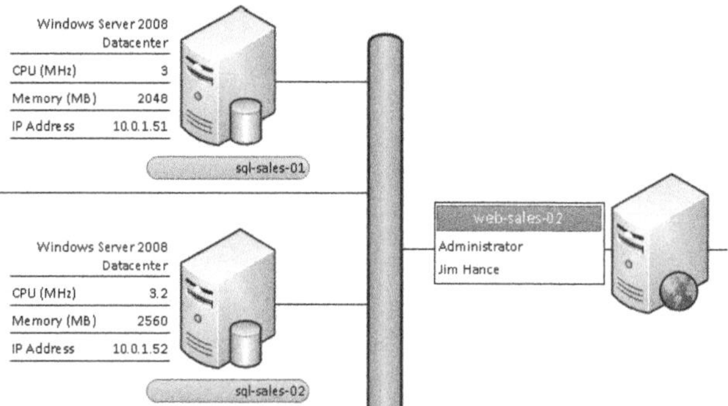

The servers on the left display a subset of the shapes' data using one style of presentation, whereas the servers on the right show different data in an alternate format:

- For the servers on the left, most of the data is displayed as underlined text to the left of the server icon, but the server name is displayed with a green background under the server.
- For the servers on the right, the name is displayed to the left of the PC shape with a blue background and the administrator name is displayed as plain text. In contrast with the servers on the left, there is also a border around the data graphic on this server.

You control all of these formatting options when you edit or create a data graphic as you will do in the exercises that follow.

Tip **You can only apply one data graphic to any one shape at any one time. However, as the figure above shows, you can apply different data graphics to different shapes on the same page.**

CLEAN UP Save your changes to the *Network with Data Graphics* drawing but leave it open if you are continuing with the next exercise.

The data graphics used in this section all display text callouts in various formats. In upcoming exercises, you will see several types of data graphic icons.

Important **Data graphics are applied to a single page at a time. If you want to apply the same data graphic to multiple pages, you must either apply it to each page separately, or write a Visio macro. You will learn about macros in the Appendix.**

Tip **Visio data graphics are automatically assigned to a special layer in a diagram. (See the "Understanding Layers" section in Chapter 3, "Adding Sophistication to Your Drawing.") If you want to hide data graphics without removing them, you can change the view properties for the data graphics layer.**

Editing Data Graphics

The placement and appearance of data graphics are controlled by an editable set of parameters. Although you can't control every attribute of a data graphic without resorting to writing code, the Visio 2010 user interface provides tools to effect a surprising number of changes.

In this exercise, you will modify the data graphics that you applied in the preceding section. First you will change the placement of one data graphic, and then you will alter the display attributes of several elements within a second data graphic.

SET UP If you completed the preceding exercise, continue working with the *Network with Data Graphics* drawing. Otherwise, click the File tab, and then click New. In the Other Ways To Get Started section, click Sample Diagrams, and then double-click the IT Asset Management thumbnail. Save the drawing as *Network with Data Graphics*.

Data Graphics

1. On the **Data** tab, in the **Display Data** group, click the **Data Graphics** button to open the gallery. (To see a graphic of the Data Graphic gallery, see Step 2 in the preceding exercise.)
2. Right-click the **Topology 2** thumbnail, and then click **Edit**. The Edit Data Graphic dialog box for Topology 2 opens.

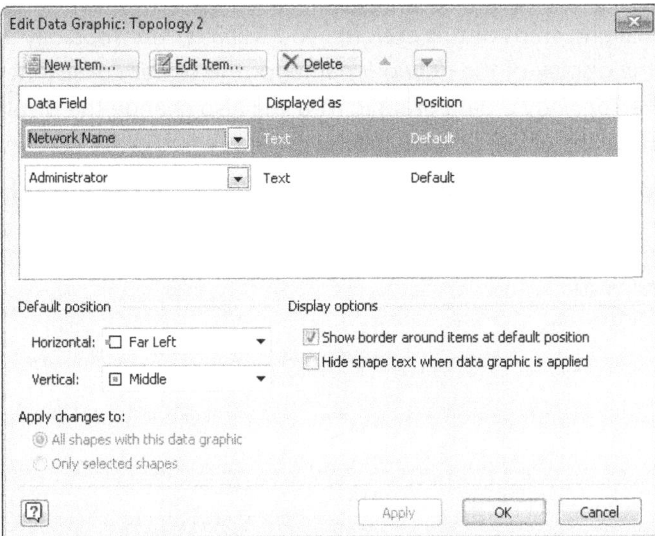

In the upper half of the Edit Data Graphic dialog box, you can add, edit, or delete individual items within the data graphic. In the lower half, you can modify the characteristics of the data graphic as a whole. You will use the lower half for this exercise.

Important You establish the default position for a data graphic in the lower-left corner of the Edit Data Graphic dialog box. (Both the horizontal and vertical position are relative to the shape to which the graphic will be attached.) Data graphic items in the upper half of the dialog box whose Position is set to Default will appear at this location.

3. In the **Default position** section of the **Edit Data Graphic** dialog box, click the arrow next to **Horizontal**, and then click **Center**.
4. Click the arrow next to **Vertical**, and then click **Above Shape**.

   Tip You will need to scroll up to locate Above Shape in the list.

5. Click **OK**. You have relocated the data graphic so it appears above the center of the server shape.

Tip The data graphic in the preceding graphic has a border around it. You can turn the border off by clearing the Show Border Around Items At Default Location check box in the Display Options section of the Edit Data Graphic dialog box shown in Step 2.

In the remaining steps of this exercise, you will alter the *Topology 1* data graphic to make the display of the network name for the server consistent with the format used in the *Topology 2* data graphic. You will also change the display of CPU speed from text to a graphical presentation.

6. On the **Data** tab, in the **Display Data** group, click the **Data Graphics** button to open the gallery, right-click the **Topology 1** thumbnail, and then click **Edit**.

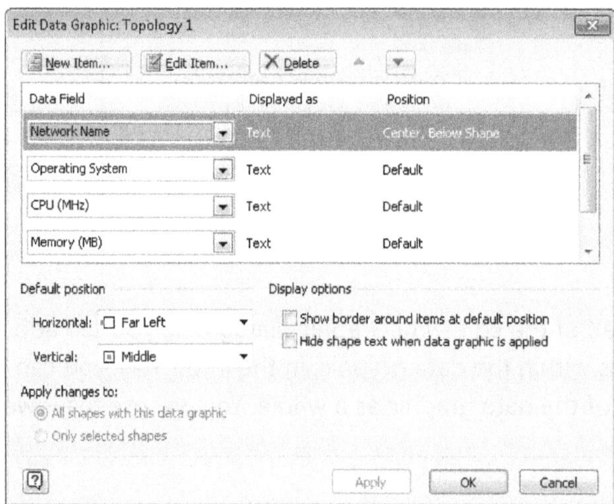

The upper half of the Edit Data Graphic dialog box shows the parameters for the items contained in this data graphic. Looking at the row for the Network Name data field, you see that it is displayed as Text and is positioned in the Center, Below (the server) Shape. Similarly, the CPU (MHz) field is displayed as Text in the Default location for the data graphic.

7. With **Network Name** already selected in the **Data Field** list (notice the highlight on that item), click the **Edit Item** button. The Edit Item dialog box opens.

Tip **You can also double-click anywhere in an item row to open the dialog box.**

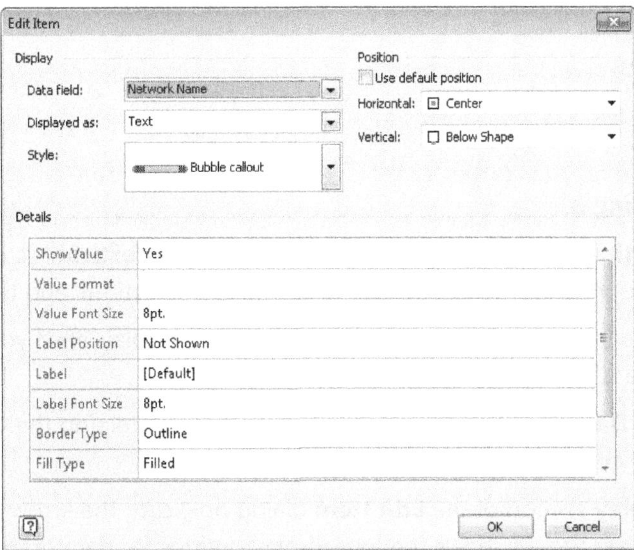

In the upper left of the Edit Item dialog box, you see the shape data field name, the display type of Text, and a predefined style called Bubble Callout.

In the upper-right corner of the dialog box, note that the Use Default Position check box is cleared. As a result, the positions set in this dialog box for Horizontal and Vertical override the default position of the data graphic as a whole. (You saw the result of this setting in the graphic in Step 8 of the previous section's exercise. The main part of the data graphic is to the left of the server shape, but the name is below the shape.)

The lower half of the dialog box displays customizable parameters for this data graphic item. Be sure to notice the scroll bar in the parameter list; there are additional parameters that are not currently visible.

8. In the **Display** section of the **Edit Item** dialog box, click the arrow next to **Style**. The list shows a set of predefined text callout styles. (Scroll to see all of them.)

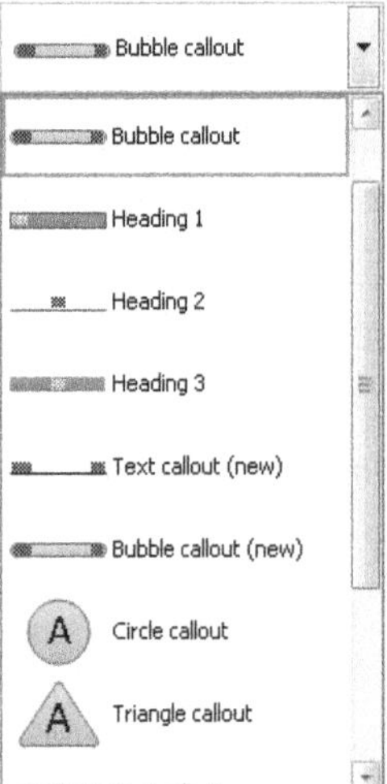

9. Click **Heading 3**.
10. In the **Position** section of the dialog box, display the **Vertical** list, click **Above shape**. (You might need to scroll up to locate this selection), and then click OK.

    You have changed the location of the server name display. Next you will change the way that CPU speed is presented.
11. In the **Edit Data Graphic** dialog box, click the row containing the **CPU (MHz)** item, and then click the **Edit Item** button.
12. In the **Display** section of the **Edit Item** dialog box, click the arrow next to **Displayed as**. The list shows the four display options for data graphic items.

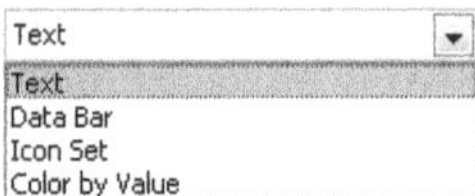

Tip You will use Icon Set and Color By Value in the next exercise in this chapter.

13. Click **Data Bar**.
14. In the **Display** section of the of the **Edit Item** dialog box, click the arrow next to **Style**.

The list shows the predefined data bar types. As you can see, data bars are designed for showing relative values in a variety of ways.

Tip **The collection of data bars offers a variety of interesting ways to display numeric data. You will use one of them in this exercise but you should take a few minutes to explore some of the other choices for potential future use.**

15. Click **Data bar 3**.
16. In the **Details** section of the **Edit Item** dialog box, type **5** in the **Maximum Value** field.

    Important **The Minimum Value and Maximum Value fields are critical for data bar graphic items. These two values set the boundaries for the values in the selected shape data field and allow Visio to scale the data bar graphic accordingly.**

17. In the **Details** section, click in the **Label Position** field, and then click **Not Shown** from the list. This action turns off the display of the shape data field name.
18. In the **Position** section of the dialog box, clear the **Use default position** check box.

    The Edit Item dialog box should now look like the following graphic.

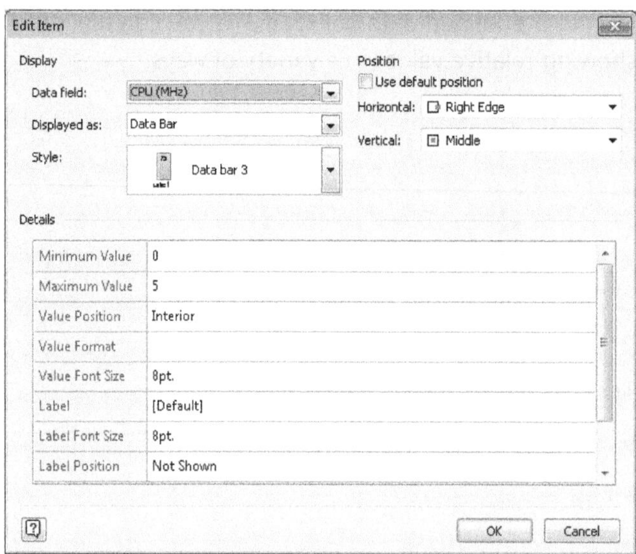

19. Click **OK** in both the **Edit Item** and **Edit Data Graphic** dialog boxes.

Your revised diagram has several advantages over the initial version:

- It uses a consistent presentation style for the server names; they are displayed above the server in white text on a blue background.
- The display of CPU speed is much more effective as a proportionally sized icon than it was as text. It's easy to tell at a glance that several of the servers on the left of the diagram may be underpowered.

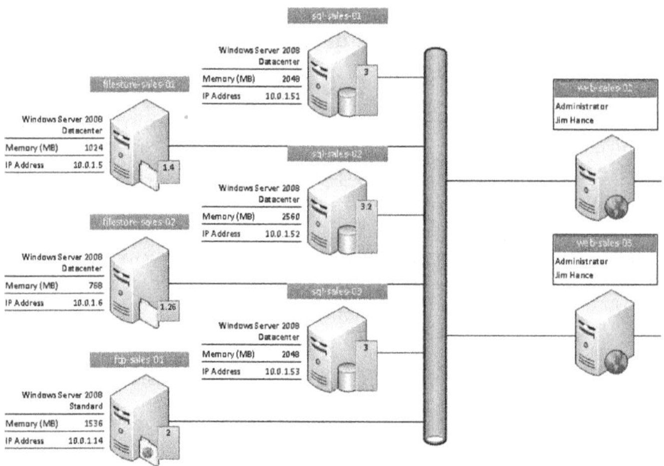

CLEAN UP Save your changes to the *Network with Data Graphics* drawing, and then close it.

Creating New Data Graphics

In the preceding exercise, you learned how flexible data graphics are and how easy it is to edit existing graphics.

In this exercise, you will create a new data graphic that contains two graphic elements and apply it to a flowchart that is similar to the one you created in Chapter 4, "Drawing the Real World: Flowcharts and Organization Charts."

Your new data graphic will automatically apply color to process shapes based on who is responsible for them, making it very easy to see who does what in the process. The graphic will also use icons to display the risk associated with each step in the process.

Important Each process shape in this diagram contains several data fields, two of which you will use in your data graphic. One field is called *Owner* and identifies who is responsible for the process step. The other is called *Risk* and expresses the relative risk, on a scale of 1 (low) to 5 (high), of successfully completing that step in the process.

SET UP You need the *HR Process Map with data_start* drawing located in the Chapter10 practice file folder to complete this exercise. Open the drawing in Visio and save it as *HR Process Map with data graphics*.

Tip When you open this diagram, you'll notice that it was saved with gridlines turned off. It was saved this way because you won't be dropping or nudging shapes. In essence, the drawing is nearly complete, so it was saved in a state suitable for using it in a presentation.

Data Graphics

1. On the **Data** tab, in the **Display Data** group, click the **Data Graphics** button to open the **Data Graphics** gallery.
2. In the **Data Graphics** gallery, click **Create New Data Graphic**. An empty version of the dialog box you used in the preceding exercise appears and is titled New Data Graphic.
3. In the **New Data Graphic** dialog box, click **New Item**. The New Item dialog box appears.

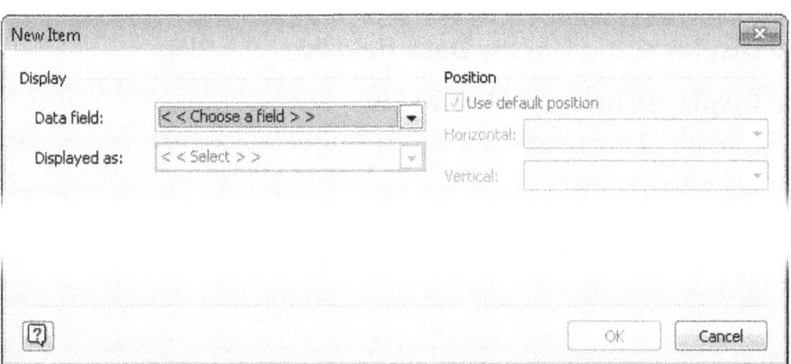

4. In the **Display** section of the **New Item** dialog box, display the **Data field** list, and then click **Owner**.
5. In the **Displayed as** list, click **Color by Value**. Visio creates a list of all of the values for Owner on this page and assigns a color to each one.

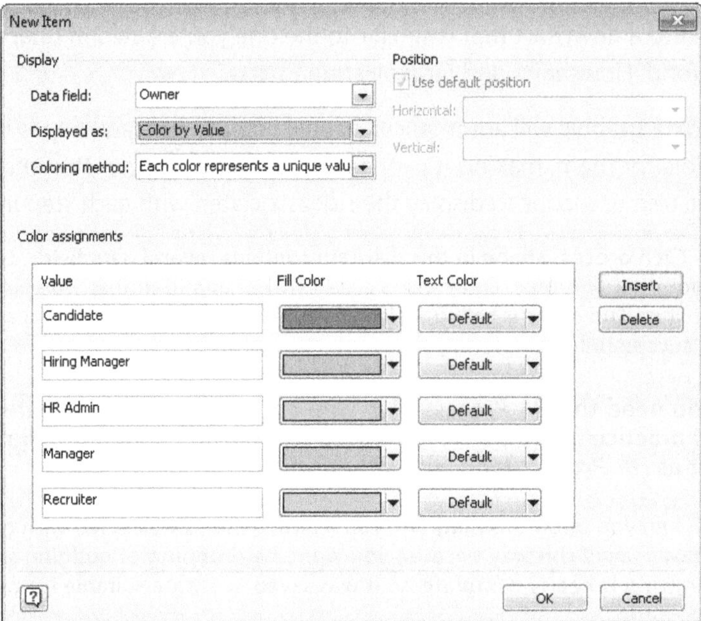

Tip The choice of colors Visio provides can be very suitable for some purposes but may be too bold for other purposes. In the latter case, you can display the Fill Color list for any field and change the color setting. You can also leave the Text Color of affected shapes at the default setting (as shown in the previous graphic) or you can manually change it. Finally, notice the Insert and Delete buttons to the right of the Color Assignments section. You can delete any field values or add new ones depending on what you want to highlight in the drawing.

6. Click **OK**.
7. In the **New Data Graphic** dialog box, click **New Item**.
8. In the **Display** section, in the **Data field** list, click **Risk**.
9. In the **Displayed as** list, click **Icon Set**.

10. Click the **Style** arrow to display a list of icon sets. (Scroll down to see all of them.)

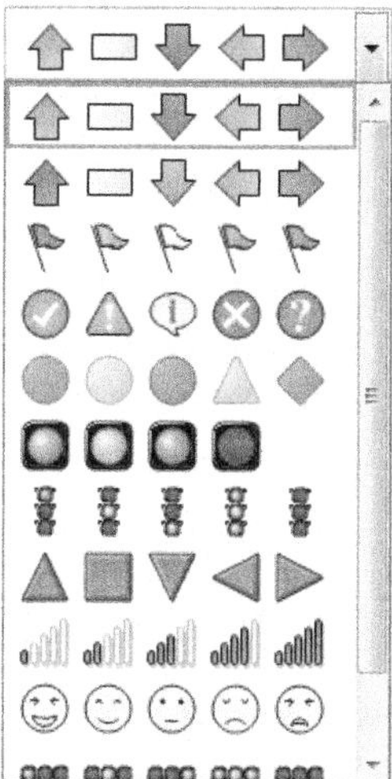

11. Click the set of colored pennants (flags) to select that icon set. The New Item dialog box should look like the following graphic.

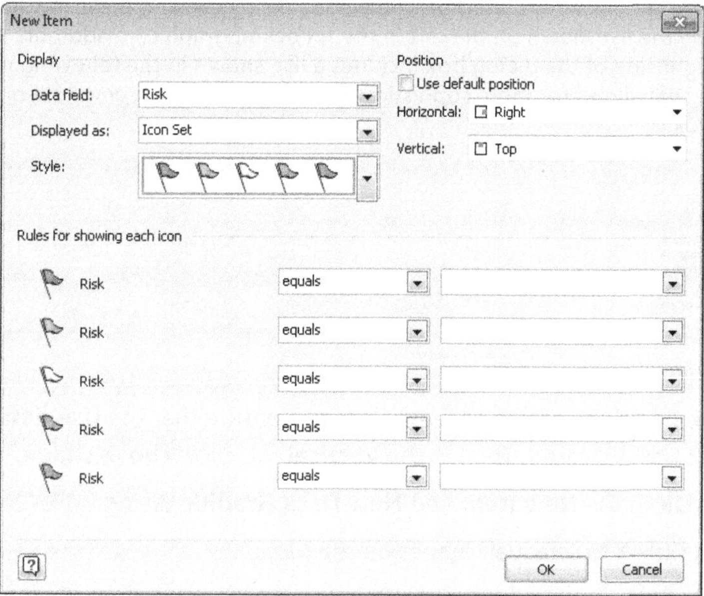

12. Type the following values in the empty text boxes to the right of the colored flags:
    - Red flag: **5**
    - Orange flag: **4**
    - Yellow flag: **3**
    - Green flag: **2**
    - Blue flag: **1**

    The center of the dialog box should look like the following graphic.

    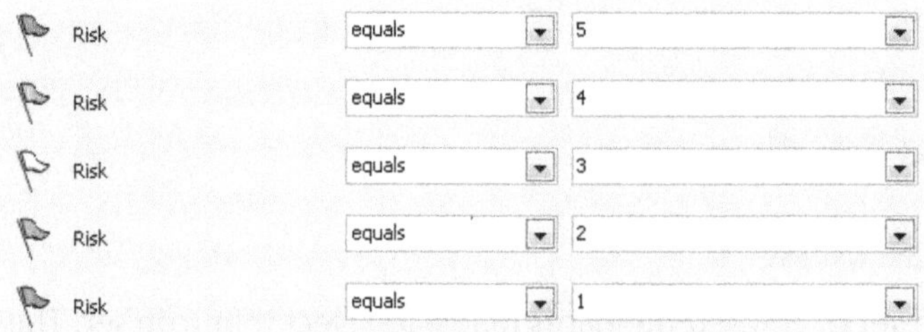

    Tip In this step, you left all five condition lists set to Equals. Realize, however, that you can create nearly any condition you would like by clicking the arrow in that field to expose the list shown on the left in the following graphic. In addition, the text box on the right side of the dialog box includes a list, shown in the following graphic on the right, that allows for more sophisticated values than just typing text or a number into the box.

    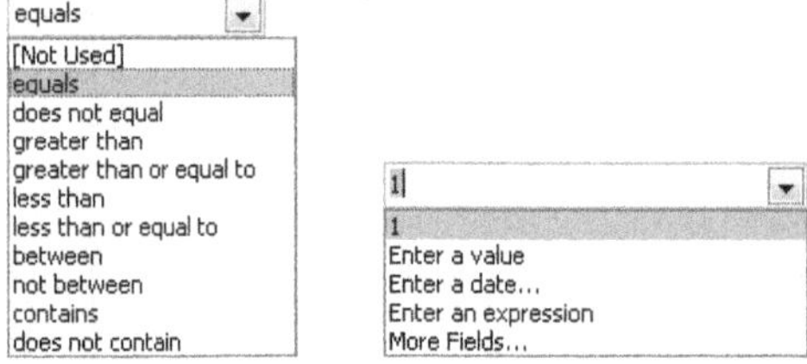

13. In the **Position** section of the dialog box, ensure that the **Use default position** check box is cleared. Then in the **Vertical** list, click **Above shape**.
14. Click **OK** in the **New Item** and **New Data Graphic** dialog boxes to close them.
15. Press Ctrl+A to select all shapes on the page.
16. On the **Data** tab, in the **Display Data** group, click the **Data Graphics** button, and then click on your new data graphic.

    Tip You'll notice when you rest on the thumbnail for your data graphic that it has been assigned the generic name *Data Graphic*. You can change the name by right-clicking on the thumbnail and selecting Rename.

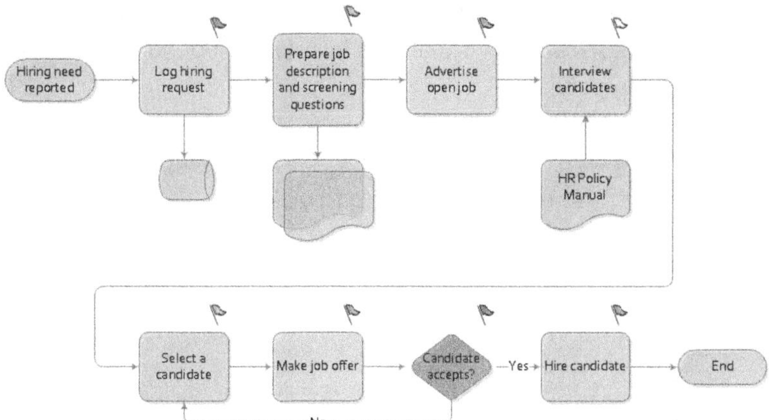

The process blocks in your diagram have been colored to reflect the owner of each task. In addition, each step in the process shows a colored flag that indicates the relative risk associated with that step. At the moment, you don't know which owners or risks are associated with which colors, but we'll solve that problem in the next section of this chapter.

CLEAN UP Save your changes to the *HR Process Map with data graphics* but leave it open if you are continuing with the next exercise.

The display of data graphics is dynamic, which means that if the underlying data values change, the data graphics will change. You can prove this to yourself by opening the shape data window and changing the risk value for any shape. The pennant in the upper-right corner of the shape will immediately change color.

Tip If you want to copy a data graphic from one Visio drawing to another, merely copy a shape displaying the data graphic from the first drawing and paste it into the second one. You can then delete the shape. The data graphic will remain behind.

Creating Data Graphic Legends

In the preceding exercise, you created a diagram in which the color of the flowchart shapes and the color of an icon signify data values in the shapes. However, there's no way to tell what each color means.

In this exercise, you will add a ***data graphic legend*** to the page.

SET UP You need the *HR Process Map with data graphics* drawing that you created in the preceding section in order to complete this exercise.

Insert Legend

1. On the **Data** tab, in the **Display Data** group, click the **Insert Legend** button, and then click **Horizontal**. Visio always inserts the legend in the upper-right corner of the drawing page.

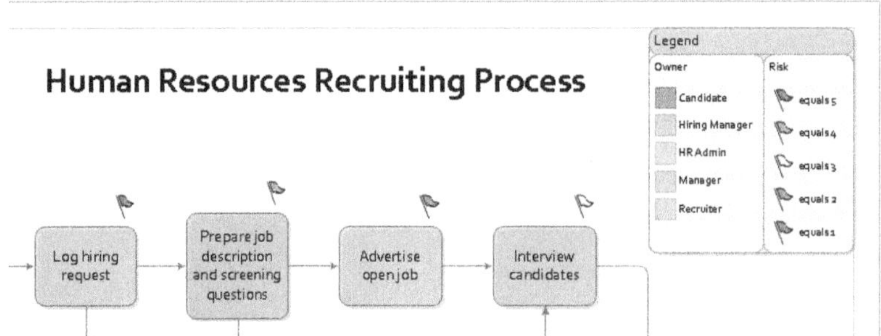

See Also Visio constructs the legend from a combination of containers and lists. See Chapter 11, "Adding Structure to Your Diagrams," for details about containers and lists.

Once Visio has placed a legend on the page, you can edit it. In the next three steps, you will edit the legend to make it more descriptive.

2. Click once on the red pennant that displays **equals 5** and type **High**.
3. Click once on the orange pennant that displays **equals 4** and type **Medium High**.

   Notice that Visio automatically expands the size of the legend shape because your replacement text is longer.

4. Continue typing descriptions for the remaining risk flags:
   - Yellow: **Medium**
   - Green: **Medium Low**
   - Blue: **Low**

   Because the width of the legend increased when you typed longer text labels, you will want to move it to the left so it remains within the page margins.

5. Click the legend heading (the word *Legend*) to select it.

   Tip You cannot select the legend by clicking anywhere in its interior; this behavior is characteristic of a list or container, as explained in Chapter 11.

6. Press the Left Arrow key to nudge the shape until it is once again aligned with the page margins. The upper part of your finished drawing should look like the following graphic.

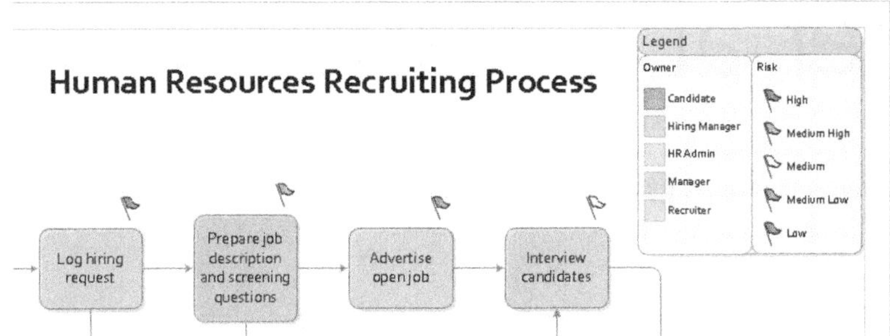

 **CLEAN UP** Save your changes to the *HR Process Map with data graphics* drawing, and then close it.

Tip After placing a data graphic legend on the page, Visio never updates it. Consequently, if you change the attributes of a data graphic in a way that affects the legend, you must delete the existing legend and insert a new one.

Key Points

- Visio data graphics provide a powerful tool for visualizing the data behind the shapes on your page. Data graphics help you tell more of your story by:
  - Displaying text on or near a shape.
  - Highlighting data with data bars, star ratings, progress indicators, speedometers and other dynamic symbols.
  - Presenting an icon from an icon set, where each icon represents a specific data value or value range.
  - Changing the color of a shape based on a data value.
- If your diagram is linked to a live data feed or a near real–time data source, you can use data graphics to turn an otherwise ordinary Visio drawing into a dashboard for process monitoring, activity management, and status review.
- You can apply existing data graphics at any time by selecting one or more shapes and then choosing a graphic from the data graphics gallery.
- The appearance and location of data graphics are controlled by parameters that you can modify, making it easy to change any existing data graphic. It's also very easy to create a new data graphic by choosing the type and style from drop-down lists and then setting a handful of parameter values.
- It requires only two clicks to create a legend for the data graphics on your drawing page.

Chapter at a Glance

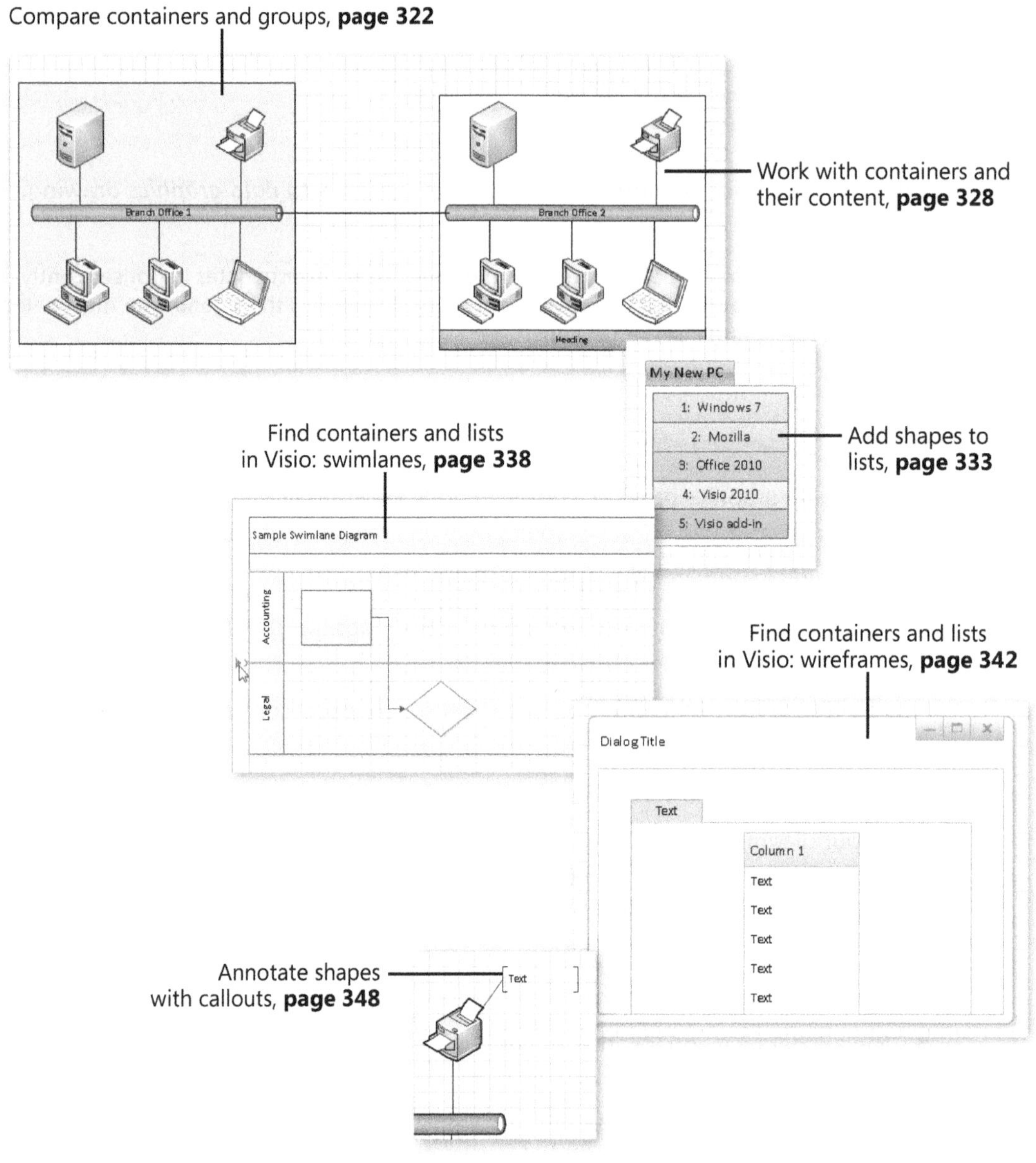
Compare containers and groups, **page 322**
Branch Office 1
Branch Office 2
Heading
Work with containers and their content, **page 328**
My New PC
1: Windows 7
2: Mozilla
3: Office 2010
4: Visio 2010
5: Visio add-in
Add shapes to lists, **page 333**
Find containers and lists in Visio: swimlanes, **page 338**
Sample Swimlane Diagram
Accounting
Legal
Find containers and lists in Visio: wireframes, **page 342**
Dialog Title
Text
Column 1
Text
Text
Text
Text
Text
Annotate shapes with callouts, **page 348**
Text

11 Adding Structure to Your Diagrams

In this chapter, you will learn how to

- ✔ Compare containers and groups.
- ✔ Work with containers and their contents.
- ✔ Format and size containers.
- ✔ Add shapes to lists.
- ✔ Format and size lists.
- ✔ Find containers and lists in Visio.
- ✔ Annotate shapes with callouts.

In many types of Microsoft Visio diagrams, it is useful to create visual or logical relationships among a set of shapes. In previous versions of Visio, you could use background shapes and groups for this purpose. These capabilities are still available in Visio 2010, as you saw when you created a network diagram in Chapter 9, "Drawing the Real World: Network and Data Center Diagrams." However, Visio 2010 introduces three new ways to establish relationships and add structure to diagrams:

- **Containers** A ***container*** provides a visual boundary around a set of objects, but it also establishes a logical relationship among the objects in the container. To wit, shapes know when they are members of a container and containers know which shapes they contain.

  The key advantage of a container is that while you can move, copy or delete it and its members as a unit, each contained shape maintains its independence. It's easy to select container members with a single click and to access their shape data and other properties.

  Tip A container can contain shapes, other containers, and lists.

- **Lists** A ***list*** is a special type of container that maintains an ordered relationship among its members. Each object in a list knows its ordinal position; new objects are not merely added to a list but are added to a specific position in a list.

Tip A list can contain shapes and containers but cannot contain other lists.

- **Callouts** In previous versions of Visio, a callout was merely a shape that you glued to another shape to add a comment. A Visio 2010 ***callout*** still provides a way to add annotation to a shape, but the callout knows the shape to which it is attached, and the shape can identify any attached callouts.

In this chapter, you will experiment with and learn the value of containers, lists, and callouts in Visio diagrams.

Practice Files Before you can complete the exercises in this chapter, you need to copy the book's practice files to your computer. The practice file you'll use to complete the exercises in this chapter is in the Chapter11 practice files folder. A complete list of practice files is provided in "Using the Practice Files" at the beginning of this book.

Comparing Containers and Groups

You can use either groups or containers to visually connect a set of shapes. However, the two have key behavioral differences that are likely to lead you to use one or the other depending on your needs.

In this exercise, you will create both a group and a container, and then you will perform the same set of actions on each in order to examine the differences.

SET UP You need the *Containers, Lists and Callouts_start* drawing located in the Chapter11 practice file folder to complete this exercise. Open the drawing in Visio and save it as *Groups vs. Containers.*

1. Create a colored rectangle and group it with the network shapes on the left side of the page.

   See Also For a refresher on using a group with a background shape to organize a set of shapes, see "Organizing Network Shapes in a Diagram" in Chapter 9.

2. Draw a bounding box around the **Branch Office 2** network shapes on the right side of the page.

Container

3. On the **Insert** tab, in the **Diagram Parts** group, click the **Container** button. The container gallery opens.

   As you move your mouse over the thumbnails in the container gallery, note that ***Live Preview*** shows how each container style will look with your selected shapes.

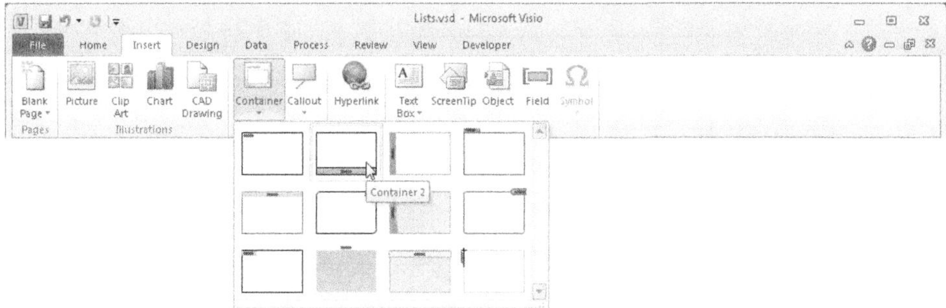

4. Click **Container 2** (as shown in the previous graphic).

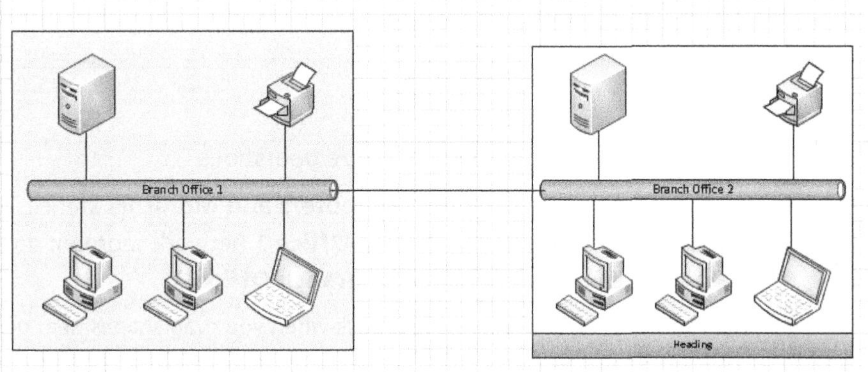

Your diagram now shows a set of grouped shapes on the left and a container on the right.

5. Click the **Branch Office 1** group once to select it, and then drag the bottom resize handle down to the bottom of the page.

6. Click the edge or heading of the **Branch Office 2** container once to select it, and then drag the bottom resize handle down to the bottom of the page.

Important **One immediate difference to note: you can select a group by clicking anywhere on its edge or interior, but you can only select a container by clicking its edge or its heading.**

In the following graphic, you can see that what you've previously learned about groups applies here: resizing the group resizes the shapes in the group. Look at the container on the right, however. The container is taller but its member shapes are unchanged.

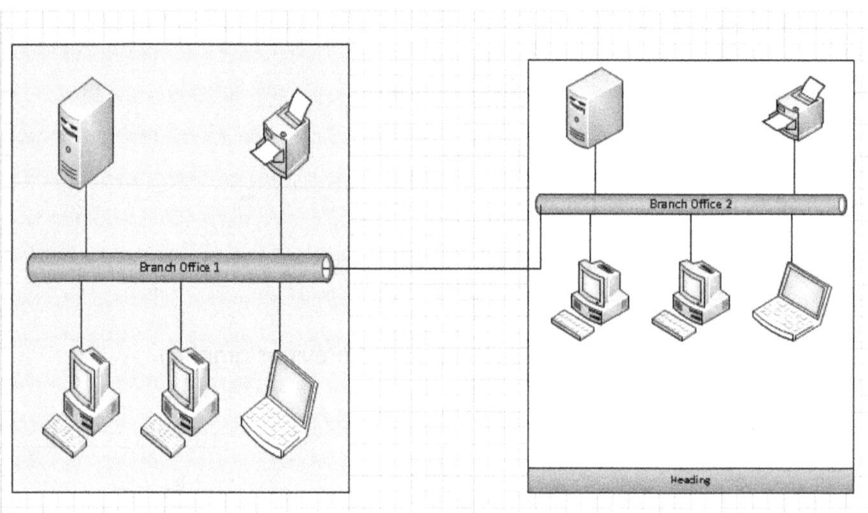

7. Press Ctrl+Z twice to undo both resize operations.
8. Drag two **PC** shapes from the **Computers and Monitors** stencil, dropping the first in the open area above the **Branch Office 1** network segment and the second in the open area of the container for **Branch Office 2**.

   Tip Containers provide visual feedback when you drag shapes near or into them. (This is one way to distinguish a container from a group or an ordinary shape.) The border of the container on the right in the following graphic shows an orange color that is very similar to the coloring used for Dynamic Grid lines.

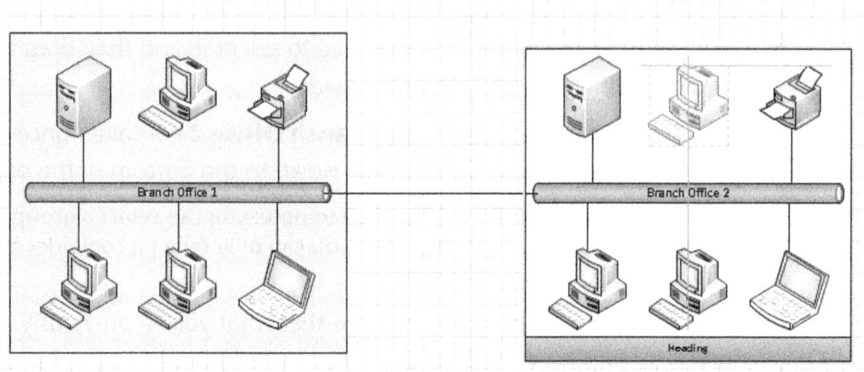

9. Hold down the Shift key and click on both the group and the container to select them. Then drag the selection down to the bottom of the page.

As you can see in the following graphic, dropping a shape on a group does not add it to the group—it is left behind when you move the group. In contrast, dropping a shape into a container does add it to the container, so it moves when you move the container.

Tip **By default, shapes dropped on a group are not added to the group. However, if you run Visio in developer mode, you can change the behavior of a group so it will accept dropped shapes. For more information about developer mode, see the Appendix.**

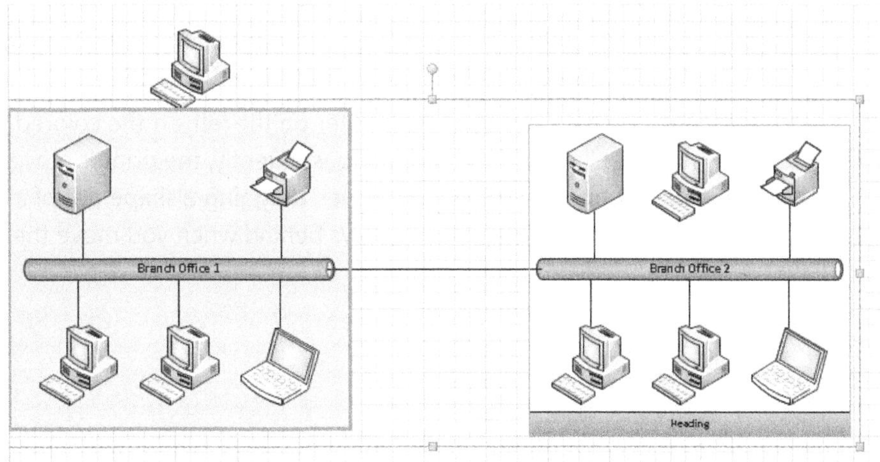

10. Press Ctrl+Z three times to undo the move operation and delete the two PCs you added.
11. Click once to select the **Branch Office 1** group, and then click the printer in the group. Drag it out of the top of the group rectangle.

    Tip **The default behavior for groups is that the first click selects the group; you must click a second time to select a shape in the group. If you run Visio in developer mode, you can alter the selection characteristics of a group. For more information about developer mode, see the Appendix.**

12. Click once to select the printer in the **Branch Office 2** container, and then drag it out of the top of the container. The results of both this step and the previous one are shown in the following graphic.

    Tip **One click is sufficient to select any shape in a container because, by design, the fill of the container can't be selected with a mouse click.**

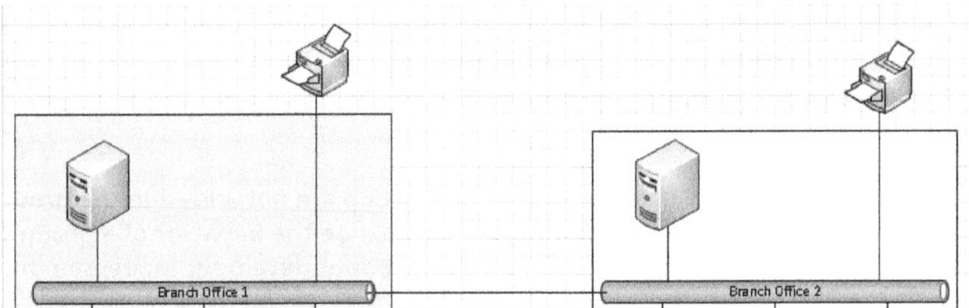

13. Hold down the Shift key and click both the group and the container to select them. Then drag the selection down to the bottom of the page.

    Although you have dragged the printer on the left off the colored group rectangle, the shape is still part of the group. Consequently, the printer moves when you move the group. On the right, however, dragging a shape out of a container removes it from the container so it stays behind when you move the container.

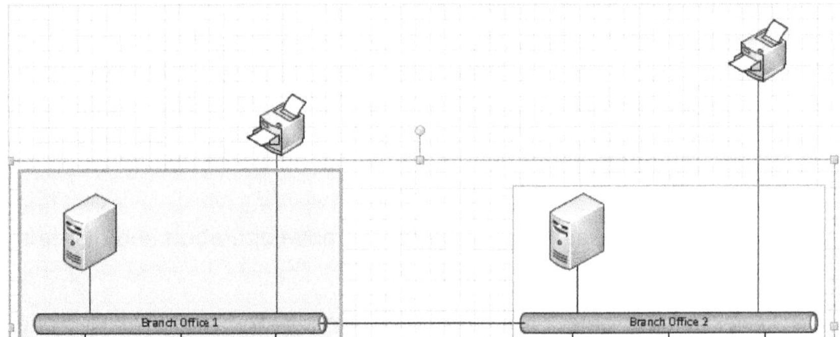

14. Press Ctrl+Z three times to undo the move operation and return the printers to their original locations.
15. Click and drag in the interior of the group and attempt to draw a bounding box around the two PCs below the network segment.

    The result will not be what you intended. You cannot select the two PCs with a bounding box because clicking and dragging within the group shape moves the group (see the graphic in the next step).

    Tip **You can select shapes in a group with a bounding box—but only if you start the bounding box outside of the group.**

16. Click once in the interior of the container and attempt to draw a bounding box around the two PCs below the network segment.

    A bounding box inside a container does select contained shapes for the same reason that you could select a contained shape with a single click in Step 13: the container background is "invisible" to mouse clicks.

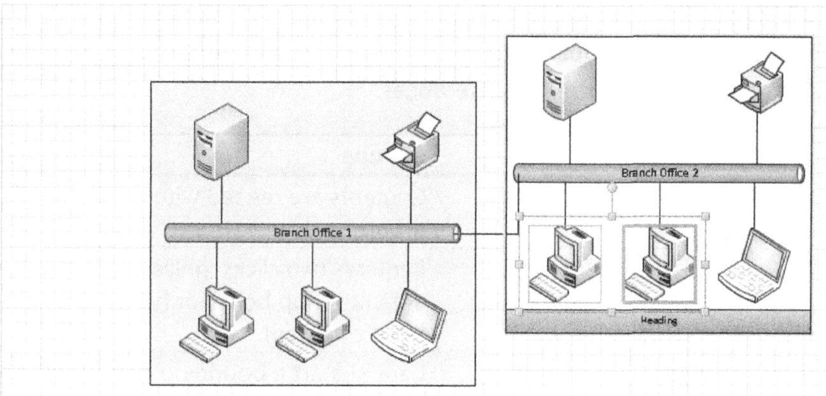

17. Click once to select the **Branch Office 1** group, type **San Francisco**, and press Esc. Then format the text to **14 pt.** and **Bold** to make it more visible.
18. Click once to select the container, type **Boston**, and press Esc. Then format the text to **14 pt.** and **Bold** to make it more visible.

    As you can see in the following graphic, the text you added to the group on the left is positioned in the center of the group by default. Unfortunately, this places the new text on top of the words *Branch Office 1*. You will need to use the text manipulation skills you learned in Chapter 3, "Adding Sophistication to Your Drawing," to move the text to a better position.

    In contrast, a container has a built-in header. When you add text to a container, the text automatically appears in the header.

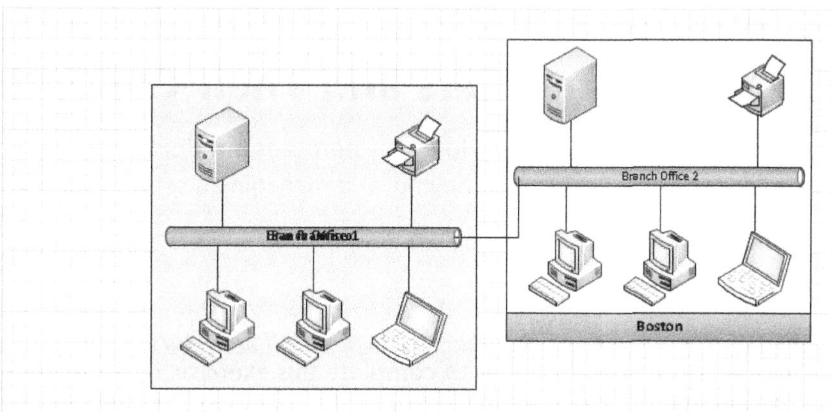

 **CLEAN UP Save your changes to the *Groups vs. Containers* drawing, and then close it.**

After completing this exercise, you should have a good working knowledge of the properties of groups compared to containers. For future reference, the following table contains a summary of the key differences.

Action	Groups	Containers
Resizing	Contents are resized with the group	Contents are not changed
Selecting an interior shape	Requires two clicks (unless default group behavior has been changed)	Requires one click
Selecting interior shape(s) with a bounding box	Cannot start a bounding box by clicking inside a group	Can start a bounding box anywhere
Dropping a new shape inside	Dropped shapes are not added to the group (unless default group behavior has been changed)	Dropped shapes are added to the container
Dragging a shape out	Shape is physically outside the group but remains part of the group	Shape is removed from the container
Typing text	Text is placed in the center of the group	Text is placed in the container's heading

See Also For more information about containers, see the Visio development team blog at *blogs.msdn.com/b/visio/archive/2009/08/25/organizing-diagrams-with-containers.aspx* and *blogs.msdn.com/b/visio/archive/2009/08/27/details-on-container-behaviors.aspx*.

Working with Containers and Their Contents

Group shapes are still valuable for many purposes but Visio 2010 containers offer numerous advantages for grouping, moving, and managing a set of related shapes.

In this exercise, you will continue working with containers to learn more about their unique properties.

SET UP You need the *Containers, Lists and Callouts_start* drawing located in the Chapter11 practice file folder to complete this exercise. Open the drawing in Visio and save it as *Container Properties*.

1. Draw a bounding box around the **Branch Office 1** network shapes.

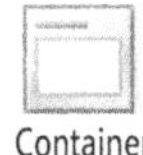

2. On the **Insert** tab, in the **Diagram Parts** group, click the **Container** button, and then click **Container 11**.
3. Right-click the edge or heading of the container to select it.

   Notice that whenever you select a container, the Container Tools ***contextual tab set*** appears and includes the Format ***contextual tab***, as shown in the following graphic.
4. In the **Container Tools** contextual tab set, click the **Format** contextual tab to activate it.

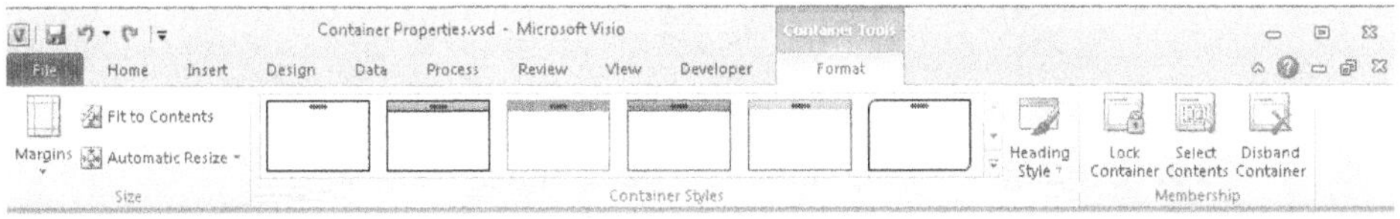

5. On the **Format** tab, in the **Membership** group, click the **Select Contents** button. All contained shapes are selected.

   Tip You can also right-click the edge or heading of the container, click Container, and then click Select Contents to achieve the same result.
6. Draw a bounding box to select the **Branch Office 2** network segment and the PCs below it; do not select the server and printer above it.
7. On the **Insert** tab, in the **Diagram Parts** group, click the **Container** button, and then click **Container 11**. You have created a container around part of the Branch Office 2 network components.

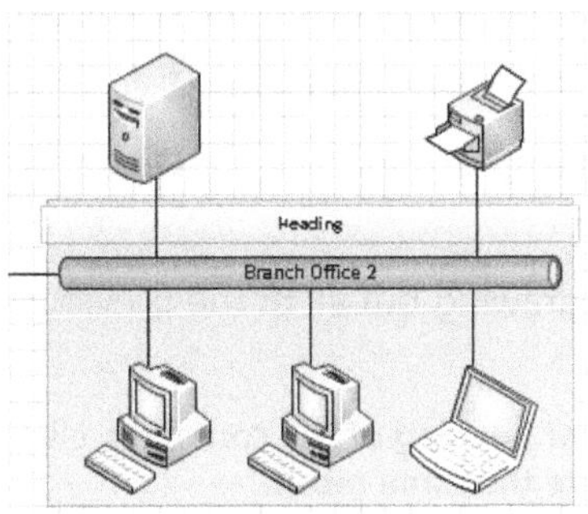

8. Click the edge or heading of the container you just created and drag the top resize handle up until the container surrounds the server and printer.
9. On the **Format** tab, in the **Membership** group, click the **Select Contents** button.

   Notice that the server and printer are not selected. Surrounding shapes with an existing container does not add them to the container.

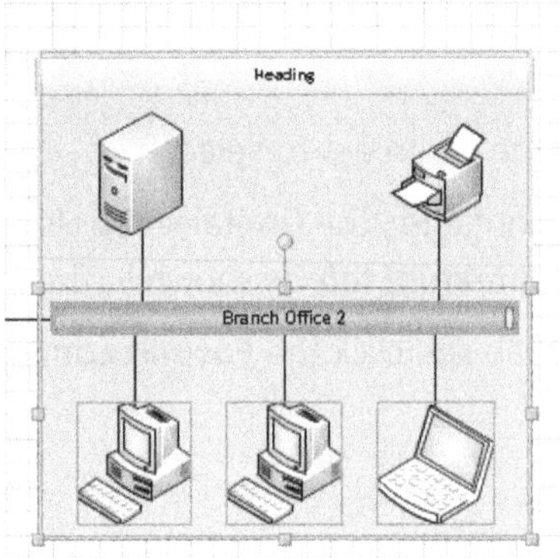

10. Click once on the server shape to select it.
11. Right-click the selected server, click **Container**, and then click **Add to Underlying Container**.

    The server shape is now a member of the container.

    Tip When you select any shape that is a member of a container, the orange outline appears on the border of the container.

12. Click once on the edge or heading of the **Branch Office 2** container to select it, and then press Delete.

    The container and its contents are deleted.

    If you want to remove the container but leave the contents, you must use a different technique. In the next two steps you will disband the container.

13. Click once on the edge or heading of the **Branch Office 1** container to select it.
14. On the **Format** tab, in the **Membership** group, click the **Disband Container** button.

Disband Container

    The container is removed from the drawing but all of the previously contained shapes remain on the page.

    Tip You can also right-click the edge or heading of the container, click Container, and then click Disband Container to achieve the same result.

CLEAN UP Close the *Container Properties* drawing without saving changes.

In this exercise and the preceding one, you selected a set of existing objects and created a container around them. You can also create an empty container and later add objects to it. To do so, ensure that nothing on the drawing page is selected. On the Insert tab, in the Diagram Parts group, click the Container button, and then click a container style in the gallery. The new container will be added to the center of the drawing window. You can then drop in new or existing shapes, lists, or other containers.

Tip You can copy a container and paste it elsewhere in the same or a different drawing. A copy of the container and all its members will be pasted into the new location.

The Lock Container button in the Membership group of the Format contextual tab prevents shapes from being added or removed; it also locks the container against deletion.

Formatting Containers

When you drop a new container onto the page, it includes a set of style attributes. You can change a container's formatting at any time by selecting it and then using the commands on the Format contextual tab of the Container Tools contextual tab set. The style gallery in the Container Styles group provides Live Preview so you can decide which new style you prefer. Note the drop-down arrows at the right end of the container gallery; use them to view additional container styles.

After you have selected a container style, you have additional flexibility in choosing alternate heading styles. Click the Heading Style button in the Container Styles group (the button to the right of the arrow in the following graphic) to preview and select any of 20 heading styles.

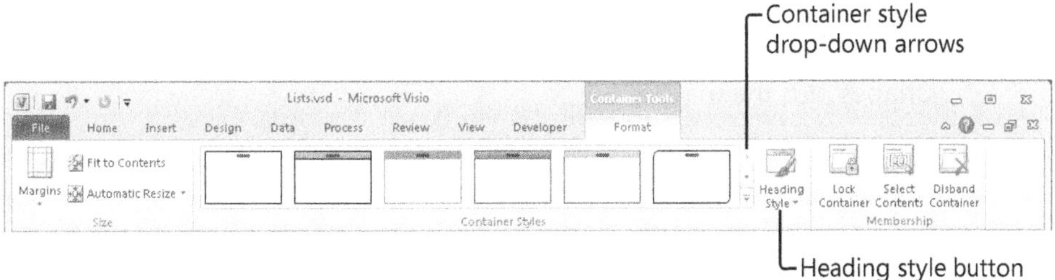

You can also change the fill, line, and shadow attributes of a container in the same way you can for any Visio shape; on the Home tab, in the Shape group, click the Fill, Line or Shadow buttons.

Sizing Containers

The predesigned containers in Visio 2010 expand automatically when you add shapes near the edge of the container. You can change the default behavior on the Format contextual tab of the Container Tools contextual tab set: in the Size group, click the Automatic Resize button to see three mutually exclusive options.

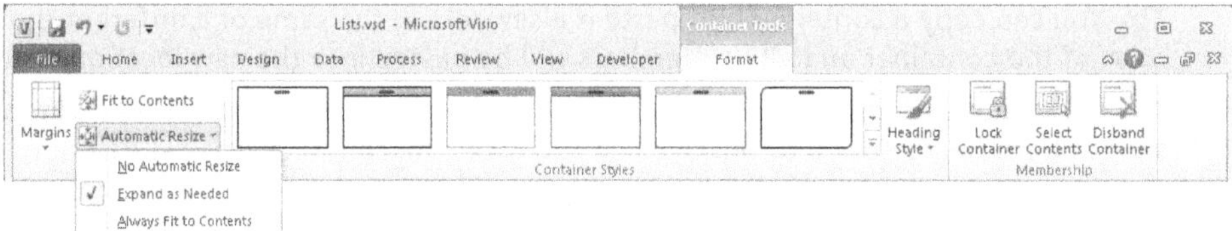

- **No Automatic Resize** The container will not expand when you drop shapes near the edge.
- **Expand as Needed** The container will expand when you drop shapes near the edge. The opposite is not true, however; the container will not shrink when you remove shapes.
- **Always Fit to Contents** The container will expand and contract automatically when you add or remove shapes.

You can also affect container size with the two buttons located above and to the left of the Automatic Resize button:

- **Margins** Sets the spacing between the edges of the container and the contained shapes.
- **Fit to Contents** Sets the container size to the minimum required for the contained shapes plus the margin.

On the Border

As you have already learned, when you drag a shape into a container, an orange outline appears on the border of the container. This is true even when you drag most but not all of the shape into the container. In the following graphic, the router will be added to the container when the mouse button is released, even though it is not fully within the borders of the container. (Depending on the resize options described just before this sidebar, the container may expand to encompass the new shape.)

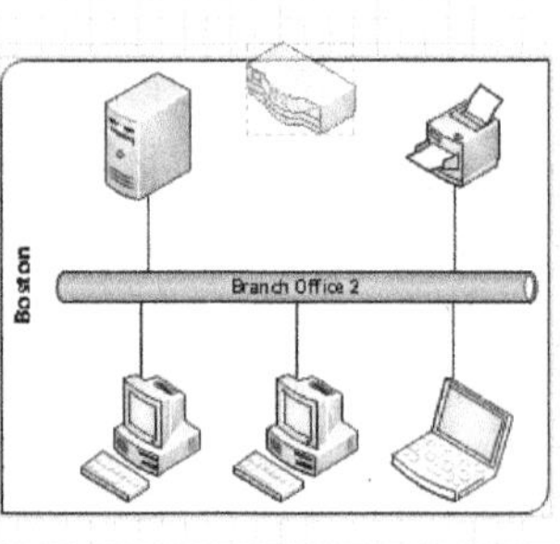

The following graphic on the left shows a different container behavior that you might use from time to time. In contrast to the previous graphic, the router has not been dragged quite as far into the container. The container signals the difference by displaying an orange outline only on the top border and not all the way around. When the mouse button is released, the router will become a member of the container, but it will be attached to the edge of the container.

The key difference in behavior of a boundary shape like the router is that when the container is resized, the router stays on the border. The following graphic on the right shows the same container after the router was dropped on the top border and the container's resize handle was dragged upward to enlarge the container.

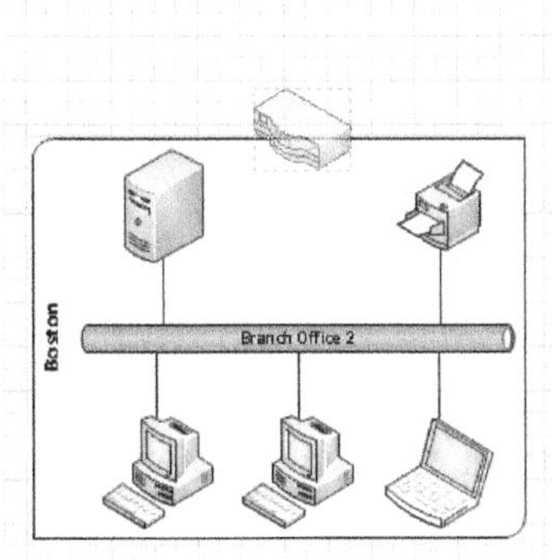

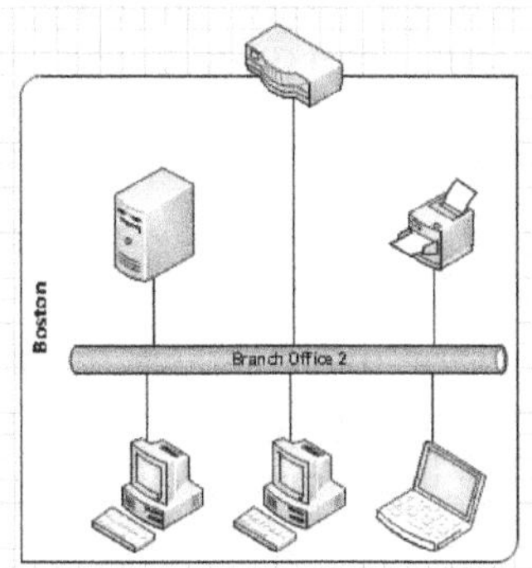

You might use border shapes for a situation like the one shown in this network diagram: the router is attached to the branch office network but is also attached to other networks so it makes sense to locate it on the border rather than in the interior of the container. You'll see another use for border shapes in the "Wireframes" section of "Finding Containers and Lists in Visio" later in this chapter.

Adding Shapes to Lists

A list is a special type of container that maintains its members in ordered sequence. When you drop an object into a list, it takes a specific place before, between, or after existing members. Each list member knows its relative position in the list.

Visio 2010 doesn't provide a list gallery on the Visio 2010 Insert tab in the same way that it provides a container gallery. Consequently, creating a list either requires reusing an existing list shape or having enough technical knowledge to make changes to the ***ShapeSheet***. (For more information about modifying the ShapeSheet, see the Appendix.)

In this exercise, you will add shapes to a list, and then reorder the shapes within the list. For this hypothetical scenario, the list shape is called *My New PC*; you will add rectangular shapes that represent the software you will load onto your new PC. Your goal for this exercise is to create a list that shows the installation sequence for your new PC.

The shapes you will drop into the list have been prepared with two special attributes:

- Each shape displays the name of a software product. (The name of the product is stored in the shape as shape data.)
- Each shape displays its relative position in the list when it is in a list. When the shape is not in a list, it doesn't display any number.

SET UP You need the *Containers, Lists and Callouts_start* drawing located in the Chapter11 practice file folder to complete this exercise. Open the drawing in Visio and save it as *Lists*. Then go to the Lists page.

1. Drag **Visio 2010** into the list.

   Tip A list provides the same visual feedback—an orange border—as a container when a shape approaches its interior.

   The graphic on the left shows the list outlined as the Visio 2010 shape approaches. The graphic on the right shows the shape inside the list. Notice that the shape now displays its ordinal position in the list in front of the product name.

   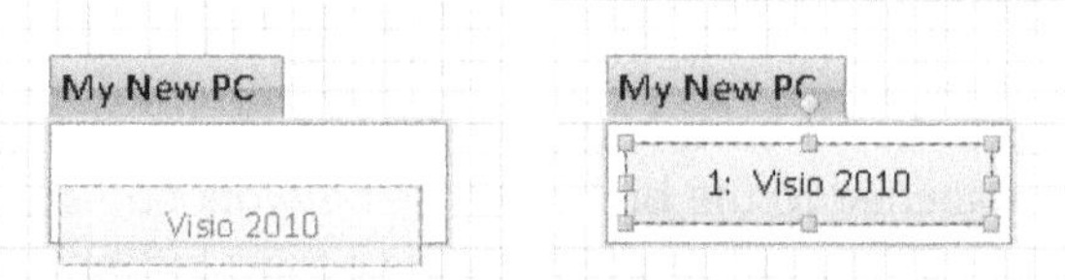

2. Because you can't install Visio until after you've installed Windows, drag **Windows 7** into the list, above **Visio 2010**.

   As you approach the list with the Windows 7 shape, notice that an orange insertion bar appears to tell you where you can add a new list member. In this example, you can insert the new shape after the existing shape (the following graphic on the left) or before the existing shape (graphic in the center).

   When you drop Windows 7 above Visio 2010, notice that each rectangle displays its current position in the list. Visio 2010 is now #2.

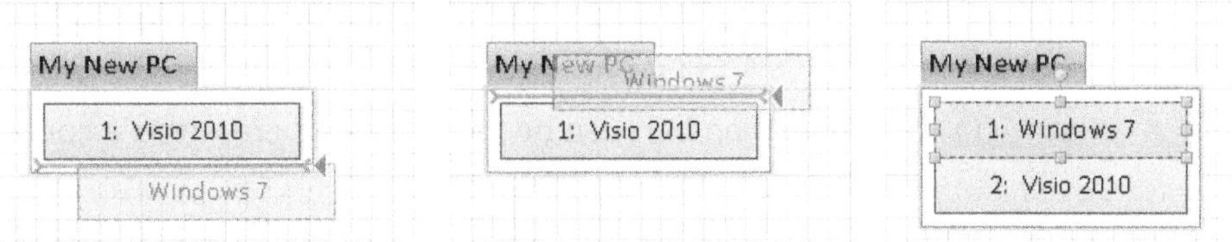

Tip The blue triangle that appears at the end of the orange insertion bar in the previous left and center graphics and in several of the following graphics will be explained in the next section.

3. Insert **Office 2010** between **Windows 7** and **Visio 2010**.

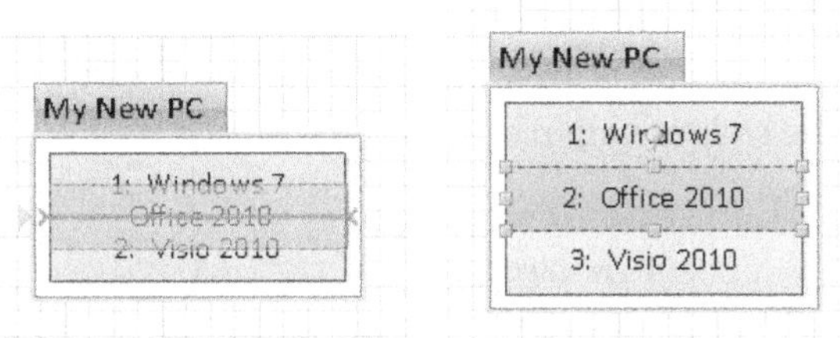

4. Drop **Mozilla** at the end of the list.
5. Drag **Visio add-in** until the orange insertion bar appears below Mozilla, but stop when most of the shape is still outside the list, as shown in the following graphic on the left.

   As you can see, moving a very small portion of a shape into a list is sufficient to trigger membership in the list.
6. With **Visio add-in** in the position shown on the left in the following graphic, release the mouse button. When you release the mouse button from this position, the shape jumps into the list as shown on the right.

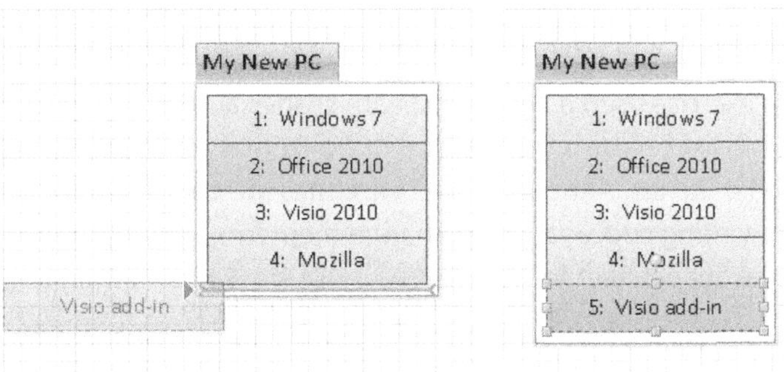

The behavior demonstrated by the *Visio add-in* shape highlights two differences between containers and lists:

- Container members can be located anywhere within a container; list members are always in fixed positions.
- Shapes that are dragged onto the border of a container can be attached to the border; shapes cannot be attached to the border of a list.

7. Drag **Mozilla** up so it is located between **Windows 7** and **Office 2010**.

   The following graphic on the left shows the Mozilla shape as it is being dragged up the list; the graphic on the right shows the result. Notice that when you release the mouse button each shape immediately reflects its new position in the list.

   As this step illustrates, you can not only add shapes to specific positions in a list, you can rearrange the shapes within a list.

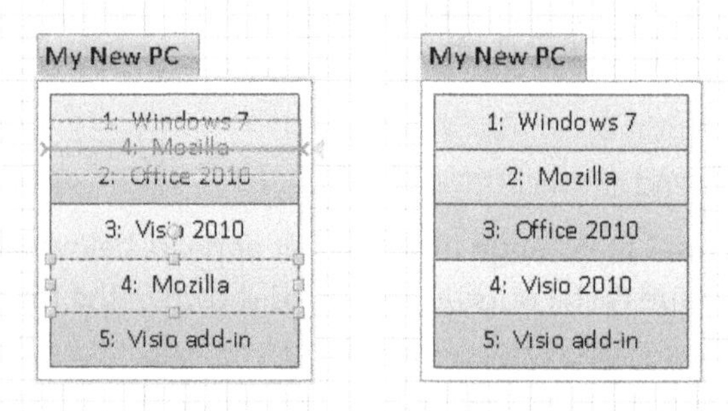

 **CLEAN UP Save your changes to the *Lists* drawing, and then close it.**

Although you aren't likely to use a Visio list for the specific purpose suggested by this exercise, you can probably imagine your own applications for position-aware shapes. If you would like to see several ways that lists are used in Visio 2010, see the sections in "Finding Containers and Lists in Visio" later in this chapter.

The previous exercise used a vertical list with shapes automatically placed from top to bottom. A Visio list can be either vertical or horizontal and can order shapes in either direction within the list. Although these attributes are controlled by parameters and don't require writing code, you can't change them from the Visio ribbon; you must make changes to the ShapeSheet for the list.

See Also **You will learn about the Visio ShapeSheet in the Appendix.**

If you would like to experiment with a horizontal list, the Lists page in the *Containers, Lists and Callouts_start* drawing located in the Chapter11 practice file folder also includes a horizontal list called Store Shelf. Drag shapes from the Computers And Monitors or

Network And Peripherals stencils to create a list like the following example. The Store Shelf list is configured to add shapes from left to right.

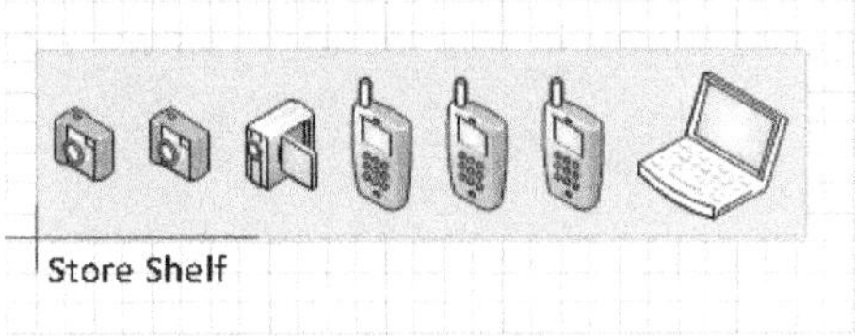

See Also If you would like to know more about lists, go to *msdn.microsoft.com/en-us/library/ff959245.aspx*, which offers a comprehensive MSDN article on structured diagrams written by Mark Nelson of Microsoft.

Formatting and Sizing Lists

The Format contextual tab in the Container Tools contextual tab set provides most of the same functions for lists that it does for containers.

In the Size group:

- Because Visio controls the size of a list shape, Fit To Container and Automatic Resize are disabled.
- You can use the Margins button to adjust the spacing between the edges of the list and the contained shapes.

In the Container Styles group:

- From the style gallery, you can select 1 of 12 preformatted list styles.
- The Heading Style gallery provides 20 heading placement and style alternatives.

In the Membership group:

- The Lock Container, Select Contents, and Disband Container buttons provide the same functions for lists that they do for containers.

You cannot change the size of a Visio list shape. Visio expands and contracts each list shape so it is the exact size of its member shapes plus the margin around the shapes.

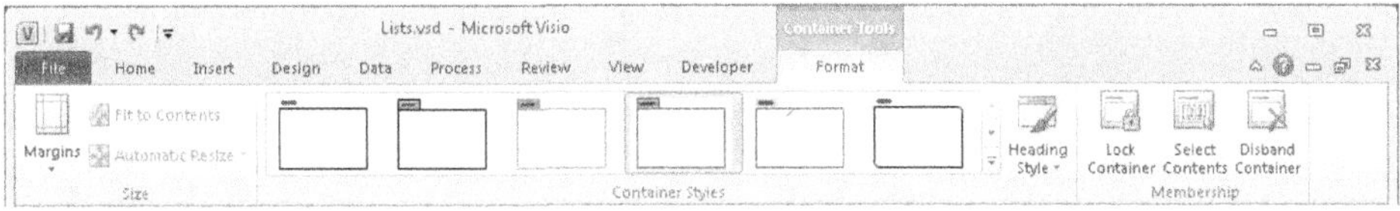

Finding Containers and Lists in Visio

Several Visio 2010 templates take advantage of the properties of containers and lists to enhance ease-of-use and to add valuable features. In this section, you will discover three examples.

Swimlanes

One of the most prominent examples of list and container usage is for ***cross-functional flowcharts***, also known as ***swimlane*** diagrams. (See Chapter 4, "Drawing the Real World: Flowcharts and Organization Charts," for more information about this type of diagram.)

The Visio 2010 swimlane add-in was completely redesigned to take advantage of both lists and containers, with the net effect that a cross-functional flowchart (CFF) is a "list of containers"!

- The framework that holds swimlanes is a list.
- Each swimlane is a container.

In this exercise, you will create part of a swimlane diagram to understand how lists and containers are used.

SET UP Click the File tab, and then click New. In the Template Categories section, click Flowchart, and then double-click the Cross-Functional Flowchart thumbnail to create a new drawing.

1. Click the top edge of the CFF, and then type **Sample Swimlane Diagram**.

   Because the CFF structure is a list, the text you typed appears in the list heading.

2. Click the rectangle at the left end of the upper swimlane, and then type **Accounting**.

   Because the swimlane is a container, your text appears in the container heading.

3. Click the rectangle at the left end of the lower swimlane, type **Legal**, and then press the Escape Key.

   The following graphic shows the results of Steps 1, 2, and 3.

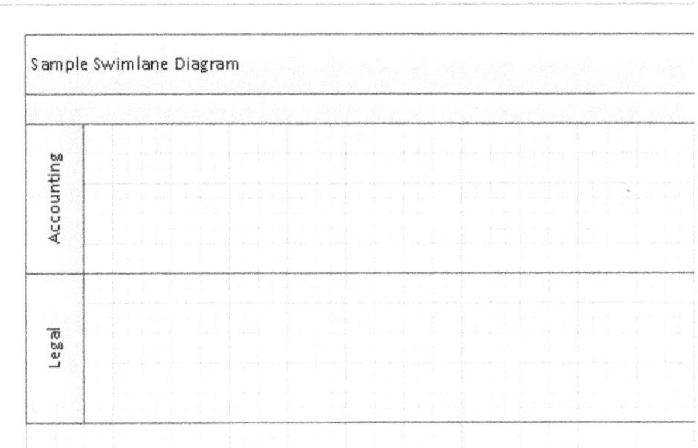

4. Drag a **Process** shape into the **Accounting** swimlane.

   Notice that the swimlane shows the orange border that you previously learned was characteristic behavior for containers.

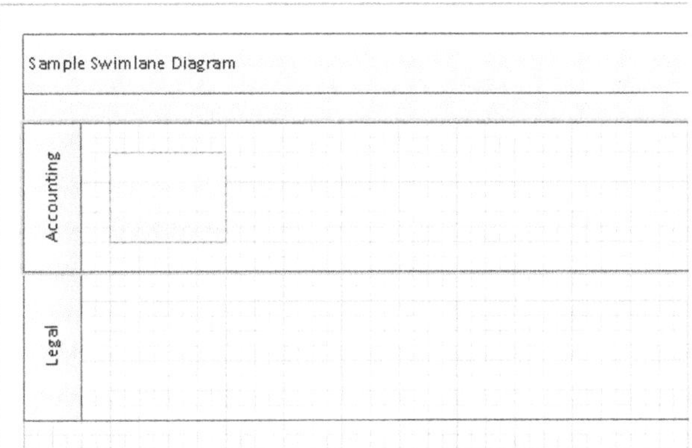

5. Drag a **Decision** shape into the **Legal** swimlane and position it to the right of the process shape in the **Accounting** lane.
6. Drag the **AutoConnect** arrow on the right side of the process shape to link that shape to the Decision shape.

   See Also See Chapter 2, "Creating a New Diagram," for a refresher on using AutoConnect.

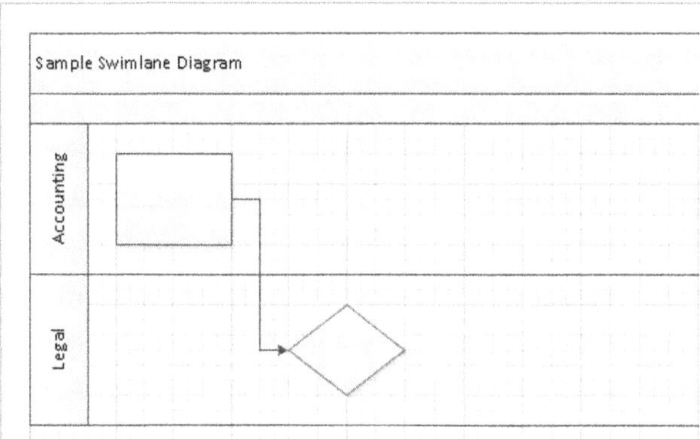

7. Rest the cursor just outside the CFF frame at the junction between the **Accounting** and **Legal** swimlanes (see the cursor in the following graphic).

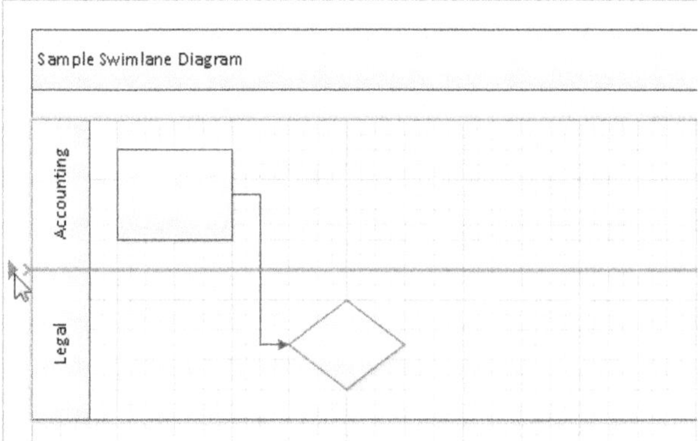

Once again, you see evidence that a cross-functional flowchart is a list: the list insertion bar appears on the boundary between the Accounting and Legal lanes. Also, be sure to note the blue insertion triangle that appears at the end of the insertion bar. Clicking the blue insertion triangle automatically adds the default insertion object at the insertion bar location.

Tip **Not all lists have a default insertion object. If you click the blue insertion triangle on a list without a default, Visio will insert a copy of one of the adjacent list members.**

8. Click the blue insertion triangle, shown in the previous graphic.

   Visio inserts a new swimlane between the other two and maintains all existing connections between shapes in the lanes.

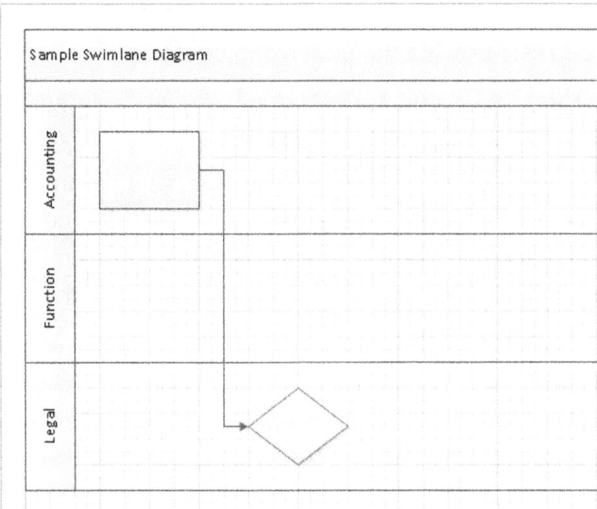

9. Click in the heading area of the **Accounting** swimlane and drag it down below the **Legal** lane.

   Visio moves the Accounting lane to the end of the list and maintains the connections between shapes within and across all swimlanes.

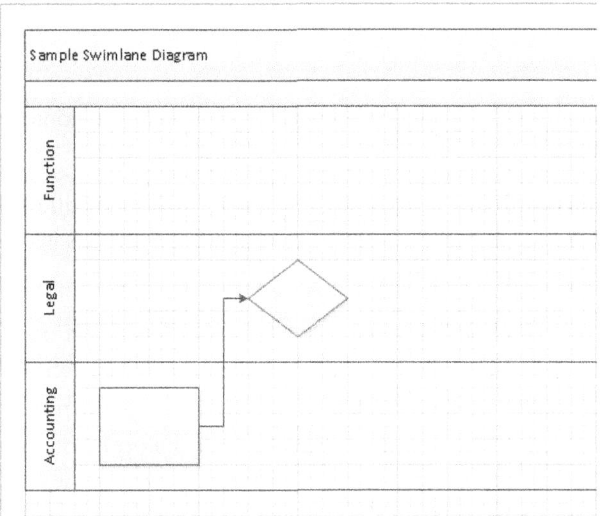

CLEAN UP Save and close your diagram if you want to keep it; otherwise, just close it.

Adding, deleting, and rearranging swimlanes is more predictable and logical in Visio 2010 because containers and lists provide the underlying structure.

Swimlane diagrams derive another benefit from being built as containers: shapes in the container know they are contained. To see evidence of this, examine the Function field in the shape data for any flowchart shape in a swimlane. As an example, the following graphics show the shape data for the process shape (on the left) and decision diamond shape (right) from the preceding graphic. The value in the Function field is derived dynamically from the swimlane heading; if you change the value of the swimlane title, the Function field will be updated for all contained shapes.

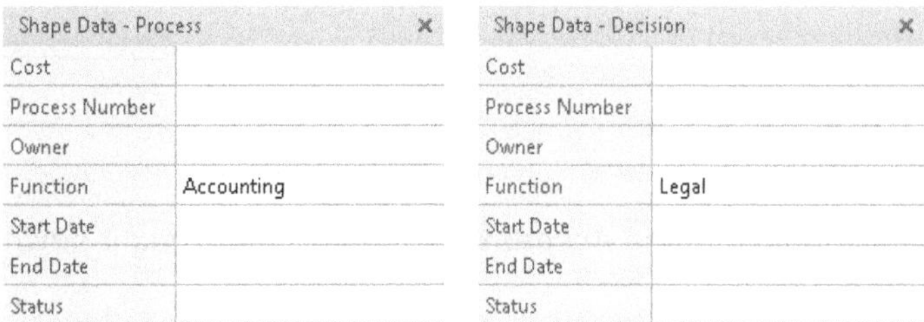

See Also **For more about swimlane containers, go to the Visio development team blog at** ***blogs.msdn.com/b/visio/archive/2009/09/01/cross-functional-flowcharts-in-visio-2010.aspx.***

Wireframes

Important **The information in this section applies only to the Professional and Premium editions of Visio 2010.**

Visio 2010 includes a completely revamped set of user interface (UI) design shapes. For this chapter, the key point of interest about the redesigned shapes is that many of them are either containers or lists.

Software designers use wireframe shapes to create mockups of dialog boxes and other visual elements that will be displayed by their applications. When you use Visio 2010 to create a mockup of a dialog box, you will find that the Dialog Form shape is a container. Consequently, as you add buttons and controls to your dialog form, they become container members. If you move, copy, or delete your dialog box, all of the contained shapes are included. If you have ever created a UI mockup using a previous version of Visio, it won't take more than a moment or two of experimentation to realize how significant an improvement this is.

Some Visio 2010 UI shapes are lists, including, not surprisingly, the List Box control. When you drop one into a dialog form container, the list is prepopulated with three list members. You can add, delete, and resequence list members by dragging them, as you learned in "Adding Shapes to Lists" earlier in this chapter.

In this exercise, you will use the Wireframe template to build a prototype of a simple dialog box that looks like the one in the following graphic. Even if you aren't a UI designer, you should find this exercise useful in learning more about the behavior of containers and lists.

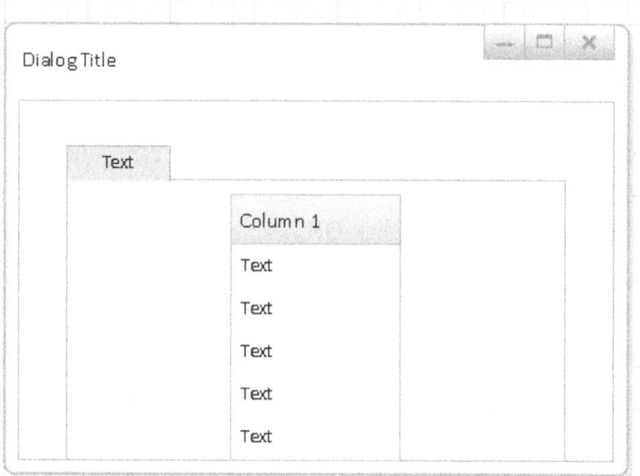

SET UP Click the File tab, and then click New. In the Template Categories section, click Software And Database, and then double-click the Wireframe Diagram thumbnail to create a new drawing.

1. Drag a **Dialog form** shape from the **Dialogs** stencil and drop it on the page. In order to work effectively with this shape, you need to zoom in.
2. Change the zoom level for the drawing page to **150%**. If the dialog form is not centered on the screen, use the scroll bars to center it.
3. Drag a **Dialog button** shape from the **Dialogs** stencil and glue it to a connection point in the upper-right corner of the dialog form.

Tip **As soon as you drag the dialog button shape into the dialog form shape, notice that the edges of the dialog form shape are marked with the orange outline that characterizes a container.**

When you drop a dialog button shape onto the page, it automatically opens the Shape Data dialog box.

4. In the **Shape Data** dialog box, click **OK** to accept the default value for **Type**.

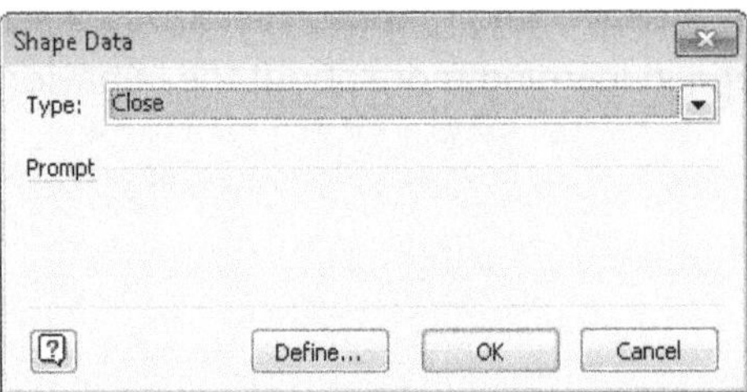

5. Drag another **Dialog button** shape into the dialog form container and glue it to the left end of the previous one; when the **Shape Data** dialog box opens, click **Maximize** in the **Type** list, and then click **OK**.

Tip The dialog button shape is a *multi-shape*; the data value you select in the Shape Data dialog box determines the appearance of the shape.

6. Drag one more **Dialog button** shape into the dialog form container and glue it to the left end of the previous one. When the **Shape Data** dialog box opens, click **Minimize** in the list, and then click **OK**.

The top of your dialog form container now looks like the following graphic.

7. Drag a **Panel** shape from the **Dialogs** stencil and drop it onto the page below (not inside) the dialog form. You need to drop it outside the dialog form because it is too large to fit inside. You must resize it first.

8. Use the resize handles or the **Size & Position** window to change the width of the panel shape to approximately 3 inches (75 mm) and its height to about 1.25 inches (30 mm).

9. Drag the **Panel** shape into the dialog form and position it in the bottom center.

Important The Panel shape is a container, so you can only select and drag it by its edges.

10. Drag an **Upper tab item** shape from the **Dialogs** stencil and position it as a boundary shape at the upper-left corner of the panel container.

Important You want the upper tab item shape to be on the boundary of the panel shape and not inside it. Consequently, when you position the upper tab item shape, make sure that only the top border of the panel container shows the orange outline, as shown in the following graphic. See the sidebar "On the Border" earlier in this chapter for more information about border shapes.

By attaching the upper tab item shape to the boundary of the panel container, you have "welded" them together. If you reposition the panel container, the tab follows along.

Tip Notice that the top border of the panel container is not the only thing with an orange outline in this graphic. There is also an orange outline surrounding the dialog form container. This is because you are adding the tab shape to a container that is nested inside another container; both containers reflect your action.

11. Drag a **List box** from the **Controls** stencil and position it in the upper center of the panel container as shown in the following graphic.

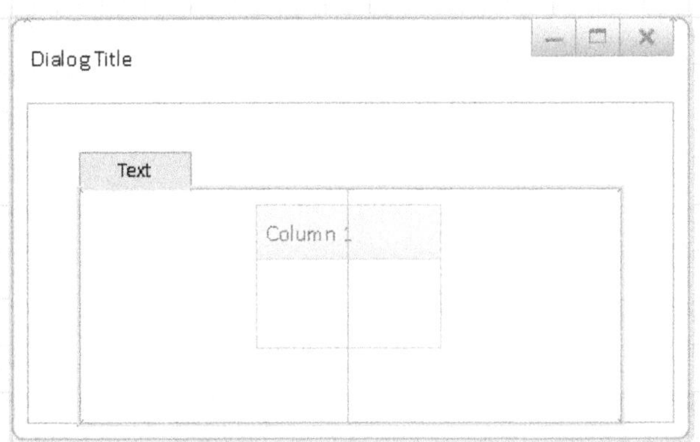

Tip The list box shape exhibits behavior you haven't seen yet in this chapter. When you release the mouse button to drop the new list, it automatically adds several list items, as shown in the following graphic. A list shape that automatically adds list entries can be very useful, but creating one is beyond the scope of this book.

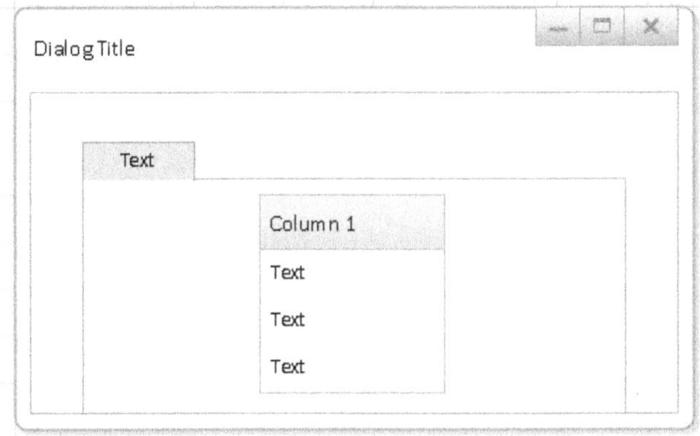

12. Position the cursor just to the left of the **Column 1** list shape and between the first and second **Text** labels.

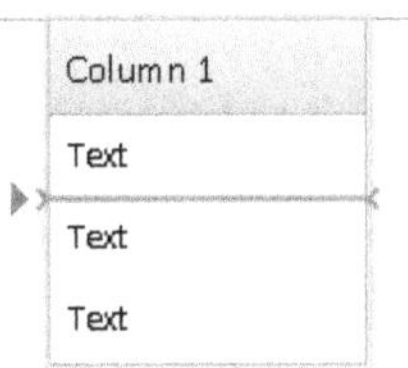

13. Click the blue insertion triangle twice to add two entries to the list box shape.

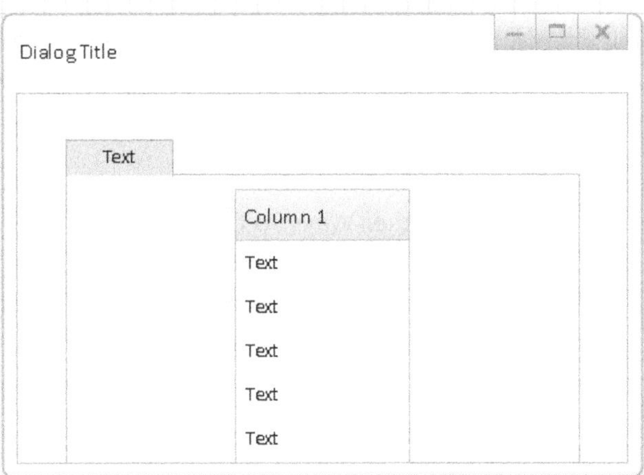

Tip The dialog form shape in this graphic is taller than the ones in Step 12. That's because the list box, panel container, and dialog form container are all configured for automatic expansion. When you added new list items, the list expanded, which, in turn, caused both containers to expand.

CLEAN UP Save and close your diagram if you want to keep it; otherwise just close it.

The dialog box mockup you've created in this exercise isn't going to win any design awards. If you wanted to create a real mockup, you would add additional controls, text, colors, and themes. However, by completing this exercise you have seen a practical application for nested containers and lists, and an example of a container with a border shape.

See Also For more information about wireframe design, see the Visio development team blog at *blogs.msdn.com/b/visio/archive/2009/12/22/wireframe-shapes-in-visio-2010.aspx.*

Legends

In Chapter 10, "Visualizing Your Data," you learned about ***data graphics*** and created a legend for your data graphics. A data graphics legend is actually a structure consisting of an outer list, one or more containers as list members, and lists within those containers.

If you return to the data graphics diagram you created in Chapter 10, you will find that you can add, delete, rename, and move legend components. Throughout your changes, however, the legend maintains its overall structure because of the nested containers and lists.

If you haven't completed Chapter 10 but would like to see a sample legend, click the File tab, and then click New. In the Other Ways To Get Started section, click Sample Diagrams, and then double-click Sales Summary. There is an existing legend in the upper-right corner. If you would like to add a different one, on the Data tab, in the Display Data group, click Insert Legend, and then click either Horizontal or Vertical.

Annotating Shapes with Callouts

In previous versions of Visio, you could add a callout to a page from the Callouts stencil in the Visio Extras group. The Callouts stencil still exists: in the Shapes window, click More Shapes, click Visio Extras, and then click Callouts to see more than three dozen callout types. The following graphic shows one example.

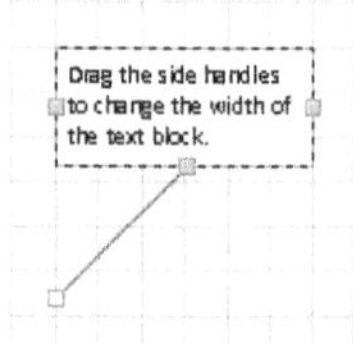

Old-style callouts are useful for their intended purpose: you can type text into the text box and glue the tail onto another shape. Some even have attractive or clever designs.

The underlying problem with the older callouts, however, is that they are just shapes. Although you can attach them to other shapes, they aren't associated with those shapes in any useful way. For example, look at the printer and callout on the left in the following graphic:

- Moving the printer to the right (center image), doesn't change the location of the callout.
- Deleting the printer shape doesn't affect the callout as you can see in the rightmost graphic.

It's also easy to accidentally detach the callout from the printer by dragging the text box portion of the callout while trying to relocate it.

In this exercise, you will discover that Visio 2010 callouts are associated with the shapes to which they are attached in ways that make sense. You will see that the callout and its attached shape act in tandem.

SET UP You need the *Containers, Lists and Callouts_start* drawing located in the Chapter11 practice file folder to complete this exercise. Open the drawing in Visio and save it as *Callouts*.

1. Go to the **Callouts** page.
2. Click once on the printer shape to select it.

Callout

3. On the **Insert** tab, in the **Diagram Parts** group, click the **Callout** button. The Callout gallery opens.
4. Move your mouse through the gallery and notice that Live Preview shows what each callout will look like when attached to the printer shape.

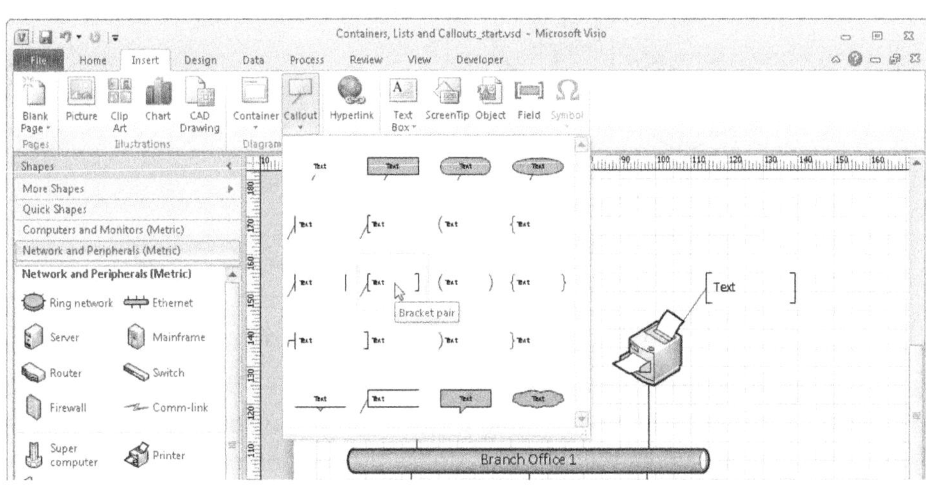

5. Click **Bracket pair** (as shown in the previous graphic). The callout is added to the page and attached to the printer.

6. With the callout still selected, type **Located in Accounting Department**, and then press Esc to exit text edit mode.

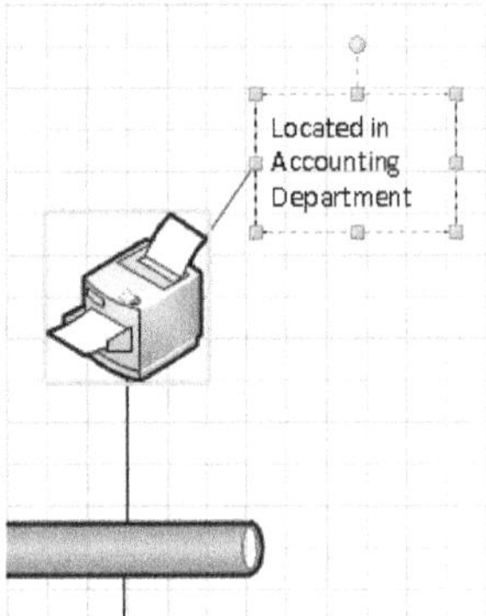

Tip **Notice that when the callout is selected, there is an orange border around the printer to signal the association between the two shapes. The reverse is not true: if you select the printer, the callout does not have any kind of border.**

7. Select and drag the printer to the right (shown on the left in the following graphic), and then release the mouse button (graphic on right). The callout moves with the printer.

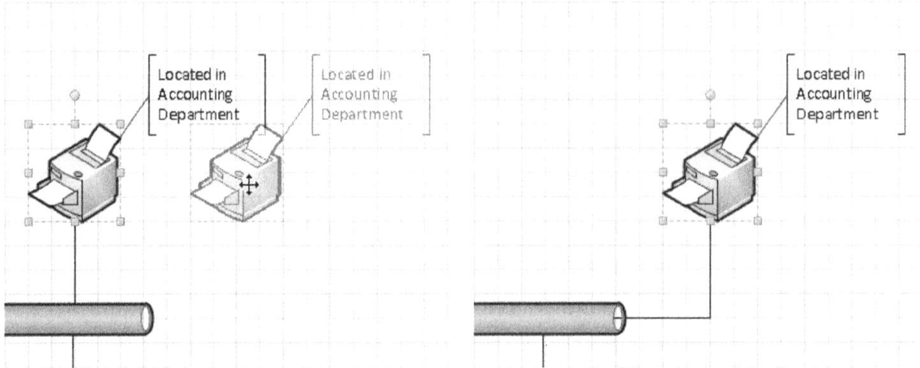

8. Select and drag the callout to the left side of the printer.

   As you drag the callout, it looks like it's been detached from the printer (left graphic on the following page). However, as soon as you release the mouse button, you can see that it is still attached to the printer (right graphic).

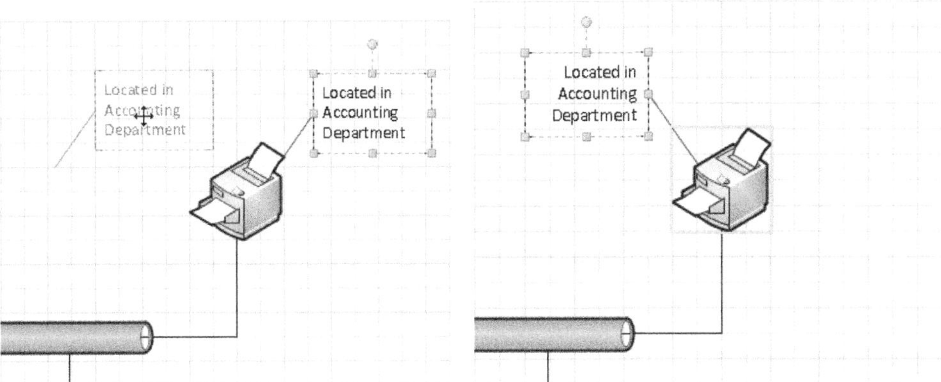

CLEAN UP Save and close your diagram if you want to keep the changes; otherwise just close it.

Unlike containers and lists, callouts do not have a context tab on the Visio ribbon. However, you can change the characteristics of a callout. When you right-click a callout, you will see the cascading menus shown in the following graphic that allow you to select a different callout style (left), change the orientation (center), and set the line type (right).

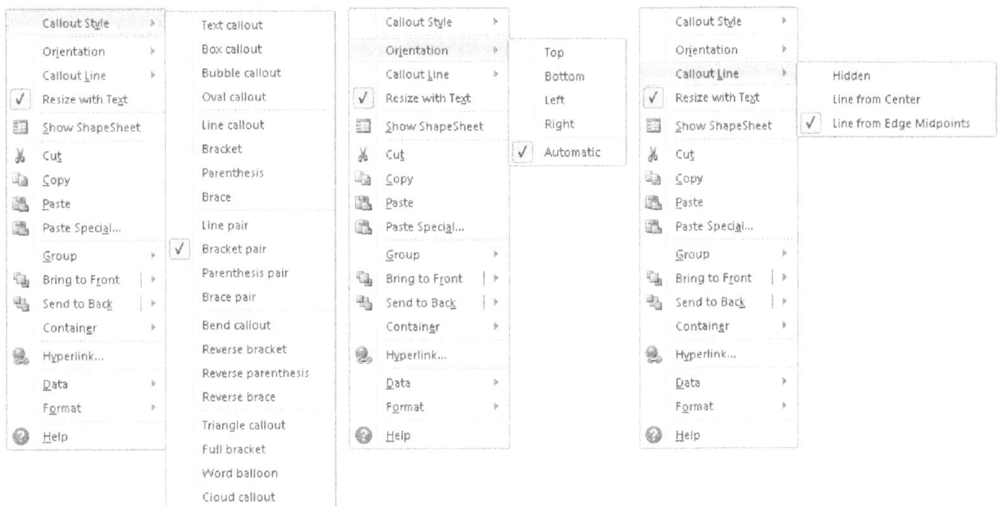

There are a few other useful things to know about callouts:

- If you delete a callout, it doesn't affect the shape to which it was attached. However, if you delete the shape, the callout is also deleted.
- If you copy a shape that has a callout attached, both the shape and the callout are copied.

- You can attach more than one callout to a shape.
- If you do not have any shapes selected when you insert a callout, Visio inserts the callout in the center of the drawing window.
- If you select more than one shape before inserting a callout, Visio will attach a callout to each selected shape.

See Also For more information about callouts, see the Visio development team blog at *blogs.msdn.com/b/visio/archive/2009/10/06/annotating-diagrams-with-callouts-in-visio-2010.aspx*.

Key Points

- You can use containers and lists to achieve many of the same results that you can by creating a background shape and grouping it with a set of shapes. However, containers offer considerable advantages over grouped shapes:
    - When you move, copy, or delete a container or a list, the member shapes in the container/list are also moved, copied, or deleted.
    - Even though the previous statement is true, each shape in a container or list maintains its independence. It's easy to select a container member with a single click and to access its shape data and other properties.
    - Shapes in containers and lists know they are contained and can derive data from the parent container. (See the example at the end of the "Swimlanes" topic in "Finding Containers and Lists in Visio" earlier in this chapter.)
- Visio 2010 lists are a special type of container in which shapes are maintained in a specific sequence. Each shape knows its ordinal position in the list even when shapes are added, deleted, or rearranged.
- Visio 2010 uses containers and lists for cross-functional flowcharts, wireframe diagrams, data graphic legends, and other purposes. Visio also provides generic containers that you can use for any purpose you would like.
- Visio 2010 callouts are much more intelligent than the callouts provided with previous versions of Visio. In Visio 2010, each callout is associated with a specific target shape and is copied, moved, or deleted with that shape.

Chapter at a Glance

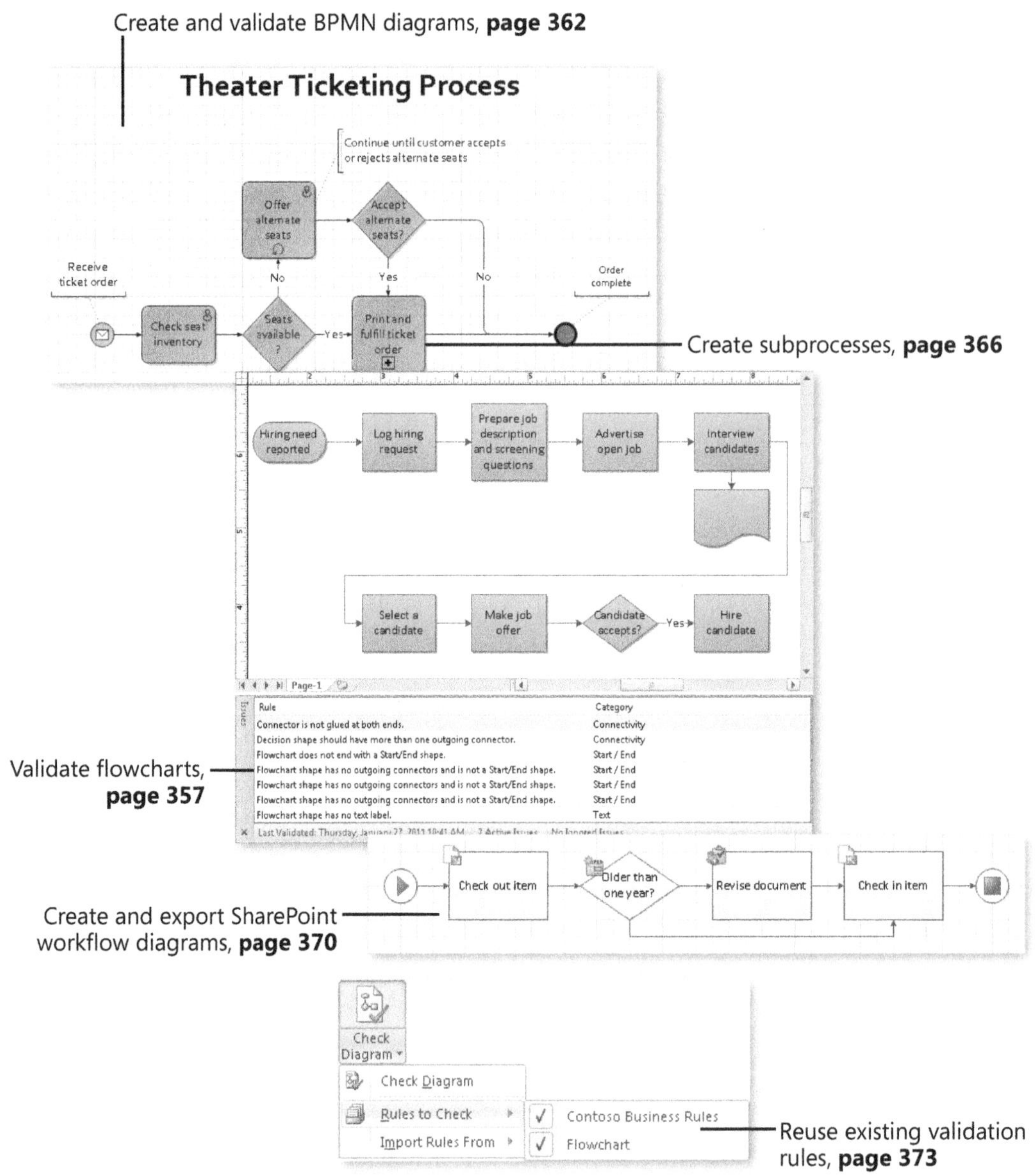

12 Creating and Validating Process Diagrams

In this chapter, you will learn how to

- ✔ Understand Visio rules.
- ✔ Validate flowcharts.
- ✔ Understand BPMN.
- ✔ Create and validate BPMN diagrams.
- ✔ Create subprocesses.
- ✔ Create and export SharePoint Workflow diagrams.
- ✔ Reuse existing validation rules.
- ✔ Create new validation rules.

A ***business process***, also known as a ***work process***, or just a ***process***, is a collection of ***tasks*** or ***activities*** that leads to a desired result. A diagram of a work process is often referred to as a ***process map***. In Chapter 4, "Drawing the Real World: Flowcharts and Organization Charts," you created and worked with ***flowcharts*** and ***swimlane diagrams***, both of which can be used to create process maps.

Microsoft Visio 2010 includes a significant set of enhancements related to diagramming work processes and to ensuring that those diagrams are correct. In fact, enhancing the process-related capabilities of Visio was a high enough priority for Microsoft, that they created a new edition of Visio—the Premium edition—to package all of the product's new process-related features. The Premium edition includes a Process tab on the Visio ribbon.

In this chapter, you will use a new facility in Visio Premium 2010 to validate a Visio diagram against a set of rules. You will also learn about two new process-oriented templates that are included with Visio Premium: ***Business Process Modeling Notation*** (***BPMN***) and SharePoint Workflow.

Important The information in this chapter applies only to the Premium edition of Visio 2010.

Tip The default font size for shapes in the drawings you will create in this chapter is 8 pt. To improve the readability of the figures in this chapter, the shapes in most screenshots use either 12 pt. or 14 pt. text. Consequently, the text in the shapes on your drawing page will be smaller than what you see in this chapter.

Practice Files Before you can complete the exercises in this chapter, you need to copy the book's practice files to your computer. The practice files you'll use to complete the exercises in this chapter are in the Chapter12 practice files folder. A complete list of practice files is provided in "Using the Practice Files" at the beginning of this book.

Understanding Visio Rules

The diagram validation capabilities of Visio 2010 are built around collections of rules. A Visio ***rule*** can check a diagram for a very simple or a very complex condition. For example, a rule developer might create a rule to answer any of the following questions:

- Are there any shapes on the page that have one connection but not two?
- Are there any unconnected shapes on the page?
- Does every ***2-D shape*** contain text?
- Are there more than three blue shapes on any one page or more than five red shapes in the entire diagram?
- Are there any containers with fewer than three or more than seven shapes?
- Are there any shapes of type X, containing a field named Y with a value of Z?

These are just representative questions. Visio rules are sufficiently flexible that the real question becomes: "What problem do you need to solve?"

Validation rules are packaged into ***rule sets***. Four Visio 2010 templates include predefined business rules:

- Basic Flowchart
- Cross-functional Flowchart
- Business Process Modeling Notation
- SharePoint Workflow

It's also possible to create your own custom rule sets for validating process diagrams, or, for that matter, for validating any kind of Visio diagram. Although the specific techniques for editing or creating custom rule sets are beyond the scope of this book, you will find links to appropriate resources in the sections titled "Reusing Existing Validation Rules" and "Creating New Validation Rules" later in this chapter.

Validating Flowcharts

One of the easiest ways to understand and begin using Visio validation is to work with something familiar: a flowchart you created in Chapter 4. The difference between the flowchart you'll create in this exercise and the one in Chapter 4 is that this version contains deliberate errors.

In this exercise, you will use flowchart validation rules to discover and correct errors in a flowchart.

SET UP You need the *HR Recruiting Flowchart Validation_start* drawing located in the Chapter12 practice file folder to complete this exercise. Open the drawing in Visio and save it as *HR Recruiting Flowchart Validation*.

Check Diagram

1. On the **Process** tab, in the **Diagram Validation** group, click the **Check Diagram** button to run the default set of flowchart validation rules.

   Visio opens an Issues window to display the problems it found in the diagram. In addition to displaying the rule and rule category for each validation error, the bottom of the Issues window shows the date and time of the most recent validation.

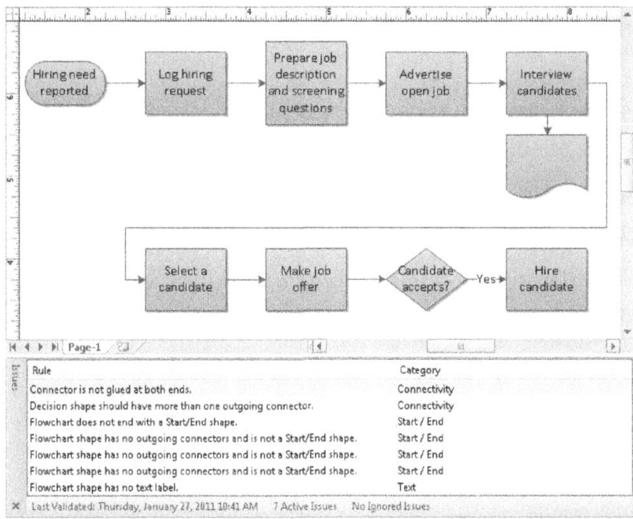

Tip You can re-sort the list of issues by clicking the Rule or Category column headings. You can also right-click anywhere in the Issues window, click Arrange By, and select Rule, Category, or Original Order.

2. In the **Issues** window, click once on **Connector is not glued at both ends.** The unlinked connector is highlighted.

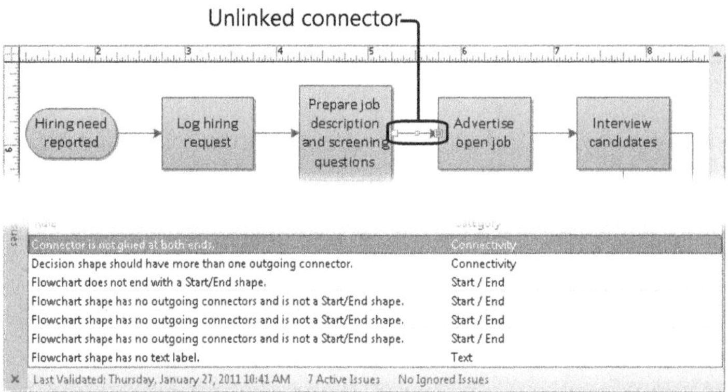

This error is an excellent example of the value of diagram validation. When you look at the flowchart image in Step 1, it's not at all obvious that there is an unlinked connector.

3. In the **Issues** window, click once on **Decision shape should have more than one outgoing connector.**

   The *Candidate accepts?* shape is highlighted, demonstrating yet another valuable reason to use validation: as you're creating a flowchart, it's easy to forget a path. This rule ensures that decisions always have at least two outcomes.

4. In the **Issues** window, click once on **Flowchart does not end with a Start/End shape.**

   Because this rule is about a missing shape, there is nothing highlighted in the drawing, but it's easy to see that the message is correct—there is no end shape.

5. In the **Issues** window, click once on the first instance of **Flowchart shape has no outgoing connectors and is not a Start/End shape.**

   The *Prepare job description and screening questions* shape is highlighted because of the unlinked connector described in Step 2.

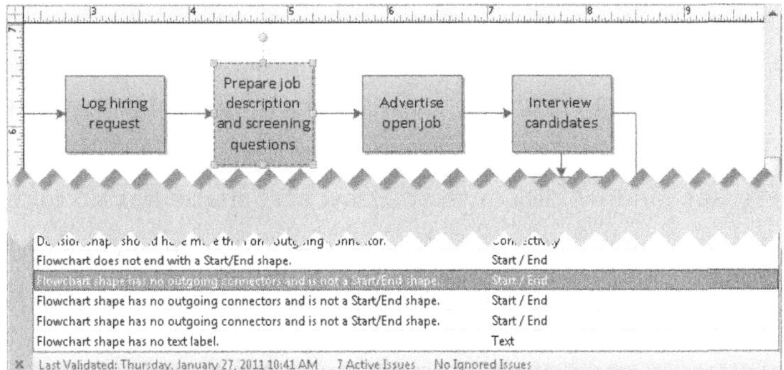

6. In the **Issues** window, click once on the second instance of **Flowchart shape has no outgoing connectors and is not a Start/End shape.**

   The *Hire candidate* shape is highlighted because there is no end shape.

7. In the **Issues** window, click once on the third instance of **Flowchart shape has no outgoing connectors and is not a Start/End shape.** The document shape is highlighted.

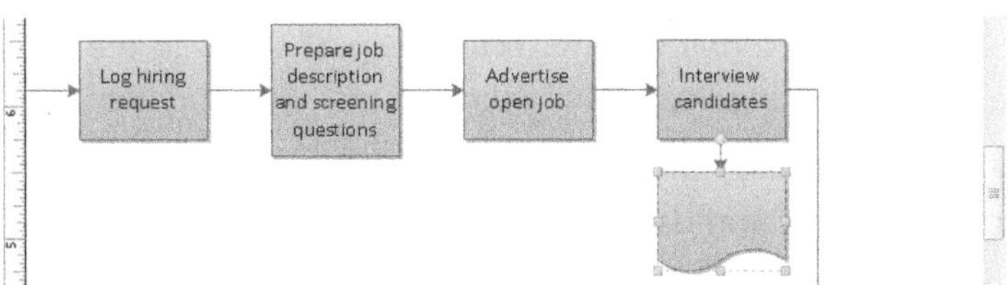

   The error message is correct. The document shape does not have any outgoing connectors. For this shape, however, that is acceptable because a document isn't a process step but is a representation of a process artifact. Consequently, you will tell Visio to ignore this rule for this shape.

8. Right-click the already-selected issue description, and then click **Ignore This Issue**.

   Important When you right-click, be careful of the distinction between Ignore This Issue and Ignore Rule. The former ignores a single issue; the latter ignores all issues created by a rule. Use Ignore Rule very carefully or you may inadvertently hide important issues.

Issues

Rule	Category
Connector is not glued at both ends.	Connectivity
Decision shape should have more than one outgoing connector.	Connectivity
Flowchart does not end with a Start/End shape.	Start / End
Flowchart shape has no outgoing connectors and is not a Start/End shape.	Start / End
Flowchart shape has no outgoing connectors and is not a Start/End shape.	Start / End
Flowchart shape has no text label.	Text

Last Validated: Thursday, January 27, 2011 10:41 AM 6 Active Issues 1 Ignored Issues

Notice that the third occurrence of the *Flowchart shape has no outgoing connectors and is not a Start/End shape* issue has disappeared from the Issues window. Also, the status bar at the bottom of the window now indicates that there is one ignored issue.

9. In the **Issues** window, click once on **Flowchart shape has no text label.**

   This issue also applies to the document shape. If you don't want to put text on this shape, you can ignore the issue as you did in the preceding step. However, for this exercise, you will add text to the shape.

10. Double-click the document shape, type **HR Policy Manual**, and then press Esc.

    In the remaining steps of this exercise, you will resolve more of the diagram issues you reviewed in the previous steps.

11. Click once on the connector between the **Prepare job description and screening questions** shape and the **Advertise open job** shape, and then glue its ends to the adjacent shapes.

    Tip You can click the Check Diagram button at any time to refresh the Issues window.

12. Draw a connector from the **Candidate accepts?** shape to the **Select a candidate** shape. While the connector is still selected, type **No**, and then press Esc.

13. Add a **Start/End** shape after the **Hire Candidate** shape, and then draw a connector from the **Hire Candidate** shape to the start/end shape.

14. On the **Process** tab, in the **Diagram Validation** group, click the **Check Diagram** button. There is one remaining issue, which you can choose to resolve by adding text to the end shape or you can ignore it.

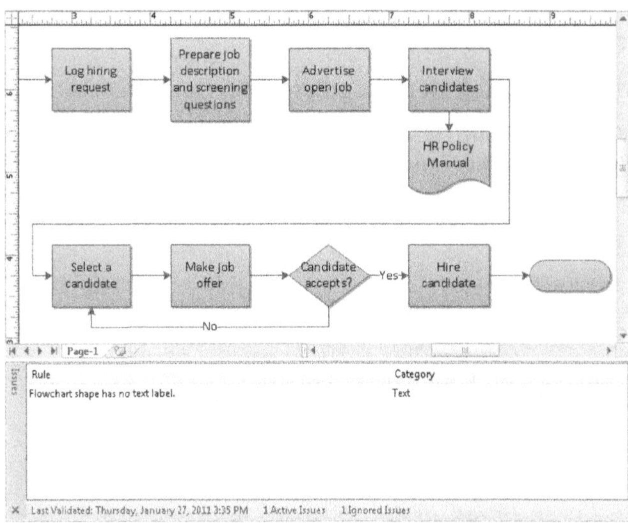

 **CLEAN UP** Save your changes to the *HR Recruiting Flowchart Validation* drawing, and then close it.

Tip You can close the Issues window at any time by clicking the *X* in the lower-left corner or by clearing the Issues Window check box in the Diagram Validation group on the Process tab.

Understanding BPMN

Business Process Modeling Notation (BPMN) was created to represent work processes in diagrams that are readily understandable by business people, yet are rich enough in detail to allow IT departments to translate process maps into technical specifications. The goal for BPMN is to enhance communication about processes across an organization. For automated processes, BPMN diagrams can serve as a bridge between process participants and the IT staff that build systems to support their work.

At one level, a BPMN diagram is like a flowchart or swimlane diagram. However, the symbol set is significantly larger than the one used for a conventional flowchart or swimlane diagram. This one fact leads both to strong advocacy for and strong resistance to BPMN.

Advocates assert that it is the combination of visual richness and underlying data attributes that allows BPMN diagrams to convey complex system and human interactions. Critics complain that the sheer number of symbols and symbol variants is off-putting to many people; they feel it makes diagrams more complex and less understandable to the business people who are half of the intended audience for BPMN.

The creators of BPMN have worked hard to make BPMN usable by a larger number of people. One result is that BPMN 2.0 defines a smaller working set of shapes and symbols that will be familiar to anyone who has created traditional flowcharts. However, Visio Premium 2010 implements BPMN 1.2 and does not, therefore, include the smaller working set. Having more shapes available in BPMN 1.2 is not inherently a bad thing, but the number of shape variations can be confusing.

The first thing to know about creating BPMN 1.2 diagrams from the Visio Premium 2010 template is that there are four core shape types: ***Events***, ***Activities***, ***Gateways***, and ***Connecting Objects***, with multiple variations of each.

The BPMN 1.2 symbol set includes the following:

- Three types of Events, classified as Start, Intermediate, and End, and represented by different kinds of circles.

There are five subtypes of Start events, eight Intermediate events, and seven End events; each subtype is represented by a symbol inside one of the circle variants.

- Two Activity types, tasks and subprocesses, each of which has multiple variations.
- Six Gateway types.
- Three Connector types, representing sequence flows, message flows, and associations between shapes, with several condition attributes for sequence flows and direction attributes for associations.

If you create process documentation in any form today, or expect to in the future, it is worth learning more about BPMN. The next two exercises in this chapter will guide you through creating and validating a BPMN diagram, but they barely scratch the surface of what BPMN is about. The websites, documents, and books in the following list provide further details:

- Object Management Group/Business Process Management Initiative: *www.bpmn.org*.
- BPMN 2.0 examples non-normative document: *www.omg.org/cgi-bin/doc?dtc/10-06-02*.
- Silver, Bruce. 2009. *BPMN Method and Style: A levels-based methodology for BPM process modeling and improvement using BPMN 2.0*. Cody-Cassidy Press.
- White, Stephen A., and Derek Miers. 2008. *BPMN Modeling and Reference Guide*. Future Strategies Inc.

Creating and Validating BPMN Diagrams

Important The Visio BPMN template supports version 1.2 of the BPMN standard.

Microsoft provides five stencils with the Visio 2010 BPMN template. The key masters in the first stencil, *BPMN Basic Shapes*, include the primary Event types described in the previous section, a generic Gateway, and a basic Activity type called a *task* (see the graphic on the left). The other four templates present all of the variations of one shape category. In the center and right graphic, you see the Gateways and Connecting Objects, respectively.

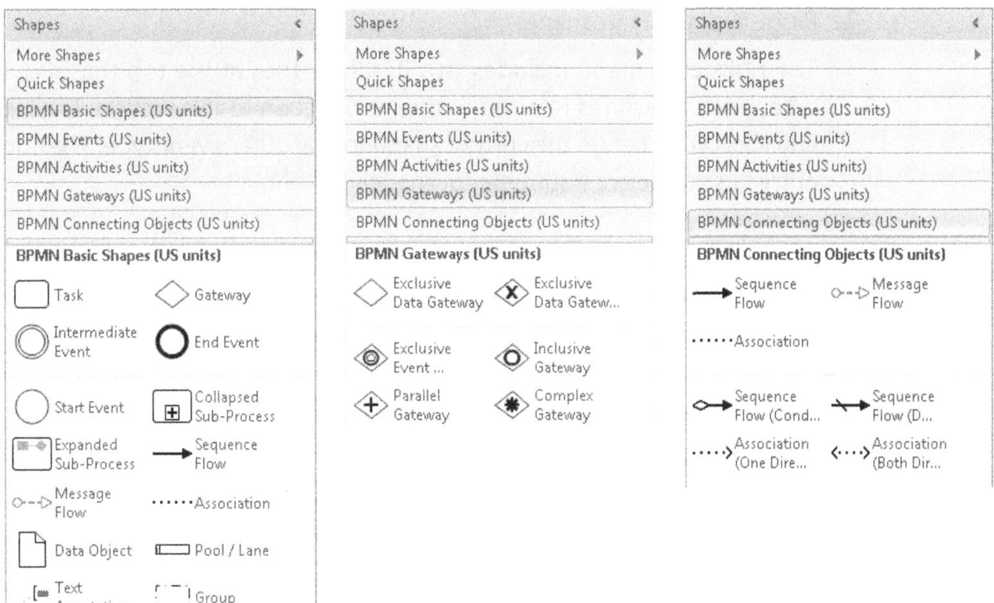

Although the five templates provide every possible BPMN map variant as a separate master in a stencil, it's important to know that all of the BPMN shapes are chameleon-like shapes. For example, you can right-click any Activity shape to transform it into any other Activity type. The same is true for Events, Gateways, and Connectors.

In this exercise, you will start with a partially completed BPMN diagram of a theater box office ticketing process. You will set a trigger for the start event that launches the process, add a task and a gateway to offer the purchaser alternatives if the requested seats are unavailable, and set BPMN subtypes for various shapes.

SET UP You need the *Theater Ticketing Process_start* drawing located in the Chapter12 practice file folder to complete this exercise. Open the drawing in Visio and save it as *Theater Ticketing Process*.

> **Tip** In the document you just opened, the masters in the stencils have colored backgrounds, unlike those in the previous graphics. This is because the diagram for this exercise includes a theme. Refer to Chapter 5, "Adding Style, Color, and Themes," for information about themes.

1. Right-click the Start shape.

   The right-click menu includes two BPMN entries at the top that provide the "chameleon" features referred to the introduction to this section. The Event Type entry lets you change the current shape to any other event type. The Trigger/Result entry lets you select a subtype for the Start event.

   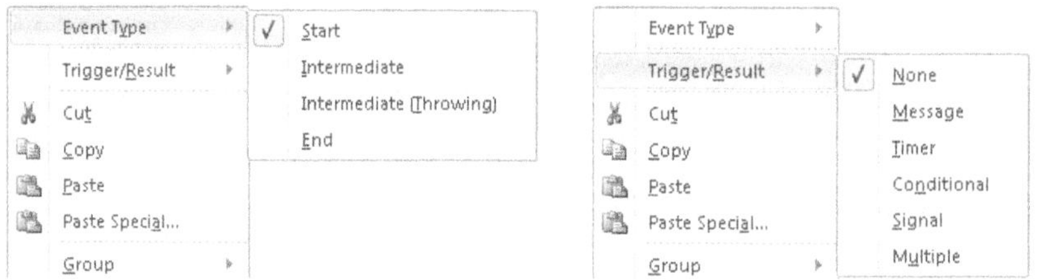

   Each type of BPMN shape has its own set of right-click menus.

2. With the right-click menu open, point to **Trigger/Result**, and then click **Message**. The start shape displays a white envelope, indicating that a message triggers the launch of this process.
3. Drag a **Task** shape from the **BPMN Basic Shapes** stencil, position it above the **Seats available?** shape, and drop it on the connector labeled **No**. The Visio 2010 *AutoAdd* feature splits the connector and inserts the new shape.

   See Also For information about AutoAdd and *AutoDelete*, see Chapter 2, "Creating a New Diagram."

4. With the new task still selected, type **Offer alternate seats**, and then press Esc.
5. Drag a **Gateway** shape from the **BPMN Basic Shapes** stencil, position it above the **Print tickets** shape, and drop it on the unlabeled connector.
6. With the new gateway still selected, type **Accept alternate seats?** and then press Esc.
7. Use the **AutoConnect** arrow under the **Accept alternate seats?** shape to draw a connector to the top of the **Print tickets** shape.

   See Also For information about AutoConnect, see Chapter 2.

8. With the new connector still selected, type **Yes**.
9. Click once on the connector from the **Accept alternate seats?** shape to the End shape, type **No**, and then press Esc.

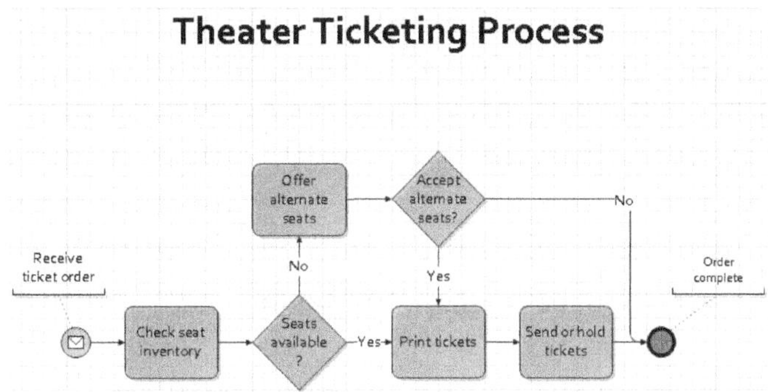

To finish this exercise, you will mark each task with a BPMN symbol to designate the task type.

10. Right-click the **Check seat inventory** shape, point to **Task Type**, and click **User**.
11. Right-click **Offer alternate seats**, move to **Task Type**, and click **User**.
12. With the **Offer alternate seats** shape still selected, point to **Loop**, and click **Standard**.

    A loop symbol appears in the task shape, indicating that this task will be repeated until certain conditions are met. You will describe those conditions with a text callout in the next step.

13. Drag a **Text Annotation** shape from the **BPMN Basic Shapes** stencil, attach it to the **Offer alternate seats** shape, and type **Continue until customer accepts or rejects alternate seats**.

    Tip You can resize and reposition the Text Annotation shape to suit your taste. Note that the Text Annotation shape is a Visio 2010 callout, so it exhibits the callout behaviors described in Chapter 11, "Adding Structure to Your Diagrams."

14. Right-click the **Print tickets** shape, point to **Task Type**, and click **Service** to indicate that this activity is performed by a system.
15. Right-click the **Send or hold tickets** shape, point to **Task Type**, and click **User**.

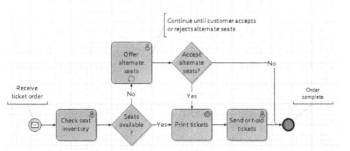

Theater Ticketing Process

Continue until customer accepts or rejects alternate seats

Offer alternate seats

Accept alternate seats?

No

Receive ticket order

No

Yes

Order complete

Check seat inventory

Seats available ?

Yes

Print tickets

Send or hold tickets

Earlier in this chapter, you validated a flowchart using built-in rules supplied by Visio 2010 Premium. There is also a set of rules provided for validating BPMN diagrams. Many of the same connectivity rules are included in the BPMN rule set; however, because BPMN diagrams can be more complex, there are many additional rules.

In the final step of this exercise, you will validate your BPMN drawing.

Check Diagram

16. On the **Process** tab, in the **Diagram Validation** group, click the **Check Diagram** button.

    Visio displays a dialog box reporting "Diagram validation is complete. No issues were found in the current document."

CLEAN UP Save your changes to the *Theater Ticketing Process* drawing but leave it open if you are continuing with the next exercise.

The ticketing process used in this exercise is deliberately very simplistic. You could easily argue that more of the steps are automated in most theater box offices and that there should be other tasks involved. All of that is true, but the purpose of this exercise is to learn a bit about BPMN and not to create the ultimate theater ticketing process.

Creating Subprocesses

As you document, define, and refine a business process, you will typically add more detail and additional steps to your process map. At some point, your map is likely to become unwieldy and difficult to read and maintain.

One common solution for a cluttered process map is to select a group of related process steps and replace them with a single ***subprocess*** symbol. You then move the selected steps to another page where you have room to spread them out and continue to work on that section of the overall process. Visio Premium 2010 includes several subprocess buttons that automate much of the work of creating subprocesses.

In this exercise, you will add additional detail to the theater ticketing example by defining a subprocess for two of the existing tasks.

SET UP You need the *Theater Ticketing Process* drawing for this exercise. Either continue with the open copy from the previous exercise or open the *Theater Ticketing with Subprocess_start* drawing located in the Chapter12 practice file folder and save it as *Theater Ticketing Process*.

1. Draw a bounding box to select both the **Print tickets** and **Send or hold tickets** shapes.

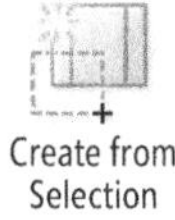

2. On the **Process** tab, in the **Subprocess** group, click the **Create from Selection** button.

   Visio replaces your selected shapes with a subprocess shape; adds a new page to the drawing; places your selected shapes on the new page; and builds a hyperlink from the new subprocess shape to the subprocess page.

   Tip The plus sign at the bottom of the new shape is the BPMN notation for a subprocess.

3. With the subprocess shape still selected, type **Print and fulfill ticket order**.

Theater Ticketing Process

Continue until customer accepts or rejects alternate seats

Offer alternate seats

Accept alternate seats?

Receive ticket order

No

Yes

No

Order complete

Check seat inventory

Seats available ?

Yes

Print and fulfill ticket order

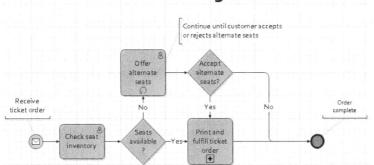

4. Hold down the Ctrl key and click the **Print and fulfill ticket order** shape to move to the subprocess page. You will see your two original activities on the new page.

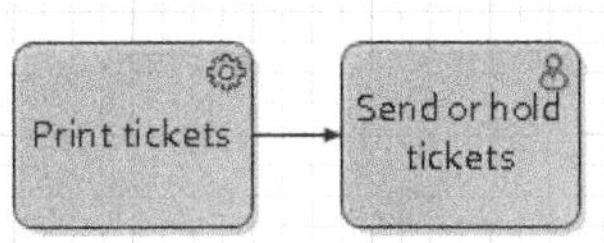

   In the remaining steps of this exercise, you will define a more complete subprocess.

5. Delete the **Send or hold tickets** shape.

6. Point to the **AutoConnect** arrow on the right side of the **Print tickets** shape, and from the **Quick Shapes** menu, add a **Gateway**.

   See Also For information about *AutoConnect* and *Quick Shapes*, see Chapter 2.

   Troubleshooting If the AutoConnect arrow doesn't appear, that option may be turned off in this drawing. To activate AutoConnect, on the View tab, in the Visual Aids group, select AutoConnect.

7. With the gateway still selected, type **More than 7 days 'til show?**.

8. Point to the **AutoConnect** arrow on the right side of the gateway, and from the **Quick Shapes** menu, add a **Task**.

9. Hold down the Shift key and drag the task up so its bottom edge is just above the top edge of the gateway.

   Tip **Holding down the Shift key while dragging a shape constrains shape movement to a single direction.**

10. Point to the **AutoConnect** arrow on the right side of the gateway, and from the **Quick Shapes** menu, add a **Task**.
11. Hold down the Shift key and drag the new task down so its top edge is just below the bottom edge of the gateway.
12. Click the connector to the upper task and type **Yes**. Then click the connector to the lower task and type **No**.
13. Click the task on the **Yes** path, and type **Ship tickets**.
14. Click the task on the **No** path, and type **Hold tickets at box office**.
15. Drag an **End Event** shape from the **BPMN Basic Shapes** stencil and drop it to the right of the two new tasks.
16. Drag the **AutoConnect** arrow on the right of the **Ship tickets** task and connect it to the end shape; then do the same thing for the **Hold tickets at box office** task.
17. Drag a **Text Annotation** shape from the **BPMN Basic Shapes** stencil, attach it to the end shape, and type **Tickets processed**.

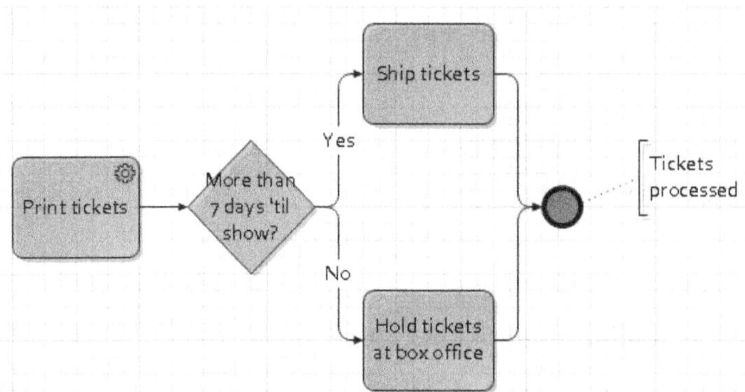

18. Double-click the **Page-1** page name tab and type **Main Process**. Then double-click the **Page-2** page name tab and type **Print and Fulfill**.

Check Diagram

19. On the **Process** tab, in the **Diagram Validation** group, click the **Check Diagram** button.

    The messages that appear in the Issues window result from a deliberate omission in this exercise: there is no Start event. A BPMN subprocess that includes an End event should also include a Start. You can resolve the error by adding a Start event.

Tip Because of the potential complexity of BPMN diagrams, the text of many BPMN issue descriptions is longer than the width of the Issues window. However, if you position the cursor over any item in the Issues window, Visio displays the full text in a pop-up message.

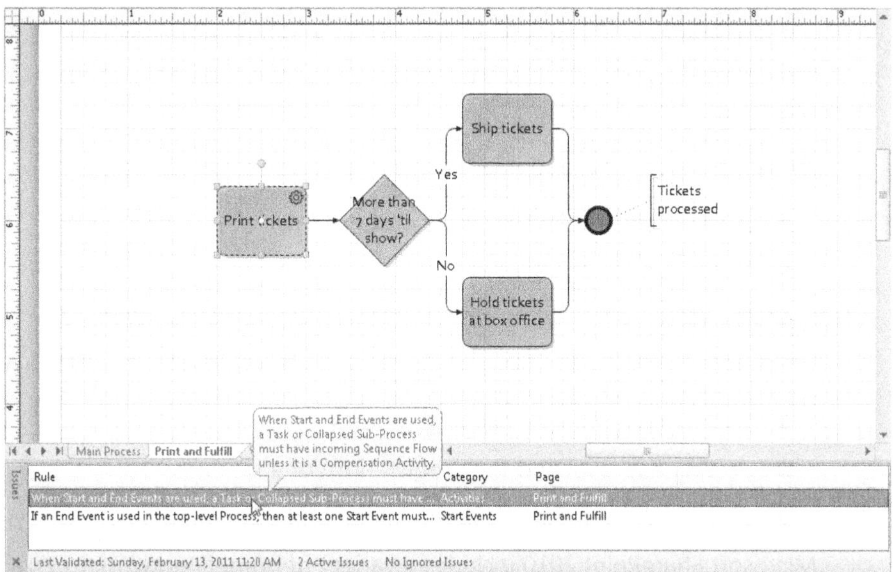

CLEAN UP Save your changes to the *Theater Ticketing Process* drawing, and then close it.

Your completed BPMN diagram now shows the main process flow on Main Process and the detailed subprocess on Print and Fulfill.

Tip In this exercise, you created a subprocess from existing tasks. The Subprocess group on the Process tab includes two additional subprocess functions:

- **Create New** To create a new, blank subprocess page, select any existing Task. When you click the Create New button, Visio inserts a new page and names it using the text from the selected Task. Visio also creates a hyperlink from the selected shape to the new page.
- **Link to Existing** You can create a hyperlink to any existing subprocess page, whether it's located in the current drawing or another one. To do so, select any Task, and then click the Link To Existing button. Visio presents a list of the pages in the current diagram as well as two options: Browse To Other Document and Edit Link. The former lets you link to any existing document; the latter opens the Hyperlinks dialog box so you can edit an existing link. The end result of selecting any of the Link To Existing menu items is a hyperlink to a page or document.

The subprocess functions described in this chapter are not restricted to BPMN. They are also available in conventional flowcharts and swimlane diagrams.

Creating and Exporting SharePoint Workflow Diagrams

A ***workflow*** is a set of process steps, some or all of which have been automated. For the automated parts of a workflow, documents and files are stored and moved electronically, according to a set of predefined rules, so that they are available to participants as required.

To define a workflow, you need to identify three things:

- The participants (both people and systems)
- The sequence of activities
- The documents, databases, and other required work items

Common workflow examples in many organizations include the following:

- Approving employee expense reports
- Getting approval and then registering for a seminar
- Writing, editing, getting approval for, and publishing a new policy manual

Microsoft SharePoint 2010 includes a variety of predefined workflows, and you can both customize the existing workflows and define new workflows using SharePoint Designer. However, SharePoint Designer is a text-oriented tool. Many people, especially those who are already familiar with creating flowcharts in Visio, prefer to define workflows visually.

Because of that desire, Visio Premium 2010 includes a SharePoint Workflow template. You can use it to build graphical workflow layouts and you can move workflow definitions in both directions between Visio and SharePoint Designer. For example, you can create a workflow definition in Visio, export it to SharePoint to add required parameters, test and revise the workflow, and then bring it back to Visio to see the new visual representation.

See Also For detailed information, including exercises for building workflows with SharePoint Designer, see Chapter 8, "Understanding Workflows," in *Microsoft SharePoint Designer 2010 Step by Step* by Penelope Coventry (Microsoft Press, 2010).

For an overall description of creating and editing workflows with SharePoint Designer 2010, go to *office.microsoft.com/en-us/sharepoint-designer-help/introduction-to-designing-and-customizing-workflows-HA101859249.aspx.*

With SharePoint Designer, you can also publish the Visio rendering of the workflow to SharePoint Server and view live status information as the workflow executes. Although there are no exercises covering workflow visualization in this book, the second of the following Visio Insights blog articles demonstrates this feature. Both articles include instructions and screenshots for both Visio and SharePoint Designer:

- *blogs.msdn.com/b/visio/archive/2009/11/23/sharepoint-workflow-authoring-in-visio-premium-2010-part-1.aspx*
- *blogs.msdn.com/b/visio/archive/2010/01/19/sharepoint-workflow-authoring-in-visio-premium-2010-part-2.aspx*

In this exercise, you will create a simple workflow to check a document out of a SharePoint repository, verify the creation date of the document, and revise the document if it is more than one year old. You will create the workflow by using the Visio SharePoint Workflow template, validate it against the SharePoint Workflow rules, and then export it in SharePoint Designer format.

SET UP Start Visio, or if it's already running, click the File tab, and then click New. In the Template Categories section, click Flowchart, and then double-click Microsoft SharePoint Workflow. Save the drawing as *Document Revision Workflow*. If the Shapes window does not display two columns of masters, adjust its width.

> **Tip** **Take a moment to explore the three stencils that open with this template. In addition to the Quick Shapes stencil, you will see SharePoint Workflow Actions, SharePoint Workflow Conditions, and SharePoint Workflow Terminators.**

1. From the **Quick Shapes** stencil, drag a **Start** shape and drop it near the left page margin.
2. Point to the start shape's **AutoConnect** arrow, and from the **Quick Shapes** menu, add a **Terminate** shape.

   See Also **For information about AutoConnect and Quick Shapes, see Chapter 2.**

3. From the **SharePoint Workflow Actions** stencil, drag a **Check out item** shape onto the connector between the start and terminate shapes.

   Tip **You will need to scroll down to find *Check out item*.**

   Visio moves the terminate shape to make room for the task shape.

   See Also **For information about AutoAdd and AutoDelete, see Chapter 2.**

4. From the **SharePoint Workflow Conditions** stencil, drag a **Created in date span** shape onto the connector between the **Check out item** shape and the terminator.
5. With the new condition shape still selected, type **Older than one year?**.

6. From the **SharePoint Workflow Actions** stencil, drag a **Start custom task process** shape onto the connector between the **Older than one year?** shape and the terminator.
7. With the new task shape still selected, type **Revise document**.
8. From the **SharePoint Workflow Actions** stencil, drag a **Check in item** shape onto the connector between the **Check out item** shape and the terminator.
9. Drag the **AutoConnect** arrow under the **Older than one year?** shape and connect to the **Check in item** shape.

Important When you glue the connector to the Check in item shape, be sure to glue it to the *connection point* on the bottom of the shape in order to create *static glue*. Do not create *dynamic glue*. Although this distinction does not affect the workflow for SharePoint, in this particular case, it creates a better layout for the connector.

See Also For information about static and dynamic glue, see Chapter 2.

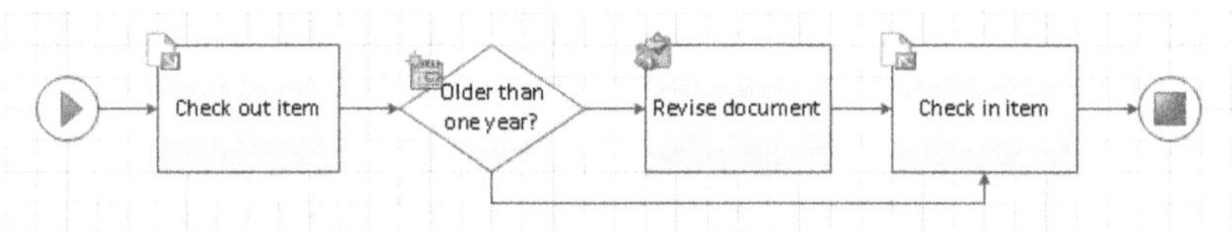

You are now ready to try exporting your SharePoint workflow.

10. On the **Process** tab, in the **SharePoint Workflow** group, click the **Export** button.

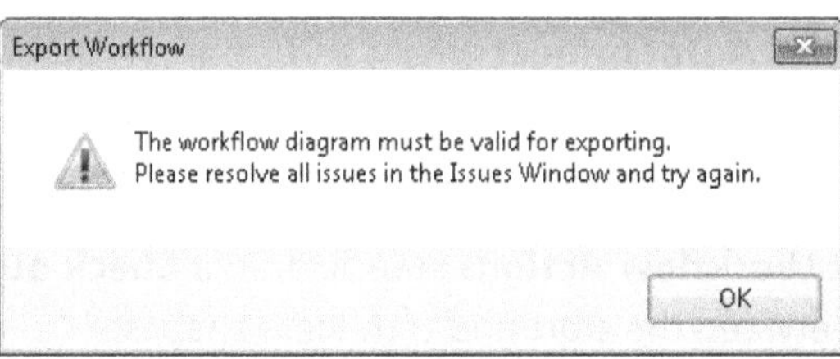

Important Visio will not let you export a SharePoint workflow if it contains errors. Consequently, Visio always runs a diagram validation check when you click Export.

11. Click **OK** to close the **Export Workflow** dialog box.

Visio opens the Issues window and reports two issues, both related to the connectors on the *Older than one year?* condition shape.

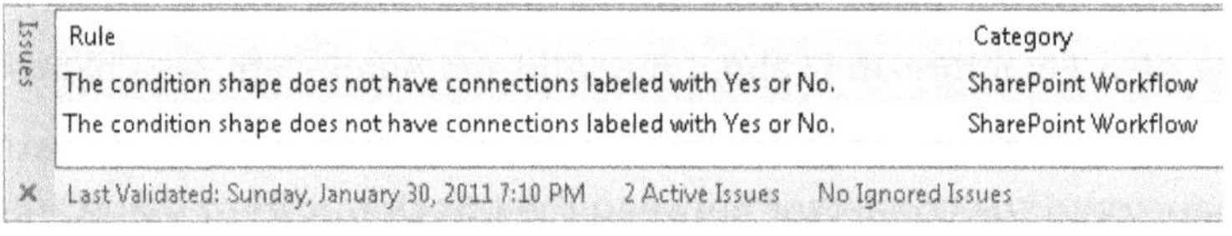

Issues
Rule
Category
The condition shape does not have connections labeled with Yes or No.
SharePoint Workflow
The condition shape does not have connections labeled with Yes or No.
SharePoint Workflow
Last Validated: Sunday, January 30, 2011 7:10 PM
2 Active Issues
No Ignored Issues

You need to add Yes/No labels to the condition's outgoing connectors. Unlike the flowchart shapes, the connectors in the SharePoint Workflow stencil have been given right-click menu options for exactly this purpose.

12. Right-click the connector between the **Older than one year?** shape and the **Revise document** shape. Then click **Yes**.
13. Right-click the connector from the **Older than one year?** shape to the **Check in item** shape. Then click **No**.
14. On the **Process** tab, in the **SharePoint Workflow** group, click the **Export** button. Visio clears the Issues window and opens the Export Workflow dialog box.
15. In the **Export Workflow** dialog box, type **Document Revision Workflow** as the file name, navigate to your desired folder, and click **Save**.

    Visio creates a ***Visio Workflow Interchange*** file with a file extension of ***.vwi***.

CLEAN UP Save your changes to the *Document Revision Workflow* drawing, and then close it.

The .vwi file you've created can be imported directly into SharePoint Designer.

Important Creating a workflow in Visio Premium 2010 does not eliminate the need to use SharePoint Designer. Although you can use Visio to define and illustrate the flow of the work in a process, you must still use SharePoint Designer to provide the rest of the information that is required to execute the workflow.

See Also The Channel 9 Learning Center on MSDN contains a 15-minute video overview of Visio Premium and SharePoint Designer. To view the video, go to *channel9.msdn.com/learn/courses/Office2010/ClientWorkflowUnit/VisioSharePointDesignerWorkflow/*.

Reusing Existing Validation Rules

As you've already learned in this chapter, four Visio 2010 templates include predefined validation rule sets. Their existence raises a number of questions, such as the following:

- Is it possible to use those rule sets with other documents?
- Is it possible for a diagram to have more than one rule set?
- How do you find out what rules comprise an existing rule set?
- Is it possible to modify an existing rule set?
- Is it possible to create new rules?

In this exercise, you will learn the answer to the first two questions by importing a rule set into a flowchart created with Visio 2007. You will learn the answer to the third question in the text at the end of this section, and will learn about modifying and creating rule sets in the next section.

SET UP You need the *Visio 2007 Flowchart_start* drawing located in the Chapter12 practice file folder to complete this exercise. Open the drawing in Visio and save it as *Visio 2010 Flowchart*.

1. On the **Process** tab, in the **Diagram Validation** group, click the **Check Diagram** button.

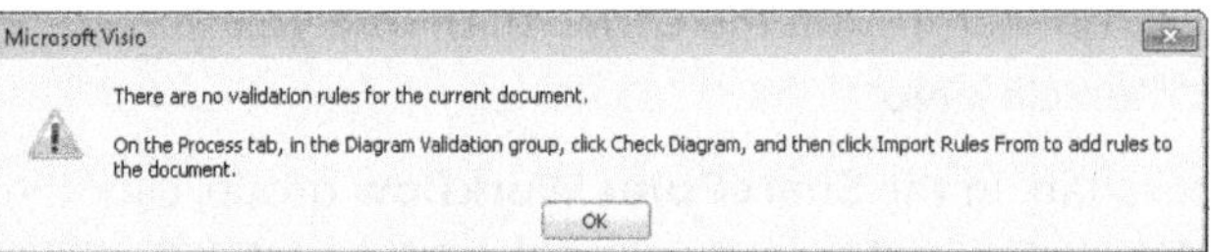

Visio tells you that the document does not contain any rule sets and also tells you what to do about it. Because you've opened a flowchart created in an older version of Visio, you will import the flowchart rule set.

2. On the **Process** tab, in the **Diagram Validation** group, click the **Check Diagram** arrow (not the button), and then point to **Rules to Check**. The submenu confirms that there are no rules in this document.

3. Point to **Import Rules From**, and click **Flowchart Rule Set**. Visio displays a dialog box confirming that one rule set was copied to the current document.

Tip The flowchart rule set is available to import into any diagram. In addition, if you have other diagrams open that contain rule sets, you will see them listed and can import their rules.

4. On the **Process** tab, in the **Diagram Validation** group, click the **Check Diagram** button. Visio runs the imported rule set against your diagram and reports the results in the Issues window.

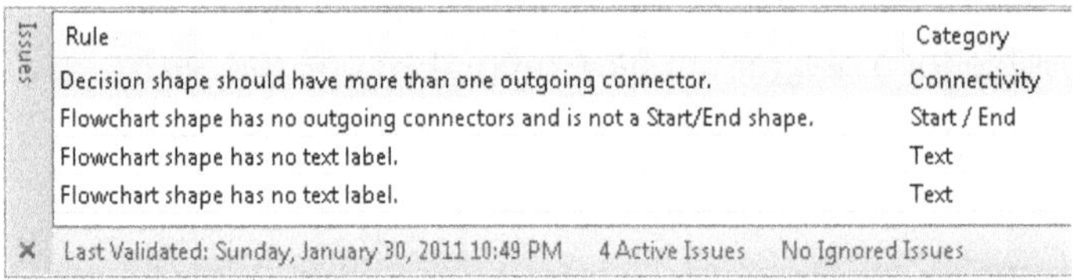

Issues
Rule
Category
Decision shape should have more than one outgoing connector.
Connectivity
Flowchart shape has no outgoing connectors and is not a Start/End shape.
Start / End
Flowchart shape has no text label.
Text
Flowchart shape has no text label.
Text
Last Validated: Sunday, January 30, 2011 10:49 PM
4 Active Issues
No Ignored Issues

CLEAN UP Save your changes to the *Visio 2010 Flowchart* drawing but leave it open if you are continuing with the next exercise.

Now that you know you can import a rule set into a diagram, you have probably guessed the answer to the second question in the list at the beginning of this section: you can have more than one rule set attached to a Visio diagram.

The following graphic indicates that the current diagram uses two rule sets. The check marks in front of both Contoso Business Rules and Flowchart indicate that both rule sets are active. Consequently, when you click the Check Diagram button, the diagram will be validated against both of them.

Tip **You can clear the check box for any rule set to remove it from the active list.**

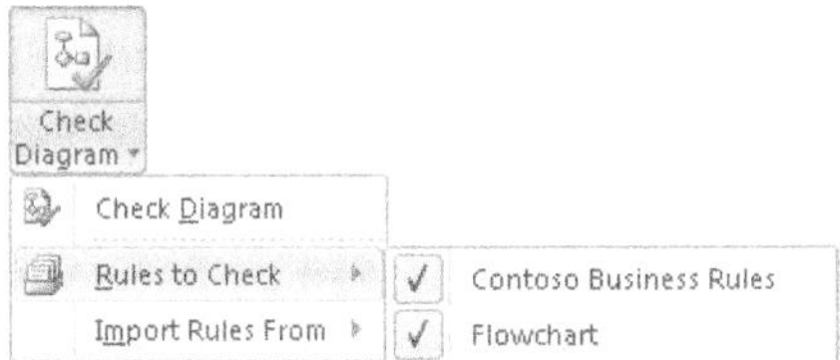

The answer to the third question posed at the beginning of this section is a bit trickier because the Visio 2010 user interface does not provide a way to list the rules in a rule set. However, an experienced Microsoft ***Visual Basic for Applications (VBA)*** programmer can write a short program to list the rules contained in a rule set. Even better, Visio MVP David Parker has already done the work for you by including code samples for this and other diagram validation purposes in an article he wrote for MSDN.

See Also **To read David Parker's article, "Introduction to Validation Rules in Visio Premium 2010," go to** ***msdn.microsoft.com/en-us/library/ff847470.aspx.***

You will find listings of all of the rules in each of the four Visio 2010 rule sets in the Chapter12 practice file folder. Look for the four .html files whose names start with the word ***RuleSets.*** **The listings were produced using David Parker's Rules Tools, which is described in the next section.**

Creating New Validation Rules

Now that you've seen the value of the predefined rule sets in Visio 2010, you're probably beginning to think of other diagram types and ways that you would like to validate aspects of those drawings. Perhaps you want to do one of the following:

- Verify network connectivity.
- Ensure that the number of connections per network device doesn't exceed the maximum allowable for that brand and model of equipment.
- Confirm that each piece of furniture in an office floor plan was selected from an approved list and meets budget guidelines.

- Verify that all parts of an electrical schematic meet minimum and maximum power thresholds.
- Ensure that a building plan conforms to local building codes.

Regardless of the type of validation you want to perform, the good news is that you can both edit existing rules and create new rules. The bad news is that Visio does not provide an easy means to accomplish either task. In addition, doing so requires technical skills that are beyond the scope of this book.

The best resource for learning more about editing and designing validation rules is a book written by David Parker, who is mentioned at the end of the previous section. His book, *Microsoft Visio 2010: Business Process Diagramming and Validation* (Packt Publishing, 2010) provides extensive, technical coverage of many of the topics in this chapter, as well as details about many parts of Visio that touch, or are touched by, diagram validation. In addition, David has filled a significant gap left by Microsoft: he wrote software called *Rules Tools* that provides a user interface for exploring and working with validation rules.

If you install David's Rules Tools and run Visio in ***developer mode***, you'll find an additional group of buttons on the right end of the Process tab.

See Also **You will learn about running Visio in developer mode in the Appendix.**

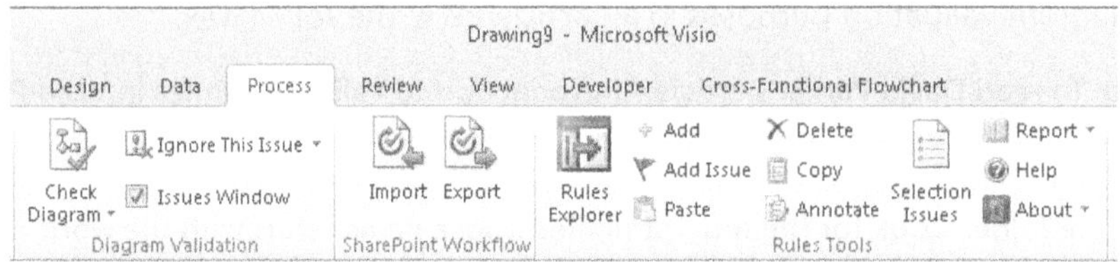

See Also **For information about David Parker's book and about Rules Tools, go to** ***www.visiorules.com.***

In addition to David's book and MSDN article referred to in the previous section, the Visio development team wrote a brief article on custom rule development, which can be found at ***blogs.msdn.com/b/visio/archive/2009/09/10/creating-custom-validation-rules-for-visio-2010.aspx.***

Key Points

- Microsoft added a collection of new features and created the Premium edition of Visio 2010 to emphasize the value of Visio for business process functions.
- Four Visio Premium 2010 templates include predefined rule sets that you can use to validate new drawings. In addition, you can import those rule sets into existing drawings (including drawings created with previous versions of Visio) to enhance the validity of older diagrams.
- You can use the BPMN template to create business process maps that comply with version 1.2 of the BPMN standard. The Visio BPMN stencils contain dozens of shapes that conform to the standard, and the template includes validation rules.
- With the subprocess feature in Visio 2010 Premium, you can select one or more tasks in a drawing and automatically create a subprocess definition on a new page. You can also create blank subprocess pages with the click of a button.
- You can create graphical workflow maps in Visio and export them to SharePoint Designer in order to have them executed by the SharePoint workflow engine. You can also import definition files created by SharePoint Designer into Visio to see the workflow layout visually.

Chapter at a Glance

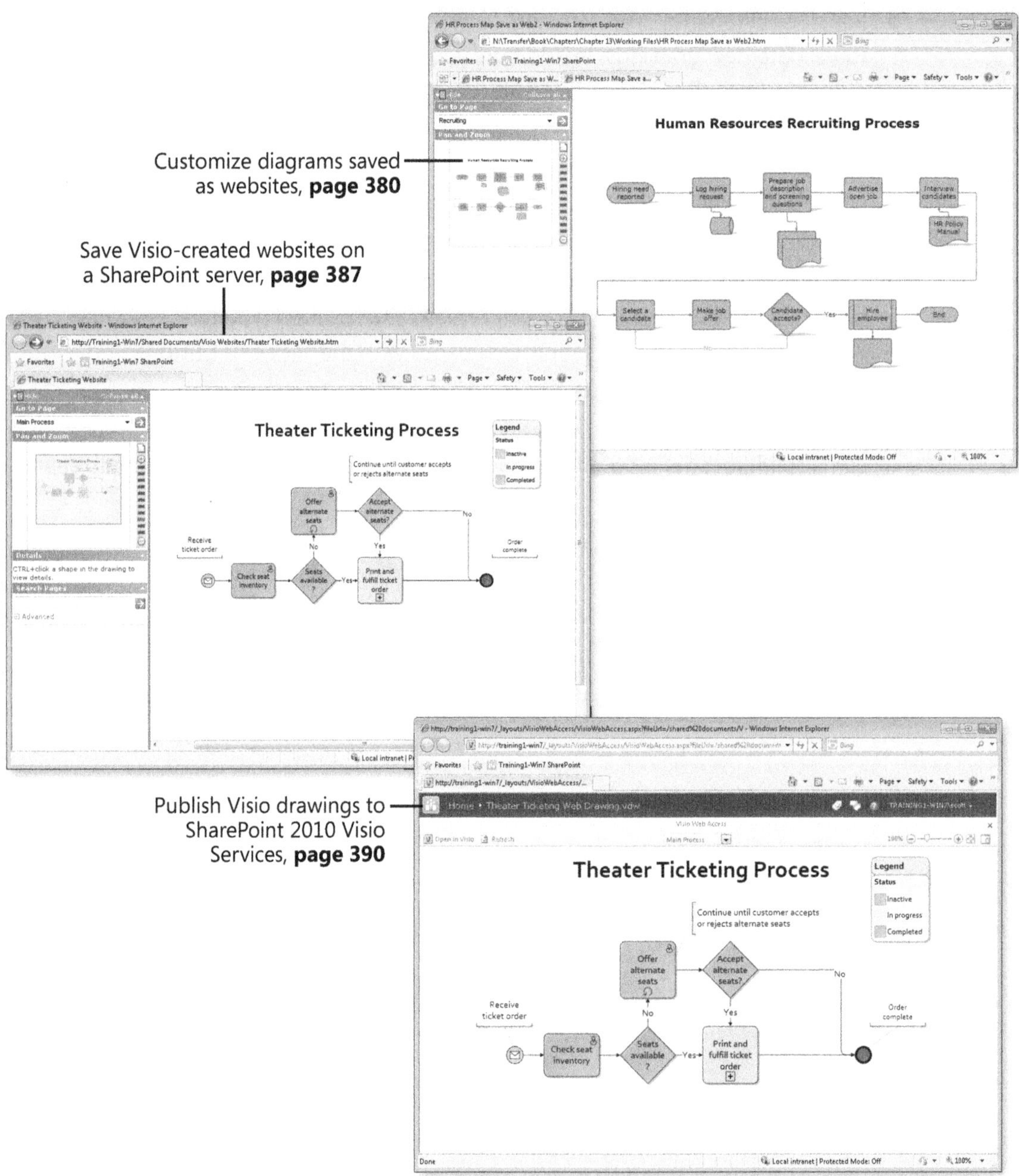
Customize diagrams saved as websites, **page 380**
Save Visio-created websites on a SharePoint server, **page 387**
Publish Visio drawings to SharePoint 2010 Visio Services, **page 390**
Human Resources Recruiting Process
Theater Ticketing Process
Theater Ticketing Process

13 Sharing and Publishing Diagrams: Part 2

In this chapter, you will learn how to

- ✔ Customize diagrams saved as websites.
- ✔ Save Visio-created websites on a SharePoint server.
- ✔ Understand Visio Services.
- ✔ Publish Visio drawings to SharePoint 2010 Visio Services.

In Chapter 8, "Sharing and Publishing Diagrams: Part 1," you learned how to save Microsoft Visio 2010 drawings in a variety of formats, including as collections of webpages.

In this chapter, you will learn advanced techniques for customizing the websites you can create with Visio. You will learn about the structure of the resulting website, allowing you to move it to an intranet or other location when you want to share your drawing with people who don't have Visio.

You will also learn about ***Visio Services***, which is part of Microsoft SharePoint 2010. Visio Services provides another technique for sharing diagrams with people who don't have Visio, and, it offers several advantages over conventional web-published diagrams. Unlike websites created using Save As Web Page, drawings published with Visio Services can be updated dynamically as the underlying data changes.

> **Practice Files** Before you can complete the exercises in this chapter, you need to copy the book's practice files to your computer. The practice files you'll use to complete the exercises in this chapter are in the Chapter13 practice files folder. A complete list of practice files is provided in "Using the Practice Files" at the beginning of this book.

Customizing Diagrams Saved as Websites

Important The option to customize webpage output does not exist in the Standard edition of Visio 2010. Consequently, if you are using Visio Standard 2010, you will not be able to complete this exercise.

Web-published Visio drawings already include full support for embedded hyperlinks along with rich navigation and search capabilities, as you learned in Chapter 8. However, you don't necessarily need all of those capabilities in every Visio-generated website, so it is convenient to be able to change the publishing options.

In addition, you might want to change the format in which Visio creates your website. By default, Visio 2010 creates webpages using the ***Extensible Application Markup Language (XAML)***, which is a different format from earlier Visio versions. XAML requires that you install Microsoft Silverlight on your computer to view Visio-created websites. If you prefer a different webpage format that doesn't require Silverlight, you can select one of the five alternatives described later in this section.

In this exercise, you will use the Publish button in the Save As dialog box to customize Visio webpage output.

SET UP You need the *HR Process Map Save as Web2_start* drawing located in the Chapter13 practice file folder to complete this exercise. Open the drawing in Visio and save it as *HR Process Map Save as Web2*.

1. On the **File** tab, click **Save & Send**, and then click the **Change File Type** button.
2. In the **Other File Types** section, click **Web Page (*.htm)**, and then click the **Save As** button.

   Tip Visio defaults to saving webpages in the folder that contains your Visio drawing file.

   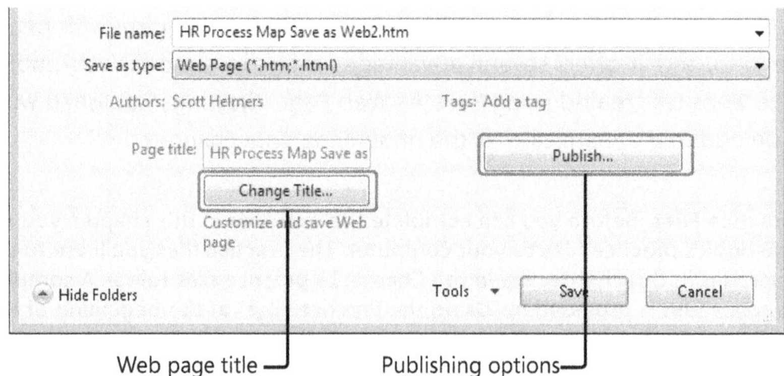

   The Publish button offers multiple options that you will explore in subsequent steps.

The lower portion of the Save As dialog box includes two buttons for customizing webpage output. You can click the Change Title button to modify the text that will be displayed in the title bar of the web browser. The default page title is the file name of the Visio drawing.

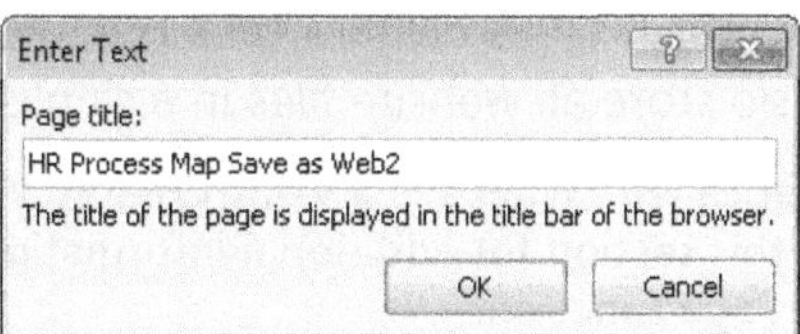

3. In the **Save As** dialog box, click the **Publish** button. The Save As Web Page dialog box opens.

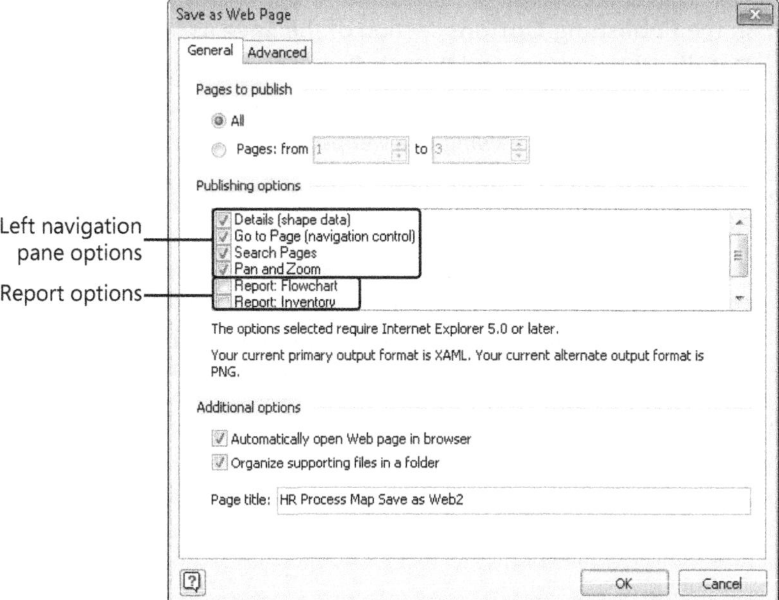

The Save As Web Page dialog box provides various ways to customize your website:

- In the Pages To Publish section, you can select a subset of the diagram's pages to include in the web-published output.
- In the Publishing Options section, you can select which navigation pane options, and which reports, if any, should be included in your website.

  Important **The only way to view reports in your web-published drawing is via the Go To Page navigation panel. Consequently, if you include reports as part of your website, you must leave the Go To Page check box selected.**

- When Visio creates a website from your drawing, it automatically opens it in your browser. You can clear the Automatically Open Web Page In Browser check box in the Additional Options section to prevent this from occurring.
- By default, Visio creates a folder to store the majority of website files. You can clear the Organize Supporting Files In A Folder check box\ in the Additional Options section to have Visio store all website files in a single folder.

  See Also **Refer to the sidebar called "What's in a Visio-Created Website and Where Is It Stored?" later in this section for additional information about the files created by the Save As Web Page function.**

- In the Additional Options section, you can type a different title in the Page Title text box. (This is an alternate method to using the Change Title button mentioned in Step 2.)

4. In the **Publishing Options** section of the **Save as Web Page** dialog box, clear the **Details (shape data)** and **Search Pages** check boxes.

   Tip **Visio remembers the settings for these options; you will see the same settings the next time you save a drawing as a webpage.**

5. In the **Publishing Options** section of the **Save as Web Page** dialog box, select the **Report: Flowchart** check box.

   Tip **Visio *does not* remember the settings for the reports you choose; none of the report check boxes will be selected the next time you save a drawing as a webpage.**

   If your Visio drawing includes more than two reports, use the scroll bar in the Publishing Options section to view the full list of reports.

6. Click **OK**. You will see one or more progress indicators before your browser displays your new website.

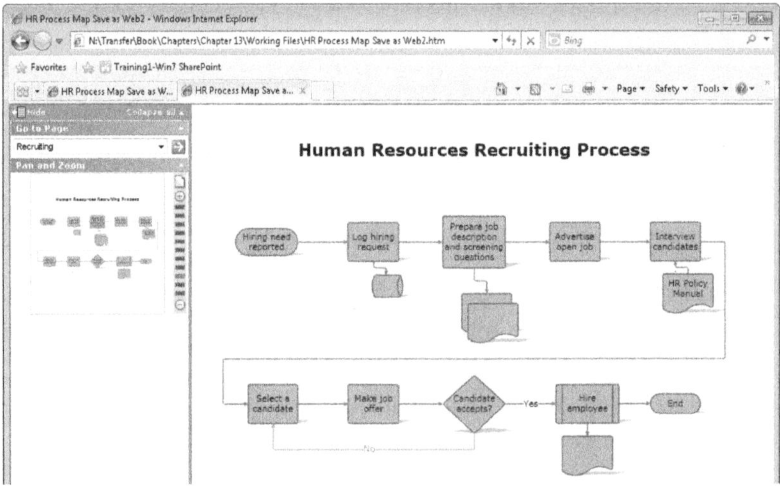

On the left side of the browser window, you see the result of the navigation pane choices you made in Step 4: only the Go To Page and Pan And Zoom panels appear.

See Also If you need to review the full set of navigation pane options in web-published Visio drawings, see "Publishing Visio Diagrams to the Web" in Chapter 8.

7. In the **Go to Page** section, click the arrow next to **Recruiting**. The Go To Page list includes entries for each page in the diagram and for each report you selected.

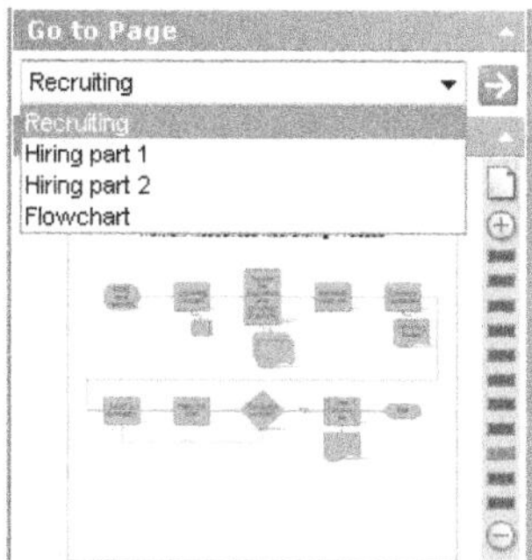

8. To view the flowchart report, click **Flowchart** in the drop-down list, and then click the green button containing the white arrow.

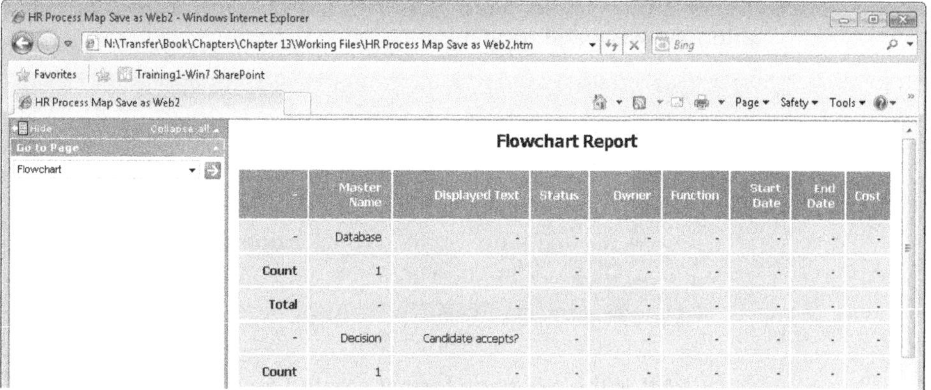

Tip To view other reports or to return to viewing the drawing pages, use the Go To Page list. You can also click the browser's back button to return to the previous page.

CLEAN UP Save your changes to the *HR Process Map Save as Web2* drawing, and then close it.

You may have noticed in Step 3 that the Save As Web Page dialog box includes a second tab labeled Advanced.

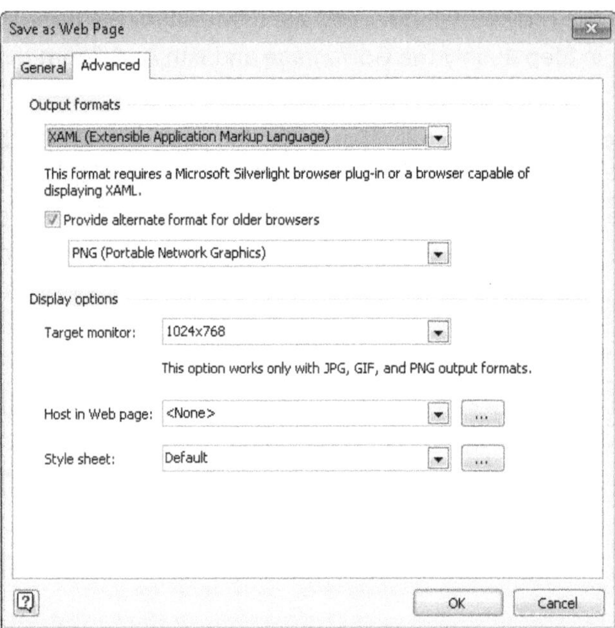

The Advanced tab provides additional customization options, such as the following:

- In the Output Formats section, you can use the drop-down list to select one of the alternate webpage formats.

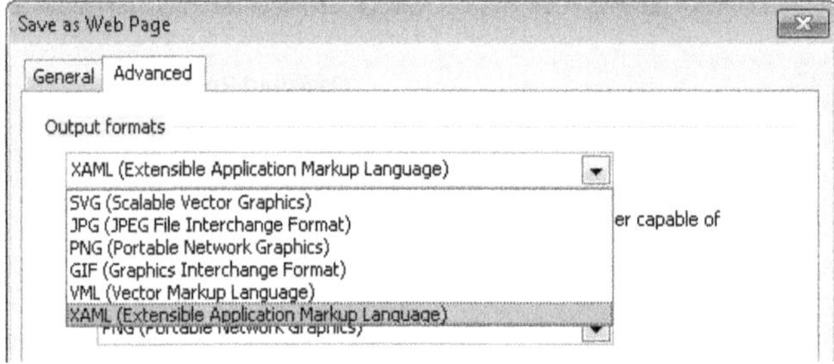

  - ***VML*** is the webpage format created by previous versions of Visio. The features of VML websites are very similar to websites created with XAML.
  - ***SVG*** is a specialized format that is supported by some but not all browsers. Like the three image formats described in the following bullet point, SVG websites display fixed-size pages with no Pan And Zoom panel.

- ***GIF***, ***JPG***, and ***PNG*** provide fewer capabilities than either VML or XAML. For example, the viewing window for these formats is a fixed size and does not include the Pan And Zoom panel in the left navigation pane. However, websites produced in these formats retain all hyperlinks and are likely to be compatible with a wider range of web browsers. (Note that you can have the best of both worlds—full navigation functions in Windows Internet Explorer and support for older browsers; see the following bullet point.)

- If you select XAML, VML, or SVG as the Output Format, Visio defaults to selecting the Provide Alternate Format For Older Browsers check box. You can use the drop-down list under this heading to select GIF, JPG, or PNG output as a backup to your primary choice.

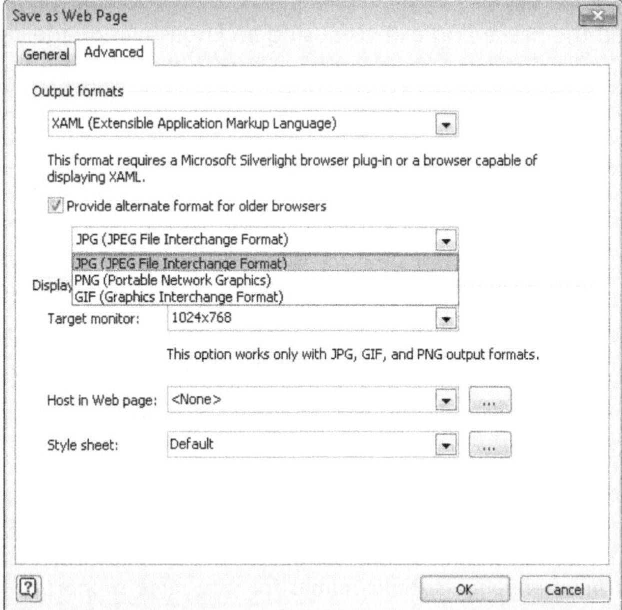

- In the Display Options section, you can use the Target Monitor, Host In Web Page, and Style Sheet settings to further customize your webpages. The second and third settings, in particular, are intended to help you integrate a Visio-created website with another, existing website.

What's in a Visio-Created Website and Where Is It Stored?

When you use the Save As Web Page function, Visio generates a webpage that is loaded into your browser and that provides access to the rest of your website. It also creates a supporting files folder that contains various graphics and webpages for each page in the drawing, as well as ***JavaScript***, ***Extensible Markup Language (XML)***, and other files that comprise the website.

By default, the Visio-generated files are stored in the same Windows folder that contains your Visio drawing. Visio gives the webpage file the same name as the drawing plus an ***.htm*** file extension. For English versions of Visio, the name of the supporting files folder is the same as the drawing name followed by *_files.*

If you completed the preceding exercise using an English language version of Visio, for example, the folder that contains *HR Process Map Save as Web2.vsd* also contains the following:

- A file called *HR Process Map Save as Web2.htm*
- A folder called *HR Process Map Save as Web2_files*

If you want to copy or move your new website, it's important to copy/move both the .htm file and the supporting files folder to the new location. Windows helps you do this: in Windows XP, Windows Vista, and Windows 7, if you copy, move, or delete either the file or the folder, the other goes with it. (In Windows XP and Windows Vista, you can disassociate the file from the folder by using a Windows Explorer setting. Windows 7 does not offer this option.)

Important The default name for the companion subfolder varies based on the language version of Microsoft Office that is installed on your computer. For a complete list of default names for various language versions, go to *office.microsoft.com/en-us/excel-help/language-specific-names-for-web-page-supporting-folders-HP001049381.aspx*. Even though the article applies to Microsoft Office Excel 2003, the list is also correct for the Visio 2010 website folder.

You can copy your website to a shared drive, to your organization's intranet, or to any web server in order to provide access to your Visio diagram.

Saving Visio-Created Websites on a SharePoint Server

Important Using the Save As Web Page feature to publish a website to a SharePoint server produces a very different result than publishing Visio drawings to Visio Services on a SharePoint server. For the latter topic, see the section titled "Publishing Visio Drawings to SharePoint 2010 Visio Services" later in this chapter.

In the previous exercise, you used the Save As Web Page feature in Visio to create a website that you stored on your computer. The sidebar in that section described how to move the published website to another location. With the increasing popularity of SharePoint, you might choose to move your website to a SharePoint server. However, it isn't necessary to publish the website locally first and then move it to SharePoint—you can publish directly to SharePoint.

In this exercise, you will save a website to a SharePoint server. You will use a modified version of the *Theater Ticketing with Subprocess* diagram that you created in Chapter 12, "Creating and Validating Process Diagrams." The modified diagram includes the following changes:

- Each BPMN activity and gateway shape contains a value to indicate its status: Inactive; In progress; Completed.
- The diagram includes a color-by-value data graphic to visualize process status.

  See Also For information about data graphics, see Chapter 10, "Visualizing Your Data."
- Each page contains a data graphic legend.
- The diagram uses a different theme than the version in Chapter 12.

  See Also For information about themes, see Chapter 5, "Adding Style, Color, and Themes."

SET UP You need the *Theater Ticketing Diagram_start* drawing located in the Chapter13 practice file folder to complete this exercise. Open the drawing in Visio and save it as *Theater Ticketing Website*.

Data Graphics

1. Press Ctrl+A to select all shapes on the **Main Process** page. Then on the **Data** tab, in the **Display Data** group, click the **Data Graphics** button.
2. In the **Available Data Graphics** section of the gallery, click **Color by Process Status**. Visio applies the color-by-value data graphic to the shapes on this page.

   See Also For information about data graphics, see Chapter 10.
3. Click the **Print and Fulfill** page name tab, select all shapes on that page, and apply the same data graphic.

4. On the **File** tab, click **Save & Send**, and then click the **Change File Type** button.
5. In the **Other File Types** section, click **Web Page (*.htm)** [do not click Web Drawing (*.vdw)], and then click the **Save As** button.
6. At the top of the **Save As** dialog box, click in the address box and type the URL for your SharePoint Server.

   Tip Often the easiest way to select the desired folder on the correct SharePoint site is to navigate to it first in your web browser. After locating the correct folder, copy and paste its URL into the address bar at the top of the Save As dialog box.

7. In the **Save As** dialog box, click the **Save** button.

   Visio creates your website on the SharePoint server, where it is now accessible by anyone with access to the server and appropriate permission. Visio also opens the website in your browser.

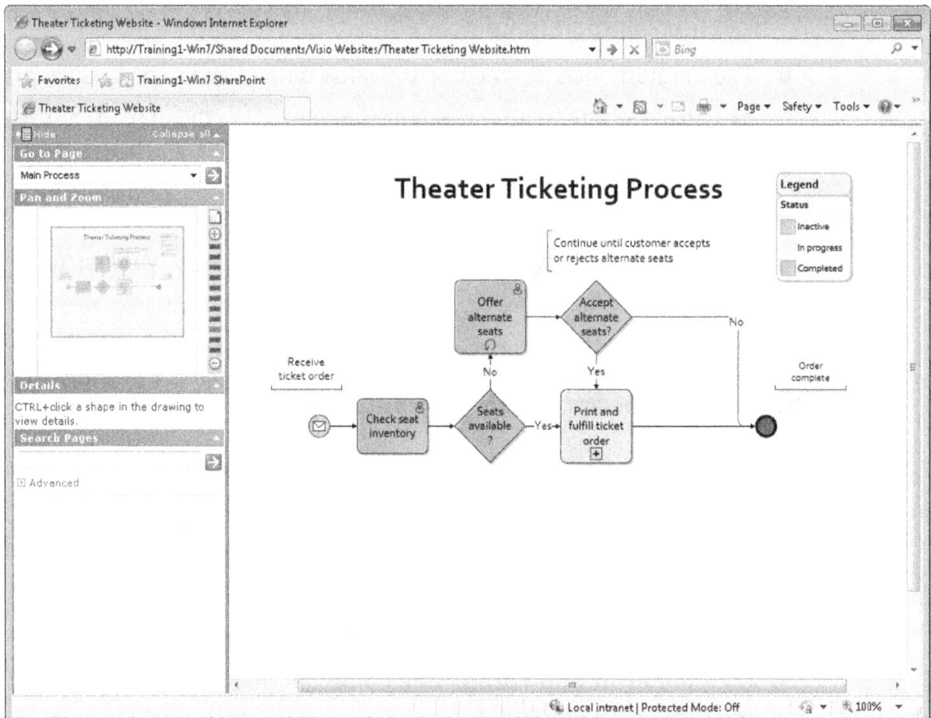

The webpage shown in this graphic displays the color-by-value data graphic that you applied to this page. It's important to understand, however, that this is a static webpage. If the data values in the Visio drawing change, causing the data graphics to change, you will need to repeat Steps 4 through 7 to see the changes.

CLEAN UP Save the changes to the *Theater Ticketing Website* drawing, and then close it.

With this webpage layout in mind, you will now learn about Visio Services so you can compare the static website you created here to a dynamic web drawing you will create in an upcoming exercise.

Understanding Visio Services

Important The information in this section applies only to the Professional and Premium editions of Visio 2010.

Visio Services is a new feature set in SharePoint Server 2010 that you can use to share diagrams with people who don't have Visio. Using either the Professional or Premium editions of Visio 2010, you can save diagrams to SharePoint in a new ***Visio web drawing*** format. Web drawings have the *.vdw* file extension.

There are two key advantages to sharing diagrams via Visio Services instead of the Save As Web Page function described in the preceding sections and in Chapter 8:

- The browser view is dynamic. The web view can be updated manually by the user or automatically by a program.
- You can incorporate Visio diagrams into SharePoint applications:
  - You can embed a Visio web drawing in a SharePoint web part.
  - You can create dynamic connections between web parts that contain Visio web drawings as well as between them and other Web Parts.
  - You can use the Visio Services Mash-up API to program dynamic changes in the browser as the user navigates around a drawing or takes other actions in a SharePoint page.

In addition to the advantages just listed, the user experience in the web browser is enhanced in Visio web drawings when compared to Visio websites:

- Navigation (zoom and pan) is easier and more effective.
- Shape data is easier to view via a floating properties window.

- The properties window that displays shape data also lists the hyperlinks, if any, that are attached to the selected shape.
- There are no warning messages to answer before viewing the document.

Tip One key feature is missing from Visio web drawings: full-text search. It is an important part of Visio-created webpages but is not part of web drawings saved to Visio Services.

See Also For the best browser viewing experience, you need to install Silverlight. Information about Silverlight is available at *www.microsoft.com/silverlight/*. If you do not install Silverlight, Visio web drawings will be rendered as PNG images and you will have fewer viewing options.

There is a wealth of information available from Microsoft and other sources about Visio Services. Some of the best are listed here, in increasing order of technical detail:

- An animated Microsoft PowerPoint presentation that walks through saving a Visio diagram to SharePoint: *www.microsoft.com/downloads/en/details.aspx?FamilyID=4c4dc6c8-c53c-4b4b-b6b4-a1dca251d597*
- An Office help page that contains instructions and important details: *office.microsoft.com/en-us/visio-help/save-diagrams-to-sharepoint-as-web-drawings-HA010357073.aspx*
- A 3½ minute video overview of Visio Services is on a page that also includes text instructions and additional links: *office.microsoft.com/en-us/visio-help/roadmap-publish-visio-drawings-to-a-sharepoint-site-HA101835144.aspx*
- An excellent collection of links to videos and documents about Visio Services, including the setup required on SharePoint Server 2010 to enable Visio Services: *blogs.msdn.com/b/visio/archive/2010/09/10/roundup-of-visio-services-documentation.aspx*
- A technical article describing how to write VBA code to set publishing options and publish to SharePoint: *msdn.microsoft.com/en-us/library/gg133643.aspx*

Publishing Visio Drawings to SharePoint 2010 Visio Services

Important Publishing Visio drawings to Visio Services on a SharePoint server produces a very different result than using the Save As Web Page feature to publish a website to a SharePoint server. For the latter topic, refer to the section titled "Saving Visio-Created Websites on a SharePoint Server" earlier in this chapter.

The information in this section applies only to the Professional and Premium editions of Visio 2010.

In "Saving Visio-Created Websites on a SharePoint Server" earlier in this chapter, you applied a data graphic to a diagram and published it to a SharePoint server. You will perform similar steps here, using the same diagram, but the end result will be very different.

In this exercise, you will publish a diagram to SharePoint as a Visio web drawing by using Visio Services. You will then update the Visio diagram and refresh the web drawing.

SET UP **You need the *Theater Ticketing Diagram_start* drawing located in the Chapter13 practice file folder to complete this exercise. Open the drawing in Visio and save it as *Theater Ticketing Web Drawing*.**

> **Important** **You need access to Visio Services on a SharePoint 2010 server to complete this exercise. Visio Services are available only with a SharePoint Server 2010 Enterprise Client Access License (ECAL). Contact your SharePoint administrator to determine whether Visio Services have been provisioned and enabled.**

1. On the **File** tab, click **Save & Send**, and then click **Save to SharePoint**.

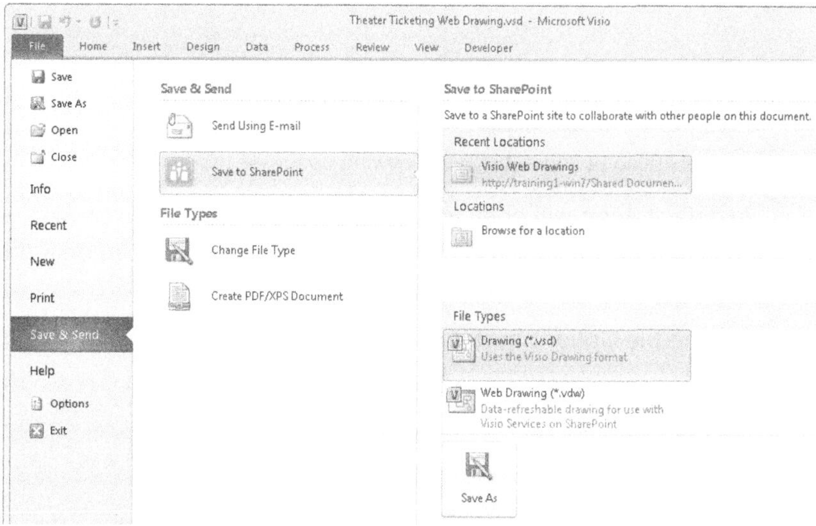

If you have previously saved to SharePoint, the Recent Locations section in the right column may contain one or more paths to SharePoint locations. Either way, the Browse For A Location button will always be available in the Locations section.

2. In the **Locations** section, click **Browse for a location**; in the **File Types** section, click **Web Drawing (*.vdw)**, and then click the **Save As** button. The Save As dialog box opens and the Save As Type entry is preset to Web Drawing (*.vdw).

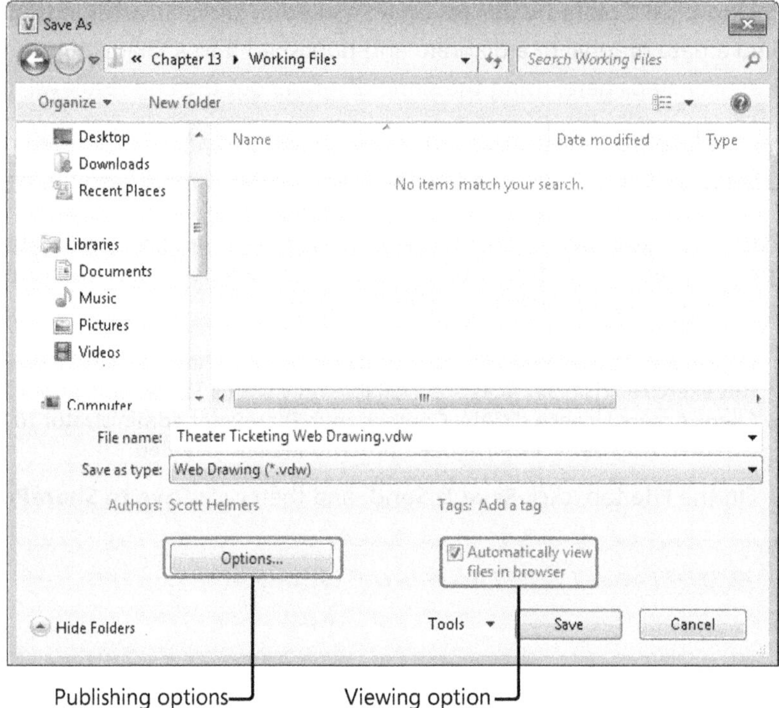

By default, Visio will open your new web drawing in your browser when you click the Save button. If you don't want this to happen, you can clear the Automatically View Files In Browser check box.

Clicking the Options button displays the Publish Settings dialog box.

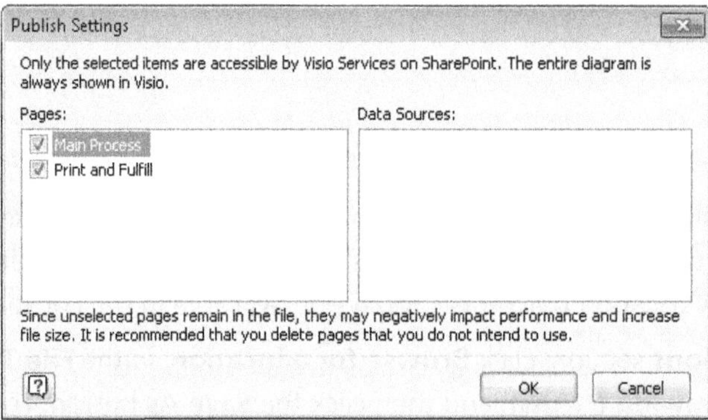

In the Pages section on the left, you can select a subset of the diagram's pages if you don't want to include all of them in your web-published drawing.

Important Be sure to notice the warning at the top of the Publish Settings dialog box: unchecking pages in this dialog box eliminates them from the browser view of the drawing. However, the unchecked pages are still in the .vdw file and are available to anyone who elects to edit the drawing while viewing it in a browser.

If your diagram is linked to one or more data sources, you can use the Data Sources section on the right to select which ones will refresh their data to the browser. Visio Services is capable of refreshing data from Microsoft SQL Server tables and views, SharePoint Lists, Excel workbooks stored in SharePoint, and OLEDB/ODBC data sources.

Important In order for Visio Services to have access to data in an Excel workbook, the workbook must be stored in SharePoint prior to linking to it from your Visio drawing.

3. Either use the left side of the **Save As** dialog box to navigate to a folder on your SharePoint site, or type the ***URL*** for a SharePoint folder in the address box at the top of the **Save As** dialog box.

   Tip Often the easiest way to select the desired folder on the correct SharePoint site is to navigate to it first in your web browser. After locating the correct folder, copy and paste its URL into the address bar at the top of the Save As dialog box.

4. Click **Save**. You may see several progress indicators as Visio creates your web drawing, and then the drawing will open in Internet Explorer.

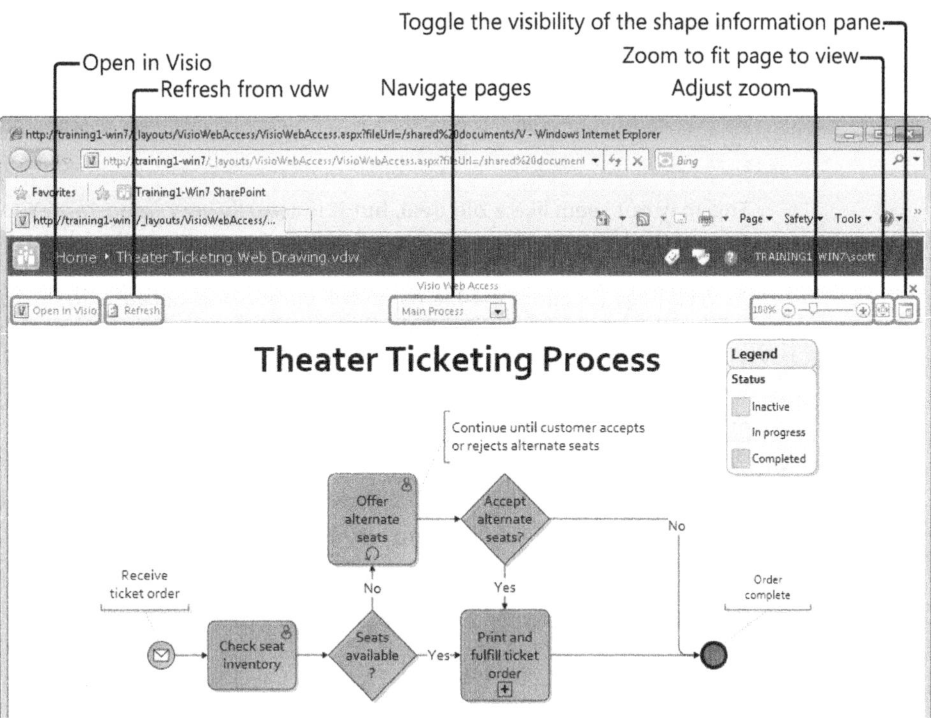

In the web drawing view, you can drag the diagram in any direction to change which portion of the page you see. In addition, you can use the controls in the top center and top right of the browser window to change your view of the drawing.

You can use the page list in the top center to view a different page.

You can change the zoom setting in four ways:

- Click the displayed percentage and type a new percentage.
- Click the plus or minus signs to increase or decrease the zoom level.
- Use the zoom slider to change the zoom level.
- Click the Zoom To Fit Page To View button to see the entire Visio page in the browser window.

You can click Toggle The Visibility Of The Shape Information Pane to show or hide the shape data pane.

In the upcoming steps, you will apply data graphics and make other changes in Visio and will see how those changes are applied to the published drawing.

5. Return to Visio (do not close the web browser).

   Important **Before you start making changes, look at the title of the Visio window. You will see that the title has changed from Theater Ticketing Web Drawing.vsd to Theater Ticketing Web Drawing.vdw.**

   This may not seem like a big deal, but it is actually very important. You are no longer editing the Visio diagram you started with but are editing the Visio web drawing that is stored in SharePoint. (For a comparison, look at the Visio title bar after you use the Save As Web Page function; the file name still ends in .vsd because, in that case, you are still editing the original diagram.) This distinction is particularly important if you close the Visio drawing and want to edit it later. If you edit the .vsd file, it will have no effect on the published web drawing. Instead, you must open the .vdw file from the SharePoint server.

Data Graphics

6. Press Ctrl+A to select all shapes on the **Main Process** page. Then on the **Data** tab, in the **Display Data** group, click **Data Graphics**. In the **Available Data Graphics** section of the gallery, click **Color by Process Status**. Visio applies the color-by-value data graphic to the shapes on this page.

   See Also **For information about data graphics, see Chapter 10.**

7. Click the **Print and Fulfill** page name tab, select all shapes on that page, and apply the same data graphic.

Save

8. On the *Quick Access Toolbar*, click the **Save** button.

Refresh

9. Return to your open web browser and click the SharePoint **Refresh** button (do not click the browser refresh button). The browser view now reflects the current state of the Visio diagram.

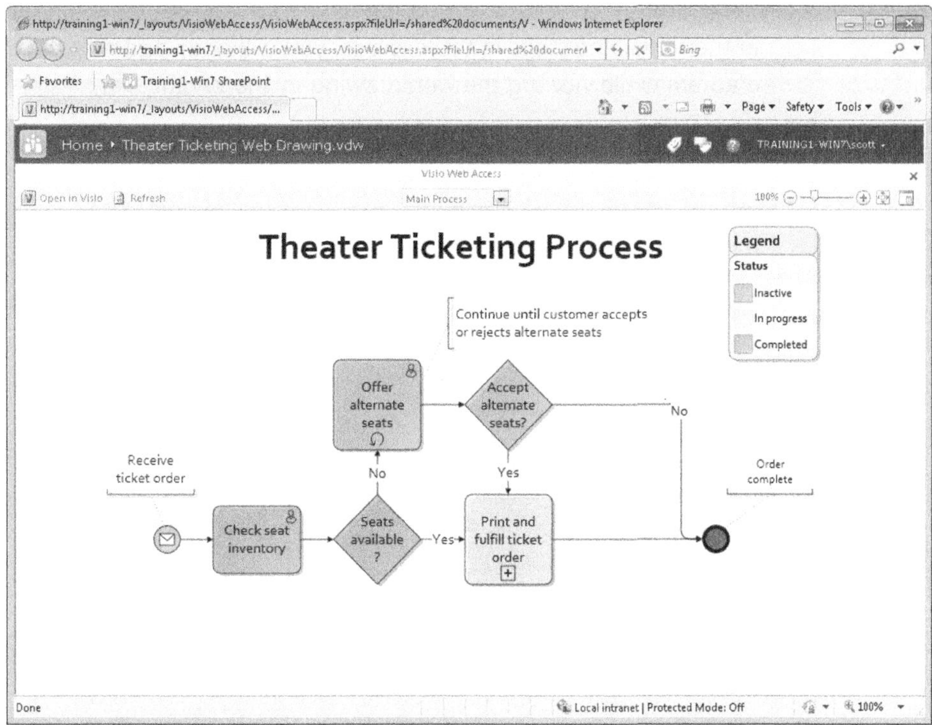

Tip To understand the user interface differences between the two web publishing methods, compare this graphic with the one following Step 7 in the exercise titled "Saving Visio-Created Websites on a SharePoint Server" earlier in this chapter.

10. Return to Visio and click **Print and Fulfill** to change to that page.

11. Right-click the **Ship tickets** shape, point to **Data**, and then click **Shape Data** to open the **Shape Data** window.

12. In the **Shape Data** window, click the arrow to the right of **Status**, and then click **Completed** (do not click Completing) in the drop-down list. The *Ship tickets* shape turns green to reflect its new status.

13. On the Quick Access Toolbar, click the **Save** button, and then close Visio.

14. Return to your open web browser, and click the **Print and fulfill ticket order** shape to follow its embedded hyperlink to the subprocess page.

    The *Ship tickets* shape on the Print And Fulfill page is already green in the browser rendering.

    Tip It isn't necessary to click the Refresh button because changing pages automatically triggers a refresh of the web drawing.

    In the remaining steps in this exercise, you will open and edit the underlying Visio diagram while viewing the web drawing in SharePoint.

Open in Visio

15. In the upper left of the browser window, click the **Open in Visio** button. The Open Document dialog box opens.

    Tip You can also open the Visio web drawing directly from Visio, but be sure to open the .vdw file stored on SharePoint and not the original .vsd file.

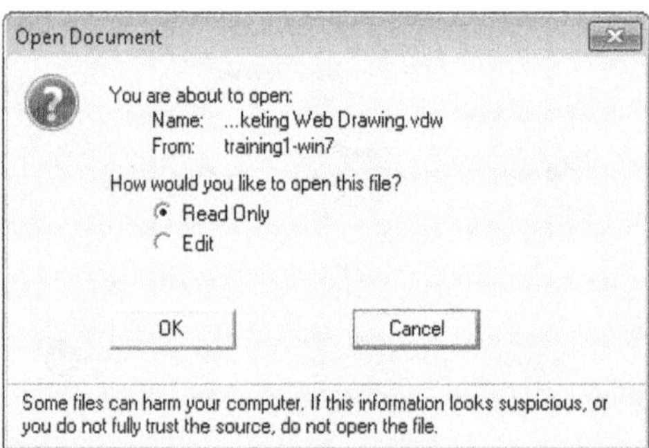

16. In the **Open Document** dialog box, click **Edit**, and then click the **OK** button. The .vdw file opens in Visio.

    Tip Note that the default in the Open Document dialog box is to open the Visio drawing in Read Only mode. You must select Edit if you want to make changes to the drawing.

17. Click the **Main Process** page name tab to go to that page.

18. Right-click the **Print and fulfill ticket order** shape, point to **Data**, and then click **Shape Data** to open the **Shape Data** window.

19. In the **Shape Data** window, click the arrow to the right of **Status**, and then click **Completed** (do not click Completing) in the drop-down list. The *Print and fulfill ticket order* shape turns green to reflect its new status.

20. On the Quick Access Toolbar, click the **Save** button.

21. Return to your open web browser and navigate to the **Main Process** page. The color of the *Print and fulfill ticket order* shape reflects its new status.

    Important Under some circumstances, there may be a small delay before the web drawing refreshes.

CLEAN UP Save your changes to the *Theater Ticketing Web Drawing* file and close it. Close your web browser.

Although you didn't explore shape data in this exercise, all shape data is available in web-published drawings. To view shape data in your browser, click the Toggle The Visibility Of The Shape Information Pane button in the upper right of your web browser. The shape information pane displays both shape data and the names of any hyperlinks that are embedded in a shape. For example, the shape information pane for the *Print and fulfill ticket order* shape is shown in the following graphic.

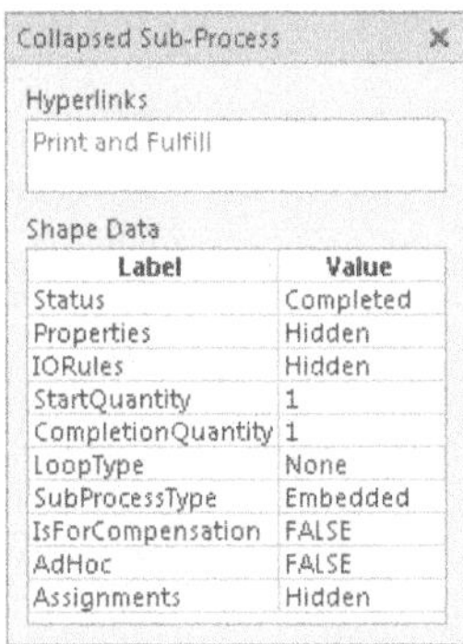

There are a number of online examples available that will give you a chance to explore Visio Services if you don't yet have it installed in your organization:

- A large-format diagram of the 2010 Soccer World Cup that was published to Visio Services: *www.visioworldcup.com*
- A 7-minute video overview of using Visio Services and System Center Operations Manager (SCOM) to monitor system status (there are additional Visio Services examples beneath the SCOM video): *www.microsoft.com/showcase/en/us/details/18ea5032-532c-4d85-a2cd-fdf4adf3acec*
- Detailed installation and configuration instructions for SCOM: *technet.microsoft.com/en-us/library/ff872146.aspx*

Key Points

- When you use the Save As Web Page function, you can customize the website that Visio creates. You can include or exclude navigation features, include reports, and even change the format and style of the website.
- You can use the Save As Web Page function to publish a web site directly to a SharePoint server.
- Visio web drawings are new in Visio 2010. Web drawings are stored on SharePoint 2010 servers using Visio Services. The web drawing format provides higher fidelity rendering of Visio drawings and enhanced user navigation controls. Even more important, Visio web drawings can be refreshed manually or automatically whenever there are changes in the underlying Visio diagram or in data sources linked to the diagram. Unlike websites created by the Save As Web Page feature, web drawings do not require republishing to reflect changes.

Appendix: Looking Under the Hood

Microsoft Visio 2010 serves two distinct communities that sometimes overlap. On one hand, there are people who create diagrams using just the tools on the standard user interface. The diagrams they create may be very simple or very sophisticated, but this group of people completes their diagrams without needing to look "under the hood." The second group of people loves to push Visio beyond its off-the-shelf capabilities by exploring and modifying the ShapeSheet or by writing code to drive the behavior of Visio.

The purpose of this appendix is not to turn members of the first group into coders and ShapeSheet developers. However, there is so much more you can accomplish with Visio if you have just a little bit of extra knowledge. Consequently, the goal for this appendix is to equip you with a few extra tips, techniques, and tools so you can customize Visio and create even more interesting, attractive, and functional diagrams.

Customizing the Visio User Interface

Because Visio 2010 employs the second generation ***fluent user interface***, you can customize both the ribbon and the ***Quick Access Toolbar*** very easily. The purpose of the Quick Access Toolbar, which resides in the upper-left corner of the Visio 2010 window, is exactly as its name suggests: to provide easy access to commonly used buttons.

The nicest feature of the Quick Access Toolbar is that you can easily add whatever additional buttons you would like. One convenient combination of file and window management functions includes Save, Save as, Open, Recent, Undo, Redo, and Switch Windows.

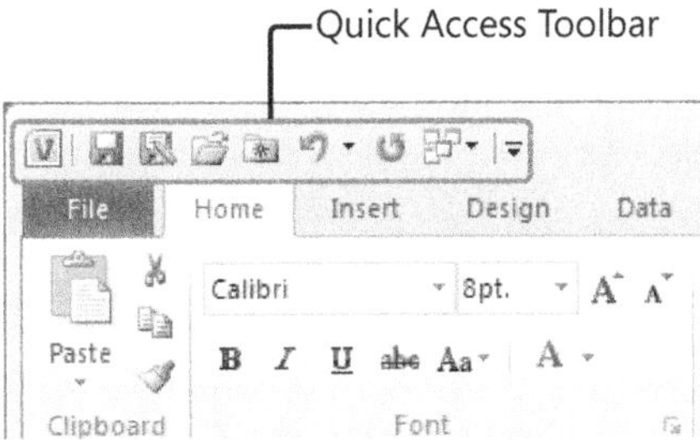

Although the Quick Access Toolbar usually shows file and window management functions, don't restrict your thinking to those categories. Do you use a certain fill color regularly? Do you frequently open and close the Shape Data window? Do you use the Check Diagram button (Visio Premium only) multiple times per day? You can add those and almost any other buttons to the Quick Access Toolbar.

To customize the Quick Access Tool bar, on the File tab, click Options. Then on the left side of the Visio Options dialog box, click Quick Access Toolbar. Use the right side of the dialog box to add, remove, or rearrange the buttons on the toolbar.

See Also **To learn more about customizing the Quick Access Toolbar, go to** ***office.microsoft.com/en-ca/help/customize-the-quick-access-toolbar-HA001234105.aspx.***

In addition to customizing the Quick Access Toolbar, you can customize the built-in tabs on the Visio ribbon by adding or removing buttons. You can also create your own tab so that all of your most frequently used buttons are arranged as you would like them.

To customize the ribbon, on the File tab, click Options. Then on the left side of the Visio Options dialog box, click Customize Ribbon. Use the right side of the dialog box to add, remove or rearrange buttons on any existing tab.

To create your own tab, open the same Visio Options dialog box described in the preceding paragraph and click Customize Ribbon. On the lower-right side of the dialog box, click the New Tab button, and then add and arrange buttons from the built-in tabs.

See Also **For more information on customizing ribbon tabs, go to** ***office.microsoft.com/en-ca/visio-help/customize-the-ribbon-HA010355697.aspx.***

Running in Developer Mode

When you decide to step beyond the ranks of ordinary Visio users, one of the first things you should do is run Visio in ***developer mode***. Don't let the name frighten you; there are no programming or hardcore technical requirements for running Visio in this mode.

The primary advantage of developer mode is easy access to a number of very useful features. In developer mode, you can perform the following functions:

- Create and run macros to automate Visio functions.
- Manage add-in programs.
- Add custom controls to Visio shapes.
- Design new shapes and alter the appearance and behavior of existing shapes.
- Create new stencils.
- View "behind the scenes" parts of Visio documents, most notably, the ShapeSheet.

To activate developer mode, on the File tab, click Options. Then on the left side of the Visio Options dialog box, click Customize Ribbon. On the right side of the dialog box, select the Developer check box.

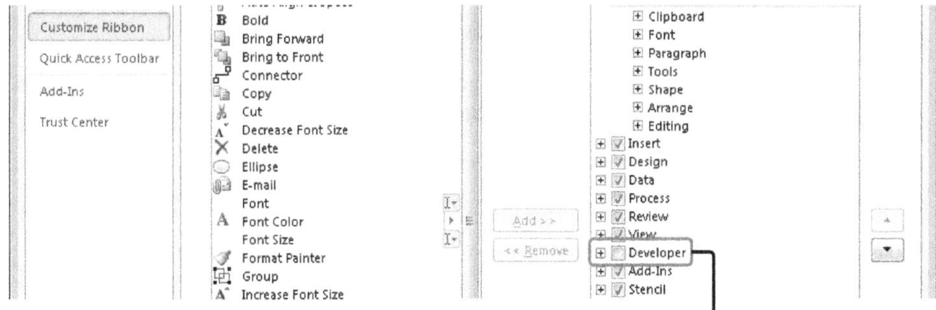

Select to activate developer mode

After you activate developer mode, you will see two visible differences in the user interface: the addition of a Developer tab on the ribbon and a right-click menu option for accessing the ShapeSheet.

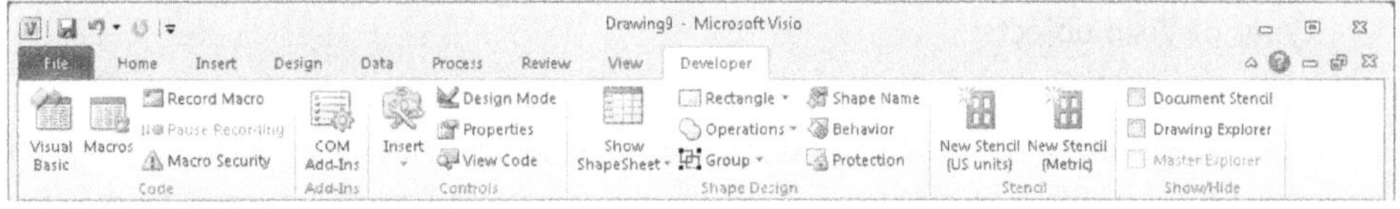

Several of the upcoming sections use functions that are enabled in developer mode.

Tip There is no downside to running Visio in developer mode, even if you don't regularly use the features it provides.

See Also For more details on Developer tab functions, go to ***blogs.msdn.com/b/visio/archive/2009/09/02/the-developer-tab-in-visio-2010.aspx.***

Viewing and Modifying the ShapeSheet

Important You must be running in developer mode to access the ShapeSheet.

There are three elements that combine to give Visio its power and versatility:

- **Visio engine** The ***Visio engine*** is the preprogrammed heart of Visio.
- **Add-in programs** ***Add-ins*** typically extend Visio by providing features that the Visio engine does not. They are created by Microsoft, other software development companies, or individuals.

- **ShapeSheet** The ***ShapeSheet*** is a spreadsheet-like data store that exists behind every object in Visio: every two-dimensional shape, every line, every container, every page, even the document itself. The values and formulae in the ShapeSheet, in conjunction with the Visio engine and add-in code, control every aspect of the appearance and behavior of Visio objects.

  Tip For the technically inclined, you might prefer to think of the ShapeSheet as a window into parts of the Visio object model.

The focus for this section is the ShapeSheet.

The remarkable thing about the ShapeSheet when you first start to explore it—or, for that matter, after you've been working with it for 10 years—is that changing one value or formula can have a profound effect on what you see on the page.

To view the ShapeSheet for any shape on the drawing page, select the shape, and then on the Developer tab, in the Shape Design group, click the Show ShapeSheet button. To view the ShapeSheet for the page or the document, click the lower half of the same button (do not click the icon) and choose an entry from the menu.

Tip There is a quick alternative method for opening the ShapeSheet for the three primary types of Visio objects:

- **Shape Right-click the shape and click Show ShapeSheet.**
- **Page Right-click the page background and click Show ShapeSheet.**
- **Document Right-click the page background, hold down the Shift key, and click Show ShapeSheet.**

The cells in the ShapeSheet are organized into sections and each section has a specific format. In the following graphic, some sections are open and visible, such as Shape Transform, and some are closed, such as Protection. You can open or close any section by clicking the blue section header.

Tip Notice the contextual tab at the top of the Visio window. The ShapeSheet Tools Design contextual tab provides ShapeSheet-specific functions.

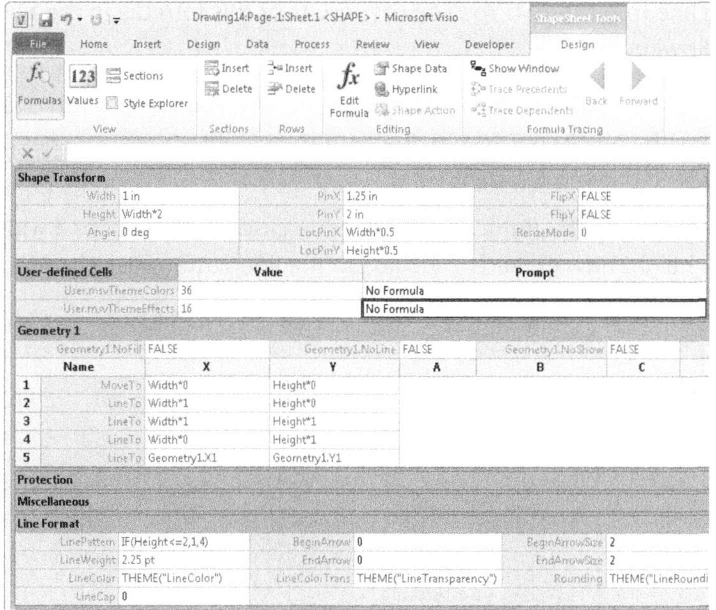

You can type either a constant or a formula into a ShapeSheet cell. The previous sample ShapeSheet describes a simple rectangle and contains examples of both types of entries. If you look in the Shape Transform section, you see that the Width cell has been set to a constant value of 1 inch. In contrast, the Height cell contains a formula that sets the height to two times the width. As a result of this formula, if you change the width of the shape by dragging the resize handle or typing a new number into the Width cell, the height of the shape will adjust automatically.

"Width*2" is obviously a very simple formula. Many Visio shapes employ much more complex formulas. In addition, there are dozens of ShapeSheet functions that can do things like perform sophisticated calculations; read data from other cells in this ShapeSheet; read data from the ShapeSheets of other objects in the document; set a value based on an "if" condition; trigger actions in the drawing; and respond to events.

As one example, look at the formula in the LineColor cell in the Line Format section. The THEME() function retrieves the default line color used in the current theme and applies it to the line on this shape.

See Also For information about Visio 2010 themes, see Chapter 5, "Adding Style, Color, and Themes."

As a second example, look at the formula for LinePattern in the Line Format section. The IF() function is interpreted this way: if the height of the shape is less than or equal to 2 inches, set the line around the shape to pattern number 1; if the height is greater than

2 inches, set the line to pattern 4. You see the results of this formula in the two shapes shown in the following graphic:

- In the ShapeSheet cells for the rectangle on the left, you see a width of 1 inch, which means the height is 2 inches. Because the height equals 2 inches, the line pattern is set to pattern 1 (a solid line).
- For the rectangle on the right, you can see the cascading effect of a width of 1.25 inches: the height now exceeds 2 inches, so the line pattern has changed.

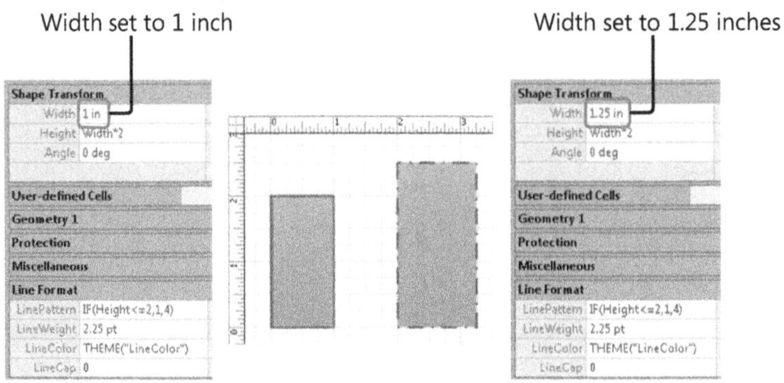

Tip If you would like to experiment with a rectangle configured like the one just described, open the *ShapeSheet_start* drawing located in the Appendix practice files folder.

The preceding example is a very simple one, but it should help you to understand the central role played by the ShapeSheet. It should also help you realize that one section in the appendix to a book like this can barely scratch the surface of the uses and functions of the ShapeSheet. Use the following references to continue your exploration of the Visio ShapeSheet:

- United Kingdom–based Visio Most Valuable Professional (MVP) John Goldsmith started his Visio blog in 2007 with a concise, nicely organized tutorial on the ShapeSheet. To read his blog, go to *visualsignals.typepad.co.uk/vislog/2007/10/just-for-starte.html.* Be sure to check out other posts on John's blog for additional ShapeSheet-related examples.
- Two other Visio MVPs blog regularly about a broad array of topics and frequently describe very clever manipulations of the ShapeSheet:
    - **Chris Roth, aka The Visio Guy** *www.visguy.com*
    - **David Parker** *davidjpp.wordpress.com*
- The aforementioned David Parker wrote a book on business process validation that is cited in Chapter 12, "Creating and Validating Process Diagrams." Chapter 3 of David's book, *Microsoft Visio 2010 Business Process Diagramming and Validation*, is

available at *msdn.microsoft.com/en-us/library/gg144579.aspx*. The first third of the chapter is an excellent ShapeSheet overview.

- The ultimate reference for the ShapeSheet is contained in the Visio 2010 Software Development Kit (SDK), which is available both online and in downloadable form at *msdn.microsoft.com/en-us/library/ff768297.aspx*.

Inserting Fields: Advanced Topics

In Chapter 3, "Adding Sophistication to Your Drawings," you learned how to display the value of a ***shape data*** field on a shape. Although that simple action is very helpful, you can do so much more than that with the Field dialog box.

The first thing to notice about the Field dialog box is that the Category section of the dialog box includes seven entries underneath Shape Data. Each of these categories contains multiple data fields. The Date/Time category, for example, shows four types of dates.

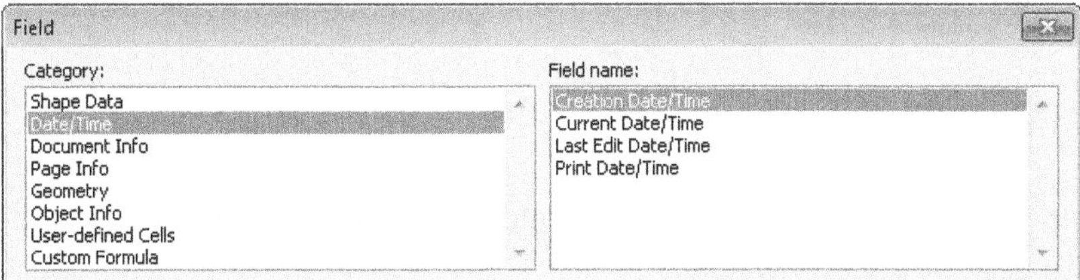

You can use the other categories to display data about the document (shown in the following graphic), the page, or various attributes of the selected object.

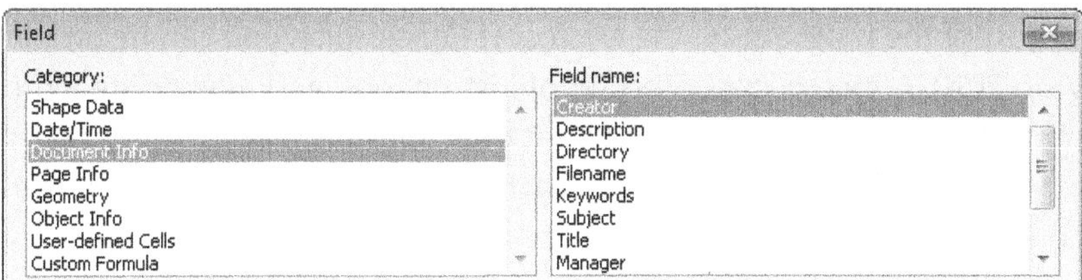

Finally, you can insert just about anything you'd like by selecting the Custom Formula category. A custom formula can include math and text functions, references to any of the data elements in the other seven field categories, and almost any ShapeSheet cell or function.

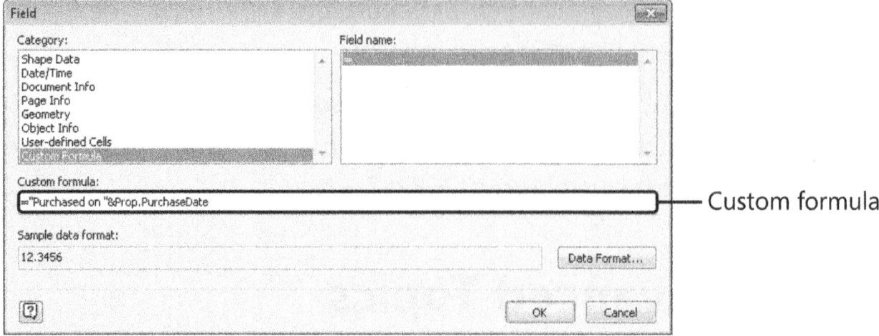

As one example, the custom formula shown in the previous graphic consists of two parts: a text label, "Purchased on", concatenated with a value stored in the PurchaseDate shape data field. The result, inserted on a conference table shape from the Office Layout template, is shown in the following graphic.

The Field dialog box offers a rich set of options for making the data in your document visible to users of your drawings.

Recording and Running Macros

As with most of the programs in the Microsoft Office suite, you can record and run macros in Visio 2010. A ***macro*** is a stored set of instructions, and macros are a great way to perform repetitive actions: you record a set of actions once and can replay it as many times as you'd like. To start recording a macro, click the Macro button on the left side of the Visio status bar (see the following graphic on the left).

In the Record Macro dialog box that appears, click OK to begin recording. Note that the appearance of the button changes to a square stop button, as shown on the right.

When you have completed the steps you want to capture, click the same button again.

Important The macro recorder does not record mouse movements; it just records the results of those movements.

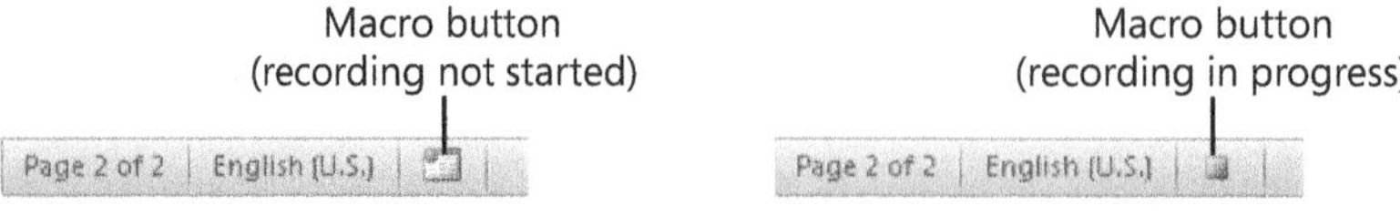

Macros

To run a macro that you've recorded, on the View tab, in the Macros group, click the Macro button. Select the appropriate macro in the Macros dialog box, and then click Run.

Although you are not required to be in developer mode to record and run macros, you can do both things very easily using buttons in the Code group on the Developer tab.

See Also **See the section titled "Running in Developer Mode" earlier in this appendix.**

Macro Security in Visio

The default security setting for macro code is Disable All Macros With Notification, which means that Visio opens any diagram containing macros in protected mode and displays a security warning bar above the drawing page.

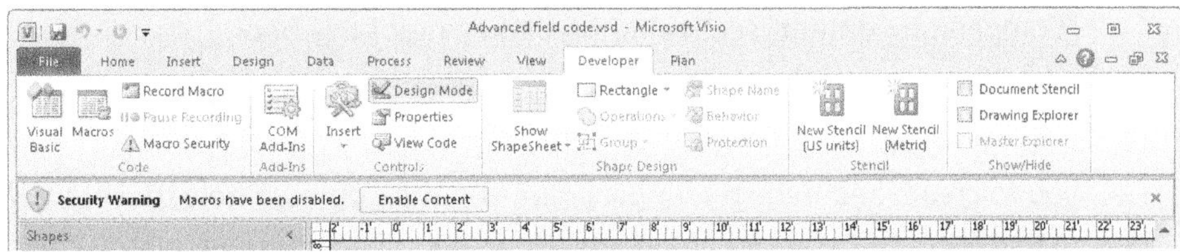

If you ignore the warning, you will be able to edit the drawing but not run macros. If you click Enable Content, the drawing will close and reopen with macros enabled.

To change macro security settings, on the File tab, click Options. Then on the left side of the Visio Options dialog box, click Trust Center, and then click Trust Center Settings. When the Trust Center dialog box opens, click Macro Settings if it's not already selected.

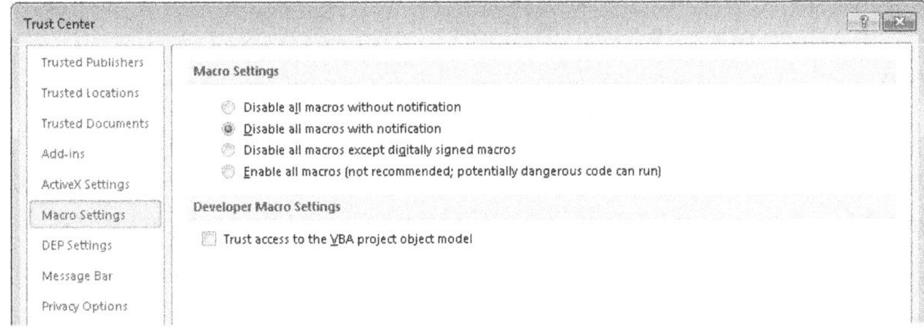

Click whichever of the other three settings meets your needs, and then click OK.

Macro Security

Tip If you are running Visio in developer mode, you can view the Macro settings with a single click. On the Developer tab, in the Code group, click Macro Security.

Programming Visio by Using Visual Basic for Applications

Microsoft ***Visual Basic for Applications*** (***VBA***) is the built-in programming language that accompanies most Microsoft Office applications. With VBA, you can extend or change the way that an Office application functions. In Visio, for example, you can automate tasks, add new features, or integrate Visio with other members of the Office suite.

Using VBA to integrate one Office application with another can yield very interesting results. For example, you can write Visio VBA code that creates a Microsoft Excel workbook and writes data to it, or saves all drawing pages as images and creates a Microsoft PowerPoint presentation from them. These are just two examples among many other possibilities. You will find several sample VBA programs in the companion content that accompanies this book. For more information about companion content, see the "Companion Content" section at the beginning of this book.

Visual Basic

To write a VBA program, you need to open the ***Visual Basic Editor*** (***VBE***): on the Developer tab, in the Code group, click Visual Basic. The VBE window opens, allowing you to create and debug your program. You will not learn how to write VBA programs in this book, but you can find many books and online tutorials about VBA. The following links will get you started:

- To get started with VBA in Office 2010, go to *msdn.microsoft.com/en-us/library/ee814735.aspx*. Note that Visio is not included in the "Applies to" list of products, but the material is relevant to Visio nevertheless.
- To learn about automating Visio 2010 with VBA, go to *msdn.microsoft.com/en-us/library/ee861526.aspx*.
- If you are already familiar with writing Visio VBA programs and want to learn what's new for developers in Visio 2010, go to *msdn.microsoft.com/en-us/library/ff767103.aspx*.
- The Visio SDK contains dozens of code samples that are excellent starting points for writing programs. Go to *www.microsoft.com/downloads/en/details.aspx?FamilyID=1cdbb7e7-6bd4-488f-91bd-7bd732dbf378*.

If you've never created a macro or written a VBA program, you might be wondering about the difference between the two because they sound similar. The answer is that a Visio macro is nothing more than a VBA program created for you by Visio. To see this for yourself, record a macro by using the instructions in the preceding section, and then open the Visual Basic Editor window and look in a module called NewMacros for the code.

Because VBA and macros are closely related, recording macros is one of the best ways to learn how to write VBA programs. Let Visio generate the code for a task that you want to perform, examine the code, and then incorporate it into your VBA program. Although this is an excellent strategy, you should be aware that macro code tends to be very verbose. Over time, you will learn which parts of the macro you need, which parts you don't need, and which parts you need to modify.

Creating Containers and Lists

In Chapter 11, "Adding Structure to Your Diagrams," you learned about containers, lists, and callouts. You learned how to insert preformatted containers from the container gallery, and learned how to add callouts from the callout gallery. You also learned that there isn't a corresponding list gallery, which means that you can't create a list by using the Visio user interface.

So how do you create a list? Or a custom container? The answer is surprisingly simple: you add one entry to the ShapeSheet for any shape and it becomes a structured diagram component.

See Also If you're not familiar with modifying the ShapeSheet, see the section titled "Viewing and Modifying the ShapeSheet" earlier in this appendix.

Important You must be running in developer mode to access the ShapeSheet.

To create a list, follow these steps:

1. On the Home tab, in the Tools group, click the Rectangle tool and draw a rectangle.
2. Right-click the rectangle, and then select Show ShapeSheet.
3. Right-click anywhere in the ShapeSheet window, and then click Insert Section.
4. In the Insert Section dialog box, select User-defined Cells, and then click OK.

User-defined Cells	Value	Prompt
User.Row_1	0	""

5. Click User.Row_1, type *msvStructureType*, and then press Enter.
6. Click in the Value cell, type "List" (include the quotation marks), and then press Enter.

You've just created a list! It isn't fancy and doesn't have any of the niceties like margins, a header, color, or style, but it is a list.

To try your new list, close the ShapeSheet window and drag a shape into the list. Drag several more shapes into the list. As you add each shape, you'll see that your rectangle behaves exactly like the lists you worked with in Chapter 11.

Creating a container is as easy as creating a list: simply type "Container" in the Value cell for msvStructureType. Creating a callout requires a few extra steps but can also be done fairly easily.

See Also If you would like to enhance the appearance and behavior of your list, container, or callout, you will need to add additional rows to the User-defined Cells section of the ShapeSheet. For an excellent summary of the user-defined rows and values required for structured diagram components, go to *blogs.msdn.com/b/visio/archive/2010/01/12/custom-containers-lists-and-callouts-in-visio-2010.aspx*. For additional technical details, including sample code for working with structured diagram components in VBA, go to *msdn.microsoft.com/en-us/library/ff959245.aspx*.

Glossary

1-D shape A Visio shape that has two endpoints and behaves like a line, sometimes in spite of its physical appearance.

2-D shape A Visio shape that has a border and an interior and behaves like a polygon.

absolute link A type of hyperlink that contains all of the information required to locate the linked object. Examples: D:\MyFolder1\MyFolder2\MyDocument.docx or *http://www.taskmap.com/Downloads.html*. See *relative link*.

active page The drawing page that has the focus within the drawing window.

active window Of the windows inside the Visio window, this is the one that has the focus; most often the active window is the drawing window.

Activity (BPMN) One of a set of rectangle shapes that represents a step in a BPMN diagram.

Activity (General) A task or step in a *work process*.

add-in Software written by Microsoft, other companies, or individuals that adds features and capabilities to Visio.

add-in tab A tab on the Visio ribbon that is present only when a Visio add-in is running. Example: the Org Chart tab for the Organization Chart add-in.

anchor shape The primary shape when multiple shapes are selected. If you select multiple shapes at one time using a bounding box, the anchor shape is the one farthest to the back (see *Z-order*). If you select multiple shapes one at a time, the anchor shape is the first one you select. The anchor shape affects the results of alignment and spacing operations.

area select A Visio technique for selecting multiple shapes within a rectangular area. See *bounding box*; compare with *lasso select*.

Auto Size A Visio option that automatically expands or contracts the drawing page as you move shapes across current page boundaries. New in Visio 2010.

AutoAdd Occurs when you drop a shape onto an existing dynamic connector that is glued to two shapes. Visio disconnects the dynamic connector from shape #2, glues it to the shape you dropped, and automatically adds a new dynamic connector, which it then glues to the new shape and to shape #2. See *AutoDelete*.

AutoConnect A Visio feature that glues a dynamic connector from one shape to another with a single click; AutoConnect arrows are small blue triangles that appear when you point to a shape.

AutoDelete Occurs when you delete a shape that is connected to two other shapes with dynamic connectors. Visio removes the deleted shape, deletes the dynamic connector glued to shape #2, and then glues the remaining dynamic connector to shape #2. See *AutoAdd*.

background An area of the drawing page that does not contain any shapes.

background page A Visio page that can be attached both to foreground pages and to other background pages. Shapes on a background page appear on other pages to which the background page is attached; however, the shapes can only be selected or altered when the background page is the active page.

Backstage view A central location for managing files and setting options that control how Visio 2010 operates; you access the Backstage view by clicking the File tab.

bounding box A temporary rectangular shape created by clicking the background of a page and dragging the mouse to select one or more shapes. By default, Visio selects all shapes that are fully contained within the area of the bounding box. Also referred to as *area select*.

BPMN See *Business Process Modeling Notation*.

business process A collection of tasks and activities that leads to a desired result; also known as a *work process*, or just a *process*.

Business Process Modeling Notation (BPMN) A standard for graphically representing business processes.

callout A shape you use to annotate other shapes in a drawing. Visio 2010 callouts exhibit more intelligent behavior because they maintain a logical association with the shapes to which they are connected.

canvas See *drawing canvas*.

color by value A type of data graphic that applies color to shapes based on data values within the shapes.

comment A Visio annotation object that can be attached to the drawing page. Compare with ***ScreenTip.***

Connecting Object One of a set of arrow shapes that links other shapes in a BPMN diagram.

connection point A location on a Visio shape to which other shapes can be glued; represented by a small blue X that appears when you point to a shape.

Connector tool A Visio tool that lets you add dynamic connectors to a drawing by dragging from one shape to another or from one connection point to another.

container A Visio 2010 structured diagram shape that can contain other shapes. Containers know which shapes are members; member shapes know the identity of their container.

contextual tab A tab on the Visio ribbon that appears only when you select an object for which it is relevant; contextual tabs are organized in contextual tab sets.

contextual tab set A collection of one or more contextual tabs that appears only when you select an object for which it is relevant. Example: the Container Tools contextual tab set appears when you select a container or a list.

control handle A yellow diamond-shaped object that you use to alter the appearance or function of a shape. Most shapes do not have control handles; when they do exist, you see them when you select a shape.

cross-functional flowchart A type of flowchart in which each process step is placed into a horizontal or vertical lane based on which person, department, or function is responsible for that step. Commonly referred to as a *swimlane diagram*.

custom properties Data values that are stored inside a Visio shape. Starting with Visio 2007, custom properties are known as *shape data*.

data graphic A Visio feature that lets you annotate a shape with icons and text callouts based on data in the shape.

data graphic legend A key to the data graphics used on a Visio drawing page.

data linking The act of building a dynamic connection between a Visio diagram and an external data source; the data in the diagram can be refreshed manually or automatically whenever the linked data changes.

developer mode A special Visio operating mode that provides additional features and tools beyond the normal user interface. When you turn on developer mode, Visio activates a Developer tab on the ribbon.

diagram See *drawing*.

drawing A Visio document that contains a drawing window and may contain other open windows. Also referred to as a diagram. Visio drawings use the .vsd file extension.

drawing canvas The space in the drawing window that is outside the Visio drawing page. If the Visio 2010 Auto Size option is turned on, when you place an object on the drawing canvas, Visio automatically expands the page size to include the shape. If the Auto Size option is turned off, you can store shapes on the canvas; they are saved with the drawing but do not print.

drawing page The printable drawing surface within the drawing window. In most templates, the drawing page displays a grid to aid in positioning and aligning shapes. Compare with *drawing canvas*.

drawing scale A ratio that expresses the size of an object in a drawing compared to its counterpart in the real world. In a metric drawing, 1:10 means that 1 cm on the page represents 10 cm in the real world. In a U.S. units drawing, 1":1′ means that 1 inch in the drawing represents 1 foot in the real world.

drawing window The Visio window that contains the drawing page.

dynamic connector A special type of line that adds and removes bends as the shapes to which it is glued are moved or resized. Each end of a dynamic connector can be glued to another shape.

dynamic glue The result of attaching a dynamic connector to the body of a shape. When you move dynamically glued shapes, the point of attachment of the connector can change. See *static glue*.

Dynamic Grid A feature of previous versions of Visio that aided in aligning and position shapes relative to other shapes. See *enhanced dynamic grid*.

enhanced Dynamic Grid A Visio 2010 feature that provides visual alignment and positioning feedback when you move shapes near other shapes or near the page margins.

Events One of a set of circle shapes that mark start, intermediate, and end events in a BPMN diagram.

Extensible Application Markup Language See *XAML*.

Extensible Markup Language See *XML*.

Flowchart A diagram that illustrates the activities, decisions, and events that occur in a work process or the logic of a program.

fluent user interface The official name of the user interface style introduced in selected Microsoft Office 2007 products. Commonly referred to as the *ribbon*, it was added to Visio 2010.

Foreground page A Visio drawing page. Can be attached to a background page.

functional band A vertical or horizontal rectangle in a cross-functional flowchart that contains process steps. Also known as a *swimlane*.

Gateway One of a set of diamond shapes that identify divergence and convergence in a BPMN diagram; gateways often represent decisions.

GIF Graphic Interchange Format; a common format for storing graphics and images on computers.

Glue A property of a Visio shape that lets it remain attached to another shape. See *dynamic glue* and *static glue*.

gravity In Visio, a mathematical function that gives the appearance of gravity; rotating a shape or text that contains the gravity function will keep the shape/text upright.

grid The background pattern of intersecting, perpendicular lines on a drawing page. By default, shapes on a Visio drawing page snap to the grid lines as you move the shapes across the page.

guide A Visio shape you create by dragging either the horizontal or vertical ruler onto the drawing page; used to align other shapes.

handle See *selection handle*.

htm/html File extension for web pages; short for *Hypertext Markup Language.*

hyperlink base The starting point for determining the path to a hyperlink target; Visio documents include a hyperlink base field, which is blank by default.

Hypertext Markup Language (HTML) A markup language used to define and render webpages.

JavaScript An object-oriented scripting language used by Visio to implement some navigation functions for websites created using Save As Web Page.

JPG/JPEG Joint Photographic Experts Group; a common format for storing graphics and images on computers.

lasso select A Visio technique for selecting multiple shapes within a freeform area drawn by the user; compare with *area select.*

layer A means for organizing sets of shapes in a drawing; layers have properties that affect all shapes in the layer at once. For example, with one or two clicks, you can show or hide all shapes on a layer, prevent shapes on a certain layer from printing, and recolor all shapes on a layer.

list A Visio 2010 structured diagram shape that can contain other shapes. A list maintains its member shapes in ordered sequence; member shapes know their ordinal position within the list.

Live Preview An Office 2010 feature that shows the results of many operations before you implement the change. Used in Visio for many font, size, color, alignment, theme, and data graphic operations.

macro A stored set of instructions; in Visio you can record a macro and play it back to repeat a set of actions.

master An object in a Visio stencil. Dragging a master from a stencil onto the drawing page creates a shape.

metric A system of measurement used in Visio drawings and templates in most countries outside North America. See *US Units.*

multi-shape A Visio shape whose appearance changes as data or attributes of the shape change.

org charts See *organization chart.*

organization chart A diagram that represents the structure of an organization.

page controls A collection of buttons and tabs at the bottom of the Visio drawing window that you can use to navigate from one page to another within the drawing.

page name tab A tab at the bottom of the Visio drawing windows that displays the name of a page. Right-clicking the tab provides access to page management functions.

pan To change which part of a drawing is visible by moving the page horizontally, vertically, or both.

pin The center of rotation for a shape.

PNG Portable Network Graphics; a common format for storing graphics and images on computers.

Pointer Tool A Visio tool that you can use to select shapes on the drawing page.

print tile The portion of the drawing page that is the size of a physical printer page; tiles are marked by dashed lines in print preview mode and on the drawing page if the Page Breaks check box is selected in the Show group on the View tab.

process See *business process.*

process map A diagram that shows the tasks and activities that comprise a business process.

Quick Access Toolbar A collection of buttons for frequently used functions that appears in the title bar of the Visio window and is always visible; can be customized.

Quick Shape One of up to four masters that appear on a Mini Toolbar when you point to the AutoConnect arrow for a shape on the drawing page; click on a Quick Shape to add it to the drawing page.

rack unit A unit of measure for the space occupied by equipment mounted in a network or data center equipment rack. Each rack unit or U equals 1.75 inches (44.45 mm); equipment height is described as a multiple of U's, for example, 3U or 5U.

relative link A type of hyperlink that contains only part of the information required to locate the linked object. The remainder of the required information is derived from the location of the document containing the hyperlink. Example: MyFolder2\MyDocument.docx or Downloads.html. See *absolute link*.

report A Visio feature that you can use to generate a summary of the data on one or more pages in a drawing. A report can be exported in html, Excel, or XML format or can be dropped on the drawing page as a Visio shape.

resize handle One of up to eight squares that appear when you select a shape; two handles adjust the width; two adjust the height; the four corner handles adjust both dimensions proportionally.

ribbon Common name for the fluent user interface. The ribbon consists of a collection of tabs, each of which contains a set of buttons that provide related functions. See *fluent user interface*.

ribbon UI Ribbon user interface; see *ribbon*.

rotation handle A circle that appears when you select a shape using the Pointer Tool, or select text with the Text tool; dragging the handle rotates the shape or text.

rule A condition to be validated in a Visio drawing. For example, a Visio validation rule might specify that all 1-D shapes must be connected on both ends.

rule set A collection of Visio validation rules, for example, the flowchart rule set or the BPMN rule set.

ScreenTip Text annotation that can be added to a shape; the ScreenTip appears when you point to the shape on the drawing page. Compare with *comment*.

selection handle Small circles, diamonds, or squares that appear when you select a shape; used to resize or adjust the appearance of a shape. See *control handle, resize handle*, and *rotation handle*.

shape An object on a Visio drawing page. You create shapes in three ways: 1) using tools from the Tools group on the Home tab to draw them; 2) dragging masters from stencils; or 3) pasting objects from the Clipboard. Alternatively, a program can create shapes for you.

shape data Data values stored inside a Visio shape; known as custom properties prior to Visio 2007. See *custom properties*.

Shape Data window A window that displays shape data names and values for a selected shape. See *shape data*.

shape name Internal name of a Visio shape.

shape text Text that is part of a shape and appears on or near the shape.

Shapes window A Visio window that contains one or more stencils.

ShapeSheet A spreadsheet-like data store that exists behind every object in Visio: every 1D or 2D shape, every container, every page, even the document itself. The values and formulas in the ShapeSheet, in conjunction with the Visio engine and add-in code, control every aspect of the appearance and behavior of Visio objects. See *Visio engine* and *add-in*.

sheet Internal Visio term for a shape.

static glue The result of attaching a dynamic connector to a connection point on a shape. When you move statically glued shapes, the point of attachment for the connector remains fixed. Compare with *dynamic glue*.

status bar A region at the bottom of the Visio window that displays information about the drawing page and selected shapes; also contains buttons and controls to adjust the page and selected shapes.

stencil A Visio document that contains a collection of masters. Stencils use a .vss file extension.

subprocess A subset of a process. In Visio, a subprocess shape on one page represents a collection of process steps that are typically located on another page; the subprocess shape is usually hyperlinked to the other page.

SVG (Scalable Vector Graphics) An XML-based format for describing and rendering vector graphics.

swimlane A vertical or horizontal rectangle in a swimlane diagram that contains process steps.

swimlane diagram A type of flowchart in which each process step is placed into a horizontal or vertical lane based on which person, department, or function is responsible for that step. Sometimes known as a *cross-functional flowchart*.

tab On the Visio 2010 ribbon, a set of buttons that provide related functions.

task pane A small, special-purpose window within the main Visio window.

task A step or activity in a process map.

template A Visio document that includes one or more drawing pages with preset dimensions and measurement units. A template may also include one or more stencils; it may include background pages and designs; its pages may contain shapes or text. A template may also include special software that only operates in that template. Templates use a .vst file extension.

text block The part of a shape that contains text.

Text tool A Visio tool that you can use to manipulate shape text when you use the tool to select a shape; also lets you create a text-only shape by dragging across the background of the drawing page.

theme A combination of theme colors and theme effects designed to enhance the presentation of a Visio diagram.

theme color A coordinated set of background, fill, line, and accent colors.

theme effect A coordinated set of fonts, fill patterns, shadows, and line styles.

tile See *print tile*.

U See *rack unit*.

URL (Uniform Resource Locator) Used to identify the location of a document or other object.

US Units A system of measurement used in Visio drawings and templates in the United States and parts of Canada and Mexico. See *metric*.

user-defined cells Data names and values that can be stored in the *ShapeSheet* for a Visio shape.

validation A Visio Premium 2010 feature that you can use to verify that a drawing meets certain predefined requirements; see *rule* and *rule set*.

VBA See *Visual Basic for Applications*.

.vdw File extension for a Visio web drawing; see *Visio web drawing*.

Visio engine The core software that provides Visio features and functions. See *add-in*.

Visio Services A service provided by SharePoint Server 2010; you can use it to publish dynamically updateable Visio drawings so they can be viewed by people without Visio.

Visio web drawing A new Visio 2010 file format that you can use to publish Visio drawings to SharePoint sites using Visio Services; Visio web drawings can be viewed by anyone with Internet Explorer; web drawings can be dynamically updated when the data in the Visio drawing changes. Uses .vdw file extension.

Visio Workflow Interchange A new Visio 2010 file format that you can use to exchange Visio SharePoint Workflow drawings with SharePoint Designer. Uses .vwi file extension.

Visual Basic for Applications (VBA) A programming language built into many Microsoft Office products.

VML (Vector Markup Language) A markup language used to define and render web pages created using Save As Web Page. VML was the primary Save As Web Page output format in versions of Visio before Visio 2010; it is still available in Visio 2010 as an alternate output format.

.vwi See *Visio Workflow Interchange*.

work process See *business process*.

workflow A set of process steps, some or all of which have been automated. For the automated parts of a workflow, documents and files are stored and moved electronically, according to a set of predefined rules, so that they are available to participants as required.

workspace A collection of Visio windows and window settings. At minimum, the workspace consists of the drawing window and the zoom settings for the pages in the drawing; frequently, it also includes a Shapes window containing one or more stencils.

X The X coordinate; defines the horizontal position of a shape on the drawing page.

XAML (Extensible Application Markup Language) A markup language based on XML that was created by Microsoft. Used by many Microsoft products; Visio creates XAML documents when you use the Save As Web Page function.

XML (Extensible Markup Language) A text-based markup language for defining objects and their values.

Y The Y coordinate; defines the vertical position of a shape on the drawing page.

zoom To magnify (zoom in) or shrink (zoom out) the display of a drawing.

Z-order Defines the relative front-to-back position of a shape on the drawing page. The first shape you add to a page is at the back and each subsequent shape is in front of all previous shapes. You can change the Z-order by using the Send Forward/Send Backward or Send To Front/Send To Back buttons.

Index

Symbols

A

B

C

D

E

F

G

H

I

J

K

L

M

P

Q

R

S

T

U

V

W

X

Y

Z

About the Author

Scott A. Helmers is a Microsoft Most Valuable Professional (MVP) for Microsoft Visio and is the primary Visio expert at Experts-Exchange.com. He has helped companies create custom Visio add-ins to enhance organizational efficiency and employee productivity, and has taught thousands of people how to use technology more effectively.

He is Vice President of Product Planning and Support at the Harvard Computing Group (HCG), a software and consulting firm that assists organizations with understanding relevant technologies and making decisions about business applications and processes. Scott is a co-inventor of TaskMap (*www.taskmap.com*), a Visio add-in that allows anyone to document all of the important aspects of any business process.

Scott has worked with clients in Afghanistan, Egypt, India, Ireland, Jordan, Malaysia, Saudi Arabia, Singapore, Canada, and the United States on projects involving knowledge management, specification of new IT systems, process mapping and redesign, and technology training. He is the author of *Data Communications: A Beginner's Guide to Concepts and Technology* (Prentice-Hall) and has been an Adjunct Professor at both Northeastern and Boston Universities.

When not working or spending time with his family in Andover, Massachusetts, Scott can usually be found on his bicycle or working with a local community theater company.